AIA

Capstone Level

Multi-Disciplinary Case Study
LEARNING & PRACTICE
WORKBOOK

In this 2025 edition:
- A **user-friendly format** for easy navigation
- **Exam-centred topic coverage**, directly linked to AIA's syllabus
- **Questions** to test your understanding
- **Exam** standard questions with answers
- A full index

FOR EXAMS FROM MAY 2025

Second edition 2024

ISBN 9781 0355 2570 6

eISBN 9781 0355 2598 0

British Library Cataloguing-in-Publication Data

A catalogue record for this book is available from the British Library

Published by

BPP Learning Media Ltd
BPP House, Aldine Place
142–144 Uxbridge Road
London W12 8AA

learningmedia.bpp.com

Printed in the United Kingdom

> Your learning materials, published by BPP Learning Media Ltd, are printed on paper obtained from traceable sustainable sources.

All rights reserved. No part of this publication may be reproduced, stored in a retrieval system or transmitted in any form or by any means, electronic, mechanical, photocopying, recording or otherwise, without the prior written permission of BPP Learning Media.

The contents of this book are intended as a guide and not professional advice. Although every effort has been made to ensure that the contents of this book are correct at the time of going to press, BPP Learning Media makes no warranty that the information in this book is accurate or complete and accept no liability for any loss or damage suffered by any person acting or refraining from acting as a result of the material in this book.

We are grateful to the Association of International Accountants for permission to reproduce past examination questions. The suggested solutions in the exam answer bank have been prepared by BPP Learning Media Ltd.

BPP Learning Media is grateful to the IASB for permission to reproduce extracts from IFRS® Accounting Standards, IAS® Standards, SIC and IFRIC. This publication contains copyright © material and trademarks of the IFRS Foundation®. All rights reserved. Used under license from the IFRS Foundation®. Reproduction and use rights are strictly limited. For more information about the IFRS Foundation and rights to use its material please visit www.IFRS.org.

Disclaimer: To the extent permitted by applicable law the Board and the IFRS Foundation expressly disclaims all liability howsoever arising from this publication or any translation thereof whether in contract, tort or otherwise (including, but not limited to, liability for any negligent act or omission) to any person in respect of any claims or losses of any nature including direct, indirect, incidental or consequential loss, punitive damages, penalties or costs.

Information contained in this publication does not constitute advice and should not be substituted for the services of an appropriately qualified professional.

©
BPP Learning Media Ltd
2024

A note about copyright

Dear Customer

What does the little © mean and why does it matter?

Your market-leading BPP books, course materials and e-learning materials do not write and update themselves. People write them on their own behalf or as employees of an organisation that invests in this activity. Copyright law protects their livelihoods. It does so by creating rights over the use of the content.

Breach of copyright is a form of theft – as well as being a criminal offence in some jurisdictions, it is potentially a serious breach of professional ethics.

With current technology, things might seem a bit hazy but, basically, without the express permission of BPP Learning Media:

- Photocopying our materials is a breach of copyright
- Printing our digital materials in order to share them with or forward them to a third party or use them in any way other than in connection with your BPP studies is a breach of copyright.

You can, of course, sell your books, in the form in which you have bought them – once you have finished with them. (Is this fair to your fellow students? We update for a reason.) Please note the e-products are sold on a single user licence basis: we do not supply 'unlock' codes to people who have bought them secondhand.

And what about outside the UK? BPP Learning Media strives to make our materials available at prices students can afford by local printing arrangements, pricing policies and partnerships which are clearly listed on our website. A tiny minority ignore this and indulge in criminal activity by illegally photocopying our material or supporting organisations that do. If they act illegally and unethically in one area, can you really trust them?

NO AI TRAINING. Unless otherwise agreed in writing, the use of BPP material for the purpose of AI training is not permitted. Any use of this material to 'train' generative artificial intelligence (AI) technologies is prohibited, as is providing archived or cached data sets containing such material to another person or entity.

Copyright © IFRS Foundation

All rights reserved. Reproduction and use rights are strictly limited. No part of this publication may be translated, reprinted or reproduced or utilised in any form either in whole or in part or by any electronic, mechanical or other means, now known or hereafter invented, including photocopying and recording, or in any information storage and retrieval system, without prior permission in writing from the IFRS Foundation. Contact the IFRS Foundation for further details.

The Foundation has trade marks registered around the world (Trade Marks) including 'IAS®', 'IASB®', 'IFRIC®', 'IFRS®', the IFRS® logo, 'IFRS for SMEs®', IFRS for SMEs® logo, the 'Hexagon Device', 'International Financial Reporting Standards®', NIIF® and 'SIC®'.

Further details of the Foundation's Trade Marks are available from the Licensor on request.

Contents

Page

Introduction

The introductory pages contain lots of valuable advice and information. They include tips on studying for and passing the exam, also the content of the syllabus and what has been examined.

1	Introducing Multi-disciplinary Case Study (MDCS)	1
2	Understanding the business environment	9
3	Financial statement analysis	53
4	Developing data analysis	75
5	Research and analysis of the MDCS pre-seen and exam	95
6	Sustainability	103
7	Risk management	173
8	Impact of emerging technology	235
9	Managing ethical issues in MDCS	295
10	Practice Case Study 1: Pre-seen material	327
11	Effectively reading and planning using Pre-seen information for Case 1	335
12	Practice Case Study 1: Unseen case information and exam requirements	343
13	Effectively reading and planning using unseen Case 1 information and exam requirements	347
14	Demonstrating professional judgement, commercial awareness, effective writing and time management	353
15	Practice Case Study 1: Suggested solution with tutorial commentary	373
16	Practice Case Study 2: Pre-seen material	383
17	Practice Case Study 2: Unseen case information and exam requirements	393
18	Practice Case Study 2: Suggested solution	399
19	Practice Case Study 3: Pre-seen material	409
20	Practice Case Study 3: Unseen case information and exam requirements	423
21	Practice Case Study 3: Suggested solution	435
22	Practice Case Study 4: Pre-seen material	445
23	Practice Case Study 4: Exam requirements and unseen material	455
24	Practice Case Study 4: Suggested answer	463
25	Practice Case Study 5: Pre-seen material	477
26	Practice Case Study 5: Exam requirements and unseen material	493
27	Practice Case Study 5: Suggested answer	503
28	Practice Case Study 6: Pre-seen material	515
29	Practice Case Study 6: Exam requirements and unseen material	529
30	Practice Case Study 6: Suggested answer	537
Index		547

INTRODUCTION

How the BPP Learning Media Learning & Practice Workbook can help you pass

> It provides you with the knowledge and understanding, skills and application techniques that you need to be successful in your exams

This Learning & Practice Workbook has been targeted at the Multi-disciplinary Case Study capstone.

- It is **comprehensive**. It covers Multi-disciplinary Case Study syllabus content and provides activities, end of chapter questions and practice case studies to try.

- It is written at the **right level**. Each chapter is written with AIA's Multi-disciplinary Case Study syllabus in mind.

- It is aimed at the **exam**. We have taken account of format and style of Multi-disciplinary Case Study exams n preparing the four case studies, guidance the examiner has given and the assessment methodology.

> It allows you to study in the way that best suits your learning style and the time you have available, by following your personal Study Plan (see page vi)

You may be studying at home on your own or you may be attending a course. You may like to read every word, or you may prefer to do a fast read through and learn through doing practice questions the rest of the time. However you study, you will find the BPP Learning Media Learning & Practice Workbook meets your needs in designing and following your personal Study Plan.

Help yourself study for your Multi-disciplinary Case Study exam

The AIA Multi-disciplinary Case Study is different from those you have already taken. You will be under **greater time pressure before** the exam as you may be combining your study with work and you will be under time pressure during the exam to create case study report in a professional way. Here are some hints and tips.

The right approach

1. **Develop the right attitude**

Believe in yourself	Yes, there is a lot to learn, but thousands have succeeded before and you can too. The case study is about responding to the task in the appropriate way within the context of the case study scenario, so only through practice and more practice will you be case study exam ready

2. **Focus on the exam**

Read through the Syllabus	This tells you what you are expected to know.
Study the Exam paper section	The sample paper is a good guide to what you should expect in the exam as well as the four practice cases in this Workbook.

3. **The right method**

See the whole picture	Keeping in mind how all the detail you need to know fits into the whole picture will help you understand it better. • The **Introduction** of each chapter puts the material in context. • The **Syllabus content** and **Exam focus points** show you what you need to **grasp**.
Use your own words	To absorb the information (and to practise your written communication skills), you need to **put it into your own words**. • Answer the **questions** in each chapter. • Try **presenting** an answer to a case study requirement to a colleague or friend.
Give yourself cues to jog your memory	The Learning & Practice Workbook uses bold to highlight key points. Try colour coding with a highlighter pen.

4. **The right recap**

Review, review, review	Regularly reviewing a topic in summary form can **fix it in your memory**. The Learning & Practice Workbook helps you review in many ways. • **Chapter roundups** summarise the 'Fast forward' key points in each chapter. Use them to recap each study session. • The **Quick quiz** actively tests your grasp of the essentials. • Go through the **Examples** in each chapter a second or third time.

INTRODUCTION

Developing your personal Study Plan

BPP recommends that you follow a study plan. Planning and sticking to the plan are key elements of learning successfully.

Step 1   **How do you learn?**

What types of intelligence do you display when learning? You might be advised to brush up on key knowledge from your AIA Professional Level 1 and AIA Professional Level 2 studies before launching into your Multi-disciplinary Case Study studies using this Learning & Practice Workbook. Key revision areas to refresh are Audit and Financial Reporting. As you practice the case studies in this Workbook, it is a good idea to have your AIA Professional Level 1 and AIA Professional Level 2 learning materials to hand for reference.

Step 2   **Follow a tried and tested pathway**

This workbook is designed to work through from Chapter 1 onwards, to provide the additional knowledge and key analytical and report writing skills you will require in order to pass Multi-disciplinary Case Study. It is essential to apply these skills as you learn, so read through the detail in each chapter, and then concentrate on the examples and end of chapter questions before working through each of the four practice case studies.

Step 3   **How much time do you have?**

Work out the time you have available per week, given the following:

- The standard you have set yourself
- Splitting that time between reading and case study question practice
- Practical matters such as other commitments, such as travel, exercise, sleep and social life

		Hours
Note your time available in box A.	A	

Step 4   **Allocate your time**

- Take the time you have available per week for this Learning & Practice Workbook shown in box A, multiply it by the number of weeks available and insert the result in box B.   **B** ☐
- Divide the figure in box B by the number of Chapters in this text and insert the result in box C.   **C** ☐

Remember that this is only a rough guide. Some of the chapters in this book are longer and more complicated than others, and you will find some subjects easier to understand than others.

Step 5   **Implement**

Set about studying each chapter in the time shown in box C, following the key study steps in the order suggested by your particular learning style.

This is your personal **Study Plan**. You should try to combine it with the study sequence outlined below. You may want to modify the sequence to adapt it to your **personal style**.

INTRODUCTION

Tackling your studies

The best way to approach this Learning & Practice Workbook is to tackle the chapters in order. Taking into account your individual learning style, you could follow this sequence for each chapter.

Key study steps	Activity
Step 1 **Topic list**	This topic list helps you navigate each chapter; each numbered topic is a numbered section in the chapter.
Step 2 **Introduction**	This sets your objectives for study by giving you the big picture in terms of the context of the chapter. The content is referenced to the syllabus, and Exam guidance shows how the topic is likely to be examined. The Introduction tells you **why** the topics covered in the chapter need to be studied.
Step 3 **Explanations**	Proceed methodically through each chapter, particularly focusing on areas highlighted as significant in the chapter introduction, or areas that are frequently examined.
Step 4 **Key terms and Exam focus points**	• Key terms are definitions of important concepts that you really need to know and understand before the exam. • Exam focus points highlight areas or topics that may be examined.
Step 5 **Note taking**	Take brief notes if you wish. Don't copy out too much. Remember that being able to record something yourself is a sign of being able to understand it. Your notes can be in whatever format you find most helpful; lists, diagrams, mind maps. However, save the bulk of your time for question practice as this is where you will practice and develop the skills you will need to pass MDCS.
Step 6 **Examples**	Work through the examples very carefully as they illustrate key knowledge and techniques.
Step 7 **Questions**	Attempt each one, as they will illustrate how well you've understood what you've read.
Step 8 **Review answers**	Check yours against ours, and make sure you understand any discrepancies.
Step 9 **Chapter roundup**	Review it carefully, to make sure you have grasped the significance of all the important points in the chapter.
Step 10 **Quick quiz**	Use the Quick quiz to check how much you have remembered of the topics covered and to practise questions in a variety of formats.
Step 11 **End of Chapter Question practice**	Attempt the quick quiz and end of chapter questions (where relevant) suggested at the very end of each chapter. These are designed for you to confirm some of the key concepts set out in each chapter. Some of these questions are designed to cover more than one topic area to develop your ability to apply syllabus learning. You are then ready to attempt the questions related to this chapter which are contained in the question bank at the end of this Learning & Practice Workbook.
Step 12 **Practice Case Studies 1–6**	There are seven practice Case Studies in this Workbook which are becoming progressively more complex. It is advised you work through Practice Case Study 1 initially, and do not skip any before you attempt Practice Case Studies 5 and 6, which are MDCS recent exams. Use the AIA MDCS Coursebook Programme guidance to help you judge when to attempt each practice case study.

AIA Achieve Academy

AIA provides an interactive course of study AIA Achieve Academy, which offers students the tools, resources and learning environment to study for the exams. The study tools include a course of study e-book, marked practice questions, marked mock exam paper and feedback and technical advice via an e-Tutor. Contact the Study Support team at: Achieve@aiaworldwide.com

Moving on...

When you are ready to start revising, you should still refer back to this Learning & Practice Workbook.

- As a source of **reference** (you should find the index particularly helpful for this)
- As a way to review (the Fast forwards, Exam focus points, Chapter roundups and Quick quizzes help you here)

Relationship to Qualification Structure

In addition to having knowledge of and practical competence in a number of specific areas of professional expertise, for example financial accounting, auditing, taxation and management accounting, a qualified professional accountant should be able to integrate such different areas of expertise when dealing with real life situations and assignments in practice.

The role of the MDCS is to develop and test that ability to integrate knowledge, technical competence and other skills developed in separate specific areas of the curriculum and thus to provide an effective means of evaluating their ability to cope with complex situations and to operate at a level commensurate with what should be expected for a professionally qualified accountant.

The MDCS provides an opportunity for assessment of higher skills of analysis, synthesis and evaluation, consistent with the level of the AIA qualification being equivalent to Masters level.

Aims

In order to successfully complete in Multi-disciplinary Case Study candidates also have to demonstrate that they are be able to:

1. Apply and integrate knowledge gained from other papers in the AIA professional qualification to a case scenario representing a practical context. **(Learning Outcome 1)**

2. Analyse diverse information in order to determine what is relevant, and communicate the interaction between different factors (such as ethics, law, taxation, auditing and financial accounting) in order to provide a comprehensive synthesis of a practical case, with appropriate recommendations where relevant. **(Learning Outcome 2)**

3. Apply appropriate professional judgement in the context of complex practical situations. **(Learning Outcome 3)**

INTRODUCTION

Structure of the Paper

Assessment is by a three-hour 15-minute examination (including 15 minutes reading time). A simulated case setting is presented to candidates with a series of questions structured to reflect the learning outcomes. The scale of the case is significantly greater than the kind of scenario represented in questions in other examination papers in order to more fully represent a realistic practical situation.

A case scenario will be made available via a cloud-based platform six weeks before the date of the examination. Candidates will be free to read and study the materials provided, to research the background to the entity's circumstances and to discuss the materials with colleagues. Candidates are not permitted to take research notes and/or pre-seen materials into the examination.

The content of the scenario will not indicate the precise form that the final requirement will take, although it is recognised that candidates will be able to think ahead and to anticipate the requirements to some extent.

The pre-seen materials will be supplemented by an unseen component which will not be made available until the examination itself. This will provide further facts that will be required to satisfy the requirements of the examination. It will not be possible to predict all the technical areas or issues to be examined from the seen material alone.

The requirements will entail the preparation of a specific document such as a report or a memorandum that is addressed to a specific reader or readers. The requirements will involve reference to the specifics of the case and will require the ability to make use of the background information gleaned from the pre-seen material as well as the ability to assimilate new information from the unseen material.

Marks will be awarded for technical knowledge, synthesis of information and professional judgement evidenced by communication of a knowledgeable overview on complex issues, identification of alternative options and choices and appropriate recommendations.

Further detailed about the pre-seen and unseen case material are covered in Chapter 1

Syllabus

There is no separate syllabus linked to a specific area of technical knowledge or expertise for this paper. Rather, the main competence to be developed by students in studying this paper relates to skills of analysis, ability to synthesise information, communication and the exercise of professional judgement.

1. **Understanding of the business environment (Learning Outcome 1)**

    Topic weighting: 15%

    - Applying an understanding of the business, economic and political environment to the scenario and issues raised within the case study

    - Demonstrating the application of appropriate ethical standards to issues raised within the case study

    - Demonstrating an awareness of the significance of the financial management of an undertaking on the risk facing the organisation and the governance responses resulting from this

    - Demonstrating the application of knowledge of the internal workings of a company including culture and management structure and how these would impact on the accounting, governance or audit environment and risks

    - Demonstrating an understanding of the impact of the UN Sustainable Development Goals and emerging CSR international legislation and regulations and reporting requirements on the case study organisation

- Demonstrating an understanding of the issues around change and innovation in an organisation, the factors promoting or compromising change and the role of change management processes in supporting change projects

2. **Application and integration of knowledge from other areas of the curriculum (Learning Outcome 1)**

   Topic weighting: 20%

   - Responses apply relevant knowledge from prior learning from all aspects of the syllabus
   - Analysis of issues is based upon relevant and appropriate technical, legal and professional knowledge

3. **Analysis and synthesis of varied and complex information (Learning Outcome 2)**

   Topic weighting: 20%

   - Critique and synthesis of responses uses appropriate technical and commercial knowledge from prior learning in a valid and reasoned manner
   - Answers reflect information from all relevant sources within the case study material – both seen and unseen
   - Answers reflect research into issues raised in the seen aspects of the case study
   - Issues reflect a balanced consideration of alternative responses and interpretations of information within the case study
   - Justification of professional judgement

4. **Communication of issues, choices and alternative courses of action (Learning Outcome 2)**

   Topic weighting: 15%

   - Report is presented in a style suitable for the professional audience identified in the scenario
   - Structure of the paper is logical and clearly articulated to enable ease of navigation and discussion
   - Ideas are expressed clearly and in language accessible to the identified audience
   - Technical terms are used accurately and explained where appropriate
   - Issues are appropriately prioritised within the structure of the report and the body of discussion
   - Rationale behind assessment of issues and recommendations of responses is clearly articulated and alternative actions explored where appropriate

5. **Professional judgement reflected in identifying issues and appropriate recommendations for action together with supporting reasoning (Learning Outcome 3)**

   Topic weighting: 30%

   - Planning appropriate responses to Professionally related assignments
   - Issues assessed in a balanced and reasoned manner with reference to appropriate technical, ethical or theoretical norms
   - Issues discussed are supported with technical authority
   - Issues discussed are supported with reference to evidence from the Case Study
   - Analysis of issues and suggested recommendations are informed by commercial knowledge
   - Suggested recommendations and responses are informed by an appropriate ethical consideration and ethical codes

Ethics

Students are advised that the standards outlined in The Code of Ethics for Professional Accountants issued by the International Ethics Standards Board for Accountants (IESBA *Code*) are implicit in, and examinable throughout, the AIA syllabus. In this paper, a brief question relating to ethics could be included in any of the five questions but will typically be included as part of the compulsory Question 1 and the coverage of the paper is consistent with the relevant learning outcomes in IES 4 *Professional Values, Ethics and Attitudes*.

The Code can be accessed via the AIA website at www.aiaworldwide.com.

Command words

The following list contains active command words appropriate for use at the Capstone Level of the AIA qualification. Reference to the command words is essential to understanding how the assessment is applied in AIA exams.

Cognitive Levels of Learning	Command Words	Definitions
MDCS Synthesis and Evaluation 20% Application and Analysis 70% Knowledge and Comprehension 10%	Appraise	Assess the worth, value, or quality of
	Assess	Determine the strength, weakness and significance
	Calculate/compute	Select the appropriate method and techniques and apply your knowledge and understandings to work out and show how figures were arrived at
	Critically analyse	Examine in detail using arguments for and against, and develop a view
	Develop	Elaborate or expand in detail
	Evaluate	Determine the value in light of arguments for and against
	Integrate	Combine information and/or standards and theory from different accounting disciplines or different parts of the case study to provide holistic professional recommendations or conclusions
	Justify	Demonstrate the correctness of an action, claim or conduct
	Prepare	To make or get ready for use
	Recommend	Advise the appropriate action in terms the recipient will understand
	Report	Give an account of the results of the investigation

INTRODUCTION

Introducing Multi-disciplinary Case Study (MDCS)

Topic list	Syllabus reference
1 Introduction to MDCS	All

Introduction

This chapter introduces the syllabus requirements and format of the AIA Multi-Disciplinary Case Study (MDCS) examination.

An AIA professional accountant is expected to have practical competence in a number of specific areas of professional expertise, for example, financial accounting, auditing, taxation, strategy and management accounting.

A qualified AIA professional accountant should be able to integrate such different areas of expertise when dealing with real-life situations and assignments in practice. The role of the Multi-disciplinary Case Study (MDCS) module and exam is to develop and test that ability to integrate knowledge, technical competence and professional skills developed in separate specific areas of the AIA Professional Qualification syllabus.

The MDCS exam aims to provide an effective means of evaluating the ability to cope with complex situations and requirements, provide credible and well-reasoned advice and to operate at a level commensurate with what should be expected for an AIA professional accountant.

1 Introduction to MDCS

The MDCS exam provides an opportunity for assessment of higher skills of analysis, synthesis, and evaluation, consistent with the fact that the level of the AIA qualification is equivalent to Masters level.

The aims of MDCS are to develop the ability to integrate and consolidate knowledge and skills developed in other Professional Stage 1 and 2 exams, and to be able to apply that knowledge and skill in the context of complex practical (encountered in real-life contexts) settings at the level of competence expected of a professionally qualified accountant.

1.1 Aims of MDCS

In order to successfully complete this paper, candidates will demonstrate that they are able to:

(a) Apply and integrate knowledge gained from other papers in the AIA Professional Qualification to a case scenario representing a practical context

(b) Analyse diverse information in order to determine what is relevant, and communicate the interaction between different factors (such as ethics, law, taxation, auditing and financial accounting) in order to provide a comprehensive synthesis of a practical case, with appropriate recommendations where relevant

(c) Apply appropriate professional judgement in the context of complex practical situations.

1.2 Assessment of MDCS

> **MDCS Assessment Key Points**
>
> - The length is 3 hours, plus 15 minutes reading time.
> - Pre-seen material is provided approximately six weeks before the exam.
> - Additional unseen material and exam requirements are provided in the exam.
> - To pass the MDCS module, candidates must get 50 marks out of 100 to pass.
> - Refer to exam calendar on AIA website for pre-seen release and MDCS exam dates.

The MDCS assessment is a three-hour 15-minute examination which includes 15 minutes reading time. A simulated case setting is presented to candidates in a pre-seen document which is updated during the exam with further unseen information and a series of requirements structured to reflect the learning outcomes. The scale of the case is significantly greater than the kind of scenario represented in questions in other AIA examination papers in order to more fully represent a realistic practical situation.

A case scenario will be made available via a cloud-based platform six weeks before the date of the examination. Candidates will be free to read and study the materials provided, to research the background to the entity's circumstances and to discuss the materials with colleagues.

Please note: Candidates are not permitted to take research notes and/or pre-seen materials into the examination.

The content of the pre-seen information will not indicate the precise form that the final exam requirements will take, although it is recognised that candidates will be able to think ahead and to anticipate the requirements to some extent, based on information in the pre-seen. Therefore, spending time researching and thinking about the pre-seen information is recommended.

The pre-seen materials will be supplemented by an unseen component which will not be made available until the examination itself. This will provide further facts that will be required to satisfy the requirements of the examination. It will not be possible to predict all the technical areas or issues to be examined from the pre-seen material alone.

The exam requirements will entail the preparation of a specific document such as a report or a memorandum that is addressed to a specific reader or readers. The requirements will involve reference to the specifics of the case and will require the ability to make use of the background information gleaned from the pre-seen material, as well as the ability to assimilate new information from the unseen material.

Marks will be awarded for technical knowledge, synthesis of information and professional judgement evidenced by communication of a knowledgeable overview on complex issues, identification of alternative options and choices and appropriate recommendations.

1.3 MDCS detailed learning outcomes

There is no separate syllabus linked to a specific area of technical knowledge or expertise for this paper. Rather, the main competence to be developed by students in studying this paper relates to skills of analysis, ability to synthesise information, communication, and the exercise of professional judgement. Below are the MDCS syllabus learning outcomes and how each is covered in this L&P Workbook.

1. UNDERSTANDING OF THE BUSINESS ENVIRONMENT (LEARNING OUTCOME 1)	
Topic weighting 15%	Chapter
Applying an understanding of the business, economic and political environment to the scenario and issues raised within the case study.	Chapters case studies 1–4
Demonstrating the application of appropriate ethical standards to issues raised within the case study	Chapter 9
Demonstrating an awareness of the significance of the financial management of an undertaking on the risk facing the organisation and the governance responses resulting from this	Chapters 2, 3, 4, 6, 7, 8, 9, 10, 11
Demonstrating the application of knowledge of the internal workings of a company, including its culture and management structure and how these would impact on the risk facing an organisation	Chapters case studies 1–4
Demonstrating an understanding of the impact of the UN Sustainable Development Goals and emerging CSR international legislation and regulations and reporting requirements on the case study organisation	Chapter 6
2. APPLICATION AND INTEGRATION OF KNOWLEDGE FROM OTHER AREAS OF THE CURRICULUM (LEARNING OUTCOME 1)	
Topic weighting 20%	
Responses apply relevant knowledge from prior learning from all aspects of the syllabus	Practice case studies 1–6
Analysis of issues is based upon relevant and appropriate technical, legal and professional knowledge	As above
3. ANALYSIS AND SYNTHESIS OF VARIED AND COMPLEX INFORMATION (LEARNING OUTCOME 2)	
Topic weighting 20%	
Critique and synthesis of responses uses appropriate technical and commercial knowledge from prior learning in a valid and reasoned manner	Practice case studies 1–6
Answers reflect information from all relevant sources within the Case Study material – both seen and unseen	As above

Answers reflect research into issues raised in the seen aspects of the Case Study	As above
Issues reflect a balanced consideration of alternative responses and interpretations of information within the Case Study	As above
Justification of professional judgement	Chapter 17 and practice case studies 1–6
4. COMMUNICATION OF ISSUES, CHOICES AND ALTERNATIVE COURSES OF ACTION (LEARNING OUTCOME 2)	
Topic weighting 15%	
Report is presented in a style suitable for the professional audience identified in the scenario	Chapter 17 and practice case studies 1–6
Structure of the paper is logical and clearly articulated to enable ease of navigation and discussion	As above
Ideas are expressed clearly and in language accessible to the identified audience	As above
Technical terms are used accurately and explained where appropriate	As above
Issues are appropriately prioritised within the structure of the report and the body of discussion	As above
Rationale behind assessment of issues and recommendations of responses is clearly articulated and alternative actions explored where appropriate	As above
5. PROFESSIONAL JUDGEMENT REFLECTED IN APPROPRIATE RECOMMENDATIONS	
Topic weighting 30%	
Planning appropriate responses to audit related assignments	Practice case studies 1–6
Issues assessed in a balanced and reasoned manner with reference to appropriate technical or theoretical norms	As above
Issues discussed are supported with technical authority	As above
Issues discussed are supported with reference to evidence from the Case Study	As above
Analysis of issues and suggested recommendations are informed by commercial knowledge	As above
Suggested recommendations and responses are informed by an appropriate ethical consideration and ethical codes	Chapter 12 and practice case studies 1–6

It is important that all chapters and practice case studies are completed to ensure you are prepared to meet all syllabus learning objectives.

1.4 The pre-seen information

The pre-seen material will be provided at least six weeks before the exam. The pre-seen could be up to 15 pages or more in length. It is intended to tell the history of a fictitious organisation with information about its people, its commercial activities and provide recent performance information and initial information about the industry sector in which the company is operating.

This fictitious organisation may be based on a real-world company; however, there are no benefits in trying to identify the company or companies. You must base your answers in the exam on the information provided in the pre-seen and unseen material.

The pre-seen material may include some or all of the following:

- Industry
- The company, its vision, mission, goals/objectives, its trading history and recent financial performance information
- Product range
- Customers
- Operational processes and internal controls
- Current challenges faced by the company
- Information about the accounting function, accounting policies and any current issues relating to how the accounting function operates
- Information about existing internal control, internal audit, external audit and assurance processes
- Information about the tax and legal function

1.5 The unseen information and exam requirements

The unseen material will be provided during the exam and will continue to tell the story of a fictitious organisation. It will provide updated or additional information and a series of tasks (requirements) for students to complete in the timeframe. This requirement will explain the required format to present your answer, for example, a report format, presentation, email response, or other prescribed format. In providing an answer, you will be expected to use information from both the pre-seen and the unseen. The unseen will contain between 4 and 8 requirements.

1.6 Answer format and mark allocation

The report should include a title page and contents page and clearly guide the reader through your conclusions/advice/recommendations. The examiner will expect you to follow answer format, such as a report, specified in the unseen.

Technical marks (85 marks) will be awarded for accuracy and validity in solving the issues arising from the case. The remaining 15 marks will be awarded for professional communication as follows:

Professional Marking Criteria (15 marks):

The Answer is presented in a style suitable for the audience articulated in the scenario.   **(2 marks)**

Structure of the paper is logical and clearly articulated to enable ease of navigation and discussion.
(2 marks)

Ideas are expressed clearly and in language accessible to the audience identified in the scenario.   **(2 marks)**

Technical terms are used accurately and explained where appropriate.   **(2 marks)**

Issues are appropriately prioritised within the structure of the report and the body of the discussion.
(2 marks)

Issues are assessed in a balanced and reasoned manner.   **(3 marks)**

Rationale behind assessment of issues and recommendations of responses is clearly articulated and alternative actions explored where appropriate.   **(2 marks)**

The professional marks represent the professional skills which each student will need to demonstrate in the report submission required by the MDCS exam, such as professional use of language and presentation, logical flow, prioritisation of issues and providing a rationale when dealing with issues and making recommendations. Like any skill, these can only be developed through practice, and therefore this

Learning and Practice Workbook provides four case studies for you to practise as well as other exercises to complete in each of the chapters.

Once you have attempted a practice Case Study, we advise you to self-assess your performance against the table of professional marks above in order to determine areas for improvement. Alternatively, you can ask a friend or colleague to review your attempt and provide you with feedback against the criteria above. You can then work on these areas for improvement when you attempt the next practice Case Study.

1.7 Introduction to MDCS exam technique

Using the right technique in the real exam can make all the difference between success and failure. Before you begin studying, it is a good idea to consider your approach to the MDCS exam, as this will determine how you study for MDCS and develop the skills you will need to demonstrate in the exam.

Consider the following exam success factors and reflect on how this will impact on your studies and exam preparations:

(a) **Use the reading time effectively.** During the 15-minute reading time at the start, read through the exam requirement and decide in what order you are going to attempt the exam.

(b) **Read the requirements carefully.** Read each requirement carefully once, and then read it again to ensure that you have picked everything up. Make sure that you understand what the question wants you to do rather than what you might like the question to be asking you. You are strongly advised to read and understand the requirement before you read the new unseen scenario material.

(c) **Read the new unseen material.** Consider each new piece of information against information in the pre-seen, as it is likely to provide an update or provide further detail, and against the exam requirement. You will then find yourself considering each requirement as you read the data in the scenario, helping you to focus on exactly what you have to do.

(d) **Allocate time.** Having established the order that you are going to attempt the exam and the nature of each of the requirements, allocate the time available to the questions and work out at what time you will need to stop working on one question and move on to the next. When you reach the end of the allocated time for the question that you are working on, STOP. It is much easier to gain the straightforward marks for the next question than to spend a long time working on the previous question in the hope of gaining one or two final marks.

(e) **Plan your answer.** Plan each requirement by creating an outline of the report sections/heading you will include in your report submission. This will ensure your answers respond to the requirements only, avoid irrelevance and help you manage your time, so that you provide a full and detailed answer to each requirement within the time allocated. For some requirements, you will need to plan the calculations needed to complete a requirement. Make sure that your calculations are not excessive and leave the majority of available time for report writing and not calculating. As part of planning, consider how you will achieve the 15 professional marks which are available.

(f) **Writing up your answer.** Stick to your plan, as this will ensure your report is requirement-focused and avoid being distracted by less relevant areas. As you are writing your report and presenting your work, don't forget the 15 professional marks which are available.

(g) **Time management.** Make sure you keep to your planned timing for each requirement. This will help you ensure you attempt every requirement, which will maximise your chances of passing the exam.

(h) **Keep it relevant.** Try to make sure that your answer relates to the specifics of the question itself. To achieve high marks, your answer will need to be relevant and customised totally to the MDCS scenario and respond directly to the task outlined in each requirement.

(i) **Aim to answer all of the exam requirements.** Even if you cannot complete all of a requirement, or correctly recall the relevant accounting or auditing standard, or do all the calculation elements, you will still be able to gain marks in the discussion parts of the requirement and deliver sensible advice, based on the information given in the pre-seen and unseen. If you finish the exam with time to spare, use the rest of the time to review your answers and to make sure that you answered each requirement within each question.

The MDCS Learning and Practice Workbook will explain and demonstrate required professional skills and exam techniques through a series of skill development chapters and practice case studies with suggested answers. MDCS does not introduce new technical syllabus content, as this is all prior learning from Foundation and Professional Skills Levels 1 and 2.

MDCS is a skills-based exam which requires you to demonstrate that you can apply your existing technical knowledge in a practical and professional manner. It is very important that you adopt an approach of learning through Case Study question practice in order to develop the necessary reading, planning, analytical and writing skills required to be successful in the Case Study examination.

1.8 MDCS study advice

Passing MDCS is all about Case Study question practice. Use the MDCS Coursebook Guidance to plan your MDCS studies and exam preparations so that you can maximise the benefits from the learning resources in this Learning and Practice Workbook and from the study time you have available.

In addition to the learning resources in this L&P Workbook, AIA provides a specimen MDCS Case Study for you to attempt as part of your exam preparations. This is available on the AIA website. Please make sure you include attempting the MDCS specimen Case Study in your MDCS studies, as doing so will help to make sure you are fully prepared to be successful in the exam.

Understanding the business environment

Topic list	Syllabus reference
1 Introduction	LO1
2 Analysis of strategic position	LO1
3 Analysis of the general business environment: PESTEL analysis	LO1
4 SWOT analysis	LO1
5 Value chain	LO1
6 Strategic choice	LO1
7 Marketing strategy	LO1
8 Operational analysis	LO1
9 Analysing business risk	LO1
10 Managing stakeholder conflict	LO1
11 Summary guide to completing strategic analysis in the MDCS	LO1

Introduction

For the MDCS examination, you may be required to carry out strategic analysis for an organisation, probably a company. (However, similar principles and methods also apply to other types of organisation, such as not-for-profit organisations.) Your analysis will consider the strategic issues and problems facing the company, and it is possible that you will be required in your report to make a recommendation about the **strategy** that the company should pursue in the future.

The approach you should take to strategic analysis and strategy formulation which is, described in this chapter is similar to the approach of senior business executives in practice.

1 Introduction

Strategy can be defined as a high-level plan for achieving a goal or objective under conditions of risk and uncertainty. The basic elements in formulating a strategy are to:

- Set the goal or objective over a given future period of time
- Decide on actions (the strategy) for achieving this goal or objective
- Mobilise the resources that will be needed to put these actions into effect. Some resources will be in limited supply and this may restrict what a company can realistically achieve.

The **process of strategy formulation** for a company can be described in simple terms as:

- Recognising the current position of the company, and also the risks, opportunities and uncertainties about its future
- Deciding on objectives for achievement over the period of the strategic plan, and setting quantified targets for achievement
- Deciding on the best way of getting from where the company is now to where it needs to be in the future, in order to achieve the planned objectives

Strategy formulation

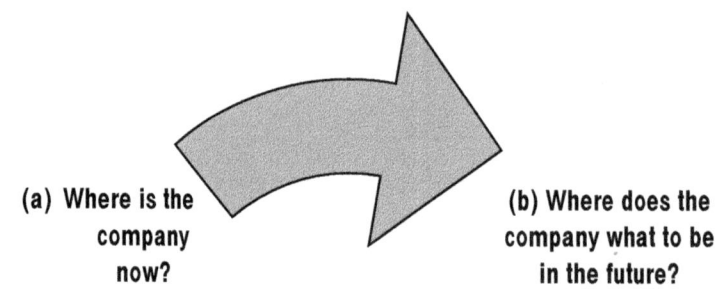

This chapter looks at techniques that may be used to analyse strategic position and formulate strategy. Financial issues are an important part of this process, and these will be considered separately in the next chapter.

2 Analysis of strategic position

A structured approach to **strategic planning** begins with an analysis of a company's current **strategic position** – 'Where are we now?' This involves analysis of:

- The general business environment in which the company operates and the risks and uncertainties in this environment. What are the factors in the environment that are having, or may have, a significant influence on the company and its operations?
- The specific industrial and competitive environment in which the company operates. What is the state of the industry? Who are the main competitors and what are they doing?
- The resources that the company has at its disposal
- What can the company do well – what are its competences? And what does it not do well?

This analysis leads to an assessment of strengths and weaknesses in the company's resources and competences, and of opportunities and threats in the business environment (SWOT analysis, which is explained later in this chapter). This assessment of 'Where are we now?' leads on to the next stages of formulating strategy – 'Where do we want to get to?' and 'How do we get there from where we are now?'

For the purpose of the MDCS examination, you should be able to carry out much of a SWOT analysis using the pre-seen provided.

2.1 Researching the industry

The pre-seen for the MDCS examination will provide details about the company and the industry in which it operates. You may, in addition, have some knowledge of the industry from your own work experience, or from what you have read in the media. However, it is likely that whatever knowledge you may have about the industry will be fairly limited.

You are therefore encouraged to use the internet to carry out some initial research into the industry, by reading about one or more companies or by looking for relevant articles and items of business news. You can search for companies by name or search the industry sector and take notes on what you find.

If you visit the website of a company in the industry, look for its most recent annual report and accounts. There may be useful information in the narrative statements and reports, such as statements of the chairperson or the chief executive officer or the directors' report, about the company's business and its strategies. The notes to the financial statements also have valuable information in addition to other narrative in the annual report and this is sometimes missed.

How much research do I need to do? This is for you to decide. However, you need to have a basic understanding of the industry at an operational level. You should be aware of local developments (such as technology advances, social policy, government involvement, industry standards, and community expectations), and industry-wide trends and market forces. But analysing the pre-seen methodically and meticulously should be your number one priority.

3 Analysis of the general business environment: PESTEL analysis

Companies operate within a complex and continually changing business environment. The general business environment refers to the environment within which all companies operate. Companies are affected by conditions in the environment and they need to adapt to changes that occur in order to succeed or survive. To do this, they should identify changes that are happening, or that might happen, and develop strategies in response to them – by exploiting emerging opportunities or responding to new threats.

The purpose of **PESTEL** analysis for a company is to organise thinking about changes in the general business environment that are happening or may happen in the future. It provides a structured analysis of the general business environment and potential future developments that may be of significance for the company.

PESTEL analysis involves thinking about the general business environment and future developments in each of six broad categories:

- **P**olitical
- **E**conomic
- **S**ocio-cultural
- **T**echnological
- **E**nvironmental
- **L**egal

The value of this structured approach is to ensure that all aspects of the environment are considered, and none are overlooked.

Important factors in the business environment will vary according to circumstances, but the outcome of the analysis should be to produce a list of potentially significant influences and developments. An illustrative example is shown in the following table.

PESTEL analysis	
Political factors: Examples • Change of government or change of government policy • Political unrest in a country • Threat of nationalisation of company's business • Corruption in government • Changes in tax policy (eg tax rates, tax incentives) • Trade restrictions imposed by the government	**Economic factors:** Examples • Economic conditions: growth or recession? What is the rate of economic growth? • Distribution of wealth in the economy • Rate of inflation • Interest rates, value of domestic currency in foreign exchange markets • Nature of taxation: types of taxation • Labour costs and supply of labour • Unemployment

Socio-cultural factors: Examples
• Age distribution of the population
• Population growth trends
• Changing cultural habits
• Changing popular tastes: Lifestyle
• Levels of literacy, standards of education
• Level of immigration
• Religious factors
	Technological factors: Examples
	• New technology: Implications for:
	  – Rate of technological change
	  – Product innovation and product design
	  – Processing methods
	  – Productivity
	  – Skills needed for technology in use
	  – Job creation or loss of jobs
	• IT, communications, robotics, developments in medicine and health, food production, water treatment, and so on

PESTEL analysis	
Environmental factors: Examples • Water shortages • Climate change • Loss of non-renewable scarce resources • Environmental pollution • Methods of recycling waste • Methods of improving use of scarce resources	**Legal factors:** Examples • Changes in company law • Changes in employment law • Changes in health and safety law • Changes in consumer protection law • Changes in voluntary codes of practice, such as a code of corporate governance

There are no 'rules' about which category each factor belongs to. For example, high levels of taxation and the risk of further tax increases may be categorised as either a political or an economic factor. Similarly, the possibility of stricter laws or regulations may be categorised as either a political or a legal issue. The purpose of PESTEL analysis is simply to make sure, as far as possible, that nothing is overlooked and everything of potential significance is recognised.

Although PESTEL analysis should consider current conditions in the business environment, it is primarily a forward-looking exercise to predict how conditions may change in the future and how this might affect the choice of business strategy.

Having categorised the influences in the business environment in this way, management can then go on to prioritise them, and to identify which factors present:

- The best opportunities to develop the business; and
- The biggest threats to the strategic aims of the business.

3.1 PESTEL analysis and the pre-seen

As part of your pre-seen analysis, you can use a simple table to enter elements from the case study that you think could be relevant. For each item that you enter in the table, it can be helpful to make a cross-reference to the pre-seen page number where the relevant information can be found.

PESTEL analysis

PESTEL analysis	
Political factors	**Economic factors**
Socio-cultural factors	**Technological factors**
Environmental factors	**Legal factors**

As you complete your analysis, you should aim to write at least one point in every box.

3.2 Competition within an industry (Porters' Five Forces model)

There may also be developments or conditions in the environment that are **specific to a particular industry or market**, and may therefore affect companies that operate within it. These should be identified. The purpose of this analysis is to assess the potential of the market for growth and profitability, and to assess the nature and strength of the competition.

You should read the pre-seen, looking for items that are specific to the company's industry or the nature of the competition that it faces. Further research into the industry more generally may also give you some ideas about the state of the industry and competition within it.

A framework or model that may be useful for assessing competition within an industry or market is **Porter's Five Forces model** (Porter, 1980). Porter argued that **some industries offer opportunities for bigger profits than other industries**, because of differences in the nature of competition within the industries. When competitive forces are strong, the opportunities for making large profits are reduced. This should affect the strategic thinking and planning of companies within the industry, or that may be planning to diversify into a new market.

Five competitive forces influence the state of competition in an industry, and collectively determine the profit potential of the industry as a whole.

- The threat of **new entrants** to the industry
- The threat of **substitute** products or services
- The bargaining power of **customers**
- The bargaining power of **suppliers**
- The **rivalry** amongst current competitors in the industry

Porter's Five Forces model

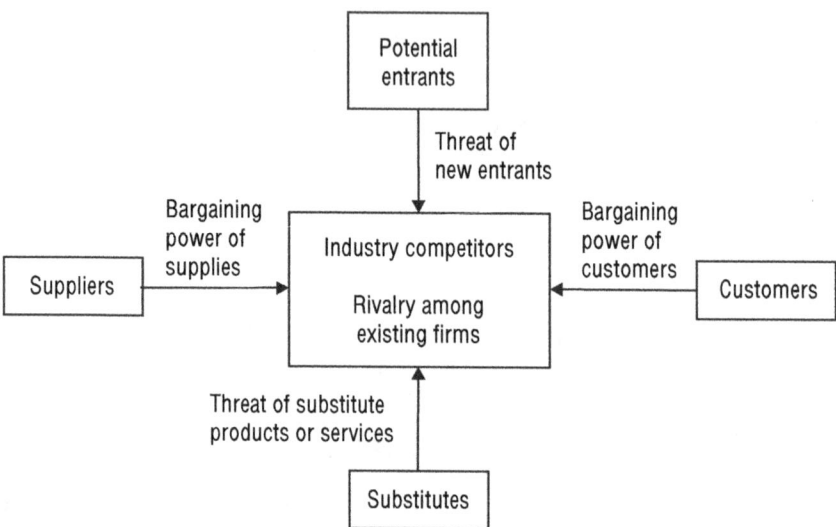

Where any of the Five Forces are strong, companies within the industry will find it difficult to make large profits.

Analysis using this model should consider each of the Five Forces and then make an overall assessment of the combined effect of all Five Forces on competition, pricing and profitability within the market or industry.

It may be possible to obtain supporting evidence for your assessment by looking at the profitability of the company and its competitors (using published financial statements).

The main focus of the analysis should be on opportunities to make profits in the future. Where the competitive forces are strong, it is unlikely that any strategy for expansion within the market will generate high profits.

Strategically, where any of the Five Forces are strong, companies might therefore consider:

- Ways of reducing the strength of the force or effect on the industry and market
- Avoiding investment in industries or markets where any of the Five Forces are strong and the profit potential is low
- Investing in an industry or market where there seem to be opportunities for bigger profits

When preparing notes from the pre-seen for the MDCS examination, you may find it useful to make notes on competition and profitability within the company's industry or markets, using a simple table based on the Five Forces model.

Illustrative example of notes based on analysis using the Five Forces model

	Threat of new entrants What are the barriers to entry to the market for new entrants? Does the economic environment make new entrants likely?	
Power of suppliers Are there many suppliers, or just a few? Is there a dominant supplier? What would be the costs of switching to a new supplier?	**Strength of existing competition in the market** Numbers and strength of competitors Local, national or global competition? Open market, monopoly oligopoly? Specialist/niche market?	**Power of customers** Are there many customers, or just a few? Is there a dominant buyer in the market who determines demand and prices? Are customers very price sensitive?
	Threat from substitute products or services Are there close substitutes for the company's products or services? Are the company's products or services different from those of competitors? Are there alternative technologies?	

4 SWOT analysis

The analysis of the general business environment, industry and competitive environment, resources and competences should lead on to an overall assessment of the organisation's strategic position. Having made this strategic analysis, it becomes possible to consider alternative strategies for the future, to achieve the organisation's goals and objectives.

SWOT analysis is the analysis of strengths, weaknesses, opportunities and threats. It brings together environmental analysis and the analysis of resources and competences.

The purpose of SWOT analysis is to identify (and perhaps prioritise) the following:

- The most significant factors in the business environment that provide opportunities to develop and grow the business
- The most significant external threats to the company's business
- The core competences and unique resources that the company can exploit strategically
- The weaknesses in resources and competences that will restrict the ability of the company to succeed, unless measures are taken to deal with them

SWOT analysis includes assessing competitors' willingness to win contracts at all costs. You must be aware of this issue and help your clients or your employer identify this unavoidable disadvantage. Without compromising on professional ethics, you will need to help find alternate ways to win.

You can make notes of the strengths, weaknesses, opportunities and threats that may be mentioned in the pre-seen for the MDCS examination, using the following simple chart.

Illustrative example of SWOT analysis chart

Strengths (resources and competences)	Weaknesses (resources and competences)
Examples:	Examples:
Does the company have a unique selling point for its products/services?	What part of the company's activities adds little or no value?
What does the company do better than its competitors?	What does the company do worse than its competitors?
What do customers see as the company's strengths?	What do customers see as the company's weaknesses?
What do employees see as the company's strengths?	What do employees see as the company's weaknesses?
What do suppliers see as the company's strengths?	What do suppliers see as the company's weaknesses?
What are the company's financial strengths?	What are the company's financial weaknesses?
Opportunities (environment, including competition)	**Threats (environment, including competition)**
Examples:	Examples:
What changes in the general environment (PESTEL factors) could be favourable to the company?	What changes in the general environment (PESTEL factors) could be damaging to the company?
Are there any developments or potential market opportunities for the company?	Are there any restrictions on the market for the company and its products/services?
Is there any unfulfilled demand in the market for the company's products/services?	What is the competition doing that could make it more difficult for the company to sell its products or services profitably?
Are there any (realistic) new markets for the company's products/services?	

SWOT analysis does not provide an assessment of the relative importance of each strength, weakness, opportunity or threat. It provides a basis for developing strategies for the future, but strategy formulation also requires an assessment of what strategic measures are most likely to succeed in helping the organisation to achieve its objectives.

Methods of strategy formulation should therefore include quantitative assessments of the expected impact of various different strategies on the organisation's objectives.

Question

StyleSpecs has a reputation for quality products. It has a group of optician shops from which it sells spectacles and performs eye tests. Recently, it has suffered intense competition and eroding customer loyalty which has resulted in shareholder dissatisfaction and a fall in the share price.

To combat this, StyleSpecs has brought in a new chief executive from a rival company, Rapidvision. Rapidvision has recently partnered with a national supermarket in whose branches it has installed mini-labs; prescriptions for spectacles are dispensed from these within an hour. Another competitor is making use of 3D printing technologies to design and produce bespoke spectacles. StyleSpecs has continued to operate as it always has in the past, and has failed to utilise advances in technology. Fortunately, StyleSpecs is financially secure and has large cash reserves, although production costs are high. Also, the country's most popular sports star was recently seen attending an awards night wearing a pair of StyleSpecs spectacles.

The new chief executive has established the need for improved financial performance as a priority, in order to appease shareholders and prevent the share price from falling further. Following a review, she discovers that:

(1) Site profitability varies enormously, and fixed costs are increasing in city centres as rentals rise.

(2) Staff turnover rates are high, so many staff in the shops are new and inexperienced.

(3) All staff, regardless of individual performance, receive a small bonus dependent on group financial performance.

The market that StyleSpecs operates in has an ageing population and increased disposable income amongst 18–30 year-olds. The economy is currently slowing down with the effects of a global recession.

Required

Produce a SWOT analysis of StyleSpecs

Answer

Strengths

- New CEO with good industry track record and knowledge of major competitor
- Reputation for quality products to help maintain customer loyalty
- Celebrity exposure increasing awareness and sales
- Strong financial position, including large cash reserves, permits investment

Weaknesses

- Failure to use new technology that could cut costs and improve service
- High production costs that erode profit margins and prevent price reductions
- Failure to use reward system for motivation to build customer focus
- High staff turnover resulting in stores being staffed by inexperienced employees

Opportunities

- Formal celebrity endorsement via a sponsorship contract
- Use of new production technology to cut costs and improve service
- Ageing population leading to an increased need for spectacles, as sight can deteriorate with age
- Increased spending power among 18-30 year-olds, especially on fashion products
- Staff retention scheme to reward good staff and reduce staff turnover

Threats

- Effects of economic slowdown on discretionary spending such as fashion goods
- Increasing competition from rivals using innovative technology
- Online providers able to make up and provide prescription spectacles at lower cost

5 Value chain

Michael Porter (1985) developed the value chain to analyse a firm's activities – ways in which they add value. You could break down the company in the pre-seen into its value chain components and then consider how value is generated within the area of product delivery and support.

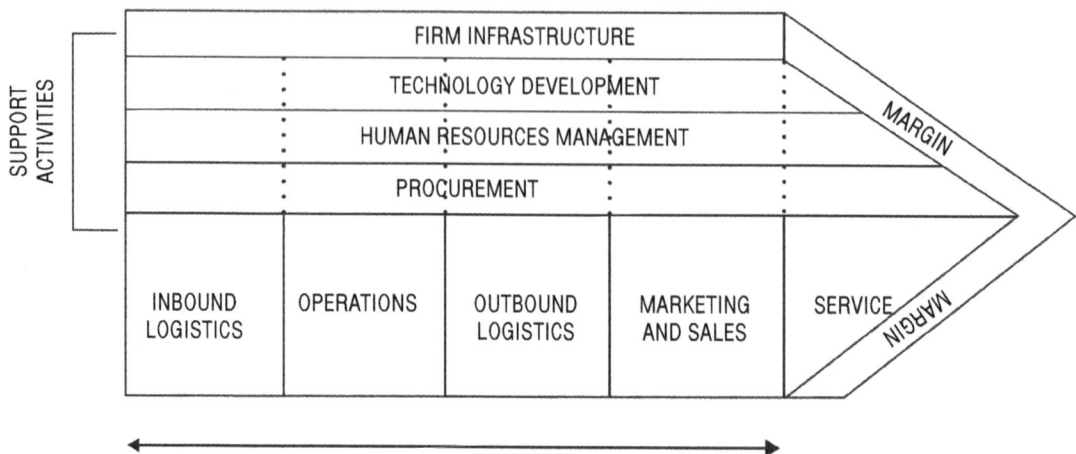

5.1 Components of the value chain

The **margin** is the excess the customer is prepared to **pay** over the **cost** to the firm of obtaining resource inputs and providing value activities. It represents the **value created** by the **value activities** themselves and by the **management of the linkages** between them.

Key term

> **Value activities** are the means by which a firm creates value in its products.
>
> The primary activities are predominantly involved in the production of goods, and support activities provide necessary assistance. **Linkages** are the relationships between activities.
>
> **Primary activities** are directly related to production, sales, marketing, delivery and service.

	Comment
Inbound logistics	Receiving, handling and storing inputs to the production system: warehousing, transport, inventory control and so on
Operations	Converting resource inputs into a final product: Resource inputs are not only materials. People are a resource, especially in service industries.
Outbound logistics	Storing the product and its distribution to customers: Packaging, testing, delivery and so on. For service industries, this activity may be more concerned with bringing customers to the place where the service is available; an example would be front-of-house management in a theatre.
Marketing and sales	Informing customers about the product, persuading them to buy it, and enabling them to do so: advertising, promotion and so on
After-sales service	Installing products, repairing them, upgrading them, providing spare parts and so forth

Support activities provide purchased inputs, human resources, technology and infrastructural functions **to support the primary activities**. It may seem an obvious point that support activities need to support the primary activities, but do not overlook it. For example, staff recruitment and training need to be appropriate for the item being produced in the operations. Support activities can also play a crucial role in helping organisations to meet their obligations in respect of corporate social responsibility and sustainability. For example, an organisation which claims that the packaging used in its products is recyclable, needs to ensure that its procurement activities are geared towards purchasing environmentally-friendly packaging.

Activity	Comment
Procurement	All of the processes involved in acquiring the resource inputs to the primary activities (eg purchase of materials, subcomponents equipment)
Technology development	Product design, improving processes and resource utilisation
Human resource management	Recruiting, training, managing, developing and rewarding people; this activity takes place in all parts of the organisation, not just in the HRM department
Firm infrastructure	Planning, finance, quality control, the structures and routines that make up the organisation's culture

Linkages connect the activities of the value chain:

(a) **Activities in the value chain affect one another**. For example, costlier product design or better quality production might reduce the need for after-sales service.

(b) **Linkages require co-ordination**. For example, just-in-time (JIT) requires smooth functioning of operations, outbound logistics and service activities such as installation.

Question

You are a management consultant currently undertaking an assignment at Carriages, a world-renowned, high quality restaurant which is located in the capital city of a developed European country. The owner of the restaurant is keen to gain understanding of how the restaurant's activities have contributed to its success. You are due to give a presentation to the owner and their senior management team, and are currently working on a slideshow and supporting notes that will illustrate Carriages' value-adding activities. As this is your firm's first assignment for Carriages, you are keen to impress the client's management team and want to make your slides interesting and attention-grabbing. To assist you in your work, your colleague has conducted a brief analysis (**Exhibit 1**) of Carriages' current activities.

Required

Using the information outlined in **Exhibit 1**, prepare one presentation slide and supporting notes which show the key value-adding activities of Carriages restaurant.

Exhibit 1 – Carriages' current activities

Carriages is currently ranked as one of the top restaurants in the world. It has won many awards for culinary excellence and often appears in the 'best restaurant' guides. Carriages has appeared in every edition of the annual Michelin guide for the last 20 years. The majority of its chefs have experience of working in Michelin star restaurants. A large team of waiting staff report to five highly trained maître d's. Carriages prides itself on only employing waiting staff who have three or more years' experience of working in 5-star hotels or restaurants.

All hiring decisions go through the owner who also acts as the restaurant's senior manager. The head chef, however, has complete autonomy over the running of the kitchen and food-related decisions. The current head chef insists on only purchasing the very finest ingredients, as this allows her team to cook the most creative and exciting dishes. The kitchen staff maintain very tight control over the food preparation and food storage facilities. They always check the freshness of the ingredients taken from storage before they are used for cooking. The kitchen facilities are at the cutting edge of food preparation and use the very best utensils, ovens and refrigeration units.

Carriages regularly advertises in quality newspapers which are aimed at customers in its target market. This is the only type of direct advertising undertaken. Diners are able to make dinner reservations using the automated, online booking system. To ensure the reliability of the booking system, the software used is reviewed every two years and, if needed, upgraded. To enhance the dining experience, soft classical music is played into the restaurant to improve the ambience. The tables and chairs used in the dining area were made especially for the restaurant by a world-famous designer and, as such, are made of highest quality wood and fabric. Carriages' owner prides himself on the car parking service the restaurant offers diners when they arrive, as this is a feature that other local restaurants are currently unable to provide.

Answer

Slide: Value-adding activities at Carriages restaurant

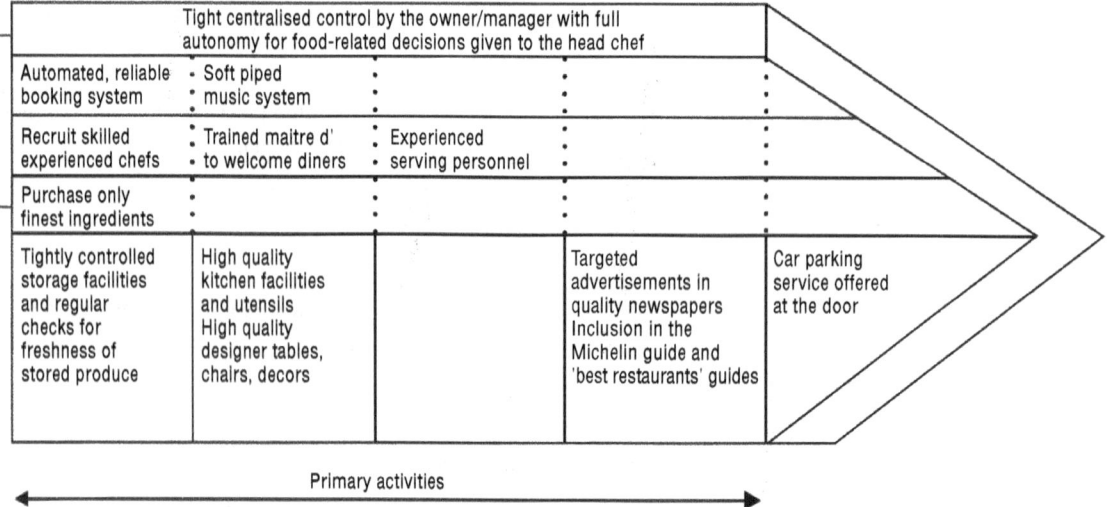

Supporting notes: Value adding activities

Firm infrastructure is characterised by the tight control which the Carriages owner has over the business. This is evident as all hiring decisions are decided by the owner. This level of control is crucial in ensuring only the very best staff are employed. The autonomy provided to the head chef is key in ensuring that only best ingredients are purchased, and most creative dishes made.

Inbound logistics are characterised by the role that the reliable automated booking system plays, as in this sense, diners are viewed as an input into the restaurant. The skills provided by appointing only experienced chefs adds value as only the highest quality dishes are prepared. The focus on only ordering the finest ingredients, supported by regular freshness checks, helps to add value as all food served is guaranteed to be as fresh as possible.

Operations relate to the running of the kitchen, and the restaurant environment which diners are exposed to, such as the service provided by the large numbers of attentive waiting staff and the ambience created by the use of classical music. These activities help to create an enjoyable dining experience.

Outbound logistics at Carriages relate to the physical delivery of dishes from the kitchen to the diners. The use of experienced waiting staff helps to create a sense of occasion while at the restaurant.

Marketing and sales activities help to reinforce the quality of the experience. Inclusion in the Michelin guide over the last 20 years has helped to distinguish the dining experience at Carriages from a standard restaurant. This ultimately adds value to the diners.

Service activities in this case relate to the activity of parking the diner's cars and then retrieving them at the end of the meal. This helps to support the entire dining experience, and crucially, is something which cannot be matched by other local restaurants.

Using the value chain allows you to consider the following questions as part of your pre-seen analysis:

- Which part(s) of the value chain offers a source of competitive advantage? Is the company clear about this and its focus?
- Are there any parts of the value chain not working well that could be reviewed for improvement?
- Are there parts of the value chain which are not central to the company's competitive edge and could be outsourced for cost savings and efficiency gains (eg logistics)?
- Do the different parts of the value chain operate in line with the company's strategic focus, such as cost leadership or differentiation?

6 Strategic choice

You may be required in the MDCS examination to consider alternative business strategies, and to recommend a strategy for the company. It will be difficult to prepare in advance for this aspect of the exam, but the pre-seen is likely to include some references to the company's current strategies and whether or not they are successful.

There are different ways of analysing and formulating business strategy. You may find any of the following approaches useful.

6.1 Organic growth or growth by mergers and acquisitions

Companies can grow by developing their own business organically. Alternatively, they can grow by acquiring or merging with other businesses.

A problem with **organic growth** is that it is usually a slow process. New finance for further growth often comes from retained profits, and there are also limitations on the company's resources and competences that it develops internally.

Companies seeking faster growth should consider growing through **acquisitions** or **mergers**. This strategy will often require large amounts of new external financing. Alternatively, acquisitions may be paid for in new shares of the company, with the purchase price for an acquisition in the form of a share-for-share exchange.

Organic growth and **growth through acquisitions** are not mutually exclusive strategies. Companies can pursue both. However, companies must also decide on the extent to which they hope to grow organically and the extent to which they plan to grow by acquiring other companies.

6.2 Cost leadership and differentiation strategies

Porter (1985) argued that companies should seek competitive advantage. This can be achieved in one of two ways:

- **Cost leadership:** Becoming the lowest-cost producer in the industry, so that the company can charge the lowest prices and hope to gain the biggest market share
- **Differentiation:** Developing a strategy to differentiate the company's products or services from those of competitors, typically by offering variations in quality (including product design and service content) for which an appropriate price is charged

Although several companies may compete to be the **least-cost producer** in a market, in theory only one company should be able to achieve this objective. Many companies therefore pursue a differentiation strategy, through a combination of product or service features and a selling price at which customers believe they are getting good value.

Porter argued that a company may also focus on a particular segment of the total market and seek to be the least-cost producer, or to pursue a differentiation strategy within that segment of the market, rather than in the market as a whole. For example, a catering firm that provides services at parties and functions may specialise in the most expensive segment of the market, catering for wealthy individuals and businesses; within this segment of the market, it may seek to offer the best prices, or it may seek to offer special service features (differentiated service features) that will have particular appeal to some customers.

6.3 Growth strategies: Ansoff's growth model

Ansoff (1957) suggested that when a company intends to grow its business, there should be a connection between its current markets, products and services and its future products/services and markets. Strategy should give a clarity to the direction in which the company intends to move in the future in order to grow successfully.

Ansoff summarised strategies for growth into four types, which can be shown in a 2 × 2 matrix.

Ansoff's growth strategies

	Existing products	New products
New market	Market development strategy	Diversification strategy
Existing market	Market penetration strategy	Product development strategy (or innovation strategy)

(Products or services across top; Market on left side)

These strategies for growth are not mutually exclusive. A company may choose to pursue two, three or four of them at the same time, should it decide that this would be the most appropriate way forward.

6.3.1 Market penetration strategy

With a **market penetration strategy**, a company seeks to grow by selling more of its existing products or services in its existing markets. This can be a very successful strategy if the company is operating in a market that is growing rapidly and has good potential for future growth. With a growing market, all competitors can hope to benefit from the rising sales demand.

In a market where there is little or no growth, a market penetration strategy is more difficult because, in order to gain market share, a company needs to take sales away from its competitors. Rivalry within the market could be intense, and the scope for profits – and growth – could be limited.

In order for a market penetration strategy to succeed, a company must be able to achieve one or more of the following outcomes:

- Persuade existing customers to use more of the product or service, and so buy more
- Persuade individuals or firms that have never bought the product or service before to start buying it
- Persuade customers to switch from buying the products or services of competitors

The first two outcomes seek to increase the total size of the market and the third seeks to increase market share.

To achieve success with this type of growth strategy, a company may need to pursue an aggressive advertising or sales promotion campaign.

There can be significant risks with a market penetration strategy.

- The company may not succeed in increasing sales as much as hoped, as a result of which it will lack any strategic direction for growth and may suffer from '**strategic drift**' – not knowing what to do.

- A strategic decision to 'continue with the same' products or services could be a high-risk strategy, because competitors may be much more innovative.

- Competitors may be more successful at winning market share, and the company's own share of the market may fall, rather than increase.

6.3.2 Market development strategy

Market development strategy involves growth through finding new markets for the company's existing products or services. New markets could be:

- Different geographical areas, such as different countries
- Different segments of the same overall market (eg an established airline company deciding to expand by creating a low-cost airline subsidiary)

Another example of market development strategy may be an attempt by a company to reach a wider geographical market by selling its products online.

Yet another example of market development in recent years has been a decision by many farmers in the USA to sell corn to energy companies for the production of bio-fuels, as well as selling corn to 'traditional' food producers.

6.3.3 Product development strategy

Product development strategy involves selling new products or services to customers in an existing market where the company is already selling an existing product or service.

There are several reasons why a company may decide on this strategy:

- A producer of consumer goods may have a strong and popular **brand image** and it may consider that it can use the strength of its brand to develop new products and sell these to customers.

- Technological advances may make it essential for companies to develop new products or services, and by innovating, there may be opportunities for growth. New technology will also occasionally

create huge opportunities for growth – as we have seen in recent years with the development of the smartphone and IT tablets.
- Customers may expect continual changes in product design: Examples are found in the fashion industry and in the software development industry.

Problems with a product development strategy may be that:

- Developing new products, involving expenditure on R&D and possibly also capital expenditure on new equipment, could be expensive.
- A large proportion of new product ideas are unsuccessful.

6.3.4 Diversification strategy

Diversification is a strategy of selling new products or services in new markets.

- **Concentric diversification** involves diversifying into product and market areas that are related in some way to the existing products or markets of the firm. For example, an accountancy firm that specialises in bookkeeping for small sole trader businesses may decide to expand by offering tax advice for corporate clients.
- **Conglomerate diversification** involves expanding into product-market areas that are unrelated to the company's current products or markets, such as a tobacco company expanding by taking over an insurance company.

Vertical integration is a form of concentric diversification strategy. Vertical integration involves taking over a business at an earlier or a later stage in the supply chain. The supply chain is the chain of production that begins with the production or growing of raw materials and ends with the sale of a final consumer product to customers.

For example, a supply chain may start with producers of rubber, continue with the processing of rubber into rubber compounds, and the use of rubber compounds to make tyres for cars, the production of cars, and the sale of cars (and replacement tyres) to customers. A producer of tyres may decide to expand by acquiring a producer of rubber compounds for tyres. This would be growth through vertical integration. The tyre producer would have no experience of rubber production, but there would be a connection between producing rubber and producing tyres.

In a similar way, a television company may decide to expand its business by acquiring or setting up its own film production company. This would be another example of **concentric diversification**.

Conglomerate diversification, growth by entering new markets with different products, is a high-risk strategy for companies. The company's lack of experience would create a high risk of failure with the strategy. However, in some countries there are very large and successful conglomerate groups of companies, so the model can work if managed well.

6.4 Functional/operational strategies

Functional strategies are strategies for particular aspects of a company's operations, such as:

- Purchasing strategy or supplier strategy for the company's raw material purchases
- Inventory strategy
- Manufacturing strategy
- Marketing and sales strategy
- IT strategy
- Strategy for business organisation and management structure
- Research and development strategy: product development strategy

Functional strategies are subsidiary strategies that should be developed to enable the organisation to achieve its overall strategic objectives and goals. It is likely that the pre-seen will contain operational information that may require improvement, which an operational strategy will seek to put in place.

6.5 Evaluating strategic options – suitability, acceptability and feasibility analysis

In practical terms, it is essential that any proposed strategy satisfies all three elements of the model – if there is one requirement that will not be met, then the strategy will not work. However, for the purposes of this exercise, we will consider how each of the three elements could be applied to a range of strategies. So, taking each one in turn:

Suitability

This considers whether or not the proposed strategy takes us where we want to go – 'Does it deal with the problem we currently have?' We could also consider if the strategy is consistent with our previous strategies, but the first question – 'Does it do what we need it to do?' – is perhaps more important.

Acceptability

Here, we look at whether or not the proposal will be acceptable to the key stakeholders. Notice that in just about any area of human activity, there will always be someone who objects to what we are intending to do – so don't expect that any strategy will be acceptable to all stakeholders. What matters is the opinion of the key players, those stakeholders with high power and high interest; if they oppose the company's plan, then it won't happen. The other stakeholders can, in theory, mobilise enough parties to be able to threaten the proposal.

Feasibility

Can we do it?' Here you need to be looking at the resources and competences of the organisation.

(a) **Resources** – this is the stuff companies have access to. Money is nearly always considered from this standpoint. If an organisation has large cash reserves at the bank, then that's a good thing; it can simply take money out of its bank account and use it to fund investment or acquisition or whatever it wants to do. If it doesn't have money in the bank, it may want to consider borrowing money, so in a question you need to look at what assets it may have that will facilitate borrowing – does it have land and buildings that can be used to secure borrowings and so get a lower rate of interest? Something else to consider here would be whether the company is listed on a stock exchange. Banks will almost always be more willing to lend to a listed company than an unlisted one.

(b) **Competences** – this looks at the skills that can be found within the organisation. By that, we mean the skills that the organisation's staff possess, so as part of this analysis, you need to be on the lookout for individuals or teams mentioned in the scenario. It might be, for instance, that the question identifies a particular department in the organisation as being acknowledged as an industry leader, or that a person has been recruited because of their experience in a particular location or industry. In practical terms, there has been an enormous increase in the application of IT over the last twenty years, so having a department with expertise in IT is often a very useful point to consider.

Suitability, acceptability and feasibility analysis can be effective when evaluating options in the MDCS exam. Of course, what matters is that the elements you discuss are actually relevant to the situation in the exam and the facts presented in the scenario.

7 Marketing strategy

You may be required in the MDCS examination to discuss **marketing strategy**. Marketing strategy is an important aspect of business strategy, especially for companies that operate in a competitive environment.

'Marketing is the management process responsible for identifying, anticipating and satisfying customer requirements profitably' (Chartered Institute of Marketing).

'The Marketing Concept holds that the key to achieving organisational goals lies in determining the needs and wants of target markets, and delivering the desired satisfactions, more efficiently and effectively than competitors' (Kotler, 1993).

Kotler identified four key concepts in marketing:

1.   Identifying target markets
2.   Determining the needs and wants of those markets
3.   Delivering a product offering which meets the needs and wants of those markets
4.   Meeting the needs of the market profitably – more efficiently and effectively than the competition

7.1 Market size

Market size refers to both actual and potential (forecast) size of the market for a product or service. A company cannot know whether its market share objectives for winning a share of the market are commercially feasible unless it knows the market's overall size and the position of competitors.

Forecasting growth and decline in a market is also important.

A distinction should be made between the overall expected size of the market and the portion of the market that the company can access. This is the **addressable market** that the company can plan to reach.

For a product to be made (or a service to be provided) and marketed by a company, there needs to be:

- A sizeable total market
- A sizeable addressable market and so, a share of the market that the company can hope to win
- Ideally, a reasonable rate of expected growth in the market
- An attractive profit pool in the selected market segment

Without a sizeable target market, it will be difficult for a company to achieve satisfactory profits (or even make a profit) with its products or services.

Analysing the addressable market and the company's share of the market may require segmentation into distinct and possibly related product and service revenue streams to fully understand strategic options and potential growth.

For example, a travel company will seek to understand the possible market for air travel separately to hotel accommodation even though customers often purchase these together. Furthermore, services such as car hire, travel insurance and airport transfers are related areas of value which customers often require, and which are capable of generating sizeable revenue and profit.

Further insight into understanding value within an addressable market can be gained using **profit pool mapping** (Harvard Business Review, 1998). Here, the **value chain analysis** is used to identify which activities are generating disproportionately large or small shares of profits. Additionally, a profit pool map opens a window onto the underlying structure of the industry.

The first step to completing a profit pool map is to identify all value chain activities. Then, the size of the attributed revenue and the profitability of the value generated are analysed. This process relies on the quality of the underlying financial information related to the industry and the company. However,

a high-level analysis is often sufficient for initial strategic thinking and decision making, as the activities which are generating most value and those which are not, can be identified.

7.2 Positioning strategies

Once a company has identified the different segments in a market, and selected its target market (customer segmentation), it then has to position its product or service in the market place. The objective of positioning is to create, and maintain, a distinctive place for the company and its products/services in its target market.

Positioning is 'the act of designing the company's offer and image so that it occupies a distinct and valued place in the target customers' mind' (Kotler and Keller, 2011).

Positioning strategies are based on the results of two key sets of choices:

- **Target markets** – **Where** a firm or brand wants to compete
- **Differential advantage** – **How** a firm or brand wants to compete (What advantages can it offer its customers that competitors cannot replicate?)

According to Kotler (1993), a brand is 'a name, term, sign, symbol or design or combination of them, intended to identify the goods or services of one seller or group of sellers and to differentiate them from those of competitors.'

Brands convey messages to customers, for example denoting quality or reliability, fashionability or tradition. Branding messages are usually qualitative rather than focusing on price. One advantage of branding is that by creating an 'identity' for a product, an organisation can reduce the importance of price differentials between their product and rival products and increase customer loyalty. The power of a brand is that it can facilitate premium pricing for a product, increase market share or even act as a barrier to entry, preventing potential entrants from entering a market. So branding is a form of product differentiation.

A 21st-century success story is the creation of the Red Bull brand, which projects an image of excitement, energy and increased performance. The Red Bull brand image is sustained by its marketing which includes sponsorship of extreme sports such as Formula One and the Air Race World Championship.

7.3 The marketing mix

The marketing mix consists of four core elements: product, price, place and promotion; supplemented by an additional three for the marketing of services: people, processes and physical evidence. Companies should develop operational plans for the marketing mix that are consistent with the unique selling proposition that the company wants to put to customers and its target position in the market.

A marketing mix for a company's products or services should be developed within broad strategies for pricing, distribution and promotion.

You may be required to demonstrate how a company could use the different elements of the mix (product, price, place and promotion – the 4Ps; plus, people, process, and physical evidence – the 7Ps) to help generate competitive advantage. The 4Ps apply to companies that make and sell products: the 7Ps apply to companies that sell services.

An important point to note here is that applying a unique (and appropriate) mix of the elements of the marketing mix within a given market allows a firm to compete more effectively, thereby helping it to generate sustainable profits.

The elements of the mix are summarised briefly here:

The 4Ps (products) and 7Ps (services) of the marketing mix

Element in the mix	Comment
Product	There is no point in making a product or trying to provide a service that nobody wants.
	The product (or service) is best considered as a collection of benefits, offered by the features that it provides. What features of the product or service are most critical to satisfying the customer's needs and providing customers with value?
Price	The only element of the mix to bring in revenue.
	Price is not solely determined by the cost of producing a good or service, but the value that the customer is prepared to pay for it. Price can be used to 'position' a product or service in the market, since customers often associate high prices with better quality or rarity value. Pricing must support the overall positioning of the product.
	Price includes rebates and discount schemes to incentivise the different distribution channels.
	Price also needs to reflect overall marketing objectives: For example, profit maximisation, or market share leadership; and needs to consider the strength of competition in the market and competitors' positions.
Place	'Place' covers:
	- Distribution channels (sales channels): Ways in which the company's products are sold to customers
	- Direct selling
	- Through intermediaries
	- Logistics between the producer and the end consumer. Logistics deals with transportation and storage.
	Companies need to decide how they plan to get their products to the buying public. Selling music or films online through downloads or streaming, for example, is an example of 'place' in the marketing mix.
Promotion	This includes advertising, public relations, personal selling and direct mail – in other words, all aspects of marketing communications.
In addition, for services:	
People	These include the people delivering a service. Inclusion of 'people' in the marketing mix reflects the fact that the consumer's perceived quality depends heavily on those providing the product/service. Staff selection, motivation of staff and customer care training are critically important for many companies.
Process	This is the process by which a product/service is provided. The process is sometimes referred to as the 'whole customer experience'. A customer of a top class restaurant, for example, experiences the food, the atmosphere, the surroundings, the service, and so on. Process can also refer to the efficiency of the service, and issues such as waiting times for service, the provision of information to customers and the helpfulness of staff.

Element in the mix	Comment
Physical evidence	A service is intangible. Physical evidence suggests that there is something to show for it. Examples of physical evidence include: • Evidence that the service has been performed. For financial services, you may receive a certificate notifying you that you have joined a scheme – a legal document entitling you to the service but not, usually, the service itself. • Testimonials or recommendations from someone who has used the service. For instance, feedback on the quality of nursing care provided in a hospital. • The environment of the service encounter. Layout and cleanliness are important physical aspects of the service and reinforce a family-friendly or caring image.

8 Operational analysis

It is likely you will be given information in the pre-seen of products and services provided by a business, the business processes which are undertaken to provide the business or service, details of the different departments involved and how they relate to each other, and how the business processes and controls its sales orders and the costs of providing its goods or services. This information can be analysed to develop a picture of transaction types and how well the company is controlling its business processes.

Operational analysis should be completed as part of your review of the pre-seen as it provides a structure to identify the key points and current issues relating to the internal operations of the company, the personnel responsible in each area of the business and the potential impact on the internal control and audit environment of any weaknesses identified.

This analysis is a starting point in evaluating the appropriateness and adequacy of business processes and assessing the effectiveness of elements of the internal control environment.

The pre-seen may also provide information from the company's internal and external auditors which can be used to identify internal control, audit and governance-related issues.

Operational analysis does not have a set format. However, one idea is to structure your operational analysis by considering the following five categories:

1. **Business transactions:** Types of business undertaken and, if provided, how related transactions are processed

2. **People:** The roles and responsibilities of the directors in the pre-seen scenario and any other key personnel identified in the scenario

3. **Internal control:** Significant internal controls in place, potential gaps in internal control and, if provided, details of any existing internal control issues

4. **Governance:** Details of significant industry regulation which the company in the scenario must comply with, where relevant, and details of any governance-related issues (such as evidence of board conflict or non-compliance with corporate governance codes)

5. **Audit:** Internal and external audit arrangements and details of any existing audit or governance-related issues

Completing operational analysis of the pre-seen will put you in a better position to understand and respond more quickly to new financial, internal control, governance or audit issues which arise in the unseen material provided with the exam requirements.

9 Analysing business risk

You may be required in the MDCS examination to comment on risk management as an element in business strategy formulation. For example, you may be required to identify significant risks facing a company and recommend an approach to managing the risk.

Companies cannot avoid risk. Some risk must be accepted in order to make a profit and return on investment. As a general rule, companies and investors should expect a higher investment return for accepting higher risks. The board of directors of a company should be aware of the risks facing their company and should decide the level of risks that they consider appropriate and acceptable.

Although some risk is unavoidable, business risks can be managed. Measures can be taken that reduce a company's exposure to risks. Some of these risk management measures have a cost, and decisions have to be taken about whether the cost of these measures is justified by the benefits of reduced risk.

9.1 Categories of business risk

Business risk is a general term for all risks facing a business. For the purpose of risk management, it is useful to analyse risks into different types or categories. A reminder about various categories of business risk is provided below.

Business risk can be divided into two main sub-categories: strategic risk and operational risks.

Strategic risk is the risk that arises from the nature of the business in which a company operates and its business environment (including its competitive environment). Factors that determine the level of strategic risks include:

- The types of industries/markets within which the business operates
- The state of the economy
- The actions of competitors and the possibility of mergers and acquisitions
- Product risk: The risk that customers will stop buying the company's products because they no longer provide value for the price
- The stage in a product's life cycle, with higher risks in the introductory and declining stages
- The dependence upon inputs with fluctuating prices, such as oil and other commodities
- The flexibility of production processes to adapt to different specifications or products
- The organisation's research and development capacity and ability to innovate
- The significance of new technology
- For companies that trade internationally, volatility in currency exchange rates
- For companies that have extensive debts, volatility in the level of interest rates
- Risks of losses from legal disputes

Companies cannot avoid strategic risks, because these risks are inherent in the business environment in which the company operates.

Operational risks are risks that arise from the possibility of errors or failures in operational systems.

Operational risks include:

- Losses from failures in the internal control system
- Non-compliance with regulations or internal procedures
- Information technology failures
- Human error and mistakes
- Loss of key-person risk
- Fraud
- Business interruptions, for example, due to a fire or flooding

Whereas strategic risks for a company arise in its business and competitive environment, operational risks are mostly risks of failure and loss arising within the company itself and its operations.

Procedures and controls can be designed to prevent failures due to operational risks, or to detect and correct failures that have occurred. Operational risks can therefore be controlled more effectively by management than strategic risks.

9.2 Financial risks

Financial risks are risks of a financial nature, and these may be operational risks or strategic risks.

Operational financial risks, arising from poor systems and procedures, IT failures, human error and criminal activity, include:

- Fraud
- Unintentional errors in recording accounting transactions in the accounting ledgers, leading to inaccurate financial statements
- Failure to collect money owed by credit customers
- Making unauthorised payments to suppliers
- Running out of cash to pay for expenditures

Some financial risks are longer-term and so, strategic in nature. Examples of **strategic financial risks** include credit risk, currency risk (or exchange risk) and interest rate risk.

9.3 Risk management systems

Risks should be managed. A risk management system may be described in terms of the '7Rs and 4Ts'. This system may be applied to both strategic risks and operational risks.

However, the total risk that a company is exposed to should be at a level that the board of directors considers appropriate.

The board should decide the amount of risk exposure that the company is prepared to accept in order to make the target return or profit. The level of risk that the board is prepared to accept is known as the company's **risk appetite**. Risk appetite usually refers to strategic risk, rather than operational risk.

A company should also have an established and formal system for managing its risks.

A risk management system is sometimes described in terms of the 7Rs and the 4Ts that make up the elements of the system.

An approach to risk management: The 7Rs and 4Ts

1	**R**ecognition or identification of risks
2	**R**anking or evaluation of risks: Prioritising risks to decide which require urgent treatment. Risks may be assessed on the basis of the probability that an adverse event will happen and the impact or loss that would result if an adverse event occurred
3	**R**esponding to, or treating, significant risks: • **T**olerate or accept: Do nothing new or different, or continue with present arrangements • **T**rim: Action to control or reduce the risk • **T**ransfer • **T**erminate or avoid
4	**R**esourcing controls: Providing resources for risk management
5	**R**eaction planning: Management must prepare plans for dealing with adverse events should they occur. Extreme forms of reaction planning include disaster recovery measures
6	**R**eporting and monitoring risk performance
7	**R**eviewing the risk management framework

9.4 Risk management policies

Risk management policies should be part of the strategic management for a company.

A suitable risk management policy should contain the 7Rs, as described above. An examination question may, however, focus more on the various methods of treating risks, and in particular, trimming or reducing risks to an acceptable level.

Appropriate measures for reducing risks vary with the type or nature of the risk. Examples of risk management or risk control methods include:

- More effective internal controls for reducing the risk of fraud and other operational irregularities, or detecting them when they have occurred
- Marketing policies to deal with competition risk
- Product/market diversification to deal with product risk

9.5 Enterprise risk management (ERM) system

The Committee of Sponsoring Organizations of the Treadway Commission COSO) is dedicated to providing thought leadership through the development of frameworks and guidance on enterprise risk management, internal control and fraud deterrence.

The COSO Enterprise Risk Management (ERM) guidance for organisations provides the framework to implement an integrated system for managing risk which covers the entire enterprise. This guidance is non-mandatory but is used by many organisations globally to implement a system to identity, evaluate and mitigate risk. The COSE framework has the following component elements which provide a good recommendation for companies that are finding it challenging to manage risk effectively.

- **Internal environment.** The internal environment is the culture of the organisation, its ethical values and its management philosophy and risk appetite. A control culture must start at the top of the organisation, with the directors and senior management.
- **Objective setting.** Objectives must be set for the organisation so that management can identify events that will affect their achievement.
- **Event/risk identification.** There must be procedures for regular identification of events that could affect the achievement of the organisation's objectives. COSO uses the term 'events' rather than 'risks', to cover both strategic opportunities as well as strategic threats and business risks.
- **Risk assessment.** There must be procedures for assessing risk – deciding how significant they are and prioritising them for treatment.
- **Risk response.** There must be a response to the risks that have been identified: Tolerate, trim, transfer or terminate.
- **Control activities.** Controls must be designed and implemented for managing risks.
- **Information and communication.** Relevant information about risk should be captured and communicated to the individuals responsible for managing them.
- **Monitoring.** The entire ERM system should be monitored continually, its effectiveness reviewed, and modifications made as and when necessary.

These components of risk management should be applied to **strategic risks** and also to **operational risks**, **reporting risks** (including financial reporting risks) and **risks of non-compliance** with relevant legislation and regulations.

This risk management framework should also operate, not only at the level of the organisation as a whole ('entity level'), but also at divisional, business unit and subsidiary level within a group of companies.

10 Managing stakeholder conflict

FAST FORWARD The fundamental objective of any organisation should be the maximisation of shareholders' wealth. In its purest sense, this means pursuing the maximum amount of profit from the organisation's operations. A threat to this objective is conflicting shareholder objectives.

Organisations must consider the interests of managers and owners may conflict so areas of conflict can be effectively managed. Shareholder wealth may be maximised by reducing the local workforce or changing the nature of the work done due to new technology being available. This would be perceived as a conflict with the goals of employee.

Separation of ownership from control

In most modern organisations the owners do not actually manage the company. Whilst the equity shareholders own the company, the day-to-day operations are managed on their behalf by the board of directors.

The directors and managers within the organisation have their own personal goals that may conflict with those of the shareholders. The problem that shareholders have is that they are seen as being passive stakeholders: that is, they do not (and are not expected to) contribute to business decisions that affect the company.

Whilst managers are privy to privileged information about the company, shareholders have to rely on publicly available details such as annual reports and press articles, a situation known as information asymmetry. As a result, managers are very much left to their own devices when making business decisions.

The relationship between management and shareholders is sometimes referred to as an agency relationship, in which managers act as agents for the shareholders. Here, there is separation of ownership from management is sometimes characterised as the 'agency problem' which is where shareholder conflict arises as a difference between the interests of managers and those of owners.

For example, if managers hold none or very little of the equity shares of the company they work for, what is to stop them from working inefficiently, not bothering to look for profitable new investment opportunities, or giving themselves high salaries and perks?

The goal of agency theory is to find governance structures and control mechanisms that minimise the problem caused by the separation of ownership and control. In that sense agency theory is the cornerstone of the theory of corporate governance. More specifically agency theory tries to find means for the owners to control the managers in such a way that the managers will operate in the interest of the shareholders.

Examples of conflicts of interest between managers and shareholders include:

Short-termism: There is evidence that in many companies the primary driver of decision-making has been to increase share prices and hence managerial rewards in the short term. The longer-term benefits of investment in research and development may be ignored in the short-term drive to cut costs and increase profits thus jeopardising the long-term prospects of the company.

Sales maximisation: This strategy is often employed by managers to increase market share and therefore the importance of the company within its sector. An increase in importance for the company will mean greater status for management but will not necessarily be in the best interests of the shareholders.

Overpriced acquisitions: Takeovers is another manifestation of the non-alignment of the interests of shareholders and managers. Managers have motives other than shareholder value maximisation and may choose to acquire another business to seek growth and status.

Resistance to takeovers: The management of a company may tend to resist takeovers if they feel that their position is threatened even if in doing so shareholder value is also reduced.

Relationships: Many companies' pursuit of short-term cost reduction may lead to difficult relationships with their wider stakeholders. Relationships with suppliers may be disrupted by demands for major improvements in terms and in reduction of prices. Employees may be made redundant in a drive to reduce costs and customers may be able to buy fewer product lines and have to face less favourable terms. These policies may aid short-term profits, but in the long-term suppliers and employees are able to take full advantage of market conditions and move to other companies, and customers can shop elsewhere or over the internet.

Avoiding risk: In order to maximise shareholder wealth in the long-term a company needs to evolve which means some risk must be taken. When managers' attitudes are conservative and risk-averse they are seeking the easiest path. Risk-averse managers seeks to avoid conflict or change because of the disruption it could cause. However, this may not be in the best interests of the shareholders.

Dividend policy: Managers may decide to maintain high dividend pay-outs in order to avoid resistance from the shareholders. This is not necessarily the best thing for shareholder wealth maximisation in the long-term as it may be better to invest in new technology so that new products can be made, or existing products made more effectively and efficiently.

10.1 Conflict between stakeholders

Although we discussed the conflict between managers and owners, there are other areas of potential conflict between managers, owners and other stakeholders who provide capital, namely the debt holders. The relationship between the long-term creditors of a company, the management and the shareholders of a company encompasses the following factors:

- Management may decide to raise finance for a company by taking out long or medium-term loans.

- Investors who provide debt finance will rely on the company's management to generate enough net cash inflows to make interest payments on time, and eventually to repay loans. Long-term creditors will often take security for their loan, perhaps in the form of a fixed charge over an asset (such as a mortgage on a building). Debentures are also often subject to certain restrictive covenants, which restrict the company's rights to borrow more money until the debentures have been repaid.

- The money that is provided by long-term creditors will be invested to earn profits, and the profits (in excess of what is needed to pay interest on the borrowing) will provide extra dividends or retained profits for the shareholders of the company. In other words, shareholders will expect to increase their wealth using creditors' money.

Sometimes, the needs of shareholders and debtholders may conflict:

- Managers may be tempted to take risky decisions using debtholders' money to finance them, knowing that the benefits of these decisions will accrue to the shareholders. If the projects go badly and the company fails, the debtholders may suffer a greater loss than the equity shareholders.

- In many jurisdictions there are rules limiting the proportion of company assets that can be paid out as dividends. However, it may still be possible to pay out lawfully considerable sums as dividends, enough to jeopardise the company's future and hence the amounts that the debtholders have advanced, should trading results turn bad in the near future.

- Shareholders and managers may wish to prolong the company's life as long as possible, whereas debtholders may wish to safeguard the amount loaned and realise their security as soon as the company appears to be getting into difficulties.

- Managers may attempt to undermine the position of debtholders by seeking further loan capital, committing the company to an increased interest burden and hence greater risk of insolvency. The additional loan capital may also have superior claims on the company's assets to the original amounts borrowed.

10.1.1 Strategies to manage stakeholder conflict

We will now show how ensuring goal congruence and enforcing corporate governance best practice can help manage conflict between different groups of stakeholders.

- **Reward systems:** Agency theory sees employees of businesses, including managers, as individuals, each with their own objectives. Within a department of a business, there are departmental objectives. Goal congruence between managers, directors and shareholders may be better dealt with by giving managers some profit-related pay, or by providing incentives which are related to profits or share price.

    Examples of such remuneration incentives are:

    – **Profit-related/economic value-added pay**

        Pay or bonuses related to the size of profits or economic value added

    – **Rewarding managers with shares**

        This might be done when a private company 'goes public' and managers are invited to subscribe for shares in the company at an attractive offer price. This means that directors and employees, as well as shareholders, have a stake in the long-term profitability of an organisation.

    – **Executive share options plans**

        In a share option scheme, selected employees are given a number of share options, each of which gives the holder the right after a certain date to subscribe for shares in the company at a fixed price. The value of an option will increase if the company is successful, and its share price goes up.

- **Separation of roles and corporate governance:** Complying with corporate governance principles ensured that not too much power accrues to a single individual within an organisation which increases the risk of disagreement between a chief executive offers and the board of directors, the company shareholders and the employees. Also, the adoption of a corporate governance framework of decision making will restrict the power of managers and increase the role of independent non-executive directors in key decisions.

- **Negotiation:** Stakeholder conflict between shareholders and directors can be resolved by negotiating contracts that allow the principal to control the agent in such a way to ensure that the agent will operate in the interests of the principal. Also, a board of directors may schedule regular investors updates which allow key investors to voice their concerns and to provide feedback on strategic decisions made by a board of directors. Differences of opinion between a company and its customers or suppliers can also be resolved by negotiation of contractual terms, price or deliverables.

- **Self-regulation:** A voluntary code of conduct is a statement by an organisation of the standards by which it seeks to do business. Codes are usually developed by a trade association and individual members incorporate the code into the dealings they have with their customers. Organisations in some business sectors self-regulate their dealings by voluntary codes of conduct. Voluntary codes usually include a mechanism for resolving disputes through arbitration.

10.2 Enhancing stakeholder engagement

Key term

> **Stakeholder engagement:** Stakeholder engagement is the process of involving all parties affected by a company's operations in its decision-making processes.

Each stakeholder group has different expectations about what it wants and different claims on the organisation, and therefore, it is essential that organisations engage in active dialogue, assess these diverse needs, and implement strategies that balance these interests while aligning with their ethical and corporate responsibilities.

Integrating sustainability into business practice requires a robust framework of corporate accountability and proactive stakeholder engagement.

Organisations that embrace these principles not only enhance their reputations and build trust but also drive long-term sustainable value for all stakeholders. By doing so, they contribute to a more sustainable and equitable world, addressing critical global challenges such as climate change, social inequality, and environmental degradation.

10.2.1 Donaldson and Preston's stakeholder engagement theory

According to Donaldson and Preston's stakeholder engagement theory, businesses have a duty to consider the interests of all their stakeholders, not just shareholders and argue that organisations have a responsibility to balance the needs and expectations of these diverse groups of stakeholders to achieve sustainability. (Source: Donaldson, T., and Preston, L. E. (1995) The Stakeholder Theory of the Corporation: Concepts, Evidence, and Implications. *Academy of Management Review*, 20(1), 65–91.)

Donaldson and Preston (1995) theory to stakeholder engagement is divided into three interrelated perspectives:

Perspectives of stakeholder engagement	Description
Normative approach	The **normative approach** asserts that considering stakeholders' interests is inherently the right thing to do. It is based on ethical principles and the intrinsic value of treating all stakeholders with respect and fairness.
Descriptive Approach	The **descriptive approach** describes how companies actually operate, showing that businesses naturally interact with various stakeholders and that these interactions influence corporate behaviour.
Instrumental Approach	The **instrumental approach** perspective suggests that attending to stakeholders' interests can lead to better business outcomes, such as increased loyalty, improved reputation, and long-term profitability.

10.2.2 Enhancing stakeholder engagement

Effective stakeholder engagement enhances corporate accountability by ensuring that boards of directors take stakeholder expectations and feedback seriously which means a company actions are much more likely to align with stakeholder needs and wider societal values.

Conversely, by implementing corporate accountability practices delivers the drivers for organisations to invest in meaningful stakeholder engagement.

Therefore, organisations require a methodology to achieve effective stakeholder engagement. Donaldson and Preston (1995) theory of stakeholder engagement recommends the following three stages.

1. **Identify key stakeholders**

    Organisations must recognise the diverse groups affected by their actions, including employees, customers, suppliers, local communities, and investors.

2. **Deploy stakeholder engagement strategies**

    Effective stakeholder engagement involves open communication, transparency, and responsiveness. Organisations use various methods such as surveys, public consultations, and social media platforms to engage with stakeholders.

3. **Integrate stakeholder feedback to organisation's strategic and operational objectives**

   Organisations should evaluate then incorporate feedback from stakeholders into their strategic planning and operations.

10.3 Stakeholders and social responsibility

FAST FORWARD

An organisation's ethical stance relates to how it **views its responsibilities** to shareholders, stakeholders, society and the environment and is intertwined with the principle of corporate accountability.

Remember, corporate accountability is the principle that organisations (and their directors) should act ethically and be answerable to their stakeholders for the consequences of their actions, decisions, policies and impacts on society and the environment.

Key terms

Social costs: Are defined as the tangible and intangible costs and losses sustained by third parties or the general public as a result of economic activity, for example pollution by industrial effluent.

Social responsibility: Is the principle that organisations should act in a manner which benefits society as well as meeting strategic and financial objectives.

The primary purpose of a business organisation is to make profits, thereby increasing the wealth of its owners, the shareholders. Businesses do not, however, exist in splendid isolation; they are dependent on the society in which they operate, and they should therefore contribute to that society. Businesses make use at least in part of the infrastructure of the country or countries in which they operate, for example roads, utilities and other social goods paid for through taxation. For this reason, it can be seen as only fair that businesses are aware of their social responsibility, and their ethical reputation can depend on the extent to which they take this responsibility seriously.

By implementing corporate accountability and social responsibility principles, organisations can make a positive impact on local and global communities by addressing identified social costs.

Businesses that implement a social responsibility initiative that's in line with their values can benefit by improve reputation and increased customer loyalty.

10.4 Social responsibility stances – Gray, Owen and Adams (1996)

Gray, Owen and Adams in their book *Accounting and Accountability* (1996) identify seven viewpoints of social responsibility. Gray, Owen and Adams social responsibility framework can be applied to analyse the potential viewpoints and reactions of key stakeholders.

The seven viewpoints are:

1. Pristine capitalists
2. Expedients
3. Proponents of the social contract
4. Social ecologists
5. Socialists
6. Radical feminists
7. Deep ecologists

Viewpoint	Explanation
1. **Pristine capitalists**	**The private property system** is the best system; companies exist to **maximise profits** and **seek economic efficiency**. Businesses therefore have **no moral responsibilities** beyond their obligations to shareholders and creditors. Pursuing the objectives of stakeholders other than shareholders, and thus reducing shareholder wealth, is theft from shareholders. Shareholders have risked their money to become legal owners, and therefore they should determine objectives and strategies.
2. **Expedients**	Economic systems do generate some **excesses**; therefore businesses have to accept some (limited) **social legislation and moral requirements** if such behaviour is in **the business's economic interests**.
3. **Proponents of the social contract**	Organisations should behave in a way that is broadly in conformance with the ethical norms in society because there is effectively a **contract or agreement** between the **organisations** in power and those who are **affected by the exercise of this power**. A business effectively enjoys a licence to operate. However, this licence will only continue to be granted by society if the business's actions deserve it. A business may therefore have to deliver benefits (or avoid causing harm) to society in general. It may also be responsible for delivering benefits to the specific groups from whom it derives its power (such as customers or employees).
4. **Social ecologists**	Businesses leave a social and environmental footprint. In particular, problems exist with the human environment that large organisations have created and need to eradicate. Economic processes that result in **resource exhaustion, waste and pollution** must be **modified**. Organisations must adopt socially responsible positions accordingly. This may involve going beyond what is required or regarded as desirable by society.
5. **Socialists**	Socialists see the business framework as one class (capitalists) manipulating and oppressing another class (workers and the socially oppressed). Business therefore acts to **concentrate wealth** in society. Business decision making should no longer be determined by the requirements of capitalism and materialism but should **promote equality**. Policies to enhance corporate social responsibility will fail if they continue to take place in the existing framework. Business should be conducted in a fundamentally different way, to redress the imbalances in society and provide benefits to many stakeholders, not just finance providers.
6. **Radical feminists**	Economic and social systems privilege masculine qualities such as aggression, conflict and competition over **feminine values such as co-operation and reflection**. Developing corporate social responsibility in the existing masculine framework will not work. A fundamental readjustment is required in the culture and structure of society with potentially far-reaching implications for accountability relationships. Society needs to emphasise qualities traditionally seen as feminine, such as equality, dialogue, compassion and fairness.
7. **Deep ecologists**	Human beings have **no greater right to resources or life** than other species and do not have the rights to subjugate social and environmental systems. Economic systems that trade off threats to the existence of species against economic objectives are **immoral**. Arguably, businesses cannot be trusted to maintain something as important as the environment. Existing economic systems are beyond repair as they are based on the wrong values, privileging humans over non-humans. A full recognition of all stakeholders would mean that business had to be conducted in a completely different way. This viewpoint is connected with ideas on sustainability which are covered next.

The examination team may ask you to discuss situations using Gray, Owen and Adams' positions, for example asking you how different positions would rank stakeholder concerns about a business development.

Step 1 Analysing the scenario

You need to look out in the scenario for key information that is relevant to each position, such as:

Viewpoint	Explanation
1. Pristine capitalists	The financial implications of the decision, and the extent to which each stakeholder can influence the level of profits made
2. Expedients	Society's current views on social responsibility, also what the impact on profits will be of not being seen as socially responsible (the significance of reputation risk and strategic positioning)
3. Proponents of the social contract	Impact on the community as a whole, groups of different stakeholders within the community, the position of local or national government, importance of relationships with the local community
4. Social ecologists	Impact (footprint) on the environment, the problems caused by the business
5. Socialists	Indications that the owners are benefiting at the expense of the employees
6. Radical feminists	Adverse impact of competition or aggressive behaviour by businesses, signs feminine values are being exploited for profit
7. Deep ecologists	Adverse impact on any aspect of the natural environment, signs of the natural world being exploited for profit, suggestions that economic objectives are being compared with environmental objectives

Step 2 Constructing your answer

Your answer will need to focus on factors that are relevant to each position.

Viewpoint	Explanation
1. Pristine capitalists	Concentrate on how shareholders' wealth can be maximised – other stakeholders will only be important if they threaten shareholder wealth
2. Expedients	Demonstrate how business will gain advantages for itself if it responds to corporate responsibility concerns; show how business should cope with trading off economic values with social responsibilities
3. Proponents of the social contract	Bring out society's norms and beliefs and the need for business to act in accordance with them; show how the business can serve interests of different groups in society and, if necessary, reconcile competing interests
4. Social ecologists	Concentrate on how the business should solve the human and environmental problems its activities cause and the changes necessary in business, economic and accounting practice
5. Socialists	Focus on ways workers are being treated unfairly; suggest methods of remedying inequalities including political and organisational change
6. Radical feminists	Highlight problems with pursuit of economic advantage and conflict, ways competition is unfairly promoted over co-operation/nurturing/family, or ways that feminine qualities (non-confrontation, co-operation) are being exploited for profit
7. Deep ecologists	Concentrate on showing how business activities inevitably impact on the natural environment and that they wrongly prioritise human needs over other needs

The question below is an example of a scenario which applied Gray, Owen and Adams social responsibility viewpoints.

Question

Leavis is a well-established firm of recruitment consultants, operating in the capital city of its home country. At its most recent board meeting, the human resources director raised several alarming concerns regarding the company's workforce. Over the past few months, Leavis has experienced an unexpected surge in the resignation of experienced staff, particularly among female employees. Upon investigation, it was suggested that these employees had been pressured into taking on additional work outside of their standard duties, often during antisocial hours that conflicted with the terms of their employment contracts. Several female employees reportedly undertook these tasks out of fear for their job security, feeling that refusal could result in the termination of their employment.

Adding to these concerns, a growing number of female staff have voiced frustrations over pay inequality. Skilled female consultants have raised complaints that they are being compensated at lower rates than their male counterparts for performing the same tasks. The HR director, while acknowledging the disparity, justified the difference by explaining that male employees had taken on additional responsibilities. This rationale, however, has sparked friction between staff, contributing to a rising wave of absenteeism and a noticeable drop in both productivity and, more critically, the quality of work. There is growing concern that this deterioration in work standards could threaten Leavis' reputation for excellence.

The issue has caught the attention of the chief executive, who is particularly concerned about the potential impact on Leavis' ability to defend its coveted 'Consultant of the Year' title, an accolade the firm earned primarily due to its stellar quality of service. Both the CEO and the director of quality management are heavily invested in maintaining this title, as they received substantial bonuses for the achievement last year. Failing to maintain the firm's high standards, therefore, poses a direct threat not only to the firm's reputation but also to executive rewards.

Additionally, the country in which Leavis operates has been compliant with the European Union's social chapter for several years, meaning that the company is expected to uphold strict regulations regarding workers' rights, gender equality, and fair treatment in the workplace. This adds a legal dimension to the company's growing HR issues, as failing to comply with these regulations could expose Leavis to legal risks, regulatory fines, or reputational damage.

Required

Compare and contrast how Gray, Owen and Adams' seven stakeholder positions on social responsibility would affect responses to stakeholder concerns about this situation.

Answer

In the case of Leavis, the recruitment consultancy facing staff retention issues, pay disparities, and concerns over antisocial working hours, we can evaluate stakeholder concerns and the possible responses to the situation by using the seven stakeholder positions on social responsibility proposed by Gray, Owen, and Adams. Each viewpoint provides a different lens through which to analyse the issues of employment conditions, gender pay inequality, and the conflict between business profitability and employee well-being.

Each of the seven stakeholder positions would offer different responses to the issues at Leavis:

- **Pristine capitalists** would prioritise profit and compliance only when legally necessary.
- **Expedients** would take a pragmatic approach, seeking to balance legal, reputational, and economic concerns.
- **Proponents of the social contract** would encourage balancing employee welfare with business objectives.
- **Social ecologists** would advocate for a sustainable, long-term approach that values employee well-being.
- **Socialists** would call for a shift in power, advocating for collective worker decision-making.

- **Radical feminists** would focus on restructuring the workplace to ensure gender equality and work-life balance.
- **Deep ecologists** would advocate for a more holistic, sustainable approach to business that promotes harmony between work and personal life.

Viewpoint	Explanation
1. **Pristine capitalists**	Pristine capitalists view employees as economic assets whose primary function is to serve the company's economic objectives. From this perspective, Leavis' management would focus solely on the company's financial success and efficiency. Female employees leaving, lower pay rates for women, and poor working conditions are not moral or ethical concerns, but purely economic ones.
	Pristine capitalists would likely argue that Leavis should continue the practice of demanding additional hours from staff if it maximises productivity and reduces labour costs. They would not be concerned with complaints of gender pay disparity unless legal risks or fines related to non-compliance with equality laws would lead to greater costs than simply maintaining the current structure. Therefore, they might advocate compliance with anti-discrimination and labour laws only to the extent that the penalties for violating such laws outweigh the economic benefits of cost-cutting.
2. **Expedients**	Expedients act based on pragmatism. They will follow ethical or legal guidelines if these have clear consequences for business survival, but are less likely to do so out of a sense of moral duty. They are focused on preserving the company's reputation and avoiding public backlash.
	From the expedient perspective, Leavis would be concerned about maintaining its public image and defending its 'Consultant of the Year' title, which directly contributes to business success. They might advocate addressing the complaints about pay disparity and antisocial hours only because these issues could lead to poor employee morale, productivity declines, or even bad press, which could tarnish the company's reputation. Leavis would likely introduce superficial changes to ensure that they meet the minimum legal and ethical standards, without fully addressing the root causes of employee dissatisfaction.
3. **Proponents of the social contract**	Proponents of the social contract believe that businesses exist within society and should act in accordance with the implicit agreement that they have obligations to society, including their employees. This viewpoint balances economic success with social responsibility.
	From this position, Leavis would be encouraged to address the complaints of gender inequality and poor working conditions seriously. The company would view the fair treatment of employees as a necessary part of maintaining the social contract with its workforce. Management would consider revising employment contracts to ensure fair pay for all employees, regardless of gender, and ensure that working hours align with the work-life balance expectations of their staff. They would also implement measures to prevent fear of job loss from being used to coerce employees into unfair working conditions.

Viewpoint	Explanation
4. **Social ecologists**	Social ecologists focus on the interdependence between society, business, and the environment. They advocate for sustainable practices that benefit both people and the planet, emphasising long-term impacts over short-term gains. Social ecologists would likely argue that Leavis' current business practices, such as requiring antisocial hours and maintaining gender pay disparities, are unsustainable in the long run. They would recommend fostering a healthier, more balanced working environment by promoting gender equality and ensuring that employees have sufficient time for personal well-being and family life. They would also suggest that creating a fairer, more inclusive workplace would enhance employee satisfaction and productivity, ultimately leading to better long-term business performance.
5. **Socialists**	Socialists emphasise worker rights and advocate for equal distribution of power and decision-making in the workplace. They see unequal treatment and labour exploitation as consequences of capitalist structures that prioritise profits over people. From a socialist viewpoint, Leavis' issues stem from an imbalance of power between management and workers. The company's ability to impose unfair working hours and unequal pay on its employees is seen as an abuse of its economic power. Socialists would argue for a fundamental shift in decision-making processes, giving employees – especially female employees – a direct role in setting their own working conditions. They would advocate for collective bargaining or worker representation to ensure that pay and working hours are determined democratically, rather than imposed unilaterally by management.
6. **Radical feminists**	Radical feminists critique the existing capitalist structures that lead to gender inequality and exploitation in the workplace. They argue that businesses often prioritise economic goals over the well-being of women, family life, and other non-economic values. Radical feminists would argue that the gender pay disparity at Leavis is a direct result of patriarchal structures within the workplace. They would advocate for a complete restructuring of the company's priorities, placing greater emphasis on equality, fairness, and work-life balance. Rather than treating the issue as a simple matter of compliance with anti-discrimination laws, they would call for a cultural change within the company, promoting flexibility, family-friendly policies, and equality. They would also push for policies that value personal well-being and discourage excessive work hours, particularly when these conflict with personal responsibilities.
7. **Deep ecologists**	Deep ecologists focus on a holistic view of business and society, promoting harmony between people and the environment. They believe that businesses should support natural systems and human well-being, not disrupt them for short-term gains. Deep ecologists would view Leavis' practices of overworking employees and ignoring their well-being as inherently unsustainable and harmful to the broader social ecosystem. They would argue that the company needs to adopt practices that respect the natural rhythms of life, such as ensuring adequate rest, promoting mental and physical health, and valuing personal time. The current focus on productivity at the expense of employees' well-being would be seen as destructive. Deep ecologists would advocate for a complete rethinking of the company's goals, suggesting that long-term success can only be achieved by aligning the business with the well-being of its workers and the broader community.

11 Summary guide to completing a review of the business environment

You will be required to demonstrate your ability to assess the business environment and appraise the current business strategy for an organisation, based on information provided in a pre-seen case study. This section contains advice in the form of a checklist to help you improve your skills in this area before you practise the end of chapter question.

First, identify the facts in the case study that may be important, and which you may be expected to comment on in a report. It is assumed here that the organisation in the case study is a company operating a commercial business.

Establishing the facts: Extract facts from the case study that may be important		
What is the company's business?	How many products or services does it sell? Does it have more than one operating division?	If there are two or more divisions in the business, in what ways do they differ?
	Does the business have any foreign operations or foreign subsidiaries? If so, in what countries?	Managing foreign businesses can be difficult, because people and operations in another country may be difficult to control effectively. There may also be problems with foreign currency risk.
	What are conditions in the company's markets?	Is the market growing in size? Or is it reaching peak level for sales demand and at risk of going into decline? How is the market changing? How are economic conditions affecting the state of the market? Is there anything unique about the company's markets and products? (For example, commodity markets are exposed to volatile prices – large increases or falls in price in a relatively short time.)
	Product portfolio	How many different products or services does the company sell? Where are they in their product life cycle? (New, growth, maturity, decline?) Are some products more profitable than others?
	The business environment	Is there any significant factor in the general business environment that affects the company? Political conditions? Technological change? Legal and regulatory conditions?
	Who are the main competitors?	Are competitors performing better or worse? Are there reasons why competitors are performing better or worse? Is there a risk of a new competitor entering the market?

Establishing the facts: Extract facts from the case study that may be important		
	Does the case study indicate any other problems for the company and its business operations?	Are there any problems in the company's value chain – for example, problems with IT systems, purchasing methods, delivery systems, marketing, manufacturing operations?
		Are there any problems with suppliers and the company's supply chain?
		Are there any problems with the work force, such as shortage of key skills, high labour turnover, poor productivity?
		Is the company operating at or near capacity levels? If so, it will need new investment to expand further.

Second, establish whether the company appears to have a strategic objective. It is often assumed that a company will want to grow its business, increasing sales and profits. However, this is not always the main issue.

What are the current business objectives?		
Growth?	How may the company achieve growth successfully?	By selling more of existing products in existing markets. This is likely to be a suitable strategy when the overall market is growing in size, or if the company can see a way of gaining market share.
		By selling existing products in new markets? Foreign expansion is a possibility, although possibly a risky strategy.
		By selling new products to existing customers? How would this be achieved? Which new products? Will there be sufficient demand from customers?
		By diversifying into new products and new market areas? Likely to be a risky strategy.
		Through acquisition or organic growth of the business? Is organic growth a realistic possibility? An acquisition strategy can be risky: In practice, many fail to achieve the intended benefits.
Cost leadership or differentiation strategy?	If cost leadership, how can the company remain the least-cost producer? If differentiation, how successful is the company in differentiating its products from those of competitors?	
	Strategy to avoid making a loss?	Consider selling off or closing down unprofitable operations. Consider ways of reducing costs.

Third, consider whether the case study data contains anything about risk, risk management and governance.

What are the risks in the business and how are they being managed?		
What may go wrong (or what opportunities may arise) externally?	What are the threats and opportunities in the company's markets?	
What may go wrong (or what may be exploited to better effect) internally?	What are the weaknesses and strengths in the company's resources?	
Are there problems with governance?	Who are the company's leaders? Who makes the key decisions?	Are there any potential problems with corporate governance? A dominant leader? Potential problems with an ageing leader and no obvious successor? Inadequate risk management?

End of chapter question

Well Being Ltd (WBL) is a UK based company that has enjoyed strong growth since it was founded twelve years ago by Janet Hunter. It originally consisted of a single beauty clinic, but has since expanded to provide a range of health and beauty services and products in a number of clinics, health spas, fitness centres and retail outlets.

Janet Hunter herself is WBL's chief executive officer (CEO) and much of the success of the company has been attributed to her drive, personality and public image.

The company obtained a stock market listing three years ago and Janet Hunter retained 34% of the company's shares during the IPO and she still holds these shares.

WBL's operations are organised into four operating divisions, as follows:

- **Beauty clinics.** The company has a number of beauty clinics within the UK, where treatments are provided to predominantly female clients although demand from men is increasing. All clinics are equipped with advanced technology and provide treatments that range in complexity. Most staff are employed within a single clinic, but the company employs two cosmetic surgeons who carry out low-risk operations at a number of clinics within the division.

- **Health spas.** WBL also operates a small number of up-market health spas, where clients can relax and receive massage treatments or instruction in yoga, in luxurious surroundings. All health spas have hydrotherapy jet baths.

- **Fitness centres.** For the more physically active, WBL operates a number of fitness centres, with gym facilities and Pilates classes. Some of the fitness centres have a swimming pool.

- **Retail products.** Three years ago, WBL acquired a chain of retail shops selling health and beauty products. Retail sales have grown strongly in the three years since acquiring the stores, but there has been no addition to the number of stores. The retail products division, as well as selling products to the public, also acts as central purchaser and supplier of products for the beauty clinics and health spas within WBL.

Three of these divisions have been achieving growth in sales and profits in the past three years. Beauty clinics and health spas have both been growing at about 5% per year for the past three years, and revenue growth in retail products has been 8% per year. However, revenue at fitness centres has fallen by 5% per year in the same period, and this division made a small loss in 2019.

The market for health and beauty services and products

WBL is the largest health and beauty services company in the UK, and the only listed company in its industry. The market in general is very fragmented, and most competitors are fairly small businesses operating just one centre or clinic, or a small chain of salons. Janet Hunter is surprised that some competitors have not copied the example of WBL and sought to grow their business by increasing the number of salons that they operate. The board of directors of WBL has already had strategy discussions about expanding the business into one or more other countries, possibly Bulgaria and Thailand.

WBL has established a reputation for very high-quality services, and its services are priced at the high end of the market range. In general, this does not appear to have had any effect on sales or sales growth; but in the past year or so, sales revenue in WBL's fitness centres has fallen. Management are not aware of any competitor gaining market share, and they are of the opinion that falling revenues are attributable to difficult economic conditions. Customers, they believe, are reducing their discretionary spending and visiting fitness centres less frequently.

Sales revenue for the other three divisions, however, does not seem to have been adversely affected by changing economic conditions. Beauty clinics and retail sales have even shown strong growth in the past financial year. As the number of wealthy families in the UK continues to grow, demand for beauty

treatments and products has increased and increasing demand is expected to continue over the next few years. WBL faces a potential capacity problem at its clinics and spas, because it will be unable to meet the growth in demand without opening new centres or expanding capacity at existing ones.

The high quality of WBL's services, combined with the strong brand recognition that the company enjoys, explains why the company's beauty centres and health spas operate at full capacity for most of the year. Some clinics and health spas have taken bookings up to 18 months ahead.

Staff turnover in WBL is quite high. The company trains its staff to a high standard but opportunities for career development within the company are limited. Skilled employees may therefore leave to join another health and beauty company, or to set up their own business. The median length of service among current employees, excluding management, is less than three years.

Men's grooming

Over the past decade, the UK has developed a booming beauty industry, and this has the potential to boost consumer interest in related services such as health spas and cosmetic procedures. The interest is mainly with women, but interest is growing amongst men too.

Major global producers of beauty and health products see the UK as a hub for the redistribution of their products to other countries in the region. It has been estimated that in spite of slow economic conditions, the cosmetics and beauty industry in the UK is set to grow by about 4% each year for the next few years – and even faster if the economy picks up.

With the industry's immense growth potential, there are huge opportunities for providers of both health and beauty services and products.

Trends

- Consumers are opening up and accepting the idea of men's skin care. Men are more image-conscious and showing a greater interest in personal grooming. In addition, companies are expanding into men's grooming as female grooming is increasingly fragmented and mature.

Competitive landscape

- Procter & Gamble remains the top player. This reflects the large presence of Gillette in men's shaving. The brand has retained its leading place in men's shaving due to its strong brand positioning and wide distribution network. In addition, Gillette offers an extensive range of men's razors and blades to meet the needs of different consumers.

Prospects

- Men's grooming is projected to see a constant value growth of 1% over the forecast period. With the higher demand for men's grooming products, companies are expected to expand their men's lines, especially skin care products, over the forecast period.

Information about Bulgaria's spa industry

It's no longer unusual to seek out a favourite spa to enjoy a relaxing massage after a day of sitting behind a desk at work. To many professionals living and working in corporate Bulgaria, the many spas in the country offer a quick respite to their stressful corporate lives.

The spa industry is now considered one of the fastest growing economic sectors in Bulgaria, as it has grown 16% in the last five years, according to industry estimates.

With that in mind, the Ministry of Tourism is expecting the spa industry to help make tourism the fifth largest income earner for the country by the year 2025.

The ministry wants to increase its tourism receipts by getting tourists to spend more. Currently, tourists spend about BGN56 billion a year in Bulgaria and the aim is to increase that spending to BGN168 billion by 2023. Two years ago, the Bulgaria Spa Council, which is made up of members of the spa industry and related government agencies, was established to address matters concerning the remaking of the local spa industry.

In the process, the Bulgaria Spa Council created an official criteria rating for spas which is now used by the Ministry of Tourism and Culture. The idea is to elevate the local spa industry to one that meets international standards and attract higher tourist volumes.

Email from Janet Hunter to the other members of the board of directors, 30 March 2019

As you know, I want the board to carry out a strategic review. The company needs to take some new initiatives if it is going to continue growing, and I think it is time that we made some strategic decisions. For our next board meeting, I would like us to discuss the following four strategic options.

Strategy 1: WBL to open a new range of clinics for men. As you know, WBL's beauty clinics are exclusively for women. We probably agree that women will not want to share treatment facilities with men. However, market research indicates that there is a growing demand for hair and facial treatments, foot reflexology and a range of massage services among men. WBL could tap into the potential of growing male demand.

Strategy 2: Expand by opening beauty clinics in one or more other countries. WBL has a strong reputation here in the UK, and we can use this to expand internationally. To internationalise our business and establish operations in Bulgaria, and possibly even China, WBL should look for a suitable acquisition target.

Strategy 3: In view of the falling profits at our fitness centres, WBL should sell them or shut them down. Any cash from sales should be reinvested by acquiring new properties to open more clinics in the UK.

Strategy 4: Economic conditions are not ideal for expansion and growth at the moment and WBL should therefore focus on efficiency improvements and cost reductions until the economy shows signs of revival. If the company can achieve better profits and cash flows, it will be in a better position to undertake a growth strategy in the future when the economy begins to recover.

I shall be interested to hear what you think.

Janet

Requirement

Assess the pros and cons for each of the strategies proposed by Janet and briefly suggest any alternative strategies (without providing justification) that the board may wish to consider.

Suggested answer

The first step in preparing an answer to the requirements is to extract information that might be of some relevance.

Establishing the facts: Extract facts from the case study that may be important	
What is the company's business?	Four operating divisions: 1. Beauty clinics for women 2. Health spas 3. Fitness centres, some with swimming pools 4. Retailing health and beauty products. Division also acts as central buyer of products/materials for other divisions. Materials purchased from fashion houses in Hong Kong and France.
	At the moment, the company does not appear to have any operations outside the UK.
	Conditions in the market: Growth in beauty clinics, spas and retail. Decline in fitness centres, and small loss in this division.
	The business environment: Growth in three divisions may be connected to increasing numbers of wealthy individuals. Growing interest in skin care and grooming for men: Growth in spas in Bulgaria. Forecast growth of 4% per year in cosmetics industry in UK.
	The company's products and services: (a) Product differentiation: High-end prices (b) Strong reputation and brand awareness (UK)
	Who are the main competitors? WBL is the market leader in UK for clinics: Competitors are small and do not seem to be pursuing growth strategies. Possible threat of new (foreign company) entrants into the market.
	Problems with business operations: (a) Loss-making fitness centres division (b) High rate of staff turnover. Trained staff join competitors

What are the current business objectives?	
Growth?	The company is considering growth in its clinics and spas divisions. Not clear what the strategy is for retailing division. Two growth strategies are suggested: • Strategy 1. Open clinics for men. New customers, probably also new products/services. Therefore, a form of diversification – risky strategy? • Strategy 2. Expansion into Bulgaria or China, through acquisitions. Existing products, but new markets.
Cost leadership or differentiation strategy?	Differentiation
Strategy to avoid making a loss?	Consider selling or closing down fitness centres Consider ways of reducing costs

What are the risks in the business and how are they being managed?	
Are there problems with governance?	Janet Hunter is chairperson, CEO and major shareholder. Possible concentration of power bad for governance. Will other shareholders support a risky growth strategy?

Your own ideas may differ from those suggested briefly here.

Assessment of strategies

Strategy 1: WBL to open a new range of clinics for men

This will involve providing new products/services to new customers. Although WBL has experience in health services, it has not offered them to men. This is a form of diversification that could be risky, unless started on a fairly small scale (to limit the risk).

WBL should try to learn more about the market potential first (market research).

Strategy 2: Expand by opening beauty clinics in one or more other countries

Entering foreign markets is a way of growing the business.

However, foreign expansion can be difficult for management to control. For example, cultural problems can arise when acquiring foreign subsidiaries.

Successful acquisitions can also be difficult to achieve: In many cases, buyers pay too much for target companies. Are there any suitable acquisition targets?

Also lack of knowledge of foreign markets. Market research needed, to assess prospects.

Strategy 3: WBL to shut down or sell off fitness centres

Is there a potential buyer?

Costs of shutting down, if no buyer can be found?

Are current losses a short-term problem, and are there good prospects for recovery in sales and profits?

Strategy 4: WBL should seek to consolidate its position

The business has been growing in three of its divisions: Why are growth prospects believed to be poor?

It is possible to seek productivity improvements and grow the business at the same time?

Cutting costs should not be achieved by reducing the quality of services provided to customers.

Alternative strategies

Here are three suggestions:

1. The company has been growing successfully in three divisions, in its UK operations, but is near full capacity. There should be opportunities for growth by expanding capacity in the UK, with new or larger clinics, spas and retail outlets. Growth in the UK may be less risky than foreign acquisitions.

2. Retailing strategy. Expand the range of products sold through WBL retail outlets. If Procter & Gamble products are the market leaders, consider stocking and selling these products, in addition to the current product ranges.

3. Employee strategy. High labour turnover among trained staff may be a problem. Consider a strategy for retaining staff, such as remuneration incentives. Higher pay may encourage staff to stay with the company.

Financial statement analysis

Topic list	Syllabus reference
1 Financial statement analysis	LO1
2 Approach to financial statement analysis for the MDCS examination	LO1
3 Initial analysis	LO1
4 Analysing sales and profitability	LO1
5 Analysing the statement of financial position	LO1
6 Analysing cash flow	LO1
7 Accounting choices, judgments and estimates	LO1
8 Differences between actual performance and expected financial performance	LO1
9 Performance for shareholders	LO1
10 Summary advice for financial statement analysis in MDCS	LO1

Introduction

The MDCS pre-seen will include historical financial information about the company and additional financial information is likely to be provided in the unseen providing more detailed and/or up to-date financial data.

The unseen may indicate a significant change in the company's financial performance and position or provide detailed financial insight into a particular issue or opportunity which you will be expected to analyse and discuss in your answer.

1 Financial statement analysis

One of your tasks in the MDCS examination may be to present in your report an analysis of the financial position and prospects for the company.

Financial statement analysis is an evaluation and explanation of the financial and other information contained in the financial statements (including summary statements, management accounts, budgets and forecasts) of a business. The analysis covers the following areas of performance and financial position:

- **Financial performance**: Analysis of information in the statement of profit or loss and other comprehensive income. The statement of profit or loss may be shown separately from other comprehensive income.
- **Financial position**: Analysis of the statement of financial position
- **Cash flow**: Analysis of the statement of cash flows
- **Notes**: Further detailed analysis of a particular balance or relevant disclosures

Analytical procedures involve the assessment of relationships between different items of data in the financial statements, often using ratio measurements. The purpose of the analysis is to identify areas of strength or weakness and increasing or decreasing trends over time. Investigation may also identify fluctuations in a ratio between one period and the next, or relationships that seem inconsistent with other relevant information, or that differ from their expected value by a significant amount.

Analysing financial statements is therefore an investigation into the financial performance and position of the business.

2 Approach to financial statement analysis for the MDCS examination

Accounting information will be presented in both the pre-seen and in the exam unseen information.

This information may be presented in the form of management accounts or abridged financial statements. This is for practical reasons; to avoid the need for unnecessarily detailed disclosures that would be required if statements compliant with IFRS Accounting Standards were provided. However, you will be given sufficient information to allow you to undertake appropriate financial analysis.

You should prepare for the MDCS examination by making a **thorough analysis of the historical financial data in the pre-seen. This analysis should include the use of ratio analysis**. Organise your analysis into notes for reference as you prepare to sit the MDCS exam. If you have already practised suitable ratio analysis as part of your pre-seen analysis, then you will be able to efficiently update this analysis using updated financial performance information in the unseen.

In the MDCS examination you will then be required to continue your financial statement analysis using the new information provided in the exam.

2.1 What are you looking for in the financial statements?

The challenge is to know how to carry out a thorough financial analysis and identify issues that may be of significance for the MDCS examination. You will not be told which financial ratios to calculate. It is for you to decide how to analyse the information – deciding which ratios to calculate and identifying trends or other features that may be important.

Look for unusual features or trends in the data.

Be prepared to analyse the following aspects of financial performance and position in the pre-seen.

Aspect of performance or position	
Revenue and profitability	Growth or decline in the business
	Revenue and sales mix
	Gross profit, net profit, cost/sales ratios
Statement of financial position	Gearing
	Working capital
	Funding/financing
	Liquidity
Cash flow	Is cash flow positive or negative?
	Reasons?
	Where does the most cash come from – operating, financing, or investing activities?

If you are given historical information over a period of two, three or four years, calculate ratios for each year and look for rising or falling trends in the ratios over time.

You may possibly also need to analyse the following aspects of performance:

Aspect of performance or position	
Difference between actual performance and expected performance	Variance analysis or similar analysis comparing actual and expected results (such as against plans, budgets, industry benchmarks, etc)
Performance for shareholders	Dividend payments
	If the company is a listed company, the share price

2.2 Initial analysis and detailed analysis

Before analysing financial performance and financial position in detail using ratio analysis, you should first take an initial 'overview' or **initial analysis of the information available**. This overview can be performed quickly, but you should:

- Try to gain an understanding of the business from its financial statements
- Look for identifiable or unusual features in the statements that 'stand out'
- Use your prior qualitative analysis to enhance your first impressions of the financial data

When you have completed your initial analysis, you should move on to a detailed analysis of the financial statements. Ratio analysis enables you to make comparisons between:

- Current financial results and past results
- Current results and forecasts or budgets
- The results of the business and an industry standard or other external business standard
- The results of different subsidiaries within the group
- The results for different business segments or revenue streams
- The results of the company and the results of a competitor, eg when the MDCS examination deals with a proposed takeover bid

When analysing the pre-seen, you should make organised notes of your calculations (ratios and percentages) and your more general observations.

3 Initial analysis

An initial analysis of the financial statements should be a quick review to establish the 'financial headlines' of the business. You should try to assess the business, from first impressions, with reference to the following.

Nature of the business	Ownership: Is the organisation for-profit, not-for-profit, government-owned?
	Is the business in the manufacturing sector, service sector, retailing or another type of business?
	Does the available information indicate whether this business sector is growing or declining?
	To what extent is the business sector dependent on technology and innovation?
Growth	Is the business growing or shrinking (or static), in terms of revenue?
	How is it growing – through organic growth or by means of acquisitions?
	Does it appear to be making good profits, or is it making losses?
	Does its past performance indicate that its performance has been fairly stable? Or have profits (or losses) changed by large amounts from one year to the next?
Size	Is it a private or public/quoted company?
	Does it seem to be a small, medium-sized or large company?
	Are the financial statements for a single company or a group of companies?
	Does the company have international operations?
Stability	From an initial review, does the company appear to have a sound financial structure, with a balance of equity and debt finance?
	From an initial review, does the company appear to be solvent and capable of meeting its current liabilities (See ISA 570 *Going Concern*)?
	How old is the business? Is it a new start-up business or is it well-established?
	Does the information indicate that the company may be achieving its budget targets and its longer-term business objectives?
Wider business context	Is the general economy in a state of growth or recession?
	Is the rate of inflation in the economy significant?
	Are you aware of any other factors in the business environment that could be relevant to the company's financial position and performance?

You may find from your initial analysis that one or two issues could be of significance for the company. You may now be in a position to consider the financial strengths and weaknesses of the company that a more detailed analysis may confirm.

4 Analysing sales and profitability

The following ratios and trends should be calculated for each year for which information is available from the pre-seen. It is assumed for the purpose of this Toolkit that you are familiar with basic financial ratio analysis.

Ratio or trend	Comment
Growth or decline in sales	Measure the annual growth or decline in total revenue. Is the rate of growth or decline high or low? Are there any apparent reasons for the change? Is there any information about the sales mix? Is the company now selling more of one type of product or service and less of another?
Gross profit	Calculate the gross profit margin (%) = Gross profit/revenue Is the gross profit margin (%) improving or deteriorating? Is the gross profit margin (%) in the range expected for this industry?
Net profit	Calculate a net profit margin (%) = Net profit/revenue The most suitable ratio is likely to be the operating profit/sales percentage. In other words, look at profits before interest and taxation. However, look for any unusual features in interest income or costs, or in taxation. Is the net profit margin similar to competitor margins and if not, can reasons for this be explained?
Cost: Sales ratios	Measure cost/sales ratios. Typically these are: • Sales and distribution costs/sales • Administration costs/sales If the pre-seen provides the detail, you may also be able to calculate other cost/sales ratios such as: • Direct materials costs/sales • Direct labour costs/sales This ratio helps provide insights into the company's productivity versus the market inflation.
Return on capital employed (ROCE)	It may also be useful to calculate ROCE in previous years, to identify any growth or decline in this ratio. ROCE = Operating profit/capital employed ROCE depends on both: • Profitability: Profit/sales ratio, and • Asset utilisation: Sales/capital employed ratio **Notes** 1 You may also come across the term 'return on investment' (ROI). This is similar to ROCE, in the sense that it is a measure of the average annual financial return on one or more assets (an investment). However, generally ROI applies to individual investments, rather than a company's entire business. It is also a term used in investment appraisal to measure the expected return on a specific new investment. 2 If capital employed consists of total assets minus current liabilities. 'Profit = Operating profit or profit before interest and tax.

If you can identify a trend in the ratios from one year to the next, or if you can identify possible reasons for a change in a ratio from one year to the next, make a note of this.

Be prepared to calculate similar ratios in the MDCS examination, using the up-to-date financial information provided. Check to see whether trends that you identified in the pre-seen have continued, and whether the rate of change is now faster than it was before.

You should also look for any unusual features in the revenues or costs of the business, such as an unusually high allowance for impairment of trade receivables (previously called 'provision for bad debts'), or large amounts of deferred income.

4.1 Taking a view about sales and profitability

It is not sufficient for the MDCS examination simply to calculate ratios and look for trends. You also need to consider the performance of the company in terms of what might be expected, given other information in the pre-seen or exam.

Can profitability and sales growth (or decline) be explained by anything in the exam?

Is sales growth satisfactory? If not, why not? You may need to express an opinion about whether the rate of growth in sales is satisfactory. To do this, you should consider:

- The 'real' growth in sales after allowing for inflation and sales price increases that may have occurred during the year
- The rate of sales growth achieved by competitors, if information about this is provided
- Whether the rate of sales growth is consistent with company targets, if information about targets or objectives is provided (or in line with industry norms and expectations, which may be available on the internet)
- Volume growth, which is a good indicator of the strength of the business
- The average price per unit trend line, as this may provide insights into the company's pricing power or heavy discounting position to obtain volume
- The overall shape of the profit and loss line item increases and demonstrate a profound understanding of the inter-relationship between the ratios in the context of the company operating in the industry (eg Attempt to understand if costs are growing faster than the general cost inflation; Is the company able to pass down its raw material cost inflation/deflation in its price of goods and services?; Is the company a price setter or price taker?)
- Whether the growth in sales is strong in one part of the business but weak (or even in decline) in another

Is profitability satisfactory? If not, why not? Which aspect of performance appears to have caused the decline in performance? For example, could a decline in the Net profit: Sales possibly be attributable to management failures to control costs?

Case Study

ABC Ltd has reported the following results in the most recent three years. What might these figures indicate about the company's financial performance?

	20X6	20X5	20X4
	£m	£m	£m
Sales	29.3	28.0	25.7
Cost of sales	11.7	10.5	10.3
Gross profit	17.6	17.5	15.4
Other operating costs	15.5	14.8	13.3
Operating profit	2.1	2.7	2.1

Analysis

	20X6	20X5	20X4
	%	%	%
Growth in sales	4.6	8.9	
Gross profit margin	60.1	62.5	59.9
Operating profit margin	7.2	9.6	8.2
Other operating costs: Sales ratio	52.9	52.9	51.8

These figures do not provide complete evidence about performance, but they provide a useful guide to direct further investigation.

(a) The rate of sales growth fell in 20X6 compared with 20X5. This could indicate that sales growth in the future may be even lower. However, it would be useful to check whether price inflation affects the comparison and what the 'real' growth in sales might be. For example, if the rate of inflation was above 4.6% in 20X6, this would suggest that the real volume of sales fell during the year.

From your research into the industry, you may be able to identify falling sales revenues for all companies in the industry. Alternatively, there may be a specific reason why the company's sales are falling that is attributable to the company itself, rather than to the industry in general.

(b) The gross profit margin has remained fairly stable over the three years, but was higher in 20X5 than in 20X4 or 20X6. Could this indicate that some improvement in control over the cost of sales was achieved in 20X5, but the benefits of these improvements were subsequently lost in 20X6?

(c) The operating profit margin was lower in 20X6 than in either 20X5 or 20X4. Operating costs as a percentage of sales have increased since 20X4, accounting for most of the difference between 20X4 and 20X6. The fall since 20X5 is attributable to the fall in the gross profit margin.

(d) Taken as a whole, sales revenue increased by 14% over the period 20X4 to 20X6, but operating profit remained stable at £2.1 million. This would seem to indicate disappointing profit performance.

This example may suggest to you that fairly extensive analysis of profitability can be made with a relatively small amount of data.

Students should bear in mind that some changes in profit margin may not be able to be explained due to manipulation of accounting information or human error. The concept of using your professional judgement to question and challenge information provided is covered later in Chapter 11.

5 Analysing the statement of financial position

Statements of financial position provide information about:

- Non-current assets and changes in non-current assets
- Working capital
- Liquidity
- Financial gearing (leverage)
- Financing of the business

When financial ratios are calculated for items in the statement of financial position, it is usual for ratios to be based on estimated average values for the year, such as average non-current assets, average inventory levels, average trade receivables, and so on.

For the purpose of the MDCS examination, however, **you will be expected to use year-end values** to calculate financial ratios.

Item	Comment
Non-current assets	Look for distinctive features in the make-up of the company's non-current assets, such as a large proportion of intangible assets.
	If the company has a large amount of intangible assets, could these have a market value?
	For tangible non-current assets, check the basis for their valuation in the accounts: are they recorded at historical cost less cumulative depreciation, or at a revalued amount? Consider whether the basis of valuation may have implications for the financial position of the company.
	Compare non-current assets values with depreciation and expenses recorded in the profit and loss account, for example, as assets age, we would expect expenses to rise. This may also indicate evidence of asset impairment.
Changes in non-current assets	Study changes in non-current assets from one year to the next.
	Measure the **ratio of sales: non-current assets** (or non-current assets: sales). Is there any significant change in this ratio over time?
	As a general rule, if the company's business is growing, we should expect non-current assets to increase each year: Net purchases of non-current assets should exceed the annual depreciation charge.
	However, new investments in non-current assets must be financed, so look for large increases in non-current assets (and a corresponding increase in liabilities too, current or non-current).
	• Do the large increases in non-current assets appear justified by the growth in the company's business?
	• How are the investments financed?
	Is the company failing to invest sufficiently in new non-current assets? (Are non-current assets declining in amount, rather than increasing?)

Item	Comment
Working capital	Working capital ratios are used to monitor the management of working capital, and in particular inventory, trade receivables and trade payables. You should be familiar with the following turnover ratios. • **Inventory**: (Inventory/cost of sales) × 365 days • **Trade receivables** average collection period: (Trade receivables/sales) × 365 days. If sufficient information is available, use the figure for total credit sales rather than total sales (cash and credit) and exclude items such as prepayments from the figure for receivables. • **Trade payables**: Average time taken to pay: (Trade payables/cost of sales) × 365 days Look for unusually long or short turnover periods, as well as for changes in the turnover periods over time, from one year to the next.
Liquidity	Useful measures of liquidity are: Current ratio = current assets: current liabilities Quick ratio = current assets excluding inventory: current liabilities Changes in these ratios over time may be significant, suggesting: • **Lack of liquidity** (cash flow from operations), and possibly **overtrading**; or • **Over-investment in working capital**. (**Overtrading** is carrying on too much business with insufficient long-term capital. **Over-investment in working capital** should be indicated by long working capital turnover periods for inventory and/or trade receivables, and large amounts of cash and cash equivalents.) Look at the extent to which current liabilities are financing current assets. In an extreme case, current liabilities may also be partly financing non-current assets as well as current assets.
Financial gearing	Financial gearing measures the proportion of debt capital in the company's long-term capital structure. (Debt capital includes preference share capital, if any.) The gearing ratio is measured as debt capital: equity capital or as Debt capital: (Equity capital plus debt capital). There are no rules about the 'ideal' level of financial gearing. Points to note are that: • An increase in gearing over time indicates increasing use of debt capital to finance the business • An increase in debt finance should correspond to an increase in interest expense. If this is not the case, then this may be evidence of error, although it is possible the interest rate has changed due to refinancing • High levels of gearing could make it difficult for the company to borrow additional amounts of capital, except perhaps at high rates of interest to compensate the lending bank (or other lending entity) for the higher credit risk Another ratio that may be useful for assessing the level of debt financing for a company is the **interest cover ratio**. This is the ratio of operating profit (profit before interest) to finance charges for the period. This ratio should be sufficiently high to ensure that the company will be able to meet its finance charges out of operating profits. An interest cover ratio below about 4.0 times may be a cause for concern, especially if the ratio is getting worse over time.

Item	Comment
Financing	You may need to take a view about the financing structure of the company, and changes in this structure over time. • Does the company have sufficient equity capital? • Is the gearing ratio satisfactory? • To what extent is the company financed from short-term sources? • If the company needed to raise new capital, could there be problems, given the current financing structure? • Is the company bound by any bank covenants?

You should consider the quality of the items in the statement of financial position, and whether there is any information that may help you to assess the:

- Quality and age of tangible non-current assets
- Nature of the long-term and current liabilities
- Quality and liquidity of the current assets

In the MDCS examination itself, you may need to consider the effect that any proposal by the company's management may have on the structure of the statement of financial position.

Analysing the pre-seen should enable you to assess the current financial position of the company. This may provide the basis for assessing the financial implications of any such proposal. Remember that the financial numbers on their own are unlikely to give a clear picture about the financial position, but they indicate possibilities or probabilities that should be investigated more closely.

Case Study

Comment on the following figures reported by a company for the most recent financial year and the corresponding previous year.

	20X6 £m	20X5 £m
Revenue	35.8	31.7
Trade receivables at end of year	6.2	3.9
Receivables written off as uncollectable	2.2	1.0

Analysis

Revenue increased by 12.9% in 20X6, but there has been a bigger proportional increase in both trade receivables and uncollectable debts.

		20X6		20X5
Average days to collect	(6.2/35.8) × 365	63 days	(3.9/31.7) × 365	45 days
Written off as a % of sales		6.1%		3.2%

Assuming that the end-of-year figures for trade receivables are representative of average receivables during the year, and **assuming** also that sales revenue is earned at an even rate over the course of the year, the average time taken to collect payment from credit customers has increased from about 45 days to 63 days. We do not know what the 'normal' credit periods are in the industry, but 30 days is commonplace as an initial point of comparison and also, usual credit terms may be given in the pre-seen or the unseen. However, such a large increase indicates that the company is either having greater difficulty in collecting payments, or it has become much more inefficient at collecting payments. (Note that the word '**assuming**' has been bolded, this is because these statements are **key assumptions**.)

Amounts owed to the company written off as uncollectable have increased substantially from 3.2% of sales to 6.1% of sales. Again, this could indicate either that the company is having greater difficulty in collecting payments, or that it has become much more inefficient at collecting payments.

It is possible, for example, that worsening economic conditions may have affected the ability of customers to pay. Another possibility is that the increase of 12.9% in sales revenue is the result of selling more to customers with a lower credit status. Yet another reason for the increase in trade receivables at year-end may be that the company wanted to clear its stock pending the release of a new model, so offered extended credit terms to entice buyers.

Further information is needed in order to establish the reasons for the deteriorating ratios.

6 Analysing cash flow

Companies need adequate cash flows and liquidity. Any company that seems to have insufficient inflows of cash (particularly from operating activities) could be in a serious financial situation.

Unless you are given a statement of cash flows in the pre-seen, you can check cash flows and liquidity by looking at:

- Changes in the cash balance over time, from one year to the next
- Whether the company has an overdraft (and if there is an overdraft, how large is it?)
- Management of the cash cycle (the working capital turnover ratios, taken together: Cash cycle = Inventory turnover period + Trade receivables collection period − Trade payables payment period)

If you are given statements of cash flows in the pre-seen, you should study these to establish reasons for the change in net cash flows each year. Where is cash coming from, and how is it being spent? A statement of cash flows divides cash flows into three broad categories.

- **Cash flows from operations.** These are the cash flows from the business. Is there a positive cash flow from operations?
- **Cash flows from investing activities.** These include spending on capital investment and cash received from selling off assets or part of the business. Are the net cash flows from investing activities positive or negative? (We should normally expect them to be negative, if the company is growing and investing in growth.)
- **Cash flows from financing activities.** These include cash obtained from issuing shares or borrowing, cash paid to repay amounts borrowed, and dividend payments to shareholders, as well as government grants. Are the net cash flows from financing activities positive or negative? What have been the changes in financing during the year?

If the case study involves **a company with potential cash flow problems**, the key items of information to consider are as follows.

- The change in cash position – by how much has the cash position deteriorated, and within what period of time has this happened?
- What are the possible implications of the deterioration in the cash position for the company's financial position and financial security?
- Is the problem significant enough to result in going concern implications which management and the external auditor will need to address in the auditor's report in the annual financial statements?

6.1 Estimate of free cash flow

It may be useful, for the purpose of analysis, to estimate the free cash flow that the company is generating. Free cash flow is cash flow over which the company has discretion in how to spend. There are different approaches to estimating free cash flow.

A simple model for calculating annual free cash flow is as follows (ignoring expenditure to replace non-current assets):

	£
Earnings (profit) before interest and tax (EBIT)	X
Add back: Depreciation and other non-cash items such as amortisation of intangible assets	X
	X
Subtract	
Taxation paid	(X)
Increase (cash outflow) or reduction (cash inflow) in working capital investment	(X) or X
Free cash flow	X

Information about free cash flow might help to indicate whether the company will be able to generate sufficient cash from its operations to cover its operational requirements, at least in the short term, or whether additional external financing might be required. (A company should normally be expected to generate net cash inflows from operating activities, even when making a loss.)

7 Accounting choices, judgments and estimates

When analysing financial statements, it is important to recognise the accounting choices or judgments and estimates that have been made in preparing them.

The scope for making choices in accounting treatment has been narrowed significantly in recent years due to the development of more prescriptive accounting standards. Nevertheless, significant choices still exist in a number of areas, and it is important to bear in mind the policies that have been used, and the judgments and estimates that have been made, in preparing the financial statements in the pre-seen or the exam.

Even though accounting standards set out detailed requirements in many areas of accounting, management still needs to exercise judgment and make significant estimates in preparing the financial statements.

Examples of judgments and estimates required of management include:

Financial statement area	Judgment or estimation required
Property, plant and equipment	• Depreciation methods • Residual values • Useful lives • Revaluations/impairments
Intangible assets	• Allocation of consideration in a business combination • Future cash flows for impairment tests • Amortisation periods
Inventories	• Inclusion of overheads and the normal level of activity • Inventory valuation methods
Leases	• Method of allocating finance charges

Financial statement area	Judgment or estimation required
Provisions, contingent liabilities and contingent assets	• Provisions: Probability of outflow of economic benefits • Measurement of liabilities
Revenue recognised over time	• Estimates of future costs • Estimation of stage of completion
Financial instruments: Recognition and measurement	• Trade receivables: Collectability and impairment
Operating segments	• Allocation of common costs to segments • Setting of transfer prices between segments **Note:** Don't forget to look at the relevant IFRS Accounting Standards and Guidance Notes to refresh your memory about how these items may be treated in the financial statements and the choices that management can make.

The preparation of financial statements requires a great deal of professional judgment, honesty and integrity. The financial statements and the associated ratio analysis could be affected by pressure on the preparers of those financial statements to improve the financial performance, financial position or both. Managers of organisations may try to improve the appearance of the financial information to:

- Increase their level of bonus pay or other reward benefits
- Deliver specific targets such as earnings per share (EPS) growth to meet investors' expectations
- Reduce the risk of corporate insolvency, eg by avoiding a breach of loan covenants
- Understate revenues and overstate expenses to reduce tax liabilities
- Improve the appearance of the company prior to an initial public offering (IPO) or a takeover bid for the company.

7.1 Financial ratios interpretation

Ratios are based on financial information from published financial statements, but as indicated above, the information may be manipulated by the management of the company. Attention should therefore be paid to the accounting quantities (non-dollar values, such as quantity of inventory, direct labour hours, wastage, on-time production, etc) as well as the financial ratios.

In order to analyse some ratios meaningfully, it is necessary to have an understanding of the underlying business operation. For example, a large sale, or a large receipt, immediately before the year-end may distort the calculation of the trade receivables average collection period. Furthermore, the year-end receivables figure is likely to depend on the sales in the final month of the year. If the final month is unusual, for example due to high or low seasonality or very high sales revenue growth, the calculation of an average collection period may be misleading. In practice, companies often use a 12-month moving average (MAT) to overcome the problem of seasonality.

The average period of credit taken for trade payables can also be misleading. Trade payables occur from material purchases (and some other expenses) rather than cost of sales. For manufacturing companies, the cost of sales includes not only raw material costs but also production labour costs and overheads, many of which are unrelated to trade payables. The trade payables turnover period is therefore an unreliable measurement for manufacturing companies.

Another is the gearing ratio. Both non-current assets and liabilities should reflect fair values, but do not necessarily do so. In addition, the gearing ratio is meaningless unless the nature of the company's operations is well understood. For example, many service-based companies are 'asset light', which means that their gearing ratios may seem unusually high if they borrow to fund their operations. This may give

the impression that the risk of insolvency is higher than it actually is. To assess solvency from capital structure, much more information is needed, such as:

- The realisable value of assets
- Timing of debt redemption; probability of re-financing
- Additional financing capacity

Intangible assets. In accordance with *IAS 38 Intangible Assets,* internally-generated goodwill is not recognised in the statement of financial position. Intangible assets will only be recognised if:

- It is probable that the expected future economic benefits that are attributable to the asset will flow to the entity; and
- The cost of the asset can be measured reliably.

Case Study

The German airline Lufthansa reports in its financial statements that it depreciates its aircraft over 12 years on a straight-line basis using an estimated residual value of 15% of the original cost.

In comparison, some other airlines depreciate their new passenger aircraft over 15 years to a residual value of 10%, and its new freight aircraft over 15 years to a residual value of 20%.

British Airways has reported in the past that it depreciated its aircraft over 20 years on a straight-line basis using an estimated residual value of 8% of the original cost.

The differences could reflect differences in asset replacement policies for the airlines. However, to make a meaningful comparison between the performance of these companies, it may be appropriate to make adjustments to depreciation charges and net asset values in order to make a like-with-like comparison. However, if the differences in depreciation policies reflect differences in commercial substance (such as differences in replacement cycles for aircraft), no adjustment would be needed to the depreciation charge or asset values to make valid comparisons.

8 Difference between actual performance and expected financial performance

You may be given information suggesting that a company's actual financial performance is worse than (or better than) expected. It may be possible to identify the reasons for the change, using a method of analysis that is similar to variance analysis in flexible budgeting.

The following example suggests a method of analysis that may be useful.

Case Study

A company expected to achieve an operating profit of £6,000,000 for the financial year on sales revenue of £90,000,000, as follows.

	£
Revenue	90,000,000
Cost of sales	36,000,000
Gross profit	54,000,000
Other operating costs	48,000,000
Operating profit	6,000,000

Actual results were disappointing. Although total revenue was higher than expected (£95m), the company made a loss of £5 million. The cost of sales was £48 million and other operating costs were £52 million.

Analysis

For the purpose of financial analysis, we might assume that:

- The cost of sales varies with sales revenue
- Other operating costs are fixed costs

Other assumptions are possible, such as an assumption that other operating costs also vary with sales revenue.

Given these assumptions, we can set out the comparison of actual and expected performance as follows.

		Expected performance £m	Actual performance £m
Sales		90.0	95.0
Cost of sales	(40% of sales)	36.0	48.0
Gross profit	(60% of sales)	54.0	47.0
Other costs		48.0	52.0
Operating profit		6.0	(5.0)

Note: In the analysis that follows, (F) indicates a favourable variance (favourable difference) where actual performance is better than expected; and (A) indicates an adverse variance (adverse difference) where actual performance is worse than expected.

	£m
Expected sales	90.0
Actual sales	95.0
Sales volume variance in £ revenue	5.0 (F)
Expected gross profit margin	60%
Sales volume variance in £ gross profit	3.0 (F)

	£m
Expected cost of sales (40% of sales £95 million)	38.0
Actual cost of sales	48.0
Cost variance, cost of sales	10.0 (A)

	£m
Expected other costs (fixed)	48.0
Actual other costs	52.0
Other costs expenditure variance	4.0 (A)

Summary of variances	£m
Expected profit	6.0
Sales volume variance	3.0
Cost variance, cost of sales	10.0 (A)
Other costs expenditure variance	4.0 (A)
Actual profit	(5.0)

The analysis shows that actual profits were below expectation by £11 million (the budget was a profit of £6 million, but the result was a loss of £5 million). In spite of higher-than-expected sales, costs exceeded expectation. The cost of sales was much higher than expected and other costs were also higher than expected.

If more information is provided in the pre-seen, it may be possible to analyse the cost variances in more detail, and estimate a materials cost variance or a labour cost variance.

9 Performance for shareholders

9.1 Unlisted companies (Private companies)

If the company in the MDCS examination is a private company, financial performance from the perspective of shareholders can be measured by:

- Earnings and earnings per share
- Dividends and dividends per share

In a growing company, shareholders will often expect growth in the annual earnings per share. This can probably be measured simply as profits after taxation divided by the number of ordinary shares in issue. (An adjustment will be required if new shares were issued during the year.)

In a private company, dividends are the only method of providing a measurable return to shareholders.

9.2 Listed companies (quoted companies)

If the company in the MDCS examination is a quoted company, and its shares are traded on a stock exchange, the financial performance from the shareholders' perspective should also take into consideration any change in the share price over time.

Share prices can be volatile, and short-term gains or losses from a rise or fall in the share price should be analysed with caution. However, a long-term rise or fall in the share price over a number of years should be measured.

10 Summary advice for financial statement analysis in MDCS

10.1 Financial statement analysis and the pre-seen

It is not possible to predict what the MDCS examination will require you to do and what further financial statement analysis may be required. You should therefore be fully prepared for any possibility, and you should understand the company and its business (from the information in the pre-seen) in great detail.

When you have completed your preparation work on the pre-seen for historical financial analysis, you should have the following items.

- A table of financial ratios for every year for which financial data is available
- Ratios organised in a way that you find easy to access. This chapter recommends that you organise ratios into categories – revenue, profitability and costs; balance sheet items; cash flows; and shareholder issues

- Notes on any other facts that you consider may be relevant for the examination, such as reasons for differences between actual and expected results; and possible reasons for changes in the rate of revenue growth or in profit margins
- Notes on your research into the industry

10.2 Performing financial statement analysis in the MDCS examination

In the MDCS examination, you may be given up-to-date financial information about the company, and you will then be expected to calculate suitable financial ratios for the most recent data. By pre-preparing ratios for the pre-seen, you will be ready to efficiently analyse any significant change in financial performance or financial position, by comparing the ratios for the most recent financial data with the ratios for previous years.

Remember that you are not being examined on your ability to calculate financial ratios. You need to demonstrate an **ability to analyse financial statements** and to **use your analysis** (and judgment) to carry out the requirements of the MDCS examination.

You will also need to **communicate** your financial analysis within the report that you write. Remember, the MDCS examination is a test of your ability to identify what is significant, and to communicate your understanding and analysis. If the financial information in the exam indicates a significant change in the company's financial performance or position, you will need to explain the likely reasons for the changes in the numbers. Clarity of explanation will be essential.

- Detailed calculations, such as tables of financial ratios, should be included in an **Appendix to the report**, and not in the main body of the report itself. Too many numbers in the main body of a report will distract and confuse the reader.
- In your written answer, you should draw attention to the significant aspects of financial performance or financial position, and consider the implications for the future. **Be selective** in the issues that you discuss or emphasise.

Importantly, keep your report **relevant to the requirements of the question**. This means that much of the work you have done on the pre-seen will not be included in either the body of your report or in the appendices to the report.

End of chapter question

This exercise continues the Well Being case study, which was introduced in Chapter 2.

Email from WBL's finance director, to the senior members of the accounts team, 18 August 2019

As you know, last week we announced our results for the financial year that's just ended, and I can give you a summary of these. You may have seen Janet Hunter being interviewed on television about them. She isn't very pleased that the company's share price fell by 5% on the day of the announcement, so she seems keen to make improvements and take new initiatives.

Janet wants answers from me about what is going right and what is going wrong.

Well Being Ltd: Summary financial statements 2019
Statement of profit or loss for the year ended 30 June 2019

	2019 £'000	2018 £'000
Sales revenue	106,100	101,200
Cost of inventory sold	3,100	2,900
Employee benefit expenses	54,500	50,500
Building occupancy costs	17,100	17,100
Building management	2,200	2,200
Depreciation	4,500	4,400
Advertising and marketing	2,000	1,700
Bank charges	5,000	4,800
Other operating expenses	8,700	7,300
Total operating costs	97,100	90,900
Profit before tax and interest	9,000	10,300
Interest income	1,200	1,000
Profit before taxation	10,200	11,300
Income tax expense	1,700	1,900
Profit after taxation	8,500	9,400

Well Being Ltd
Statement of financial position at 30 June 2019

	2019 £'000	2019 £'000	2018 £'000	2018 £'000
Property, plant and equipment		41,400		39,700
Current assets				
Inventory	1,800		1,700	
Receivables and prepayments	3,300		2,700	
Cash and bank	56,900		53,400	
		62,000		57,800
		103,400		97,500
Equity and liabilities				
Share capital and reserves		41,000		41,500
Liabilities				
Trade payables and accruals	10,100		9,300	
Deferred revenue	50,300		44,700	
Taxation	2,000		2,000	
		62,400		56,000
		103,400		97,500

Notes

1. Most sales are paid for by credit card. Most customers are required to pay in advance, and due to the popularity of WBL's clinics and centres, payments in advance for packages are substantial. They may cover courses of treatment that last for 12 months or even longer. On receipt of payments, WBL places the money on deposit with its banks. Payments in advance are shown as deferred revenue in the statement of financial position above.

2. Not all sales are made in advance, however. Due to late cancellations, WBL has some late vacancies at its centres and clinics. Customers taking up these vacancies are allowed 30 days' credit before payment is required. WBL allow this credit as a way of attracting customers to fill the vacancies.

Well Being Ltd
Summary statement of cash flows for the year ended 30 June 2019

	£'000	£'000
Profit before interest and tax		9,000
Depreciation	4,500	
Increase in inventory	(100)	
Increase in receivables, deposits and prepayments	(600)	
Increase in trade payables and accruals	800	
Increase in deferred revenue	5,600	
	10,200	
Interest received	1,200	
Tax paid	(1,700)	
		9,700
Net cash from operating activities		18,700
Net purchase of property, plant and equipment		(6,200)
Dividends paid		(9,000)
Increase in cash		3,500

Extracts from segmental performance, year to 30 June 2019

	Beauty clinics	Spa centres	Fitness centres	Product sales	Total
	£'000	£'000	£'000	£'000	£'000
External sales	78,300	15,800	5,500	6,500	106,100
Internal transfers	–	–	–	2,900	2,900
Total sales	78,300	15,800	5,500	9,400	109,000
Operating profit	6,400	1,400	(200)	1,400	9,000
Sales in year to 30 June 2018, excluding internal transfers	71,900	15,100	8,400	5,800	101,200

Requirement

Review the performance of the company as a whole in the year to 30 June 2019 and its position as at the end of the year. Conclude your review with an assessment of whether the company appears to be in a strong position to pursue a growth strategy over the next year.

Suggested answer

The first step in preparing an answer to the requirements is to extract information (mainly financial ratios) that might be of some relevance.

	2019	2018	Comment
Sales revenue growth	((106,100 – 101,200)/101,200) 4.8%		Reasonable but need to compare with strategic targets.
Operating profit margin	(9,000/106,100) 8.5%	(10,300/101,200) 10.2%	There has been a substantial fall in profit margin, which is attributable mainly to the £4 million increase in employee benefit expenses. No reason for this has been given.
Fall in operating profit since previous year	(1,300/10,300) (12.6%)		A significant contraction in operating profit, due to cost increases exceeding the effect of 4.8% revenue growth.
Employee costs/sales	(54,500/106,100) 51.4%	(50,500/101,200) 49.9%	Increase in employee costs as % of sales explains most of fall in operating profit margin.
Other operating expenses/sales	(8,700/106,100) 8.2%	(7,300/101,200) 7.2%	Another reason for the fall in operating profit margin. No information about what these costs are.
Return on capital employed (ROCE)	(9,000/103,400) 8.7%	(10,300/97,500) 10.6%	Also down. Capital employed here has been calculated as total assets, but other definitions should also be acceptable.
Asset turnover	(106,100/103,400) 1.03 times	(101,200/97,500) 1.04 times	Small decline in sales revenue per £1 capital.
No borrowing			This suggests opportunities to borrow if required.
Seems cash rich, but after setting deferred revenue against cash	(56,900 – 50,300) £6,600,000	(53,400 – 44,700) £8,700,000	Does this suggest that the company's cash position is not as good in 2019 as in 2018?
Dividends (9,000 paid)	= 100% of operating profit and 105.9% of profit after tax		Why were dividends so high? Can the company afford such a generous dividend policy?

	2019	2018	Comment
Increase/(fall) in revenue for each business segment			Highlights the effect of poor fitness centre performance on company profits.
Beauty clinics	+ 8.9%		
Health spas	+ 4.6%		
Fitness centres	(34.5%)		
Retail: Product sales	+ 12.1%		
Three divisions excluding fitness centres	(106,100 – 5,500) compared to (101,200 – 8,400) + 8.4%		This compares with expected future growth of 4% per year in the cosmetics industry.

Assessment of the overall position of WBL

- Revenue has grown by 4.8% in the year to 30 June 2019. This compares well with expected annual growth in the cosmetics industry of 4%. Taking out the (decline in) revenue from fitness centres, revenue growth was 8.4%, which seems very strong.

- Some operating costs have increased, suggesting that there may be scope for improvements in cost control. However, the reasons for the increase in employee costs and other operating expenses are not apparent.

- Cash and bank has increased by £3,500,000 to £56,900,000 providing the company with the financial power to exploit strategic market opportunities. The absence of any debt finance further strengthens WBL's ability to finance expansion through debt and equity funding.

- The decline in revenue of the fitness centres was significant, suggesting a need for further investigation.

- Zero gearing (no borrowings) suggests the company is not fully taking advantage of the low interest rate environment, which may continue into 2020. Banks will be more willing to lend for existing business and expansion of business. Is the company and its chairperson/CEO too risk averse, and missing opportunities to invest in growth?

Is the company in a strong position to pursue a growth strategy?

Yes. The overall conclusion is that the company is in a strong financial position and should be able to invest in growth – but only if suitable opportunities for growth exist and if the board of directors considers that the risks are acceptable.

- WBL has significant cash (£56,900,000). It is debt-free and so could probably borrow a substantial amount of money to finance growth.

- The generous dividend policy means that overall equity in the company has fallen. To pursue a growth strategy, the company should probably seek to retain a greater proportion of profits for reinvestment in growth. A change in dividend policy should be communicated to shareholders.

- Given the success of the IPO three years ago, there may be market demand for a further issue of equity shares if the proposed strategy is positively received by the stock market.

- The excess of cash balances over deferred revenue is low in June 2019. This may indicate that the company is vulnerable to cancellation and withdrawal of customer contracts for whatever reasons (eg reputation damage over certain health products sold and used by the company).

Developing data analysis

Topic list	Syllabus reference
1 Introduction to data analysis	LO1
2 Estimates and assumptions	LO1
3 Cost structure and decision-making	LO1
4 Preparing a financial forecast	LO1
5 Performance analysis	LO1
6 Reliability of information	LO1
7 Interpretation of results	LO1
8 Improving data analysis	LO1

Introduction

In your MDCS examination, you will be required to give advice or make a recommendation, based on your assessment of strategic issues and financial data. New information will be given to you in the exam, and you will need to combine this with your pre-prepared analysis of the pre-seen.

The previous chapters have looked at the approach to formulating strategy and at the analysis of historical financial information. This chapter suggests techniques for analysing data for the purpose of reaching a decision or point of view.

1 Introduction to data analysis

In order to make a recommendation or give advice, you need to understand the objective that you are trying to achieve. The objective may simply be to improve profitability or to add value to the organisation by making a new investment.

The **objective** should be something that:

- Adds value
- Over a given period of time
- Within an acceptable level of risk
- Is ethical in character.

You also need to be aware of the **options** that are available. When you provide advice or make a recommendation, you should ensure you are putting forward the best available option. In some cases, this choice may be simple: Whether or not to undertake a specific acquisition or investment. In other cases, there may be a number of different options to choose from.

Remember that any recommendations you make or advice that you give should be:

- **Suitable**: Appropriate for the problem or situation under review
- **Feasible**: Realistically capable of achievement
- **Acceptable**: A course of action that would be acceptable to key stakeholders, or that key stakeholders can be persuaded to accept

The MDCS examination will often require you to evaluate possible options by analysing data from the case study. You should provide a meaningful solution which provides evidence to support the recommendation provided.

2 Estimates and assumptions

The pre-seen and the additional information in the exam will not give you sufficient information to reach an appropriate answer to the problem. You may be required to make assumptions and estimates.

- You may be expected to make certain **assumptions**, for example about cost structures or future working capital turnover periods, in order to make your analysis or produce a forecast.

  You should include your assumptions in the appendices to your report, unless it is a critical assumption (in which case, you should explain this in the body of the report). If possible, in the time available, you should prepare a separate appendix listing all your assumptions, as this will make it easier for the marker to identify the judgments that you have made. It will also help you to direct your reader to the appropriate assumption: 'Please refer to Appendix 1 Point 3,' for instance.

- You may be required to make predictions or forecasts based on **estimates**, such as estimates of future growth in sales demand or sales revenue; or estimates of profit margin or cash flows. When you make an estimate, specify any assumptions you are making if the necessary information is not specified in the pre-seen or exam.

- Recognise the uncertainty in estimates, especially when the estimates have been provided by managers with a vested interest in a proposal being accepted. You may need to demonstrate **professional scepticism** in your analysis, as well as state the rationale behind your opinion.

You should understand that assumptions and estimates are necessary to make forecasts and predictions. They should be reasonable, but they could be wrong. There is no magic formula for making a correct forecast! However, the reader of your report needs to understand how you have arrived at your predictions, so you should state your assumptions and estimates clearly.

2.1 Estimates and rounding

The MDCS examination also tests your common sense and professional judgement.

Since forecasts are based on estimates and assumptions, do not be afraid to round estimates to convenient whole numbers. For example, if you calculate that the unit cost of sale for a product is £45.67, do not be afraid to round this figure to £46. If you estimate that a gross profit margin will be 53.729%, do not be afraid to round this to 54%.

However, be judicious in your rounding (and dropping off decimal places) because rounding at every step in a calculation has a cumulative effect, that might considerably alter the final result.

3 Cost structure and decision-making

The pre-seen is unlikely to reveal the nature of a decision or a problem that you will be required to discuss in your MDCS examination report. The problem or recommendation required will only be revealed to you in the exam requirement.

The pre-seen may, however, provide you with data that may be useful for making estimates of costs or profits.

3.1 Fixed and variable cost estimates

You should consider whether the pre-seen provides you with enough data to make a distinction between fixed costs and variable costs, making whatever assumptions you consider to be reasonable. Always be aware of the assumptions that you are making. You should state what they are in your MDCS examination report, if they seem important.

For the purpose of analysis, it is often reasonable to assume that:

- The cost of sales (revenue minus direct costs) is a variable cost
- Gross profit is a good approximation for contribution.

Question

A manufacturing company makes a product for which the current production cost is as follows:

	£
Materials	21.85
Production labour	16.46
Other production costs	32.92
Factory cost per unit	71.23

The product sells for £120 per unit.

Answer

In the absence of information to the contrary, you should assume that the materials cost per unit is a variable cost. (However, state this as an assumption in an appendix to your report.) The other production costs seem to be absorbed by factory overhead costs (absorbed at a rate of 200% of production labour cost) and it may be reasonable to assume that most of these costs are fixed costs.

Production labour could be either a fixed cost or a variable cost, and the pre-seen may give some indication as to which of these possibilities is more likely. You should make an assumption, and state what this is, if required, for your MDCS examination report.

Let us assume that production labour is a variable cost. This means that the variable production cost per unit is £38.31 (= £21.85 + £16.46) and the contribution per unit is £81.69 (= £120 – £38.31).

- For the purpose of forecasting, this estimate of the contribution per unit might be rounded to £82.
- Alternatively, you could calculate the contribution/sales ratio as 68.1% (= 81.69/120) and round this to 68%.

Let us assume instead that production labour is a fixed cost. This means that the variable production cost per unit is £21.85 and the contribution per unit is £98.15 (= £120 – £21.85).

- For the purpose of forecasting, this estimate of the contribution per unit might be rounded down to £98.
- Alternatively, you could calculate the contribution/sales ratio as 81.8% (= 98.15/120) and round this up to 82%.

These two alternative assumptions produce significantly different figures. This is why it is important to state your assumptions in an appendix to your MDCS examination report, if you want to use the estimates of cost or contribution that you produce. Clearly stating your assumptions also helps the reader to understand your logic and reasoning.

You should remember that it is important to state all of your assumptions, usually in an appendix to your report, unless they are given to you in the pre-seen or exam. Even if you think they are obvious, you should state all your assumptions, to show the marker that you are aware of what you are doing.

3.2 Cost-volume-profit analysis

If you have sufficient information, you may be able to analyse costs into fixed and variable cost elements, you may be able to apply cost-volume-profit (CVP) analysis (also called breakeven analysis) for the purpose of giving financial advice or making a recommendation. For example, you may be able to make any of the following estimates.

- Amount of sales revenue required to break even
- Amount of sales revenue required to achieve a minimum target profit or return on capital
- Margin of safety between breakeven sales and planned sales (as a percentage of planned sales)
- The effect on profit of any proposed change in sales price (and consequent change in sales volume/sales demand)
- Product/sales mix analysis: CVP analysis can be used to estimate the effect of changing the sales mix, where the company makes and sells more than one product

CVP calculations of this type should be straightforward for you, provided that you have analysed costs into fixed and variable elements correctly.

You may need to be aware, however, of step increases in fixed costs ('step costs'), where information about these is provided in the pre-seen or exam.

CVP analysis draws on the knowledge you gained as part of your academic base.

4: Developing data analysis

Question

Let's assume that the company in the previous example makes and sells just one product. The company's finance director is concerned about declining sales and profitability. Budgeted production and sales for next year are 800,000 units but actual sales could be lower than this. Administration, selling and distribution costs are expected to be £28,000,000. (Factory costs are those given in the previous example.)

Required

Advise the finance director on the basis of the information available.

Answer

It will be assumed here that production labour is a variable cost and the contribution/sales ratio is 68%.

If budgeted production is 800,000 units, this indicates that production overhead costs will be £26,336,000 (= 800,000 units × £32.92 per unit). If we assume that administration and selling and distribution costs are fixed costs, total annual fixed costs will be about £54,336,000 (= £26,336,000 + £28,000,000).

Budgeted sales revenue is £96,000,000 (= 800,000 units × £120 per unit).

Breakeven sales revenue = £54,336,000/0.68 = £79,905,882 – say £80,000,000

The margin of safety is £16,000,000, or 16.7% of expected sales.

If the finance director is concerned that actual sales will fall short of the budget, the company should still make an operating profit, provided that actual sales are within 16.7% of budget.

A point to note from this analysis is that by separating costs into fixed and variable elements, if this is possible, there are opportunities for making financial forecasts and predictions.

A further point to note is that this is a simple example and it therefore disregards issues such as obsolescence or impairment of any unsold inventory, and the implications this might have for profitability.

Note on rounding. In this example, only the final figures are rounded, rather than the factory costs individually. Although the answer in this particular example does not change, when there are multiple factors of production (for example, numerous different elements in the raw materials cost) the final answer is different if rounding is applied to each factor individually.

3.3 Fixed overheads and capacity

By separating costs into fixed and variable elements, it may also be possible to make forecasts based on production capacity or sales capacity.

Case Study

A company manufactures a range of products, and the average contribution/sales ratio last year was 40% and sales revenue was £72 million. The company is currently operating at 90% production capacity. It is believed that if the company could increase its output, it would be able to sell all the additional output. The production manager believes, however, that for various operational reasons, it would not be possible to increase actual production to more than 94% of maximum (full capacity).

The separation of costs into fixed and variable elements enables us to predict by how much profits would increase if output and sales increased from the current 90% to 94% of full capacity.

The increase in sales would be (4/90) × £72 million = £3,200,000.

If the contribution/sales ratio is 40%, the expected increase in annual operating profit would be 40% × £3.2 million = £1,280,000.

The example above relates to a manufacturing company. Similar principles would apply to a **service company**. However, in a service company where material costs are low and labour costs are usually fixed salary costs, the contribution/sales ratio can be much higher than in manufacturing companies. So, if the contribution/sales ratio is 90%, this means that additional profit of £0.90 would be earned for each additional £1 of sales.

Surprisingly perhaps, the distinction between fixed and variable costs is not so obvious in published financial statements, where gross profit percentage margins are often fairly constant from one year to the next, in spite of sales revenue growth.

4 Preparing a financial forecast

You may find it useful to prepare a year-by-year financial forecast based on estimates and assumptions, to assess whether a proposed investment will meet certain criteria in order to be acceptable.

A basic form of financial forecast can be produced from:

- Annual sales revenue in a base year, and assumptions about future annual revenue growth
- Assumptions about the gross profit margin, and whether the cost of sales is 100% variable cost
- Assumptions about other expenditures, and whether these can be assumed to consist of fixed costs
- The future rate of taxation
- Dividend policy

An example will illustrate this forecasting method.

Question

In the year just ended, PLE Company achieved the following results:

	£'000
Sales revenue	10,000
Cost of sales	4,000
Gross profit	6,000
Other operating expenditure	3,000
Operating profit	3,000
Taxation (15%)	450
Profit after tax (earnings)	2,550
Dividends paid	1,275
Retained earnings	1,275
Net assets employed	21,000

The company has no debt. Management estimates that the company needs to have net assets of at least 200% of annual sales revenue, in order to support sales revenue growth in the future. An investment is under consideration that will provide 10% annual sales revenue growth for at least the next three years.

Required

Provide a year-by-year financial analysis for the next three years.

Answer

In order to make a financial projection, it is necessary to make some assumptions. These should be sensible, and they should be clearly explained. However, they could be incorrect, and you should recognise this fact in your subsequent discussion of the forecast.

Here, the following assumptions will be made:

- The same cost structure will apply to the new investment as to existing operations.
- The costs of sales are 100% variable costs and are 40% of sales revenue.
- Other operating expenditure consists of 100% fixed costs.
- Taxation will be 15% throughout the three years.
- The company will pay 50% of after-tax profits in dividends.

Information that is given is that:

- Sales revenue will increase by 10% each year.
- There is no debt, so no debt interest.
- Net assets employed must be at least 200% of annual sales revenue.

A three-year analysis is set out below. Check to make sure that you can see how the figures have been obtained.

	Year just ended £'000	Year 1 £'000	Year 2 £'000	Year 3 £'000
Sales revenue	10,000	11,000	12,100	13,310
Cost of sales	4,000	4,400	4,840	5,324
Gross profit	6,000	6,600	7,260	7,986
Other operating expenditure	3,000	3,000	3,000	3,000
Operating profit	3,000	3,600	4,260	4,986
Taxation (15%)	450	540	639	748
Profit after tax (earnings)	2,550	3,060	3,621	4,238
Dividends paid	1,275	1,530	1,811	2,119
Retained earnings	1,275	1,530	1,810	2,119
Net assets employed	21,000	22,530	24,340	26,459
Minimum requirement	20,000	22,000	24,200	26,620

The forecast predicts that by Year 3, the company may not have enough finance for the minimum net assets that it requires, if it relies entirely on retained profits as the source of new finance. The company may need to consider:

- Raising some additional finance from an external source; or
- Paying a lower dividend – even 49% would achieve the desired outcome in this example.

However, the forecast is only a rough guide to what may happen. Some of the assumptions may be incorrect – such as the assumption that all other operating expenditure is a fixed cost, and these costs will remain unchanged each year, in spite of a 33% increase in sales revenue. The assumption that dividends will always be 50% of profit before tax is also questionable, and so on.

So, when you make predictions, recognise how these may be incorrect and how a small change can have a big impact.

Note. Your forecast should be included as an appendix to your report. The body of the report should contain your analysis and conclusions based on the forecast that you have made, together with some commentary about the uncertainty in the forecast due to the assumptions and estimates that have been used.

4.1 Financial forecasting: Factors to consider

When preparing a financial forecast, it is important to bear in mind the following factors.

Financial forecasting: Issues to consider

Context of the forecast	Is the forecast for a project, an activity or the company's operations as a whole?
The materiality of the subject matter	The error tolerance level for the forecast The degree of accuracy that is possible
Reliability of the information	Can the information be relied upon and are the assumptions valid?
The timeframe for the forecast	Inevitably, forecasts for the longer term will be much less reliable than shorter-term forecasts.
Missing information	Try to identify any information that is missing that would improve the quality of the forecast.
Making your own assumptions	It is often necessary to make forecasts with incomplete information. If this is the case, you should make your own assumptions in order to complete a calculation. State any assumptions that you make in the Appendix to the report that provides the detailed computations.

5 Performance analysis

Key term

Key performance indicators are quantifiable measures used to evaluate the success of a business or individual in meeting a set objectives.

Quantitative information can be expressed in numbers and for the most part, is based on fact or actual events and can be independently verified.

Qualitative information is information which cannot be expressed in numbers, but still has considerable value to an organisation.

An important part of data analysis is creating evidence to measure the performance of a business against a strategy, budget or targets. This process uses data collected by the business, which may be financial, operational, qualitative or quantitative, which is then analysed into key performance indicators (ratios, percentages and other measures) so how a company is performing can be evaluated. The MDCS examination may require you to comment on aspects of operational performance within the business.

5.1 Identifying critical success factors to create suitable KPI's

A process of defining measurable KPIs based on known critical success factors (CSFs) is used by many organisations as an effective tool to measure strategic performance. Given this is such an important technique to help determine useful performance measures, we will look at two examples that demonstrate this process.

Case Study

One of the objectives of an organisation may be to maintain a high level of service direct from inventory without holding uneconomic inventory levels. The organisation has determined a goal to ensure that 95% of orders for goods can be satisfied directly from inventory, while minimising total holding costs and inventory levels. The following identifies the CSFs of the organisation which then links to relevant KPIs that measure whether these are being achieved.

CSFs might be identified as the following:	KPIs identified to measure the ability of the organisation to demonstrate its CSFs
Supplier performance in terms of quality and lead times	• Percentage of supply defects or goods returned • Percentage late deliveries after due date
Items are stock when ordered which requires good inventory management	• Percentage of orders satisfied directly from inventory vs 95% target • Frequency of stock outs, production stoppages or value of monthly stock write-offs
Forecasting of demand variations	• Value of unprocessed orders • Sales volume variances

This process of using CSFs to determine the most important KPIs for an organisation to measure will also help to determine the information needs of the organisation.

5.2 The balanced scorecard

The balanced scorecard was devised in the 1990s by Robert Kaplan and David Norton (1996). It is an approach to setting targets and measuring performance that adds strategic non-financial measures to 'traditional' financial measures.

The basis for this approach was that traditional financial targets and measures of performance are generally short-term in nature. KPI's are measures of what a business has achieved, and do not indicate necessarily whether it is on course to achieve its strategic objectives over the longer term.

Kaplan and Norton therefore recommended that measures and targets should be established for four perspectives of performance.

The balanced scorecard's four perspectives of performance

Perspective	
Financial	How does the company create value for its shareholders? To succeed financially, how should the company appear to its shareholders? What measures of performance will therefore provide an indication to shareholders, whether or not the company has been successful in achieving its objectives?
Customer	What do customers value? For the company to achieve its vision, how should it appear to customers? What measures of performance will provide an indication of whether customers are satisfied with the products or services of the company, and the value they derive from them?

Perspective	
Internal business processes	What operations must the company excel at?
	For the company to satisfy its shareholders and its customers, what business processes must it excel at?
	The focus of this perspective is on operational performance and excellence.
Learning and growth (or **Innovation and learning**)	How can the company continue to improve and create value over time?
	To achieve its strategic vision, how will the company sustain its ability to change and improve?
	Over time, a company can only maintain its competitive position by innovating and developing, and by improving the knowledge and skills of its work force.

A similar balanced set of perspectives of performance can be applied, with some modifications, to a non-profit-making organisation.

Three of these perspectives are non-financial in nature, but they are intended to identify key aspects of performance over the longer term that will be essential for the company to succeed in achieving its strategic objectives. Performance measures linked to these perspectives of performance are concerned more with the longer term than with short-term profit.

5.3 Using the balanced scorecard to create suitable KPI's

The significance of the balanced scorecard is that it focuses on longer-term strategy and vision, as well as on shorter-term financial performance. When considering a proposal, or when making recommendations about an investment, it is **appropriate to consider the strategic implications, as well as profit and financial return**. You should be aware of the strategic and non-financial implications of any recommendations or suggestions that you make.

The balanced scorecard is not a specific set of performance measures. Targets and measures that are appropriate for one company may not be relevant to another. Each company using a balanced scorecard should select measures that are relevant to its own circumstances and strategies.

There will be occasions when balanced scorecard targets are not fully consistent with each other. In particular, actions taken to improve non-financial strategic objectives (such as spending money on staff training or research and development) may have a negative impact on profit in the short term. The scorecard of performance targets should provide a suitable balance between the differing perspectives.

A guide to performance measures that may be used in a balanced scorecard are set out in the table below. For each perspective, there should usually be no more than four performance targets/measures: One or two for each perspective may be sufficient.

Balanced scorecard: Illustrative measures of performance

Perspective	
Financial	Total return on shareholder capital: (Total return = dividends plus increase in share price)
	Return on investment
	Profitability
	Positive net cash flows from operations
	Sales revenue growth
	Cost control; productivity improvements

4: Developing data analysis

Perspective	
Customer	Measures of customer satisfaction (eg from market research)
	Proportion of customers buying more than once/regularly
	Number of new customers
	On-time delivery
	Market share
Internal business processes	Percentage of orders met within a specified time, or percentage met from existing inventories
	Production cycle time: Speed of production
	Success rate of sales team in winning new orders
	Product reliability
Learning and growth (or Innovation and learning)	Employee productivity
	Labour turnover rate/employee retention rate
	Training hours per employee; rate of successful qualifications in examinations
	Number of new products developed for market launch
	Percentage of sales revenue earned from new products

Key performance indicators (KPIs) within a balanced scorecard should have the following characteristics:

- They should provide a measure that allows management to see whether the strategy is working.
- They should focus attention on what matters most to success.
- They should seek to measure accomplishment achieved, not just the amount of work done.
- Measures should be defined in terms of: Who is responsible for their achievement; unit of measure; frequency of measurement; expected targets (for comparison).
- Measurements should be reliable (based on data that is sufficiently accurate for its purpose).

In your MDCS examination, you will not be required to discuss the balanced scorecard directly. The important point to recognise is that when setting strategic performance objectives, or measuring actual performance, you should give due consideration to strategic and non-financial perspectives, and not focus exclusively on financial matters. As a professional accountant advising the CEO, you need to be able to understand non-financial strategic benefits and demonstrate the skill to weigh them against the financial cost.

Question

Dynamic Deliveries plc started out 100 years ago with two brothers delivering packages by bicycle. It is now one of the largest listed delivery companies in the world, operating in 20 countries, with over 40,000 employees and 9,000 vehicles, delivering more than 2 million parcels and documents each day. It is in a highly competitive market, but the board of Dynamic Deliveries plc have a strategic aim of growing the business in its core territories.

Required

Using the balance scorecard, identify critical success factors (CSFs) for Dynamic Deliveries and for each, suggest one suitable KPI to monitor its performance.

Answer

CSFs for Dynamic Deliveries	KPIs identified to measure the ability of Dynamic Deliveries to demonstrate its CSFs
Customer focus	
Reliable pickups at the time booked	Percentage of late pickups per day
Competitive prices	Competitor price/current price percentage. Here, use a standard delivery, by item, by weight, by distance to benchmark to competitor prices.
Good, polite service provided by delivery and support staff	Frequency of complaint per month Request for customer feedback surveys • Track satisfaction ratings per month • Review of individual customer comments
Internal operations focus	
Delivering goods on time and in good condition	Percentage of late deliveries per day Percentage of damaged or lost deliveries per day
Use of most efficient delivery routes	Actual distance/target distance percentage
Training focus	
Expert and knowledgeable staff resolve customers' requirements and issues quickly	Number of training days per quarter vs target
Finance focus	
Deliver optimal return for shareholders	Net margin, ROCE, annual increase in share price vs targets

5.4 Economy, efficiency and effectiveness

A further useful performance evaluation model to help create key performance indicators is economy, efficiency and effectiveness. When commenting on a business operation, you may find it useful to consider whether the operation is successful in achieving economy, efficiency and effectiveness.

- **Economy** is concerned with controlling costs and avoiding unnecessary spending, such as paying too much for raw materials.

- **Efficiency** is concerned with using resources in a productive way. Efficiency in the use of materials means avoiding excessive waste. Labour efficiency is concerned with avoiding idle time as much as possible and with improving labour productivity. Improvements in efficiency should reduce the costs of operations.

- **Effectiveness** means operating in a way that succeeds in achieving the intended purpose or target for the operations. For example, the purpose of spending money on advertising may be to increase sales. Effectiveness can therefore be measured by the increase in sales following an advertising campaign.

Question

A dry cleaning company will only retain loyal customers and attract new customers if the cleaning process is effective, completed on time and priced competitively. It is important the business owner understands the CSFs of the business and then gathers data which measures whether the business is achieving its CSFs.

Required

Using the three E's, identify critical success factors (CSFs) for Dynamic Deliveries and, for each, suggest suitable KPI's to monitor performance.

Answer

The following table identifies the CSFs of a dry cleaning business which then links to relevant KPIs that measure whether the CSFs are currently being achieved.

CSFs might be identified as the following:	KPIs identified to measure the ability of the organisation to demonstrate its CSFs
The cleaning process is **effective**	Percentage damaged items Percentage lost items Percentage not satisfactorily cleaned garments
The cleaning process is **efficient** and completed on time	Percentage capacity of machine utilised Percentage garments not ready for collection on due date
The cleaning process is **economic** and priced competitively	Variation to budget or target profit margin percentage Percentage Price variation (over/under) vs local competition (**Note:** A comparison with an external competitor is called benchmarking)

5.5 Flexing the numbers: Sensitivity analysis

Forecasts prepared by means of financial data analysis are inevitably subject to approximation and inaccuracy.

An important part of financial data analysis should therefore be to re-assess the forecast, given a change in items in the forecast. You should be able to 'flex the numbers'.

One of the techniques you may use is sensitivity analysis. This involves:

- Identifying the critical factors in the financial calculations
- Considering the effect of a change in the assumption or estimate for each of these factors

For example, if you think that the estimate for the rate of sales revenue growth is a critical factor in your financial forecast, you can prepare a revised forecast using an alternative assumption of lower sales growth.

In the MDCS examination, you will not be required to carry out sensitivity analysis on all the items in a financial forecast. You should identify the critical factors with care and restrict your sensitivity analysis to these factors.

If you do not have time in the examination to make detailed computations for the purpose of sensitivity analysis, you should at the very least:

- Indicate what you consider to be the critical factors.
- Be specific. Do not try to cover all eventualities and possible critical factors. Covering everything could bring your competence and understanding into question.
- Explain in general terms how any change in the value of the critical factor you have identified could affect your financial forecast. (Always make your explanation with authoritative words.)

Do not ignore uncertainty analysis in your report. Whatever time pressure you are under in the MDCS examination, **it will be insufficient** to state briefly that 'sensitivity analysis should be undertaken' or 'the numbers should be flexed and reviewed for accuracy'. This would be admitting that you have not done something that you should have done. However, as a general guide, you should avoid doing sensitivity analysis on more than two key assumptions, as it will become overly complicated and distract you from the main issue.

5.6 Sensitivity analysis matrix table

Sensitivity analysis matrix table

Often, a business case will contain a sensitivity analysis matrix table for key risks or uncertain variables that presents the impact of increasing key uncertainties. Often, the combined effect of all variables is summarised to estimate the impact if the uncertainties identified occur simultaneously.

In the following illustration, the expected NPV from a business opportunity is £750,000. However, by applying various levels of sensitivity to key uncertainties, we can see that the fall in product price and the increase in cost of finance have the greatest impact on the expected return. Each of the scenarios require the NPV to be separately calculated, only the result is shown in the table below for illustration purposes.

A cumulative position, incorporating all variable uncertainties, can also be provided to show a worse position.

Key uncertainties	0%	1%	2%	5%	10%
	£'000	£'000	£'000	£'000	£'000
Reduction in expected product price	750	748	746	735	602
Reduction in expected product volumes	750	745	735	690	628
Additional cost inflation	750	749	744	745	739
Additional costs of finance	750	722	690	643	544
Cumulative impact of uncertainties	**750**	**714**	**669**	**563**	**263**

A sensitivity analysis matrix table can be constructed by applying the following steps:

(a) Identify the key uncertainties, or variables, in your business case.

(b) Re-calculate the outcome for each variable change identified.

(c) Determine the cumulative impact of all variables. The important assumption here is that there is no relationship between each variable.

Be aware that constructing a sensitivity matrix table is time consuming and is often completed using a spreadsheet. In the MDCS exam, you may be required to use this technique on a simple and limited range of variables to demonstrate how returns may change as key assumptions change.

6 Reliability of information

The financial data analysis that you make in the MDCS examination may be based on assumptions given to you in the pre-seen or the exam. It is not possible to specify what these assumptions might be. However, as examples, the pre-seen may contain data about historical growth rates in sales revenue, or data about gross profit margins or operating costs. Information that you prepare for your report may then be based on such assumptions.

You should always be prepared to question and evaluate any of the assumptions that you have been given.

- You need to identify what the assumptions are that you are using and recognise that they may not be 'correct'. (For example, they may be too optimistic, or too pessimistic; or the assumption may have a logical flaw/weakness.)

- You then need to question whether these assumptions are valid, or whether they can be challenged. If you challenge any of the assumptions that you use, you should consider the possible consequences of making a different assumption for your financial analysis.

- If you feel that the assumptions in the pre-seen or exam are not valid, or are not the most appropriate, you should state the assumptions that you are using instead. If you do this, make sure that you explain clearly your reasons for making these different assumptions. It is not sufficient to state your different assumptions: You must justify your opinion.

- If you make any additional assumptions of your own, you will need to explain these (and **justify** these) in your report. Your report for the MDCS examination will be marked on the quality of the assumptions that you have made – and explained.

- When making an analysis of financial data, it is essential to demonstrate a suitable degree of professional scepticism. You should question the information and the assumptions or estimates that you have used in your analysis. Where has the basic information come from? Who provided the estimates? Professional scepticism is covered in more detailed in Chapter 11.

7 Interpretation of results

Financial data analysis does not end with the calculations. The results must be explained to the readers of your report.

If your data analysis is provided to support advice or a recommendation that you are giving in your report, you need to explain:

- Why you are giving your chosen advice or recommendation, on the basis of the analysis you have prepared

- What the expected consequences will be, if your advice or recommendation is accepted or even if it is rejected

8 Improving data analysis

The data analysis skills you will need to demonstrate in the MDCS examination itself are as follows:

- Recognise the need for financial data analysis and the purpose of the analysis: What will be the purpose of the advice you give or recommendation that you make?

- Choose the technique or techniques to use for making the analysis.

- Exercise your judgment, especially in terms of materiality, in selecting the appropriate level of detail for the analysis.

- Construct a clear appendix (or appendices) based on the information provided, using any additional assumptions you consider necessary and appropriate. You need to do the calculations before you can write your report!

- Identify and evaluate all the assumptions that are made in the information provided in the pre-seen or exam.

- Apply your professional scepticism to the reliability of the figures.

- Consider using or suggesting sensitivity analysis and flexing the numbers to provide a range of outcomes which will help to evaluate risk.

- State clearly any reservations that you have about the recommendations that you make, or any assumptions made.

- Overall, aim to ensure the advice or decision provided is consistent with your financial data analysis, and your data analysis is based on sound judgment and sensible assumptions – then you will be given credit in the marking of your MDCS examination report.

Data analysis skills must be practised in order to develop and improve. Therefore, it is important you work through the four practice case studies in this L&P Workbook.

End of chapter question

This question continues the Well Being Case Study, which was introduced in Chapters 2 and 3.

Memo from Janet Hunter circulated to board members: Feel Good Clinics

From: Janet Hunter
Date: 8 April 2019

Subject: Feel Good Clinics

I have just received a report from our investment bank about a health clinic company, Feel Good Clinics, which is available for sale in Bulgaria. It is privately owned, and I understand that its owner, who is also the chairperson and chief executive, wishes to retire. As their sons and daughters do not want to run the business, they think that selling is their only realistic option.

I am unaware of how many other potential bidders there are.

The owner of Feel Good Clinics has supplied the following most recent financial information. They say it was prepared two weeks ago and is still in draft form.

Draft summary statement of financial position as at 31 December 2018

	BGN'000
Non-current assets	39,060
Inventory	1,260
Trade receivables	140
Prepayments	840
Cash	8,400
	49,700
Trade creditors and other liabilities	1,540
Equity capital	48,160
	49,700

Notes

1. The non-current assets include leasehold premises. These are included in the statement of financial position at a value of BGN25.2 million, but the lease interest is thought to be worth about BGN35.0 million in the open market.
2. The trade receivables relate to three long-standing debts that are unlikely to be paid but have not yet been written off or impaired.
3. The owners plan to take out all the cash from the business before selling it.
4. The current exchange rate is the Bulgarian Lev and is currently quoted at BGN 2.80 = £1. The exchange rate has been fairly stable for the past year or so.

Draft summary statement of profit or loss for year to 31 December 2018

	BGN'000
Revenue	47,240
Employment benefit expenses	22,680
Depreciation	5,040
Administrative and other expenses	13,300
Operating profit	6,220
Finance income	280
Profit before tax	6,500
Income tax	1,625
Profit after tax	4,875

Feel Good Clinics pays Bulgarian corporate tax of 25%.

The annual operating profit of Feel Good Clinics has been increasing at about 3% per year.

Other relevant information

Our investment bank has advised that the acquisition would be high-risk, since revenue growth for Feel Good Clinics has been less than for the industry sector as a whole in Bulgaria. It suggests that a cost of capital of about 12% to 15% might be appropriate for evaluation of the company as an acquisition investment.

Requirement

Estimate a price that might be offered for the acquisition of Feel Good Clinics and state what you consider to be the main risks associated with this strategy.

Suggested answer

There are only two types of valuation that seem possible with the available information:

(a) A net assets valuation
(b) A present value of future free cash flows

Net assets valuation (See Exhibit 1)

	BGN'000
Net assets as in statement of financial position (49,700 – 1,540)	48,160
Adjust for:	
Cash (to be taken out of the business)	(8,400)
Non-recoverable receivables	(140)
Property valuation adjustment (35,000 – 25,200)	9,800
Net assets	49,420

Net assets valuation (BGN 49,420,000/2.8) = £17,650,000

However, this valuation is based on a draft and relates to 31 December 2018. A more up-to-date statement of financial position should be obtained. Since the acquisition of a private company will require the agreement of its current owners, the acquisition needs to be 'friendly', and the owner(s) and board of directors of Feel Good Clinics should be prepared to produce the up-to-date information required.

An independent valuation of the leasehold premises should also be obtained. The estimate used here seems to be based on 'guesswork' by an unidentified person or persons.

Free cash flow valuation (PV of future free cash flows in perpetuity)

What are the free cash flows of Feel Good Clinics?

- Assumptions need to be made about essential non-current asset replacements and the rate of taxation.
- One view is that depreciation should be added back on to profits, because it is a non-cash expense. However, depreciation may represent an amount that the company needs to spend each year on replacement non-current assets. This means that although depreciation is a non-cash expense, it is a reasonable approximation to the cash payments required to replace worn-out non-current assets each year.

The assumptions here are:

(a) Operating profit is a reasonable approximation to operating cash flow.
(b) The depreciation charge is a reasonable approximation of the amount of essential non-current asset replacement each year; therefore, do not add depreciation back in calculating free cash flows.
(c) Ignore future interest income, since cash will be taken out of the business.
(d) The rate of Bulgarian tax will remain at 25% and will be applied to the company's annual free cash flows.
(e) Value the company on the basis of no annual growth in free cash flows and valuation of annual cash flows in perpetuity. You may choose to assume that the business will continue to grow by 3% per year in perpetuity, or for a limited number of years in the future (for which forecasts may be considered reasonably reliable), after which the assumption is that there will be no further growth in perpetuity. The assumption about growth is very important; whatever assumption you use, it can be challenged!

The following valuation is an estimate of the present value of the free cash flows in perpetuity of Feel Good Clinics.

(a) **Annual free cash flow (BGN'000), assuming zero growth and 12% required return (cost of capital)**

Annual free cash flow (FCF) = 6,220 – (25% of 6,220) = 4,665

Present value of annual FCF in perpetuity, using 12% discount rate (in BGN'000):

Current FCF/Cost of capital = 4,665/0.12 = 38,875

Using an exchange rate of 2.8 BGN = £1: Value in £ = 38,875,000/2.8 = £13,883,929

Say £14,000,000

(b) **Annual free cash flow (BGN'000), assuming 3% annual growth in perpetuity and 12% required return (cost of capital)**

Valuation = Current FCF × (1+ growth rate)/(Cost of capital – growth rate)

(In BGN'000) = 4,665 (1.03)/(0.12 – 0.03) = 53,388

Using an exchange rate of 2.8 BGN = £1: Value in £ = 53,388,333/2.8 = £19,067,262

Say £19,000,000

(c) **Annual free cash flow (BGN'000), assuming zero growth and 15% required return (cost of capital)**

Valuation in BGN'000 = 4,665/0.15 = 31,100

Using an exchange rate of 2.8 BGN = £1: Value in £ = 31,100,000/2.8 = £11,107,143

Say £11,000,000

(d) **Annual free cash flow (BGN'000), assuming 3% annual growth in perpetuity and 15% required return (cost of capital)**

Valuation in BGN'000 = 4,665 (1.03)/(0.15 – 0.03) = 40,041

Using an exchange rate of 2.8 BGN = £1: Value in £ = 40,041,250/2.8 = £14,300,446

Say £14,300,000

Overall, the value of the cash flows from the business appears to be worth less than the company's claimed net assets of £17.65 million. Future annual growth would need to be in excess of 3% annually to exceed this value. The board of directors of WBL should not consider an acquisition for Feel Good Clinics unless its owners agree with a valuation below the company's draft net asset value, or unless the board is confident that WBL would be able to achieve annual growth in excess of 3% if it were to acquire the business of Feel Good Clinics.

Main acquisition risks

The main risks would seem to be:

(a) Paying too much for a company that does not have particularly strong growth prospects

(b) Problems with assimilating an acquired company: Clash of cultures, getting the acquired company to adopt WBL's methods and achieve the same quality standard as WBL

(c) Problems with managing a subsidiary in a different country. How much senior management time will be needed?

(d) How much cash would WBL need to put into the acquired business, in addition to the purchase price – in order to provide working capital (since the current owner will take out all the cash that the company has)?

(e) Potentially volatile currency

Research and analysis of the MDCS pre-seen and exam

Topic list	Syllabus reference
1 Research and analysis of pre-seen material	LO 2
2 Use of unseen material and planning exam requirements	LO 2

Introduction

In this chapter, we consider how to make best use of the pre-seen material in the Case Study and how to utilise the clues in it to prepare for the exam and the unseen material. You will find the guidance in Chapters 2 to 4 very useful here. We also consider how to use your time wisely in the exam, in reading the unseen material and planning and writing your answer. We will apply this guidance in Chapters 8 to 10, using the information in our first Case Study, Sophie McCloud (Chapter 7).

1 Research and analysis of pre-seen material

FAST FORWARD The better your knowledge and understanding of the pre-seen material when you go into the exam, the better your chances of achieving a good score.

The Case Study is likely to be structured to give you some clues about what's in the exam but without giving the game away completely. You can use the pre-seen material to research the industry a bit so as to gather background knowledge that could be useful when you come to do your exam. You will also be able to revise key accounting and auditing standards that you may have forgotten but that you think may be relevant to information contained in the pre-seen.

Although the content varies by case study, the following table gives you some typical content of pre-seen material and suggestions as to what you might do with that information.

Content	Suggestion
Information about the type of business/industry	Try to get some **background information** about the industry, the **key players**, the key **competitive issues** and think about the key **accounting issues**. BUT don't forget that you're answering **questions on the case study company**, not a real life company; this is just to help you understand the case study company.
	An **internet search** is a good place to start. For example, Sophie McCloud (Case Study 1) is a luxury chocolate maker. If you do an internet search using the keywords, 'luxury chocolate maker UK,' a range of company names come up, together with a few blogs and news stories.
	Having found the names of major companies in that industry, try and find one that's a listed company. You can then access their **annual report** (look in the investor relations section of their website). As well as the financial statements, the annual report will usually contain lots of information on the company and its internal and external environment which can be useful. If the real-life company is part of a diversified group, which is very common, there is likely to be **segmental information** in the financial statements and in the other information in the report, which can be useful.
	Now try a brief **internet news search** on the real-life company. This will give you information on important events affecting that company which are likely to affect the case study company too and may help in discussions of risk.
Financial and operating data/KPIs	This gives a real clue as to the key issues in the company.
	Look for **trends** to see if the company is growing or struggling, look at **margins** to get an idea of how vulnerable the company will be to downturns in revenue. The **choice of specific KPIs** given to you is also likely to be a clue as to the key issues affecting the business.

Content	Suggestion
Extracts from financial statements	These obviously give you information about the financial performance of the company. They could give you a clue that there are issues for you to discuss in **a risks question,** or could indicate **accounting or auditing issues** that could be examined. Although you can't take anything with you into the exam, it's a good idea to perform some **financial analysis** on the figures in advance, as it may highlight risks that will inform how you read the rest of the case. Even if you don't remember, say, inventory days when you go into the exam, you might remember there is slow moving inventory. We'd suggest as a minimum a **trend analysis** on the statement of profit or loss and some **ratio analysis**. Some case studies may give you certain of the **notes to the financial statements**. Notice the accounting issues that these notes cover, as these could be clues as to what the question will be about.
Details of key personnel	You could be given **names of directors/senior management**, and other information referring to these individuals will appear in different exhibits. It might be worth taking **notes on each key individual** as their name arises, in order to build up a list by person of their qualifications, competence, tasks and issues as the case progresses. This will make it much easier to get a picture of what is happening in the company and enable you to tailor your communication appropriately.
Minutes of board meetings Emails/memos Press articles	Information about the company may be presented to you in the form of a **direct scenario** or via a **series of exhibits**. It can be a little overwhelming, so as you read, think of the information as relating to: • **Strategy/operational issues/risks** • **Accounting/auditing** • **Tax**

You need to know the pre-seen information thoroughly. You'll be given the information again when you get into the exam, but you have limited time and you also need to absorb the unseen information and plan and write your answer.

In order to help organise your thoughts, you could try drawing some sort of mind maps/diagrams. The creation of these drawings will help to cement in your mind the information and how the different aspects relate to one another. You could draw a mind map using specialised mapping software or an app such as MS Word, or by writing different information on sticky notes and organising them into themes.

Although the structure of your mind map will obviously vary according to the question, and could be a lot more complicated than this, an example of a structure is given below.

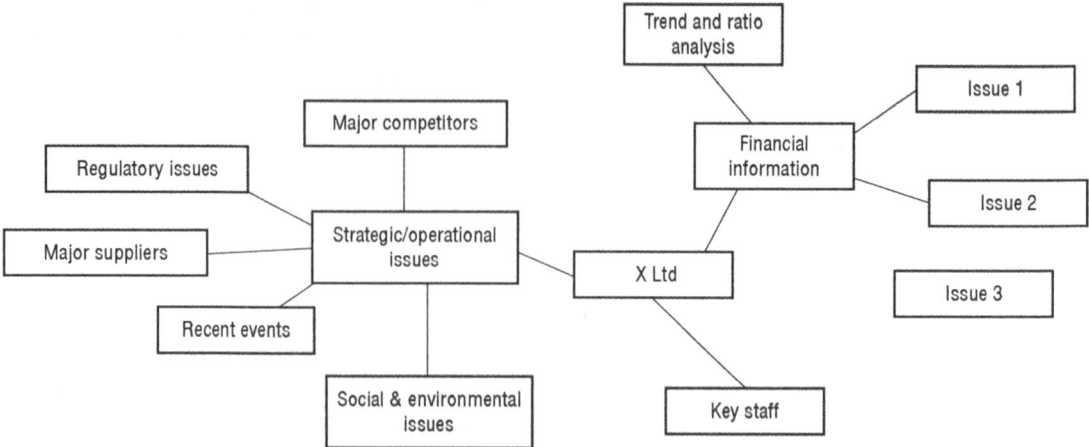

Having gathered and organised all this information, do the following.

Research the **accounting and auditing standards** relating to the accounting issues that you have identified. There's a good chance that the issues raised will be examined as part of accounting, tax or auditing questions and, especially if it's been a while since you studied these subjects, you may need to refresh your technical knowledge. If the pre-seen material raises **corporate governance** issues, then you should revise those too. If there are any hints of **tax issues,** then you should revisit your tax studies.

We'd also suggest that you prepare some kind of brief **risk assessment**. Past case studies invariably involve some kind of risk question, whether it be business risk (identification, assessment, or management) or audit risk (identification and response). Even if the question in the exam is not on risk, thinking about a risk assessment will be useful in most questions on strategic or operational management.

Remember, the better you know the pre-seen material going into the exam, the better your answer is likely to be.

Case Study

ABC plc has disclosed the following KPIs in its annual report. What might the choice of these KPIs tell you about the company?

Cost of products donated to healthcare charities	$130,000
Number of new product licences during year	87
Number of serious accidents in the workplace	2 serious accidents
Number of days of training by staff	1,260

The company appears to have some kind of production facility in that reducing serious accidents is an important issue and serious accidents are arguably more likely to occur in a manufacturing setting. Innovation appears to be important to the company, given that the number of new product licences is measured and there is a focus on staff training, which is likely to lead to more innovation. The company seems to be developing medical products, maybe equipment or pharmaceutical products, and is keen to demonstrate its social conscience by donating products to healthcare charities.

Relevant financial reporting topics that you might identify and choose to revise are intangible assets and corporate social responsibility reporting. From a tax perspective, the treatment of spending on research and development and charitable donations may be relevant.

2 Use of unseen material and planning exam requirements

> **FAST FORWARD**
> A key skill in the MDCS exam is being able to organise a large quantity of information and pick out the important parts for answering the question requirements.

2.1 Reading the information

You are not allowed to take any of your notes on the pre-seen material or the material itself into the exam (although you will be given another copy), but if you know the material well and have performed a thorough analysis as suggested above, then you will be well prepared to face the exam.

Although you will undoubtedly need to refer back to the pre-seen material to confirm details in order to write your answer, you should already know it well enough that you don't need to read it in depth.

The information in the unseen material is likely to provide further details on some issues raised in the pre-seen material, in order to give you a fuller picture, or narrow down the number of options or alternatives that were introduced in the pre-seen material. There may be totally new information introduced but it is likely to form only a small part of the exam.

It is a good idea to read the exam requirements before reading the unseen material as it will provide valuable context. For example, the pre-seen material may have given some information about challenges facing the company and so you have performed a risk assessment as part of your pre-exam work. If the requirement then asks you to discuss audit risks, then you know that you need to focus on those risks rather than business risks when you're reading the unseen material.

When you read the unseen material, think about how it may impact on the knowledge you have gained from your analysis of the pre-seen material. For example, the pre-seen material may raise various financing options and then the unseen material concludes as to which option is to be pursued.

2.2 Organising and synthesising the information

In the first half of this chapter, we suggested that you draft a mind map of the information in the pre-seen material. When you first get into the exam, it's a good idea to roughly draft out the bare bones of the mind map as part of your workings and then you can briefly add information from the unseen material. The emphasis here is on brief: you don't have to include lots of information – just a pointer as to where the additional information can be found.

For example, the mind map above has a textbox that says 'Key staff.' It may be that the unseen material includes details of the finance director, Melody Grey, leaving suddenly in disputed circumstances just before the year end. You wouldn't need to record all that information, but you might write, something like 'FD leaving, p18' next to the textbox, so that you know where to look later.

At the end of this reading and organising process, you'll have an overview of all the information you've been given. At this point, read the requirements again, because you may then realise that some of the information laid out in the mind map is not needed to answer the question. If that's the case, put a light line through that branch of your map.

2.3 Planning your answer

On a workings sheet, write out brief headings based on the requirements and jot down the sub-headings that you will need in your answer and the location of the information that you will use in your answer. For example, if the question is about audit risk, you may write, 'FD leaving, possible fraud/unfair dismissal, p18'.

By having this plan, you'll be able to take what may seem like an overwhelming task and break it down into smaller, more 'doable' chunks.

And then you can start writing!

We will illustrate the processes discussed in this chapter using the first of our case studies, Sophie McCloud, in Chapters 7 to 10, and then look at how to write this all up in Chapters 11 and 12.

End of chapter question

You are the audit manager in charge of the audit of Poinsetta Publishing plc, a new client for your firm with a year end of 31 December 20X3.

The company publishes a series of lifestyle magazines. The company's major titles are *Scandi Interiors*, *Modern Housekeeping*, and *Renter Style*. The typical readership of these titles is female, married, aged 35-45, and has a household income of £35,000 – £50,000 per annum.

A new chief executive, Damian Morse, was appointed a year ago. Damian sees his mission as being the modernisation of the company. As a result, the company's printing department was closed down and the staff made redundant. Printing is now outsourced.

Damian is keen to widen the demographics of the company's readership due to poor economic conditions. A new magazine, *Grey Nomad*, aimed at those over 60, is scheduled to be launched on 1 January 20X4. Damian has also entered into negotiations for the purchase of E-solutions, an electronic publishing company, with the intention of launching an interactive electronic magazine, *EDIY*. E-solutions is based in Taiwan, where your firm does not have an affiliated office.

Requirement

Prepare brief notes on the business risks and possible financial reporting issues facing Poinsetta Publishing, such as would be useful in preparing for the MDCS exam.

Suggested answer

Business risks

(a) Due to the current economic recession, less people will have money to renovate their property, and so fewer copies of the interiors magazines will be sold, reducing readership and therefore, revenue and profits.

(b) Advertising revenue is also likely to fall. This will be because companies will have reduced advertising budgets and so will be more selective in the way they spend their money. Also, as mentioned above, the circulation of the magazines will probably fall, so advertisers will be less keen to advertise, and if they do, they will probably expect to pay lower rates.

(c) Damian is new to the job, and may have problems with 'change management' issues. Staff at the company may be resentful of him, and his mission to modernise the company may lead to him antagonising existing staff. Key staff might leave the company, or work behind Damian's back to sabotage his plans.

(d) The closure of the printing department and the redundancy of the staff will increase the potential resentment t Damian. Other staff may be fearful of losing their jobs and may be tempted to start looking for other sources of employment. Poinsetta Publishing will then lose good staff, which will adversely affect the business operations.

(e) Following the closure, the printing function has now been outsourced. This means that Poinsetta Publishing is unable to control the quality of the printing output in the same way that it would if it was performed by Poinsetta Publishing.

(f) The new magazine, *Grey Nomad*, is operating in a very competitive business segment. Customers may be more likely to purchase existing, established magazines which will limit sales and advertising revenue, as explained above.

(g) The new magazine is operating in a different market segment to the company's existing magazines. The company's staff may not have expertise in this area, and may not know what areas are of interest to such a readership.

(h) Interactive electronic publishing is a new area for the company to move into. It is also a new technology, which may experience operational problems. It is also unclear whether there is a market for such an interactive electronic magazine.

Financial reporting issues

(a) Magazines may be sold on a subscription basis, possibly with a bundle discount built in, giving rise to revenue recognition issued (IFRS 15 *Revenue recognition*).

(b) The printing department has been closed and may qualify to be reported as a discontinued operation (IFRS 5 *Discontinued operations*).

(c) Property, plant and equipment used by the printing department is likely to have been disposed of, giving rise to a profit or loss on disposal (IAS 16 *Property, Plant and Equipment*).

(d) The closure of the printing department may have resulted in some of the company's assets being impaired (IAS 36 *Impairment of assets*).

(e) Staff in the printing department have been made redundant and therefore accounting for termination benefits is relevant (IAS 19 *Employee benefits*).

(f) Poinsetta Publishing is in negotiations to buy E-solutions and therefore, acquisition accounting and consolidation accounting are relevant (IFRS 3 *Business combinations* and IFRS 10 *Consolidation accounting*).

(g) E-solutions is located overseas, which is likely to make foreign currency exchange an issue (IAS 21 *The Effects of Changes in Foreign Exchange Rates*)

6: Sustainability

Topic list	Syllabus reference
1 Introduction to sustainability	All LOs
2 An unsustainable world?	"
3 Sustainable development	"
4 Development of sustainability awareness, guidelines and regulation	"
5 Sustainability and environmental, social and governance	"
6 Sustainability strategy setting and management decision making	"
7 ESG risk management and metrics for sustainability performance monitoring and reporting	"
8 Sustainability reporting	"
9 International Sustainability Standards Board (ISSB) IFRS® Sustainability Disclosure Standards	"
10 Assurance engagements related to disclosures in sustainability reporting	"
11 The role of accountants and management in developing sustainability within organisations	"

Introduction

As the world's eyes are focusing on the adverse effects of climate change, the awareness of ESG issues has increased and there has been a rising trend for global stock exchanges to impose mandatory sustainability reporting for listed companies.

Board of directors are now expected to consider their ESG impact of their products and operations when they are developing business strategies and making business decisions. The monitoring and reporting of ESG's key performance indicators are designed to improve business sustainability and provide transparency of ESG and related performance to stakeholders and particularly, investors.

This chapter on sustainability investigates different aspects of sustainability such as sustainability strategy setting, sustainability management and decision making, sustainability performance measuring and monitoring and sustainability reporting requirements. As sustainability becomes more important to stakeholders and long-term success, the ability to apply sustainability knowledge in multi-disciplinary case study scenarios is essential.

This chapter investigate different aspects of sustainability such as strategy setting, management and decision making, sustainability performance measuring and monitoring and sustainability reporting requirements. The ability to apply sustainability knowledge in multi-disciplinary case study scenarios is essential.

1 Introduction to sustainability

Sustainability is a multifaceted concept aimed at improving people's lives and safeguarding the planet for future generations. Stemming from the 1987 Brundtland report, sustainable development is defined as 'development that meets the needs of the present without compromising the ability of future generations to meet their own needs.'

The scope of sustainability has evolved beyond environmental concerns to encompass a wide range of issues, including increasing disparities in wealth, population growth, biodiversity loss, deteriorating air and water quality, climate change, human rights, and bribery and corruption.

In recent years, heightened awareness of environmental, social, and governance (ESG) issues has prompted global stock exchanges to mandate sustainability reporting for listed companies. Consequently, board directors are now expected to integrate ESG considerations into their business strategies and decision-making processes.

This chapter delves into various aspects of sustainability, including:

- **An unsustainable world?** This section examines empirical evidence highlighting the challenges and consequences of unsustainable practices, such as resource depletion, environmental degradation, and social inequalities, underscoring the urgent need for sustainable solutions.

- **Sustainable development:** This section explores the concept of sustainable development, which seeks to meet the needs of the present without compromising the ability of future generations to meet their own needs, encompassing economic prosperity, social equity, and environmental stewardship.

- **Development of sustainability awareness, guidelines, and regulation:** This section explores the evolution of sustainability awareness, the establishment of guidelines and regulations, and their impact on corporate practices.

- **Sustainability and environmental, social, and governance (ESG):** This section examines the interconnectedness of sustainability with environmental, social, and governance factors and their significance in driving long-term value creation.

- **Sustainability strategy setting and management decision making:** This section discusses the formulation and implementation of sustainability strategies and their integration into organisational decision-making processes.

- **ESG risk management and metrics for sustainability performance monitoring and reporting:** This section explores the identification, assessment, and management of ESG risks, as well as the development of metrics for monitoring and reporting sustainability performance.

- **Sustainability reporting:** This section examines the principles and practices of sustainability reporting, including the disclosure of ESG-related information to stakeholders and investors.

- **International Sustainability Standards Board (ISSB) IFRS Sustainability Disclosure Standards:** This section provides an overview of the ISSB's role in developing global sustainability disclosure standards aligned with International Financial Reporting Standards (IFRS).

- **Assurance engagements related to disclosures in sustainability reporting:** This section discusses the role of assurance engagements in enhancing the credibility and reliability of disclosures in sustainability reporting.

- **The role of accountants and management in developing sustainability within organisations:** This section explores the roles and responsibilities of accountants and management in driving sustainability initiatives and embedding sustainability principles into organisational culture and practices.

These themes collectively underscore the importance of sustainability in fostering resilience, transparency, and responsible business practices in today's interconnected world.

In addition to understanding the various aspects of sustainability outlined in this chapter, it is imperative for students to be able to respond effectively to sustainability strategy setting, reporting, and assurance in multi-disciplinary case study scenarios.

As sustainability considerations become increasingly integral to organisational decision-making and stakeholder expectations, students must develop the skills necessary to provide informed advice to organisations on these matters in real-world scenarios.

This includes not only grasping the technical aspects of sustainability reporting frameworks and assurance standards but also understanding the strategic implications of sustainability initiatives on business operations, reputation, and long-term value creation.

Sustainable enterprise is crucial in today's world due to its potential to drive economic growth, enhance social well-being, and protect the environment. By adopting sustainable practices, businesses can mitigate risks associated with resource scarcity, regulatory changes, and reputational damage, while also tapping into new markets and opportunities for innovation.

Sustainable development is closely intertwined with economic resilience and prosperity. Unsustainable consumption and production patterns, coupled with resource depletion and environmental degradation, pose risks to long-term economic stability. Transitioning to sustainable business models and investing in clean technologies can spur innovation, create new job opportunities, and drive economic growth while minimising environmental impacts. Moreover, sustainable finance mechanisms such as green bonds and impact investing can mobilise capital towards environmentally and socially beneficial projects.

Achieving global sustainability requires collaborative efforts from diverse stakeholders, including governments, businesses, civil society organizations, and individuals. Governments play a crucial role in setting regulatory frameworks, implementing policies, and mobilising resources to support sustainability initiatives. Businesses have a responsibility to integrate sustainability into their operations, supply chains, and corporate strategies, driving innovation and promoting responsible practices. Civil society organizations and grassroots movements play a vital role in advocating for change, raising awareness, and holding stakeholders accountable for their actions. Individuals also have a role to play through their consumption choices, lifestyle habits, and active participation in community initiatives.

Businesses and enterprises play a critical role in delivering a sustainable world through responsible practices, innovation, and collaboration, which we will explore further in this chapter. By integrating sustainability into their core strategies, businesses can drive positive social and environmental impact while also generating long-term value for shareholders and stakeholders.

Achieving global sustainability is not only a moral imperative but also an economic and social necessity. The interconnected challenges of climate change, environmental degradation, and social inequality require urgent and concerted action from all sectors of society.

By embracing sustainable practices, fostering collaboration, and prioritising the well-being of people and the planet, we can pave the way towards a more resilient, equitable, and prosperous future for generations to come.

For MDCS students, being equipped with the knowledge and expertise to navigate complex sustainability challenges means you will be able to contribute meaningfully to sustainable development goals contained in multi-disciplinary case study scenarios.

2 An unsustainable world?

In recent years, the concept of sustainability has gained significant traction across various sectors, from business and finance to environmental conservation and social development. The pressing challenges of climate change, resource depletion, and social inequality have underscored the urgent need for a paradigm shift towards sustainable practices on a global scale. This discussion paper aims to explore the critical importance of achieving global sustainability and the implications for stakeholders worldwide.

Global sustainability refers to the ability to meet the needs of the present without compromising the ability of future generations to meet their own needs. It encompasses environmental, social, and economic dimensions, often referred to as the three pillars of sustainability. Achieving global sustainability requires addressing interconnected issues such as climate change mitigation, biodiversity conservation, poverty alleviation, and equitable economic growth.

In the following section we consider the specific issue of climate change and planetary boundary limits.

2.1 Climate change

Key term

> **Climate change:** Refers to the long-term alteration of global or regional climate patterns, primarily driven by human activities that disrupt the Earth's natural systems and processes.

Climate change encompasses shifts in temperature, precipitation, sea levels, and weather patterns, with profound consequences for ecosystems, societies, and economies worldwide.

2.1.1 Evidence for climate change

The scientific evidence for action on climate change and environmental damage is compelling, with various indicators showing significant degradation of Earth's systems. For example:

- **Increase in global temperature:** The Earth's average temperature has risen by approximately 1.2 degrees Celsius above pre-industrial levels, primarily due to human activities such as burning fossil fuels and deforestation (Source: IPCC).

- **Rise in sea levels:** Global sea levels have risen by about 20 centimetres since the late 19th century, with an accelerating rate of increase in recent decades (Source: NASA).

- **Increase in air pollution:** Air pollution is responsible for an estimated 7 million premature deaths worldwide every year, with particulate matter and ozone pollution being the leading causes (Source: WHO).

- **Loss of natural forests:** The world has lost over 420 million hectares of forest since 1990, primarily due to deforestation for agriculture, urbanisation, and logging (Source: FAO).

- **Reduced biodiversity:** Species extinction rates are currently estimated to be 1,000 times higher than the natural background rate, with an estimated 10,000 species going extinct every year (Source: IPBES).

- **Atmospheric CO2 levels:** The concentration of carbon dioxide (CO_2) in the atmosphere has increased from pre-industrial levels of 280 parts per million (ppm) to over 415 ppm in 2021, the highest level in at least 800,000 years (Source: NOAA).

- **Melting ice caps and glaciers:** Polar ice caps and glaciers are melting at unprecedented rates. For example, Greenland's ice sheet lost an average of 268 billion metric tons of ice per year between 2002 and 2019, contributing to global sea level rise (Source: NASA). Similarly, Antarctica's ice loss has tripled in the last decade, with significant impacts on sea level rise and coastal regions (Source: Nature).

- **Changing precipitation patterns:** Climate change is altering precipitation patterns worldwide. Regions like the Sahel in Africa and parts of the Mediterranean experience increased drought frequency and severity, leading to water shortages and food insecurity (Source: IPCC). Conversely, other regions, such as South-East Asia, face heavier rainfall and flooding events, disrupting agriculture and infrastructure (Source: NOAA).

- **Extreme weather events:** The frequency and intensity of extreme weather events have risen due to climate change. For instance, hurricanes in the North Atlantic have become more powerful, with stronger winds and heavier rainfall, posing significant risks to coastal communities (Source: NOAA). Heatwaves have also become more frequent and intense, leading to heat-related illnesses and deaths (Source: IPCC).

- **Ocean acidification:** The absorption of carbon dioxide by the oceans is causing ocean acidification, impacting marine ecosystems globally. Coral reefs, crucial marine habitats, are particularly vulnerable, with approximately 75% of coral reefs projected to suffer severe bleaching by 2070 under current emissions scenarios (Source: Nature Climate Change). Acidification also affects shell-forming organisms like molluscs and plankton, disrupting marine food webs and fisheries (Source: NOAA).

World scientists and climate experts, along with many governments, concur that urgent action is needed to mitigate greenhouse gas emissions, adapt to changing climatic conditions, and build resilience in vulnerable communities to address the challenges posed by climate change.

2.1.2 Consequences of climate change

The following main consequences of climate change are multifaceted and pose significant challenges across various aspects of Earth's systems:

(a) **Greenhouse gas concentrations and climate system functions**

Elevated levels of greenhouse gases, such as carbon dioxide and methane, disrupt Earth's energy balance by trapping heat in the atmosphere. This leads to global warming, resulting in changes to climate system dynamics. For example, altered ocean currents and atmospheric circulation patterns impact weather phenomena like El Niño and La Niña events, with far-reaching consequences for regional climates and ecosystems.

(b) **Precipitation**

Climate change alters precipitation patterns, leading to shifts in rainfall intensity, frequency, and distribution. Some regions experience more frequent and severe droughts, while others face increased rainfall and flooding events. These changes affect water availability for agriculture, drinking water supplies, and hydropower generation. Additionally, altered precipitation patterns disrupt freshwater ecosystems, leading to habitat loss and species decline.

(c) **Storm frequency and intensity**

Warmer ocean temperatures provide energy for more intense and frequent tropical storms, hurricanes, and cyclones. These extreme weather events pose significant risks to coastal communities, increasing the likelihood of storm surges, flooding, and erosion. Infrastructure damage, loss of livelihoods, and human casualties result from these intensified storms, exacerbating the challenges of climate adaptation and disaster resilience.

(d) **Growing zones of instability and inhabitability**

Climate change exacerbates environmental stressors, creating zones of instability and inhabitability in vulnerable regions. Competition over dwindling resources, such as water and arable land, escalates tensions and conflicts among communities and nations. Displacement of populations due to climate-induced events, such as sea-level rise and desertification, strains social cohesion and exacerbates humanitarian crises. Moreover, loss of biodiversity and disruptions to ecosystems undermine the capacity of natural systems to provide essential services, further compromising societal resilience and adaptation efforts.

These consequences highlight the interconnectedness of climate change with various aspects of human and environmental well-being, emphasising the urgent need for comprehensive and collaborative action to mitigate its impacts and build resilience for a sustainable future.

Current examples of the consequences of climate change

The Arctic region is experiencing accelerated warming due to elevated greenhouse gas concentrations. This has led to the rapid melting of polar ice caps and glaciers, disrupting global climate patterns. The loss of Arctic sea ice is altering ocean currents and atmospheric circulation, impacting weather systems worldwide. For instance, changes in the polar jet stream have been linked to extreme weather events, such as prolonged heatwaves and severe winter storms, in regions far beyond the Arctic.

Precipitation

The Indian subcontinent has witnessed erratic precipitation patterns in recent years, with alternating periods of drought and intense rainfall. These changes have affected agricultural productivity and water availability, leading to crop failures, water shortages, and socioeconomic disruptions. Additionally, increased rainfall intensity has resulted in devastating floods, such as the Kerala floods in 2018, which submerged vast areas, displaced millions of people, and caused widespread destruction of infrastructure and livelihoods.

Storm frequency and intensity

The Atlantic hurricane season has become increasingly active and destructive due to rising sea surface temperatures fuelled by climate change. Hurricanes like Harvey, Irma, and Maria in 2017 demonstrated unprecedented intensity and destructive power, causing widespread devastation across the Caribbean and southeastern United States. These extreme weather events highlight the heightened risks faced by coastal communities, including storm surges, flooding, and infrastructure damage, underscoring the urgent need for climate-resilient infrastructure and disaster preparedness measures.

Growing zones of instability and inhabitability

The Lake Chad Basin region in Africa is experiencing environmental degradation and resource depletion exacerbated by climate change, leading to conflicts over dwindling water and land resources. Competition among pastoralists, farmers, and fishing communities for access to water and grazing lands has intensified, fuelling tensions and violence. This has resulted in population displacement, food insecurity, and humanitarian crises, highlighting the interconnectedness between environmental degradation, social instability, and conflict in vulnerable regions.

These real-world examples illustrate how climate change is already impacting communities and ecosystems, underscoring the urgent need for concerted global action to mitigate its effects and build resilience for a sustainable future.

2.2 Planetary boundary framing

Given the extensive evidence of degradation to our planetary environment and ecosystems, urgent action to reduce and reverse these impacts is imperative. Planetary boundary framing provides a compelling framework for understanding these complex interactions and guiding human development towards a more sustainable future.

Planetary boundary framing, as outlined by Steffen et al. (2015) in their seminal work *Planetary boundaries: Guiding human development on a changing planet*, refers to a framework for understanding and managing the complex interactions between human activities and Earth's natural systems.

This framework identifies nine key planetary boundaries that define the safe operating space for humanity within which we can thrive and maintain a stable Earth system.

The Holocene Epoch, spanning from approximately 11,700 years ago to the present, represents a period characterised by stable environmental conditions and the flourishing of modern humanity. During this time, human societies developed and thrived within the confines of a relatively stable planetary system.

In contrast, the Anthropocene Epoch marks a significant shift in Earth's history, where the collective activities of human beings, particularly since the Industrial Revolution, have substantially altered the planet's surface, atmosphere, oceans, and nutrient cycles.

The Anthropocene era is characterised by unprecedented rates of environmental change driven by human actions, leading to profound impacts on Earth's systems and ecosystems. While the precise start date of the Anthropocene is subject to debate among scientists, many argue for its commencement around the mid-20th century, symbolising the dawn of the 'age of man.'

2.2.1 Why worry about breaching planetary boundary limits?

The following arguments present a compelling case for humanity to change course and take action to avoid breaching planetary boundary limits or reversing trends where there is evidence that humans have already done so.

- **Acceleration of change:** Human activities have accelerated environmental change to a level comparable to geological processes, exerting significant pressure on Earth's systems and ecosystems. This rapid pace of change poses unprecedented challenges for biodiversity, ecosystem functioning, and human well-being.

- **Shift from the Holocene era:** Breaching planetary boundary limits risks pushing Earth's systems beyond the stable conditions that have supported life during the Holocene Epoch. This shift into uncharted territory threatens the resilience and sustainability of human societies and ecosystems.

- **Tipping points:** Crossing planetary boundary limits may trigger irreversible tipping points, leading to abrupt and catastrophic changes in Earth's systems. Once these thresholds are crossed, recovery becomes increasingly difficult, if not impossible, leading to long-term consequences for biodiversity, climate stability, and ecosystem services.

- **Unsustainability of the Anthropocene era:** The Anthropocene era, characterised by unprecedented human impacts on the planet, may not be conducive to sustaining human life at its current scale in the longer term. Continued disregard for planetary boundaries jeopardises the Earth's capacity to support human societies and ecosystems in a manner that ensures long-term resilience and well-being.

Adopting a planetary boundary framing approach is essential for guiding human development toward a more sustainable and resilient future, where humanity can thrive within the safe operating space of our planet.

The following diagram from a 2015 studies, summaries scientific evidence, where humanity is exceeding safe planetary boundaries, in different risk areas:

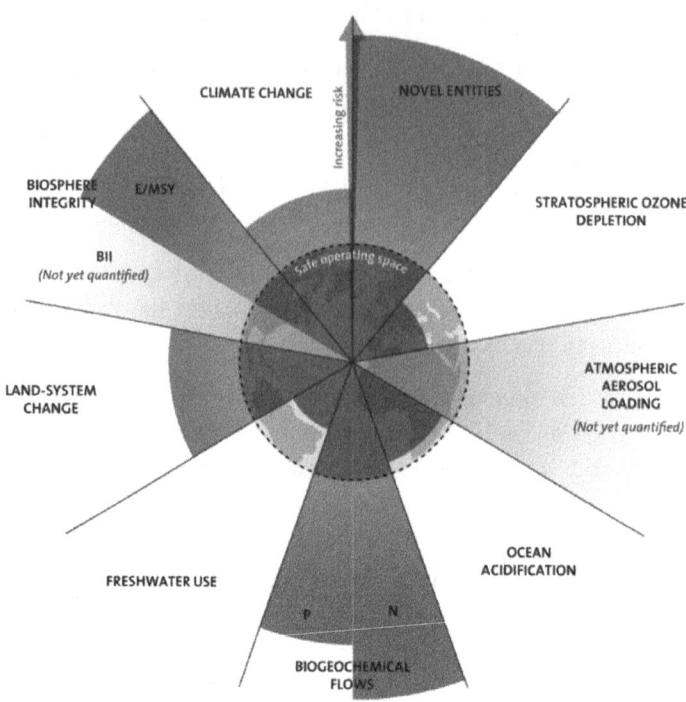

(**Source:** Steffer, W., Richardson, K., Rockström, J., Cornell, S. E., Fetser, I., Bennett, E. M., Biggs, R., Carpenter, S. R., de Vries, W., de Wit, C. A., and Folke, C. (2015) Planetary boundaries: Guiding human development on a changing planet. *Science.* 347 (6223): 1259855)

As evidence of human-induced environmental changes mounts, particularly in areas such as rising global ocean temperatures, there is a growing imperative for accountability and stewardship of the Earth by states and corporations.

3 Sustainable development

3.1 What is sustainable development?

Key term

> **Sustainable development:** Development that meets the needs of the present without compromising the ability of future generations to meet their own needs (Brundtland Report, 1987).

In essence, sustainable development encompasses the idea of balancing economic growth, environmental protection, and social equity to ensure a prosperous and harmonious future for all, across the world.

Sustainable development acknowledges the interconnectedness of economic, environmental, and social factors, emphasising the importance of long-term thinking and responsible stewardship of resources. It seeks to address current challenges while safeguarding the well-being of future generations.

For example, initiatives promoting renewable energy sources like solar and wind power contribute to sustainable development by reducing reliance on finite fossil fuels and mitigating climate change impacts for future generations.

Sustainable development recognises the complexity of social, economic, and environmental systems and seeks to address development challenges holistically. It emphasises the need for integrated solutions that consider multiple factors and stakeholders.

At its core, sustainable development acknowledges the dependence of human societies on healthy ecosystems for essential resources and services. It emphasises the conservation and restoration of ecological systems to ensure the continued availability of resources for current and future generations.

Sustainable development promotes justice, equity, and fairness both within and between generations. It advocates for a balance between meeting the needs of the present generation without compromising the ability of future generations to meet their own needs (inter-generational equity) and ensuring equitable distribution of resources and opportunities within the current generation (intra-generational equity).

Sustainable development also calls for the transformation of economic systems to align with environmental and social objectives. It advocates for the adoption of economic models that prioritise environmental sustainability, social inclusivity, and ethical business practices. This includes transitioning towards circular economies, where resources are used efficiently, waste is minimised, and social well-being is prioritised alongside economic growth.

Individuals, organisations, and governments can foster a more resilient, equitable, and prosperous future for all by implementing sustainable development goals (SDG)

3.2 Principles of sustainable development

Corporate sustainability starts with a company's value system and a principles-based approach to doing business. This means operating in ways that, at a minimum, meet fundamental responsibilities in the areas of human rights, labour, environment and anti-corruption.

Responsible businesses should consistently apply the same values and principles wherever they operate in the world to ensure their good practices in one region of the world do not offset the harm they incur in another part of the world.

The United Nations Global Compact is a non-binding United Nations pact of countries to persuade businesses and firms worldwide to adopt sustainable and socially responsible policies, and to report on their implementation. The UN Global Compact call on companies to align their strategies and operations with ten universal principles related to human rights, labour, environment and anti-corruption, and take actions that advance societal goals and the implementation of the strategic development goals

The Ten Principles of the United Nations Global Compact cover human rights, labour, the environment and anti-corruption, and have been developed from a number of sources, including.

(a) The Universal Declaration of Human Rights.
See: https://www.un.org/en/about-us/universal-declaration-of-human-rights

(b) The International Labour Organisation's Declaration on Fundamental Principles and Rights at Work.
See: https://www.ilo.org/ilo-declaration-fundamental-principles-and-rights-work

(c) The Rio Declaration on Environment and Development.
See: https://sustainabledevelopment.un.org/rio20/futurewewant

(d) The United Nations Convention Against Corruption.
See: https://www.unodc.org/unodc/en/treaties/CAC/index.html

The Ten Principles of the United Nations Global Compact are as follows

3.2.1 Human rights

Principle 1: Businesses should support and respect the protection of internationally proclaimed human rights.

For example, a multinational corporation operating in a country where freedom of speech is restricted ensures that its employees are aware of their rights to express themselves freely within the company's premises, even if they cannot do so publicly in the broader society.

Principle 2: Businesses should ensure they are not complicit in human rights abuses.

For example, a clothing manufacturer conducts thorough audits of its supply chain to ensure that none of its subcontractors engage in practices such as forced labour or human trafficking. If any instances of abuse are found, the company takes immediate action to address them and terminates contracts with offending suppliers.

3.2.2 Labour

Principle 3: Businesses should uphold the freedom of association and the effective recognition of the right to collective bargaining.

For example, a technology company allows its employees to form labour unions and actively engages in collective bargaining negotiations to ensure fair wages, benefits, and working conditions for its workforce.

Principle 4: Businesses should strive for elimination of all forms of forced and compulsory labour.

For example, a construction company prohibits the use of forced labour in all its projects and conducts regular inspections to verify compliance. It also provides training and support to workers to empower them to report any instances of coercion or exploitation.

Principle 5: Businesses should strive for the effective abolition of child labour.

For example, a global agriculture corporation implements strict policies to prevent child labour in its supply chain. It verifies the age of workers in its farms and cooperates with local authorities and NGOs to provide education and alternative livelihood opportunities for affected children.

Principle 6: Businesses should strive for the elimination of discrimination in respect of employment and occupation.

For example, an automotive manufacturer promotes diversity and inclusion in its hiring practices by actively recruiting women, minorities, and individuals from underrepresented communities. It also provides equal opportunities for career advancement and ensures a non-discriminatory work environment for all employees.

3.2.3 Environment

Principle 7: Businesses should support a precautionary approach to environmental challenges.

For example, an energy company invests in research and development to explore renewable energy sources and adopts a precautionary approach by implementing measures to mitigate environmental risks associated with its operations, such as carbon emissions and water pollution.

Principle 8: Businesses should undertake initiatives to promote greater environmental responsibility.

For example, a retail company implements recycling programs in its stores and offices, reduces packaging waste by using sustainable materials, and encourages customers to opt for reusable shopping bags. It also partners with environmental organisations to support conservation projects and raise awareness about environmental issues.

Principle 9: Businesses should encourage the development and diffusion of environmentally friendly technologies.

For example, an automobile manufacturer develops hybrid and electric vehicles to reduce carbon emissions and dependence on fossil fuels. It also licenses its environmentally friendly technologies to other companies and collaborates with suppliers to improve the sustainability of its supply chain.

3.2.4 Anti-corruption

Principle 10: Businesses should work against corruption in all its forms, including extortion and bribery.

For example, a pharmaceutical company adopts a zero-tolerance policy towards corruption and bribery in its business dealings. It conducts regular training sessions for employees and partners on ethical business practices and implements robust internal controls and reporting mechanisms to detect and prevent corruption. Additionally, the company refuses to engage in bribery or kickback schemes to secure contracts or regulatory approvals.

(**Source:** United Nations Global Compact. [Online] Available from: https://unglobalcompact.org/what-is-gc/mission/principles [Accessed 3 October 2024])

By incorporating the Ten Principles of the UN Global Compact into strategies, policies and procedures, and establishing a culture of integrity, organisations are not only upholding their basic responsibilities to people and planet, but also setting the stage for long-term success.

3.3 United Nations Sustainability Development Goals

> **Key term**
>
> **Sustainable Development Goals (SFGs):** Are specific, stated, objectives which aim to transform our world. SDG's are a call for action to end poverty and inequality, protect the planet, and ensure that all people, everywhere, enjoy health, justice, and prosperity.

The 2030 Agenda for Sustainable Development, adopted by all United Nations Member States in 2015, is a comprehensive blueprint for achieving a better and more sustainable future for all. At its heart are the 17 Sustainable Development Goals (SDGs), which are an urgent call for action by all countries in a global partnership. The 2030 Agenda recognises that eradicating poverty in all its forms and dimensions, accelerating sustainable development, and ensuring that no one is left behind are among the greatest global challenges and priorities.

The UN Sustainable Development Goals (UN SDGs), also known as the Global Goals, are a universal call to action to end poverty, protect the planet, and ensure that all people enjoy peace and prosperity by 2030.

The seventeen UN SDGs address a wide range of interconnected issues, including poverty, inequality, climate change, environmental degradation, peace, and justice. Each goal has specific targets to be achieved over the next decade, with the aim of addressing the root causes of global challenges and promoting sustainable development in all its dimensions.

The UN SDGs can be broadly categorised into three dimensions:

(a) **Planet (biosphere):** Goals related to environmental sustainability, including climate action (Goal 13), responsible consumption and production (Goal 12), and the conservation and sustainable use of terrestrial and marine ecosystems (Goals 14 and 15). These goals aim to protect and preserve the planet's natural resources, mitigate climate change, and promote sustainable management practices that ensure the well-being of current and future generations.

(b) **Society:** Goals focused on social progress and inclusion, such as ending poverty (Goal 1), achieving gender equality (Goal 5), ensuring quality education for all (Goal 4), and promoting health and well-being (Goal 3). These goals aim to eradicate poverty, reduce inequality, improve access to essential services, and promote social cohesion and inclusivity within communities and societies.

(c) **Economy:** Goals related to economic growth, employment, and sustainable development, including decent work and economic growth (Goal 8), industry, innovation, and infrastructure (Goal 9), and building sustainable cities and communities (Goal 11). These goals aim to foster inclusive and sustainable economic growth, promote innovation and infrastructure development, and create opportunities for prosperity and employment while minimising negative environmental impacts.

As we stated at the beginning of this chapter, in 1987, the United Nations Brundtland Commission defined sustainability as 'meeting the needs of the present without compromising the ability of future generations to meet their own needs.'

In response, in 2015, the United Nations published 17 Sustainable Development Goals to transform the world for all humans by achieving sustainable development for all. This is an important set of principles and goals which underpins the current progress towards sustainability and addresses ESG related issues.

The 17 Sustainable Development Goals provide a shared framework and roadmap for governments, businesses, civil society organisations, and individuals to work together towards a more equitable, resilient, and sustainable future.

By aligning their strategies, policies, and actions with the 17 UN SDGs, companies and their stakeholders can contribute to global efforts to address pressing challenges and achieve a world where no one is left behind. Some organisations specifically align their published strategic and operating objectives to the 17 UN Sustainable Development Goals.

The 17 UN SDG's are as follows:

  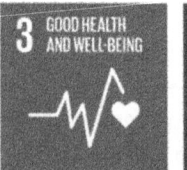  

(**Source**: United Nations. [Online] Available from: https://www.un.org/sustainabledevelopment/sustainable-development-goals/ [Accessed 3 October 2024])

United Nations Sustainable Development Goals		
(1) **No poverty** Economic growth must be inclusive to provide sustainable jobs and promote equality.	(2) **Zero hunger** The food and agriculture sector offer key solutions for development and is central for hunger and poverty eradication.	(3) **Good health and well-being** Ensuring healthy lives and promoting the well-being for all at all ages is essential to sustainable development.
(4) **Quality education** Obtaining a quality education is the foundation to improving people's lives and sustainable development.	(5) **Gender inequality** Gender equality is not only a fundamental human right, but a necessary foundation for a peaceful, prosperous and sustainable world.	(6) **Clean water and sanitation** Clean, accessible water for all is an essential part of the world we want to live in.

United Nations Sustainable Development Goals		
(7) Affordable and clean energy Energy is central to nearly every major challenge and opportunity.	**(8) Decent work and economic growth** Sustainable economic growth will require societies to create the conditions that allow people to have quality jobs.	**(9) Industry, innovation and infrastructure** Investments in infrastructure are crucial to achieving sustainable development.
(10) Reduced inequality To reduce inequalities, policies should be universal in principle, paying attention to the needs of disadvantaged and marginalised populations.	**(11) Sustainable cities and communities** There needs to be a future in where cities provide opportunities for all, with access to basic services, energy, housing, transportation and more.	**(12) Responsible consumption and production** Sustainable consumption and production can contribute substantially to poverty alleviation and the transition towards low-carbon and green economies.
(13) Climate action Climate change is a global challenge that affects everyone, everywhere.	**(14) Life below water** Careful management of this essential global resource is a key feature of a sustainable future.	**(15) Life on land** Sustainably manage forests, combat desertification, halt and reverse land degradation, halt biodiversity loss.
(16) Peace and justice strong institutions Access to justice for all, and building effective, accountable institutions at all levels.	**(17) Partnerships to achieve the goal** Revitalise the global partnership for sustainable development.	

(**Source:** United Nations. [Online] Available from: https://www.un.org/sustainabledevelopment/sustainable-development-goals/ [Accessed 3 October 2024])

Case Study

The following are examples of companies aligning their operations with the United Nations' 17 Sustainable Development Goals.

Unilever: Unilever operates in the consumer goods and food manufacture industry sectors.

Unilever has integrated sustainability into its business strategy, aligning with multiple SDGs such as Goal 2 (Zero Hunger) through initiatives to improve food security and nutrition, Goal 6 (Clean Water and Sanitation) by reducing water usage in its manufacturing processes, and Goal 12 (Responsible Consumption and Production) by promoting sustainable sourcing and reducing waste.

For further reading, see the Unilever's pages on sustainability.

https://www.unilever.com/news/news-search/2023/leading-and-delivering-on-sustainability-through-our-compass-commitments/

Tesla, Inc: Tesla operates in the electric vehicle automotive industry sector.

Tesla is contributing to Goal 7 (Affordable and Clean Energy) by producing electric vehicles and renewable energy solutions, Goal 9 (Industry, Innovation, and Infrastructure) by pioneering advancements in electric vehicle technology and renewable energy infrastructure, and Goal 13 (Climate Action) by advocating for the transition to sustainable transportation and energy systems.

For further reading, see the Tesla's pages on sustainability:

https://www.tesla.com/en_gb/impact

IKEA: IKEA operates in the furniture and homeware retail industry sector.

IKEA supports Goal 11 (Sustainable Cities and Communities) by promoting sustainable urban development through affordable and energy-efficient home furnishing solutions, Goal 12 (Responsible Consumption and Production) by implementing initiatives to reduce waste and promote recycling, and Goal 17 (Partnerships for the Goals) by collaborating with stakeholders to drive sustainability initiatives.

For further reading, see the Ikea's pages on sustainability:

https://www.ikea.com/gb/en/this-is-ikea/climate-environment/the-ikea-sustainability-strategy-pubfea4c210

Patagonia: Patagonia operates in the outdoor apparel industry sector.

Patagonia aligns with Goal 14 (Life Below Water) by advocating for marine conservation and supporting initiatives to protect oceans and coastal ecosystems, Goal 15 (Life on Land) by promoting biodiversity conservation and sustainable land management practices, and Goal 16 (Peace, Justice, and Strong Institutions) by advocating for social and environmental justice.

For further reading, see the Patagonia's pages on sustainability:

https://www.patagonia.com/our-footprint/

Danone: Danone operates in the food and beverage manufacturing sectors.

Danone contributes to UN SDG 2 (Zero Hunger) by promoting food security and nutrition through sustainable agricultural practices and nutritious food products, UN SDG 3 (Good Health and Well-being) by producing healthy and environmentally friendly food and beverage products, and UN SDG 6 (Clean Water and Sanitation) by implementing water stewardship initiatives across its operations.

For further reading, see the Danone's pages on sustainability:

https://www.danone.com/impact/un-sustainable-developement-goals.html

3.4 Possible implications of a resource-constrained world

In a resource-constrained world, the unsustainable depletion of finite resources such as minerals, energy, water, and food production pose significant challenges to global sustainability. Addressing these challenges requires a shift towards resource-efficient technologies, circular economy models, and sustainable consumption patterns.

The risk of increased tension and conflicts over scarce resources further exacerbates the urgency of addressing resource constraints. Competition for access to essential resources could lead to geopolitical instability, economic disruptions, and social unrest, underscoring the need for collaborative and equitable solutions to resource management.

Millions of people worldwide still lack access to basic necessities such as clean water, food, healthcare, and education. Gender inequality, discrimination, and marginalization further exacerbate social disparities, hindering efforts to build resilient and inclusive societies. Global sustainability demands actions to eradicate poverty, promote human rights, and foster social cohesion and inclusivity.

Poor social conditions, including poverty, inequality, and lack of access to basic services, exacerbate vulnerabilities and undermine sustainable development efforts.

Sustainability cannot be achieved without addressing social inequities and promoting social justice. Addressing social inequities is therefore essential for building resilient communities, fostering social cohesion, and promoting inclusive growth.

3.5 Challenges of creating a sustainable world

The challenges of creating a sustainable world are multifaceted and include addressing finite global resources, ensuring energy security, promoting water conservation, enhancing food production, and tackling poverty. For example:

- Finite global resources, including minerals, fossil fuels, and freshwater, are being depleted at an unsustainable rate, threatening ecosystems and human well-being.
- Energy security is a pressing issue as dependence on fossil fuels contributes to climate change and geopolitical tensions.
- Water scarcity and pollution jeopardise access to clean water for drinking, sanitation, and agriculture, exacerbating social inequalities and environmental degradation.
- Food production is under pressure from population growth, land degradation, and climate change, necessitating sustainable agriculture practices to ensure food security and nutrition for all.
- Also, poverty remains a persistent challenge, with millions of people worldwide living in extreme poverty and lacking access to essential services, education, and economic opportunities.

All these challenges require comprehensive solutions at a global level that integrate economic, social, and environmental considerations.

3.6 Potential solutions to create a more a sustainable world

Potential solutions to move toward a sustainable world encompass various environmental, social, and economic initiatives. These include transitioning to renewable energy sources, implementing water conservation measures, reducing greenhouse gas emissions, promoting sustainable agriculture practices, and addressing poverty.

- **Transitioning to renewable energy sources** involves adopting solar, wind, and hydroelectric power to diminish reliance on fossil fuels. Investment in research and development of innovative technologies such as tidal energy and geothermal power can further advance this transition. Policy implementation and incentives are crucial to promote the deployment of renewable energy systems, while collaboration with international partners facilitates technology transfer to developing countries.
- **Implementing water conservation measures** is imperative, including promoting water-efficient irrigation techniques and rainwater harvesting systems. Investment in water recycling and reuse technologies, along with the implementation of pricing mechanisms and regulations, can incentivise conservation practices. Watershed management strategies are also essential to protect and restore natural water sources.
- **Greenhouse gas emission reduction initiatives** can be developed and implemented on a global scale, such as CO2 emission caps, carbon trading, and carbon capture. These measures aim to mitigate the impact of greenhouse gases on the environment and climate change.
- **Promoting sustainable agriculture practices** involves encouraging organic farming, supporting agroforestry, and implementing agroecological techniques. Additionally, sustainable livestock management practices and investments in agricultural extension services contribute to sustainable agriculture.
- **Addressing poverty through inclusive economic development** entails implementing social protection programs, investing in education and vocational training, and promoting microfinance initiatives. Creating job opportunities in emerging sectors like renewable energy and eco-tourism fosters economic growth and social inclusion.

Coordinated political action at local, national, and global levels is required to address these challenges. Governments, businesses, civil society organizations, and individuals must work together to implement innovative solutions and transformative policies to achieve global sustainability.

4 Development of sustainability awareness, guidelines and regulation

4.1 The Paris agreement

The Paris Agreement is an international treaty on climate change that was signed by nearly 200 countries in 2015 at the United Nations Framework Convention on Climate Change's 21st Conference of Parties.

This agreement is generally regarded as the framework for international action towards mitigating climate change and its impacts through a global commitment to collective action on climate change, with the goal of achieving a sustainable and resilient future for all.

The Paris Agreement set the ambition to a maximum of 2°C global temperature change, with the preferred goal of 1.5°C above pre-industrial levels.

Note, the term 'net Zero' refers to the global reduction of greenhouse gas emissions to net Zero by 2050 and is the action required to limit temperature rise to 1.5 degrees celsius.

The Paris Agreement also includes provisions for financial assistance to developing countries and promotes transparency and accountability through regular reporting mechanisms.

4.2 Integrated reporting framework for sustainable development

The Integrated Reporting Framework for Sustainable Development introduces the concept of the 'six capitals,' which represent the various forms of resources and relationships that organisations utilise and affect through their activities.

4.2.1 Six capitals

The six capitals model provides a basis for understanding the long-term sustainability of a business. Organisations use six types of capital to deliver their products or services.

The six types of capital are as follows and are explained further below:

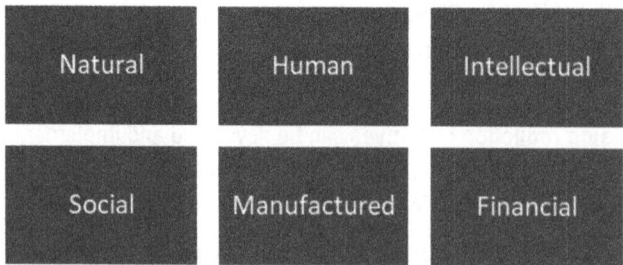

1. **Financial capital**

    This includes the monetary resources available to an organisation, such as cash, investments, and income. Financial capital represents the financial value generated or consumed by the organisation's activities.

    For example, Apple, with its vast cash reserves, investments in various financial instruments, and steady income from product sales and services, Apple possesses substantial financial capital resources that fuel its operations, investments in research and development, and strategic initiatives.

2. **Manufactured capital**

    Manufactured capital encompasses the physical infrastructure, equipment, and technology that organisations use to produce goods and services. Manufactured capital includes assets like buildings, machinery, and intellectual property.

    For example, Toyota Motor Corporation exemplifies manufactured capital through its extensive physical infrastructure, advanced manufacturing facilities, and cutting-edge technology used in vehicle production. With state-of-the-art factories, machinery, and patented manufacturing processes, Toyota relies heavily on its manufactured capital to maintain its position as a leading global automobile manufacturer.

3. **Intellectual capital**

    Intellectual capital refers to the knowledge, expertise, and intellectual property owned or developed by an organisation. Intellectual capital includes patents, trademarks, copyrights, and the skills and capabilities of employees.

    For example, Microsoft Corporation showcases intellectual capital through its vast portfolio of patents, trademarks, and copyrights, along with the expertise and skills of its employees. As a technology giant, Microsoft owns valuable intellectual property rights to software products like Windows and Office, while also leveraging the knowledge and innovation of its workforce to develop new technologies and solutions.

4. **Human capital**

    Human capital represents the skills, experience, and capabilities of an organisation's workforce. Human capital encompasses factors such as employee education, training, health, and well-being.

    For example, Google demonstrates strong human capital through its highly skilled and diverse workforce, comprised of talented engineers, developers, and professionals across various fields. With a focus on employee education, training, and well-being, Google invests in nurturing its human capital to drive innovation, creativity, and productivity across its diverse range of products and services

5. **Social capital**

    Social capital encompasses the relationships and networks that organisations have with stakeholders, including employees, customers, suppliers, communities, and society at large. It includes aspects such as trust, reputation, and social license to operate.

    For example, Starbucks Corporation exemplifies social capital through its extensive network of relationships with stakeholders, including employees, customers, suppliers, and communities. Through initiatives like ethical sourcing, community outreach programs, and employee welfare initiatives, Starbucks builds trust, fosters positive relationships, and earns social license to operate, enhancing its brand reputation and long-term sustainability.

6. **Natural capital**

    Natural capital refers to the environmental resources and ecosystems that provide essential services and benefits to organisations and society. Natural capital includes elements such as clean air and water, biodiversity, ecosystems, and natural resources like minerals and forests.

    For example, the Body Shop, a cosmetics company, emphasises natural capital through its commitment to sustainable sourcing, environmental conservation, and biodiversity preservation. By using natural ingredients, supporting fair trade practices, and advocating for environmental causes, The Body Shop relies on natural capital to create eco-friendly products and contribute to the preservation of natural resources and ecosystems.

4.2.2 Integrated reporting

Key term

> **Integrated reporting:** Is a reporting approach that aims to provide a holistic view of an organisation's performance, value creation, and impact across the six capitals.

Unlike traditional financial reporting, which focuses primarily on financial capital, integrated reporting considers the organisation's broader value creation process and its interactions with various forms of capital.

Integrated reporting encourages organisations to communicate how they create value over time by utilising and affecting the six capitals. It emphasises the interdependencies between financial, environmental, social, and governance factors and their influence on organisational performance and sustainability.

Integrated reporting is highly relevant to sustainable development as it provides a comprehensive framework for organisations to assess and communicate their sustainability performance and impact. By considering the interconnectedness of financial, environmental, social, and governance factors, integrated reporting enables organisations to:

Evaluate their contribution to sustainable development goals and objectives.

- Identify opportunities to enhance value creation while minimising negative impacts on society and the environment.
- Engage stakeholders in meaningful dialogue about sustainability issues and performance.
- Enhance transparency, accountability, and trust by providing a more complete picture of the organisation's activities and impacts.
- Explanation of the IFRS International Integrated Reporting Framework.

The International Integrated Reporting Framework (IFRS Framework) provides guidance and principles for organisations seeking to adopt integrated reporting practices. It outlines the fundamental concepts, content elements, and guiding principles of integrated reporting, helping organisations effectively communicate their value creation story.

The IFRS Framework emphasises the importance of connectivity, materiality, conciseness, and reliability in integrated reporting. It encourages organisations to tailor their reports to reflect the unique circumstances, strategies, and impacts relevant to their operations and stakeholders.

The diagram provided by the IFRS Framework illustrates the key components of integrated reporting, including the organisation's business model, governance structure, performance measures, and outcomes across the six capitals. It serves as a visual representation of how organisations can integrate financial and non-financial information to communicate their value creation process and impact on sustainable development.

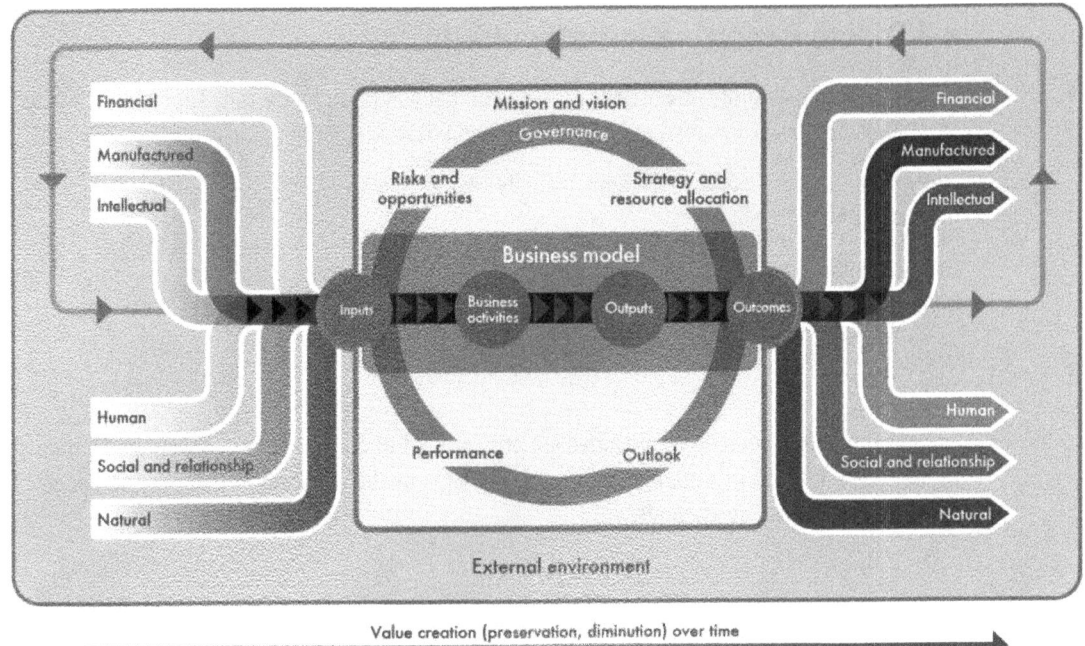

(**Source:** IFRS. [Online] Available from: https://integratedreporting.ifrs.org/resource/international-ir-framework/ [Accessed 3 October 2024])

4.3 Other global initiatives

Globally, there is now much greater awareness of the adverse effects of climate change and the negative impact an organisation's operations can have on the environment. Over the past two decades there may been many initiates and organisations formed to provide guidance to organisations how to improve their sustainability performance reporting. Some of the more impactful, are including in the following table.

Initiative	Description
Global Reporting Initiative (GRI) (2000)	GRI is an independent international organisation that provides guidelines for sustainability reporting, helping organisations communicate their impacts transparently.
Principles for Responsible Investment (PRI) (2005)	PRI is a UN-supported initiative that encourages investors to integrate environmental, social, and governance factors into their investment decisions and practices.
Task Force on Climate-related Financial Disclosure (TCFD)	TCFD was established in 2015 to develop recommendations for voluntary climate-related financial disclosures, aiding stakeholders in assessing climate-related risks and opportunities.
United Nations Sustainable Development Goals (SDGs) (2016)	The SDGs are a set of 17 global goals developed the United Nation in 2016 and adopted by UN Member States to address various challenges and guide efforts towards sustainable development worldwide.
International Sustainability Standards Board (ISSB)	ISSB aims to develop globally accepted sustainability reporting standards, facilitating consistent and comparable information for stakeholders.

Each of these in explained further in the following sections.

4.4 Global Reporting Initiative (GRI)

The Global Reporting Initiative (GRI) provides guidelines for sustainability reporting, helping organisations communicate their economic, environmental, and social impacts transparently.

Many organisations use the GRI sustainability reporting framework as a basis for their sustainability reports to their stakeholders.

GRI guidelines cover various aspects of sustainability performance, including governance, environmental impacts, labour practices, human rights, and community involvement.

GRI's reporting framework is based on principles of stakeholder inclusiveness, materiality, completeness, and accuracy.

Organisations following GRI guidelines are encouraged to disclose their sustainability impacts and performance metrics in a standardised format, enabling stakeholders to compare and assess their sustainability efforts consistently.

Case Study

As an example, National Grid plc sustainability report follows the GRI Standards. The 2023/23 providing comprehensive information on its environmental, social, and governance (ESG) performance.

On page 49 is the reference to the application of GRI Standards.

'Global Reporting Initiative (GRI)

This report has been prepared in accordance with the GRI Standards. We believe that all the requirements to claim alignment have been met. Further details on the requirements and our disclosures can be found in our GRI index. While we have used the GRI Standards as our primary resource in developing our Responsible Business Report, we have also prepared separate sustainability reporting disclosures described below [...]'

The full Responsible Business Report can be viewed here:

https://www.nationalgrid.com/document/149761/download

4.5 Principles for Responsible Investment (PRI)

The Principles for Responsible Investment (PRI) offers a framework for incorporating environmental, social, and governance (ESG) factors into investment decision-making and ownership practices.

These principles guide signatories in integrating sustainability considerations across their investment processes, including asset allocation, manager selection, and active ownership.

The six PRI principles outline commitments to incorporate ESG issues into investment analysis and decision-making, engage with companies on ESG matters, and disclose ESG activities and progress.

PRI encourages investors to consider long-term sustainability impacts alongside financial returns, promoting responsible investment practices that align with broader societal and environmental goals.

The six principles for responsible investment are as follows:

Principle	Description
Principle 1: Incorporate ESG into investment analysis and decision-making	Integrate environmental, social, and governance (ESG) factors into investment processes to understand and manage risks and opportunities.
Principle 2: Be active owners and incorporate ESG issues into ownership policies and practices	Actively engage with investee companies to encourage improved ESG performance and transparency through dialogue and voting.
Principle 3: Seek appropriate disclosure on ESG issues by the entities in which we invest	Advocate for greater transparency and disclosure from companies on their ESG performance, enabling informed investment decision-making.
Principle 4: Promote acceptance and implementation of the principles within the investment industry	Collaborate with stakeholders to promote the adoption and implementation of responsible investment practices across the industry.
Principle 5: Work towards the adoption of appropriate reporting and assurance practices	Adopt standardised reporting and assurance practices to enhance transparency and accountability in responsible investment activities.
Principle 6: Advocate for effective governance structures and implementation	Support policies and practices that facilitate sustainable development.

(**Source**: PRI. [Online] Available from: https://www.unpri.org/about-us/what-are-the-principles-for-responsible-investment [Accessed 3 October 2024])

4.6 The Task Force on Climate-related Financial Disclosures (TCFD)

The G20 is an intergovernmental forum comprising 19 countries and the European Union. It works to address major issues related to the global economy, such as international financial stability, climate change mitigation, and sustainable development.

Climate-related reporting is an important part of sustainability and environmental, social responsibility and governance reporting as scientists and governments agree that the impacts of climate change are now being realised across the planet.

In 2017, the Task Force on Climate-related Financial Disclosures (TCFD) released its recommendations on climate-related financial disclosures. The Task Force consists of 31 members from across the G20, representing both preparers and users of financial disclosures.

TCFD recommendations are designed to help organisations provide better information to support informed investment capital allocation to those organisations which are taking steps to mitigate against climate related threats.

The UK Government is the first in the G20 to mandate that the largest UK-registered companies provide disclosures, on a 'comply or explain' basis, in line with the recommendations of the Task Force on Climate-related Financial Disclosures (TCFD).

The TCFD structure their recommendations around four core elements

- Governance
- Strategy
- Risk management
- Metrics and targets

Each of these core elements include reporting requirements and additional guidance for disclosing organisations.

In particular, the TCFD focus on forward-looking financial disclosure. They ask organisations to identify climate-related risks and opportunities, to consider the financial implications, and to assess the resilience of the business strategy to future climate outcomes.

TCFD recommends organisations use scenarios to explore future business risks arising from climate change and present the findings in the narrative report.

TCFD recommends seven principles for effective disclosure to achieve high-quality disclosures regarding the impact of climate change on organisations:

1. **Relevance:** Disclosures should represent information that is pertinent to stakeholders and relevant to understanding the organisation's exposure to climate-related risks and opportunities.

2. **Specificity and completeness:** Disclosure should be specific and comprehensive, providing a detailed account of the organisation's climate-related risks and opportunities without omitting material information.

3. **Clarity, balance, and understandability:** Disclosures should be clear, balanced, and easily understandable to stakeholders, ensuring that the information provided is accessible and comprehensible to a wide audience.

4. **Consistency over time:** Disclosure should maintain consistency over time, allowing stakeholders to track changes and developments in the organisation's climate-related performance and strategies.

5. **Comparability:** Disclosure should enable comparability among companies within the same sector, industry, or portfolio, facilitating benchmarking and analysis of climate-related performance across entities.

6. **Reliability, verifiability, and objectivity:** Disclosure should be reliable, verifiable, and objective, based on accurate data and methodologies that are subject to independent verification to enhance credibility and trustworthiness.

7. **Timeliness:** Disclosure should be provided on a timely basis, ensuring that stakeholders have access to up-to-date information to inform decision-making and risk assessments related to climate change.

In terms of specific disclosures for an organisation, TCFD provide eleven disclosure recommendations structured around four thematic areas – (1) Governance, (2) Strategy, (3) Risk management, and (4) Metrics and targets.

Each of these core elements include reporting requirements and additional guidance for disclosing organisations. (**Source:** TCFD. [Online] Available from: https://www.fsb-tcfd.org/recommendations/)

1. **Governance** – the organisation's governance around climate-related risks and opportunities
2. **Strategy** – the actual and potential impacts of climate-related risks and opportunities on the organisation's businesses, strategy, and financial planning where such information is material
3. **Risk management** – how the organisation identifies, assesses, and manages climate-related risks
4. **Metrics and targets** – the metrics and targets used to assess and manage relevant climate-related risks and opportunities where such information is material

The eleven disclosure recommendations can be summarised as follows:

Governance:

Describe the board's oversight of climate-related risks and opportunities.

1. Describe the board's oversight of climate-related risks and opportunities
2. Describe management's role in assessing and managing climate-related risks and opportunities

Strategy:

3. Describe the climate-related risks and opportunities the organisation has identified over the short, medium, and long term
4. Describe the impact of climate-related risks and opportunities on the organisation's businesses, strategy, and financial planning
5. Describe the resilience of the organisation's strategy, taking into consideration different climate-related scenarios, including a 2°C or lower scenario

Risk management:

6. Describe the organisation's processes for identifying and assessing climate-related risks
7. Describe the organisation's processes for managing climate-related risks
8. Describe how processes for identifying, assessing, and managing climate-related risks are integrated into the organisation's overall risk management

Metrics and targets:

9. Disclose the metrics used by the organisation to assess climate-related risks and opportunities in line with its strategy and risk management process
10. Disclose (Scope 1, Scope 2, and, if appropriate, Scope 3) greenhouse gas (GHG) emissions, and the related risks
11. Describe the targets used by the organisation to manage climate-related risks and opportunities and performance against targets

These disclosures are recommendations only. They only become mandatory for an organisation if adopted in full or in part by a global listing authority on which shares are listed.

TCFD disclosures are now mandatory for UK listed companies.

Also, TCFD disclosure requirements have been adopted by the following IFRS Sustainability Disclosure Standards, which you have seen in your previous studies.

- Standard 1: IFRS S1 *General sustainability-related disclosures*
- Standard 2: IFRS S2 *Climate-related disclosures*

4.7 International Sustainability Standards Board (ISSB)

The International Sustainability Standards Board (ISSB) was established in response to investors' demand for high-quality, transparent, reliable, and comparable reporting on climate and other Environmental, Social, and Governance (ESG) issues. Announced by the IFRS Foundation Trustees on 3 November 2021, the ISSB aims to develop sustainability reporting requirements under the IFRS umbrella. These standards will complement conventional financial reporting, providing non-financial information on company performance, risk profiles, and economic decisions within sustainable business development contexts. By doing so, they will facilitate sustainability disclosure to investors and stakeholders.

The ISSB's Sustainability Disclosure Standards will furnish investors and capital market participants with insights into organisations' sustainability-related risks and opportunities, enabling informed investment decisions. These standards will align with the Integrated Reporting Framework, bridging financial statements with sustainability-related financial disclosures. The ISSB, alongside the IFRS Foundation's International Accounting Standards Board (IASB), jointly oversees this framework.

In March 2022, the ISSB and the Global Reporting Initiative (GRI) entered into a memorandum of understanding (MOU) to collaborate on global financial reporting. ISSB will focus on disclosing sustainability information relevant to enterprise value and share prices through annual reports. Its first two proposed standards, IFRS S1 *General Requirements for Disclosure of Sustainability-related Financial Information* and IFRS S2 *Climate-related Disclosures*, were published in July 2023.

Concurrently, GRI will continue to offer standards for sustainability reports, covering issues significant to stakeholders but not necessarily material to enterprise value. This includes reporting on human rights, environmental matters, and sector specific ESG impacts. Additionally, GRI will provide topic standards listing recommended disclosures for specific ESG themes.

Furthermore, the Sustainability Accounting Standards Board (SASB) Standards, now published under the IFRS, provide industry-specific guidance to 77 sectors, supporting organisations in their sustainability reporting efforts. These standards offer valuable insights to companies aiming for comprehensive and standardised reporting on ESG matters within their respective industries.

You can read more about the role of the ISSB and the status of new sustainability reporting standards here: https://www.ifrs.org/groups/international-sustainability-standards-board/

Also, Sustainability Accounting Standards Board (SASB) Standards which are also now published by the IFRS Foundation, which provide specific guidance to 77 industries to provide helpful guidance to support their sustainability reporting.

Industry specific SASB Standards can be found here: https://sasb.ifrs.org/standards/

5 Sustainability and environmental, social and governance (ESG)

5.1 Defining environmental, social and governance (ESG)

Environmental, social and governance (ESG) is also referred to as the three pillars of sustainability. ESG issues derive from increasing political and stakeholder concerns on the growing adverse effect of business operations on human sustainability.

There are no standard definitions of ESG issues, however, the Principles of Responsible Investment (PRI) define ESG issues as follows:

Key terms

Environmental: These are issues relating to the quality and functioning of the natural environment and natural systems. These include biodiversity loss; greenhouse gas (GHG) emissions, climate change, renewable energy, energy efficiency, air, water or resource depletion or pollution, waste management, stratospheric ozone depletion, changes in land use, ocean acidification and changes to the nitrogen and phosphorus cycles.

Social: These are issues relating to the rights, well-being and interests of people and communities. These include human rights; labour standards in the supply chain; child, slave and bonded labour; workplace health and safety; freedom of association and freedom of expression; human capital management and employee relations; diversity; relations with local communities; activities in conflict sones; health and access to medicine; HIV/AIDS; consumer protection; and controversial weapons.

Governance: These are issues relating to the governance of companies and other investee entities. In the listed equity context these include, board structure, size, diversity, skills and independence, executive pay, shareholder rights, stakeholder interaction, disclosure of information, business ethics, bribery and corruption, internal controls and risk management, and, in general, issues dealing with the relationship between a company's management, its board, its shareholders and its other stakeholders. This category may also include matters of business strategy.

(**Source:** PRI. [Online] Available from: https://www.unpri.org/sustainability-issues/environmental-social-and-governance-issues [Accessed 3 October 2024])

5.2 Sustainability versus ESG

Sustainability describes a world of thriving economies and just societies based on what nature can afford. It incorporates consideration of both the impacts and dependencies of an organisation and so includes those factors that are material both to the organisation but also to society.

Environmental, social and governance (ESG) approaches this issue through a corporate lens and considers only how these risks and opportunities affect a business and its enterprise value.

Whilst sustainability includes the concept of environmental and social limits (planetary limits and a social foundation) within which there is a safe operating space, ESG does not.

ESG focusses on enterprise value and does not include consideration of planetary limits and a social foundation, together considered the 'safe operating space' within which companies, governments and individuals can sustainably operate. Therefore, ESG is separate from the overall concept of sustainability.

Note, organisations tend to consider only how ESG related risks and opportunities affect a business and its enterprise value.

6 Sustainable business practices

In today's business environment, sustainability is a critical factor for long-term success and viability. Companies are increasingly recognising the importance of integrating sustainability into their core business practices, which involves a commitment to corporate accountability and proactive stakeholder engagement.

6.1 Corporate accountability

As we learned from the previous chapter, corporate accountability is the principle that companies should act ethically and be answerable to their stakeholders for their actions, decisions, policies and impacts on society and the environment.

Corporate accountability extends beyond financial performance to include social and environmental dimensions, ensuring that businesses contribute positively to sustainable development.

Gray and Adams (2014) argue that s sustainable business practices is essential for achieving long-term success and sustainability. Therefore, sustainable business practices are intrinsically linked to corporate accountability.

6.2 Sustainability accounting

Sustainability accounting focuses on expanding traditional accounting practices to incorporate environmental and social impacts, requiring businesses to measure and report their impacts on the environment and society as well as their financial performance.

Sustainability accounting aims to provide a more comprehensive view of an organisation's performance by including the impacts of its activities on society and the environment, alongside the traditional financial metrics.

Gray and Adams (2014) define the three components which provide a comprehensive approach to sustainability accounting; environmental accountability, social accountability and economic accountability. Each of these is explained further below.

6.2.1 Environmental accountability

Key term

> **Environmental accountability:** Is where organisations take responsibility for their environmental impacts by implementing sustainable practices and reducing their ecological footprint.

An example of environmental accountability is US company Tesla, which has been at the forefront of promoting electric vehicles to reduce carbon emissions over the past decade. Also, Apple, a US computer and smart device manufacturer, has committed to using 100% recycled aluminium in its products to reduce the environmental impact of its products.

6.2.2 Social accountability

Key term

> **Social accountability:** Involves ensuring that business operations respect human rights, provide fair labour conditions, and contribute to the well-being of its employees and wider society.

An example of social accountability is US shoe manufacturer Nike's efforts to improve labour conditions in its supply chain after facing criticism for sweatshop practices. As a result, Nike regularly audits its factories and publishes detailed reports on labour conditions.

6.2.3 Economic accountability

Key term

> **Economic accountability:** Is where companies are required, or voluntarily, demonstrate that their economic activities support sustainable development. This can include investing in local economies, supporting small businesses, and fostering inclusive growth.

An example of environmental accountability is Danone, a French multinational food-products corporation. Its operations fund the 'Danone Communities' initiative which supports social businesses that address issues like malnutrition and access to clean water, creating economic opportunities in communities where access to food and clean water is challenging.

Environmental, Social and Economic accountability provide a comprehensive approach to sustainability accounting which provides transparency to stakeholders so they can fully understand the scope and impact of a company's operations and its commitment to meeting its sustainability objectives.

(**Source:** Gray, R., Adams, C. A., and Owen, D. (2014). *Accountability, Social Responsibility and Sustainability: Accounting for Society and the Environment.* Pearson Education Ltd)

6.3 Sustainable business practices

Key term

> **Sustainable value creation:** Is where organisation engage with stakeholders helps organisations identify opportunities for creating sustainable value.

By considering the needs and interests of all stakeholders, companies can create long-term value and achieve sustainable growth. This approach not only benefits the company but also contributes positively to society and the environment.

Donaldson and Preston suggest that when organisations engage with their stakeholders and uphold corporate accountability then sustainable business practices follow and an organisation's sustainability performance improves.

The following are examples of sustainable business practices:

(a) Inclusive decision-making
(b) Transparency and reporting
(c) Ethical practices
(d) Responsiveness and responsibility

Each of these sustainable business practices are explained further in the table below.

	Sustainable business practice	Description	Example
(a)	Inclusive decision-making	Companies are encouraged to involve a wide range of stakeholders in their decision-making processes. This inclusivity ensures that diverse perspectives are considered, leading to more balanced and sustainable business strategies.	Ben & Jerry's actively engages with local communities and social justice organisations to guide their business practices and ensure they align with broader societal goals.
(b)	Responsiveness and responsibility	Organisations that are responsive to stakeholder concerns demonstrate their commitment to accountability.	After receiving feedback from environmental groups, Coca-Cola pledged to reduce plastic waste by increasing the use of recycled materials in its packaging, showing responsiveness to stakeholder concerns.
(c)	Transparency and reporting	To be accountable, companies must transparently report their sustainability efforts and impacts. This includes disclosing information on environmental performance, social initiatives, and governance practices to stakeholders. Transparency in reporting and operations builds trust with stakeholders.	Nestlé applies Global Reporting Initiative (GRI) standards to provide comprehensive sustainability reports that cover various stakeholder concerns.
(d)	Ethical practices	Businesses are expected to adopt ethical practices that respect stakeholder interests and promote sustainability. This includes reducing environmental footprints, ensuring fair labour practices, and contributing to community development.	

Case Study

The following organisations demonstrate corporate accountability practices through their sustainability and corporate responsibility initiatives:

Ben & Jerry's (US)

Ben & Jerry's is a US-based ice cream manufacturers and retailer. This company has developed a reputation for strong social and environmental commitments, Ben & Jerry's engages with various stakeholders, including local communities, suppliers, and customers. The company uses fair trade ingredients and supports social justice causes, demonstrating a robust model of corporate accountability and stakeholder engagement.

Starbucks (US)

Starbucks engages with its stakeholders through its ethical sourcing practices, community involvement, and environmental initiatives. The company's 'Starbucks C.A.F.E. Practices' ensure that coffee is ethically sourced, benefiting farmers and promoting sustainable farming practices.

Unilever (Netherlands/UK)

Launched in 2010, Unilever's Sustainable Living Plan aimed to decouple strategic business growth from its environmental impact while increasing positive social impact. The company focuses on improving health and well-being, reducing its environmental footprint, and enhancing employee and supplier livelihoods. Unilever actively engages with various stakeholders, including customers, employees, suppliers, and communities, to realise their aims and to understand and address their concerns, and Unilever publishes detailed sustainability reports, providing transparent data on their environmental and social impact.

IKEA (Sweden)

IKEA commitment to sustainability and ethical practices is contained in its 'People & Planet Positive Strategy'. IKEA's sustainability strategy aims to use resources efficiently, promote renewable energy, and contribute to a circular economy by 2030. IKEA is also known for its efforts in ensuring ethical sourcing and working conditions throughout its supply chain and it audits suppliers regularly to ensure compliance with its code of conduct. Also, the IKEA Foundation supports numerous global initiatives to improve children's education and support refugee families.

Siemens (Germany)

Siemens has committed to becoming carbon-neutral by 2030. The company focuses on energy-efficient products and solutions, contributing significantly to reducing global emissions. Siemens actively promotes diversity and inclusion within its workforce, implementing policies to ensure equal opportunities for all employees and it has implemented a robust compliance framework to prevent corruption in its business practices, such as bribery and money-laundering, which ensures ethical conduct in all business activities.

Novo Nordisk (Norway)

Novo Nordisk aims to have zero environmental impact by 2030 through initiatives like recycling and reducing waste. The company follows GRI standards for sustainability reporting, ensuring transparency in their social and environmental impact and it runs several programs to make diabetes care affordable and accessible in low- and middle-income countries.

Each of these organisations exemplify corporate accountability through various initiatives, including rigorous sustainability practices, ethical supply chain management, transparent reporting, and proactive engagement with stakeholders. They set benchmarks in their respective industries, demonstrating that business success and corporate responsibility can go hand in hand.

7 Sustainability strategy setting and management decision making

In the pursuit of sustainability excellence, organisations must strategically set and effectively manage their sustainability initiatives. This section delves into the critical aspects of sustainability strategy setting and management decision making, exploring how companies can align their goals, policies, and actions with sustainability principles to drive positive environmental and social impact while maintaining operational resilience and competitiveness. Let's delve into the key considerations and best practices for crafting and implementing sustainability strategies within organisational decision-making frameworks.

7.1 Features of a sustainability strategy

Many organisations are developing new strategies to meet ESG objectives and implement new ways of working in their service provision, product delivery, supply chain and operations, as follows.

Organisations are increasingly recognising the critical importance of integrating Environmental, Social, and Governance (ESG) aspects into their overall strategy and operations. This integration is driven by the need to attract and retain customers and providers of finance who are demanding improvements in corporate sustainability practices.

To truly benefit from portraying themselves as socially responsible, organisations must be genuinely committed to governance, environmental, and ethical principles, fostering trust with stakeholders and planning for long-term of sustainability within value creation strategies.

The following table includes examples of ESG strategies which organisations may adopt.

Category	Explanation	Examples ESG Strategies
Environmental (E) Neutralising the impact of economic activity on the environment	Promote resource and product sustainability by using renewable energy sources, using recycled materials and designing products which can be recycled. Innovate greener production technologies and minimise waste and pollution. Reduce CO_2 emissions levels, reduce energy consumption and improve air quality. Reduce waste, minimise use of natural resources and aim to use renewable sources, impacts of product use. Go beyond minimum compliance with environmental legislations.	Renewable energy investments, supply chain sustainability, climate risk assessment and management, water and waste management
Social (S) Acting in a fair, just and honest way is a universal human expectation of each other and from organisations	Engage with local communities. For example, by supporting local charities and social events, employing local people, investing in the local economy. Apply health and safety, workers' rights (in the business itself and its supply chain), pay and benefits, diversity and equal opportunities, responsible marketing, data protection and privacy, community impact and investment, supply chain impact, bribery/corruption principles. Also, consider economic stability and growth, provision of sustainable employment opportunities, local economic development, healthy competition, compliance with governance structures, transparency, long-term viability of businesses and investment in innovation/new product development.	Diversity and inclusion initiatives, community engagement and philanthropy, product innovation for sustainability

Category	Explanation	Examples ESG Strategies
Governance (G) Complying with the law is a requirement in all societies, and this applies to organisations as well as individuals	Apply mandatory and best practice legal and regulatory governance frameworks. Set strategic objectives which aim to provide long term sustainable benefits to all stakeholders which includes environment, social and ethical objectives. Prevent short term profit motives overriding the exploitation of stakeholders and the environment. Adopt good governance and responsible business practices, for example, by eliminating self-interest, fraud, bribery, money laundering and other forms of corruption. Understand the benefits of diversity and shared decision making on the board and comply with employee health and safety regulations.	Ethical governance practises

7.2 Integration of sustainability objectives into the overall strategy

To achieve sustainable development, organisations must integrate ESG issues into their conventional strategic objective setting. This involves aligning strategic objectives with ESG and sustainability considerations to meet stakeholder expectations and promote responsible business practices.

A company's sustainability strategy typically encompasses many features aimed at addressing environmental, social, and governance (ESG) issues while promoting long-term value creation and responsible business practices. These include, but are not limited to, the following areas

- Vision and commitment
- Materiality assessment
- Strategic goal setting and targets
- Product development and innovation
- Supply chain management
- Marketing strategy
- Financing strategy
- Human resource strategy
- Managing stakeholder relationships
- Measuring investment appraisal
- ESG risk management
- Integration with corporate governance
- Codes of conduct and ethics
- Continuous improvement
- ESG performance monitoring
- Community involvement

Each of these is explained in the following sections.

7.2.1 Vision and commitment

A sustainability strategy requires a clear vision statement and commitment to sustainability, outlining the company's goals and aspirations for environmental stewardship, social responsibility, and ethical governance.

For example, a global consumer goods corporation, has a clear vision and commitment to sustainability outlined in its corporate mission statement. The company pledges to minimise its environmental footprint, support community development initiatives, and uphold ethical business practices. This commitment is demonstrated through the integration of sustainability principles into the company's core values, strategic planning processes, and decision-making frameworks.

7.2.2 Materiality assessment

A sustainability strategy includes identification of material ESG issues that are most relevant to the company's operations, stakeholders, and long-term value creation, based on stakeholder engagement, risk assessments, and industry benchmarks.

For example, an organisation conducts a comprehensive materiality assessment to identify key environmental, social, and governance (ESG) issues that are most relevant to its business and stakeholders. Through stakeholder engagement sessions, industry research, and risk assessments, the company determines that reducing carbon emissions, ensuring responsible sourcing practices, and enhancing employee diversity and inclusion are the most critical material issues that could impact its long-term success and reputation.

7.2.3 Strategic goal setting and targets

A well-developed sustainability strategy includes the establishment of specific, measurable, and time-bound goals and targets to drive progress towards sustainability objectives, such as reducing greenhouse gas emissions, promoting diversity and inclusion, or enhancing supply chain transparency.

For example, a company sets strategic sustainability goals and targets to drive progress towards its environmental and social objectives. As part of its sustainability strategy, the company commits to achieving a 30% reduction in greenhouse gas emissions by 2030, sourcing 100% of its electricity from renewable energy sources by 2025 and increasing gender diversity in its leadership positions to 40% by 2023. These specific, measurable, and time-bound targets provide a roadmap for the company to align its actions with its sustainability aspirations and track progress over time.

7.2.4 Product development and innovation

Integrating ESG and sustainability objectives into product development involves designing products and services that minimise environmental impact, promote social responsibility, and meet stakeholder expectations.

For example, a clothing company may develop a line of sustainably sourced and ethically manufactured apparel made from organic cotton and recycled materials to reduce water usage and support fair labour practices.

7.2.5 Supply chain management

Incorporating ESG and sustainability considerations into supply chain management entails selecting suppliers and partners that adhere to responsible business practices, environmental standards, and labour rights.

For instance, a multinational corporation may implement supplier sustainability assessments and audits to ensure ethical sourcing practices, increased use of renewal or recycled materials, reducing the risks of child labour, reduced supply miles (lessening the distance to key suppliers) or reducing environmental degradation and damage in its supply chain.

7.2.6 Marketing strategy

Aligning marketing strategies with ESG and sustainability objectives involves communicating the organisation's commitment to responsible business practices, environmental stewardship, and social impact.

An example is a food company promoting its use of locally sourced, organic ingredients in its products through marketing campaigns that emphasise sustainability, health, and community support.

7.2.7 Financing strategy

Integrating ESG and sustainability considerations into financing strategies involves accessing capital markets that prioritise environmental, social, and governance criteria. An example is a renewable energy company issuing green bonds to finance solar or wind energy projects, attracting investors who prioritise investments with positive environmental impacts and sustainable returns.

7.2.8 Human resource strategy

Incorporating ESG and sustainability objectives into human resource strategies involves fostering a culture of sustainability within the organisation. Empowerment of employees through sustainability training, education, and awareness programs will build a culture of sustainability, foster employee engagement, and encourage innovation and continuous improvement.

For example, a technology company may offer sustainability training programs to employees, implement diversity and inclusion policies to promote equitable opportunities, and recognise employee contributions to environmental initiatives through rewards and incentives.

7.2.9 Managing stakeholder relationships

Integrating ESG considerations into stakeholder management involves engaging with stakeholders to understand their expectations and concerns regarding sustainability.

An example is a mining company consulting with local communities and indigenous groups to address concerns about environmental conservation, land rights, and community development in areas where it operates.

7.2.10 Measuring investment appraisal

Incorporating ESG factors into investment appraisal involves assessing the financial and non-financial impacts of investment decisions on environmental, social, and governance performance.

For instance, an infrastructure investment firm may evaluate the potential social and environmental risks and benefits of a new transportation project, considering factors such as community displacement, biodiversity impacts, and climate resilience.

7.2.11 ESG risk management

Integrating ESG considerations into risk management involves identifying, assessing, and mitigating environmental, social, and governance risks.

An example is a financial institution incorporating climate change risk assessments into its lending practices to evaluate the exposure of loan portfolios to physical risks (eg extreme weather events) and transition risks (eg policy changes, technological advancements) associated with climate change.

7.2.12 Integration with corporate governance

Integration of sustainability principles into corporate governance structures, practices, and policies, including board oversight, executive compensation, and risk management frameworks, to ensure

accountability, transparency, and ethical decision-making at all levels of the organisation. This will require the establishment of governance structures, policies, and practices that promote transparency, accountability, and responsible decision-making.

For example, a multinational corporation may appoint board members with expertise in sustainability to oversee ESG-related risks and opportunities, establish a sustainability committee to monitor performance, and integrate ESG criteria into executive compensation frameworks.

7.2.13 Codes of conduct and ethics

Embedding ESG and sustainability policies into codes of conduct involves setting ethical standards and guidelines for employee conduct, supplier relationships, and business operations.

An example is a pharmaceutical company implementing a code of conduct that prohibits bribery, corruption, and unethical marketing practices, and promotes compliance with environmental regulations and human rights standards in its global operations.

7.2.14 Continuous improvement

Implement a culture and commitment to continuous improvement and adaptation based on performance monitoring, feedback mechanisms, stakeholder engagement, and emerging trends and best practices in sustainability, to drive innovation, resilience, and long-term value creation.

7.2.15 ESG performance monitoring

Transparent reporting and disclosure of sustainability performance, initiatives, and progress against goals using standardised frameworks such as the Global Reporting Initiative (GRI) or the Sustainability Accounting Standards Board (SASB), to provide stakeholders with credible and comparable information.

Integrating ESG performance monitoring involves establishing metrics, KPIs, and reporting mechanisms to track progress towards sustainability goals.

For instance, a real estate investment trust may measure energy efficiency, water usage, waste management, and tenant satisfaction across its property portfolio to assess ESG performance and report on sustainability initiatives in annual reports and investor communications.

7.2.16 Community involvement

Integrating ESG considerations into community involvement involves engaging with local communities and other stakeholders to address social and environmental issues.

An example is a hospitality company partnering with local nonprofits to support education and healthcare initiatives in communities near its resorts, contributing to economic development and social well-being while promoting sustainable tourism practices.

Once a sustainability strategy has been development then integration of sustainability objectives and other considerations into the company's overall business strategy, decision-making processes, and operational practices to embed sustainability throughout the organisation and align with core business objectives.

The following question demonstrates how an organisation's strategic objectives are integrated and aligned with its sustainability objectives.

Question

Raw Press Juices (RPJ) is a premium UK-based soft drinks manufacturer known for its commitment to producing high-quality cold-pressed organic fruit and vegetable juices with no artificial additives. Founded on principles of health, sustainability, and ethical sourcing, RPJ has established a strong presence in the UK market, with a growing customer base that values natural, nutritious beverages. While the majority of

RPJ's sales occur within the UK, the company also exports approximately 10% of its production output to international markets, leveraging its reputation for premium quality and sustainability.

RPJ's commitment to sustainability extends beyond its product offerings to every aspect of its operations. From sourcing organic produce to reducing carbon emissions in its supply chain, RPJ aims to minimise its environmental footprint while positively impacting the communities it operates in. Additionally, RPJ prioritises employee well-being, fostering a culture of inclusivity, growth, and empowerment within its workforce. Recognising the importance of stakeholder engagement, RPJ actively involves its shareholders in decision-making processes, ensuring alignment between business goals and sustainability objectives.

The board of RPJ would like to develop new sustainability objectives which aligned and are integrated with the following strategic objectives.

(a) **Market development:** Expand market presence by increasing distribution channels and entering new geographic markets.

(b) **Product development and innovation:** Continuously innovate and diversify product portfolio to meet evolving consumer preferences and market trends.

(c) **Supply chain:** Strengthen and optimise the supply chain to enhance efficiency, reduce costs, and ensure product quality and consistency.

(d) **Employees:** Invest in employee training and development programs to foster a skilled and engaged workforce.

(e) **Shareholders:** Maximise shareholder value through sustainable growth and profitability.

Required

Suggest new sustainability objectives which align and are integrated with RPJ's existing strategic objectives.

Answer

RPJs five-point strategy each has a traditional strategic focus and a sustainability focus.

Strategic focus	Traditional strategic objective	Specific target	Sustainability objective	Specific target
(a) **Market development**	Expand market presence by increasing distribution channels and entering new geographic markets.	Increase the number of retail outlets carrying RPJ products by 20% within the next fiscal year.	Ensure expansion efforts prioritise partnerships with local farmers and suppliers, supporting sustainable agricultural practices and promoting economic development in rural communities.	Source at least 50% of raw materials from certified organic farms within a 100-mile radius of production facilities by the end of the next two years.

Strategic focus	Traditional strategic objective	Specific target	Sustainability objective	Specific target
(b) **Product development and innovation**	Continuously innovate and diversify product portfolio to meet evolving consumer preferences and market trends.	Launch at least three new juice flavours incorporating seasonal and locally sourced ingredients within the next 12 months.	Incorporate sustainable packaging solutions to minimise environmental impact and promote circular economy principles.	Transition 75% of RPJ's product packaging to recyclable materials by the end of the next fiscal year.
(c) **Supply chain**	Strengthen and optimise the supply chain to enhance efficiency, reduce costs, and ensure product quality and consistency.	Reduce transportation-related carbon emissions by 15% through route optimisation and use of low-emission vehicles within the next three years.	Implement fair trade practices and ethical sourcing standards throughout the supply chain, prioritising partnerships with suppliers who adhere to sustainable farming practices and provide fair wages and working conditions for workers.	Certify 100% of RPJ's key suppliers for compliance with recognised fair trade and labour standards by the end of the next two years.
(d) **Employees**	Invest in employee training and development programs to foster a skilled and engaged workforce.	Provide at least 20 hours of sustainability training to all employees annually, covering topics such as waste reduction, energy conservation, and ethical sourcing.	Promote employee health and well-being by offering wellness programs, flexible work arrangements, and opportunities for professional growth, creating a supportive and inclusive workplace culture.	Achieve a 10% reduction in employee turnover rates by implementing wellness initiatives and offering flexible work options within the next fiscal year.
(e) **Shareholders**	Maximise shareholder value through sustainable growth and profitability.	Increase annual revenue by 15% while maintaining profitability margins of at least 20% over the next three years.	Enhance transparency and accountability in corporate governance practices, providing shareholders with	Publish an annual sustainability report outlining key environmental, social, and governance (ESG) metrics and progress towards

Strategic focus	Traditional strategic objective	Specific target	Sustainability objective	Specific target
			regular updates on sustainability initiatives, performance metrics, and long-term value creation strategies.	sustainability goals, starting from the next fiscal year.

7.3 Sustainability management and decision making

Embedding sustainability within management decision-making processes is essential for organisations to effectively address environmental, social, and economic challenges while pursuing long-term success. By integrating sustainability considerations into decision-making frameworks, cultures, and support systems, organisations can make informed choices that align with their sustainability goals and create value for stakeholders.

This approach ensures that sustainability becomes an integral part of organisational strategy, operations, and culture, driving positive environmental and social impact while enhancing business resilience and competitiveness.

The process of sustainability-led management decision making is supported by the following four components, each of which is explored in greater detail in the following sections:

1. Sustainability-led decision-making culture
2. Sustainability-led decision-making frameworks
3. Sustainability-led decision support systems
4. Sustainability-led decision support systems

7.3.1 Sustainability-led decision-making culture

A culture that prioritises sustainability in decision – making fosters organisational values, norms, and behaviours that support environmental and social responsibility. Building a sustainable decision – making culture requires leadership, collaboration, and a commitment to continuous improvement.

- **Sustainability led leadership** – Organisations foster a culture of sustainability leadership, where senior executives champion sustainability initiatives and integrate sustainability into the organisation's values and vision.

  For example, a clothing retailer may appoint a chief sustainability officer (CSO) to oversee sustainability efforts and ensure alignment with business objectives.

- **Cross-functional collaboration** – Sustainability requires collaboration across departments and functions to address complex challenges.

  For example, a technology company may establish cross – functional sustainability task forces comprised of representatives from different departments, such as R&D, procurement, and marketing, to develop and implement sustainability initiatives.

- **Continuous improvement culture** – Organisations promote a culture of continuous improvement in sustainability performance, encouraging employees to identify opportunities for innovation and efficiency.

For example, a hospitality company may implement employee suggestion programs to solicit ideas for reducing energy consumption, waste generation, and water usage, fostering a culture of sustainability innovation.

7.3.2 Sustainability-led decision-making frameworks

The application of sustainability focused decision-making frameworks provide the structure and guidance necessary for organisations to integrate sustainability considerations into their strategic planning and operational processes. These frameworks outline the principles, goals, and criteria that guide decision-making, ensuring alignment with sustainability objectives.

- **Sustainable strategy formulation** – This involves developing strategies that align with the organisation's sustainability goals and objectives.

    For example, an energy company may decide to invest in renewable energy projects as part of its strategy to reduce greenhouse gas emissions and transition to a low-carbon economy.

- **Sustainable operations planning** – Organisations need to consider sustainability principles when planning day-to-day operations.

    For example, a manufacturing facility may implement energy-efficient technologies and processes to minimise resource consumption and waste generation, aligning with sustainability objectives.

7.3.3 Sustainability-led decision-making processes

Effective decision-making processes enable organisations to assess the environmental, social, and economic impacts of their actions and make informed choices that support sustainability. These processes involve methodologies and tools that facilitate thorough analysis and stakeholder engagement to ensure holistic decision-making.

- **Life cycle assessment (LCA)** – Organisations conduct LCAs to evaluate the environmental impacts of products or services throughout their life cycle.

    For example, a food manufacturer may conduct an LCA to assess the carbon footprint of its products from sourcing raw materials to distribution and consumption, informing decisions to reduce emissions.

- **Triple bottom line analysis** – This approach considers environmental, social, and economic (ESG) impacts when evaluating alternatives. This is also known as the Three P's analysis – planet, people, profit.

    For example, a construction company may use a triple bottom line analysis to assess the sustainability of different building materials, considering factors such as environmental impact, social equity, and long-term cost-effectiveness.

- **Stakeholder engagement** – Organisations are advised to engage stakeholders, including employees, customers, suppliers, and communities, to gather feedback and incorporate diverse perspectives and sustainability expectations into sustainability decision making processes.

    For example, a retail company may consult with local communities and environmental NGOs when selecting suppliers to ensure alignment with sustainability goals and address stakeholder concerns.

7.3.4 Sustainability-led decision support systems

Decision support systems provide sustainability related expertise and people resources and IT technologies necessary for organisations to collect, analyse, and visualise data related to sustainability performance and impacts. These systems enable organisations to make evidence-based decisions and monitor progress towards sustainability goals.

- **Environmental management systems (EMS)** – EMS help organisations manage and track their environmental performance, compliance obligations, and sustainability initiatives.

    For example, a manufacturing company may implement an EMS to monitor energy consumption, waste generation, and emissions, enabling data-driven decision-making to improve environmental performance.

- **Sustainability impact assessment tools** – Sustainability impact assessment tools evaluate the potential environmental and social impacts of decisions and projects.

    For example, before launching a new product line, a consumer goods company may use a sustainability impact assessment tool to identify potential risks and opportunities related to resource use, supply chain practices, and social equity.

- **Sustainability reporting platforms** – Organisations use sustainability reporting platforms to track and communicate their sustainability performance to stakeholders.

    For example, a financial institution may use a sustainability reporting platform to disclose its carbon footprint, social investments, and community engagement initiatives, demonstrating transparency and accountability in sustainability management.

Incorporating sustainability into management decision-making processes is vital for organisations to navigate environmental, social, and economic challenges while ensuring long-term success. By integrating sustainability considerations into decision-making frameworks, cultures, and support systems, organisations can make informed choices that align with their sustainability goals and create value for stakeholders.

This approach ensures that sustainability becomes ingrained in organisational strategy, operations, and culture, driving positive environmental and social impact while enhancing business resilience and competitiveness. Through the four components of sustainability-led decision-making explored in this discussion – cultures, frameworks, processes, and support systems – organisations can effectively navigate complex sustainability issues and contribute to a more sustainable future for all.

Question

EcoThreads is a leading clothing retailer based in the UK, known for its commitment to sustainability and ethical sourcing practices. Under the leadership of CEO Emma Green, EcoThreads has established a reputation for offering environmentally friendly and socially responsible fashion to its customers. The company sources its products from both UK-based suppliers and manufacturers located in India, China, and other South-East Asian countries.

In response to growing consumer demand for sustainable fashion and increasing regulatory pressure on businesses to address environmental and social issues, CEO Emma Green has tasked the board of directors with embedding sustainability principles throughout EcoThreads' organisational decision-making processes. The goal is to ensure that sustainability becomes ingrained in the company's culture, operations, and strategic direction, enabling EcoThreads to meet its sustainability objectives and targets while maintaining its competitive edge in the market.

Required

Advise the board on the steps it should take to established sustainability-led management decision making processes throughout EcoThreads.

Answer

Introduction

EcoThreads, a prominent clothing retailer headquartered in the UK, has garnered recognition for its unwavering commitment to sustainability and ethical sourcing practices. Spearheaded by CEO Emma Green, EcoThreads has positioned itself as a leader in offering environmentally friendly and socially responsible fashion to its clientele. With supply chains extending to both UK-based suppliers and manufacturers in regions like India, China, and South-East Asia, EcoThreads faces a complex landscape of sustainability challenges and opportunities.

Given the escalating demand for sustainable fashion among consumers and mounting regulatory pressures on businesses to address environmental and social issues, CEO Emma Green has charged the board with the pivotal task of embedding sustainability principles across EcoThreads' organizational decision-making processes. The overarching goal is to seamlessly integrate sustainability into the company's culture, operations, and strategic direction, thereby enabling EcoThreads to achieve its sustainability objectives while maintaining its competitive advantage in the market.

To establish sustainability-led management decision-making processes throughout EcoThreads, the board must take strategic steps tailored to the company's unique scenario and objectives. To realise this vision, the board should implement a tailored approach encompassing several key steps:

Cultivate a sustainability-led culture

The board must foster a culture within EcoThreads that prioritises sustainability in decision-making. This involves instilling values and behaviours that champion environmental and social responsibility. Board members should lead by example, actively championing sustainability initiatives and integrating sustainability into the company's core values and vision. Cross-functional collaboration should be encouraged, fostering synergy across departments to address complex sustainability challenges. Additionally, the board should promote a culture of continuous improvement in sustainability performance, empowering employees to innovate and drive efficiency in sustainability initiatives.

Develop tailored sustainability-led decision-making frameworks

EcoThreads requires decision-making frameworks specifically tailored to its sustainability goals and operational processes. The board should formulate sustainable strategies aligned with the company's overarching sustainability objectives. This may involve investing in renewable energy projects, adopting sustainable sourcing practices, or implementing waste reduction initiatives. Sustainable operations planning should be integrated into day-to-day activities, with a focus on minimising resource consumption and waste generation across the supply chain.

Implement holistic decision-making processes

Effective decision-making processes are crucial for EcoThreads to assess the environmental, social, and economic impacts of its actions comprehensively. The board should advocate for methodologies such as life cycle assessments (LCAs) to evaluate the environmental footprint of products throughout their life cycle. Triple bottom line analysis should be employed to assess alternatives based on their environmental, social, and economic implications. Stakeholder engagement should be prioritised, ensuring that diverse perspectives are considered in sustainability decision-making processes.

Leverage decision support systems

Decision support systems equipped with sustainability-related expertise and technologies are indispensable for EcoThreads to make informed decisions and monitor progress towards sustainability goals. The board should invest in environmental management systems (EMS) to track and manage environmental performance effectively. Sustainability impact assessment tools can aid in evaluating the potential environmental and social impacts of decisions and projects. Sustainability reporting platforms should be utilised to communicate EcoThreads' sustainability performance transparently to stakeholders.

Conclusion

By adopting these strategic measures, the board can navigate EcoThreads through the complexities of sustainability management, ensuring that sustainability becomes deeply embedded within the company's DNA. Through concerted efforts to integrate sustainability considerations into decision-making processes, EcoThreads can realise its vision of becoming a beacon of sustainable fashion, driving positive environmental and social impact while maintaining its competitive edge in the global marketplace.

8 ESG risk management and metrics for sustainability performance monitoring and reporting

In today's rapidly changing business landscape, organisations are increasingly recognising the critical importance of proactive risk management, particularly in relation to Environmental, Social, and Governance (ESG) factors.

ESG risks encompass a wide range of environmental, social, and governance issues that can significantly impact an organisation's long-term sustainability, reputation, and financial performance.

These risks include climate change impacts, supply chain disruptions, human rights violations, regulatory non-compliance, and ethical misconduct, among others. In light of growing stakeholder expectations, regulatory pressures, and market dynamics, organisations are under increasing scrutiny to effectively identify, assess, and mitigate ESG-related risks.

ESG risk management is considered to be an essential for organisations seeking to navigate the complex and interconnected challenges of the modern business environment and meet stakeholder expectations. By taking a proactive approach to identifying, assessing, and mitigating ESG risks, organisations can enhance resilience, protect reputation, ensure regulatory compliance, attract investment, and drive sustainable growth in the long term.

8.1 Benefits of ESG risk management

Implementing risk management processes within an organisation are beneficial for several reasons:

- **Enhanced resilience:** Proactively addressing ESG risks enables organisations to build resilience and adaptability in the face of evolving environmental, social, and regulatory challenges. By identifying and mitigating potential risks early on, organisations can better anticipate and respond to disruptions, safeguarding their operations, supply chains, and stakeholder relationships.

- **Protection of reputation:** ESG risks have the potential to significantly impact an organisation's reputation and brand value. Proactive risk management helps organisations protect their reputation by addressing ESG issues before they escalate into crises. By demonstrating a commitment to responsible business practices and sustainability, organisations can enhance trust and credibility with stakeholders, safeguarding their brand reputation in the long term.

- **Regulatory compliance:** Many ESG risks are subject to regulatory requirements and reporting obligations. Proactive risk management ensures that organisations stay compliant with applicable laws, regulations, and industry standards related to environmental protection, labour practices, data privacy, and corporate governance. By staying ahead of regulatory developments, organisations can avoid costly fines, legal penalties, and reputational damage associated with non-compliance.

- **Investor confidence**: Investors and financial stakeholders are increasingly integrating ESG considerations into their investment decisions. Proactively managing ESG risks and disclosing sustainability performance can enhance investor confidence and attract capital from socially

responsible investors. By demonstrating a commitment to ESG risk management and transparency, organisations can access new sources of financing and improve their access to capital markets.

- **Operational efficiency:** effective ESG risk management can drive operational efficiencies and cost savings by identifying opportunities for resource optimisation, waste reduction, and energy efficiency improvements. By implementing sustainable practices and reducing environmental impacts, organisations can lower operational costs, enhance resource efficiency, and improve overall profitability.

8.2 ESG risk management processes

An effective approach for organisations to manage sustainability and ESG risk involves the following steps:

- **ESG risk identification and assessment:** Begin by identifying and assessing sustainability and ESG risks relevant to your organisation's operations, supply chain, and stakeholders. This involves conducting comprehensive risk assessments to identify potential environmental, social, and governance risks that could impact the organisation's long-term viability, reputation, and performance.

- **ESG risk prioritisation:** Once risks are identified, prioritise them based on their likelihood and potential impact on the organisation's objectives and stakeholders. Focus on risks that pose the greatest threats to the organisation's sustainability goals, reputation, regulatory compliance, and financial stability.

- **Integration into existing risk management processes:** Integrate sustainability and ESG risk management into existing risk management processes and frameworks, such as enterprise risk management (ERM) systems. Ensure that sustainability and ESG risks are considered alongside traditional financial and operational risks, and that they are adequately addressed in risk mitigation strategies and action plans.

- **ESG metric measurement and monitoring:** Establish ESG metrics such as key performance indicators (KPIs) and other metrics to measure and monitor sustainability and ESG risks over time. Track progress against KPIs regularly and adjust risk management strategies as needed based on changes in risk exposure, stakeholder expectations, and regulatory requirements.

- **Stakeholder engagement:** Engage with stakeholders, including investors, customers, employees, suppliers, and communities, to understand their expectations and concerns regarding sustainability and ESG issues. Incorporate stakeholder feedback into risk management processes and decision-making to ensure alignment with stakeholder interests and values.

- **Transparency and reporting:** Communicate transparently with stakeholders about the organisation's sustainability and ESG risk management efforts, including the identification, assessment, and mitigation of risks. Provide regular updates and disclosures on sustainability performance, ESG initiatives, and progress towards risk management goals through internal reporting, sustainability reports, annual filings, and other communication channels.

- **Continuous improvement:** Commit to continuous improvement in sustainability and ESG risk management practices by regularly reviewing and updating policies, procedures, and controls. Stay informed about emerging sustainability trends, regulatory developments, and best practices in ESG risk management, and adapt strategies accordingly to maintain relevance and effectiveness.

By following this approach, organisations can effectively manage sustainability and ESG risks, enhance resilience to environmental, social, and governance challenges, and create long-term value for stakeholders.

8.3 Determining ESG risk materiality

Whether a particular ESG issue is material is a matter of judgment that depends on the facts involved, the circumstances of the specific issuer with reference to the views of its key stakeholders. Prioritisation of the risks and opportunities that have been determined by the board may be achieved through conducting a materiality assessment exercise.

Materiality can have different meanings for different stakeholder groups, and should disclose the board's involvement, the identification process and the criteria for the selection of material ESG factors in the ESG report.

Since stakeholder engagement on ESG matters to aid determination of materiality should be part of an organisation's everyday operations, it is not necessary to conduct a stakeholder engagement specifically for the purpose of preparing an ESG report. The absence of a specific stakeholder engagement need not be disclosed in the ESG report in a given year.

However, if a stakeholder engagement was conducted then organisations should disclose the significant stakeholders identified, the process and results.

Double materiality means considering two aspects.

(a) The sustainability issues that might create **financial** risks for the company (financial materiality)

(b) Also, those sustainability issues where a company's activities materially impact on **people** and the **environment** (impact materiality)

8.4 Climate-related risks

The risks private organisations and the public sector will face due to climate change can be categorised into two areas:

(a) **Physical risks**, which arise from the physical effects of climate change such as storms, extreme temperatures, wildfires, flooding.

(b) **Transition risks**, which relate to social and economic shifts to a low-carbon economy such as changes to policy, regulation, technology and market.

As a result, business needs to consider potential impairment of assets which have become economically stranded as a result, having suffered from unanticipated or premature write-downs or devaluation. These assets are referred to as stranded assets. Stranded assets can be caused by a range of environmental-related risks including:

- Climate change
- New ESG related regulations
- Changing societal norms and stakeholders expectations
- Litigation from third parties

8.5 Response strategy to climate-related risks

In the face of increasing climate-related risks, organisations need to focus on both mitigation and adaptation activities.

8.5.1 Climate change mitigation

Climate change mitigation means avoiding and reducing emissions of greenhouse gases into the atmosphere to prevent the planet from warming to more extreme temperatures. This involves a transition away from fossil fuels to clean, renewable energy; halting deforestation; and restoring natural habitats to reach net zero emissions.

8.5.2 Climate change adaptation

Climate change adaptation refers to adjustments of strategies and actions in response to the effects and future risks of climate change. These risks may be linked to the physical impacts of climate change; but also, the economic impact of a transition towards net Zero. Identifying, managing and adapting to these risks is key for the development of a resilient business that can survive, and even thrive in the unprecedented physical and transitional changes ahead.

8.6 Environmental, social, and governance (ESG) metrics

Environmental, social, and governance (ESG) metrics are instrumental in monitoring and reporting sustainability performance for organisations.

The purpose of ESG metrics is multifaceted:

- **Performance monitoring:** ESG metrics serve as key performance indicators (KPIs) for measuring an organisation's progress towards its sustainability goals and objectives. By tracking ESG metrics over time, organisations can assess their environmental impact, social responsibility, and governance practices, identifying areas of improvement and success.

- **Risk management:** ESG metrics help organisations identify and mitigate environmental, social, and governance risks that may impact their long-term viability and reputation. By monitoring ESG performance, organisations can proactively address issues such as climate change risks, supply chain disruptions, labour controversies, and regulatory compliance challenges.

- **Stakeholder engagement:** ESG metrics provide valuable information for engaging with stakeholders, including investors, customers, employees, regulators, and communities. Transparent reporting of ESG performance builds trust and credibility with stakeholders, demonstrating the organisation's commitment to responsible business practices and sustainability.

- **Investor decision-making:** ESG metrics are increasingly used by investors to evaluate the sustainability performance of companies and make informed investment decisions. Investors are integrating ESG factors into their investment analysis to assess risk, identify opportunities, and align their portfolios with environmental and social values.

- **Regulatory compliance:** ESG metrics help organisations comply with regulatory requirements related to sustainability reporting and disclosure. Many jurisdictions now mandate ESG reporting for listed companies, requiring them to disclose environmental impacts, social practices, and governance structures.

- **Competitive advantage:** Organisations that effectively monitor and report their ESG performance can gain a competitive advantage in the marketplace. Sustainability leadership and responsible business practices can enhance brand reputation, attract customers, and differentiate the organisation from competitors.

Overall, the purpose of ESG metrics for sustainability performance monitoring and reporting is to drive continuous improvement, mitigate risks, engage stakeholders, meet regulatory requirements, attract investment, and enhance long-term value creation for the organisation and society as a whole.

In the next table are examples of ESG Metrics which organisations could implement to improve their sustainability performance and reporting.

Area	Suggested ESG metric	Measured by
Environment		
Greenhouse gas emissions (GHG)	Absolute emissions	CO_2e CO_2e/unit of production
Energy consumption	Absolute energy consumption Energy consumption intensity	Megawatt hours (MWhs) Megawatt hours (MWhs)/unit of production
Water consumption	Total water consumption Water consumption intensity	Metric litre or m^3 Metric litre or m^3/unit of production
Waste generation	Total waste generated	Tonnes Tonnes/time unit or unit of production
Social		
Gender diversity	Current employees by gender New hires and turnover by gender	Percentage (%) or M:F ratio
Age-based diversity	Current employees by age New hires and turnover by age	Percentage (%) or M:F ratio
Employment	Total turnover Total number of employees	Number of employees with joiners and leavers Percentage (%) or M:F ratio
Development and training	Average training hours per employee Average training hours per employee per gender	Training Hours/numbers of employees
Occupational health and safety	Fatalities High-consequence injuries Recordable injuries Recordable work-related ill health cases	Number of incidents Percentage change (%)
Governance		
Board composition	Board independence Women on the board	Percentage (%) Percentage (%) or M:F ratio
Management diversity	Women in the management team	Percentage (%) or M:F ratio
Ethical behaviour	Anti-corruption disclosures Anti-corruption training for employees	List Number of days and Percentage completed (%)
Certifications	List all sustainability or ESG-related certification	List
Alignment with frameworks	The issuer needs to give priority to using globally recognised frameworks and disclosure practices to guide its sustainability reporting.	Disclosure of frameworks Exceptions Non-compliance

Area	Suggested ESG metric	Measured by
Assurance	Disclose whether sustainability report has undertaken: (a) External independent assurance (b) Internal assurance (c) No assurance Provide scope of assurance if organisation has undertaken external or internal assurance.	Case-by-case disclosure Number of assurance engagements undertaken

Organisations can choose to support KPI disclosures with independent assurance to strengthen the credibility of ESG information disclosed, although currently, there are no mandatory audit of a company's sustainability reporting disclosures.

Case Study

(a) Unilever

Each year, Unilever publish the basis of preparation of each of its ESG performance metrics for transparency, so stakeholders can understand how each measure is determined.

See Sections 4.1 to 4.8 for the basis of preparation for each sustainability performance measure.

https://www.unilever.com/files/bd7239b8-a13b-483b-83a3-b9ea6e6148d8/unilever-basis-of-preparation-2023.pdf

Unilever also publish its ESG performance metrics performance in the same report. For example, for climate, the following performance is disclosed for 2023:

Indicator	Performance measure	Reported performance result
Climate:		
Total greenhouse gas emissions	Total greenhouse gas (GHG) emissions, measured in metric tonnes of CO2-equivalent (tCO2e), between the period from 1 October 2020 to 30 September 2021.	121.12 million tonnes CO2e
100% renewable electricity by 2030	Percentage of electricity generated from renewable resources at operational sites in 2023 (covers the period 1 October 2022 to 30 September 2023).	92%
Replace fossil-fuel derived carbon with renewable or recycled carbon in all our cleaning and laundry product formulations by 2030	The total number of newly contracted partnerships to develop renewable or recycled carbon surfactants or renewable or recycled precursor feedstocks, between 1 January 2023 and 31 December 2023.	4

Other Unilever ESG performance metrics for 2023, can be viewed in the report.

(b) Tesco

Tesco is a UK based supermarket chain. It publishes its sustainability report each year. The board at Tesco's has applied stakeholder feedback (employees, customers, suppliers, and shareholders) to identify it four most material sustainability areas: (i) Climate change, (ii) Healthy sustainable diets (iii) Diversity and Inclusion, and (iv) Waste and packaging. These four areas provide a framework for its sustainability reporting.

Key headlines from Tesco's sustainability objectives are as follows:

- Tesco state they were the first business to set a zero-carbon goal back in 2009. Since 2015 Tesco claim to have reduced Group Scope 1 and 2 green-house gas emissions by 55%. Also, Tesco aim to be carbon neutral by 2035 and they are working with suppliers and partners to be net zero from farm to fork by 2050.
- In terms of community support, Tesco state that since 2015 we have supported tens of thousands of community projects with more than £100m in grants and through their partnerships with food banks they have donated over 52 million meals in unsold food from our stores.
- In terms of promoting healthy eating, Tesco state they have removed over 71 billion calories from the food we sell since 2018 through our product reformulation programme. Tesco is also encouraging our customers to try more plant-based diets that are kinder on the planet.
- In terms of diversity, Tesco say that 85% of Tesco colleagues agree that there is an inclusive culture at Tesco.

You can read more about Tesco's sustainability performance here which links to its sustainability reporting in its Annual Report here: https://www.tescoplc.com/sustainability

8.7 Environmental, social, and governance (ESG) metrics measuring strategies

One of the difficulties faced by many organisations is knowing how to measure specific ESG-related key performance indicators (KPIs), such as CO_2 emissions. This challenge arises due to the complexity of measuring and monitoring environmental, social, and governance impacts accurately and consistently.

However, there are several strategies and suggestions that organisations can employ to address this issue:

- **Standardised measurement protocols:** Organisations can utilise standardised measurement protocols and methodologies developed by recognised institutions and industry bodies. For example, the Greenhouse Gas Protocol provides a widely accepted framework for measuring and reporting greenhouse gas emissions, including CO_2 emissions, across different sectors and industries.
- **Data collection and reporting tools:** Implementing specialised software and tools for data collection, management, and reporting can streamline the process of measuring ESG-related KPIs. These tools often include features for data aggregation, analysis, visualisation, and reporting, making it easier for organisations to track and monitor their performance over time.
- **Third-party verification:** Engaging third-party auditors or verification services can help ensure the accuracy and credibility of ESG data and KPIs. Independent verification provides stakeholders with confidence in the reliability and integrity of the reported information, enhancing transparency and trust.
- **Collaboration and knowledge sharing:** Organisations can benefit from collaborating with industry peers, stakeholders, and experts to share best practices, challenges, and lessons learned in measuring and reporting ESG-related KPIs. Participating in industry forums, working groups, and partnerships facilitates knowledge exchange and capacity building.

- **Capacity building and training:** Investing in employee training and capacity building programs can enhance internal expertise and capabilities in measuring and reporting ESG-related KPIs. Providing staff with training on data collection methodologies, analytical techniques, and reporting standards equips them with the skills needed to effectively manage ESG performance.
- **Continuous improvement and adaptation:** Recognising that ESG measurement is an evolving discipline, organisations should commit to continuous improvement and adaptation. Regularly reviewing measurement processes, updating methodologies in line with emerging standards and best practices, and incorporating stakeholder feedback are essential for staying relevant and responsive to changing ESG requirements.

By leveraging these strategies and suggestions, organisations can overcome the challenges associated with measuring specific ESG-related KPIs like CO2 emissions and enhance their ability to effectively monitor and report their sustainability performance.

8.8 ESG impacts and ESG dependencies

This section looks further into the complexities of ESG risk management by further analysing ESG risks into impacts and dependencies. This provides further insights into how organisations can analyse, manage, and improve their sustainability practices.

8.8.1 ESG impacts

Key term

> **ESG impacts:** Considers how the decisions an organisation makes or its actions either positively or negatively affect environmental, societal and governance issues

Assessing and managing these impacts allows companies to align their practices with sustainable development goals, regulatory requirements, and stakeholder expectations. An organisation's impacts can be financially material due to reputational impacts such as reduced consumer demand or removal of license to operate.

Examples of impacts include worker rights, human rights, health and safety policy, waste, greenhouse gas emissions, water usage, land usage and biodiversity.

8.8.2 ESG dependencies

Key term

> **ESG dependencies:** Are the external factors and influences that affect a company's business operations, performance, and reputation.

These dependencies can stem from various sources such as regulatory changes, consumer preferences, availability of resources, stakeholder demands, and societal trends. Understanding these dependencies enables companies to anticipate risks, identify opportunities, and adapt their strategies and practices accordingly.

Information on dependencies is generally more useful for investors, who want to assess how well a company is managing it is exposure to long-term ESG risks, and hence assess the value of the company to inform investment decisions. This relates to financial materiality.

Examples of dependencies which may affect an organisation are worker health, workplace diversity, climatic conditions, resource availability, regulation, consumer expectations, other stakeholder expectations and risks to organisational reputation.

By effectively managing ESG impacts and dependencies, companies can enhance their reputation, attract investment, build customer loyalty, mitigate risks, and drive innovation. Also, reporting ESG related risks in terms of impact and dependencies provides greater transparency to an organisation's stakeholders.

The International Federation of Accountants has prepared a useful visual of impact information and dependencies, **which can be** found here:

https://www.ifac.org/knowledge-gateway/contributing-global-economy/publications/enhancing-corporate-reporting-sustainability-building-blocks

Question

As an ESG analyst at a sustainability consulting firm, you've been tasked with conducting an ESG risk assessment for ToughGear Ltd, an outdoor clothing manufacturer. Your analysis will utilise the ESG impacts and dependencies framework to evaluate the company's ESG risks.

ToughGear is a multinational corporation engaged in the design, production, and distribution of clothing and accessories. With a diverse supply chain spanning multiple countries, they source materials globally and sell their products through various channels, including retail stores and an e-commerce platform.

Required

Analyse ToughGear most significant ESG impacts and dependencies.

Answer

ToughGear's ESG impacts are expected to include the following:

- **Environmental impacts:** tough Gear's operations contribute to carbon emissions primarily through manufacturing processes and transportation. They can reduce their environmental impact by adopting renewable energy sources, optimising logistics and transportation efficiency, implementing sustainable waste management practices, and exploring eco-friendly materials.

- **Social impacts:** ToughGear should ensure fair labour practices throughout their supply chain, addressing issues like child labour, forced labour, and working conditions. Employee well-being can be enhanced through health and safety programs, diversity and inclusion initiatives, and employee training and development opportunities. Community engagement efforts may include supporting local initiatives, promoting sustainable practices, and fostering positive relationships with local communities.

- **Governance impacts:** ToughGear government policies and practices can have a significant impact on stakeholder returns, employee well-being and fair treatment of its suppliers. ToughGear should enhance its corporate governance structure by ensuring transparency, accountability, and ethical business practices throughout the entire organisation. This can involve implementing robust risk management policies, maintaining an independent and diverse board of directors, setting up independent committees to monitor ESG performance, ethics and corporate social responsibility and establishing clear channels for stakeholder engagement and feedback.

ToughGear's ESG dependencies are expected to include the following:

- **Regulatory changes:** Changes in environmental regulations, labour laws, and consumer protection regulations can impact the company's operations, supply chain, and market access.

- **Consumer preferences**: Shifting consumer preferences towards sustainable and ethically produced products can influence purchasing decisions and brand reputation.

- **Resource availability:** Access to water, raw materials, and energy sources can be affected by environmental and geopolitical factors, impacting the company's supply chain and cost structure.

- **Reputation management:** Negative incidents related to ESG issues can harm the company's reputation and brand image, affecting customer loyalty and investor confidence.

9 Sustainability reporting

Sustainability reporting is of growing importance to investors and other stakeholders as they use it to help inform their decisions. Investors are driving the pressure for more consistent and comparable reporting in this area as they need reassurance about the resilience of their investments.

If an organisation is not adequately considering the sustainability of their business, then what does this say to its stakeholders about the future success of the organisation?

There are two aspects to sustainability reporting: one is organisations reporting how their business affects society, the planet and the economy; and the other one is reporting how these factors affect an organisation's business value.

The trend from voluntary guidance to mandatory compliance for ESG reporting requirements in sustainability reports continues as stakeholder awareness of climate-related issues increase.

Beyond regulatory compliance, stakeholders are increasingly expecting a board of directors to increase the corporate transparency through voluntary disclosures and consider the impacts of its operations on the climate and on the resource sustainability

9.1 Increasing importance of ESG disclosure in sustainability reports

Corporate attitudes have changed in recent years recognising that sustainability practices and reporting creates business value, especially as climate change awareness increased following the Paris Agreement, which is a legally binding international treaty on climate change adopted by 196 countries in November 2016.

ESG and sustainability are now widely reflected in corporate governance and strategy setting, risk management, and ESG related key performance indictors monitored against targets as well as ESG and sustainability reporting to stakeholders. More requirements on ESG reporting and/or sustainability reporting are attributed to:

- Stakeholder pressure to address ESG related issues and to adopt sustainable business practices.
- Shift from voluntary to mandatory regulatory requirements.
- Influence from corporations with advanced ESG practices down the international supply chain to suppliers.
- Increased awareness of corporate leaders to be accountable for action; and
- Increased pressure from lenders to support more ethical and sustainable business practices.

In response, some global stock exchanges, including HKEX now mandate that listed companies to prepare an annual sustainability report, in addition to the financial report. Sustainability reporting is now as a routine part of corporate reporting for many listed entities worldwide.

A sustainability report is a report published by an organisation about the economic, environmental and social impacts caused by its business activities and operations. The report also presents the organisation's value and governance model and demonstrates the link between its strategy and its commitment to a sustainable global economy.

Whilst sustainability reporting is currently voluntary for some stock exchanges, such as those in the UK and the US, some forms of sustainability reporting has been compulsory for listed companies for a few years, for example, in Hong Kong and Singapore.

9.2 Companies Act 2006 Strategic Report disclosure for environmental information

All companies that are required to produce a Strategic Report must include a s.172(1) statement, with the exception of companies qualifying for the medium-sized companies' regime.

The Companies Act 2006 (Strategic Report and Directors' Report) requires quoted companies to report on environmental matters within the Strategic Report section of their Annual Report, to the extent that this environmental information is necessary for an understanding of the development, performance or position of the company's business.

This requirement comes under one of the seven general duties directors have to the company, commonly referred to as the 's.172 duty' to 'promote the success of the company'. Part 1 of that duty notes that:

'[…] A director of a company must act in the way [they] consider, in good faith, would be most likely to promote the success of the company for the benefit of its members as a whole, and in doing so have (amongst other matters) regard to […] the impact of the company's operations on the community and the environment.'

9.3 Summary of Sustainability Reporting Requirements under UK Listing Rules:

UK Financial Conduct Authority set the UK Listing Rules for companies listed on the London Stock Exchange. UK Listing Rules mandate that every listed company must prepare an annual sustainability report alongside its financial reports, detailing its business conduct and sustainability practices.

The UK Listing Rules require that the board of directors has the overall responsibility for their ESG strategy and reporting. The ESG Reporting Guide comprises two levels of disclosure obligations:

- Mandatory disclosure requirements
- 'Comply or explain' provisions

For mandatory disclosure, it means that the organisation must include such information in its ESG report.

For 'comply or explain provisions,' it means that if an organisation does not report on one or more of these provisions, the organisation must provide its reasons in its ESG report.

Failure to disclose the required information without explanation is a breach of the UK Listing Rules.

In assessing ESG issues, the UK Listing Rules encourage organisations to engage with stakeholders on an ongoing basis in order to understand their views and better meet their expectations.

The following is a brief summary of the main sustainability reporting requirements for UK listed companies.

9.3.1 Overall reporting sustainability reporting requirements for UK listed companies

The following overall sustainability reporting requirements must be included by a UK listed company in its annual sustainability report.

- **'Comply or explain' basis:** Companies unable to report on primary components must disclose this and provide explanations for their actions, adhering to the regulatory framework set by the UK Listing Rules.
- **Focus areas:** Sustainability reports must address environment, social, and governance factors, in alignment with the sustainability reporting guidelines outlined by the UK Listing Rules.
- **Timing:** Sustainability reports must be issued within 4 months after the end of the financial year, as specified by the UK Listing Rules.

9.3.2 Primary components to be included in the Sustainability Report

The following primary components must be included by a UK listed company in its annual sustainability report.

- **Material ESG factors:** Companies must identify factors critical for business continuity, explain their significance, and outline the selection process, as required by the UK Listing Rules.
- **Climate-related disclosures:** Report on climate risks and opportunities annually, based on the Task Force on Climate-related Financial Disclosures (TCFD) recommendations, as mandated by the UK Listing Rules.
- **Policies, practices, and performance:** Provide descriptive and quantitative information on material ESG factors, including performance against targets, in accordance with the UK Listing Rules.
- **Key performance indicators and targets:** Set targets for the forthcoming year related to each material ESG factor, following the guidelines outlined by the UK Listing Rules.
- **Sustainability reporting framework:** Select an appropriate framework such as the Global Reporting Initiative's (GRI) Sustainability Reporting Standards, and explain the choice and extent of application, in compliance with the UK Listing Rules.
- **Board statement:** Confirm board consideration of sustainability issues in strategy formulation, determination of material ESG factors, and oversight of management and monitoring, as required by the UK Listing Rules.

9.4 Integrated reporting

Integrated reporting combines in a single communication to stakeholders on its strategic objectives of how it will create value for its shareholders in the short-term and long-term, its approach to corporate governance and regulatory compliance, its recent financial performance and its futures prospects and risks in the business and economic environment in which it operates.

The International Integrated Reporting Council framework has laid down the following seven guiding principles to outline what an integrated report should contain:

- Strategic focus and future orientation
- Connectivity of information
- Stakeholder relationships
- Materiality
- Conciseness
- Reliability and completeness
- Consistency and comparability

Integrated reports provide a commentary to providers of equity and debt finance how an organisation has performed and how it will create value over the short-term and long-term. In contrast, sustainability reports communicate to a wide group of stakeholders with a focus on ESG goals, strategies, and related impacts. The differences are summarised in the following table.

	Integrated reporting	Sustainability reporting
Objective	Explain financial performance, strategy, risk management and value creation against challenges	Summarise ESG goals, strategies, impacts, targets and performance
Audience	Shareholders and other finance providers	Range of interested stakeholders

Scope	<ul><li>Company overview</li><li>Review of external business environment</li><li>Corporate governance compliance</li><li>Key risks and opportunities</li><li>Recent company performance and business review</li><li>Strategic objectives and future prospects</li></ul>	<ul><li>Significant impacts from economic issues such as global inflation and supply</li><li>For environmental and social issues, a summary of impact and disclosure of current performance (KPIs) with commentary against its own targets</li><li>Governance related matters including explaining areas of non-compliance and adopted best practices</li></ul>

Question

Be More Beautiful Company plc (BMB) recently became listed on the UK Stock Exchange, marking a significant milestone in its journey as a manufacturer and distributor of skincare products sold worldwide. BMB's product line is crafted from raw plant-based ingredients sourced from Indonesia and India, with manufacturing operations based in Sri Lanka through sub-contractor arrangements.

The manufacturing plants in Sri Lanka are situated in remote areas characterised by high levels of poverty, where children often travel long distances to access education. Media reports have surfaced, indicating the possible employment of children as young as fourteen by the subcontractor manufacturers. While education is compulsory until the age of 14, many children leave school at this age with the expectation of seeking employment.

The CEO of BMB holds the belief that ESG reporting, and compliance are merely additional costs, assuming that BMB shareholders prioritise financial returns over sustainability efforts. However, the chairperson and several non-executive directors of BMB express concerns regarding the company's lack of compliance with sustainability reporting requirements for UK listed companies. Despite being due to issue its inaugural sustainability report in six months, BMB has yet to develop a system to monitor environmental or social key performance indicators for shareholder reporting.

The board of BMB is now faced with uncertainties regarding the implications of non-compliance with sustainability reporting requirements and the contents of a compliant sustainability report under UK listing rules.

Required

Explain the main ESG reporting issues arising from BMB's current position.

Answer

Environmental issues

The sourcing of raw materials from Indonesia and India raises significant concerns about the impact on forests and farmlands. BMB must adopt sustainable practices to mitigate environmental degradation, such as implementing initiatives like replanting forests at a rate exceeding depletion and utilising recycled materials for packaging. It's imperative for the leadership to recognise environmental sustainability as an opportunity for long-term brand enhancement and profitability rather than viewing it solely as a cost.

Social issues

Addressing social issues within BMB's supply chain requires a commitment to ensuring fair wages, safe working conditions, and access to essential services like healthcare and education for all workers. Conducting wage reviews and ensuring fair compensation based on local living standards is crucial to prevent exploitation and promote social equity.

Additionally, BMB must thoroughly evaluate its subcontractor's employment practices, particularly regarding the utilisation of fourteen-year-olds post-education and ensure compliance with legal standards in Sri Lanka on minimum working age while also offering fair wages. BMB must also consider the ethics of employing fourteen-year-olds, as it wouldn't do so in the UK. If BMB informs its subcontractors not to employ those under, say, sixteen years of age, to be consistent with UK practices, then it may be denying an important source of income to many families in Sri Lanka. It may be better for BMB to support these employees with funding for further education opportunities rather than removing employment opportunities. The board should discuss the position with subcontractors to understand further before a decision is taken.

Governance and sustainability reporting issues

The CEO and board should undergo sustainability reporting training to change the mindset of the CEO; sustainability reporting is perceived as a benefit rather than a cost. This change in cultural mindset will reduce the risk of sustainability reporting non-compliance with UK listing rules.

Understanding UK sustainability reporting requirements is essential for BMB's board to ensure timely compliance and transparency. Leveraging the 'comply or explain' mechanism will enable BMB to address any current non-compliance transparently and take corrective actions.

With the impending issuance of its first annual report, BMB has a prime opportunity to establish ESG metrics and targets for monitoring and disclosure, demonstrating a commitment to sustainable practices. Clarifying these metrics and outlining actions to address non-compliance will be crucial for BMB to align with UK listing rules and build trust among stakeholders.

10 International Sustainability Standards Board (ISSB) IFRS Sustainability Disclosure Standards

10.1 About the International Sustainability Standards Board (ISSB)

The Trustees of the IFRS Foundation announced the formation of the International Sustainability Standards Board (ISSB) on 3 November 2021 at COP26 in Glasgow, following strong market demand for its establishment. The ISSB is developing – in the public interest – standards that will result in a high-quality, comprehensive global baseline of sustainability disclosures focused on the needs of investors and the financial markets.

Sustainability factors are becoming a mainstream part of investment decision-making. There are increasing calls for companies to provide high-quality, globally comparable information on sustainability-related risks and opportunities, as indicated by feedback from many consultations with market participants.

There is also a strong desire to address a fragmented landscape of voluntary, sustainability-related standards and requirements that add cost, complexity and risk to both companies and investors.

The ISSB has international support with its work to develop sustainability disclosure standards backed by the G7, the G20, the International Organisation of Securities Commissions (IOSCO), the Financial Stability Board, African Finance Ministers and Finance Ministers and Central Bank Governors from more than 40 jurisdictions.

The ISSB has published four key objectives:

1. To develop standards for a global baseline of sustainability disclosures
2. To meet the information needs of investors

3. To enable companies to provide comprehensive sustainability information to global capital markets

4. To facilitate interoperability with disclosures that are jurisdiction-specific and/or aimed at broader stakeholder groups

The ISSB builds on the work of market-led investor-focused reporting initiatives, including the Climate Disclosure Standards Board (CDSB), the Task Force for Climate-related Financial Disclosures (TCFD), the Value Reporting Foundation's Integrated Reporting Framework and industry-based SASB Standards, as well as the World Economic Forum's Stakeholder Capitalism Metrics.

The ISSB is committed to delivering standards that are cost-effective, decision-useful and market informed.

- The standards are developed with efficiency in mind, helping companies to report what is needed globally to investors across markets globally.
- The standards are designed to provide the right information, in the right way, to support investor decision-making and facilitate international comparability to attract capital.
- A company can avoid double-reporting by applying the ISSB's standards. When jurisdictional requirements build on the global baseline, companies are able to meet jurisdictional requirements while benefiting from the efficiency and comparability of the global baseline.

10.2 ISSB issued IFRS Sustainability Disclosure Standards

International investors with global investment portfolios are increasingly calling for high quality, transparent, reliable and comparable reporting by organisations on climate and other ESG issues.

The standards being developed by the International Sustainability Standards Board (ISSB), which governs the development of Sustainability Accounting Standards Board (SASB) Standards, is embedding the industry-based approach of the SASB Standards into its standard-setting process, as well as addressing the international applicability of the SASB Standards as a priority.

New ISSB Sustainability Disclosure Standards will provide investors and other capital market participants with information about organisations' sustainability-related risks and opportunities to help them make informed investment decisions.

In June 2023 the International Sustainability Standards Board (ISSB) issued its first two IFRS Sustainability Disclosure Standards, IFRS S1 *General Requirements for Disclosure of Sustainability-related Financial Information* and IFRS S2 *Climate-related Disclosures*, to encourage organisations to improve their sustainability performance and to ensure investors are provided with sustainability risk-focused information which is relevant to enterprise value and hence share price.

These two standards require commentaries to be included in directors commentary section of the annual report for organisations with accounting period starting after 1 January 2024.

10.3 IFRS S1 *General Requirements for Disclosure of Sustainability-related Financial Information*

IFRS S1 is effective for annual reporting periods beginning on or after 1 January 2024 with earlier application permitted as long as IFRS S2 *Climate-related Disclosures* is also applied.

The objective of IFRS S1 is to require an entity to disclose information about its sustainability-related risks and opportunities that is useful to users of general-purpose financial reports in making decisions relating to providing resources to the entity.

IFRS S1 requires an entity to disclose information about all sustainability-related risks and opportunities that could reasonably be expected to affect the entity's cash flows, its access to finance or cost of capital over the short, medium, or long term (collectively referred to as 'sustainability-related risks and opportunities that could reasonably be expected to affect the entity's prospects').

IFRS S1 prescribes how an entity prepares and reports its sustainability-related financial disclosures. It sets out general requirements for the content and presentation of those disclosures so that the information disclosed is useful to users in making decisions relating to providing resources to the entity.

IFRS S1 sets out the requirements for disclosing information about an entity's sustainability-related risks and opportunities. In particular, an entity is required to provide disclosures about its sustainability related governance, strategy, processes and performance, as follows:

(a) The **governance** processes, controls and procedures the entity uses to monitor, manage and oversee sustainability-related risks and opportunities

(b) The entity's **strategy** for managing sustainability-related risks and opportunities

(c) The **processes** the entity uses to identify, assess, prioritise and monitor sustainability-related risks and opportunities

(d) The entity's **performance** in relation to sustainability-related risks and opportunities, including progress towards any targets the entity has set or is required to meet by law or regulation

In June 2023, the ISSB issued IFRS S1 *General Requirements for Disclosure of Sustainability-related Financial Information*. IFRS S1 lays the groundwork for sustainability reporting, applicable to all organisations. Its scope encompasses fundamental requirements for disclosing:

- **Organisational profile:** Offering insights into the organisation's structure, governance, operations, and markets, alongside how sustainability is integrated into decision-making processes

- **Materiality assessment:** Identifying and prioritising sustainability topics crucial to stakeholders and long-term success through a materiality assessment

- **Sustainability strategy:** Communicating the sustainability strategy, including objectives, targets, and actions to address material issues, demonstrates the organisation's commitment to sustainable practices

- **Governance and risk management:** Disclosing the governance structure, responsibilities for sustainability, and approaches to identifying, assessing, and managing sustainability risks at different levels

- **Targets and performance:** Reporting sustainability targets, performance data, and progress towards objectives aids stakeholders in evaluating the organisation's sustainability progress

- **Verification:** Considering third-party assurance or verification of sustainability disclosures enhances credibility and accountability

- **Stakeholder engagement:** Disclosing stakeholder engagement practices ensures diverse perspectives are considered in sustainability decision-making

By adhering to IFRS S1, organisations can establish a solid foundation for comprehensive and credible sustainability reporting, promoting consistency and comparability across various entities.

IFRS S1 *General Requirements for Disclosure of Sustainability-related Financial Information* can be found here:

https://www.ifrs.org/issued-standards/ifrs-sustainability-standards-navigator/ifrs-s1-general-requirements.html/content/dam/ifrs/publications/html-standards-issb/english/2023/issued/issbs1/

10.4 IFRS S2 *Climate-related Disclosures*

IFRS S2 *Climate-related Disclosures* is effective for annual reporting periods beginning on or after 1 January 2024 with earlier application permitted as long as IFRS S1 *General Requirements for Disclosure of Sustainability-related Financial Information* is also applied.

The objective of IFRS S2 is to require an entity to disclose information about its climate-related risks and opportunities that is useful to users of general-purpose financial reports in making decisions relating to providing resources to the entity.

IFRS S2 requires an entity to disclose information about climate-related risks and opportunities that could reasonably be expected to affect the entity's cash flows, its access to finance or cost of capital over the short, medium, or long term (collectively referred to as 'climate-related risks and opportunities that could reasonably be expected to affect the entity's prospects').

IFRS S2 applies to:

- Climate-related risks to which the entity is exposed, which are:
    - Climate-related physical risks
    - Climate-related transition risks
- Climate-related opportunities available to the entity

IFRS S2 sets out the requirements for disclosing information about an entity's climate-related risks and opportunities. In particular, IFRS S2 requires an entity to disclose information that enables users of general-purpose financial reports to understand:

(a) The governance processes, controls, and procedures the entity uses to monitor, manage, and oversee climate-related risks and opportunities.

(b) The entity's strategy for managing climate-related risks and opportunities.

(c) The processes the entity uses to identify, assess, prioritise, and monitor climate-related risks and opportunities, including whether and how those processes are integrated into and inform the entity's overall risk management process.

(d) The entity's performance in relation to its climate-related risks and opportunities, including progress towards any climate-related targets it has set, and any targets it is required to meet by law or regulation.

In June 2023, the ISSB issued IFRS S2 *Climate-related Disclosures*. IFRS S2 is dedicated to climate-specific risks and opportunities. It mandates organisations to disclose the following:

- **Climate governance:** Details on governance structures and processes related to climate issues, including board oversight and management responsibilities

- **Climate strategy:** Disclosure of the organisation's approach to addressing climate risks and opportunities, aligning with long-term goals

- **Climate risk management:** Information on how climate-related risks is identified, assessed, and managed, encompassing physical and transition risks

- **Climate-related metrics and targets:** Reporting climate-related metrics and targets, such as greenhouse gas emissions and renewable energy usage, to assess progress

- **Scenario analysis:** Conducting scenario analysis to assess the potential impact of different climate scenarios on the business and disclosing the outcomes

- **Low-carbon transition plans:** Disclosing plans for transitioning to a low-carbon economy, signalling a commitment to sustainable practices

- **Climate disclosures in financial statements:** Integrating climate-related disclosures into financial statements, reflecting the financial implications of climate risks and opportunities

By adhering to IFRS S2, organisations can increase transparency and consistency of their sustainability objectives and ESG performance disclosures, empowering stakeholders to evaluate organisations' climate resilience and sustainability strategies effectively.

IFRS S2 *Climate Related Disclosures* can be found here:

https://www.ifrs.org/issued-standards/ifrs-sustainability-standards-navigator/ifrs-s2-climate-related-disclosures.html/content/dam/ifrs/publications/html-standards-issb/english/2023/issued/issbs2/

11 Assurance engagements related to disclosures in sustainability reporting

11.1 IFRS S1 and IFRS S2 impact on the statutory audit

Disclosures made under IFRS S1 and S2 are not yet subject to any form of assurance.

However, the auditor has a statutory duty to review all other information supplied in the same document as the audited financial statements under ISA (UK) 720 *The Auditor's Responsibilities Relating to Other Information*.

As part of this review of other information supplied, the auditor will evaluate whether there are any:

(a) Inconsistencies between the other information, the auditor's understanding of the entity and the audited financial statements; and

(b) Material misstatements in the other information.

Again, the disclosures made under IFRS S1 and S2 are not yet subject to any form of assurance but as part of their responsibilities under ISA (UK) 720, auditors would be required to evaluate matters such as:

(a) The integrity of any data presented.
(b) Its consistency with the organisation's business; and
(c) Other disclosures in the other information supplied.

Should the other information relate to disclosures made under IFRS S1 and S2, the auditor would need to confirm:

(a) That information disclosed under IFRS S1 and S2 is consistent with anything ESG-related in the audited financial statements as well as any other ESG information that the auditor may have obtained during the course of the audit; and

(b) That no material misstatements exist in the ESG information (which is likely to include some form of evaluation of whether this information complies with IFRS S1 and S2).

For example, an auditor may review the audited entity's risk identification and evaluation process, the internal control environment relevant to the measurement of sustainability or other ESG metrics or targets, or the suitability of the method of measurement undertaken (for example, CO_2 emissions or energy consumption).

Such work could be complex as evaluation of the IFRS S1 and S2 disclosures may require expertise beyond that of the auditor, possibly requiring the services of an expert.

Should either inconsistent or materially misstated other information be identified, the auditor would request the management of the audited entity to correct the inconsistency or misstatement. Should this request be refused, the auditor would then be required to disclose this within the auditor's report under the heading 'Other information'. However, the auditor's opinion on the financial statements would not be modified in respect of this matter.'

11.2 ESG voluntary assurance of ESG information disclosed in sustainability reports (or other reports)

Sustainability reports encompass diverse environmental, social, and governance (ESG) matters, leading to variability in content, and therefore, so currently, a standard on sustainability assurance engagements does not exists.

Absence of formal assurance framework

While there is no standardised assurance framework, staying alert to developments in key areas is crucial. These include:

- The IFRS Sustainability Disclosure Standards, IFRS S1 and S2
- The TCFD and SECR approaches followed in the UK
- The EU's CSRD
- The US SEC proposals on climate-related disclosures
- The IAASB project on assurance for sustainability reporting

Voluntary frameworks and considerations

Organisations must weigh the costs and benefits of voluntary assurance on sustainability disclosures. The World Business Council for Sustainable Development (WBCSD) advocates for assurance, emphasising credibility and trust.

Benefits of undertaking sustainability assurance engagements

Assurance enhances credibility, trust, and decision-making. It can also identify areas for improvement and prepare organisations for potential future requirements.

Drawbacks of undertaking sustainability assurance engagements

Potential pitfalls include additional costs, scrutiny of systems, and time requirements.

Reasons for non-mandatory status of sustainability assurance engagements

The absence of defined, formal, assurance standards issued by global audit and assurance standards issuers and challenges in their implementation. However, projects like the IAASB's indicate there will be change.

11.3 Types of sustainability related assurance services

11.3.1 Assurance on sustainability reporting

Auditors can provide a spectrum of assurance services related to environmental and social issues present in sustainability reporting. These services encompass evaluating the accuracy, completeness, and reliability of information disclosed in sustainability reports, ensuring alignment with relevant standards and principles.

11.3.2 Relevant standards

ISAE 3000 (Revised), issued by the International Auditing and Assurance Standards Board (IAASB), offers guidance on assurance engagements other than audits or reviews of historical financial information. Additionally, AA1000AS, developed by AccountAbility, provides a comprehensive framework for organisations to assess and enhance their sustainability reporting practices.

11.3.3 AccountAbility's reporting principles

AccountAbility's four reporting principles, (a) Inclusivity, (b) Materiality, (c) Responsiveness, and (d) Impact. These principles can serve as a framework for evaluating effective voluntary assurance

engagements on reported sustainability disclosures, and other aspects, such as sustainability processes, measurement, risk management and review of ESG metrics appropriateness.

(a) **Inclusivity** emphasises the participation of stakeholders in the reporting process.

(b) **Materiality** focuses on identifying issues that significantly influence decision-making for both the organisation and its stakeholders.

(c) **Responsiveness** entails addressing stakeholder concerns and feedback promptly.

(d) **Impact** evaluates the effects of organisational behaviour and performance on various stakeholders and aspects of sustainability.

These criteria can help organisations to decide on the type and scope of any assurance undertaken sustainability risks, processes, measurements and/or disclosures.

11.3.4 Assurance statement

A detailed assurance statement for each sustainability engagement should include information on intended users, responsibilities, assurance standards used, scope, methodology, limitations, criteria used, level of assurance, findings, conclusions, observations, competencies, independence, and provider details.

There is no set wording for the assurance statement, but the following is suggested as a minimum for consideration.

- Intended users of the assurance statement
- The responsibility of the reporting organisation and of the assurance provider
- Assurance standard(s) used, including reference to AA1000AS (2008)
- Description of the scope, including the type of assurance provided
- Description of disclosures covered
- Description of methodology
- Any limitations
- Reference to criteria used
- Statement of level of assurance
- Findings and conclusions concerning adherence to the AA1000 *Accountability Principles of Inclusivity, Materiality, Responsiveness, and Impact* (in all instances)
- Findings and conclusions concerning the reliability of specified performance information (for Type 2 assurance only)
- Observations and/or recommendations
- Notes on competencies and independence of the assurance provider
- Name of the assurance provider
- Date and place

11.3.5 Types of sustainability engagement reports

A sustainability engagement could be a Type 1 or Type 2 report, as follows.

(a) **Type 1 reports**

The assurance provider evaluates the nature and extent of an organisation's adherence to the four AA1000 Accountability Principles. The focus here is on providing stakeholders with assurance over the way an organisation manages sustainability performance and communicates this in its sustainability reporting, without verifying the reliability of the medium or long term reporting information. As such, the assurance provider focuses on the systems and processes the organisation has in place to ensure it adheres to the principles for sustainability reporting.

(b) **Type 2 reports**

For Type 2 reports, an assurance engagement provider evaluates the nature and extent of an organisation's adherence to the principles but also evaluates the reliability of specified sustainability performance information. Due diligence engagements were covered earlier but this is another area where there is increasing emphasis on environmental and other corporate responsibility issues.

12 The role of accountants and management in developing sustainability within organisations

The evolving landscape of sustainability in the accounting profession demands a more targeted approach from professionals, as the significance of integrating sustainability goals and managing associated risks continues to grow. This shift calls for a deep understanding of the implications of sustainability-related risks and issues, seamlessly integrating them into strategic planning, financial management, and business reporting. This involves not only recognising the broader implications of environmental, social, and governance (ESG) issues but also employing precise tools to accurately measure and report their impact. Such robust monitoring and reporting mechanisms enable informed decision-making and progress assessment.

12.1 Role of accountants in realising sustainable development goals

Key terms

> **Accountability:** As defined by Gray, Owen, and Adams (1996), refers to the duty to provide an account or reckoning of actions for which one is responsible. This extends beyond merely financial reporting to encompass a broader spectrum of responsibilities and actions.
>
> **Stewardship:** Entails the shared responsibility for maintaining the integrity of systems. In the context of sustainable development, stewardship involves overseeing the ecological resources (E), considering the impacts on people (S), and adhering to governance principles (G) that regulate behaviour and expectations.

The role of accountants is pivotal in assisting efforts to mitigate the impact of human activities on the planet which require the application of accountability and stewardship. This can be achieved by applying the following.

- **Responsibility and accountability:** Accounting serves as a core function in ensuring responsibility and accountability for actions taken by individuals, organisations, and societies. By providing transparent and accurate reporting, accountants facilitate accountability to stakeholders and society at large.

- **Exercising control:** In the context of dynamic systems and the interaction of the six capitals (financial, manufactured, intellectual, human, social and relationship, and natural), accountants play a crucial role in exercising control. This includes implementing measures to manage resources sustainably, mitigate risks, and optimise performance across various dimensions.

- **Understanding dynamics:** Accountants need to have a comprehensive understanding of the dynamics of sustainable development, including planetary boundaries, limits, tipping points, and resilience to impacts. This knowledge enables them to assess risks, anticipate challenges, and develop strategies to address sustainability issues effectively.

- **Competencies for accountability and stewardship:** Developing suitable competencies is essential for citizens, managers, and accountants to demonstrate accountability and stewardship in response to risks facing the planet. These competencies encompass a range of skills, including ethical decision-making, environmental literacy, stakeholder engagement, and sustainability reporting expertise.

By fulfilling their responsibilities with integrity and diligence, accountants contribute to the collective effort to safeguard the planet's resources, mitigate environmental impacts, and create a more sustainable future for all.

12.2 Role of accountants and management in developing sustainability within organisations

Accountants shoulder key responsibilities in identifying and efficiently managing ESG risks and issues. Ensuring compliance with sustainability-related laws, regulations, and corporate governance codes is crucial for maintaining ethical business practices. Additionally, accountants must adeptly measure ESG-related liabilities, assess impaired assets and financial instruments, and navigate new forms of taxation, such as renewable energy incentives or carbon emission tariffs, while providing necessary assurance as required. Equally crucial is the design and operation of risk management and internal control systems to uphold sustainable practices within organisations.

Recognising the diverse nature of sustainability challenges, accountants collaborate with sustainability experts and relevant professionals to ensure comprehensive solutions. Moreover, their role extends beyond business reporting to actively contributing to the preparation and issuance of sustainability information. This includes continuous risk management, advising on solutions to mitigate impacts, and modelling how sustainability risks may influence an organisation's strategic direction or necessitate changes to its operations and reporting requirements.

Accountants also play a vital role in advising organisations on relevant sustainability metrics to monitor and report on all ESG-related activities, implementing methodologies, systems, and solutions to accurately measure these metrics and report progress against targets set by the board. This process involves establishing robust processes and controls to ensure the reliability and verification of sustainability information, culminating in the preparation of comprehensive sustainability reports with a critical assessment of current disclosures.

Transparency and credibility are key aspects of sustainability reporting, and accountants offer valuable assurance over both mandatory and voluntary sustainability information, enhancing stakeholders' trust. Beyond reporting responsibilities, accountants actively provide sustainability information that informs strategic and operational decision-making within organisations. Their advocacy for sustainable practices and ability to influence stakeholders contribute significantly to fostering positive change and promoting an organisation's sustainable performance.

In summary, the role of accountants in implementing a credible sustainability strategy encompasses a diverse set of activities and responsibilities, from identifying and managing risks to providing reliable sustainability information.

By seamlessly integrating sustainability into core business operations, accountants play a pivotal role in driving ethical practices, informed decisions, and long-term success, thereby contributing to a more responsible and sustainable business landscape.

End of chapter questions

Question 1

Relax Hotels, a prominent private hotel chain partially owned by founding family members and private equity investors, is renowned for its properties situated in areas of remarkable natural beauty across the UK. With an esteemed brand reputation and a target demographic of individuals aged 28 to 49 with considerable disposable income, Relax Hotels boasts a significant celebrity following and frequent media features.

Presently comprising eight hotels, Relax Hotels has set a strategic goal to double its portfolio within three years. Embracing nature-inspired design principles, each hotel endeavours to bring the outdoors indoors, creating a serene ambiance throughout its rooms, restaurants, and public spaces. Offering a top-tier experience, Relax Hotels feature luxurious spa facilities, signature treatments, state-of-the-art fitness centres, and highly acclaimed dining options.

In response to feedback from a recent guest survey highlighting opportunities to enhance communication regarding its sustainability efforts, the Relax Hotels board has formulated nine new Environmental, Social, and Governance (ESG) objectives. These objectives will be publicly disclosed on the company's website, accompanied by quarterly sustainability reports detailing Relax Hotels' progress in achieving these ESG goals.

The nine new ESG objectives approved by the Relax Hotels board are as follows:

Environment objectives

1. **Climate-change related emissions**: Ensure compliance with relevant laws and regulations that have a significant impact on the issuer relating to air and greenhouse gas emissions (such as carbon dioxide, methane, nitrous oxide) and water pollutants (such as use of cleaning chemical in hotel laundry and cleaning.)

2. **Consumption of resources**: Ensure Relax Hotels' operations make efficient use of resources, including energy and water.

3. **Waste minimisation**: Ensure that actions are taken to identify and action opportunities to reduce waste, such as food waste, across all Relax Hotel operations.

Social objectives

4. **Employee wellbeing**: Ensure compliance with relevant laws and regulations that have a significant impact on the issuer relating to compensation and dismissal, recruitment, and promotion, working hours, rest periods, equal opportunity, diversity, anti-discrimination, and other benefits and welfare.

5. **Guest and employee safety**: Ensure compliance with relevant laws and regulations that have a significant impact on the issuer relating to providing a safe working environment for employees and protecting hotel guests from hazards.

6. **Employee personal and professional development**: Supporting personal and professional development for Relax Hotels employees.

Governance objectives

7. **Supply chain sustainability**: Improve procurement policies and processes to increase sustainability practices in its supply chain management.

8. **Local community support**: Improve community engagement to understand the needs of the communities where its hotels operate, and to ensure its activities take into consideration the communities' interests.

9. **Anti-bribery and corruption**: Eliminate the incidence of bribery, money laundering and other corruption practices from all Relax Hotels operations and the potential for such incidences to occur.

Required

Recommend a new key performance indicator (KPI) which will improve sustainability performance at Relax Hotels in the area specified.

Question 2: Formulate sustainability objectives

Fine Future Ltd is a premium furniture supplier that uses natural wood and carpentry to produce high quality furniture design pieces at scale, so affordable. Its CEO, Mina Patel, has recently attained training on enhancing sustainability performance and is keen to implement new sustainability objectives and ESG metrics and a framework to monitor Fine Furniture Ltd (FF) future sustainability performance. To start this process, Mina has written the following email to Sarah Tate, chief operating officer (COO) at Fine Furniture Ltd.

Email from Mina Patel explaining the need to adopt sustainability into its current operations

To: Sarah Tate, chief operating officer (COO) at Fine Furniture Ltd
From: Mina Patel, chief executive officer (CEO) at Fine Furniture Ltd
Subject: New sustainability objectives and governance framework
Date: 15 April 2024

Dear Sarah,

I want to discuss a critical development that pertains to our organisation and its future direction.

As you may be aware, there has been growing concern from various stakeholders, including the media, regarding our sustainability practices in comparison to our competitors in the kitchen and bathroom supplies industry. To address these concerns and meet the expectations of our stakeholders, I am pleased to inform you that the board of FF has recognised the necessity of introducing new sustainability objectives and a new sustainability governance framework to ensure sustainability objectives are properly implemented and monitored.

In light of this, I would like to recommend a series of sustainability objectives that are relevant to our operations in the supply, manufacture and distribution of our furniture and advise on a suitable governance framework which will help the company to monitor and improve its sustainability performance. This will help to position FF as a responsible organisation to our customers and other stakeholders.

I am eager to hear your insights and recommendations as we embark on this journey towards sustainability performance improvement.

Kind regards,

Mina Patel (CEO)

Required

Draft a response to the CEO, which recommends a series of sustainability objectives relevant to FF and advises the board of FF on a suitable sustainability governance framework in each of the following areas:

(a) Strategic decision making
(b) Measuring and monitoring of sustainability objectives
(c) Sustainability reporting

Question 3

Sustainability reporting evaluation

Greenwald Airport Services Ltd provides ground and passenger services to airports in the United Kingdom.

Extract from Greenwald Airport Services Ltd Sustainability Report for the year ended 30 June 2024

The following key environmental, sustainability and governance (ESG) metrics and the director's commentary on performance have been extracted from the Greenwald Airport Services Ltd (Greenwald) Annual Report and Sustainability Report for the year ended 30 June 2024 (Sustainability Report).

Board statement

The board recognises the importance of sustainability. It steers the board in ensuring that Greenwald long-term value creation is achieved with Environmental, Social, and Governance (ESG) factors as guiding principles at all times. Sustainability is an integral part of Greenwald operations across all levels of the organisation. In publishing this sustainability report, the board has considered sustainability issues when formulating strategies, has determined the material ESG factors, and has overseen the management and monitoring of those factors.

Balance

The board confirms that the content and data provided in this Sustainability Report are unbiased. In this consideration, Greenwald acknowledges it must make further improvements to its sustainability performance in all ESG aspects.

Sustainability reporting framework

This Sustainability Report has been prepared in accordance with UK Listing Rules This report has also been prepared in accordance with the GRI Universal Standards 2021. The GRI Standards were selected as they represent the global best practice for reporting on an organisation's sustainability impacts.

A set of disclosures on climate risks and opportunities has been included in this report based on the recommendations of the Task Force on Climate-related Financial Disclosures (TCFD) which aligns to the mandatory climate reporting for all issuers on a 'comply or explain' basis of reporting.

Reporting scope

Greenwald is organised and managed according to the nature of the services provided. All sustainability data and information presented in this report relates it ground operations for the year ended 30 June 2024.

Environmental sustainability matters at Greenwald

The disclosures on environmental aspects in this report include operations over which we exercise full management control, namely the facilities and equipment owned/controlled by Greenwald. The environmental impact of Greenwald's provided airline services is considered within the scope of this sustainability report. However, the operations of the airlines themselves, which Greenwald does not own, are outside the scope of this report.

Social sustainability matters at Greenwald

The social impact of Greenwald activities includes the impact on Greenwald employees and communities on which our activities have an impact.

Governance of sustainability matters at Greenwald

The board of directors of Greenwald (the 'board') is solely accountable for our ESG strategies and reporting and for overseeing and managing our ESG-related risks. The board formulates strategies and maintains oversight of the environmental, social and governance (ESG) performance. This sustainability report has been reviewed and approved by the board. Implementing decisions affecting ESG performance is subject to Greenwald's regular risk management programme and board scrutiny. Also, where relevant, it is independently reviewed by Greenwald internal audit function.

Materiality

The threshold for sustainability topics to become material was reviewed and confirmed by the board to ensure that they were sufficiently important to our stakeholders. All material matters identified are measured with reference to relevant ESG performance indicators.

Quantitative

We use specialist equipment to record emission data, which is recorded in our management systems. Where applicable, we compared year-to-year data and discussed its implications. Relevant standards, methodologies, assumptions, and conversion factors are disclosed if these are considered helpful.

Consistency

This report adopts consistent methodologies to allow a fair comparison of our performance year-on-year.

Comply or explain statement

Greenwald is fully compliant with UK Listing Rules, so there are no comply or explain matters requiring explanation.

ESG metrics

The following ESG metrics are monitored by Greenwald and disclosed here.

	Greenwald sustainability Target	Performance indicator	2024 KPI
Environmental factors			
Emissions	Achieve a 15% reduction in CO_2 emissions per ton of cargo transported by 30 June 2025.	Annual CO_2 emissions per ton of cargo transported	0.00045 (CO_2 per ton)
Resource efficiency	Reduce water consumption in ground service operations by 10% by 2025 through water-saving technologies.	Annual water consumption in ground service operations per day	2.2% reduction
Social factors			
Employee development	Implement an annual training program for Greenwald employees to enhance safety awareness and sustainable practices, with a target of 95% participation.	% of Greenwald employees trained annually	29.5%
Community engagement	Organise and engage in at least five community outreach events annually, involving ground service employees to contribute positively to local communities.	Number of community outreach events organised by Greenwald (no of events) Greenwald employee participation in community initiatives (days)	4 396 days
Governance factors			
Gender diversity	Have at least 40% female board members	Male (%): Female (%)	58% : 42%

Suggested answers

Question 1

Climate-change related emissions

KPI: Reduce consumption of electricity, gas and oil measured by type. For example, overall consumption of electricity, gas, or oil in the period (measured in kWh '000s) and intensity of usage per hotel for comparison. For example, usage per hotel per week.

Relax Hotels could increase usage of renewable energy and install solar panels on hotel land and roof tops. Relax Hotels could also limit the minimum air-conditioning temperatures and reduce the temperature of heated areas and pools. Energy efficient lightbulb, timers on light switches and turning off excessive external lighting are other initiatives which would reduce energy consumption.

Consumption of resources

KPI: Percentage reduction in annual water use per hotel, or average number of towels used per guest per stay.

Purchase food for hotel kitchens based on actual need to reduce order quantities and reduce the quantity of food prepared and reduce portion sizes for hotel guests where these are excessive. Also, install smart water timer systems to reduce showering times and hotel garden watering requirements of plants and lawns in the hotels gardens which will limit watering by quantity and only during dry periods.

Also, encourage hotel guests to reuse towels and limit the quantity of towel per room for each new guest, as this will reduce consumption of energy used by each hotel laundry.

Waste minimisation

KPI: Percentage reduction in food purchased per month/annum per hotel, or reduction in food waste of 5% per annum by weight or 20% reduction in plastic usage.

Reduce the quantity of food made available at mealtimes by reduce the quantity of food prepared, reducing choice so less is wasted, reducing portion sizes for hotel guests and by encouraging healthier choices or vegan based meals which emit less greenhouse gases to produce. Also, reduce the use of single of use plastic in Relax hotels, for example, plastic bottles, straws, toiletries, by switching to sustainable alternatives, such as installing water fountains, paper straws, and refillable toiletry dispensers.

Employee wellbeing

KPI: Total employees by gender vs target gender diversity, or employee turnover by gender and age group, overall and by hotel.

Implement employment policies and benefits which make it easier for women to (a) enter the workplace and work at Relax Hotels and (b) remain at Relax Hotels during life changes which will seek to improve the overall gender balance. For example, paid parental leave, provision of childcare arrangements, flexible hours or agreed absence during school holidays.

Guest and employee safety

KPI: Number of working days absent per month/annum missed due to injury, or number of hotel guest accidents per month (or per annum) by fatality, serious injury requiring hospitalization or other recordable injury.

Relax Hotels could implement an onsite safety team to focus on identifying and resolving potential safety issues at end hotel site. This will ensure consistent application of safety policy at all its hotels,

Employee personal and professional development

KPI: The average investment (£) in employee personal and professional development per annum by gender, age group, and employment category (ie management, lobby, hospitality, housekeeping), or average days of training undertaken per employee per annum, overall and split by gender, age group, and employment category.

Increase investment in a new company training and development programme for all employee categories. This will provide Relax Hotels with the knowledge, skills, and experiences it requires identified as gaps by human resources.

Supply chain sustainability

KPI: Value of supplier orders by distance in kilometres (km) in the following ranges: 1 km–10 km, 11 km–25 km, 26 km–50 km, 51 km–100 km, 101 km –200 km > 200 km, or percentage of suppliers signed up for compliance with a sustainability charter.

A supply chain management initiative can prioritise hotel industry suppliers which can supply within a 25 km radius of a Relax Hotels site. Hotel procurement can then prioritise those suppliers within a 50 km radius, then a 100 km radius and so forth. This initiative could reduce the overall delivery kilometres which will reduce energy consumption and related greenhouse gas emissions related to supply and delivery.

Also, Relax Hotels could adopt a sustainability code which sets out expected ESG practices for supplier. Compliance with this code would then provide preferred supplier state. The take-up of this charter can then be monitored to track its success.

Local community support

KPI: Frequency of Relax Hotels representatives meeting with the local community representatives per month (or per annum), or percentage volume of queries from local community responded/volume of queries from local community received.

Relax Hotels could set to a local community 'give back' scheme where it hosts focus sessions with local community representatives to listen to their concerns and understand how Relax Hotels can be more supportive to local community actions and events (eg education, environmental concerns, labour needs, health, culture, sport).

Anti-bribery and corruption

KPI: Percentage reported bribery, money laundering or other corruption cases to anti-corruption team, which are investigated and resolved within a specific time (eg 90 days).

Relax Hotels can set up anti-corruption and compliance team to allow employees to report incidences of potential corruption, independent to their managers or other employees, so provide whistleblowing protections. This KPI can help Relax Hotels measure the effectiveness of its anti-corruption measures and the efficiency of its investigative process.

Question 2

Dear Mina,

Thank you for your email and for highlighting the importance of integrating sustainability objectives into our operations at Fine Furniture Ltd (FF). We fully support this initiative and are committed to working together to enhance our sustainability performance.

Recommended sustainability objectives for FF

Environmental conservation: To reduce our carbon footprint, we will implement energy-efficient practices and promote the use of renewable energy sources in our warehouses and showrooms, such as solar panels on the roof. Additionally, we will develop waste reduction strategies through sustainable procurement practices, optimise inventory management, increase recycling efforts, and minimise the use of single-use plastics in our packaging.

- **Carbon footprint reduction**: KPI – Percentage reduction in carbon emissions compared to the previous year

- **Waste reduction**: KPI – Percentage increase in waste diverted from landfills through recycling and sustainable disposal methods

Product sustainability: We will increase the availability of environmentally friendly furniture made from sustainably sourced wood. We will prioritise suppliers that adhere to sustainable forest management practices, ensuring responsible harvesting and replanting of trees. Furthermore, we will encourage the sale of long-lasting, high-quality products to reduce the frequency of replacements.

Suitable KPIs to monitor product sustainability include:

- **Sustainable wood usage**: KPI – Percentage of furniture products made from sustainably sourced wood
- **Supplier adherence to sustainability standards**: KPI – Percentage of suppliers certified for sustainable forest management practices

Ethical practices: To ensure ethical practices throughout our supply chain, we will prioritise suppliers that adhere to fair labour standards, ensuring fair wages and safe working conditions. We will also avoid products that are associated with unethical practices or harmful materials.

Suitable KPIs to monitor ethical practices include:

- **Supplier compliance with fair labour standards**: KPI – Percentage of suppliers verified to comply with fair labour standards
- **Avoidance of unethical products**: KPI – Percentage of products in inventory that meet ethical sourcing criteria

Customer education: We will provide customers with information and resources on sustainable furniture design and maintenance, including tips for prolonging the lifespan of their furniture and responsible disposal options.

Suitable KPIs to monitor customer education include:

- **Customer awareness**: KPI – Percentage increase in customer awareness of sustainable furniture design and maintenance practices
- **Adoption of sustainable practices**: KPI – Percentage of customers implementing sustainable furniture maintenance tips provided by the company

Community engagement: We will engage in community initiatives and charitable activities that promote sustainability and environmental awareness, supporting local communities and fostering positive change.

Suitable KPIs to monitor community engagement include:

- **Community involvement**: KPI – Number of community initiatives and charitable activities participated in by the company
- **Impact on local communities**: KPI – Measurement of the positive environmental and social impact generated by community engagement activities

Suitable framework for good governance of sustainability

Strategic decision making

We will establish a dedicated sustainability committee within the board responsible for setting and overseeing sustainability objectives and strategies. The committee will present recommendations to the board of directors for approval, ensuring alignment with the company's overall strategy.

Measuring and monitoring of sustainability objectives

We will develop measurable key performance indicators (KPIs) for each sustainability objective to track progress effectively. Internal sustainability reports will be compiled for operational and senior management, with routine review and discussion by the board of directors.

Sustainability reporting

We will prepare comprehensive annual sustainability reports that highlight Environmental, Social, and Governance (ESG) performance alongside financial reports. These reports will be easily accessible to stakeholders, and the audit committee will oversee the accuracy and completeness of disclosures.

At FF, we believe that implementing these recommendations will not only enhance our sustainability efforts but also enable us to meet stakeholder expectations and address concerns raised by the media. We look forward to collaborating on the successful implementation of these sustainability initiatives.

Best regards,
Sarah COO,
Fine Furniture Ltd

Question 3

Overall comments on the body of Greenwald 2024 Sustainability Report (excluding KPI table of disclosures)

- Greenwald's Sustainability Report lacks specific and factual detail outlining Greenwald's ESG-related risks over the past year to stakeholders, the process of identifying material ESG-related related risks and actions the board has taken to improve sustainability practices and address ESG-related issues at Greenwald.

- It is noted that the board of Greenwald formulates strategies and maintains oversight of ESG performance. However, it is unlikely that the board of Greenwald (the board) has sufficient time to commit to monitoring and implementing sustainability and ESG-related improvements. It is advised that the board create a separate board level ESG and Sustainability Committee to oversee Greenwald's sustainability objectives and performance.

- Greenwald confirms that content and performance metric data provided in the Sustainability Report is unbiased. However, this may not be true as ESG data is not independently verified or audited. Whilst there is no current mandatory requirement for ESG data to be verified through assurance processes, assurance of ESG data disclosed in the ESG report is likely to provide stakeholders with greater confidence that the data, such as emissions, is accurate. The board should consider the benefits of providing independent assurance or verification of disclosed ESG performance metric data.

- Greenwald's Sustainability Report includes the required mandatory statements on materiality, quantitative data, balance, and consistency for Singapore-listed companies. However, for materiality, there is no transparency or disclosure of the materiality threshold for sustainability issues. Therefore, material sustainability topics are determined entirely by judgement made by the board rather than an agreed framework. This increases the risk that material ESG issues may not be tracked or reported to stakeholders.

- The compliance or explanation statement states, 'Greenwald is fully compliant with UK Listing Rules, so there are no comply or explain matters requiring explanation'. This is unlikely due the lack of KPI comparative data, lack of KPI measuring methodology, lack of disclosure of specific ESG risks and initiatives undertaken during the year and lack of directors' narrative of current ESG performance and future expected ESG performance. These areas should be fully addressed in the next Greenwald Sustainability Report.

Overall comments on ESG KPI disclosures

- Overall, the current range of ESG performance metrics is limiting as it only includes five KPI measures. This will likely be disappointing for stakeholders. It is advised that Greenwald could expand its ESG performance metric reporting to include further ESG performance measures in its Sustainability Report.

- The Sustainability Report states in its consistency statement that it adopts consistent methodologies to allow a fair comparison of performance year-on-year. This is not evident in the report as there is no comparative information, so stakeholders cannot evaluate Greenwald's progress. This lack of comparison is a considerable disclosure deficit.

- There is no information on how each KPI is measured. This is important, as the measurement method may not be reliable or credible.

- Whilst Greenwald includes targets for each of its disclosed ESG metrics, it does not disclose how each target will be met within the timeframe disclosed. Also, the targets are vague as they generally do not disclose a target in quantifiable terms, such as a % of reduction, when it was set, and when it is expected to be achieved.

- Also, there is no specific narrative from the board of directors to accompany each KPI, which would explain to stakeholders how progress toward the stated target has been achieved, what the risks relating to each KPI are, and how directors expect each ESG KPI to perform in the short term.

Specific comments on ESG KPI disclosures

- **Emissions: CO2 emissions per ton of cargo:** The CO2 emissions KPI of 0.00045 (CO2 per ton) fails in its objective as it does not provide a percentage reduction in CO2 emissions instead it states what the current emission level is. Also, there is no indication of whether a 15% reduction in CO2 emissions per ton of cargo transported by 2025 will be achieved. How the emission data is measured is also unknown, as this information has not been disclosed.

- **Resource efficiency:** In Ground and Cargo services, water consumption is not the most significant resource consumption. Stakeholders are much more likely to be interested in energy consumption to deliver those services and initiatives to reduce energy consumption. Regarding the 2.2% reduction in water consumption, it is unclear how much water this represented and how Greenwald plans to achieve its 10% reduction by 2025, as this information is not disclosed.

- **Employee development:** For percentage of Greenwald employees trained annually, it is unclear if the measure of 29.5% reflected employees trained during the year or cumulatively. It is also unclear how and when Greenwald proposes to meet the 95%, as the target lacks a date, and e there is no director's narrative supplied.

- **Community engagement:** From the disclosure, Greenwald has not achieved its target for arranging five community outreach events during the year as four have been achieved. However, 396 Greenwald employee days have been committed to supporting this, which is admirable, although there are no target days or industry benchmark to compare against. The community engagement KPI disclosure would be improved if the nature of each outreach event were explained and target days for employee participation were disclosed.

- **Board diversity:** The Greenwald target of a minimum of 40% representation of women on the executive board has been met at 42%. However, it is unclear why the target is 40% and not 50%, representing equal representation from men and women. Also, it is not clear why the KPI measures board members only, and not all Greenwald employees.

Risk management

Topic list	Syllabus reference
1 Introduction to risk management	All LOs
2 Shareholder responses to risk	"
3 Risk management processes	"
4 Enterprise risk management	"
5 Quality information for risk management	"
6 Role of management and internal audit in monitoring or risk and control	"
7 Governance for effective risk management	"

Introduction

Risk is an inherent aspect of every business endeavour, representing the uncertainty surrounding future outcomes. While uncertainty encompasses all potential future scenarios, risk specifically quantifies the dispersion of possibilities, encompassing both favourable and adverse outcomes. Whether viewed as opportunities or threats, risks introduce the possibility that organisational objectives may not be achieved as intended.

Therefore, effective risk management processes are essential for identifying, assessing, and mitigating these uncertainties, thereby enhancing the likelihood of achieving desired outcomes and minimising the impact of adverse events. By systematically addressing risks, organisations can navigate volatile environments, capitalise on opportunities, and safeguard against potential disruptions, ultimately contributing to their long-term success and resilience in dynamic markets. This chapter will develop your ability to demonstrate this in MDCS.

1 Introduction to risk management

In this chapter, we consider first what we mean by risk and examine different stakeholders' attitude to risk. An organisation itself cannot have an attitude to risk – it is the sum total of the stakeholders' attitudes to risk. Hence, to understand the organisation's appetite for risk we need to consider the stakeholders' varied perspectives.

We then consider formal risk management processes, typically utilised to identify, and manage risk in large established businesses. We will first look at risk management from corporate governance perspective – who does what in terms of formal roles, and also what they do. Next, we will learn that a formal risk management framework is made up of several discrete steps: risk identification (using frameworks and lists, and consulting widely), risk evaluation (using numerical and non-numerical techniques), risk response (transfer, accept, reduce, or avoid), risk controls, and risk monitoring and reporting.

In real life, all organisations, regardless of their nature or industry, face various degrees of risk that can significantly impact their operations, reputation, and overall success. From financial institutions navigating market volatility to healthcare providers managing patient safety, the ability to identify, evaluate, and mitigate risks is crucial across diverse disciplines.

Therefore, in preparing for the AIA Multi-Disciplinary Case Study Capstone exam, it is essential for students to develop a comprehensive understanding of risk management principles and practices. This ensures that they are equipped with the necessary skills to analyse and address risks effectively within complex case study scenarios spanning different fields and industries. By mastering risk management concepts, students can enhance their problem-solving abilities, decision-making skills, and overall readiness to tackle real-world challenges.

1.1 Risk management process

The following simple risk management process is applied by businesses across the world:

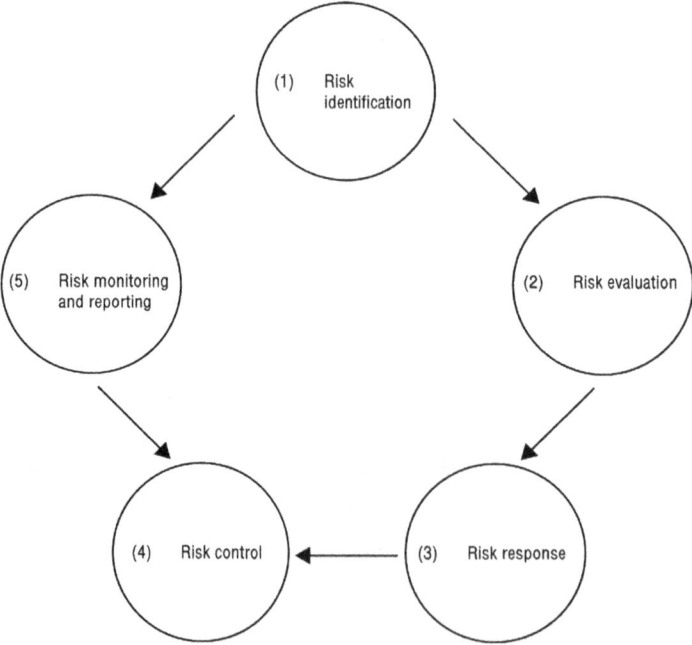

Each of these elements of the risk management cycle is explained below.

(1) **Risk identification**: Events which can adversely or positively pull the company from its strategic objectives and forecasts

(2) **Risk evaluation:** Measure the scale of the risk ie likelihood/severity of a 'risk event' occurring

(3) **Risk response:** Transfer, accept, reduce, avoid

(4) **Risk control:** Actions which mitigate against the potential risk impact (reduce probability/reduce severity)

(5) **Risk monitoring and reporting:** Organisational transparency of risk exposure as internal and external environment changes

These steps are encapsulated in best practice programs such as ISO 31000 (see below) and the COSO Enterprise Risk Management Framework (Section 4).

1.2 Risk management framework: ISO 31000

International Organisation for Standardisation (ISO) is an independent, non-governmental international organisation based in Geneva, Switzerland. ISO brings together experts to share knowledge and develop voluntary, consensus-based, market relevant international standards that support innovation and provide solutions to specific global challenges.

ISO 31000 *Risk Management* – Guidelines was developed by ISO to provide principles to manage risk for organisations around the world to follow.

The purpose of ISO 31000 is to help organisations increase the likelihood of achieving objectives, improve the identification of opportunities and threats and effectively allocate and use resources for risk treatment.

- How to proactively manage risk rather than react to risk events after they have happened
- How to oversee a system of risk management which goes beyond simply putting policy documents in place
- How to communicate risk evaluation and reports to the board to facilitate an urgent, strategic response and to provide assurance that the risk management process is operating effectively as part of its internal control environment

ISO 3100 contains a risk management framework and extends the general risk management process to the following eight elements:

1. **Establish the context:** It is necessary to understand the external and internal aspects of the organisation and its business.
2. **Identify risks:** Identify risks and their location, time frame, root causes and possible outcomes.
3. **Analyse risks:** Analyse the possible outcome of a risk event in terms of impact and likelihood.
4. **Evaluate risks:** Use risk analysis to decide which risks need treatment, and in what order of priority.
5. **Risk assessment:** This term is used as a collective description for risk identification, analysis, and evaluation. The same classifications of risk are used throughout the organisation, and similar methods for measuring and assessing the same type of risk, wherever it occurs within the organisation.
6. **Control risks:** Respond to the risk by identifying alternative ways of treating the risk and select and implement the preferred alternative.
7. **Monitor and review:** Monitoring and review relates to all the above elements or stages in the risk management cycle.
8. **Communicate and consult:** Communication to all stakeholders improves the level of understanding of risk and so improves risk treatment.

(**Source**: ISO. [Online] Available from: https://www.iso.org/iso-31000-risk-management.html [Accessed 3 October 2024])

1.3 Risk management infrastructure

For the above risk management activities to be performed, the following risk infrastructure is required:

(a) **Risk management architecture**: Committees, people – This identifies who is responsible for what in relation to risk management.

(b) **Risk management policy**: Strategy, appetite for risk – This identifies the organisation's basic approach to managing risk and how much risk is acceptable to the organisation.

(c) **Risk management protocols**: Documented processes and procedures

The risk management architecture will decide and then communicate the risk management policy in the organisation and ensure that protocols are developed to manage risk in a holistic and orderly way.

In practice, companies apply these three elements using the following tools:

Risk management architecture	Risk management policy	Risk management protocols
• Risk management information systems (RMIS) • Use of specialists: internal/external audit, risk managers, independent non-executive directors • Risk management/audit committee	• Approved risk management company policy • Approved risk management company procedures • Risk appetite statement	• Risk reports • Risk and compliance activities and procedures • Risk documentation updates • Risk and compliance training activities • Risk reporting scope, format, frequency and follow up

Ultimately, it is worth noting that risk management is not about eliminating risk as this is neither possible nor desirable – it is about managing risk to an acceptable level in the hope of making returns that compensate adequately for the risk of being taken on.

Risk management can be considered in the short term and the long term. Sometimes, managing short-term risk can lead to long-term risky consequences. For example, to manage for an exchange risk in the short term we may consider invoicing foreign customers in our domestic currency. However, in the longer term, this present as with the risk that customers may seek alternative suppliers who are prepared to invoice them in their own currency. Cost benefit analysis needs to be undertaken to ensure that on balance risk management benefits the business.

1.4 Key terms in risk management

Review the following series of key terms in risk management.

Key terms

- **Risk:** Is a range of known possibilities, with known or estimated probabilities, which may impact on an organisation's ability to reach its objectives.

- **Uncertainty:** Is a range of possibilities that is not completely known, and/or with unknown probabilities associated with some or all of those possibilities.

- **Risk exposure:** Is the degree of impact should a risk event occur (ie by how much income falls, or by how much costs rise, from the predicted level).

- **Risk attitude:** This is the general approach taken to risk by the organisation. Risk attitudes can generally be classified as risk seeking (optimist, happy to take on risk in the hope of a higher return), risk averse (pessimist, dislikes risk), or risk neutral (makes decisions based on the balance of probabilities). The attitude to risk will vary according to the size and nature of the risk being faced amongst many other variables.

- **Risk capacity:** Is the amount of risk an organisation is capable of bearing. It is the maximum amount of risk that can possibly be managed.
- **Risk appetite:** Is the degree of desire to take on risk in order to obtain a financial return. This refers to the type of risk and the amount of risk that the board of directors wants for the company. Risk appetite is constrained by risk capacity.
- **Risk tolerance:** Is the amount of risk that the company is willing to accept, expressed as a quantified measure, a threshold for deviation from a specified target, or a risk limit.
- **Risk identification:** Is a continuous (iterative) process. Once identified, risks can be included within the firm's risk register and kept under review.
- **Risk events:** Are circumstances happening which lead to risk happening.
- **Upside risks:** Upside risk is the possibility that something better than expected may occur, such as achieving more sales than plan.
- **Downside risk:** Results in negative outcomes.
- **Pure risk:** Risks which have a negative impact only (ie damage, accident, fire).
- **Speculative risk:** Risks which can have a negative, neutral, or positive impact.
- **Inherent risk:** This is the risk level before the influence of mitigating controls. Sometimes known as a 'gross risk.'
- **Residual risk:** Is the risk level after the influence of mitigating controls. Sometimes known as a 'net risk.'
- **Emerging risk:** Is a risk which currently does not affect the organisation but may do so in the future.
- **Tail risk:** Is a risk from a highly improbable event for which it is difficult to predict and where the impact is likely to be severe. A good example is COVID-19, analysed from a pre-COVID world.
- **Cliff risk:** This is a probable risk with very severe implications. These should be classed as the highest priority for an organisation to manage.
- **Unquantifiable risk:** Is a risk that cannot be measured using statistical methods as a reliable probability cannot be quantified either due to the lack of relevant data or the situation that the risk is not sufficiently understood or is too complex. Here quantitative and qualitative solutions are used to manage these risks.
- **Risk taxonomy:** Is the full list of categorised and assessed risks within an organisation and provides a reference resource in ongoing risk assessment.
- **Risk profile:** Is the resulting exposure by combining all residual and emerging risks which the organisation has identified and evaluated.

1.5 Risk cannot be eliminated entirely

The fact that risk has upside as well as downside potential is one of the main reasons why businesses do not seek to eliminate or minimise risk: rather they seek to manage it to an appropriate level.

Also, there are in fact several reasons why risk cannot be eliminated entirely:

- **Controls are designed for known possibilities:** New risk events present themselves constantly and risk management systems need to keep up with them and adapt.
- **Reducing risk costs money:** Reducing risk incrementally further costs disproportionately more money and effort each time: there comes a point where the extra cost is not worth the reduction in risk that is achieved. This is sometimes known as the ALARP principle: reducing risk to 'as low as reasonably possible.'

- **The risk of fraud:** Deliberate actions may undermine the management of risk leaving the business exposed (eg bypassing organisational controls for personal gain).
- **The risk of human error:** Many risk management systems have human elements that may make mistakes which undermines the effectiveness of the associated controls.
- **The desire to make reasonable returns:** As noted above, there is a relationship between risk and return: some risk needs to be accepted in the hope of making reasonable returns.

Given that risk cannot be entirely eliminated, it therefore needs to be accepted that risk needs to be tolerated and managed. Risk tolerance can also be described as the boundaries of risk-taking that a company sets for itself: the company should not go outside these boundaries in pursuit of its business objectives.

Risk tolerance limits should be expressed differently for different types of risk and at different management levels within the organisation.

Risk appetite is the degree of desire to take on risk in order to obtain a financial return. This refers to the type of risk and the amount of risk that the board of directors wants for the company. Risk appetite is constrained by risk capacity, which is the point beyond which the company's sustainability is put into doubt. An acceptable appetite for risk is needed for boards to satisfy shareholder expectations for return and growth.

Case Study

A major oil company has operations in four areas: exploration, extraction, refining and distribution. The highest risks are in exploration, where a large amount of money may be invested without finding oil deposits that are large enough to justify commercial extraction. However, the potential returns from successful exploration are high.

The second-highest risks are in extraction, which requires heavy investment and the security risks (such as terrorism) and costs of insurance against environmental risks are high.

The board of directors of the company must make a strategic decision about the relative size of investment in each of the four areas of activity, given the limited amount of funding available.

The risk appetite of the board may be different depending on the directors, the economy, current company performance and target and pressure from stakeholders. The risk appetite can influence the company's strategy as the following two possibilities demonstrate.

(a) **High risk appetite:** The board votes in favour of higher-risk investment, with more investment in higher risk activities of oil exploration and extraction than in oil refining and distribution.

(b) **Low risk appetite:** The board votes against excessive risk investment. Instead, the board finds consensus in pushing investment into oil refining and distribution and relying more on independent oil exploration and extraction companies for supplying oil to its refineries.

2 Stakeholder responses to risk

Stakeholder groups are not necessarily risk averse. They are likely to react adversely if a company does not conform to their return expectations.

The attitude of some stakeholder groups to risk can have a significant influence on the company's overall strategy. Shareholders can affect the market price of shares by trading them. Shareholder groups, such as institutional investors, have the power to remove directors and management. Therefore, the CEO and board of directors must be mindful of shareholders' reactions when setting risk appetite. Also,

organisations must be aware of other stakeholders' responses to risk, such as employees, creditors, customers, local communities, institutional investors, and government.

2.1 Evaluating stakeholders reaction to risk (Mendelow's matrix)

Power means who can exercise **most influence** over a particular decision (though the power may not be used). These include stakeholders who **actively participate** in decision making (normally directors, senior managers) or those whose views are **regularly consulted** on important decisions (major shareholders). It can also, in a negative sense, mean those who have the right of veto over major decisions (creditors with a charge on major business assets can prevent those assets being sold to raise money). Stakeholders may be more influential if their power is combined with:

- **Legitimacy**: The company perceives the stakeholders' claims to be valid
- **Urgency**: Whether the stakeholder claim requires immediate action

Level of interest reflects the **effort** stakeholders put in to attempting to participate in the organisation's activities, whether they succeed or not. It also reflects the amount of knowledge stakeholders have about what the organisation is doing.

Organisations should focus on delivering the needs of those stakeholders with:

(a) **High power**: Those who can influence other stakeholders, such as, investment funds; and

(b) **High interest**: Those who take a proactive interest in influencing the shareholders or commenting about the company in the public domain, such as the media or activists on social media

Therefore, an effective way of weighing stakeholder interests is to look at the **power** they exert and the **level of interest** they have in its activities.

Mendelow classifies stakeholders on a matrix whose axes are **power** held and likelihood of showing an **interest** in the organisation's activities. These factors will help define the type of relationship the organisation should seek with its stakeholders and how it should view their concerns. Mendelow's matrix represents a continuum, a map for plotting the relative influence of stakeholders.

Stakeholders in the bottom right of the continuum are more significant because they combine the highest power and influence.

Level of interest

	Low	High
Power Low	Minimal effort	Keep satisfied
Power High	Keep informed	Consult directly

Stakeholder mapping is used to assess the significance of stakeholders. This in turn has implications for the organisation.

(a) The framework of corporate governance and the direction and control of the business should recognise **stakeholders' levels** of **interest** and **power**.

(b) Companies may try to **reposition** certain stakeholders and discourage others from repositioning themselves, depending on their attitudes.

(c) Key **blockers** and **facilitators** of change must be identified.

(d) Stakeholder mapping can also be used to establish **future priorities**.

Question

Required

For each of the following stakeholder groups, evaluate the possible attitude towards risk-taking by a company by considering risk from the stakeholders' perspective.

- Shareholders
- Providers of debt finance
- Employees
- Customers
- Government, regulatory and other bodies

Answer

Shareholders are not necessarily risk averse, but they will expect higher returns from high-risk companies. They may well have acquired their shares to fit into a balanced portfolio. They will be concerned if there is an unexpected change in the organisation's risk appetite and may choose to invest elsewhere. Many of a company's shareholders are small private investors who may remain out of loyalty and may prefer a low-risk investment. Institutional investors will hold shares as part of a balanced portfolio, so will demand high returns and as a result be more willing for the organisation to take strategic risks.

Providers of debt finance are most concerned about the risk of non-payment, and they can take various actions, with potentially serious consequences such as:

- Denial of credit
- Higher interest charges,
- Applying restrictive covenants
- Requiring security (eg mortgage)
- Putting the organisation into liquidation

Employees will be concerned about threats to their job prospects (salary, promotion, benefits, and satisfaction) and ultimately threats to the jobs themselves. The variety of actions employees can take include:

- Pursuing their own goals rather than shareholder interests
- Industrial action
- Refusal to co-operate
- Resignation

Customers will be concerned with threats to their getting the goods or services that they have been promised, or not getting the value from the goods or services that they expect. The risk to a company is that they could take their business elsewhere.

Governments, regulatory and other bodies will be particularly concerned with risks that the organisation does not act as a good corporate citizen, implementing for example, poor employment or environmental policies. A number of the variety of actions that can be taken could have serious consequences. Government can impose tax increases or regulation or take legal action. Pressure groups' tactics can include publicity, direct action, sabotage or pressure on government or other stakeholders.

3 Risk management processes

Risk management involves putting resources in place with prescribed responsibilities for various aspects of the risk management process: going from the board level right the way through the business. It is important to note that, ultimately, the business as a whole needs to own the risk management process as risk happens through operations.

It is dangerous to assume that just because there is a separate risk management process in place that operational staff do not need to concern themselves with risk. Embedding risk management throughout the entire organisation, its culture and processes is a key part of risk management.

3.1 Risk management governance

Before we consider in detail what the steps are that an organisation should consider in formal risk management, we will first identify the governance around risk management, such as who is responsible for different parts and different levels of that risk management process and the governance framework which is required

- **The board of directors is responsible for risk management as a whole:** Ultimately, the board of directors as a whole is responsible for adequately identifying and managing risk on behalf of the shareholders and wider stakeholder groups. The board will agree risk policy and set the overall risk appetite (the level of acceptable risk).

    The board will usually delegate direct oversight to an appropriate risk management committee (see below), but the board will need to be kept informed, at least in a summary fashion, to enable themselves to be satisfied that risk is in fact being appropriately managed.

    Important Note. The board **cannot** delegate responsibility for risk management.

- **The audit committee:** The traditional place for oversight of risk management resides with the audit committee given their background in controls and their independence. However, many companies opt to constitute a separate and dedicated risk management committee. There are several reasons for this:

    - The audit committee already has an extensive agenda and having a separate risk management committee should mean that risk management is given (and is seen to be given) sufficient priority.

    - The audit committee is made up exclusively of independent non-executive directors. Whereas independence is useful to get an objective opinion as to whether or not the risk management process is working well, there is a strong argument for saying that those responsible for risk management need to have some detailed operational knowledge of the business as they need to know in practical terms what could possibly go wrong. A separate risk management committee can be constituted however the company likes: and will usually involve executives and senior managers to ensure sufficient practical knowledge is brought to bear on the process.

    - The audit committee will usually lead the internal audit function. Part of the internal audit department's role is to review the risk management process to ensure it is efficient and effective. The independence of this review is enhanced if a separate board committee has responsibility for the risk management process.

    - Practically a risk management committee can meet as regularly as required to ensure the risk management process is being effectively governed. The timetable of the audit committee may be affected by other priorities.

- **The risk management committee and role of the risk manager:**

    A risk management committee can be established by a board to ensure the process for effective risk management (ie risk identification, risk evaluation, risk control/response and risk monitoring) are applied across the organisation.

    A key role of a risk management committee is to ensure that after a risk management process, the residual risk is acceptable to the board and in turn is acceptable to the stakeholders of the organisation. Remember, the residual risk is the inherent risk after the effect of any mitigating controls which can be put in place.

    The risk management committee is commonly resourced by employees from many different operational functions in the organisation: finance, marketing, human resources, information technology and so on. Not only will this group of people be best placed to identify risks from within the different parts of the business, but they can also then take the risks that have been identified and associated strategies for managing those risks back to their individual departments to ensure they are managed where they need to be managed. The risk management group would typically be made up of part-time members who attend regular meetings led by the risk manager.

    The risk management committee will typically appoint a risk manager who is responsible for:

    - The design, implementation and control of formal risk management procedures which will achieve the risk policies and risk appetite set by the board of directors
    - Ensuring that risk management is embedded in the organisational culture and operations throughout

- **Managers and all other employees:** It is important that managers and employees do not relinquish responsibility for risk management on the basis there is a separate formal process for managing risk is in place. Therefore, the governance of risk management should be embedded throughout the entire culture, processes, and systems of an organisation in a number of ways:

- **Employee training:** The risk management committee can ensure all employees are trained to identify, evaluate, document and report on risk impacting in their role or department. Training needs to be updated periodically so employees are up to date.

- **Individual accountability:** The risk manager will allocate individual responsibility to an appropriate operational person to act as risk owner for managing a risk. This risk owner should be allocated individual objectives relating to the management of key risks in their area and be held to account for their performance in this regard.

- **Tone from the top down:** The board of directors as a whole have a direct responsibility for ensuring that they set the tone appropriately at the top of the organisation, and that they are seen to live by the values they express. This will include openly appreciating the importance of risk management and a risk-considered approach to conducting business.

- **Responsibility for specific risk management formally allocated across the wider business:** The risk management group will ensure responsibility for specific risks is managed by the most appropriate person in the business: this spreads ownership to the business as a whole for risk management.

3.2 Risk attitude, risk capacity and risk appetite

Here is a reminder of the explanations for risk attitude, risk capacity and risk appetite.

Key terms

- **Risk attitude:** This is the general approach taken to risk by the organisation. Risk attitudes can generally be classified as risk seeking (optimist, happy to take on risk in the hope of a higher return), risk averse (pessimist, dislikes risk), or risk neutral (makes decisions based on the balance of probabilities). The attitude to risk will vary according to the size and nature of the risk being faced amongst many other variables.
- **Risk capacity:** Is the amount of risk an organisation is capable of bearing. It is the maximum amount of risk that can possibly be managed.
- **Risk appetite:** Is the degree of desire to take on risk in order to obtain a financial return. This refers to the type of risk and the amount of risk that the board of directors wants for the company. Risk appetite is constrained by risk capacity.

The risk capacity is governed by the organisations strategy and the size of its current operations, so can be increased by strategic growth, and rise in asset values. The risk attitude and risk appetite set by the board should be communicated to the risk manager by the board sub-committee responsible for managing risk. It will shape the whole strategy and approach to risk management in the organisation.

In practice, this is a difficult process because risk attitude varies according to the situation. In addition, an organisation in itself does not in fact have a risk attitude, it is the stakeholders within that organisation that have differing risk attitudes so the board sub-committee responsible for risk management needs to distil the risk attitude of the various stakeholders into an organisational risk attitude they feel to be appropriate.

The risk manager will be responsible for ensuring a sound risk management process is in place in the organisation.

3.3 The risk management process

As we introduced earlier in this chapter, a formalised risk management process typically the following five stages:

Stage 1: Risk identification	A comprehensive list of risks needs to be identified from a broad range of internal and external sources.
Stage 2: Risk evaluation	Each identified risk needs to be evaluated. Risks are typically prioritised using the two measures of likelihood and impact.
Stage 3: Risk response	Based on the risk assessment, a risk response needs to be identified and agreed. Typical classes of response include transfer, accept, reduce, avoid (TARA). Once a risk response has been agreed, then a specific control solution should be designed and implemented to meet this response.
Stage 4: Risk control	Details of controls to be put in place are specified and individual owners to implement and monitor each control is assigned
Stage 5: Risk monitoring and risk reporting	The risk management function will monitor the risk response and associated controls to ensure they are efficient and effective and take proper corrective actions should be taken if necessary.

	Summary reporting will be routed up to the board via the appropriate sub-committee. Detailed reports will be made available as appropriate (for example, to risk owners).
Repeat stages 1 to 5	The process is repeated continuously. Risks change, and the most appropriate responses to risks can be developed and adapted over time. It is important to note that risk management is a continuous process and not a one-off exercise.

Each of the five risk management steps is considered in more detail in the following sections.

3.4 Risk identification

Risk identification involves looking at the specific internal and external events and conditions which exist which could impact on an organisation.

No one can manage a risk without first being aware that it exists. Some knowledge of perils and what items they can affect and how is helpful to improve awareness of whether familiar risks (potential sources and causes of loss) are present, and the extent to which they could harm a particular person or organisation. Managers should also keep an eye open for unfamiliar risks which may be present.

Actively identifying the risks before they materialise makes it easier to think of methods that can be used to manage them.

Risk identification is a continuous process, so that new risks and changes affecting existing risks may be identified quickly and dealt with appropriately before they can cause unacceptable losses.

Businesses also need to ensure that risks are identified:

- At an **organisational level**, particularly key risks affecting strategy such as risks relating to competition
- At a divisional **level**, for example supply shortages
- At a **day-to-day operational level**, for example the risks of machine breakdown delaying production

The risk identification process will typically be led by the risk manager, but the risk manager should consult widely given the broad-based considerations needed. For example, they could:

- **Consult the board of directors and senior management** – particularly for strategic risks (see below)
- **Consult junior management** – particularly useful for more operational risks
- **Consult industry experts** – may be consultants engaged to assist with this process
- **Learn from others** – eg consider risks that competitors have suffered from in the past and ensure that controls are in place to cater for those eventualities
- **Learn from history** – ensure that the lessons have been learned from past events in the organisation
- **Use standard lists and checklists** – particularly useful to ensure a thorough and complete assessment of the different possible types of risks that may be faced
- **Physical inspection** – will show up risks such as poor housekeeping (eg rubbish left on floors, for people to slip on and to sustain fires)
- **Enquiries** – from which the frequency and extent of product quality controls and checks on new employees' references, for example, can be ascertained

- **Checking** – checking a copy of every letter and memo issued in the organisation for early indications of major changes and new projects
- **Brainstorming** – brainstorming with representatives of different departments or against other sections within the organisation or external experiences

As well as underlying conditions, specific events can lead to the crystallisation of risks that could impact on implementation of strategy or achievement of objectives. Event analysis includes identification of:

(a) **External events**. These could be economic changes, political developments, or technological advances.

(b) **Internal events**. These could be equipment problems, human error, or difficulties with products.

(c) **Leading event indicators**. By monitoring data correlated to events, organisations identify the existence of conditions that could give rise to an event, for example customers who have balances outstanding beyond a certain length of time being very likely to default on those balances.

(d) **Trends and root causes**. Once these have been identified, management may find that assessment and treatment of causes is a more effective solution than acting on individual events once they occur.

(e) **Escalation triggers**, certain events happening or levels being reached that require immediate action. It will be important to identify and respond to signs of danger as soon as they arise. For example, quick responses to product failure may be vital in ensuring that lost sales and threats to reputation are minimised.

(f) **Event interdependencies**, identifying how one event can trigger another and how events can occur concurrently. For example, a decision to defer investment in an improved distribution system might mean that downtime increases and operating costs go up.

Once events have been identified, they can be classified horizontally across the whole organisation and vertically within operating units. By doing this, management can gain a better understanding of the interrelationships between events, gaining enhanced information as a basis for risk assessment.

In common with other aspects of risk assessment and management, risk identification procedures will have costs and require time and resources. Risk identification may therefore be influenced not by a desire to identify all risks, but rather by a focus on identifying unacceptable risks.

3.4.1 Risk categories

The following risk categories are relevant to most organisations:

Risk category	Explanation
Financial risk	Financial risk refers to the likelihood that the organisation, its shareholders, lenders, creditors, or other stakeholders of an organisation may experience variability in returns or costs, gain money from financial opportunities or lose money if the organisation gets into financial difficulties. Financial risk includes a broad set of specific risk factors that relate to an organisation's capital structure, financing strategies, sources of revenue and the broader financial industry. Almost all risk can create consequences of a financial nature. Financial risk also includes: • **Credit risk**: The risk that customers default, or the risk that the organisation's credit rating is reduced. • **Market risk:** The loss in the market value of an organisation's assets. For example, the market price of its property drops due to a downturn in the property market.

Risk category	Explanation
	• **Commodity risk**: The impact on returns of changes to the prices of commodities such as oil or gold. • **Interest rate risk**: The impact of movements in interests on the organisation. For example, an increase in interest rates may increase finance charges if the organisation is partly financed by variable rate debt. • **Liquidity risk**: The risk that the organisation fails to be able to pay its bills as and when they fall due. • **Foreign exchange risk**: The impact that changes in foreign exchange rates has on the organisation. It can be further sub-classified as: transaction risk (pay more/receive less to settle credit transactions), translation risk (impact on retranslations in financial statements) and economic risk (long-term impacts on organisation value due to long-term trends in exchange rates).
Strategic risk	Risks that affect the long run performance of the organisation as a whole as it navigates its way through the environment, working towards its mission and objectives. For example, a badly damaged reputation in a competitive market may fundamentally and permanently damage the strategic performance of an organisation.
Operational risk	Operational risks related to the day-to-day activities of an organisation. These include: • **Process risks:** The risk that a process may fail or perform sub-optimally. • **People risk:** The impact of human factors, such as loss of key personnel, poor management oversight, fraud, and error. • **IT risk:** The impact of IT systems failing causing often severe operational disruption. • **External risk:** The likelihood of an external event beneficially or adversely affecting the way in which the organisation conducts its operations. For example, trading partners fail to perform, or competition damages the organisation. It should be noted that operational risks should not be dismissed as insignificant just because they are more day-to-day in nature: operational risks can quickly escalate into strategic concerns if they are not addressed. For example, if the customers' personal data were leaked as a result of systems failure, this could badly damage the reputation of the organisation.
Hazard risk	One-off events, generally outside the control of the organisation like natural disasters, weather events, outbreaks of disease, or accidents in the workplace.
Political risk	The impact of exposure to political regimes. For example, if the organisation operates in a country that is politically unstable, a change in regime or significant civil unrest could significantly damage business operations and performance.
Compliance risk	Suffering damage and/or loss as a result of changes to, or a lack of compliance with laws, regulations, rules, and enforceable agreements.
Business risk	Business risk is a very broad term meaning anything that impacts the performance of the business. Typically, 'business risk' applies to anything that has the potential to impact on turnover or operating costs. Business risks can come from a wide variety of internal and external factors.
Cyber risk	With the widespread use of digital technology in the business world, an organisation should place more attention on cyber security. See below for more details.

7: Risk management

Risk category	Explanation

Audit risk	Audit risk can be viewed in two ways:
	• The risk that an audit process finds issues that were not expected
	• The risk that an audit process comes to the wrong conclusion. This can be subdivided into:
	   - **Inherent risk:** The risk that relates to the nature of the area being examined (eg if it involves fair value measurement or subjective estimates).
	   - **Control risk:** The risk that controls fail to detect issues in a given area.
	   - **Detection risk:** The risk that the audit process fails to detect errors missed by controls. For example, this can be exacerbated by insufficient staff or inexperienced auditors.

Taxation risk	Taxation risk refers to: • The possibility for actions to have unintended taxation consequences, for example an expense unexpectedly not being allowable for tax purposes. • The chance that taxation rules change affecting the tax charges suffered by the organisation, for example an increase in the profits tax rate. • The risk of failing to comply with taxation requirements.
Cyber risk	Cyber risk is the potential financial loss, disruption, or damage to the reputation of an organisation from some sort of failure of its information technology systems. Cybersecurity are the measures, processes and technology designed to protect an organisation from a cyber-attack. A cyber-attack is a deliberate attempt to steal, damage or disrupt information and systems operated and held electronically.

Organisations are free to classify risk as they see fit. Many widen their risk classification to the specific nature of their business and the industry it operates in. For example, foreign exchange or derivative risk, intellectual property risk, IT related risks, knowledge or talent retention or reputation risk.

Question

Scenario: FitStore Health and Fitness Centres

FitStore is a small UK-based chain comprising 15 health and fitness centres strategically located across various cities and towns. The UK health and fitness industry is highly competitive, with new entrants constantly emerging and offering 24/7 access to facilities at low prices. Despite the competitive landscape, FitStore stands out for its commitment to quality service and member satisfaction.

Each FitStore centre offers state-of-the-art gym facilities equipped with modern exercise equipment and amenities, catering to individuals of all fitness levels and preferences. Additionally, every centre boasts a well-maintained swimming pool, providing members with the opportunity to engage in aquatic workouts, swim laps, or simply relax and unwind.

The company prides itself on offering a comprehensive range of services designed to promote physical health, mental well-being, and overall fitness. In addition to access to the gym and swimming pool, members can benefit from personalised training sessions with certified fitness instructors, group fitness classes such as yoga, Pilates, and high-intensity interval training (HIIT), nutritional counselling, and wellness workshops. FitStore also offers special programs for seniors, children, and individuals with specific health goals or conditions, ensuring inclusivity and accessibility for all members of the community.

However, the competitive nature of the industry poses challenges for FitStore. With new entrants offering 24/7 access at low prices, FitStore must continually innovate and differentiate itself to maintain its competitive edge and attract and retain members.

Furthermore, staff turnover is high in the health and fitness industry, making it a continual challenge for FitStore to recruit and retain qualified employees. Despite this challenge, FitStore remains committed to investing in its staff and providing ongoing training and development opportunities to ensure a high standard of service delivery across all its centres.

FitStore's commitment to excellence extends beyond its facilities and services to encompass a supportive and motivating environment conducive to achieving fitness goals. With a team of dedicated staff members passionate about health and fitness, FitStore endeavours to inspire and empower individuals on their journey to a healthier lifestyle.

As FitStore continues to expand its presence and reach, it recognises the importance of identifying and mitigating potential risks to ensure the safety, satisfaction, and well-being of its members, staff, and stakeholders.

Required

Briefly identify and explain the following risks
- Three strategic risks
- Four operational risks
- Three ESG (sustainability risks)
- Two financial risks

Answer

Strategic risks

Increased competition: FitStore faces the risk of losing market share and profitability due to the emergence of new entrants in the highly competitive health and fitness industry. To address this risk, FitStore must continually innovate its services and offerings to differentiate itself and maintain its competitive edge.

Market saturation: With the expansion of FitStore's presence across various cities and towns, there is a risk of market saturation, where the demand for health and fitness services may plateau or decline in certain areas. FitStore needs to conduct thorough market analysis and strategic planning to identify new growth opportunities and diversify its revenue streams.

Changes in consumer preferences: Shifts in consumer preferences towards alternative fitness trends or preferences for convenience and affordability could pose a risk to FitStore's business model. To mitigate this risk, FitStore must stay abreast of industry trends, regularly gather feedback from members, and adapt its services to meet evolving customer needs.

Operational risks

Equipment malfunction or maintenance issues: Operational disruptions due to equipment breakdowns or maintenance issues can impact the member experience and lead to dissatisfaction. FitStore should implement regular maintenance schedules, invest in high-quality equipment, and have contingency plans in place to minimise downtime.

Staff turnover and training: High staff turnover rates in the health and fitness industry present challenges in maintaining consistent service standards and member relationships. FitStore should prioritise staff retention initiatives, provide ongoing training and development opportunities, and foster a positive work culture to reduce turnover and ensure a skilled workforce.

Health and safety incidents: Operational risks related to health and safety incidents, such as accidents or injuries on-site, can result in reputational damage and legal liabilities for FitStore. Implementing robust health and safety protocols, conducting regular inspections, and providing staff with proper training in emergency response procedures are essential risk mitigation measures.

Data protection and privacy laws: With the increasing reliance on technology and digital platforms for member management and data storage, FitStore faces regulatory risks related to data protection and privacy laws. Implementing robust cybersecurity measures, obtaining consent for data collection and processing, and adhering to GDPR guidelines can help mitigate the risk of data breaches and safeguard sensitive information.

ESG (sustainability) risks

Environmental impact: FitStore may face risks associated with its environmental footprint, such as energy consumption, waste generation, and carbon emissions from its operations. Adopting eco-friendly practices, investing in renewable energy sources, and implementing waste reduction initiatives can mitigate these risks and demonstrate FitStore's commitment to sustainability.

- **Social responsibility:** Risks related to social responsibility include issues such as community engagement, diversity and inclusion, and employee well-being. FitStore should prioritise social initiatives, foster a diverse and inclusive workplace culture, and offer health and wellness programs to support the holistic well-being of its employees and members.

- **Governance:** ESG risks also encompass governance and ethical considerations, including transparency, integrity, and compliance with regulatory standards. FitStore should uphold high ethical standards in its business practices, ensure transparent communication with stakeholders, and establish robust governance frameworks to mitigate risks associated with misconduct or non-compliance.

Financial risks

- **Revenue volatility:** FitStore may experience revenue volatility due to factors such as seasonal fluctuations in membership renewals, economic downturns, or unexpected disruptions like the COVID-19 pandemic. Building financial resilience through diversified revenue streams, contingency planning, and prudent financial management can help mitigate the impact of revenue fluctuations.

- **Capital investment risks:** As FitStore considers expansion and investment in new facilities or technologies, there are inherent financial risks associated with capital expenditures, including cost overruns, project delays, and potential returns on investment. Conducting thorough feasibility studies, risk assessments, and financial modelling can inform strategic decision-making and minimise investment risks.

3.5 Risk evaluation

Risk evaluation involves analysing, profiling and consolidating risks.

As well as deciding how to assess risks, organisations also need to decide how often assessment should take place. This will depend on how dynamic the environment is within which they operate, and how changes in that environment could result in significant and sudden changes in risks, which will in turn mean that the ways they are managed will change. Maybe the methods used to mitigate risks will alter, perhaps the priorities given to dealing with particular risks will change.

In some environments, risks will change very little, but in other risks will change a great deal and change quickly. The continuum below shows the two extremes and the variable state between them. On the left no risks ever change. On the right all risks are changing all the time. The two extremes do not exist in reality but situations close to them do exist.

Static   Dynamic

⟶

Increasing environmental
change and turbulence

Some changes in the environment will arise from the strategic decisions businesses make, for example launching a new product, penetrating a new market, or significantly changing their financial structure. Here the need for accurate risk assessment to support the strategic decisions may seem obvious, but there will also be changes in risk assessment once the strategy is launched to monitor the risks resulting from the new strategy.

Other significant changes to risks may arise from the decisions taken by other participants in the industry in which the business operates, in particular decisions by competitors, suppliers and customers.

In other instances businesses may face changes in risks that they do not themselves influence but are a result of external forces acting on their environment. Factors that may result in significant rapid changes in risks may include the following.

- **Technology.** Sectors where developments in new technology can quickly and significantly benefit innovators.
- **Supply.** Businesses may be dependent on sources of raw materials that are increasingly uncertain.
- **Social.** Businesses selling goods in markets where fashion is a significant influence on consumer demand.
- **Economic.** Sellers of non-essential goods or services to consumers being particularly vulnerable to adverse swings in the business cycle or even short-term losses of confidence caused by stock market volatility, such as was seen worldwide during the summer of 2011.
- **Political.** Businesses operating in unstable political environments or facing major changes in legislation.

Internal risks may alter quickly too. If for example the business is dependent on a few staff, loss of these staff may significantly increase the risk of errors occurring or loss of business to competitors if these staff join rivals.

3.5.1 Risk quantification

Organisations can calculate possible results or losses and probabilities and add on distributions or confidence limits. They can ascertain certain key figures. Commonly, two dimensions are used to evaluate risk:

(a) **Severity/impact** (how severe this risk could be or what could be impact?); and
(b) **Frequency/likelihood** (is there a high likelihood of a risk event occurring or how often?)

Severity (or **impact**) is the potential loss that may occur from an adverse risk event (or the potential gain from a favourable risk event). It may be measured either as the maximum possible loss (or benefit) or as the most likely amount of loss (or benefit).

Frequency (or **likelihood**) is a measure of how often the risk event is expected to occur. Frequency is a measure for risk events that occur with regularity, such as defaults on debt, equipment or system breakdowns or a human error. Probability is a statistical measure of the likelihood of a risk event: this may be a frequently recurring event or a once-only event, such as the probability of winning a contract for which a tender or bid has been submitted.

Risk measurement may therefore require analysis of both the severity of a risk and the frequency of a risk event and will require data analysis and statistical techniques to do so.

Measuring the severity (impact) and frequency (likelihood) of risks

There are various ways of measuring or analysing risk, either quantitatively or qualitatively.

- **Quantitative measures:** To measure this reliably:
  - Experience of the event is needed to understand how likely it is to occur.
  - Experience is also needed to understand the likely severity.
  - The nature of the risk needs to lend itself to quantification. For example, a foreign exchange loss will be a financial number. However, 'damaging staff morale' will be inherently much more difficult to quantify.
- **Qualitative measures**: Risks may be graded on a scale, for example from 'very serious' to 'insignificant.' Some companies use a colour coding system for risks in their IT systems in a 'risk dashboard', or even a subjective 'scale of 1 to 5' for example.

Once an assessment has been made of the probability and severity of the risk, this can then be used to help prioritise the risks to focus the risk management process on the most serious ones.

In the next two sections, we will see how non-analytical and analytical methods are used for evaluating risk.

3.5.2 Non-analytical methods for evaluating risk

Non-analytical tools to evaluate risk	Explanation
Employee expertise	Many organisations will use their internal specialists to analyse risk.
Past loss risk events or near misses	Risk events which have or have almost happened to a company provide the greatest likelihood of a similar risk event occurring.
Specific industry regulator information	Guidance issued by regulators will often contain the types of risk which companies should monitor and control.
Use of external experts	An external risk assessment can provide an expert perspective where a company does not possess the required expertise
Site visits and physical inspections	Sometimes, detailed risk evaluation will only emerge through observation by visiting a site or walking through a manufacturing process.
Benchmarking	Monitoring performance against an internal target or an external benchmark acts a risk early warning signal.
Stress testing	Stress testing examines a number of future potential outcomes given a situation in which one or more extreme conditions apply. For example, banks are required to carry out stress tests of their financial stability such as the impact if there is a 2% increase in loan defaults.

Non-analytical tools to evaluate risk	Explanation
Structured what if technique (SWIFT)	Structured what if technique (SWIFT) uses checklists to consider what could happen/go wrong against a wide range of different circumstances. The technique uses questioning such as 'what if' and 'how could this happen' and 'what could go wrong' questions to trigger a deeper discussion.
Root cause analysis	Root cause analysis is an approach to identify and assess the fundamental causes of a problem or a risk. The 'Five Whys' technique can be used to search for the root cause of a problem. It involves asking the question 'Why?' several times (five times is a general guide). For example: (a) Why did the injury occur – the operator was overworked (b) Why was the operator overworked – the operates is under a new shift pattern due to reduced staff numbers (c) Why is there reduced staff – staff turnover has been high, and it is difficult to recruit (d) Why is staff turnover high and it is difficult to recruit – the company offers lower than market rates, and wages have not increased in line with inflation.

3.5.3 Analytical methods for evaluating risk

There are several analytical methods available to evaluate risks such as probability analysis, sensitivity analysis, value at risk, simulation, and systems and process mapping. We consider these below:

3.5.3.1 Probability analysis

A common analytical method for analysing risk is probability analysis, which requires the calculation of an expected value of loss or an expected value of the outcome. An expected value (EV) is simply a weighted average value, where possible outcomes are weighted according to the probability that they will happen.

Expected value = $\sum p_i x_i$

p_i = the probability of event 'i' happening

x_i = the value of event 'i'

Question

A company is considering an investment to make a new product based on a new technology. The minimum amount of investment required would be $10 million. If the investment is successful, the estimated return would have a present value of $25 million before deducting the initial investment cost. If the investment is unsuccessful, there would be operating losses of $2 million and in addition the initial investment would be lost entirely. It has been estimated that the probability of success is 60%.

Required

Calculate the expected value of the investment and the expected value of the loss.

Answer

The expected value of the investment is $ [0.6 × (25 − 10)] − [0.4 × (10 + 2)] million = $4.2 million.

The expected value of the loss is $4.8 million which can be calculated by multiplying the loss of $12 million (severity) and 40% (probability).

Expected values have the advantage of allowing decision makers to perform analysis on one number.

However, expected values are inappropriate for one-off decisions as they are long run average, and they are very dependent on the estimates for probabilities and values used. By using expected values, the decision maker may have overlooked the most or least favourable outcomes since expected value only give you average results. This might influence the decision of someone who is risk averse or risk seeking.

3.5.3.2 Sensitivity analysis

Sensitivity analysis can be applied to plans and forecasts such as business plans and budgets. Sensitivity analysis can identify which items in financial or operational performance are the biggest sources of risk.

The basic approach with sensitivity analysis is to calculate under alternative assumptions how sensitive the outcome is to changing conditions. The analysis identifies:

- Those variables to which the outcome is most critical, or sensitive; and
- The extent to which the critical variables can change in value before the expected outcome reaches a critical level.

Management should review critical variables to assess whether or not there is a strong possibility of events occurring that would lead to a different decision.

Sensitivity analysis has the advantage of drawing the decision-makers attention to variables that have a significant impact on the outcome.

However, sensitivity analysis has a number of weaknesses:

- Changes in each key variable are only considered once at a time. However, management should also be interested in the combination of the effects of changes in two or more key variables.
- Looking at factors in isolation is unrealistic since they are often interdependent. The same risks may influence a number of variables in the calculation.
- Sensitivity analysis does not examine the probability that any particular variation in a key variable might occur.

Question

Calcite Company Ltd is considering a project to launch a new product. The initial investment of $6 million will generate revenues of $5 million in each of the next two years. The variable costs are expected to be $1.5 million per annum in the next two years. Calcite's cost of capital is 8%.

Required

Assess whether the project is more sensitive to the risks associated with variable costs or price.

Answer

To calculate net present value (NPV) of the project, we should calculate the difference between the present value of cash inflows and that of cash outflows. In this case, net cash inflows to be derived in the next two years should be discounted at 8% while the cash outflows should be the initial outlay of $6 million.

Project NPV: ($5m – $1.5m) × 1.783* – $6m= $0.241m positive. The project should be accepted as it has a positive NPV.

*1.783 = 0.926 + 0.857 (applying a two-year 8% annuity factor)

Sensitivity analysis = NPV/PV Variable

Revenues NPV = ($5m × 1.783) = $8.915m

Price sensitivity = 241,000/8,915,000 = 3%

Variable costs NPV = ($1.5m × 1.783) = $2.675m

Variable cost sensitivity = 241,000/2,675,000 = 9%

Therefore, we can conclude that variable costs would be needed to rise by 9% for reaching the break-even point.

Changes in the selling price of this product are a higher risk than changes in the variable costs, as revenues only need to fall by 3% (the equivalent of $241,000) to make the project only break even. Variable costs would be needed to rise by 9% for reaching the break-even point.

3.5.3.3 Value at risk

A value at risk (VaR) model is a measure of the **maximum** expected loss that will be incurred within a given period of time, at a given level of probability. VaR models are used by many banks. For example, the maximum losses of the bank within the next seven days will be $25 million with 95% certainty. The weakness of this analysis is there is a 5% chance the loss could be higher.

VaR has the advantage of being practical in nature – rather than considering theoretical extremes, it draws the decision-makers attention to worst-case scenarios on the normal operating circumstances and so is useful to help with real-world planning.

However, VaR assumes normal distributions hold true for the risky variable and that the value of standard deviations in the future can be predicted from past data.

3.5.3.4 Simulation

A simulation involves the creation of a model that is designed to simulate 'real-world' conditions. In a mathematical simulation model, a number of different variables are identified. The nature of the variables depends on the real-world situation that is being modelled, but in a simple business model, the variables may be sales volumes of different products or different items of costs or expenditures. Relationships between the variables are also built into the model.

Uncertainty is introduced into the model because for each variable there are a range of different possible values. The simulation is used many times over assigned different values to each variable. This produces a large range of possible 'real world' outcomes. The results can then be used to identify the most likely outcome and calculate statistical measures of variability in the outcome.

Simulations have the big advantage over sensitivity analysis that more than one variable is being considered at a time.

However, in reality it is very difficult to obtain an accurate probability distribution for key variables which means assumptions need to be made, limiting the usefulness of the result. In addition, simulations are not

an optimising message in the sense that they do not indicate what the best approach is – they simply inform the decision maker of the range of possibilities and how likely they are to occur.

3.5.3.5 System and process mapping

System and process mapping involves converting all processes into flow diagrams and considering where things could go wrong, and the reason why, at each point in the diagram. This is particularly useful for complex manufacturing (technology or pharmaceuticals) or dangerous or invisible processes (ie in the chemical industry).

Identified problems are known as fault trees, and they can be traced backwards through the flow diagram to establish the root cause which can then be addressed.

System and process mapping has the advantage of being a very visual, and analytical approach. However, the process maps may oversimplify complex situations making them often difficult to apply in practice.

3.5.4 Risk consolidation and risk correlation

Risk that has been analysed and quantified at the divisional or subsidiary level needs to be aggregated to the corporate level and grouped into categories (categorisation). This aggregation will be required as part of the overall review of risk that the board needs to undertake which we shall look at in more detail in later chapters.

One significant part of the risk consolidation process may be to analyse risks that are not independent of each other.

Correlation between risks is also important when considering the costs and benefits of risk management. Major expenditure on controls may reduce risks, but it could increase financial risks such as running short of funds or not being able to make profitable investments.

Organisations should also consider the relationship between business and financial risk. For example. The relationship between business risk and financial risk.

Business risk is borne by both the firm's equity holders and providers of debt, as it is the risk associated with investing in the firm in whatever capacity. The only way that either party can get rid of the business risk is to withdraw its investment in the firm.

Financial risk, on the other hand, is borne entirely by equity holders. This is due to the fact that payment to debt holders (ie interest) takes precedence over dividends to shareholders. The more debt there is in the firm's capital structure, the greater the financial risk to equity holders, as the increased interest burden coming out of earnings reduces the likelihood that there will be sufficient funds remaining from which to pay a dividend. Debt holders however know there is a legal obligation on the firm to meet their interest commitments.

3.6 Risk response strategies

Risk response strategies are the various ways in which organisations can try to mitigate risks or indeed consider whether it will be worthwhile for them to accept risks.

How controllable risks are considered to be is likely to be an important influence on management strategies. Risks that are largely uncontrollable may not be tackled effectively by risk reduction measures, so the choice may be between accepting the risk and avoiding the activity that causes the risk.

Risk management strategies can be linked into the likelihood/consequences to prioritise them. Once risks have been prioritised then thought can now turn to how best to deal with those risks. This is known as risk response and is how businesses reduce their exposure to a risk event by reducing or eliminating the likelihood that a risk will occur, or reducing the severity of the impact should a risk event occur.

A common framework to help develop a risk response strategy is known as the TARA Framework.

TARA stands for transfer, accept, reduce, or avoid.

The below table represents the TARA framework and provides guidance which risk response strategy is most appropriate depending on the situation.

	Severity or impact	
	Low	High
Likelihood, frequency, or probability — Low	Accept (Tolerate)	Transfer
Likelihood, frequency, or probability — High	Reduce (Control)	Avoid (Terminate)

Mapping identified risks by their risk evaluation of likelihood and severity on a chart, such as the one above, is known as risk mapping. This helps an organisation to visualise the most important risks which it should prioritise as part of its risk response strategy and overall risk monitoring.

From this, a risk response is determined (transfer, accept, reduce or avoid) depending on the likelihood and severity classification. This is then discussed by the risk management committee. The response can change depending on the specific nature of the risk.

Therefore, the TARA Framework is only ever advisory, and if you use it in Capstone, you need to think practically whether the approach fits the particular situation you are considering.

There are four ways of responding to identified risks using the TARA Framework:

(a) **Transfer the risk**

In some situations, and for some risks, the specified risk can be transferred to someone else. The risk remains, but someone else takes on the exposure to the risk.

Insurance transfers stated risks to an insurance company; however, buying insurance can have a high cost. Examples of business insurance include buildings, motor accidents, fire, employers' liability, professional indemnity, public liability, fraud, business interruption and customer default.

Hedging reduces the financial risk using a financial product such as a forward, future, or option contract to compensate for commodity, interest rate or foreign exchange losses.

(b) **Accept the risk**

One approach is to accept the risk because:

- It is not significant, so there is no need to be overly concerned about it.
- It is unavoidable and there is nothing that can be done about it (not even insuring against the risk).

This is also known as Tolerate. For example, the risk that a courier company may deliver a relatively unimportant document late given that the courier company has a good track record of delivering on time may be considered low probability and low impact and therefore the risk should be accepted – if it happens, which appears unlikely, the impact would be low.

(c) **Reduce (or control) the risk**

Many risks can be reduced or trimmed by taking a control action. Control actions are unlikely to eliminate the risk entirely, but they can reduce the risk to an acceptable level.

For example, the owner of a supermarket may suffer frequently from relatively small theft from the store. Although a single theft will have a low impact, the high frequency of theft will increase the cumulative impact of multiple thefts. The owner may therefore take steps to reduce the probability of theft, for example, by installing closed-circuit television cameras to monitor customers or keeping high value items in locked cabinets.

(d) **Avoid the risk**

Risks can be avoided altogether by remaining outside an area of business operations completely. A company that has invested in an area of business may decide to pull out of the business when it discovers that the risks of losses are too high and unacceptable.

For example, if a company is considering investing in a new overseas market and it is felt that the probability of business failure is high and, should they fail, they would lose a significant amount of funding, it seems sensible to consider avoiding this particular investment.

The choice of risk management policy: transfer, accept, reduce or avoid may be considered in the context of the severity-frequency matrix, as follows:

	Severity or impact	
	Low	**High**
Low	**Accept (Tolerate)** Risks are not significant. Keep under review, but the costs of dealing with the risk are unlikely to be worth the potential benefit.	**Transfer** Insure a risk. Also, reduce excessive cover of existing insured risks will reduce the cost of insurance premiums.
High	**Reduce (Control)** Take some action. For example, carry out credit checks on customers in order to reduce credit risk.	**Avoid (Terminate)** Take immediate action. For example, change major suppliers or abandon an activity.

(Likelihood, frequency, or probability)

Question

FreshMart is a well-established supermarket chain with multiple branches across urban and suburban areas, offering a wide range of fresh produce, groceries, household items, and convenience goods. Known for its commitment to quality, affordability, and customer service, FreshMart has built a loyal customer base over the years, catering to the diverse needs of local communities.

As part of its proactive approach to risk management, FreshMart's dedicated risk management team regularly conducts comprehensive risk assessments to identify potential threats and vulnerabilities to the business. Recently, FreshMart's risk manager and their team conducted a thorough analysis of FreshMart's operations and identified four significant operating risks that require attention and strategic intervention.

(a) **Inventory shortfalls:** Despite implementing various inventory control measures, FreshMart has observed a consistent level of inventory shortfall across its branches. This includes losses due to customer theft, product spoilage, damaged goods, and administrative errors. The risk manager recognises the potential impact of inventory shortfall on profitability and operational efficiency, prompting the need for targeted risk mitigation strategies.

(b) **Supplier Reliability:** FreshMart heavily relies on a network of suppliers to ensure a steady supply of goods to meet customer demand. However, recent instances of supplier delays, quality issues, and inconsistent deliveries have raised concerns about the reliability of certain vendors. The risk manager acknowledges the importance of securing dependable suppliers to maintain product availability and customer satisfaction while minimising supply chain disruptions.

(c) **Employee Theft:** While FreshMart maintains a positive work environment and promotes ethical conduct among its employees, the risk manager has identified a potential risk of employee theft. Instances of pilferage, unauthorised discounts, and mishandling of cash transactions have been reported, highlighting the need for enhanced measures to prevent internal theft and safeguard company assets.

(d) **Potential breach of customer data:** FreshMart collects personal customer data for its online delivery service. FreshMart's IT department has identified a possible risk to customer data if the firewall is breached. FreshMart's IT security software was last updated over six months ago, and an update is pending. The risk manager recognises the potential reputational damage, financial losses, and regulatory implications associated with a data breach, underscoring the importance of robust cybersecurity measures and proactive risk mitigation strategies.

Required

Recommend an appropriate risk response strategy for each of the risks mentioned above using the TARA Framework

Answer

(a) **Inventory shrinkage**

Implement a 'Reduce' risk response strategy

FreshMart should enhance its inventory control measures to minimise shrinkage. This could involve implementing stricter inventory tracking systems, conducting regular stock audits, improving security measures, and providing staff training on loss prevention techniques. By reducing the likelihood of inventory shrinkage, FreshMart can protect its profitability and operational efficiency.

(b) **Supplier reliability**

Adopt a 'Transfer' risk response strategy

FreshMart should diversify its supplier base and establish relationships with alternative vendors to mitigate the risk of supplier unreliability. Additionally, FreshMart may consider renegotiating contracts with existing suppliers to include penalty clauses for delivery delays or quality issues. By transferring the risk to multiple suppliers, FreshMart can minimise the impact of supply chain disruptions and ensure continuity of product availability.

(c) **Employee theft**

Employ a 'Reduce' risk response strategy

FreshMart should implement stringent internal controls and security measures to prevent and detect instances of employee theft. This could include implementing surveillance cameras, conducting regular audits of cash registers and inventory, segregating duties among employees, and implementing strict access controls. By controlling access to sensitive areas and implementing checks and balances, FreshMart can mitigate the risk of employee theft and safeguard company assets.

(d) **Potential breach of customer data**

Pursue an 'Avoid' risk response strategy

FreshMart should prioritise updating its IT security software and implementing additional cybersecurity measures to mitigate the risk of a data breach. This could involve investing in the latest firewall technologies, conducting regular security audits, encrypting sensitive customer data, and implementing multi-factor authentication for access to customer databases. By avoiding the risk of a data breach through proactive cybersecurity measures, FreshMart can protect its reputation, minimise financial losses, and comply with regulatory requirements.

3.7 Risk control

An organisation's internal controls should be designed to counter the risks that are a consequence of the objectives it pursues. A risk control assessment should determine which internal controls will be most effective.

Controls should be designed to be efficient and effective. The cost of implementing and operating the controls should not outweigh the potential benefit of having them.

In this section we discuss the following categories of internal control:

(a) **Preventative controls:** Preventative controls are designed to stop problems before they happen. For example, a firewall will help to prevent hackers from succeeding. Examples of preventative controls are:

- Checking invoices from suppliers against goods received notes before paying the invoices, to ensure that payments are accurately made for goods actually received
- Regular checking of goods delivery notes against invoices, to ensure that all deliveries have been invoiced
- Signing of goods received notes, credit notes, overtime records and so forth, to confirm that goods have actually been received, credit notes properly issued, overtime actually authorised and worked
- Denying access to sensitive areas of the business to unauthorised people
- Keeping cash in a safe or strong box, to protect it from theft

(b) **Detective controls:** Controls designed to detect errors once they have happened. Not all issues can be prevented. It is important therefore to detect when problems have occurred to facilitate a timely response.

Examples of detective controls in an accounting system are bank reconciliations and regular checks of physical inventory against book records of inventory. Exception reports may be used to detect when actual performance differs from expected performance, indicating that a failure of some nature may have occurred. Duties may be segregated so that if one person makes an error, someone else performing a subsequent task will be able to detect it. Fire alarms and security alarms are possibly more obvious examples of detective controls.

Note. Preventative controls are superior to detective controls as they prevent risk impact from occurring. However, detective controls should also be used as preventative controls may not be perfect.

(c) **Corrective controls:** Corrective controls are controls that are designed to minimise or negate the effect of errors or control failures. An example of a corrective control would be back-up of computer input at the end of each day, or the storing of additional copies of software at a remote location.

(d) **Directive controls:** Directive controls are controls that direct activities or staff towards a desired outcome. Examples include operational manuals or training employees in procedures for dealing with customers. Directive controls may sometimes be useful to ensure that staff follow regulatory procedures when completing a task.

A practical method to help you to generate ideas for internal control measures are the SPAMSOAP internal control categories as follows:

Control	Explanation
Segregation of duties	Having more than one person involved in any one transaction cycle to pick up on errors or deliberate fraud
Personnel	Recruiting high calibre personnel, training them, and ensuring they are suitably motivated towards organisational objectives
Authorisation	Ensuring significant transactions or events are approved at the appropriate level
Management	Remote monitoring by supervising managers or boards, who may not be present where the operation occurs. For example, via monthly management reports or incidence reports and taking appropriate action, as required
Supervision	**Directly watching staff**
Organisational	**Ensuring reporting lines and organisational structures are appropriate**
Accounting	**Ensuring accurate recording and processing of transactions. Includes, for example, control account reconciliations**
Physical	**Keypad access to sensitive areas and locking doors. Using a safe to store sensitive documents and equipment securely**

Resourcing and financing of internal controls

The risk management and internal control system within an organisation should be adequately resourced, so that it can function effectively.

- Individual managers should be given ownership of specific risks, and they should be given sufficient time within their job to give a suitable amount of attention to risks and risk controls.

    Note. Ownership of risk has little purpose if managers do not have the time to manage the risks.

- Specialist control functions within the organisation should be given adequate staff and resources, including the:
    - Health and safety function
    - Internal audit function
    - Quality control function

- If the new controls bring more benefits than costs, there is a business case to support the financing of new controls to reduce risk.

Limitations of internal controls

Any internal control system can provide only reasonable assurance about control, no matter how good the system appears to be.

There are several reasons for this:

- Some additional controls would reduce risks further, but it would be too expensive to implement them.
- The risk of human error and fraud can never be eliminated and is always present.
- The risk of collusion between two or more employees to commit fraud may reduce the effectiveness of segregation of duties or supervisory controls.
- Controls may be bypassed or over-ridden by managers. Senior managers may take an arrogant view that controls are for their employees but do not apply to them personally.
- Controls that are designed to deal with routine control problems may be unable to deal properly with unusual circumstances.
- Controls may appear well-designed 'on paper', but they may not be implemented fully or effectively.

Question

For each risk identified in the previous examples, recommend a suitable risk control response to mitigate the risk likelihood or impact.

Answer

The recommended risk control response for each identified risk are as follows.

Intense competition from new entrants

Implement a differentiation strategy by offering unique services or amenities not available at competitor facilities. Focus on enhancing member experience through personalised services, innovative fitness programs, and exceptional customer service to increase loyalty and retention.

Market saturation in existing locations

Conduct thorough market research before expanding into new locations to assess demand and competition. Implement a diversification strategy by exploring opportunities in underserved markets or targeting niche demographics. Prioritise quality over quantity to maintain brand reputation and customer satisfaction.

Reputation damage due to negative publicity or social media backlash

Develop a robust crisis management plan to address potential reputational threats promptly and effectively. Monitor online channels and social media platforms for any negative feedback or mentions and respond promptly with transparency and accountability. Invest in proactive reputation management strategies to build and safeguard the brand's image.

Equipment breakdown or maintenance issues

Implement a preventive maintenance program to regularly inspect and service fitness equipment to minimise the risk of breakdowns. Maintain adequate spare parts inventory to facilitate timely repairs. Provide staff training on equipment usage and safety protocols to prevent accidents and ensure efficient operations.

Staff shortages or high turnover rates

Implement employee retention strategies such as competitive wages, benefits, and professional development opportunities to reduce turnover rates. Conduct regular staff feedback surveys to identify concerns and address them proactively. Develop a talent pipeline through recruitment drives, internships, and partnerships with educational institutions.

Data security breaches or cyberattack

Enhance cybersecurity measures by implementing firewalls, encryption protocols, and multi-factor authentication to protect sensitive member data. Conduct regular security audits and vulnerability assessments to identify and address potential weaknesses in IT systems. Provide staff training on cybersecurity best practices to prevent phishing attacks and data breaches.

Environmental impact of facilities and operations

Implement sustainable practices such as energy-efficient lighting, water conservation measures, and waste recycling programs to minimise environmental footprint. Seek green certifications and accreditations to demonstrate commitment to sustainability. Engage with suppliers and partners who share similar environmental values and practices.

Social responsibility and community engagement

Develop community outreach programs and initiatives to support local charities, schools, and organisations. Foster a culture of inclusivity and diversity within the organisation by promoting equal employment opportunities and supporting employee volunteerism. Communicate corporate social responsibility efforts transparently to stakeholders to enhance brand reputation and loyalty.

Non-compliance with health and safety regulations

Establish comprehensive health and safety policies and procedures compliant with regulatory standards. Conduct regular inspections and audits to ensure facilities meet safety requirements and address any identified deficiencies promptly. Provide staff training on safety protocols and emergency response procedures to mitigate risks of accidents or injuries.

Non-compliance with data protection laws (eg GDPR)

Develop and implement a robust data protection policy aligned with relevant regulations such as GDPR. Obtain explicit consent from members before collecting and processing their personal data. Encrypt sensitive information and implement access controls to prevent unauthorised disclosure or misuse. Conduct regular audits and assessments to ensure compliance with data protection laws.

Revenue volatility

Diversify revenue streams by offering additional services or products to reduce reliance on membership fees. Establish contingency funds or reserves to cushion against revenue fluctuations during economic downturns or unforeseen events. Implement flexible pricing strategies and membership plans to attract and retain members across different market segments.

Capital investment risks

Conduct thorough feasibility studies and financial assessments before undertaking capital investment projects to evaluate potential risks and returns. Establish project management protocols to monitor progress, costs, and timelines closely. Consider alternative financing options such as leasing or partnerships to mitigate financial risks associated with large capital expenditures.

3.8 Risk monitoring and reporting

The risk management committee (possibly led by a risk manager) should monitor the risk management process to ensure it is efficient and effective and take corrective action as and when required.

This will involve regular reporting as follows:

- **Summary reporting:** The risk manager should ensure there are regular reporting procedures in place to keep an overview of the risk management process that is sufficiently detailed for the risk manager to be able to see if it is operating adequately. This summary reporting can also form the basis of reporting up to the board via the appropriate board sub-committee.
- **Detailed reports:** Individual risk owners will need reports that are sufficiently detailed to enable them to manage their risks adequately. For example, a treasury manager responsible for managing foreign exchange risk may need regular reports highlighting foreign exchange exposures and the effectiveness or otherwise of the risk management steps taken in relation to those exposures.
- **External reporting:** Some businesses opt to report externally on risk management processes in more detail than others to promote transparency and to engender trust with the stakeholder community.

Additionally, internal audit can play a key role in risk monitoring. Internal audit should not be involved in designing controls or operating the risk management process in the first place. This then enables them to objectively review the risk management process to see if its integrated risk operating systems operate adequately, and to recommend improvements as appropriate.

3.8.1 Integrated risk reporting systems

COSO Enterprise Risk Management advises organisations to invest in an integrated risk reporting system throughout the organisation. This allows management (risk owners) at all levels from all over the organisation to record risks in one system, using the same format, which they have identified to facilitate risk evaluation and reporting.

In developing integrated risk reporting systems, an organisation should consider the following:

(a) A standard format is used across the entire organisation.

(b) Risk registers are updated and reviewed by senior management at regular intervals.

(c) The risk reporting system is integrated when it is digitally linked to other business systems to share the same database of company information. Therefore, data can be pulled from business system in real time to populate the risk reporting system as needed.

(d) Risk registers used by business units are aggregated into a single consolidated document for the board. This is called a risk profile.

Once risks have been evaluated, they are summarised in order to report them to senior management.

This process of risk consolidation involves compiling risks together and then evaluating the overall risk profile for the organisation. The entire organisation risk profile is reported to the board on a regular basis for board discussion. Risk management should be recurring agenda point at executive board meetings.

Risk reporting should incorporate a risk classification system which will enable management to identify which strategies and operations are most exposed to risk.

The following table includes typical information which would be recorded for each risk in integrated risk reporting system. Note, this is sometimes referred to as a risk register.

Key elements of risk register	Explanation
Name or title of risk	Detailed information gathered or results of data analysis to be recorded
Scope of risk	The scope of the risk and details of possible risk events, including a description of the events, their type, size, and number

Key elements of risk register	Explanation
Nature of risk	Classification of the risk Timescale for possible impact Whether it is a hazard (negative risk), an opportunity (two-way risk) or something that adds to uncertainty
Risk category	To link to a business transition, process, or business unit (ie credit risk, IT risk, processing risk)
Stakeholders	Stakeholders both external and internal to the organisation who are affected by the risk, and their expectations
Risk metrics or trends	Information which tracks whether risk exposure is increasing/decreasing and documents relevant external information sources
Risk evaluation	The likely severity (or impact) and frequency (or likelihood) of a risk event and escalation
Loss experience	Previous incidents, and history of any losses in the past related to this risk
Potential causes	Factors which have been identified as contributing to a risk event
Risk tolerance, appetite, or attitude	Potential or anticipated financial loss and reputational damage arising from the risk Target for control of risk and desired level of performance Risk attitude, appetite and tolerance or limits for the risk
Risk response, treatment, and controls	Existing control mechanisms and activities Level of confidence in existing controls Procedures for monitoring and review of risk performance
Potential for risk improvement	Potential for cost-effective improvements or modifications Recommendations and deadlines for implementation Responsibilities for implementing any recommendations
Risk strategy and policy	Responsibility for developing strategy related to the risk Responsibility for auditing/checking on compliance with risk controls

3.8.2 Risk monitoring

To be effective, monitoring by management needs to be ongoing and involve separate evaluation of internal controls and systems. Deficiencies need to be communicated to all the appropriate people. Risk monitoring ensures that internal controls designed to mitigate identified risks continues to operate effectively. This process involves assessment by appropriate personnel of the design and operation of control on a suitable timely basis, and the taking of necessary actions. It applies to all activities within an organisation and sometimes to outside contractors as well.

If deficiencies are found, they should be **reported, assessed** and their **root causes corrected**.

Correction of root causes may address why staff have made errors. In this case correction processes may include training, discipline, or control redesign. It may involve implementing better controls when controls have been found to be inadequate. The aim of correcting **root causes** distinguishes monitoring procedures from control procedures. Control procedures seek **only** to **correct errors**.

The 2009 COSO guidance on internal control monitoring highlights two fundamental principles:

(a) **Ongoing monitoring** and **separate evaluation** enable management to determine whether internal controls continue to function over time.

    (i) **Ongoing monitoring** includes routine review of reconciliations and system action applications. It may be particularly effective in smaller companies, since their managers will have high-level first-hand knowledge of the company's activities. Their close involvement in operations should help them identify variances and inaccuracies.

    (ii) **Separate evaluation** is generally carried out by the audit committee and internal audit, and also includes annual reviews of control procedures. Separate evaluation is likely to be more difficult if a company does not have an internal audit department, as review of control effectiveness within a business unit by a manager responsible for that unit will lack objectivity.

(b) Internal control deficiencies should be **identified and communicated** to those responsible for taking corrective action, management, and the board.

The COSO guidance emphasises that monitoring should relate to **all control objectives**, not just financial reporting objectives. It should evaluate the internal control system's ability to manage or mitigate meaningful risks to organisational objectives.

If the operation of controls is not measured and monitored by management, their effectiveness may deteriorate over time as circumstances change. Different controls will need more monitoring over time as an organisation's strategy develops, and the tolerances allowed by those controls will also need to change.

3.8.3 Prioritising effective monitoring procedures

The COSO guidance stresses that the business's overall risk assessment process will also influence the scope of monitoring. Key factors will include the **size and complexity of the organisation**, the **nature of the organisation's operations**, the **purpose for which monitoring is being conducted** and the **relative importance of the underlying controls**. COSO provides helpful guidance on how organisations may vary their approach to monitoring.

Control importance	Risks controls address	Possible monitoring approach
Highest	High likelihood, high significance	Ongoing monitoring using direct and indirect information, periodic separate evaluation of direct information
Moderate in short term	Low likelihood, high significance	Ongoing monitoring using indirect information, periodic separate evaluation of direct information
Moderate in long term	High likelihood, low significance	**Ongoing monitoring using direct and indirect information, less frequent separate evaluation of direct information**
Lowest	Low likelihood, low significance	Relatively infrequent separate evaluations

To ensure monitoring has an appropriate risk-based focus, the organisation should establish a structure that firstly ensures that internal control is effective in a given area and focuses monitoring attention on areas of change. This structure will have the following elements.

Control baseline	A reasonable basis for believing internal controls operate effectively
Change identification process	Identifying changes in processes or risks that indicate controls should have changed; monitoring should focus on the ability of the risk assessment procedures to identify changes in processes or risks that should result in changes in controls and should also assess whether indicators of change in control design and operation are effective

Change management process	Verifying that the internal control systems have managed changes in controls effectively
Control reconfirmation	Reconfirming control operation through separate evaluation

3.8.4 Monitoring procedures

The **size of the organisation** and the **complexity of its operations and controls** will be key determinants.

Monitoring procedures may include:

- **Periodic evaluation and testing of controls** by internal audit
- **Continuous monitoring programs** built into information systems
- Analysis of, and appropriate follow-up on, **operating reports** or metrics that might identify anomalies indicative of a control failure
- **Supervisory reviews of controls**, such as reconciliation reviews as a normal part of processing
- **Self-assessment** by the board and management regarding the tone they set in the organisation and the effectiveness of their oversight functions
- **Audit committee enquiries** of internal and external auditors
- **Quality assurance reviews** of the internal audit department

The results of monitoring need to be reported to the right people and corrective action taken. Deficiencies in internal controls should be reported to the person **responsible for the control's operation** and **to at least one level higher**. The deficiencies need to be assessed in the same terms as risks, the **likelihood** that a control will fail to detect or prevent a risk's occurrence and the **significance** of the potential impact of the risk.

Where control deficiencies are potentially significant, additional monitoring procedures may be needed during the correction period to protect against errors.

3.9 Repeat the risk management process

The risk management process is a cycle rather than a 'one off' exercise. The risk management group should work their way through each stage of the cycle and consider if changes need to be made.

New risks may surface, old ones may disappear, and ones that remain may change their likelihood and impact. In addition, the most appropriate response to those risks may need to be reassessed in light of the experience gained and the changing landscape.

4 Quality information for risk management

Directors need information from a large variety of sources to be able to supervise and review the operation of the internal control systems. Information sources should include normal reporting procedures, but staff should also have channels available to report problems or doubtful practices of others.

4.1 Types of information

4.1.1 Strategic information

Strategic information is used to **plan** the **objectives** of the **organisation**, and to **assess** whether the objectives are being met in practice. Such information includes overall profitability, the profitability of

different segments of the business, future market prospects, the availability and cost of raising new funds, total cash needs, total manning levels and capital equipment needs.

Strategic information is:

- Derived from both **internal and external** sources
- **Summarised** at a high level
- Relevant to the **long term**
- Concerned with the **whole organisation**
- Often prepared on an **'ad hoc'** basis
- Both **quantitative and qualitative**
- Often **uncertain**, as the future cannot be accurately predicted

4.1.2 Tactical information

Tactical information is used to decide **how the resources of the business should be employed**, and to **monitor** how they are being and have been employed. Such information includes productivity measurements (output per hour), budgetary control reports, variance analysis reports, cash flow forecasts, staffing levels and short-term purchasing requirements.

Tactical information is:

- Primarily **generated internally** (but may have a limited external component)
- **Summarised at a lower level**
- Relevant to the **short and medium term**
- Concerned with **activities or departments**
- Prepared **routinely and regularly**
- Based on **quantitative** measures

4.1.3 Operational information

Operational information is used to ensure that **specific operational tasks** are planned and carried out as intended.

Operational information is:

- Derived from **internal** sources such as transaction recording methods
- **Detailed**, being the processing of raw data (for example transaction reports listing all transactions in a period)
- Relevant to the **immediate term**
- **Task-specific**
- Prepared very **frequently**
- Largely **quantitative**

4.2 The qualities of good information

The COSO guidance stresses the importance of the board and management having good quality information. 'Good' information is information that adds to the understanding of a situation. The qualities of good information are outlined in the following table.

	Quality	Example
A	Accurate	Figures should add up, the degree of rounding should be appropriate, there should be no typos, items should be allocated to the correct category, and assumptions should be stated for uncertain information.
C	Complete	Information should include everything that it needs to include, for example external data if relevant, comparative information and qualitative information as well as quantitative. Sometimes managers or strategic planners will need to build on the available information to produce a forecast using assumptions or extrapolations.
C	Cost-beneficial	It should not cost more to obtain the information than the benefit derived from having it. Providers of information should be given efficient means of collecting and analysing it. Users should not waste time working out what it means.
U	User-targeted	The needs of the user should be borne in mind; for instance, senior managers need strategic summaries, and junior managers need detail.
R	Relevant	Information that is not needed for a decision should be omitted, no matter how 'interesting' it may be.
A	Authoritative	The source of the information should be a reliable one. However, subjective information (eg expert opinions) may be required in addition to objective facts.
T	Timely	The information should be available when it is needed. It should also cover relevant time periods and the future as well as the past.
E	Easy to use	Information should be clearly presented, not excessively long, and sent using the right medium and communication channel (email, telephone, hard-copy report).

4.3 Needs of directors

We have emphasised above that board and senior manager involvement is a critical element of internal control systems and the control environment.

They will need:

- **Financial information** is important for internal purposes and to fulfil legal requirements for true and fair external reporting
- **Non-financial information** such as quality reports, customer complaints, human resource data
- **External information** about competitors, suppliers, impact of future economic and social trends

There are various ways in which management can obtain the information they need to play the necessary active part in control systems.

Managers also need to take into account the needs of internal and external auditors for accurate and precise information.

4.4 Information sources

The information directors need to be able to monitor risks and controls effectively comes from a wide variety of sources. Directors can obtain information partly through their own efforts. However, if information systems are to work effectively, it is vital that they identify particular people or departments who are responsible for providing particular information. Controls must be built into the systems to ensure that those **responsible provide that data**. This is particularly important in the context of the information that supports the contents of the financial statements and is used by internal and external audit and the audit committee.

4.4.1 The directors' own efforts

Directors will receive reports from the audit committee and risk committee. Management **walking about** and regular visits by the directors to operations may yield valuable insights and should help the directors understand the context in which controls are currently operating.

4.4.2 Reports from subordinates

There should be systems in place for all staff with supervisory responsibilities to report on a regular basis to senior managers, and senior managers in turn to report regularly to directors. The COSO guidelines comment:

'Among the most critical communications channels is that between top management and the board of directors. Management must keep the board up to date on performance, developments, risk and the functioning of enterprise risk management and other relevant events or issues. The better the communications, the more effective the board will be in carrying out its oversight responsibilities, in acting as a sounding board on critical issues and in providing advice, counsel and direction. By the same token the board should communicate to management what information it needs and provide feedback and direction.'

However, COSO's guidance also emphasises the need for the board to use information sources other than sub-board management, including internal and external auditors and regulators. There should be channels for stakeholders who have information about the effectiveness of internal controls to communicate with the company.

4.4.3 Lines of communication

Very importantly directors must ensure that staff have lines of communication that can be used to **address concerns**. There should be normal communication channels through which most concerns are addressed, but there should also be alternative channels for reporting if normal communication channels are ineffective. These include communication channels for staff to report, or **whistleblow**, particularly serious problems and perhaps active seeking of feedback through **staff attitude surveys**.

As well as channels existing, it is also important that staff believe that directors and managers want to know about problems and will deal with them effectively. Staff must believe that there will be **no reprisals** for **reporting relevant information**.

4.4.4 Reports from control functions

Organisational functions that have a key role to play in internal control systems must report on a regular basis to the board and senior management. One example is the need for a close relationship between **internal audit** and the **audit committee**. The **human resources function** should also report regularly to the board about personnel practices in operational units. Poor human resource management can often be an indicator of future problems with controls, since it may create dissatisfied staff or staff who believe that laxness will be tolerated.

4.4.5 Reports on activities

The board should receive regular reports on **certain activities**. A good example is major developments in computerised systems. As well as board approval before the start of key stages of the development process, the board needs to be informed of progress and any problems during the course of the project, so that any difficulties with potentially serious consequences can be rapidly addressed.

4.4.6 Reports on resolution of deficiencies

Similarly, the board should obtain evidence to confirm that control deficiencies that have previously **been identified** have been **resolved**. When it has been agreed that action should be taken to deal with problems, this should include a **timescale** for action and also **reporting** that the actions have been implemented.

4.4.7 Results of checks

The board should receive confirmation as a matter of course that the necessary **checks** on the operation of the controls have been **carried out** satisfactorily and that the results have been clearly reported. This includes gaining assurance that the **right sort** of check has been **performed**. For example, **random checks** may be required on high risk areas, such as unauthorised access to computer systems. Sufficient **independent** evidence from external or internal audit should be obtained to reinforce the evidence supplied by operational units.

4.4.8 Exception reporting

Exception reports highlighting variances in **budgeting systems**, **performance measures**, **quality targets** and **planning systems** are an important part of the information that management receives. Organisations should have a system of exception reporting that will trigger action if potential risks have been identified.

You will remember from your management accounting studies that adverse variances are often an important sign of problems and indicate a need to tighten internal control.

Managers may consider the following issues when deciding whether to investigate further.

(a) **Materiality. Small variations in a single period** are bound to occur and **are unlikely to be significant**. Obtaining an 'explanation' is likely to be time consuming and irritating for the manager concerned. The explanation will often be 'chance', which is not particularly helpful.

(b) **Controllability.** Controllability must also influence the decision whether to investigate further. If there is a general worldwide price increase in the price of an important raw material there is **nothing that can be done internally** to control the effect of this.

(c) **Variance trend.** If, say, an efficiency **variance** is £1,000 adverse in month 1, the obvious conclusion is that the process is **out of control** and that corrective action must be taken. This may be correct, but what if the same variance is £1,000 adverse every month? The **trend** indicates that the process is **in control** and the standard has been wrongly set.

(d) **Cost.** The likely cost of an investigation needs to be weighed against the cost to the organisation of allowing the variance to continue in future periods.

(e) **Interrelationship of variances.** Quite possibly, individual variances should not be looked at in isolation. One variance might be interrelated with another, and much of it might have occurred only because the other, interrelated, variance occurred too.

4.4.9 Feedback from customers

Customer responses, particularly complaints, are important evidence for the board to consider, particularly as regards how controls ensure the **quality of output**.

5 Role of management and internal audit in monitoring or risk and control

Management is responsible for the implementation of effective risk and control monitoring procedures. The board is responsible for ensuring a system of effective monitoring is in place, and for monitoring management's activities.

5.1 Distinction between role of management and role of board

The UK Turnbull report draws a distinction between the role of senior (operational) management and the role of the board.

5.1.1 Role of management

Turnbull emphasises that monitoring forms part of management's role to **implement board policies** on risk and control. Ongoing monitoring is an essential element of a sound system of internal control.

5.1.2 Role of board

Turnbull emphasises that the board cannot just rely on the management monitoring processes to discharge its responsibilities. It should **regularly receive and review reports on internal control** to ensure that management has implemented an effective monitoring system. It should also carry out an annual assessment that forms the basis of its report on internal controls.

Although the board need not understand the details of every management procedure, it should focus on controls performed directly by senior management, and controls designed to prevent or detect senior management override.

We shall examine the board's role further in Section 7 of this chapter.

5.2 Qualities of management

COSO stresses the need for **competence** and **objectivity** in management monitoring.

5.2.1 Competence

This relates to managers' knowledge of how controls operates and what constitutes an effective weakness. Managers must be able to identify the **root causes** and to do this they must have knowledge of the underlying control and the risks the control is designed to mitigate.

5.2.2 Objectivity

Different reviewers provide different levels of objectivity. **Self-review**, review of one's own work, is obviously the least objective. **Review by peers or superiors** is more objective. **Review by impartial evaluators** is the most objective. Impartial evaluators may include internal auditors, people from other departments or external parties. However, because impartial evaluators are distant from the operation of controls, they tend to carry out separate evaluations rather than be involved in ongoing monitoring.

5.3 Role of internal audit in risk management

Internal audit is an independent appraisal function established within an organisation to examine and evaluate its activities as a service to the organisation. The objective of internal audit is to assist members of the organisation in the effective discharge of their responsibilities. To this end, internal audit furnishes

them with analyses, appraisals, recommendations, counsel, and information concerning the activities reviewed.

The role of internal audit will vary according to the organisation's objectives but is likely to include review of internal control systems, risk management, legal compliance, and value for money audits.

This section summarises briefly the role of internal audit. It concentrates on the main issues for this exam, the **independence** of internal audit and its significance as part of the control and risk management systems.

5.3.1 Objectives of internal audit

The role of the internal auditor has expanded in recent years as internal auditors seek to monitor all aspects (not just accounting) of organisations and add value to their employers. The work of the internal auditor is still prescribed by management, but it may cover the following broad areas.

(a) **Review of the accounting and internal control systems.** The establishment of adequate accounting and internal control systems is a responsibility of management and the directors. Internal audit is often assigned specific responsibility for the following tasks.

   (i) Reviewing the design of the systems

   (ii) Monitoring the effectiveness of the operation of the systems by risk assessment and detailed testing

   (iii) Recommending cost-effective improvements

   Review will cover both financial and non-financial controls.

(b) **Examination of financial and operating information.** This may include review of the means used to identify, measure, classify and report such information and specific enquiry into individual items including detailed testing of transactions, balances, and procedures.

(c) **Review of the economy, efficiency, and effectiveness** of operations. In the public sector especially this helps to determine whether or not value for money has been achieved.

(d) **Review of compliance.** This should be carried out in relation to laws, regulations, and other external requirements, with internal policies and directives, and with other requirements including appropriate authorisation of transactions.

(e) **Review of the safeguarding of assets.** Are valuable, portable items such as computers or cash secured, is authorisation needed for dealing in investments?

(f) **Review of the implementation of corporate objectives.** This includes review of the effectiveness of planning, the relevance of standards and policies, the organisation's corporate governance procedures and the operation of specific procedures such as communication of information.

(g) **Identification of significant business** and financial **risks.** This involves **monitoring** the **organisation's overall risk management policy** to ensure it operates effectively, and **monitoring** the **risk management strategies** to ensure they continue to operate effectively.

(h) **Special investigations.** These can be carried out in particular areas, for example suspected fraud.

It is inevitable that internal audit will focus on **operational controls.** In some companies, however, the problem may be a failure of strategic level controls, due to management override of controls or poor strategic decision-making. However, internal audit's role in relation to strategic controls will be limited, as most checking procedures have been followed at board level. The board must ultimately be responsible for the operation of strategic controls.

You may need to apply your knowledge of what internal audit does to argue in favour of a particular organisation establishing an internal audit function.

5.3.2 Risk based internal audits

Risk-based internal audits are a development of systems audits. Auditors will be concerned to see that managers have put in place **risk assessment processes that are capable of identifying risks on a timely basis** and have **designed robust risk management processes and internal control systems**. Auditors will attempt to confirm that these risk management processes and controls **operate to mitigate risks** and ensure that management **receives accurate information** about risks, particularly high consequences-likelihood risks, risks outside the organisation's risk appetite or risks that have materialised due to serious deficiencies in internal control. Risk audits are not compulsory for all organisations, although in some regulated industries (banking and financial services) a form of ongoing risk assessment and audit is compulsory in most jurisdictions.

Internal audit's work will be influenced by **business objectives**, the risks that may **prevent** the organisation **achieving its objectives** and the organisation's attitude towards risk (that is, its degree of risk acceptance or risk aversion).

The main stages of the risk audit are:

(a) **Identification of risks**

Risk auditors need to identify **what risks** are relevant to the work they will be required to do.

(b) **Assessment of risks**

The auditors need to obtain evidence of the probability of those **risks crystallising** and their **likely impact**. Where the risk management framework is insufficient, auditors will have to rely on their own **risk assessment** and **recommend an appropriate framework**. Where an adequate framework for risk management and control is embedded in operations, auditors will aim to use **management assessment of risks** and concentrate on **auditing the risk management processes**.

(c) **Review of management and controls**

The auditors will assess the **operation and effectiveness** of the **risk management processes** and the **internal controls** in operation to **limit risks**. A comprehensive risk audit will extend to the risk management and control **culture**.

(d) **Reporting**

Reporting will mostly be to the board, or to the audit or risk committee. The report will concentrate on the extent of the **key risks**, the **quality of existing assessment procedures** and the **effectiveness of controls**.

If internal auditors carry out the audit, they should be familiar with the organisation, its systems and procedures, its culture and the regulations that affect it. The internal auditors should be able to carry out a well-targeted audit and report in a way that is appropriate and helpful for the organisation.

However, internal auditors may suffer from the disadvantages of **lack of independence and over-familiarity**. An internal audit may be undermined by internal politics and divisions. An external auditor can provide an unbiased, fresh view. A risk audit carried out by external auditors should give a higher degree of confidence to external stakeholders. It is also possible that external auditors' knowledge of best practice and current developments may be more up to date. The external auditor may have a better awareness of certain risks than internal auditors do.

5.3.3 Independence of internal audit

Although an internal audit department is part of an organisation, it should be **independent** of the **line management** whose sphere of authority it may audit.

Spencer Pickett in the *Internal Auditing Handbook* suggests that the concept of independence involves a number of key qualities.

Objectivity	Judgements made in a state of detachment from the situation or decision
Impartiality	Not taking sides, in particular not being influenced by office politics in determining the work carried out and the reports given
Unbiased views	Avoiding the perception that internal audit is out to 'hit' certain individuals or departments
Valid opinion	The audit opinion should be based on all relevant factors, rather than being one that pleases everyone
No spying for management	Again internal audit should serve the whole organisation. Managers who want their staff targeted might be trying to cover up their own inadequacies
No no-go areas	Being kept away from certain areas will fatally undermine the usefulness of internal audit and mean that aggressive (incompetent?) managers are not checked
Sensitive areas audited	Internal audit must have the abilities and skills to audit complex areas effectively
Senior management audited	Internal audit must cover the management process and not just audit the detailed operational areas
No backing off	Audit objectives must be pursued fully in a professional manner and auditors must not allow aggressive managers to deflect them from doing necessary work and issuing valid opinions

A lack of independence can mean that audits cannot be carried out to the extent and effectiveness desired. Internal auditors may not be able to examine all the areas they'd like to or determine how the areas selected will be audited. They may feel inhibited from carrying out certain procedures for fear of upsetting powerful or vocal managers or staff.

In addition, internal audit will be **trusted more by managers and staff**, and therefore are more likely to have **sensitive information disclosed to them**, if they are felt to be independent.

Also, internal audit's recommendations will only be valuable if they are **influenced solely by what they find**, and not biased by other factors. Factors that can distort the judgements which internal audit make include a willingness to take sides, motives of personal advantage or a desire to use the audit to confirm their own previous judgements (for example a dislike of certain individuals).

6 Enterprise risk management

COSO (The Committee of Sponsoring Organisations of the Treadway Commission) is one of the global leaders in developing guidance on risk management, internal controls, and fraud deterrence, designed to improve organisational performance and governance. COSO first published its enterprise risk management framework in 2004.

Key term

> **Enterprise risk management (ERM):** Is a process, effected by an organisation's board of directors, management and other personnel, applied in strategy setting and across the enterprise, designed to identify potential events that may affect the organisation, and manage risks to be within its risk appetite, to provide reasonable assurance regarding the achievement of organisation objectives.

ERM was a breakthrough at the time it was issued, as prior to that risk management was seen as a 'cost', performed by a separate and often isolated department.

ERM was first time that risk management was integrated with strategy setting performed at board level.

6.1 Characteristics of enterprise risk management (ERM)

ERM is usually more preferred than standard risk management due to the following three characteristics.

(a) **Holistic focus**: This means ERM principles are embedded in the organisation's culture and cover all types of risk across the entire business, recognising that risks in different business units are connected and interrelated. No department or activity is missed.

(b) **Value add focus**: Management activity creates and protects value by naturally linking risk management to strategic decision making at board level, so positive risk opportunities are actively pursued, and not avoided, and negative risk opportunities are managed before a strategic decision is made.

(c) **Formal and informal focus**: Informal factors such as culture, social networks, risk perception, views and opinions of stakeholders are as important as formal risk management tools such as risk mapping and reporting and should feed in the overall risk management process.

The COSO ERM Framework also considers the relationship between strategic, operations, reporting and compliance objectives at each level of the business and the process of effective risk management as demonstrated by the COSO cube.

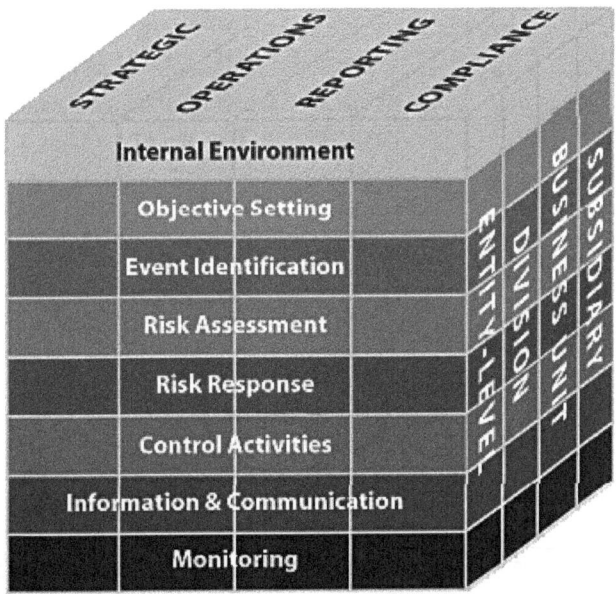

(**Source**: COSO. [Online] Available from: https://www.coso.org/erm-framework [Accessed 3 October 2024])

The top of the cube refers to the scope of risk management – strategic and operational, as well as reporting and compliance with relevant rules and regulations.

The **side** of the cube represents the level of the organisation being addressed, going from organisation level all the way down to individual subsidiaries.

The **face** of the cube shows the risk management process to be followed.

An ERM system **should be proportionate to the level of risk in the** organisation. Larger and more complex organisations have much more exposure to risk than small entrepreneurial businesses. Also, the risk management system should be cost effective for the size of the organisation.

6.2 Enterprise risk management: Process attributes

ERM processes within an organisation should demonstrate the following attributes.

Attribute	Explanation
Operate at every level	ERM operates at every level within the organisation, and it helps people to understand risk and their own responsibility for risk management.
Apply across the organisation	ERM applies to activities at all levels of business, ranging from strategic planning and allocation of resources to business unit activities and business planning.
Identify key risks and how to manage them (risk appetite)	The ERM system helps management to identify and assess the key risks affecting the organisation and to ensure that risks are kept within the tolerance levels set with the board approval, and consistent with the risk appetite of the board.
Provide reasonable assurance of acceptable risk exposure	The ERM system provides reasonable assurance that risks will remain within acceptable limits and the organisation is not exposed to excessive risks. However, risks are uncertain in nature and a risk management system cannot provide absolute or total assurance.
Be aligned with the achievement of objectives	Risk management as well as the pursuit of profit are integral parts of the organisation's management systems.
Be embedded in the culture and processes	ERM policies and procedures are embedded in the culture and operational infrastructure across the organisation.
Include reporting and escalation, and allow whistleblowing	All risks in an ERM system are included in timely, regular, and consistent risk reporting. The key is to provide a summary, holistic 'heat map' of urgent and severe risks which provide a snapshot to senior management for action, with the ability to 'drill down' into detail as required.
Considered by the audit committee and risk management committee	Audit and risk management committees consider all negative and positive risks providing independent scrutiny. This avoids conflict of interest between performance targets and effective risk management within the agreed risk appetite.
Be part of business contingency and continuity planning	For severe risk events which threaten the capacity to operate in the short term (ie IT failure, fire or flood, a business continuity plan is part of the risk response). This would aim to limit the impact of 'cliff edge' risk events.

6.3 Enterprise risk management: Integrating with strategy and performance

The COSO published an update to its ERM guidance (2017) which highlights the need for organisations to look forward and predict risk in new strategy-setting processes, and not simply analyse risk terms of its impact on existing strategies.

Traditionally, organisations have viewed ERM as consequence of strategy, and not part of strategy setting itself.

The COSO ERM 2017 Update emphasises two additional aspects of ERM which potentially impact on an organisation's value:

- Assessing whether a potential strategy aligns with an organisation's mission (its core purpose), vision (what it aims to achieve over time) and core values (its beliefs about what is good or bad, which influence its behaviour)
- Understanding the risk implications of choosing a given strategy including being consistent with the organisation's risk appetite

The COSO ERM 2017 Update has been extended to provide guidance on embedding enterprice risk management systems.

ERM component	Description
Governance and culture (mission, vision, and core values)	This component sets the 'tone at the top' of the organisation in terms of ERM oversight, what is risk and what are the acceptable organisation values and behaviours.
Strategy and objective-setting (strategy development)	This component focuses on using the ERM within the strategic planning process to operationalise the governance and culture values into business objectives, ensuring such objectives are aligned to the organisation's risk appetite.
Performance (business objective formulation)	This component focuses on identifying, assessing, and responding to all risks that can affect the organisation's business objectives (performance), while maintain a portfolio view of the total residual risk assumed by the organisation.
Review and revision (implementation and performance)	This component considers how well the ERM is operating over time and whether any improvements or revisions are necessary.
Information, communication, and reporting (enhanced value)	This component considers how the ERM shares and reports risk information obtained from internal and external sources around the organisation.

(**Source:** COSO. [Online] Available from: https://www.coso.org/_files/ugd/3059fc_61ea5985b03c4293960642fdce408eaa.pdf [Accessed 3 October 2024])

Question

PlumbFast is a plumbing company that started off as a one-person entrepreneur. The business has grown over the years into a large national operation. Over the years, PlumbFast has diversified from domestic and commercial plumbing to domestic and commercial property refit and installation of heating systems, energy efficient windows and solar energy systems PlumbFast has recently acquired a house building business, which it is struggling to integrate in terms of systems and culture. PlumbFast is now considering listing on the UK stock exchange to raise capital to finance further expansion.

Required

Advise the board of PlumbFast on the benefits and challenges of implementing enterprise risk management (ERM) throughout the organisation.

Answer

Benefits of ERM

(a) **Holistic risk management:** Implementing ERM allows PlumbFast to adopt a comprehensive approach to risk management that encompasses all aspects of its operations. By integrating risk management practices across the organisation, PlumbFast can identify, assess, and address risks more effectively, ensuring greater resilience to potential threats and opportunities.

(b) **Value creation:** ERM enables PlumbFast to proactively identify and capitalise on opportunities while mitigating potential risks. By aligning risk management with strategic objectives, the company can make informed decisions that enhance value creation and drive sustainable growth. By leveraging ERM to identify strategic risks and opportunities, PlumbFast can gain a competitive advantage in the market and position itself for long-term success.

(c) **Improved decision-making:** ERM provides PlumbFast's leadership with a structured framework for evaluating risks and making informed decisions. By systematically assessing risks and their potential impact on business objectives, management can prioritise resources, allocate investments, and implement mitigation strategies more effectively. This enhances decision-making processes, reducing uncertainty and maximising the likelihood of achieving organisational goals.

(d) **Enhanced transparency and reporting:** ERM promotes transparency and accountability by providing clear mechanisms for identifying, monitoring, and reporting risks. By establishing robust risk governance structures and communication channels, PlumbFast can ensure that stakeholders are kept informed about key risks and mitigation efforts. This fosters trust and confidence among investors, customers, and other stakeholders, enhancing the company's reputation and credibility.

(e) **Compliance and regulatory alignment:** Implementing ERM helps PlumbFast comply with regulatory requirements and industry standards related to risk management. By integrating risk management into its operations and governance processes, the company can demonstrate its commitment to compliance and risk oversight. This reduces the risk of regulatory penalties, litigation, and reputational damage, safeguarding the company's long-term viability and sustainability.

Challenges of ERM

(a) **Cultural resistance:** Integrating ERM into PlumbFast's organisational culture may face resistance from employees who are accustomed to traditional risk management practices. Overcoming cultural barriers and fostering a risk-aware culture requires strong leadership, effective communication, and ongoing training and education programs to ensure widespread adoption and acceptance of ERM principles.

(b) **Complexity and resource allocation:** Implementing ERM across a large and diverse organisation like PlumbFast can be complex and resource intensive. Allocating sufficient resources, including time, personnel, and financial investments, to develop and maintain an effective ERM framework may pose challenges, particularly during periods of organisational change or expansion. It's crucial for PlumbFast to carefully prioritise its resources and focus on areas of highest risk exposure to maximise the effectiveness of its ERM efforts.

(c) **Integration of acquired businesses:** PlumbFast's recent acquisition of a house building business introduces additional complexities in integrating risk management processes and cultures. Harmonising risk management practices across different business units and ensuring alignment with PlumbFast's overall ERM framework may require careful planning and coordination. Effective communication, collaboration, and change management strategies are essential to facilitate a smooth integration process and minimise disruption to operations.

(d) **Strategic alignment:** Ensuring alignment between PlumbFast's risk management practices and its strategic objectives can be challenging. Balancing risk-taking with risk mitigation efforts while pursuing growth opportunities requires careful consideration and proactive risk management strategies to avoid potential conflicts and inconsistencies. PlumbFast must regularly review and adjust its risk management priorities to align with changing business objectives and market conditions.

(e) **Change management:** Implementing ERM involves significant organisational change, which may encounter resistance from stakeholders accustomed to existing processes and structures. Effective change management strategies, including stakeholder engagement, communication, and training, are essential to overcoming resistance and driving successful ERM adoption. PlumbFast must invest in robust change management processes to ensure buy-in and support from employees at all levels of the organisation.

While implementing ERM offers numerous benefits for PlumbFast, including holistic risk management, value creation, and improved decision-making, it also presents several challenges that must be addressed effectively to maximise its effectiveness and ensure long-term success. By proactively addressing these challenges and leveraging the benefits of ERM, PlumbFast can strengthen its risk management capabilities and enhance its resilience in an increasingly complex business environment.

7 Governance for effective risk management

Organisational wide governance is essential to good governance is an effective board of directors to set the tone from the top, and to elevate the importance of risk and compliance management to a successful, sustainable company.

The following governance structures significantly contribute to this:

(a) UK Corporate Governance Code principles and provisions relevant to risk management
(b) UK Companies Act principle risk disclosure requirements
(c) 'Three Lines of Defence' model

Each of these is explored further in this section.

7.1 UK Corporate Governance Code risk management requirements

The UK Corporate Governance Code provides a framework for effective risk management, with principles and provisions that guide boards in fulfilling their responsibilities to oversee and manage risks in alignment with the company's long-term sustainable success.

These principles align with the Code's key provisions, which are as follows:

- **Risk leadership:** Principle A of the UK Corporate Governance Code underscores the significance of leadership in risk management. It states that 'A successful company is led by an effective and entrepreneurial board, whose role is to promote the long-term sustainable success of the company, generating value for shareholders and contributing to wider society.' This principle highlights the board's responsibility in setting the tone from the top, demonstrating a commitment to risk management and compliance.

- **Board effectiveness:** Principle B of the Code emphasises the importance of board effectiveness, stating that 'The board should establish the company's purpose, values, and strategy, and satisfy itself that these and its culture are aligned.' This principle underscores the need for the board to establish clear objectives and regularly evaluate its performance, including its oversight of risk management.

- **Board accountability:** The UK Corporate Governance Code recommends that companies have clear accountability for risk management, with roles and responsibilities defined and communicated effectively throughout the organisation. Provision 28 of the Code states, 'The board should establish procedures to manage risk, oversee the internal control framework, and determine the nature and extent of the principal risks the company is willing to take in order to achieve its long-term strategic objectives.' This provision emphasises the need for robust governance structures to manage risks.

- **Directors' remuneration:** Principle P of the Code addresses remuneration structures in the context of risk management. It states that 'Remuneration policies and practices should be designed to support strategy and promote long-term sustainable success.' This principle highlights the importance of designing remuneration structures that promote effective risk management and align with the long-term interests of the company.

- **Dialogue with shareholders:** Principle D emphasises the importance of shareholder engagement in risk management. It states that 'There should be a dialogue with shareholders based on the mutual understanding of objectives. The board should ensure that shareholders are provided with timely information about the company.' This principle underscores the board's responsibility to engage with shareholders on matters relating to risk management and provide transparent disclosure on risk-related issues, fostering trust and accountability.

While the UK Corporate Governance Code does not specifically mandate the establishment of a separate risk management group or committee, it underscores the importance of having robust governance structures in place to manage risks.

Many companies choose to establish dedicated risk management committees or groups as part of their governance framework to focus on identifying, assessing, and mitigating risks across the organisation. These committees or groups typically comprise members with relevant expertise and experience in risk management and report directly to the board of directors.

7.2 UK Companies Act principle risk disclosure requirements

Disclosure is an important component of governance around risk management, as full disclosure promotes transparency in reporting, creating trust with stakeholders.

The UK Companies Act requires companies to disclose principle risks in their annual report, providing shareholders and stakeholders with insight into the significant risks facing the company. This disclosure typically includes:

- **Identification of principle risks:** Companies must identify the key risks that may impact their business operations, financial performance, or reputation.

- **Assessment of risk management processes:** Companies should assess the effectiveness of their risk management processes in mitigating identified risks.

- **Mitigation strategies:** Companies should disclose the strategies and measures in place to mitigate the identified principle risks.

- **Forward-looking statements:** Companies may also provide forward-looking statements regarding potential risks and uncertainties that could affect future performance.

7.3 'Three Lines of Defence' model

The 'Three Lines of Defence' model is a widely recognised framework for effective risk management within organisations. It delineates the roles and responsibilities of various stakeholders in mitigating risks and ensuring robust internal controls. In this model, the organisation's risk management practices are divided into three lines, each playing a distinct role in safeguarding against potential threats.

The first line of defence involves internal controls established within each department to manage risks inherent in daily operations. This includes implementing risk management measures, conducting regular risk assessments, and aligning activities with the organisation's risk appetite.

The second line of defence comprises the risk management group, which provides oversight and support to ensure that risk management processes are effectively implemented across the organisation. This group reports to the executive committee and the audit and risk management committee, proposing enhancements to the risk management framework as needed.

The third line of defence involves internal audit, board committees, and the board of directors, which oversee the risk management and internal control systems, ensuring their adequacy and effectiveness.

Additionally, external auditors and stakeholders, such as shareholders, provide additional safeguards against excessive risks. This multi-layered approach to risk management enhances organisational resilience and facilitates compliance with regulatory requirements, fostering trust and confidence among stakeholders.

Each are further explained as follows.

7.3.1 First line of defence: Internal controls

Each department within an organisation has the duty to manage its own risks in the course of its daily operations, including:

- Establishing its own risk management measures for identifying, measuring, mitigating, and monitoring its own risks

- Completing a risk assessment template and submitting its assessment results to the risk management group at least twice a year

- Operating in a manner that is in line with the risk appetite of the Group

- Implementing any risk action plans as advised by the risk management group and/or the internal audit department and/or the audit and risk management committee to address any significant risk that may affect its operation

7.3.2 Second line of defence: Risk management processes

The risk management group is under the direct supervision of the executive committee and also accountable to the audit and risk management committee. Members of this committee comprise the two deputy managing directors, the company secretary, the head of accounting, the head of internal affairs, and the risk manager. The risk management group is primarily responsible for:

- Providing assistance to the board and the audit and risk management committee in overseeing and monitoring the operation of the risk management and internal control systems

- Reviewing the risk assessment results submitted by each department, providing support and guidance to them, and putting forward any risk action plans for implementation by them

- Reporting its work done to the audit and risk management committee at least twice a year

- Proposing any enhancement to the risk management and internal control systems for consideration by the audit and risk management committee and/or the individual department concerned

7.3.3 Third line of defence: Internal audit, board committees, and board of directors

The internal audit department is primarily responsible for:

- Performing audits to evaluate the proper functioning of the risk management and internal control systems
- Reporting its findings to the audit and risk management committee and providing the committee with an independent and objective assurance on the effectiveness of the risk management and internal control systems of the Group
- Putting forward any risk action plans for implementation by relevant departments concerned
- Proposing any enhancement to the risk management and internal control systems for consideration by the audit and risk management committee and/or the risk management group and/or the individual department concerned

The audit and risk management committee assist the board in overseeing the risk management and internal control systems of the Group, including:

- Reviewing, at least annually, the risk management and internal control systems of the Group with the internal audit department to ascertain whether management has fulfilled its responsibilities in establishing and maintaining effective systems
- Reviewing the risk assessment results, including changes in the nature and extent of significant risks since the last review and the Group's ability to respond to changes in its business and the external environment
- Discussing with management on the resources, staff qualifications and experience, training programs, and budget of the Group's accounting, internal audit, and financial reporting functions to ensure that these are adequate
- Considering major investigation findings on risk management and internal control matters as delegated by the board or on its own initiative and management's response to these findings
- Identifying any significant risks that should be drawn to the attention of the board
- Putting forward any risk action plans for implementation by relevant departments concerned
- Reviewing and considering any enhancement to the risk management and internal control systems as proposed by the risk management group and/or the internal audit department

The board of directors has the overall responsibility for establishing and maintaining sound and effective risk management and internal control systems, including:

- Setting the Group's strategies and corporate goals
- Evaluating and determining the nature and extent of the risks it is willing to take in achieving its strategic and business objectives
- Overseeing management in the design, implementation, and monitoring of the risk management and internal control systems
- Overseeing the risk management and internal control systems on an ongoing basis and ensuring that a review of the systems is conducted at least annually to ensure their effectiveness
- Reviewing the changes in the nature and extent of significant risks since the last review and the Group's ability to respond to changes in its business and the external environment
- Considering the scope and quality of management's ongoing monitoring of risks and of the internal control systems

- Considering the extent and frequency of communication of monitoring results to the board
- Considering any significant control failings or weaknesses that have been identified during the period

Additional defences which mitigate against the excessive impacts of risk are external auditors and the organisation's stakeholders, such as shareholders.

Overall, an effective risk governance framework will enhance effective risk management and risk related decision making throughout an organisation and improve transparency and accountability, enabling stakeholders to make informed decisions about the company's risk profile and resilience.

Chapter Roundup

- **Risks** can be classified in various ways, including financial, product, legal, IT, operational, fraud and reputation.

- **Strategic risks** are risks that relate to the fundamental decisions that the directors take about the future of the organisation.

- **Operational risks** relate to matters that can go wrong on a day-to-day basis while the organisation is carrying out its business.

- **Risk identification** involves looking at the specific events and conditions that could result in risks materialising.

- **Risk assessment** involves **analysing, profiling** and **consolidating risks**.

- Methods for dealing with risk include **risk avoidance, risk reduction, risk acceptance** and **risk transference** (TARA framework).

- **Diversification** limits financial risk by taking on a portfolio of different risks constructed so that, should they all crystallise, the outcome will be **neutral**. **Hedging** is the main method used to control **interest rate and exchange rate risks**.

- Internal controls can be classified in various ways including **corporate, management, business process** and **transaction, administrative** and **accounting, prevent, detect,** and **correct, discretionary** and **non-discretionary, voluntary,** and **mandated**.

  The mnemonic **SPAMSOAP** can be used to remember the main types of internal control.

- An organisation's internal controls should be designed to counter the **risks** that are a consequence of the objectives it pursues.

- Sometimes the benefits of controls will be outweighed by their costs, and organisations should compare them. However, it is difficult to put a monetary value on many **benefits** and **costs** of controls, and also the potential losses if controls are not in place.

- To be effective, risk monitoring by management needs to be **ongoing** and to involve **separate evaluation** of systems. Deficiencies need to be communicated to all the appropriate people.

- Management is responsible for the **implementation of effective monitoring procedures**. The board is responsible for **ensuring a system of effective monitoring** is in place, and for **monitoring management's activities**.

- The role of internal audit will **vary** according to the **organisation's objectives** but is likely to include **review of internal control systems, risk management, legal compliance,** and **value for money**.

- Boards should **review risks** and the effectiveness of internal controls regularly.

- Boards should carry out an annual review that looks more widely at risks faced and control systems, and also how these issues should be reported.

End of chapter questions

Question 1

Prestigious Dining Ltd (PDL) is a medium-sized private company which operates in the UK restaurant sector. The company was incorporated in in 2007 and currently operates a chain of twenty-five popular restaurants throughout under the Heritage Club brand. It enjoys a high brand recognition in with affluent, fashionable, and professional customers.

Heritage Club restaurants are often a destination for family celebrations and business dinners. Each of the Heritage Club restaurant sites is large with a seating capacity of at least 200 coupled with additional private dining rooms and events spaces.

Restaurant operations

Each restaurant has its own manager. Historically, restaurant manager attrition is low and many of the twenty-five restaurant managers have been with PDL for over five years. Each restaurant manager is given considerable autonomy to operate their assigned restaurant and to decide on the menu, food pricing, staff recruitment and training, staffing levels and raw ingredient orders which are then purchased centrally by PDL's head office function.

Each restaurant offers the standard Heritage Club choice of meals as a base menu supplemented by daily menu specials determined by the lead chef at each restaurant. Additionally, each restaurant decorated differently, which provides a unique feel to each restaurant, encouraging its customers to visit many of its restaurants to sample different menu choices and enjoy a different dining environment. This strategy has increased return customers who regularly visit different restaurants.

Each restaurant uses tablet technology to record customer orders and each order joins a queue which is displayed in the restaurant kitchen. Restaurant servers must ask the customer to confirm their choices before the order is submitted to the kitchen through the ordering system. Once meals are served, the confirmed order is used to prepare the bill at the end of the meal. All restaurant servers are allowed to amend or cancel any order on the system as customers may add additional items or cancel their orders prior to payment.

Each restaurant manager must control costs by balancing staff levels with customer demand by preparing a weekly staff schedule. The restaurant manager must also minimise raw ingredients wastage, for example, by promoting daily specials and managing raw ingredients order frequency and quantities. Kitchen and waiting staff work a minimum number of hours set by the restaurant manager with overtime work as and when required. Overtime is common as periods of high demand at each restaurant are not always predictable and often staff cover is frequently required for absent kitchen or waiting staff members. Each restaurant manager verbally agrees on overtime with each employee in advance, as and when it is needed. Once the overtime has been worked, the relevant employee will add a record of the overtime worked to the weekly overtime sheet which is kept at the cash register at each restaurant. The overtime sheet is then approved by the restaurant manager at the end of the week and submitted to the head office for payment.

Raw ingredients and beverage supply orders are completed weekly by the restaurant manager and submitted to a centralised purchasing department for order processing. Supplies are delivered directly to each restaurant by suppliers. Deliveries can be signed for by any employee when the deliveries are made to restaurants. As PDL has been using trusted suppliers for many years, deliveries are only checked for quality and quantity on a sample basis.

Raw ingredients are stored in chilled cabinets which are accessible by all employees to ensure supplies can be obtained as needed without delay.

Each restaurant has its own set of methods to manage raw ingredients inventory, in order to minimise raw ingredients wastage and ensure raw ingredients used in meal preparation is within the 'use by' dates printed on labels. It is the responsibility of each restaurant manager to ensure compliance with all food safety, hygiene, and worker related regulations. As all restaurants have passed the official food regulation compliance inspections to date, there were no specific training provided by PDL to restaurant managers in the area of food regulation.

Head office control

PDL's head office is responsible for strategic planning, financial management and legal matters. It also provides marketing support for each restaurant and purchases all raw ingredients and beverages through central purchasing arrangements.

The head office operates financial control activities. A weekly profit statement showing the performance of the restaurant is prepared by head office for a weekly discussion with each restaurant manager by the operations director. The report includes a comparison against the budget for that restaurant and a comparison with the average results for all restaurants. The report contains information such as restaurant income, gross and operating profits, and spending per customer. PDL defines gross profit as sales less the cost of raw ingredients and beverages and restaurant staff wages. Each restaurant is expected to achieve a minimum 30% gross profit margin.

The last six months have been particularly busy for PDL with the opening of two new restaurants and preparations for a possible listing on the UK Stock Exchange which has prevented the operations director from discussing individual restaurant performance with each restaurant manager. The current overall gross profit margin for the company is 41%. However, there are currently two restaurants which are failing to meet the minimum gross profit margin of 30%.

Market research and customer feedback

A market research consultancy is engaged to carry out quarterly customer satisfaction and brand recognition surveys. A customer satisfaction report is submitted each quarter to PDL's board of directors. However, there has been insufficient time to discuss the quarterly reports at recent PDL board meetings. The operations director, of PDL recently reviewed the latest customer satisfaction and brand awareness survey was surprised by some negative customer comments expressing dissatisfaction with the service and food quality at some of PDL's restaurant sites.

Restaurant promotion

Each restaurant manager actively uses social media to promote their restaurant and also uses traditional advertising on billboards, on public transport and in local magazines.

Required

Identify the risks which PDL restaurant operations are exposed to.

For each risk:

(a) Explain the risk identified.
(b) Evaluate the expected likelihood as high, medium, or low and explain your assessment.
(c) Evaluate the expected impact as high, medium, or low and explain your assessment.
(d) Describe a suitable risk control response to mitigate the risk likelihood or impact.

Question 2

Planet Airways (Planet) and Kwik Air (Kwik) both operate in the airline industry and are listed on the UK Stock Exchange.

Planet is an established global airline player that has won many prestigious global awards consistently over the years. It operates long-haul and short-haul flights and serves both full-service and low-cost segments. Beyond the air passenger business, Planet is also significantly involved in the air cargo business. Planet also owns an air engineering subsidiary that provides maintenance, repair and overhaul services for many international carriers, manufacturers, and airports. Planet and its related entities actively pursue strategic alliances with multiple players across the world.

Kwik is a new airline and serves short-haul markets and low-cost segment. It is focused on air passenger services. Kwik is much smaller in its operations as compared with Planet.

Acquisition of Kwik by Planet

There are persuasive business reasons for Planet to complete an acquisition of Kwik to create a new airline, initially named SuperAirways, as Kwik occupies a market segment combination that Planet presently does not operate in. This benefits Planet so that it can enhance its overall portfolio of businesses. There is also opportunity to create operational efficiency reasons through economies of scale, and for strategic reasons to enter new markets, or increase market share, as well as improve integrated flight connections from major cities to smaller towns and coastal resorts.

From key investor discussions, the board of Planet believe its shareholders to be supportive of an acquisition. Being the larger company, Planet will lead on the acquisition and make an acquisition offer to the board of Kwik, for its directors to present to their shareholders. The board of Kwik will make a recommendation to its shareholders whether if supports the acquisition offer, but it will up to the shareholders of Kwik to decide.

As an initial step, the directors of Planet have decided that its chief financial officer should determine a preliminary valuation of Kwik based on assumptions made by the board of directors to support an offer to merge on the basis of Kwik's current quoted market value. Following the acquisition of Kwik, it is assumed that the equity value of SuperAirways will increase by 25% from the current quoted equity values of Planet and Kwik due to revenue and costs synergies.

On-going dispute at Kwik

There have been recent news articles in the past months citing cases of disgruntled airline pilots from Kwik over remuneration packages that are not on par with competitor airlines. These articles highlighted the fallout of the first round of negotiations of salaries and benefits between the union and Kwik, which led to the resignation of a group of senior pilots. These events had resulted in a squeeze in the schedules of the remaining crew, causing them to work more shifts and operate more flights. As negotiations between management and pilots dragged on, the latest news article even carried a rumour on an impending strike at Kwik which might cause some flight disruptions to destinations served by Kwik.

Required

(a) From Kwik' perspective, identify and describe **two** risks which Kwik are exposed to in its current operations, before an acquisition with Planet, for each of the following four categories; strategic, operational, financial and compliance.

(b) From Planet's perspective as acquirer, discuss and evaluate **two** risks which Planet will need to consider as a result of acquiring Kwik, the each of the following four categories; strategic, operational, financial and compliance.

(c) For each risk identified in part (b), provide one recommendation how Planet can mitigate each risk following an acquisition with Kwik.

Suggested answers

Question 1

Covid-19 style pandemic or other similar public health emergency

The emergence of COVID-19, or something similar in the future has multiple impacts and likely to temporarily restrict trading or require government-enforced closure of restaurant sites which will reduce revenue and profits, as fixed restaurant costs, such as rent, will still be incurred by PDL.

Risk evaluation – likelihood

The likelihood is now higher as COVID-19 has shown, due to the large movement of people between cities and countries, aided by aviation. However, this may be mitigated by future government actions to control movement which may limit the spread of future pandemic diseases and the awareness and preventive measures inbuilt in our business processes As a result, likelihood of re-occurrence is considered low.

Risk evaluation – impacts

The impacts are likely to be very high, as follows:

- Reduction of customer demand as people choose to reduce public gatherings
- Enforced social distancing between customers reducing restaurant capacity
- Impact on the food supply chain increasing the scarcity of certain raw ingredients
- Reduction on available workforce restricting the ability of each restaurant to operate at full capacity

Control response

The company should establish a risk management committee whose role will be to establish company policy and procedures which are ready to act in such an event to ensure business continuity and mitigate the risk of business failure. Additionally, PDL should consider establishing an investment fund of liquid assets which would be available in a similar crisis to keep the business running by having sufficient cash to pay workers' wages, suppliers, property rent and business rates for a short-term period. PDL board will need to establish an appropriate fund value based on at least three months of expenses. This will ensure PDL has sufficient liquidity to survive a pandemic, or similar event.

Cancelled sales orders

Restaurant staff are able to cancel restaurant orders without additional authorisation after meals have been consumed. Restaurant staff could be cancelling orders and awarding free meals to friends and family members.

Risk evaluation – likelihood

There is risk that restaurant staff are routinely cancelling meals and awarding free meals resulting in lower margins for PDL as no additional authorisation is required. This risk is mitigated by the presence of the restaurant manager and lack of motivation for restaurant staff to award free meals beyond a small number of friends and family. Therefore, overall likelihood is low.

Risk evaluation – impact

The impact over the year could be material as all restaurant servers at all sites have this opportunity and the entire cost of the meal could still be incurred, and no revenue is earned. However, the overall impact is considered low as the friends and family of servers will be a very small proportion of overall customer volumes.

Control response

The restaurant must have clear policies on change and cancellation of orders, and these must be clearly communicated to the restaurant staff and customers. All cancelled restaurant orders after preparation by the kitchen must be approved by the restaurant manager. The reasons for the cancellation after the food has been prepared must be noted by the restaurant staff on the cancelled order chit and be reviewed by the restaurant manager regularly.

Misappropriation of food inventory

The lack of kitchen security provides the opportunity for restaurant employees to remove items of food for their own use without this being challenged or noticed.

Risk evaluation – likelihood

The likelihood is high as there are no controls, other than personal honesty, preventing this and this could be pervasive across all restaurant sites so the frequency of occurrence could be high.

Risk evaluation – impact

Therefore, the overall impact could be high as required raw ingredient reordering to compensate for this negatively impacts on the gross profit margin at each site.

Control response

Whilst is it possible to implement greater security at restaurant kitchens, the cost of doing so is likely to outweigh the benefit. The performance of regular inventory checks and monitoring of gross margins and food wastage at each restaurant will highlight incidences of significant theft especially where the profit margin at a particular restaurant falls below acceptable levels and is significantly lower than other restaurant sites.

Overtime recording

There is an opportunity for employees to claim more overtime hours than have actually been worked, for themselves and others, as employees are required to record overtime themselves.

Risk evaluation – likelihood

The incidence is likely to be low as employees know excessive claims are likely to lead to dismissal and claims for persistent or unrealistic hours should be noticed by the restaurant manager at the weekly overtime submission.

Risk evaluation – impact

Therefore, the impact on profit will be low given unauthorised overtime will only be a small proportion of the overall labour cost.

Control response

Staff should not be allowed to record their own overtime for payment. The weekly preparation of overtime sheets is done by the restaurant manager or a supervisor, based on overtime authorisations given during the week. This should be implemented at each restaurant to ensure all overtime recorded has been authorised.

Lack of raw ingredients delivery checks

On delivery, there is no requirement for kitchen staff to confirm the items and quantities received against the purchase order and confirm the quality of food items received is sufficient for all deliveries as PDL believes errors will not occur as suppliers are trusted. In reality, errors are likely to occur due to the volume or deliveries across all sites and will go unnoticed. This practice may result in unnecessary reordering and excessive cost if quantities are under-delivered or omitted.

Risk evaluation – likelihood

Given the number of restaurants and delivery, the incidence is likely to be frequent, so likelihood is high.

Risk evaluation – impact

However, the overall impact is mitigated as this would have been observed in lower reported gross margins, so the impact assessment is low.

Control response

The delivery of required quantities of high-quality food items, as ordered, is essential to maintain the restaurant brand. Checking of the quantity and quality of the raw ingredients and authorisation of food deliveries should be limited to senior kitchen staff or the restaurant manager only. The head office should implement food delivery training, so inspections are performed consistently by each restaurant.

Restaurant performance monitoring and reporting

The operations director is currently behind with restaurant performance monitoring and recent performance reporting indicates two restaurants are currently below the minimum required gross profit margin. Problems at these restaurants, or others, may go unnoticed or unresolved as the operations directors are not currently routinely discussing performance with each restaurant manager.

Risk evaluation – likelihood

The likelihood of poor restaurant performance is assessed as low given only 4% of restaurants (2/25) are currently reporting below the target gross margin of 30% and the overall margin is considerably higher at 41%.

Risk evaluation – impact

However, whilst operationally the impact risk is low, there is evidence of underperformance which could be more widespread that initially reported. Avoidable underperformance will certainly impact on PDL's value for its shareholders.

Control response

The monitoring and follow up of restaurant performance is a control priority in order to maximise restaurant efficiency, performance, and value. The operations director appears to be too busy and therefore a performance manager should be appointed to regularly monitor and follow up on restaurant performance. The priority should be to understand and resolve issues contributing to lower profitability at the two restaurant sites which are currently not achieving a 30% gross margin.

Customer satisfaction decline

Recently, the PDL board has not had sufficient time to discuss quarterly customer satisfaction reports. Customers who have eaten in the restaurants and been dissatisfied may not return; potential customers may be deterred by word-of-mouth reports or reviews on the internet.

Risk evaluation – likelihood

The likelihood is low as there is only minor and recent evidence of dissatisfaction in the quarterly customer satisfaction report and there is no evidence of significant dissatisfaction on social media.

Risk evaluation – impact

However, the impact could be high as adverse feedback from customer focus groups is a surprise to the board and may be a recent unnoticed trend. The sharing of adverse feedback on social media can have a wide reach in the future and therefore adversely impact customer demand and brand value.

Control response

PDL should review all social media and customer feedback on a daily basis and respond positively to any negative feedback. Furthermore, the directors should formally review focus group feedback, discuss the results as a regular agenda item at board meetings and take appropriate action as required to address service issues.

Non-compliance with food safety, hygiene, and worker related regulations

Each restaurant has its own set methods to ensure food is disposed of which is past its use-by date. Additionally, each restaurant manager is responsible to ensure compliance with all food safety, hygiene, and worker related regulations rather than a central head office responsibility. This arrangement is likely to lead to variable compliance with food safety, hygiene practices across the restaurant chain.

Risk evaluation – likelihood

The likelihood of non-compliance is high as PDL currently does not provide staff training in these important areas and it is unlikely each restaurant manager has the time to individually research and upskill themselves in all relevant areas of regulation.

Risk evaluation – impact

Should a restaurant fail a food hygiene inspection or is sued by a mistreated worker then the impact could be high as this may negatively affect all restaurants due to adverse public reaction of media reporting of poor hygiene practices or worker mistreatment.

Control response

The board should immediately appoint a food safety and hygiene compliance director who will be responsible for compliance with all food preparation related. Once appointed, a full food regulations audit should be completed at each restaurant with any areas of non-compliance identified and rectified as soon as possible. The new director should also identify any training requirements for restaurant kitchen employees to ensure ongoing regulatory compliance.

Question 2

(a) The following are the main risks of Kwik before its acquisition by Planet.

Strategic risks:

Limited end-to-end services: As a standalone short-haul airline, Kwik Air is unable to provide full end-to-end services and connecting flights to certain locations. This puts Kwik at a competitive disadvantage compared to larger rivals who can offer a more comprehensive travel experience. The inability to offer seamless connectivity may result in lower customer satisfaction and reduced market share.

Limited international presence: Kwik Air's limited international presence poses a significant strategic risk to the airline. With its focus on short-haul markets, Kwik Air may struggle to compete with larger rivals that have well-established global networks and extensive partnerships with international carriers. The lack of international reach hampers the airline's ability to tap into the immense potential of the global market and capitalise on the growing demand for international travel. For example, a limited regional route network and a lack of interest from major airlines in forming strategic alliances.

Operational risks:

Pilot retention: Kwik Air is currently facing signs of pilot dissatisfaction, which poses a risk to the company's operational stability. Retaining skilled and experienced pilots is crucial for maintaining flight schedules, ensuring safety, and providing a high level of service. Implementing effective labour retention management strategies will be essential to address this issue.

Complex global flight management: The airline industry is evolving towards managing flights in a more complex global setting. Kwik Air may face challenges in adapting to this changing landscape, including navigating diverse regulatory frameworks, coordinating with multiple air traffic control systems, and ensuring compliance with international standards. Successfully managing these complexities is essential for maintaining operational efficiency and meeting customer expectations.

Fleet and personnel expansion: Expanding services, particularly into new markets or segments, will require Kwik Air to grow its fleet and personnel. However, achieving significant fleet and personnel expansion in the short term can be challenging due to the time and investment required for aircraft acquisition, pilot training, and recruitment processes. This limitation may hinder Kwik's ability to quickly respond to market demands and capitalise on growth opportunities.

Financial risks:

High gearing: Kwik Air is highly geared compared to Planet Airways. The airline may require additional funds to support its operations, expansion plans, or debt repayment. However, due to its existing high level of leverage, Kwik may face difficulty in securing further borrowing or attracting investors. This financial constraint can impede the company's growth potential and financial stability.

Limited access to capital: Kwik Air's relatively smaller size and weaker financial position compared to Planet Airways pose a significant financial risk. This risk revolves around the airline's ability to access necessary capital for investments, expansion plans, debt refinancing, and other strategic initiatives. The limited access to capital can impede Kwik Air's ability to fuel growth, improve its financial position, and take advantage of opportunities in the dynamic aviation industry. This may manifest in some difficulty in securing favourable financing terms or lack of investor interest in small, listed companies.

Compliance risks:

Regulatory compliance: Given the scale and complexity of regulations in the highly regulated aviation sector, Kwik Air may lack the necessary resources to ensure full compliance with industry standards. Regulatory changes can be substantial and fast-moving, requiring continuous monitoring, adaptation, and investment in compliance measures. The limited resources at Kwik may pose challenges in keeping up with evolving regulatory requirements and maintaining compliance.

Route licensing challenges: As a smaller airline, Kwik Air may face greater challenges in obtaining, managing, and maintaining licenses for routes compared to larger competitors. Securing route licenses is crucial for expanding market reach, establishing competitive positioning, and attracting customers. The comparatively limited resources and influence of Kwik may make it more difficult to win and retain route licenses, further hampering its growth prospects.

(b) From the acquirers' perspective, Planet will assume different risks as compared to Kwik in its roles as acquirer and will be the majority owner and take the lead in the management of the newly merged company. Planet will need to consider the following risks which are from an acquirer's perspective.

Strategic risks:

Integration challenges: The successful integration of Kwik into Planet's operations presents a significant strategic risk. It involves aligning corporate cultures, combining workforce, integrating IT systems, and harmonising processes. Poor integration can lead to inefficiencies, customer dissatisfaction, and loss of key talent. Planet needs to carefully plan and execute the integration process to mitigate these risks and ensure a seamless transition.

Brand consolidation: Consolidating the brands of Planet and Kwik into a unified brand for the newly merged company presents strategic challenges. Maintaining brand equity, managing customer perception, and ensuring a smooth brand transition can be complex. Planet needs to carefully manage the branding strategy to ensure it resonates with customers, maintains brand loyalty, and effectively represents the merged entity's value proposition.

Operational risks:

Operational disruption: Merging two airlines with different operational processes, systems, and procedures can lead to operational disruptions. This includes challenges in managing flight schedules, reservations, baggage handling, and customer service. Planet needs to implement robust operational integration plans, conduct thorough testing, and provide appropriate training to minimise disruptions and ensure a smooth operational transition.

Workforce integration: Integrating the workforce from Kwik into Planet's existing employee base brings operational risks. Differences in company culture, work practices, and labour relations can impact employee morale, productivity, and engagement. Planet needs to develop a comprehensive integration strategy that focuses on effective communication, employee engagement, and the retention of key talent to minimise disruptions and maintain operational efficiency.

Financial risks:

Financial performance: The financial performance of the merged entity is a critical risk for Planet as the acquirer. The successful integration of Kwik's financials, aligning accounting practices, and managing financial reporting can be complex. Planet needs to ensure accurate financial consolidation, effective cost management, and the realization of synergies to maintain or enhance the financial performance of the merged company.

Increased debt and financial obligations: Assuming a majority ownership in the merged entity, Planet may take on additional debt and financial obligations. This includes servicing Kwik's existing debt, potential capital expenditures for integration, and financing growth initiatives. Planet needs to assess the impact of increased leverage, evaluate debt restructuring options, and manage financial obligations effectively to maintain a healthy financial position.

Compliance risks:

Regulatory compliance: Planet needs to ensure compliance with applicable laws, regulations, and industry standards post-merger. This includes compliance with aviation regulations, safety standards, data privacy laws, and labour regulations. Planet should conduct thorough due diligence, establish compliance frameworks, and allocate sufficient resources to mitigate compliance risks and maintain a strong compliance culture within the merged entity.

Antitrust and competition laws: Merging two airlines may attract scrutiny from antitrust authorities, particularly if the acquisition results in a dominant market position. Planet needs to evaluate potential antitrust risks, navigate regulatory approvals, and address any concerns related to competition and market concentration. Compliance with antitrust laws and regulations is crucial to avoid legal implications and potential fines.

(c) The following suggested risk control strategies will help to mitigate the risks discussed in part (b).

Strategic risks:

Integration challenges: Planet can establish a dedicated integration team comprising representatives from both Planet and Kwik. This team can develop a detailed integration plan, clearly define roles and responsibilities, and ensure effective communication throughout the process. Regular progress reviews and feedback sessions can help address any challenges promptly and ensure a smooth integration.

Brand consolidation: Planet should conduct extensive market research to understand customer preferences and perceptions regarding the merged entity's brand. Based on the findings, Planet can develop a comprehensive brand strategy that leverages the strengths of both brands and creates a unified brand identity. Careful communication and brand transition plans can help minimise confusion and maintain customer loyalty.

Operational Risks:

Operational disruption: Planet should implement a phased integration approach, allowing for gradual system integration and testing. This can help identify and address operational challenges in a controlled manner. Comprehensive training programs and workshops can be conducted to familiarise employees with new processes and systems, ensuring a smooth transition without disrupting day-to-day operations.

Workforce integration: Planet should prioritise open and transparent communication with employees from both Planet and Kwik. Establishing cross-functional teams and organising team-building activities can help foster collaboration and create a unified company culture. Recognising and addressing employee concerns promptly, offering career development opportunities, and implementing fair HR policies can promote employee satisfaction and retention.

Financial risks:

Financial performance: Planet should establish key performance indicators (KPIs) and financial targets for the merged entity. Regular financial reviews, performance tracking, and reporting can provide insights

into the financial health of the company. Identifying cost-saving opportunities, optimising operational efficiencies, and leveraging synergies can contribute to maintaining or improving the financial performance of the merged entity.

Increased debt and financial obligations: Planet should work closely with financial advisors to evaluate the optimal capital structure for the merged entity. This can include exploring refinancing options, negotiating favourable debt terms, and optimising the use of available financial resources. Careful financial planning and budgeting can help manage the increased debt and obligations while ensuring sufficient liquidity for growth initiatives.

Compliance risks:

Regulatory compliance: Planet should establish a dedicated compliance team responsible for monitoring and ensuring compliance with all applicable laws and regulations. Regular internal audits and training programs can help educate employees on compliance requirements. Collaboration with external experts and industry associations can provide insights into regulatory changes and help stay ahead of compliance obligations.

Antitrust and competition laws: Planet should engage legal experts specialising in antitrust and competition laws to conduct a thorough assessment of the potential impact of the acquisition on market competition. If required, Planet can propose remedies or divestitures to address any concerns raised by antitrust authorities. Proactive engagement with regulatory bodies and maintaining transparent communication can help mitigate antitrust risks effectively.

Impact of emerging technology

Topic list	Syllabus reference
1 Introduction to technology in MDCS	All MDCS syllabus learning outcomes
2 The role of managers and accountants in the digital world	"
3 Emerging technology	"
4 Automation in business	"
5 Data analytics	"
6 Change management	"
7 Implementing new information systems	"

Introduction

In this chapter, we will look at how the digital revolution, powered by digital technology and data, has transformed the finance function and the role of accountants, as well as businesses in general. We shall see that the role of accountants has shifted from being providers of information, to providing real business insights that can support the organisation. To a large extent, this change has been necessary due to advances in automation.

How accountants deal with new technologies (such as artificial intelligence, blockchain, data security, and the cloud) as well as how data is collected and shared is becoming increasingly important. Therefore, we shall look at the information systems that organisations need to handle and share data in the new digital world, before looking at big data and data analytics.

Finally, we will look at the costs, benefits and risks of new information systems, as well as seeing how they can be implemented.

1 Introduction to technology in MDCS

In this chapter, we will explore how changes in technology and data analysis are reshaping the finance function, the role of accountants, and businesses overall.

Understanding the evolving role of accountants and the impact of emerging technologies on finance functions and businesses is essential.

Additionally, it is crucial for students to grasp how technological developments are influencing real-world companies and may be incorporated into multi-disciplinary case study scenarios. For instance, automation has led to a transformation in the traditional role of accountants, shifting them from mere providers of information to advisors who offer valuable business insights to boards of directors, supporting organisational objectives.

As technology continues to progress rapidly, it is imperative for MDCS students to comprehend how these innovations drive change across various industries. Familiarity with emerging technologies like artificial intelligence, blockchain, data security, and cloud computing is necessary for students to effectively navigate change and make informed decisions in exam scenarios.

Exploring the costs, benefits, and risks associated with new information systems enables students to develop the skills required to evaluate technology implementations and contribute strategically to organisational success.

Furthermore, consideration of the ethical and regulatory aspects related to data privacy and security provides students with a comprehensive understanding of the challenges and responsibilities accompanying technological advancements in the digital age.

2 The role of accountants in the digital world

2.1 Basic finance activities of accountants

The white paper mentioned above identifies four basic interconnected finance activities required of accountants in the digital world.

The basic functions are:

- **Assembling information** – collecting, cleaning and connecting data into assembled information (such as financial and management accounts and returns)
- **Analysing for insights** – analysing financial and non-financial information to draw out patterns and relevant insights
- **Advising to influence** – communicating the above insights and contributing to an objective, responsible perspective which will influence decision making
- **Applying for impact** – guiding actions to help organisations achieve the required impact, including enabling and using control systems such as strategic planning, budgeting, performance measures and performance reviews
- **Acumen** – the finance function applies acumen to help it assemble valuable information (such as reports and analysis) and inform the consideration of subsequent proposals. It is acumen that connects each of the four activities above to each other.

Therefore, the basic activities of finance professionals can be thought of as the 5As (assemble, analyse, advise, apply and acumen). They are summarised in the diagram below (which is also known as the information to impact diagram).

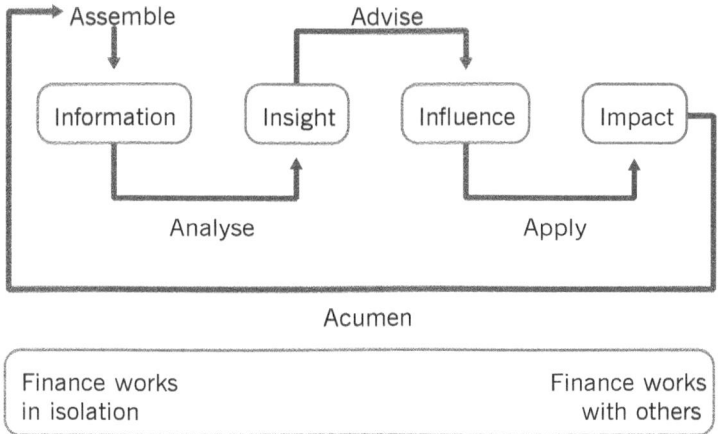

2.2 Impact of the digital world on the role of accountants

The information to impact diagram shows that there is a shift in emphasis between accounting and governance (information and insight roles) and guidance and management (influence and impact roles) as you move along the functions. The role of accountants is changing from providers of information (such as reports and accounts) to providers of business insights that supports all of the organisation's functions.

Later on, we shall see that automation is playing an important role in assembly and analysis activities. This has the effect of freeing up finance professionals to focus on advising and applying activities. This means that finance professionals must keep up to date with technology and to acquire the necessary skills to provide the influence and impact required of them.

The white paper concludes by summarising five key areas of value that accountants bring to an organisation.

- **Reporting accuracy** – a balance between effort, accuracy and relevance (linked to data integrity)
- **Partnering and decision support** – partnering helps businesses make better decisions (linked to value enabling and stewardship)
- **Controllership and risk** – robust controls which are embedded across core financial processes provide surety over figures (linked to data integrity)
- **Enterprise-wide cost management** – enables cost transparency and the identification of opportunities to reduce costs (linked to value analysis and value enabling)
- **Analysis and insight** – increased level and quality of insight provided to businesses (linked to value analysis)

Rather than this being a potential cause of the extinction of accountancy, these changes are driving substantial savings in time that enable accountants to act as internal business consultants and therefore add value to an organisation in other ways.

3 Emerging technologies

3.1 The impact of technological developments

The development of technology overtime has allowed the accountant's role to be elevated beyond the recording of transactions in the mechanical work involved in ensuring account balance and are accurate. Technology has allowed much of his historically administrative work to be automated, freeing the accountant's role up for more value adding work.

Farrar (2019) explains that technologies increase the value of workers (and in particular, accountants) in three ways:

- It enables them to work faster.
- It enables them to work more efficiently.
- It makes them more productive in developing new skills to complete new tasks.

These attributes of technology can be seen as an opportunity for accountants to elevate their role to a more strategic level, where they can have more commercial value to the business than ever before. It could also be viewed as a threat to certain roles in the finance department, such as those that historically have processed transactions as technology is increasingly making this type of role redundant for humans.

Weather in opportunity or a threat, technology is here to stay and continues to advance so the finance function needs to adapt its skill sets to keep up and make the best use of technology in the finance function and in the wider workplace.

3.1.1 Cloud computing

Key term

> **Cloud computing:** Is a model for enabling ubiquitous, convenient, on-demand network access to a shared pool of configurable computing resources (eg networks, servers, storage, applications and services) that can be rapidly provisioned and released with minimal management effort or service provider interaction (National Institute of Standards and Technology, 2011)
>
> (**Source**: NST. [Online] Available from:
> https://nvlpubs.nist.gov/nistpubs/legacy/sp/nistspecialpublications800-145.pdf [Accessed 3 October 2024])

A cloud can be private or public. A public cloud service provider provides cloud services to anybody through the Internet. A private cloud is limited in terms of who is able to access those services. An entirely private cloud will be hosted within one organisation. A hybrid of the two is a 'virtual private cloud' which is in fact hosted using public cloud resources, but looks, feels and works like a private cloud.

The goal of cloud computing is to provide easy, scalable access to computing resources and IT services.

A cloud computing service has distinct characteristics that differentiate it from traditional hosting:

Characteristic	Explanation
Sold on demand	Users pay for cloud services only when they use them (for example by the day, month or year).
Elastic	Cloud computing shifts the bulk of IT costs from capital expenditures (or buying and installing servers, storage, networking and related infrastructure) to an operating expense model, where users pay for the usage of these types of resources.
Fully managed	Users do not have to set up any machines, manage their systems, update them, or back them up as these aspects are mostly taken care of for the users by the service provider.
On-demand and self-service	Cloud computing allows for the expansion and reduction of resources according to specific service requirements.

Benefits and risks of cloud computing

Cloud computing may provide an organisation with a number of benefits; however, these need to be considered against the risks:

Benefits	Risks
Using cloud computing services may be more cost effective than operating in-house technology.	The organisation has to give up control of its data to an external party being the cloud-based service provider. Such providers may be in remote

Benefits	Risks
	locations and as a result this increases the risk should the provider suffer some form of disaster event.
Cloud computing offers greater flexibility to organisations as there are lots of service providers around to choose from.	Data held by the service provider may be stolen, lost or corrupted.
Establishing a cloud-based approach to data storage and management can be done more quickly than establishing the technology in-house.	Increased danger that the service provider's own staff may interfere with data stored on its servers.
Storing organisational data on the cloud means that it is accessible anywhere around the world where there is internet connectivity.	Failure to keep up payments to the service provider to store data on the organisation's behalf may lead to a loss of access or even the deletion of data.
Cloud computing is available to both very large organisations and smaller entities.	

Cloud computing is changing the structure and working of the finance function by:

- Allowing flexible working as staff can work in different locations at different times
- Allowing collaboration as files can be shared and updated by multiple staff in real-time
- Keeping software continuously up to date and improving compliance with data protection regulations
- Improving the integration of software as, for example, customer relationship management software can be linked to accounting software
- Improving data security as cloud providers better understand how to protect data

Finance functions use cloud computing in a similar way to other parts of the business. Files and software can be stored in cloud servers so that they can be easily shared by all users and accessed by employees whether they are located in the organisation's offices or not.

One application of cloud computing that is specific to finance functions is cloud accounting. Cloud accounting is the provision of accountancy software through the cloud. Users log in to the accountancy software to process financial transactions and produce management reports through a web browser. The software is hosted through the cloud but essentially behaves in the same way as if the software was installed on their own machine.

Examples of providers of cloud accounting software include QuickBooks, Xero and Sage.

This means accounting processing can be conducted from anywhere, at any time. All that is required is a web browser. The output can also be easily shared around without having to email what is quite possibly commercially sensitive information.

3.1.2 Process automation

Key term

Process automation: Refers to the ability of systems to perform routine activities (such as the processing of data and assembling electronic components) without the input of a human. It is important to note this is not limited to physical automation (eg of production lines), but online automation, for example processing and responding to customer queries.

Robotic process automation (RPA) is the term given to the use of technology to facilitate the automation of previously manual and often routine processes. This increases speed, reliability and efficiency of processes and reduced staff costs.

We shall look at automation again later in this chapter when we shall see how it has transformed the finance function.

3.1.3 Artificial intelligence (AI)

Key term

> **Artificial intelligence (AI):** Refers to the ability of a machine to perform cognitive functions we associate with human minds, such as perceiving, reasoning, learning and problem solving' and acting in a way that we would consider to be 'smart' (McKinsey and Co, no date).
>
> **Machine learning:** Is an application of AI in which systems or machines can learn from very large data sets, identify patterns and make decisions with minimal human intervention.

AI is a field of computer science that can mimic human intelligence. It is a technology that we can use to create systems that simulate human intelligence – eg Apple's Siri or Amazon's Alexa.

AI is driven by machine learning.

A machine's learning algorithm empowers it to recognise patterns within observed data, constructing models that elucidate these patterns or make predictions. A fundamental characteristic of machine learning is its iterative nature: as models encounter new data, they autonomously adapt, modifying the underlying algorithm based on insights gained from the data.

AI enables computers to learn from data, enabling accurate execution of novel tasks and the generation of dependable decisions and outcomes. Consequently, AI, founded on machine learning, empowers organisations to make decisions without direct human involvement.

Machine learning manifests in various forms:

- **Supervised learning:** In this approach, training data and human feedback are used to demonstrate relationships between inputs and outputs. This entails human labelling of input data and output data. The algorithm learns to correlate inputs and outputs, and upon completion, is applied to new data.

- **Unsupervised learning:** Here, an algorithm explores input data without explicit output variables. The algorithm receives unlabelled data, deduces data structures, and identifies groups of behaviour with similar patterns.

- **Reinforcement learning:** This type involves an algorithm learning to perform a task, aiming to maximise rewards for its actions. The process includes the algorithm taking an action, receiving a reward if the action aligns with the objective, and optimising its actions over time by self-correction.

Machine learning algorithms do not require explicit programming but instead learn by doing. They adapt to new data and experiences, progressively enhancing their effectiveness in performing tasks and generating dependable decisions. An illustrative example is the predictive text feature on smartphones and internet search engines, where the algorithm becomes more accurate in predicting user inputs based on their past texts or searches.

Machine learning decisions are based on three important aspects of analytics:

- **Description** ('descriptive analytics'): shows correlations between historic and current variables, and attempts to explain the correlation

- **Prediction** ('predictive analytics'): anticipating what will happen, based on the data and patterns in the data

- **Prescription** ('prescriptive analytics'): providing recommendations for what to do in order to achieve goals or objectives

Applications of AI

The following are some examples of the ways AI and machine learning can be applied:

- **Transportation** – autonomous vehicles (self-driving cars) could potentially transform the way people move around.
- **Route optimisation** – analysing real-time information to identify potential problems and traffic jams, and to suggest alternative routes, can be very important for transport and delivery companies.
- **Personalised recommendations** – websites recommend items a customer might want to buy based on buying history (eg Amazon), or Netflix recommends programmes to watch based on previous viewing.
- **Healthcare** – machines can record and process vast amounts of patient data and can analyse it using sophisticated AI algorithms. As such, technology can be used to diagnose illnesses and create personalised medicines based on a deep knowledge of a person's genetics to help clinicians do their jobs more effectively. AI can also help to predict people who are at risk from certain diseases and target them for early intervention, thereby reducing the cost of future treatments which would otherwise be required.
- **Portfolio management** – 'robo-advisors' (eg Betterment or Wealthfront) use algorithms to tailor investment portfolios to the goals and risk appetite of the investor, and to adjust these for real-time changes in the market.
- **Fraud detection** – detecting anomalies in patterns of payments or receipts.
- **Cybersecurity** – AI makes decisions very quickly. One of the problems that cyber defence teams face is that they get so many alerts it is difficult to know how to prioritise them. AI can detect anomalies, and so can alert defence teams to the specific data they need to look at.

Note. In many of these cases, the volume of data available enables algorithms to find patterns and trends. In effect, AI is being used to analyse 'big data' – so it is important to note the links between AI and big data in this context.

Benefits and limitations of AI

AI offers many benefits to organisations but does not come without problems and limitations.

Benefits of AI	Limitations of AI
AI is able to quickly process large amounts of structured and unstructured data, providing fast, accurate and reliable outputs.	Although machine learning enables machines to adapt algorithms, the technology is only as good as the data it receives. (Maintaining high-quality data is crucial to a successful AI platform.)
AI can identify complex patterns in data, to enable better decision making and strategic planning.	Machines 'learn' from the data they are given, but if there are gaps or biases in the initial 'training' data, then the models the machines learn could be incomplete or inaccurate.

Benefits of AI	Limitations of AI
Machine learning can provide consistency with regard to decision making. Machines do not suffer tiredness like humans do, and technology does not have cognitive bias like humans do. Also, crucially, machines' capacity for learning means they are able to process data and identify patterns without the need for human monitoring. Note, this is an important feature that distinguishes AI from big data analytics. Patterns and trends in data are also identified in big data analytics, but in AI the machines identify the trends and issues themselves without being prompted to do so by people.	Machine learning models can lack flexibility; they can learn to carry out specific tasks but cannot reproduce the level of multifaceted analysis carried out by the human brain. (For example, the technology in an autonomous vehicle enables it to drive a car, but it can only perform tasks related to driving the car.)

Some examples of how AI can support the finance function include:

- Simple processes can be automated, such as highlighting significant variances for further investigation.
- Predictive analytics can help forecast costs and revenues
- AI enables improved analysis of unstructured data in contacts and emails, for example sifting through an email database for discussion around certain topics.

Case Study

Ocado, is a UK-based online grocery retailer which takes customer orders through its website or mobile app, where customers browse and select items for purchase. Once an order is placed, Ocado's AI-powered systems spring into action to ensure seamless order fulfilment and delivery.

Ocado's strategic integration of artificial intelligence into its business processes has enabled the company to streamline operations, optimise logistics, improve customer service, and maintain its position as a leader in the online grocery market.

In Ocado's highly automated warehouses, AI-powered robots navigate shelves, pick and pack grocery items, and manage inventory. These robots utilise advanced machine learning algorithms to optimise their movements, ensuring efficient order fulfilment and minimising errors. By automating the picking process with AI, Ocado has significantly increased the speed and accuracy of order processing, enabling faster delivery times and enhancing customer satisfaction.

Additionally, Ocado employs AI-driven predictive analytics to forecast demand, optimise inventory management, and personalise recommendations for customers. By analysing vast amounts of data, including past purchases, browsing behaviour, and seasonal trends, Ocado's AI algorithms can anticipate customer preferences and tailor product offerings accordingly. This personalised approach not only enhances the shopping experience but also drives higher sales and customer loyalty.

Furthermore, Ocado's AI-powered routing and scheduling algorithms optimise delivery routes in real-time, considering factors such as traffic conditions, delivery windows, and vehicle capacity. By dynamically adjusting delivery schedules based on changing conditions, Ocado maximises efficiency, reduces fuel consumption, and minimises environmental impact.

Question

You are a manager working in a company's procurement department for a large organisation. The procurement team is responsible for undertaking all procurement-related business management activities and overseeing procurement forecasting, transaction recording in the financial systems, and analysis.

Required

Explain how AI might support a manager working in a company's procurement department?

Answer

By integrating AI into the procurement team's workflow, a procurement manager can enhance efficiency, accuracy, and strategic decision-making, leading to improved procurement processes and outcomes for the organisation. AI can provide the following specific support:

- **Automated data entry and processing:** AI-powered systems can automatically process incoming procurement documents, such as purchase orders, invoices, and contracts, extracting relevant data and populating procurement systems. This reduces manual effort and minimises errors in data entry.

- **Supplier performance analysis:** AI algorithms can analyse historical supplier data, including delivery times, product quality, and pricing, to assess supplier performance and identify opportunities for improvement or potential risks. This enables procurement managers to make informed decisions when selecting or negotiating with suppliers.

- **Demand forecasting:** AI can analyse historical procurement data and external factors, such as market trends and seasonality, to forecast future demand for goods and services accurately. This helps procurement managers anticipate resource requirements and optimise inventory levels to meet demand while minimising excess or shortages.

- **Price optimisation:** AI-powered analytics can analyse market trends, supplier pricing strategies, and historical procurement data to identify opportunities for cost savings and negotiate better prices with suppliers. This enables procurement managers to achieve optimal pricing and maximise value for the organisation.

- **Contract management:** AI can assist in contract lifecycle management by automating contract creation, review, and renewal processes. It can also analyse contract terms and conditions to identify potential risks or opportunities for cost savings, ensuring compliance and mitigating contract-related risks.

- **Supplier relationship management:** AI-driven tools can monitor and analyse interactions with suppliers, including communication, performance, and feedback, to assess supplier relationships and identify areas for improvement or intervention. This supports procurement managers in fostering strategic partnerships and driving supplier performance.

- **Market intelligence:** AI can gather and analyse data from various sources, such as news articles, industry reports, and social media, to provide insights into market trends, competitor strategies, and emerging risks or opportunities. This enables procurement managers to make informed decisions and adapt procurement strategies to changing market conditions.

- **Risk identification and mitigation:** AI algorithms can assess various types of risks associated with procurement, such as supply chain disruptions, regulatory compliance, and supplier financial stability, enabling procurement managers to proactively identify and mitigate risks to minimise potential negative impacts on operations.

- **Sustainability analysis:** AI can analyse supplier data and product information to evaluate sustainability metrics, such as carbon footprint, ethical sourcing, and social responsibility, helping

procurement managers make environmentally and socially responsible procurement decisions aligned with corporate sustainability goals.

- **Performance monitoring and reporting:** AI-driven dashboards and analytics tools can provide real-time visibility into procurement performance metrics, such as cost savings, supplier performance, and compliance, enabling procurement managers to track progress, identify areas for improvement, and communicate results to stakeholders effectively.

3.1.4 Distributed ledger technology and blockchain

Key term

Distributed ledger technology: Is a technology that allows organisations and individuals who are unconnected to share an agreed record of events, such as ownership of an asset.

Blockchain: Is a public form of bookkeeping that uses a digital ledger to allow individuals to share a record of transactions.

Distributed ledger technology eliminates the need for data and information to be stored and managed centrally. Furthermore, it allows an accurate, up-to-date, single, trusted and transparent record to be shared between numerous parties.

Blockchain is a type of incorruptible distributed ledger that allows information to be recorded and shared with a network of individuals. In essence, blockchain is a public form of bookkeeping which makes use of internet technologies to instantly verify and record the transactions that take place between individuals. The public nature of blockchain means that every individual can view the transactions made by participants in that network. This means that participants can view the date, time, value of transactions, and the individuals involved, thereby creating a shared record of events.

It is anticipated that blockchain will have a disruptive impact on a wide range of industries as it increases the levels of transparency over transactions. Greater use of blockchain should allow organisations including firms of accountants and auditors to more easily verify the transactions undertaken by clients when preparing (and auditing) financial statements. The use of blockchain should also make it easier for accountants to verify the background and transactional history of prospective new clients, especially when undertaking money laundering procedures. Blockchain will also be beneficial to providers of finance as they will be able to make more informed decisions about which prospective clients they should lend to.

Participants of a blockchain record transactions on an online network that is publicly available and distributed to everyone.

Details of transactions are recorded by all participants. Transactions are only accepted once all participants have updated their ledgers to reflect them.

Network computers verify the transaction to make sure the records have all been updated correctly. Once the validation work is complete, the transaction is authorised and added to the blockchain. This means that a single system cannot itself add new blocks to the chain.

Blocks are connected to a blockchain using a cryptographic hash that is generated from the previous block. This means the chain cannot be broken and each block is preserved permanently. It is only possible to amend previous blocks if the subsequent blocks are altered first.

Stages in a blockchain transaction	Description
Stage 1	A transaction is requested
Stage 2	A digital representation of the transaction is requested (a block)
Stage 3	The block is sent to all nodes in the network (distributed ledger)

Stages in a blockchain transaction	Description
Stage 4	The authenticity of the transaction is verified by each node
Stage 5	A reward for the verification is sent to each node (such as a bitcoin)
Stage 6	The completed and authorised block is added to the chain

The ICAEW's report *Blockchain and the Future of Accountancy* (ICAEW, 2018) identifies three key features of blockchain, known as the Three Ps.

(a) **Propagation.** There are many copies of a blockchain ledger, but no master copy. All versions are identical. When new transactions occur, they propagate to all copies of the blockchain.

(b) **Permanence.** Every user has their own copy of the blockchain, and past transactions cannot be edited (except by consent of the majority). Therefore, the blockchain is a permanent record. Each copy can be inspected and verified.

(c) **Programmability.** Blockchains may allow program code to be stored as well as transaction information. Such code may create ledger entries when triggered, allowing so-called smart contracts, which carry out actions automatically when certain conditions are met.

Case Study

A real-world example of a global company utilising blockchain technology is IBM. IBM has been actively exploring and implementing blockchain solutions across various industries, including supply chain management, finance, healthcare, and more.

One prominent initiative by IBM is the IBM Food Trust platform, which leverages blockchain technology to enhance transparency and traceability in the food supply chain. The platform allows food retailers, suppliers, growers, and distributors to track the journey of food products from farm to table, thereby ensuring food safety, reducing waste, and improving efficiency.

Through the IBM Food Trust platform, participants in the supply chain can access a secure and immutable record of every transaction and movement of food products. This transparency enables quick identification of the source of foodborne illnesses or contamination outbreaks, facilitating targeted recalls and minimising the impact on public health.

IBM Food Trust has been adopted by major food retailers and manufacturers worldwide, including Walmart, Carrefour, Nestlé, and Dole, among others. By implementing blockchain technology, IBM has helped these companies enhance consumer trust, streamline supply chain operations, and meet regulatory compliance requirements.

This real-world example demonstrates how blockchain technology, as implemented by IBM, is transforming traditional supply chain practices and driving innovation in food safety and traceability on a global scale.

Question

You are the accountant for a business owner who sells handmade crafts online. Your client often faces challenges with tracking inventory, managing orders, and ensuring timely deliveries to your customers.

Required

Explain how blockchain technology could help streamline and secure the business operations of this online retailer.

Answer

- **Enhanced transactional transparency:** Blockchain technology allows for a transparent and immutable record of all transactions related to inventory management, order processing, and delivery tracking. This transparency ensures that both the business owner and customers can track the movement of goods in real-time, reducing disputes and improving trust.

- **Improved inventory management:** With blockchain, each item in the inventory can be assigned a unique digital identifier or 'token' that is recorded on the blockchain. This allows for accurate tracking of inventory levels, including when items are added, sold, or restocked. By having a transparent and tamper-proof ledger of inventory data, the business owner can optimise stock levels, minimise stockouts, and prevent overstocking.

- **Secure supplier order processing:** Blockchain technology enables secure and tamper-proof order processing by recording each transaction on a decentralised ledger. This eliminates the risk of fraudulent orders or unauthorised changes to order details. Additionally, smart contracts can be implemented to automate order processing tasks, such as payment verification and order fulfilment, based on predefined conditions.

- **Traceability in supply chain:** Blockchain provides end-to-end traceability in the supply chain, allowing the business owner to track the origin and movement of raw materials, components, and finished products. This transparency helps ensure the authenticity and quality of products, which is particularly important for handmade crafts where craftsmanship and materials are valued by customers.

- **Enhanced security:** Blockchain technology uses cryptographic techniques to secure data and transactions, making it highly resistant to hacking and fraud. By storing sensitive business information on a decentralised and encrypted ledger, the business owner can mitigate the risk of data breaches and unauthorised access to customer data or financial records.

- **Streamlined customer experience:** By leveraging blockchain for order tracking and delivery management, the business owner can provide customers with a seamless and transparent shopping experience. Customers can track the status of their orders in real-time, receive notifications about shipment updates, and have confidence in the security and authenticity of their purchases.

- **Efficiency cost savings:** Implementing blockchain technology can lead to cost savings for the business owner by reducing manual errors, streamlining administrative processes, and minimising the need for intermediaries in supply chain transactions. This ultimately results in improved operational efficiency and lower overhead costs.

Distributed ledger technology and blockchain can increase the clarity and transparency in the recording of business transactions.

Key uses are in regard to measuring the value of assets and verifying asset ownership and accounting transactions, which are of interest to financial reporting and internal audit. Accurate and transparent records can be created of asset ownership and associated transactions. This helps to reduce the need for internal auditors and financial accountants to check transactions and verify the ownership of assets because they have a source of information about the assets that they can trust.

Blockchain may have the following impacts on the finance function:

- Cryptocurrency (see below) allows money to cross borders easily and seamlessly by avoiding traditional intermediaries such as banks.
- The security and traceability of transactions may impact how businesses record their dealings with third parties.
- Smart contracts can be created which are self-executing agreements that utilise cryptography, digital signatures and secure completion. If certain obligations are met, they can be automatically executed on a particular date and time.

3.1.5 Cryptocurrencies

Cryptocurrencies such as bitcoin are digital tokens that allow users to trade with each other online. They are an alternative to traditional currencies.

Many of the cryptocurrencies use distributed ledgers and blockchain technology to maintain records of transactions, and owner's currencies are kept in 'digital wallets'. Unlike traditional currencies, no third parties (such as banks or online payment agencies) are required to record transactions. This can save transaction costs and provide greater privacy to the traders.

There is still scepticism amongst individuals, and regulatory institutions concerning cryptocurrencies. Companies would be mindful of the following concerns:

- As cryptocurrencies are unregulated by a central bank, their values are often exceptionally volatile.
- Cryptocurrencies provide anonymity to traders, meaning that they can be used to finance illicit activities (eg cybercriminals often demand payment in cryptocurrency).
- A number of governments have banned the use of cryptocurrencies which may limit their acceptability as a means of payment.

3.1.6 Internet of things (IoT)

Key term

> **The internet of things:** Include physical devices with internet connectivity enabling them to interact with many other devices via the internet, as well as enabling the user to control them remotely. For example, the Amazon Echo can play music, make calls, set alarms/timers, answer user questions, manage shopping lists, control Bluetooth enabled lights and so on.

The internet of things includes smart devices, sensors and security devices which are connected over the internet to perform a range of tasks. They can record and store data as well as transferring the data over the internet to other devices. They can also be controlled remotely by other connected devices, such as apps on a smart phone.

By combining connected devices with automated systems, it is possible to gather information, analyse it and create an action to perform a task or learn from a process.

The internet of things provides businesses with more data about the products or services, thereby improving their ability to make changes.

The following are some of the potential applications of the internet of things:

- Sensors on products (or components) transmit data about how that product is performing. This can help a company identify if a product, or component, is likely to fail, meaning it can carry out preventative maintenance before the failure causes any damage.
- Real-time data generated by sensors on products can be used to make supply chains more efficient, for example by being able to track the location of freight which is being delivered. (RFID – radio frequency identification – can also be useful in inventory and supply chain management,

allowing organisations to keep track of assets by tagging them.) Sensors monitoring traffic flows can provide information about the best routes for delivery drivers to take.

- Sensors in smart buildings can adjust temperature automatically – for example, turning on air conditioning if sensors detect a conference room is occupied, or turning the heating in a building down once everyone has gone home.

3.1.7 Mobile technology

Mobile technology is concerned with technology that is portable. Mobile technology devices include laptops, tablet computers, smartphones, GPS technologies. Such devices enable users to communicate with one another in different ways, some of which may make use of the internet. Communicative features of mobile technologies include Wi-Fi connectivity, Bluetooth and 4G technologies.

Mobile technology has two types of impact on organisations:

- **New products and services:** For example, organisations can develop apps for smart devices that allow users to control home technology when away from the property (for example, smart thermostats).
- **Freedom of location:** Employees can connect to the internet and their workplace wherever they are, providing they have a mobile phone signal.

3.1.8 Cybersecurity

The following table contains examples of the common types of cybersecurity issues:

Type of cyberattack	Description
Phishing	The cyberattacker sends emails to the victim which appear to be from a trusted source, for example a bank. The emails request the victim sends back security information (such as usernames and passwords) and personal details and the cyberattacker uses this information to steal funds from the victim.
Pharming	Cyberattackers target an organisation's website by automatically redirecting visitors from the organisation's website to a bogus website. The intention is to collect data in order to commit fraud and is similar to phishing.
Hacking	The cyberattacker uses specialist software and other tools to gain unauthorised access to an organisation's computer system and take administrative control. Such control allows them to view and copy system records, as well as amend or delete information that they find. Some hackers may try to stop the system working altogether.
Distributed Denial of Service (DDoS) attack	The cyberattacker attempts to disrupt an organisation's online activities by preventing people from accessing the organisation's website. Botnets (large numbers of individual computers which have been taken over without the user knowing) are instructed to overwhelm the organisation's website with a wave of internet traffic so that the system is unable to handle it and may crash.
Webcam manager	The cyberattacker uses software to take control of the user's webcam.
File hijacker/ransomware	Cyber attackers gain access to the user's system to hijack their files and hold them to ransom.
Keylogging	The cyber attacker plants software onto the user's computer to record what the user types onto their keyboard. The objective is to learn passwords and user details to gain access to confidential information.

Type of cyberattack	Description
Screenshot manager	The cyber attacker obtains information from the victim by installing software onto the user's computer to enable screenshots of the user's computer screen to be taken. Like other cyberattacks, the purpose can be to steal information, funds, or may even be to perform corporate espionage.
Ad clicker	The cyber attacker directs the victim's computer to a bogus website by encouraging them to click on a specific link contained in online advertising.

The following table contains some common cybersecurity methods used by organisations:

Cybersecurity method	Description
Access control	These are physical and network procedures to restrict access to a system.
firewalls	Firewalls intercept data being transmitted in and out of a system.
Malware protection and virus protection	Malware protection software prevents installation and removes suspicious programs (such as trojans) and viruses from a system.
Ensure software is regularly updated	This is a system procedure rather than a hardware or software solution. The organisation should ensure that the latest software updates are installed on the system when available.
Secure configuration	The organisation should have a policy which states that systems should be set up with cybersecurity as a priority.

4 Automation in business

Three types of activities will continue to evolve in business

- **Machine-only activities:** These are activities where machines will always outperform humans. They typically involve routine processing of transactions, making rational predictions and generating answers to questions. However, some degree of human involvement is currently needed to put the output into context and resolve errors that might arise, however AI will increasingly take on this more complex role.

- **Human-only activities:** These are activities where humans will always outperform machines. They typically involve the application of knowledge across a range of different tasks and finding patterns of interest. They may also involve making predictions based on a higher level of judgement than making a rational prediction. That said, AI can increasingly take on what have historically been seen as human-only roles.

- **Human and machine hybrid activities:** These are activities where technology can augment human intelligence to make finance professionals faster, more efficient and more productive. Such activities can be significantly enhanced because of the value humans bring to machines by training, programming and maintaining the machines and because machines can amplify the work humans can do.

The automation paradox occurs as technology takes tasks out of human control, resulting in loss of skills in these areas. However, unexpected events might occur that systems are not designed to cope with or do not have the capacity to deal with. In such circumstances, the human skills may be urgently required which are no longer available as the deskilling of humans means that the tasks cannot be quickly or easily performed.

This paradox can be overcome by ensuring staff have a full understanding of how the systems work so that they can either assist the system to overcome the problem or to perform the task manually themselves.

4.1 Impact of automation on the components of the finance function

The table below summarises some examples of how automation can impact on the work of the finance function and business managers.

Function	Examples of automation
Financial reporting	Downloads of bank transactions into the accounting system
	Posting of bank transactions to nominal accounts
	Reconciliations of bank, supplier, and customer accounts
	Creation of statutory accounts
	Exception reports to identify possible errors or areas requiring professional attention
Management accounting	Generation of management accounts
	Calculation of variances and finance ratios
	In-depth analysis of results and data analytics to support theories of why performance was as it was
	Budgeting based on current actuals
	Forecasting based on assumptions set by the finance team
Treasury	Investment appraisal calculations
	Analysis of financial markets to predict costs of capital
	'What if' scenario planning to analyse potential outcomes for investments
	Monitoring of currency markets to identify the best opportunities to buy and sell different currencies
	Cash flow forecasting to identify future requirements for cash to reduce shortfalls
Internal audit	Routine monitoring of transactions to identify only suspicious transactions that need investigation
	Routine testing of controls and procedures (such as tracing invoices through the system)
	Simulations of cyberattacks to test the strength of IT systems and risk of attack
	Real-time feedback of system controls and monitoring via a dashboard
	Vulnerability testing to identify potential weaknesses and impacts on the business if they occur

Function	Examples of automation
Business management processes	Automated employee scheduling software to assign shifts based on availability and workload requirements
	Workflow automation tools for streamlining project management processes, including task assignment, progress tracking, and deadline management
	Customer relationship management (CRM) systems for automating sales and marketing activities, such as lead generation, email campaigns, and customer follow-ups
	Inventory management software for automatically tracking stock levels, reordering products when inventory runs low, and optimising warehouse operations
	Automated data entry and processing systems for capturing and processing information from various sources, such as invoices, receipts, and forms

Most of the impacts are to remove repetitive tasks which a computer can be programmed to do faster, and with greater accuracy. This increases the effectiveness of accountants and business managers because they can spend less time on simple, routine tasks and more time on value-adding services, making better use of the professional knowledge and skills that they have.

There are a number of advantages and disadvantages to finance functions of investing in process automation.

Advantages of automation

- Automation can free up staff time to focus on value-adding activities.
- Headcount can be reduced as work is automated, this helps to reduce costs.
- Introducing the system involves change which must be managed carefully and thoughtfully.
- Removal of human error will improve accuracy of information.
- Automation can be used as a catalyst to help the organisation adapt and improve in response to change.

Disadvantages of automation

- Systems may create uncertainty over job security and future prospects in staff.
- Systems are only as effective as the person who creates them. Therefore, the programmer must be competent and understand the existing process completely.
- Development costs and employee retraining can be significant.

5 Data analytics

5.1 Data and information

Key terms

Data: Consists of raw, unprocessed facts and figures.

Information: Is data that has been processed in a way that makes it meaningful for planning or decision making.

5.1.1 Types of data

Data can be categorised into three types of data. Each one is greater in scale and complexity than the previous and requires greater levels of analysis.

- **Financial data** – standard metrics which are well tracked and understood by the organisation
- **Enterprise data** – financial data plus broad operational and transactional data that bolsters analysis and forecasting
- **Big data** – enterprise data plus new types of internal and external data which can be unstructured and large in volume but could yield new insights into business performance, risks and opportunities

5.2 Data analysis and insights

Key terms

Data analysis: Is the process of evaluating data by comparison against benchmarks or yardsticks to form some sort of finding or conclusion, for example to measure the performance of an organisation compared to the prior year and the current budget.

Data insights: Is more than reporting basic financial information; they are indications of the drivers of value for the organisation.

We can see that the role of data analysis is to 'report the facts', for example, the organisation's performance in its management accounts. When finance professionals report insights, they go further, by explaining the reasons why the organisation's performance was as reported, what is happening to the business now and what might happen in the future. These insights are the building blocks that tell the organisation's value-creation story.

5.3 Data cleansing

Data cleansing is the process which identifies inaccurate or irrelevant data and modifying or deleting it as appropriate.

Question

Required

Can you think of some examples of data that would need cleansing?

Answer

Examples of data that require cleansing include:

- Duplicate (redundant) data held about customers
- Errors in data which may cause poor decisions, such as incorrect customer dates of birth held in a marketing database (may cause incorrect customers to receive marketing emails)
- Corrupt or unintelligible data due to file damage
- Out of date data, such as old price lists or standard costs

- Data which has no strategic purpose for the business
- Data which does not meet the rules set out in data protection legislation (eg data which breaches the rights of individuals, or is not permitted to be kept under law)

Methods of data cleansing include:

- Cross-checking raw data with validated data to identify data sets requiring cleansing
- Manual checks and corrections to database fields by humans
- Automated batch processing or scripting processes by computer
- Data wrangling (converting raw data from one form into another to use in a different system). At the end of the process, all raw data held in a system should be consistent and reliable.

5.4 Data visualisation

Key term

Data visualisation: Is the process of presenting report formats that represent data and information in a pictorial or graphical format that helps the recipient to understand the significance of the content more easily than if presented in a traditional report format.

Data visualisation concerns how finance communicates to influence key stakeholders. Effective communication with stakeholders is based on three factors:

(a) Audience
(b) Frequency
(c) Format

5.4.1 Audience

Who is the target of the communication and what are their information needs?

Different stakeholders have different information needs that should be met. These needs are different even if the overall message is the same. For example, a communication to close down part of the organisation's operations will impact on employees and shareholders. Employees will be concerned about potential job losses and the communication must address this for them. Shareholders will be more interested on the impact on the business's future and profitability and therefore communications to them will have a different focus.

5.4.2 Frequency

How often should stakeholders receive communications?

Different stakeholders require different frequency of communication depending on what is being communicated. For some, detailed, daily updates are expected, but others will be satisfied with a brief communication every few months. As technology develops, stakeholders may expect an almost constant flow of information that can be fed to them via tracking and analytics tools and apps.

5.4.3 Format

How and where will the stakeholders receive the communication?

Different stakeholders will have different needs and expectations of how they will be communicated with. Some will be happy with, for example, a single channel of communication such as email. Others may prefer a range of communications channels such as blogs, text message, formal reports, data visualisations, face-to-face meetings or virtual gatherings such as through Zoom or Teams.

5.4.4 Types of data visualisation

Types of data visualisation are included in the following table:

Tool	Description
Waterfall charts	These are also known as bridges and are often used to present variance analysis. The size of the steps in the bridge are scaled so that the eye naturally focuses on the most significant movements first.
Dashboards	These provide a relevant summary and are often used to provide four or five relevant drivers that give an overview of a business area. Each driver can be further analysed by drilling down into the supporting data.
Line charts	These are often used to show trend analysis or time-based results (such as product sales over the last five years).
Mapping charts	These present data geographically, eg countries or regions can be clicked on and drilled into to find information specific to those areas.
Bar and pie charts	The traditional methods of comparing data which is made up of component parts. For example, an organisation's total sales can be broken down in a pie chart into sales by region or business area.
Tables	The traditional method of presenting reference material by breaking it down into rows and columns.

The main impact of data visualisation on organisations is how information is presented. Because data presented in dashboards and mapping charts can be drilled into, they are geared to being presented on tablets and smart devices rather than on paper. This makes reporting quicker and cheaper, and it should support the quicker decision-making capabilities required in the modern business environment. It is important for organisations to provide the necessary technology and training so that staff get the most out of the visualisations and can use them for improved decision making.

To be effective, data visualisation tools should have five features.

Feature	Description
(a) **Real-time**	The tool must allow users to interact in real-time with each other and the data.
(b) **Interrogation**	The tool must have the capability to interrogate the systems and the overall business.
(c) **Decision making**	The tool must be focussed on results and support decision making.
(d) **Prompt (timely)**	The tool must display results quickly because delays may make insights or rules discovered out-of-date.
(e) **Infrastructure**	The tool must be supported by sufficient quality and quantity of data.

Data visualisation can be used by the finance function to present the information and reports that are required by management. It allows far richer information to be provided and therefore more value can be added by the finance function. For example, mapping analysis allows the recipient to drill down into sales data by region to identify the areas of the business which are having the biggest impact on sales.

It also allows the finance function to present the information in different ways depending on the audience. For example, higher levels of management may want a dashboard overview of the performance of the business areas, whereas the management team of each business area will want a greater depth of information, such as management accounts with variance analysis. These different reports can be prepared quickly and easily because they are all driven by the same data in the system.

Some key benefits of data visualisation for the finance function include:

- Accessibility in terms of visual appeal and the ability to be understood easily
- Real-time processing means the picture is always kept up to date
- Performance optimisation as clear information allows improved decision making and efficient use of resources in response
- Allows richer insights and understanding of the relationships that drive performance

5.5 Big data

Key term

Big data: Is used to describe the vast volumes of data, which is captured from various sources, both internally and externally, and includes structured data, as well as unstructured data such as social media posts, news stories, video and audio clips. This is often analysed to reveal patterns or trends, especially relating to human behaviour or interactions.

The main use of big data in organisations is to identify trends that may exist in vast quantities of data in the pursuit of value creation. These trends can then be 'commercialised' – in other words, fed into business decision that help further the organisations objectives. For example, an understanding of customer tastes can inform design decisions for the next generation of products.

Some sources of big data include:

- Human interactions with social networks, search engines, online retailers, and other digital platforms, generating vast amounts of user-generated content, clickstream data, and transaction records.
- Machines, including smart devices equipped with sensors, such as wearable fitness trackers, smart home appliances, and industrial machinery, contributing to the internet of things (IoT) ecosystem by generating real-time data on environmental conditions, performance metrics, and operational status.
- Open data sources, comprising publicly available datasets provided by government agencies, public services, research institutions, and non-profit organisations, covering a wide range of topics such as demographics, economic indicators, environmental measurements, and geographic information.
- Closed data sources, encompassing proprietary datasets held by businesses and organisations, including customer databases, sales records, marketing analytics, and internal operational data, often processed and curated by market research firms, data brokers, and specialised vendors for insights and analysis.

Big data has four characteristics:

Characteristic	Description
Volume	This refers to the quantity of data that is available. Big data is available relatively easily and in large quantities.
Velocity	This refers to the speed at which big data can be accessed by an organisation. Big data is often available to an organisation in real time rather than at intervals such as on a weekly or monthly basis.
Variety	Variety concerns the different forms that big data can take. It is often unstructured and can take many forms including free text, images and audio. This makes analysis more complex and also takes up more storage space.

Characteristic	Description
Veracity	Veracity concerns the trustworthiness or accuracy of big data. Despite an organisation's best efforts, data sets will contain inaccuracies, bias, anomalies and irrelevant 'noise'. Therefore, as much as possible needs to be done to verify the data before it can be trusted as accurate.

Finance functions use data analytics to provide insights that can add value to decision makers in the organisation. The table below considers how the characteristics and components of big data can be managed by the finance function.

5.5.1 Characteristics and components of big data and the finance function

Characteristic	Components of big data and management by the finance function
Volume (the quantity of data that is available)	Because big data is readily available and in vast quantities, a key component of big data is the infrastructure used to store it.
	The role of finance here is to assist management in determining the storage needs of the organisation. Volumes of data stored should be closely monitored and predictions run on future demand for storage.
	A key risk for the business will be running out of data storage and therefore internal audit should be involved in ensuring the ever-increasing need for data storage is met. Cloud storage would be a good solution because it can be scaled up or down as needed.
Velocity (the speed at which big data can be streamed)	Because big data can be streamed in real time, another component is the network and communications system used to distribute and view it.
	A key role for finance is to provide benchmarking insights (for example, on system speeds and downtime) to the IT function. If data cannot be streamed as fast as the business requires, then the infrastructure should be upgraded or replaced.
Variety (the different forms that big data can take)	Because big data comes from many sources and can take many forms (such as structured and unstructured), another component is the data connection and visualisation tools that can make sense of it.
	A key role for finance is to ensure that these data connection and visualisation tools enable the function to meet the organisation's need for insight.
Veracity (the trustworthiness or accuracy of big data)	Due to the volume of data held, a certain percentage of data sets will contain inaccuracies, bias, anomalies and 'noise'.
	The finance function has a key role to play in cleansing the data before it can be trusted as accurate.

5.6 Data analytics

Key term

Data analytics: Is the collection, management and analysis of large data sets with the objective of discovering useful information that an organisation can use for decision making.

To have value to an organisation, data needs to have meaning. Data analytics creates this meaning by assembling, filtering, sorting, highlighting and finally presenting the data in useful forms.

Some key impacts that big data and data analytics have on organisations are summarised as follows:

Area of impact	Description
Decision making	Large volumes of data can be analysed in real-time to help managers make better decisions that improve profitability.

Area of impact	Description
Marketing	Analysis can be performed on customer data so that the organisation can customise its marketing approach to individuals or customer groups.
Risk management	Analytics can provide management with a better understanding of the risks that the organisation faces, particularly in the business environment.
Product development	Analysis of the organisation's market and customer needs can help to identify opportunities to develop new products and services.
Knowledge	Analytics can create and enhance knowledge. For example, customer buying patterns or trends in supplier costs, which the business did not know before, might be identified.
Performance management	Deeper levels of understanding of the organisation's performance may identify previously unknown causes for poor performance that can be rectified.

Effective data analytics bring the following benefits to an organisation:

Benefit	Description
Fresh insight and understanding	Intelligent use of data can reveal patterns and insight into how a business operates and identify previously unknown issues.
Improved performance	The processing of data and the creation of relevant management information in real time can result in improvements to operations, decision making and resource utilisation.
Segmentation and customisation of markets	The needs and wants of customer groups can be increasingly refined, leading to better personalisation and customisation of products and services.
Fast decision making	Real-time processing of data results in faster decisions and advantage over the competition.
Innovation	Existing products can be improved through the organisation better understanding the aspects of the product that customers value the most. New products can also be developed.
Risk management	Data analytics can support all aspects of the risk management process.

Data analytics on big data can assist the finance function's work by looking at internal and external data.

In terms of internal data, analytics can help with the identification, quantification and management of risk within an organisation. This is of particular benefit to the internal audit function because it can help focus its work on key business risks. Analytics can identify specific areas of the business which have the most risk or have procedures and processes in place that are not performing as well as they could. The internal audit team can concentrate on these areas, which should have the greatest impact on reducing risk within the organisation.

Data analytics on external data can be used by the management accounting function to support performance management. Variance analysis will often identify areas where the organisation's performance is better or worse than planned, but the root cause of the variance might not always be apparent. Data analytics can be used as evidence to support theories as to why the organisation performed as it did. It can also help to develop efficient and insightful budgeting processes and management control systems.

For financial accounting, big data can improve the quality and relevance of financial information, improve transparency in reporting and enhance stakeholder decision making.

In terms of financial reporting, big data can support the development of more relevant and useful information that can be used to improve future accounting standards.

It is also important to appreciate that data analytics does not have to involve big data. For example, data analytics could be performed on an income statement.

5.7 Data activities: Modelling, manipulation and analysis

We shall now briefly consider the activities of data modelling, manipulation and analysis before looking at the role of the **finance** function in each.

Key term

> **Data modelling:** Is the analysis of an organisation's data needs required to support its business processes.
>
> **Data manipulation:** Is the reorganisation or transformation of data to make it easier to read or more meaningful.
>
> **Data analysis:** Is the name given to the overall process of collecting, cleansing, manipulating and modelling data to support decision making.

5.7.1 Advantages of data modelling

- **Foundation for handling data:** A well-structured data model acts as a blueprint for an organisation, allowing data to be stored, retrieved, and managed efficiently. It offers a clear view of how different data elements interrelate, facilitating better decision making.
- **Compliance with regulations:** With increasing scrutiny on data management, having a structured data model ensures that business rules are adhered to, and data security measures are in place. For finance functions, this is crucial as financial data is often regulated and audited.
- **Enhanced data quality:** An effective data model ensures that there's a system in place for consistent data entry, update, and retrieval. It reduces data redundancy and inconsistencies, thereby ensuring accurate and timely financial reporting.
- **Improved consistency:** A data model standardises naming conventions and value definitions. This is crucial in financial data where standard naming and values help in accurate data analysis and reporting, ensuring all stakeholders have a unified understanding.

In essence, data modelling is not just about creating databases. It's a strategic endeavour that ensures an organisation's data infrastructure aligns with its business goals, especially in areas as pivotal as finance.

5.7.2 The role of the finance function in data manipulation

An example of a very basic form of data manipulation would be arranging data in alphabetical order to make it easier for a user to read. In practice, a data manipulation language (or DML) will be used to automate the process and handle complex databases. DMLs search the parameters of data being held and give instructions to ensure it is held in a consistent and structured manner.

Finance professionals will also manipulate data using accounting fields, dates and values to make it easier for users to understand trends such as demand for products, certain types of cost and even predicting economic indicators such as interest rates.

5.7.3 The role of the finance function in data analysis

We have already seen how the finance function can be involved in collecting, cleansing, manipulating and modelling data. In this section, we shall briefly look at its role in the final aspect of data analysis – decision making.

Finance professionals have an increasingly important role to play in decision making. In particular, their logical skills help to make decisions more scientific and make the organisation more effective.

8: Impact of emerging technology

The following are examples of the different stages of data analysis for decision making:

Stage of data analysis	Description	Example involving a finance function
Descriptive data analysis	Examining a number of disparate hypotheses that often concern differences between subgroups	Data analysis, using tools such as tables of means and quantiles, measures of dispersion and cross-tabulations, to look into the background of customers for market segmentation purposes For example, investigating the proportion of customers in the market who have a business degree and who buy a particular brand of car
Exploratory data analysis	Finding new relationships or features in a data set	Data analysis to find a connection between sales volume and time of the year, for a seasonal business
Confirmatory data analysis	Confirming, or disproving a hypothesis	Data analysis to prove the elasticity of demand for an organisation's products
Predictive data analysis (Explained further below)	Making forecasts, based on techniques such as statistical modelling	A forecasting algorithm analyses previous sales data to predict future sales
Decision optimisation analysis	Coming to a decision that is equivalent, or better, than the other available decision options	Data analysis to determine the most profitable course of action given a number of constraints, such as budget, available capital, or other resources

The following are examples of specific data analysis tools and methodologies for decision making:

Data analysis tool/methodology	Description	Example involving a finance function
Text data analysis	Extracting and classifying data from textual sources	Data analysis to sort or arrange data alphabetically or in groups or sets (such as grouping products into named categories)
Data modelling	Utilising abstract constructs, often of a mathematical nature, to depict the data structures and interconnections within an entity	An e-tailer wants to forecast its next year's revenue. It builds a data model incorporating factors like website traffic, conversion rate of visitors to sales, average sales value, and seasonal variations to make an accurate prediction

Data analysis tool/methodology	Description	Example involving a finance function
Data manipulation (Explained further below)	Modifying, organising, or transforming raw data to make it more understandable or suitable for analysis. Cleaning and transforming raw transactional data to categorise into expense and revenue types	The loyalty card function in a large supermarket company has a vast database of customer information collected over decades in various formats. Before analysing patterns to understand what items should be stocked in their shops, they manipulate the data to standardise formats, remove duplicates, and handle missing values to categorise by product, by customer, by gender, by age, by location
Linear regression (Explained further below)	Assessing the correlation between variables. For instance, data analysis can be employed to comprehend the connection between a company's advertising expenditure and its sales revenue	A manufacturing company could assess the correlation between output and manufacturing costs. To form the basis of predicting costs given an anticipated output level
Simulations using multiple outcome variables (Explained further below)	Simulating multiple outcome variables involves predicting various results through a simulation model. This model relies on a set of input variables to generate best- and worst-case scenarios, providing an analysis that helps understand the most probable outcomes	A manufacturing firm is exploring several strategies, including launching a new product, entering new markets, or investing in new machinery. To make an informed decision, it employs simulation techniques to anticipate potential outcomes such as revenue growth, market share, and ROI for each strategy

5.7.4 Data manipulation

In today's data-centric landscape, the finance sector relies heavily on data manipulation, a pivotal process for meaningful decision making, accurate forecasting, and strategic formulation. Tailoring data structures using specialised tools and languages is imperative for handling vast datasets with precision, ensuring actionable insights.

Data manipulation involves refining data to enhance its utility and efficiency for analysis. This encompasses rectifying errors, transforming raw data into meaningful information, and preparing data for analytical processes. By optimising data structure and quality, this process guarantees that data not only meets its intended use requirements but also yields consistent and precise insights. Finance professionals frequently engage in data manipulation, employing accounting fields, dates, and values to elucidate trends such as product demand, specific costs, and even predictions of economic indicators like interest rates.

Various levels of data manipulation exist in business:

- **Basic manipulation:** Organising data alphabetically or by attributes like date or numeric value simplifies navigation and comprehension.
- **Data manipulation language (DML):** Specific to database management systems (DBMS), DMLs like SQL facilitate efficient interaction with stored data through commands such as SELECT, INSERT, UPDATE, and DELETE.

- **Consistency and structure:** Uniformity in naming conventions, data types, and formats is crucial for coherent analysis. Standardising formats, like dates, ensures consistency.
- **Manipulation of financial data:** This involves meticulous organisation, including accounting fields, chronological sorting of transactions, adjusting financial metrics for factors like inflation or currency conversion, and recognising trends or anomalies.

Finance professionals may employ advanced manipulations to derive metrics such as year-over-year growth, compound annual growth rate (CAGR), or ratios like price-to-earnings (P/E). These derived metrics, not directly present in raw data, offer valuable insights into an organisation's financial health and trajectory.

5.7.5. Predictive analytics

Key term

> **Predictive analytics:** Uses historical and current data to create predictions about potential outcomes that may happen in the future.

In the evolving landscape of business, particularly in the finance sector, the increasing volume and diversity of data, coupled with advancements in analytical tools, will further amplify the potential of predictive analytics, playing a central role in business decisions.

The significance of predictive analytics in accounting and finance encompasses various aspects:

- **Historical context:** Accountants, historically adept at forecasting, now benefit from the enhanced capabilities of predictive analytics. Traditional financial predictions, such as those related to revenue, expenses, and cash flows, have traditionally relied on time-series analysis or linear regression, where historical trends are projected into the future.
- **Big data's Influence:** The advent of Big data has revolutionised predictive analytics in finance. Data now originates not only from spreadsheets but also from diverse sources like social media sentiments, real-time market feeds, and customer behaviour on e-commerce platforms. This abundance of data provides organisations with a more comprehensive view for predicting financial outcomes, such as forecasting product demand by analysing social media trends.
- **Techniques in predictive analytics:**
  - **Linear regression models:** Utilising statistical methods to ascertain the relationship between variables and use this as a basis for forecasting. The relationship between the variables is assumed to be linear in nature. For example, forecasting future sales based on advertising spend.
  - **Multi-variable simulation:** Analysing multiple variables simultaneously to predict the distribution and likelihood of potential outcomes. For instance, simulating a company's future revenue based on factors like marketing budget, product pricing, and expected market growth.
  - **Other predictive analytics techniques:** In addition to the mentioned techniques, various others like decision trees, neural networks, clustering, etc, can be applied based on the complexity of data and the nature of predictions required.

Advantages of predictive analytics

- **Proactive decision making:** Predictive analytics leverages big data to generate accurate forecasts and identify trends, enabling organisations to make proactive decisions rather than reacting after events occur.
- **Improved and broader business analysis:** By combining statistical tools with AI and algorithms, predictive analytics enhances forecasting and what-if analysis, leading to more informed decisions and improved business outcomes.

- **Risk management:** In finance, predictive analytics assesses risk by applying probabilities to predictive models and conducting what-if analysis, such as credit scoring for loans based on borrowers' credit history and related factors.
- **Operational efficiency:** Predictive analytics helps streamline operations by forecasting high sales volumes and ensuring adequate stock and staffing levels during peak periods, thereby optimising resources.
- **Innovative opportunities:** Insights derived from predictive analytics empower businesses to identify new market opportunities, diversify product lines, and innovate in service delivery, maintaining a competitive edge.

Disadvantages of predictive analytics

- **Data quality and reliability:** Predictive analytics heavily relies on data quality and reliability, and inaccuracies or biases in the data can lead to flawed predictions and decisions.
- **Complexity and expertise requirement**: Implementing predictive analytics requires specialised skills and expertise in data science and analytics, which may pose challenges for organisations lacking in-house capabilities or resources.
- **Privacy and ethical concerns:** Predictive analytics may raise privacy and ethical concerns, especially when dealing with sensitive personal data, leading to potential regulatory and reputational risks.
- **Cost and resource implications:** Developing and maintaining predictive analytics models can be costly and resource-intensive, requiring investments in technology infrastructure, data management, and skilled personnel.

6 Change management

In developing strategies for the future of the business, organisational change becomes necessary.

Change may be planned or unplanned, and incremental or transformational in nature. For example, a position audit may reveal serious strategic weaknesses in the organisation that need to be dealt with, and the changes needed to deal with the problem may be substantial. The organisation may also identify strengths that it plans to exploit more fully, and its plans for doing this could involve big changes. Or the requirement for change can often be in response to developments in the business environment (the micro-environment or the macro-environment).

6.1 Types and reasons for change

6.1.1 Types of change

There are many types of change which can happen. Below are some examples.

(a) **Planned change** (or **proactive change**) is deliberate and intended. Management identifies the benefits that change will bring and plan how it should be introduced. Planned changes may be changes to exploit a new opportunity that has been identified.

(b) **Unplanned change** (or **reactive change**) happens in response to developments or events that have occurred. These changes are not devised as part of the planning process. Unplanned changes are often a response to new threats that have emerged in the environment.

(c) **A 'one-off' event**, so that the organisation moves from an 'old' way of doing things to a 'new' way; or

(d) **Continual**, with change occurring over a long period of time.

(e) **Incremental change** is a fairly small change. This type of change happens without the need for a major reorganisation or restructuring of the organisation. Incremental change should not be a serious problem for management.

(f) **Transformational change** is a major change that requires a substantial reorganisation or restructuring of the organisation and its systems. It will typically have a significant impact on culture, systems, processes and people.

To survive and ensure future success, organisations should respond to the challenges that environmental change presents by employing change management strategies.

Change within an organisation may involve:

(a) A change in the organisation structure and management responsibilities
(b) A change in technology, such as introducing new equipment and systems
(c) A change in the physical setting for business operations
(d) Relocating employees or changing job roles, descriptions and responsibilities

Change can have a big effect on the organisation and the people working in it, and change management skills are needed to implement the change successfully.

6.1.2 Reasons for change

External triggers for change are caused by changes in the environment. A PESTEL analysis of the macro-environment can be a useful framework for analysing external triggers for change.

(a) **Political reasons for change.** A change in strategy might be caused by an unexpected political crisis, such as a civil war or major civil unrest in a country that is either a major source of raw material supply or a major export market.

(b) **Economic reasons for change.** Economic change can have a major impact on an organisation and force it to make changes. In recent years a notable development has been the rapid growth of the economy of China. Many large companies in the US and Europe have shut down production operations in Western countries and have changed to buying products and components from Chinese manufacturers. Some companies in Western Europe have moved production facilities to countries in Eastern Europe where costs are lower.

(c) **Social and cultural** reasons for change. A change in public attitudes and opinions might persuade an organisation to alter its strategy. For example, there might be a change in public attitudes to food safety and hygiene. If this is significant, a food manufacturer might decide to change its strategy for new product development or alter its production methods to improve the hygiene in its production systems.

(d) **Technological** reasons for change. Companies need to adopt new technology to continue to succeed in their business. A clear example of the pressure for change is the rapid development of information technology and telecommunications in recent years. Unless they had adopted the new technology, it would have been virtually impossible for any competitive business (except for very small businesses) to survive.

(e) **Ecological** reasons for change. Major strategic changes might be triggered by changes in the ecological environment. Climate change may force companies to reconsider the location of their operations, perhaps because of a threat to the water supply or major changes in weather conditions.

(f) **Legal** reasons for change. Change may be triggered by important changes in the law, such as changes in employment law or new laws against pollution.

Change may be triggered by developments within the organisation itself.

(a) **Change in senior management**. When there is a change in the senior management of an organisation, the new managers may have their own ideas about strategy and will introduce big changes.

(b) **Acquisition**. When an organisation takes over another in an acquisition, and management try to merge their systems and operations, there will be major changes. For example, the merged organisations may try to use the same computer system. Switching from one computer system to another may create significant challenges.

(c) **Reorganisation or downsising**. Change might be necessary because management decides on the need to close down a loss-making organisation or relocate its operations to a different part of the country.

Some changes are less 'transformational' than others and are easier to implement. For example, change may be triggered by:

(a) A general sense that the organisation could perform better

(b) A perceived need to improve organisational flexibility, quality or to develop new customer concern

(c) A sense that skills and abilities of people are under-utilised or concerns about a lack of commitment from employees

(d) Concerns about ineffective communications or poor performance indicators

(e) Fractious relationship between managers and the managed

Some change requires strategic change where the activities of a business fundamental change. Examples of strategic change are:

(a) Companies may need to respond to the globalisation of business by changing their organisation to meet the competitive threat from foreign multinational companies that are seeking to invest in the country.

(b) There may be a serious fall in demand for the organisation's products because they are reaching the end of their life cycle, prompting the need for a strategy for survival through change.

(c) Change may be prompted by the need or desire to respond to a competitive threat. When the market is dynamic and continually changing, organisations need to adjust their competitive strategy continually, and there may be a continual process of change.

6.1.3 Balogun and Hope Hailey 'Nature and Scope of Change' model

It is necessary for organisations to consider the types of strategic change which are possible. By applying a two axis model which evaluates (a) the scope of the change and (b) the nature of change.

Balogun and Hope Hailey (2008) uses these two axes to help define the scale the change required; this then helps boards of directors to respond with sufficient resources to address the pace and scale of change.

These four types of change classifications are represented in the following diagram:

		Scope of change	
		Realignment	**Transformation**
Nature of change	**Incremental**	Adaptation	Evolution
	Big bang	Reconstruction	Revolution

(**Source**: Balogun and Hope Hailey, 2008: p.21)

The **scope of change** takes into account the breadth of the change across an organisation. Does it affect just a particular department or process or is it something that is going to affect lots of departments and revenue and costs in those departments?

The **nature of change** (also called the speed of change) could require a sudden change, as the implementation of the change all occurs at the same time. Alternately the change may be far slower and can be phased in over some time.

Balogun and Hope Hailey's define the extent of change using the following four classifications as follows:

(a) **Adaptation:** This is the most common type of change and involves a realignment of the current process on an incremental basis ie it affects the processes and systems in place relatively slowly.

(b) **Reconstruction:** This needs rapid and extensive action on existing processes that require urgent change. It relates to existing processes and systems, and this will often happen if there is a crisis for the organisation.

(c) **Evolution:** This is a slow and considered process leading to a brand-new way of doing things across a whole organisation. The organisation will have changed substantially though it will not necessarily be obvious as the change is occurring.

(d) **Revolution:** This is a very large and transformative change that happens very quickly. There may be something that has happened in the organisation's environment that requires such a big, fast change. New processes will come into place very quickly, so a revolution can be very stressful. After revolutionary change, what the organisation does and how it will go about this, are completely different to what went before.

6.2 Change management

Change management is concerned with managing the changes and developments that an organisation undertakes. It is the responsibility of managers and leaders to devise and execute a change management programme that is suitable for the circumstances.

Planned change management involves planning how to get to a desired new way of doing things from the current position. This involves planning the objective of change, and how to achieve the objective, implementing the change and making the change stick.

When change is planned, management should have an idea of what they are trying to achieve, and the future state of the organisation or business that they are trying to get to. Planned change is managed effectively when:

(a) The organisation is moved from its current state to a planned future state that will exist after the change.

(b) The transition is accomplished without excessive cost to the organisation.

(c) The transition is accomplished without excessive cost to the employees in the organisation.

(d) The planned future state, when it has been reached, meet expectations, and the change works as planned.

6.2.1 Requirements for effective change management

The following attributes are required for change management to be effective:

- Identification of the changes that should be made
- Leadership to drive and champion change
- A business case and sufficient allocated resources ie people, skills, expertise, time, money, technology

- Recognising the effect of change on:
  - People – employees, customers, suppliers and others affected by change programmes, depending on the scope and nature of the change itself
  - Organisational structures
  - Processes
  - Information technology
- Careful planning and managed implementation of the change
- Procedure to ensure that change is permanent and successfully implemented

6.2.2 Resistance to change

Change can affect what the company makes, how it makes it, and who/how it sells it to. Change can potentially affect any aspect of the organisation and its stakeholders.

It is inevitable that there will be some resistance to strategic change from key stakeholders, say the employees of an organisation not wanting to have to learn new skills or being upset that some of their colleagues have been made redundant.

Kotter and Schlesinger suggested that there are four reasons why individuals may resist change:

(a) **Parochial self-interest**. They may resist change because they are concerned about the negative consequences of the change for themselves. They are concerned with how the change will affect them, not how the change will benefit the organisation.

(b) **Misunderstanding**. Individuals may misunderstand the nature of the change or the reason why it is necessary. Misunderstanding may occur because of poor communication or failure to provide adequate information about the change

(c) **Low tolerance to change**. Some people resist change because they like stability and security in their life, and they think that change will be too disruptive.

(d) **Different assessments of the situation**. Some individuals may have a different opinion about the need for change and disagree with the proposals that have been made.

Common areas of resistance to change include:

- Fear of losing jobs, status, and income
- Contracts – employment terms
- Organisational structure – especially if the structures are formal and bureaucratic
- Influential individuals – those that are powerful and command support
- Departmentalism – defending one's department
- Myths and stories – about the 'good old days', for example
- Worry about inability to cope with the change
- Extra work – as a result of the large change happening

6.2.3 Strategies of overcoming resistance to change (Kotter's 'Six Change Approaches' model)

Kotter's Six Change Approaches model (2007) identifies six strategies to mitigate resistance to change.

(a) **Education and communication**. If the resistance to change is caused by misunderstanding, management should deal with the problem by educating and informing employees. The aim should be to remove the misunderstanding. This is the most convenient way of managing change, but it will only be effective if the resistance has been caused by misunderstanding.

(b) **Participation and involvement**. It may be possible to overcome resistance to change by involving employees in the change process. This may be appropriate when the individuals have some power to resist the change, but their resistance is not very strong. Participation and involvement may go some way to lowering their resistance, as they become familiar with what the change involves.

(c) **Facilitation and support**. Management may decide to prevent resistance by offering help and support to individuals who are worried about the change. This may be appropriate when the employees have a low resistance to change and are likely to be anxious about it. Measures to provide facilitation and support might include counselling, special training or even giving individuals some time off work.

(d) **Negotiation and agreement**. This approach may be necessary when the individuals who are resisting the change are in a position of power and may be able to resist successfully. Management might negotiate with them to reach a deal. This could involve offering them money to retire from work or to leave the company.

(e) **Manipulation and co-option**. If the organisation cannot afford to pay employees to accept change or leave the organisation, an alternative approach to change is to invite the individual to join the change management team, even though the individual would not have any skills or ability to bring to the team. This would be making a gesture, for the sake of appearances. It would only be appropriate when the individual concerned is in a position of power to resist the change.

(f) **Explicit or implicit coercion**. Coercion means forcing people to accept the change or accept the consequences if they do not. This approach is recommended only when the change has to be implemented quickly, or as a last resort when other approaches have been unsuccessful. Management may announce that the proposed change will be implemented, and they may threaten anyone who resists the change with dismissal, no promotion or transfer to another job.

6.3 Planning for change

6.3.1 Lewin's change management model

Lewin (1947) noted that resistance presents significant forcefields against change as:

(a) It is often difficult to persuade people about the benefits of change, even where change is desirable and will have a positive effect.

(b) People should be persuaded about the need for change before the change actually takes place.

(c) After a change has been made, there is a risk that people will eventually return to the 'old way of doing things', so the effects and benefits of the change are lost – in other words, the changes might not last long.

In response, Lewin suggested that in order for people to accept change, they must understand the following reasons for change:

- Why change is necessary
- What the problems are with the current way of doing things
- What opportunities there are for improvement and advancement
- Why change might be desirable
- What benefits change will bring

Lewin's change management model (1947) provides a three-stage process for introducing major change into an organisation to counter the forcefields against change, as follows:

(a) Unfreeze
(b) Change (or movement)
(c) Refreeze

Each stage is explained further below.

(a) **Unfreeze**

This is the first stage in the change process. It involves getting individuals to recognise that change is desirable. Their initial attitudes and views are 'frozen', and they do not see the need for any change. Their opinions need to be 'unfrozen'.

There are two aspects to 'unfreezing':

Individuals need to feel dissatisfied with the current state of affairs.

They should then be persuaded that the planned change will bring desirable improvements.

Changing attitudes calls for considerable 'people management' skills of communication and persuasion.

(b) **Change (or movement)**

The second stage in the process is to make the change and move from the old way of doing things to the new way. Lewin argued that this stage should not begin until the unfreezing stage is completed.

The change needs to be successful, and management responsible for implementing the change should be given all the resources they need to complete their task.

Implementing the change is more likely to be successful when the individuals affected are allowed to participate closely in the process by providing ideas and offering suggestions about how to deal with any unexpected problems that arise.

Throughout this stage of the change process, there must be continuing support for the change. If any opposition to the change re-emerges, management should not try to force through the change. Instead, they should try to understand the reasons for the new resistance, discuss the problems with the individuals affected, and look for a satisfactory solution.

(c) **Refreeze**

The third and final stage in the planned change process is 'refreeze'. After a change has been made, there may be a natural tendency for individuals to go back to their old ways of doing things and their old ways of thinking.

The attitudes of individuals must be frozen again, but this time they should be frozen into believing that the new approach is good and desirable.

Lewin suggested that one way to refreeze attitudes is to reward individuals within the new changed system, for example by paying a bonus or higher salary.

By applying this model, the probability that implemented change will be effective is increased.

6.3.2 Balogun and Hope Hailey 'Change Kaleidoscope' model (2008)

The context, or business case, for proceeding with change is provided by the organisational setting; this has many aspects and can therefore be very complex.

Organisational change can be considered the following eight general headings proposed by Balogun and Hope Hailey (2008). These headings for consider the ability to change are scope, time, preservation, diversity, capability, capacity, readiness and power, each of which is explained further below. The Balogun and Hope Hailey model is sometimes referred to as the Change Kaleidoscope.

(a) **Scope of change.** The scope of change, whether it is incremental or transformational. Transformational change, having a more profound effect, needs more detailed and careful planning.

(b) **Time available.** The time available may vary dramatically but can often be quite limited when responding to competitive or regulatory pressure. The amount of time available will also be influenced by cultural considerations, as the attitudes and perceptions of those within the organisation will largely determine whether they regard the amount of time available to achieve a change as acceptable or not.

(c) **Preservation.** The preservation of some organisational culture, characteristics and resources may be required. It is important that the overall change process does not undermine or alter core processes such as manufacturing or customer services unless these are the targets of change.

(d) **Diversity.** Diversity of general experience, opinion, and practice is likely to ease the change process; homogeneity in these factors is unlikely to do so. An organisational culture where the sharing of ideas and challenging of existing ways of working is common practice may prove useful when implementing a change programme, especially if it helps others within the organisation to understand the reason for the change.

(e) **Capability.** The capability to manage and implement change is obviously important. To a great extent, this depends on past experience of change projects, both among managers and lower-level staff. Stories told by those within the organisation about successful or unsuccessful change programmes provide a useful insight into how future change proposals will be treated by staff.

(f) **Capacity.** Capacity to undertake change depends on the availability of resources, particularly finance, the quality and capacity of information systems, and management time and skill. However, it is important to note that unrealisable or outdated systems could become a blockage in the change process.

Capacity from a cultural perspective is particularly important in relation to change projects, as it is those operational workers within the organisation who are likely to have the best understanding of whether or not a change can be successfully implemented. A lack of belief among those within the organisation about the resources and skills needed to successfully introduce a change will create resistance.

(g) **Readiness for change.** The degree of workforce readiness for change will affect its success. Readiness may be contrasted with resistance to change, which can exist at varying levels of intensity and may be widespread or confined to pockets. The workforce of an organisation with a positive attitude to change is likely to display features of readiness. Readiness and resistance may be influenced by the tone at the top of the organisation and the stories told about historical change projects.

(h) **Power.** The power to effect change may not be sufficient to overcome determined resistance among important stakeholder groups. This can apply even at the strategic apex, where, for example, major shareholders, trustees, or government ministers may constrain managers' freedom of action. Overcoming such cultural resistance to change will require senior management to adopt an appropriate leadership style to create buy-in to the change.

6.3.3 Managing the process of change

Once the nature and scope of change has been decided, Balogun and Hope Hailey (2008) set down a series of nine process steps for change that helps organisations to structure their approach to change management.

The nine steps of Balogun and Hope Hailey (2008) process for change are as follows:

Step 1: Analyse the competitive position
Step 2: Determine type of change needed
Step 3: Identify the desired future state
Step 4: Analyse the change context

Step 5: Identify the critical change features
Step 6: Determine design choices
Step 7: Design the implementation or transition process
Step 8: Manage the implementation or transition
Step 9: Evaluate the change outcomes

This framework can be applied to create a high-level change management implementation place. Each step can then be further broken down into specific workstreams, resource requirements, communication plans and project management processes.

Each step is explained more fully as follows.

Step 1: Analyse the competitive position

As we have seen with the analysis of business strategy, it is important to analyse the external environment to identify and evaluate if there are any significant opportunities and threats for an organisation to address. If it is found that there is, say, a new entrant to the market due to a technological change, then the organisation will need to consider what it needs to do to improve its competitive position and competitive advantage. This consideration will provide the foundations for the business changes needed.

Step 2: Determine the type of change needed

The speed of the change needed, and the scope, can then be decided so that it can be seen what is needed for the organisation to be able to compete. This uses Balogun and Hope Hailey's Matrix to see whether revolution, adaptation, reconstruction or evolution is needed. It may be that business process reengineering is needed, for example.

Step 3: Identify the desired future state

This considers the high-level objectives of change for the organisation. It will most likely be decided by the board of directors. It will set the target for the organisation so that more detailed plans can be put in place, to decide the response and implement it.

Step 4: Analyse the change context

Next, each of the departments, functions and product areas of the organisation are considered and objectives are set for each of them relating to the change required.

Step 5: Identify the critical change features

Then the existing systems, processes and products are looked at and consideration is made of the changes made to each to achieve the overall objective for the organisation based on the level of change required.

Step 6: Determine design choices

Once the specific changes are known, then the design of the changes can be addressed. It may be necessary to obtain assistance with this from external consultants, though it may be that there is enough expertise internally. New systems and processes are needed, so will have to be designed. Once sorted, the board of directors will have to give approval to progress.

Step 7: Design the implementation or transition process

The process to effect the change will have to be decided. This will depend on how big the changes are, and project management is probably needed to help here and reduce the risk of something going wrong. Budgets and implementation plans will have to be created and agreed.

Step 8: Manage the implementation or transition

Once decided, the process of change will begin. As we will see in Section 3 which covers project management, a project manager will have overall command of the implementation steps and there will be a project plan that states the steps, their timescales and how they will be achieved. It is important that the organisation can continue to operate in this stage of the change, so that will have to be considered in the project plan. Once the project is complete and the change implemented, then it will have to be tested and staff trained in the new processes and systems they will be using.

Step 9: Evaluate the change outcomes

Success in the change is desired, so the objectives of the change will be evaluated against the new process or system to see if the desired future state has been achieved. If some changes are required, then they can be made until the required outcome is obtained. If the objective has not been met on the change and there are no easy adjustments that can be made, a post implementation review should be undertaken to avoid similar failures in the future.

6.4 The role of leadership and culture in change management

6.4.1 The role of leadership in managing change

Leaders and managers play a central role in managing the change process. Without careful leadership organisational change is unlikely to be successful.

Kanter identified seven 'classic' skills that are useful for organisational leaders in managing change. She described these as follows:

(a) **Tuning into the environment**. Creating a 'network of listening posts', such as listening to customer complaints so that they are aware of what is going on in the environment.

(b) **Challenging the prevailing organisational wisdom**. This means getting others in the organisation to accept that the old ways of doing things are no longer necessarily the best ways.

(c) **Communicating a compelling aspiration**. You cannot change things successfully without a conviction. Change managers should have this conviction and should communicate it to others.

(d) **Building coalitions**. Change leaders need the involvement of people of people who have resources, knowledge or political clout to make things happen. They need to build coalitions with people who are prepared to support them.

(e) **Transforming ownership to a working team**. Once a 'coalition' is in place, a change leader can enlist others to implement the change. They do not need to make the change themselves. They can delegate responsibility to the team.

(f) **Learning to persevere**. Change will not go smoothly and there will be setbacks. Change managers must be able to keep on trying until they succeed.

(g) **Make everyone a hero**. Change managers should recognise, reward and celebrate the accomplishments of everyone who has contributed to the change process.

6.4.2 The role of culture in managing change

To grasp the role of culture in managing change, it's essential to understand what organisational culture entails. Organisational culture can be defined as:

- 'The collection of traditions, values, policies, beliefs, and attitudes that constitute a pervasive context for everything we do and think in an organisation' (Mullins).

- 'A pattern of beliefs and expectations shared by the organisation's members, which produce norms that powerfully shape the behaviour of individuals and groups in the organisation' (Schwartz and Davies).

- 'The way we do things around here' (Schein).

Culture in an organisation may encompass:

- The formality of the organisational structure
- Communication. the approachability of senior managers
- Office layout
- The type of people employed
- Symbols (eg corporate logo), legends, and corporate myths
- Management style
- Freedom for subordinates to take ownership and show initiative
- Attitudes to quality
- Attitudes to risk
- Attitudes to customers
- Attitudes to technology

The McKinsey seven S model illustrates the interdependence between formal organisational elements and cultural and behavioural elements in organisational management as follows:

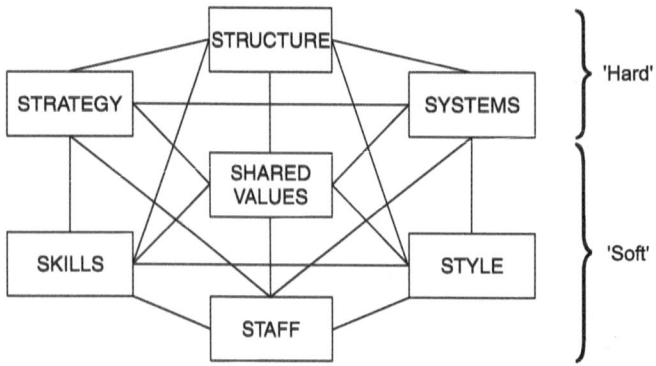

- **Shared Values.** At the centre are the organisations shared values which are its core beliefs and assumptions that guide the organisation
- **Style.** Corporate image, management style, and behavioural norms
- **Staff.** The type of people employed and their overall mindset
- **Skills.** The capabilities and competencies of the organisation's workforce
- **Structure.** The formal organisational structure and hierarchy
- **Systems.** The procedures and processes in place
- **Strategy.** The plan for achieving competitive advantage

The important points to note are:

- Culture, or shared values, occupies a central position in the model, both in terms of style (corporate image, management style, patterns, and norms of behaviour) and shared values (the underlying guiding beliefs and assumptions that shape the way the organisation sees itself and its purpose).
- All elements are inter-linked. altering any one variable will affect the others and the entire network.

Leaders must be ready to initiate change when the external business and competitive environment demands it and to ensure that change happens. A significant barrier to change can be the corporate culture that has evolved over time. In such cases, a cultural reset may be required to prepare it for new strategic goals, values, technologies, and operational processes.

Understanding what the culture needs to become and how to change it is a highly challenging undertaking that can only be achieved by truly effective leaders. Effective leaders can:

- **Diagnose the current culture.** Understand the existing cultural dynamics and how they align or misalign with the new strategic direction.
- **Communicate the vision for change.** Clearly articulate the need for change and the benefits it will bring to all stakeholders.
- **Model desired behaviours.** Exhibit the behaviours and attitudes that reflect the new cultural values.
- **Reinforce new norms.** Use systems, processes, and rewards to reinforce the new cultural norms.
- **Engage and empower employees.** Involve employees in the change process, allowing them to contribute ideas and take ownership of the change.

The role of culture in managing change is pivotal. It can either be a barrier or a facilitator of change, depending on how well it aligns with the new strategic goals.

Leaders must be adept at navigating and reshaping culture to ensure successful change implementation.

Understanding what the culture needs to become and how to change it, is a highly challenging undertaking and can only be achieved by an effective leader.

6.4.3 Change-adept organisations

Some organisations are better at making changes than others.

Kanter suggested that change-adept organisations have the imagination to innovate, professionalism to perform and openness to collaborate. Major changes may result in a change in organisational culture, especially if it results in the departure of many existing employees and the recruitment of new employees.

According to Kanter, 'change-adept' organisations have three key attributes:

(a) **Imagination to innovate.** This comes from a leadership that seeks new ideas for positive change. Management are innovators.

(b) **Professionalism to perform.** The managers of the entity are competent at introducing change. In other words, they are skilled at change management. In addition, the work force may have the experience and skills to recognise the inevitability of change. As a result, there is a culture of change within the organisation.

(c) **Openness to collaborate.** Change-adept organisations share ideas with other organisations, such as customers, suppliers and joint venture partners. They can work well with other organisations in making changes. For example, a change in product design or production methods may require support from the organisation's main suppliers. In order to make the change, there has to be collaboration with the suppliers and an agreement on how the change can be made.

6.4.4 Changing organisational culture to facilitate transformational change

Transformational change often requires a shift in the culture of the organisation. For example, if there is a change from a functional management structure to a decentralised structure with business divisions, employees will have to adapt to a new way of doing things and a new set of management attitudes.

If managers and other employees do not like the new way of operating, they might decide to leave the organisation. If they do, new people will be recruited who accept the new system. As a result, a permanent change in culture may occur.

It may become evident to the leader that the culture is not aligned with the organisation's objectives and needs to change. This misalignment could be due to a lack of success, the necessity for change, problems with the public image, or noted employee dissatisfaction. To successfully achieve transformational change, fundamental changes to the organisation's culture may be required.

There are various tools that a leader can use to change the culture of an organisation:

- A **new corporate mission** can energise employees and express the new corporate values needed for the organisation to progress.
- Expressing **new attitudes to innovation**, participation, control, and trust from the top of the organisation can set the tone for cultural change.
- **Rewards are important** so that employees can see that it is in their benefit to change and take a new direction.
- **New recruitment and selection policies** can help obtain a workforce with the right culture. Equally, there may need to be a redundancy policy if some employees are unable or unwilling to change.
- **New symbols of the organisation**, like a new logo or office design, can act as a reset and show that things have changed at the organisation.

6.4.5 Changing organisational culture to facilitate transformational change

The following question considers resistance to change and implementation of change through a planned change management process.

Question

The board of Hem Ltd (Hem), a UK-based clothing manufacturer, has agreed that changes are necessary to improve the efficiency and effectiveness of its supply chain management processes in order to remain competitive. The board has approved the implementation of a new integrated supply chain management system, which will enhance visibility of fabric orders with all suppliers and improve the coordination of ordering decisions across the supply chain.

With better information, Hem aims to increase responsiveness to customer orders and reduce errors in its supply ordering process. The directors of Hem have completed their investigation into potential system solutions and have approved the appointment of an integrated supply chain system provider. The new system will include the following technology components:

- **Supply chain sales ordering and relationship management system**: This central system will record all communications with suppliers, document all contracts, purchase order quantities, delivery details, invoicing, and payments.
- **Blockchain distributed ledger**: This will enable instantaneous, paperless purchase orders with all suppliers using cloud-based technology. It will facilitate an accurate, up-to-date, single, trusted, and transparent record of all orders shared between suppliers. Each order transaction will be entered in 'blocks' that are linked and secured using cryptography.
- **Enterprise resource planning (ERP) system**: This will integrate Hem's supply ordering, sales, and inventory systems, providing real-time visibility of inventory levels in stores and warehouses.

The new system will overhaul Hem's entire procurement, manufacturing, and warehousing processes, involving significant changes for nearly everyone in the organisation involved in sales or purchasing. Hem's operations director has identified six potential areas of employee resistance to change:

(a) Fear of the unknown
(b) Potential loss of status
(c) Potential loss of employment or reduced rewards
(d) Belief of insufficient resources leading to implementation failure
(e) Lack of faith that the proposed change will result in organisational improvement
(f) Lack of faith that suppliers will adopt the new system

8: Impact of emerging technology

The board seeks your advice on strategies to overcome resistance to change to manage employee resistance to change and an initial high-level change implementation plan.

Required

(a) Apply Kotter and Schlesinger's six management styles to advise on effective methods to overcome employee resistance to the new integrated supply chain management system.

(b) Apply Balogun and Hope Hailey's process for change model to manage the implementation of the new integrated supply chain management system.

Answer

(a) **Overcoming employee resistance to a new integrated supply chain management system**

(i) **Fear of the unknown**

The procurement and sales teams at Hem have used the same manual purchase ordering and inventory management systems for many years, making these processes deeply embedded in the company's culture. This familiarity can lead to resistance when faced with significant technological changes that are difficult to visualise.

Strategy to overcome resistance to change

To address this resistance, Hem should implement a phased communication plan that educates employees and suppliers on the proposed changes and the reasons behind them. The communication should be detailed but manageable, ensuring that information is absorbed in stages without overwhelming employees. Emphasising the benefits to both individuals and the organisation is crucial. Hem should provide a platform for employees to voice their fears and concerns, and management should respond in a measured and supportive manner.

(ii) **Potential loss of status**

Long-serving employees may fear that automation or reorganisation could diminish their decision-making responsibilities and status within the organisation.

Strategy to overcome resistance to change

To mitigate these concerns, Hem should invite key employees to participate in the system and process design, as well as involve them in the change team. This approach acknowledges their current status and provides them with a stake in the outcome, making them more willing to engage with the change.

(iii) **Potential loss of employment or reduced rewards**

Employees might fear that their roles will be diminished or eliminated by the new technology, leading to resistance.

Strategies to overcome resistance to change

Transparency is vital, so Hem should communicate the new structure as early as possible, confirming roles and responsibilities to provide certainty and time for adaptation. While roles may change, they are unlikely to be reduced. Hem's small workforce means that freed-up time from efficient technology can be allocated to other tasks. If there are genuine concerns about role reduction, Hem should negotiate compromises, such as alternative responsibilities or financial compensation.

(iv) **Belief of insufficient resources leading to implementation failure**

Employees may worry that there are not enough resources to implement the new system effectively, especially as they are already fully utilised with ongoing operations.

Strategy to overcome resistance to change

Involving employees in the system design and implementation process can demonstrate that resourcing concerns are addressed and that technology efficiencies will not overburden existing staff. This involvement allows employees to identify potential resource gaps, which can be planned for and addressed.

(v) **Lack of faith that the proposed change will result in organisational improvement**

Hem's procurement team might doubt the effectiveness of the new system, believing it will not address existing problems or might even worsen the situation.

Strategies to overcome resistance to change

Hem should thoroughly explain the objectives and design of the new system, providing accessible resources through the company intranet. This transparency can help persuade employees of the system's benefits. Additionally, involving employees in a consultation process can harness their expertise, allowing them to contribute to the system design and implementation plan.

(vi) **Lack of faith that suppliers will adopt the new system**

Suppliers, particularly smaller ones, may be reluctant to adopt the new system due to perceived effort, cost, and lack of direct benefits.

Strategies to overcome resistance to change

Hem should educate suppliers on how the system can reduce errors and operational costs. Consulting suppliers early in the design process and addressing their concerns can foster inclusion and acceptance. Hem should provide training and support to suppliers, covering associated costs. Offering incentives such as subsidised IT equipment can further ease the transition. If necessary, Hem can require system adoption as a condition of continued trade, seeking alternative suppliers if resistance persists.

(b)

Change process	Recommended change management activities
Step 1: Analyse the competitive position	• Speak to existing fabric and clothing manufacturing suppliers to understand how other clothing retailers, including competitors, use technology to manage their supply chain. • Explore how other industries manage their supply chains effectively. • Consult with supply chain software companies for cost and benefit analysis.
Step 2: Determine type of change needed	• Implementing an integrated supply chain management system introduces cutting-edge distributed ledger technology, replacing a largely manual system. • New system categorised as revolutionary change as represents a rapid and extensive change to supply chain management at Hem. • Requires careful planning and management to avoid errors and implementation failure.

Change process	Recommended change management activities
Step 3: Identify the desired future state	• Fully map existing supply chain processes to determine specific requirements for the new system. • Address current problems such as inaccuracies, late deliveries, and reorder delays. • Consult sales and procurement teams, and key suppliers to capture their needs. • Document change objectives and map out the new system design.
Step 4: Analyse the change context	• Develop a business case quantifying revenue, cost, and profit impacts of current issues such as lost sales due to late deliveries, ordering errors, delays in reacting to sales data and increased inventory write-offs. • Communicate the business case to employees to highlight the benefits of change.
Step 5: Identify the critical change features	• Ensure business continuity by maintaining existing processes during implementation. • Thoroughly test the new system before and after going live. Train all relevant employees and provide support for troubleshooting. • Engage and onboard key suppliers, ensuring they are trained and supported.
Step 6: Determine design choices	• Consult with IT systems experts to determine the best system design. • Engage with potential suppliers and possibly undertake a tender process to ensure value-for-money and an optimal design solution.
Step 7: Design the transition process – levers and mechanisms	• Consider using an expert project manager to design and implement the new system. • Document the logic and reasoning behind the system design for board approval. Develop a detailed implementation plan including a budget, resource plan, and schedule. Appoint a change team with representatives from sales, procurement, and suppliers.
Step 8: Manage the transition	• Track progress against the plan and schedule regular updates with the change team. • Perform extensive system testing with the procurement team and suppliers. • Schedule comprehensive training for employees and suppliers. • Implement supplier service level agreements to clarify responsibilities.
Step 9: Evaluate the change outcomes	• Monitor system performance post-implementation to address any unforeseen issues. • Conduct a post-implementation review to measure success against the agreed scope and objectives. • Address any unmet objectives with proposed resolutions.

6.4.6 Diffusion of Innovations theory (Everett Rogers, 1988) for successful organisation change

Everett Rogers' Diffusion of Innovations theory (1988) provides a framework for understanding how innovations – whether new ideas, processes, products, or cultural changes – spread within a social system over time.

This theory is highly relevant in an organisational context, as it outlines the stages and elements that influence how changes are adopted by individuals and groups within a company.

By focusing on how innovations are perceived against existing corporate values, communicated to influential persons and wider stakeholders, and adopted over time, leaders can better facilitate cultural shifts and ensure the successful implementation of new ideas and practices.

Therefore, Rogers' Diffusion Theory provides a practical roadmap for introducing and managing change within an organisation's culture.

The five key elements of Diffusion of Innovations theory are:

(a) Innovation
(b) Communication channels
(c) Time to adopt
(d) The social system
(e) Adopter categories

Each of these elements is explained further below.

(a) **Innovation**

Innovation is a new idea, behaviour, policy, or product being introduced into the social system. Within an organisation, innovations can include new technologies, management practices, or changes in company culture. The likelihood of adoption depends on several characteristics of the innovation:

- **Relative advantage** – How much better the new idea is perceived compared to the existing one
- **Compatibility** – How well the innovation fits with current values, needs, and past experiences of the organisation
- **Complexity** – The degree to which the innovation is seen as difficult to understand or implement
- **Trialability** – The extent to which the innovation can be tested on a small scale before full implementation
- **Observability** – The visibility of the innovation's results to others, making it easier to demonstrate its benefits

(b) **Communication channels**

Information about the innovation is communicated through various channels, including formal communications (meetings, emails, training sessions) and informal networks (word of mouth, social interactions). The effectiveness of these channels is critical in influencing the perception of the innovation. In an organisation, communication channels can be top-down (from leadership to employees) or peer-based, and both play a vital role in how quickly and positively the change is adopted.

(c) **Time to adopt innovation**

Adoption of an innovation occurs over time and typically follows an 'S-curve.' Initially, only a few members of the organisation adopt the change, but as momentum builds and more people see its

benefits, the rate of adoption accelerates. Eventually, the adoption slows as the innovation becomes a standard practice. This time element involves three main components:

- **Innovation-decision process** – The stages individuals go through when deciding to adopt or reject the innovation – knowledge, persuasion, decision, implementation, and confirmation
- **Rate of adoption** – How quickly the innovation is adopted within the organisation, influenced by its characteristics and communication strategies
- **Time of adoption** – The point in time at which individuals within the organisation choose to adopt the change

(d) **The Social System**

The social structure of the organisation, including its values, norms, hierarchy, and interpersonal networks, significantly impacts the diffusion process. An organisation's culture, values, and power dynamics determine how open it is to change. Within a company, formal leaders (eg, executives, managers) and informal influencers (eg respected employees) play pivotal roles in shaping attitudes toward the innovation. The social system can either facilitate or hinder the spread of new practices depending on how aligned the innovation is with the organisation's cultural norms and values.

(e) **Adopter categories**

Rogers categorises members of the social system based on their willingness to adopt the innovation:

- **Innovators** – Risk-takers who are the first to embrace new ideas. In organisations, these are often forward-thinking employees who are open to experimentation.
- **Early adopters** – Influential opinion leaders who adopt the innovation early and advocate for its benefits. They are crucial for gaining wider acceptance, as others often look to them for cues on whether to embrace the change.
- **Early majority** – These individuals are more cautious but will adopt the innovation once they see its success among early adopters. They represent a larger segment of the workforce and their adoption is essential for the change to become mainstream.
- **Late majority** – Sceptical and resistant to change, they will adopt the innovation only after it has been established and accepted by the majority of their peers.
- **Laggards** – The last to adopt, often due to strong ties to tradition or scepticism towards change. Their acceptance of the innovation typically occurs only when it becomes unavoidable.

Application to organisational culture

Rogers' Diffusion of Innovations theory has significant implications for managing cultural change within an organisation.

When leaders introduce a new practice, policy, or cultural shift, understanding the following five elements effectively guide successful change implementation within an organisation.

(a) **Align with organisational values** – For an innovation (such as a new cultural norm) to be adopted, it must align with the organisation's existing values and practices. Leaders need to communicate how the change is compatible with the company's goals and beneficial for both the business and its employees.

(b) **Gain key influencer engagement** – Identifying and engaging early adopters and opinion leaders within the company is critical. These individuals can act as change champions, promoting the innovation and influencing others to adopt it.

(c) **Effective communication** – The spread of information about the new change must be managed through multiple channels, including both formal announcements and informal conversations. Transparent communication helps in addressing concerns and building trust in the innovation.

(d) **Manage employee resistance** – Understanding that some individuals (late majority and laggards) may be more resistant to change allows leaders to tailor their strategies. Providing clear evidence of benefits, opportunities for trial or testing, and addressing doubts can facilitate wider adoption.

(e) **Emphasise characteristics of successful innovation (sustainable change)** – By considering the innovation's characteristics (eg simplicity, observability), organisations can encourage faster and more sustainable adoption of cultural changes. Highlighting early successes and recognising the contributions of adopters can help maintain momentum and integrate the change into the company culture.

Question

SkyHigh Airways plc, a leading UK-based airline, has been operating successfully for over 30 years, offering domestic and international flights with a strong emphasis on customer service and reliability. The company employs over 8,000 staff, including pilots, cabin crew, ground staff, and administrative personnel. As the airline industry faces increasing competition and evolving customer expectations, SkyHigh has embarked on a strategic plan to modernise its operations and increase efficiency.

SkyHigh is planning a major overhaul of its employee scheduling system, which currently relies on a manual process managed by the human resources and operations teams. The current system is time-consuming, prone to human error, and often results in disputes over shifts, vacation time, and overtime. Recognising these challenges, SkyHigh's board of directors has approved the implementation of an automated scheduling system using advanced software.

The new system promises to streamline shift assignments, optimise staffing levels, and reduce scheduling conflicts. It will use algorithms to match crew availability with flight rosters, factoring in employee preferences, legal requirements, rest periods, and union regulations. The airline expects the automated system to significantly improve efficiency, reduce costs, and enhance employee satisfaction by providing a fair and transparent scheduling process. However, the change also raises concerns among employees about potential job redundancies, reduced flexibility, and the impersonal nature of automation.

SkyHigh anticipates resistance from various stakeholder groups within the company:

- **Pilots and cabin crew:** Many employees are concerned that the new system may restrict their control over their schedules, limit flexibility, and fail to accommodate personal circumstances. Some worry that the system will not adequately consider their individual preferences or special requests, potentially leading to dissatisfaction and fatigue.

- **Operations and human resources teams:** These teams, which currently manage the manual scheduling process, fear that the automation will lead to job redundancies or significantly alter their roles within the company. They also express concern over the potential technical challenges of implementing the new system.

- **Union representatives:** Unions are cautious, emphasising the need for transparency, fairness, and compliance with employment contracts and regulations. They demand assurance that the new system will not compromise employee welfare or violate agreed-upon working conditions.

The management of SkyHigh aims to implement the automated scheduling system successfully within the next twelve months. For the change to be effective, they need to ensure buy-in from employees, smooth integration with existing systems, and minimal disruption to operations.

To guide the implementation, SkyHigh's leadership team will apply Everett Rogers' Diffusion of Innovations Theory to manage and facilitate this organisational change.

Required

Advise the board of SkyHigh on how to successfully implement the new scheduling system by applying Everett Rogers' Diffusion of Innovations Theory, ensuring the approach maximises stakeholder acceptance and minimises resistance.

(a) Innovation
(b) Communication channels
(c) Time to adopt
(d) Social system
(e) Adopter categories

Answer

SkyHigh Airways plc is set to introduce an automated employee scheduling system to modernise its operations and improve efficiency. While this change promises significant benefits, including reduced errors and enhanced transparency, it raises concerns among employees, unions, and various internal teams regarding job security, flexibility, and fairness. To implement this change successfully, the board must apply Everett Rogers' Diffusion of Innovations Theory, focusing on innovation characteristics, communication, timing, social dynamics, and adopter categories to minimise resistance and maximise acceptance, while considering the potential impacts on SkyHigh.

(a) **Innovation**

The automated scheduling system is SkyHigh's proposed innovation, intended to streamline operations and enhance transparency. To foster acceptance, SkyHigh must highlight the system's direct benefits, such as improved accuracy in scheduling, reduced disputes, and compliance with regulations. Emphasising how the system can accommodate personal preferences and address employee fatigue will help mitigate concerns, particularly from pilots and cabin crew. The perceived complexity of this system is a potential barrier, so offering hands-on training and trials will be crucial. Demonstrating that the system can improve working conditions and provide employees with more predictable schedules will help align the innovation with SkyHigh's values of employee welfare and customer service.

(b) **Communication channels**

Effective communication is vital to addressing concerns and gaining support. SkyHigh should use formal channels like company meetings, emails, and newsletters to articulate the necessity of the system, linking it to long-term organisational goals such as improved operational efficiency and market competitiveness. Informal channels, such as small group workshops and feedback sessions, will allow employees to voice concerns and contribute ideas. Early involvement of union representatives through open dialogue will demonstrate transparency and build trust. By using a range of communication methods, SkyHigh can create a sense of ownership among employees, reducing the fear of job loss and enhancing buy-in for the change.

(c) **Time to adopt**

A phased implementation approach is necessary to avoid disruption and resistance. SkyHigh should initiate a pilot phase in a smaller operational area, allowing for adjustments based on real-world feedback before a full rollout. This gradual adoption provides employees with time to adapt and reduces the anxiety associated with sudden changes. Clear timelines and regular updates on progress will help manage expectations, showing that SkyHigh is committed to a smooth transition. The company should prepare for some initial impact on productivity but position this as an investment in a more efficient future.

(d) **Social system**

SkyHigh's internal social structure plays a significant role in the change process. Identifying and engaging key influencers within the workforce, such as senior pilots, experienced cabin crew, and respected HR staff, will help shape a positive narrative around the new system. By involving these individuals in the planning and testing phases, SkyHigh can use their support to influence their peers. Additionally, fostering open communication with union representatives will help address employee concerns about fairness and job security. By creating a support network within the social system, SkyHigh can alleviate fears and encourage acceptance.

(e) **Adopter categories**

Understanding the different categories of adopters within the organisation is crucial. Innovators and early adopters, such as tech-savvy staff and those who have previously advocated for process improvements, should be the first to trial the system. Their experiences and positive feedback can then be used to influence the early majority. As the system's benefits become apparent, the late majority and laggards will be more likely to accept the change. SkyHigh should focus on providing consistent support and clear evidence of the system's advantages to encourage widespread adoption, thereby minimising the negative impact on employee morale and productivity.

Conclusion

By applying Rogers' Diffusion of Innovations Theory, SkyHigh can strategically implement the automated scheduling system in a way that considers potential impacts on its operations, employees, and brand reputation. Emphasising the system's benefits, facilitating clear and open communication, adopting a phased rollout, engaging key social influencers, and addressing different adopter categories will be key to overcoming resistance. This approach will help SkyHigh minimise disruptions, enhance operational efficiency, and maintain its standing as a responsible and progressive employer in the competitive airline industry.

7 Implementing new information systems

7.1 Cost benefit analysis and reviews

Cost-benefit analysis and cost-benefit reviews can be used to determine whether or not it is worthwhile developing a new information system and to determine whether, after a new system has been implemented, it achieves the benefits that it set out to.

Cost-benefit analysis is performed before or during the development of an information system. Its performance is complicated by the fact that many of the system cost elements are estimates or are unknown and that benefits can often be highly qualitative and subjective in nature.

A cost-benefit review is similar to a cost-benefit analysis, except that it is performed after the system has been implemented. Therefore, actual data can be used in the review.

The main analysis and review techniques are:

- The payback method
- Discounted cashflow
- Accounting rate of return/Return on investment

7.2 Costs of information systems

The costs of an information system can be categorised as development, implementation and running costs.

- Development costs are incurred before the system has been implemented.
- Implementation costs are incurred to get the developed system ready for use.
- Running costs are incurred on a day-to-day basis as the system is operated and maintained.

System costs can also be analysed under the following headings:

Cost type	Examples
Equipment costs	Computer and peripherals
	Ancillary equipment
Installation costs	New buildings (if necessary)
	The computer room (wiring, air-conditioning if necessary)
Development costs	Measuring and analysing the existing system
	Software/consultancy work
	Systems analysis and programming
	Changeover costs such as file conversion
Personnel costs	Staff training
	Staff recruitment/relocation
	Staff salaries and pensions
Operating costs	Consumable materials
	Maintenance
	Accommodation costs
	Heating/power/insurance/telephone
	Standby arrangements, in case the system breaks down

7.3 Benefits of information systems

The benefits of an information system can be categorised as direct and indirect.

- Direct benefits include reduced operating costs, for example lower staff overtime payments. These are often financial and easy to quantify.
- Indirect benefits might include better decision making and the freeing of human 'brainpower' from routine tasks so that it can be used for more creative work. These are often non-financial and hard to quantify.

General benefits from a proposed new system may include:

- Savings because an inefficient old system will no longer be operated
- Extra savings or revenue benefits because of the improvements or enhancements that the new system should bring
- Greater customer satisfaction, arising from a prompter service
- Improved staff morale from working with a 'better' system
- Better decision making is hard to quantify, but may result from better systems
- Faster processing speed of routine tasks and outputs

- Reduced scope for human error improves accuracy of input
- Increased volumes of data that can be processed
- Ability to handle more complexity in terms of the number of data streams
- Improved collaboration across all business functions due to real-time sharing of data
- Improved methods of presenting data in a user-friendly way that is easier to understand (data visualisations)

7.4 Risks of new information systems

There are a number of risks involved in implementing a new information system. Risks can occur at a number of stages, in particular at the design and development stages.

7.4.1 Risks in the design stage

A key risk is that the system is not designed appropriately so that it does not meet the needs of end-users. A common cause of dissatisfaction with new information systems is insufficient user involvement when establishing requirements for the new system.

Other risks that can cause dissatisfaction with information systems at this stage, include the following:

- Project managers are often technicians, not managers. However, technical ability of IT staff is also no guarantee of project management skill. An individual might be a highly proficient analyst or programmer, but not a good manager.
- The project manager may accept an unrealistic deadline where the timescale is fixed early in the planning process. User demands may be accepted as deadlines before sufficient consideration is given to the realism of this.
- Unrealistic deadlines would be identified much earlier if a proper planning process was undertaken.
- There is a lack of monitoring and control.
- Users change their requirements, resulting in changes to the system as it is being developed.
- Poor timetabling and resourcing. It is no use being presented on Day 1 with a team of programmers when there is still systems analysis and design work to do. The development and implementation of a computer project may take a considerable length of time (perhaps two years for a relatively large installation). Major projects require formal planning and scheduling.

7.4.2 Risks in the development process

Issues that occur when implementing a new system can usually be traced to deficiencies in the development process.

The table that follows outlines some common risks and mistakes that adversely affect the implementation process, and the systems development stage or activity they relate to.

Stage/activity	Problems
Analysis	The problem the system is intended to solve is not fully understood.
	Investigation of the situation is hindered by insufficient resources.
	User input is inadequate through either lack of consultation or lack of user interest.
	The project team is unable to dedicate the time required or insufficient time spent planning the project.

Stage/activity	Problems
Design	Insufficient user input
	Lack of flexibility – the organisation's future needs are neglected.
	The system requires unforeseen changes in working patterns.
	Failure to perform organisation impact analysis. An organisational impact analysis studies the way a proposed system will affect organisation structure, attitudes, decision making and operations. The analysis aims to ensure the system is designed to best ensure integration with the organisation.
	Organisational factors sometimes overlooked include: • Ergonomics (including equipment, work environment and user interfaces) • Health and safety • Compliance with legislation • Job design • Employee involvement
Programming	Insufficient time and money allocated to programming
	Programmers supplied with incomplete or inaccurate specifications
	The logic of the program is misunderstood
	Poor programming technique results in programs that are hard to modify
	Programs are not adequately documented
Testing	Insufficient time and money allocated to testing
	Failure to develop an organised testing plan
	Insufficient user involvement
	User management do not review and sign off the results of testing
Conversion	Insufficient time and money allocated to data conversion
	Insufficient checking between old and new files
	The process is rushed to compensate for time overruns elsewhere
Final implementation	Insufficient time, money and/or appropriate staff mean the process has to be rushed
	Lack of user training increases the risk of system underutilisation and rejection
	Poor system and user documentation
	Lack of performance standards to assess system performance against
	System maintenance provisions inadequate

7.5 Implementing new information systems

Once a new system has been through a cost benefit analysis, and has been designed and developed, it is ready to be implemented. The main steps in the implementation of an information system are as follows:

7.5.1 Installation

Installing involves setting up the computer hardware and loading the software onto it. It also involves setting up local networks and internet connections. Historically the software would have been loaded onto a central mainframe computer, although more recently, client server networks are used, whereby

programmes are loaded onto servers and accessed from 'client' PCs for shared programmes (eg the accounting system). Many programmes are loaded directly onto the users' PCs.

The growth of cloud computing means that much of the hardware and software may be located remotely on the cloud service provider's hardware, accessed via the internet. If that is the case, the installation stage will involve giving users access to the cloud-based systems.

7.5.2 Testing

A system must be thoroughly tested before implementation, to prevent the system 'going live' with faults that might prove costly. The scope of tests and trials will vary with the size and complexity of the system. To ensure a coherent, effective approach to testing, a testing strategy should be developed.

A testing strategy should cover the following areas:

Testing strategy area	Comment
Test strategy	A testing strategy should be formulated that details the approach that will be taken to testing, including the tests to be conducted and the testing tools/techniques that will be used.
Test plan	A test plan should be developed that states what will be tested, when it will be tested (sequence), and the test environment.
Test design	The logic and reasoning behind the design of the tests should be explained.
Test procedures	Detailed procedures should be provided for all tests. This explanation should ensure tests are carried out consistently, even if different people carry out the tests.
Documentation	It must be clear how the results of tests are to be documented. This provides a record of errors, and a starting point for error correction procedures.
Retesting	The retest procedure should be explained. In many cases, after correction all aspects of the software should be retested to ensure the corrections have not affected other aspects of the software.

Four stages of testing can be identified as:

Stage	Comment
(a) Testing system logic	Before any programs are written, the logic devised by the systems analyst should be checked. This process often involves the use of flowcharts or data flow diagrams. Both tools involve the manual plotting of different types of data and transactions through the system. The object is to ensure that all possibilities have been catered for and that the processing logic is correct. When all results are as expected, programs can be written.
(b) Program testing	Program testing involves processing test data through all system programs. Test data should be of the type that the program will be required to process and should include invalid/exceptional items to test whether the program reacts as it should. The testing process should be fully documented – recording data used, expected results, actual results and action taken. This documentation may be referred to at a later date, for example if program modifications are required. Two types of program testing are unit testing and unit integration testing.
(c) System integration testing	System integration testing has a wider focus than program testing. It will involve testing both before installation (known as off-line testing) and after implementation (on-line testing). As many problems as possible should be identified before implementation, but it is likely that some problems will only become apparent when the system goes live.

Stage	Comment
(d) User acceptance testing	The purpose of user acceptance testing is to establish whether users are satisfied that the system meets the system specification when used in the actual operating environment. Users process test data; system performance is closely monitored, and users report whether they feel the system meets their needs. Test data may include some historical data, because it is then possible to check results against the 'actual' output from the old system.

7.5.3 Types of tests

To ensure as many scenarios as possible are tested, testing should include the following types of tests:

- **Realistic tests.** These involve using the system in the way it will be used in reality – ie the actual environment, users and types of data.

- **Contrived tests.** These are designed to present the system with unusual events to ensure these are handled correctly, for example that invalid data is rejected.

- **Volume tests.** These present the system with large numbers of transactions to see how the system copes.

- **User acceptance tests.** These are undertaken by users to ensure the system meets user needs.

7.5.4 Training

Employee training in the use of a new system is essential if the system is to meet its full potential. Training should be provided to all staff who will use the system. Training should focus on the specific tasks the user is required to perform, such as entering an invoice or answering a query. There are a range of options available to deliver training, as shown below.

Training method	Comment
Individual tuition 'at desk'	A trainer could work with an employee observing how they use a system and suggesting possible alternatives.
Classroom course	The software could be used in a classroom environment, using 'dummy' data.
Computer-based training	Training can be provided using CDs, DVDs, over an intranet or via an interactive website.
Case studies and exercises	Regardless of how training is delivered, it is likely that material will be based around a realistic case study relevant to the user.
Software reference material	Users may find online help, built-in tutorials and reference manuals useful.

7.5.5 File conversion

File conversion means converting existing files into a format suitable for the new system.

Most computer systems are based around files containing data. When a new system is introduced, files must be created that conform to the requirements of that system. The various scenarios that file conversion could involve are outlined in the following table.

Existing data	Comment
Held in manual (ie paper) files	Data will be keyed into the new system – probably via input forms, so that data entry operators have all the data they require in one document. This is likely to be a time-consuming process. Such situations are very rare, as most new systems replace existing computerised systems rather than manual systems.
Held in existing computer files	How complex the process is in converting the files to a format compatible with the new system will depend on technical issues and the coding systems used. It may be possible to automate much of the conversion process.
Held in both manual and computer files	Two separate conversion procedures are required.
Existing data is incomplete	If the missing data is crucial, it must be researched and made available in a format suitable for the new system – or suitable for the file conversion process.

7.5.6 System changeover

Once the new system has been fully and satisfactorily tested, the final stage of implementation, changeover, can begin. There are four approaches to system changeover; each varies in terms of time required, cost and risk.

- **Direct ('Big Bang') changeover** – the old system is completely replaced by the new system in one move.
- **Parallel running** – the old and new systems are run in parallel for a period of time.
- **Pilot operation** – a part or parts of an organisation are selected to operate the new system in parallel with the existing system.
- **Phased or modular implementation** – a complete section of the system is selected for a direct changeover.

The advantages and disadvantages of the various changeover methods are outlined below.

Method	Advantages	Disadvantages
Direct ('Big Bang') changeover	Quick Minimal cost Minimal workload	Risky Could disrupt operations If fails, will be costly
Parallel running	Safe Provides a way of verifying results of the new system	Costly, two systems need to be operated Time consuming Additional workload
Pilot operation	Less risky than direct changeover Less costly than complete parallel running	Can take a long time to achieve total changeover Not as safe as complete parallel running

Method	Advantages	Disadvantages
Phased or modular changeover	Less risky than a single direct changeover	Can take a long time to achieve total changeover
	Any problems should be in one area – other operations unaffected	Interfaces between parts of the system may make this impractical

Question

Relax Hotels, a prominent private hotel chain known for its properties in areas of remarkable natural beauty across the UK, is considering implementing a new integrated hotel room sales and room booking management system to replace its current separate legacy systems. The new system aims to revolutionise how Relax Hotels handles customer bookings, manages room availability, and enhances overall guest experiences.

The new system will incorporate functionalities such as online booking portals for guests to reserve rooms conveniently, real-time updates on room availability and pricing, automated payment processing, and seamless integration with Relax Hotels' existing customer relationship management (CRM) system. Additionally, the system will feature advanced reporting and analytics capabilities to provide insights into booking trends, customer preferences, and revenue performance.

The board of Relax Hotels has requested advice on the process for implementing the new system, covering the following key areas:

The board have asked for the following advice on the process for new system implementation

(a) System implementation planning
(b) System implementation management
(c) System changeover methodology
(d) System risk management
(e) System testing

Required

Prepare a briefing paper which covers the advice requested by the board of Relax Hotels

Answer

Introduction

Relax Hotels, renowned for its picturesque properties in scenic locations across the UK, is embarking on a transformative journey by implementing a new integrated hotel room sales and room booking management system. This innovative system promises to revolutionise the way Relax Hotels handles customer bookings, manages room availability, and enhances overall guest experiences. The board of Relax Hotels has solicited advice on various facets of the implementation process to ensure a seamless and successful transition to the new system.

(a) **System implementation planning**

System implementation planning involves meticulous preparation and organisation to ensure a smooth transition to the new system. This encompasses creating a detailed project plan outlining tasks, timelines, resource allocation, and dependencies. Additionally, it entails conducting a comprehensive assessment of the organisation's current processes, infrastructure, and potential challenges. By identifying key stakeholders and establishing clear communication channels, Relax Hotels can foster collaboration and alignment throughout the implementation journey. Moreover,

developing a robust change management strategy to address employee concerns and facilitate training programs is essential for maximising user adoption and minimising resistance.

(b) **System implementation management**

Effective implementation management necessitates the appointment of a skilled project manager to oversee the execution of tasks and coordinate activities across various departments. The project manager plays a pivotal role in monitoring progress, addressing issues promptly, and ensuring adherence to timelines and budget constraints. Establishing regular progress meetings and status updates enables stakeholders to stay informed and actively participate in decision-making processes. Moreover, fostering a culture of accountability and teamwork encourages cross-functional collaboration and facilitates problem-solving efforts.

(c) **System changeover methodology**

Selecting the appropriate changeover methodology is critical for minimising disruptions and optimising the transition to the new system. Relax Hotels must evaluate various options, such as direct (big bang) changeover, parallel running, pilot operation, or phased implementation, based on factors such as organisational readiness, risk tolerance, and system complexity. Each method has its advantages and challenges, and the chosen approach should align with the organisation's strategic objectives and operational priorities. Given Relax Hotels is open 365% then a pilot operation with phased implementation is recommended, to manage costs and to minimise system risk and disruption to business operations.

(d) **System risk management**

Proactive risk management is imperative to identify, assess, and mitigate potential risks associated with the implementation process. Relax Hotels must conduct a comprehensive risk analysis to identify potential threats, vulnerabilities, and impacts on project deliverables and organisational objectives. This involves assessing technical challenges, data migration issues, user acceptance, and external factors such as regulatory compliance and market dynamics. By developing contingency plans and mitigation strategies, Relax Hotels can proactively address risks and ensure business continuity throughout the implementation journey.

(e) **System testing**

System testing is a crucial phase in the implementation process to validate the functionality, performance, and usability of the new system. Relax Hotels should conduct comprehensive testing encompassing various types, including system logic testing, program testing, system integration testing, and user acceptance testing. Rigorous testing ensures the identification and resolution of defects or issues before full deployment, minimising disruptions and ensuring a positive user experience. Moreover, involving end-users in the testing process enables feedback gathering and user validation, enhancing system usability and alignment with business requirements.

Conclusion

The successful implementation of the new integrated hotel room sales and room booking management system requires meticulous planning, effective management, rigorous testing, and proactive risk management. By following best practices in system implementation and leveraging the expertise of key stakeholders, Relax Hotels can navigate the complexities of the implementation process and unlock the full potential of the new system. With a focus on collaboration, communication, and continuous improvement, Relax Hotels can achieve its objectives of enhancing operational efficiency, improving guest experiences, and driving sustainable growth in the competitive hospitality industry.

7.6 Post-implementation review

Once the system is up and running, it is good practice to perform a post-implementation review ('postmortem'). The objective of this is to ensure that the benefits that were identified when the new system was first planned have been met, and to compare the costs of the system with what was expected. The expected benefits and costs would have been documented in the cost benefit analysis, if one was performed, before the decision to go ahead with the systems implementation was made.

A post-implementation review usually takes place a few months after the system has been implemented when the system is up and running. By this time, the staff will have become used to the system and will be able to give a better-informed view of how the system is working.

End of chapter questions

Question 1

Relax Hotels (Relax) is a prominent private hotel chain renowned for its properties situated in areas of remarkable natural beauty across the UK. Embracing nature-inspired design principles, each Relax hotel endeavours to bring the outdoors indoors, creating a serene ambiance throughout its rooms, restaurants, and public spaces. Offering a top-tier experience, Relax Hotels feature luxurious spa facilities, signature treatments, state-of-the-art fitness centres, and highly acclaimed dining options. Presently comprising eight hotels.

On booking a hotel room, Relax processes the personal data and payment details for its guests. Currently, Relax does not have formal cybersecurity risk response protocols, cybersecurity policies, or utilise automation, artificial intelligence, or data analytics in its operations or marketing.

Relax's chief financial officer (CFO) recently attended a conference entitled, 'Emerging Technology and Cyber Risk.' As a result, the CFO has become more concerned about cybersecurity risks and believes the board should consider introducing artificial intelligence to automate or improve finance, hotel booking, procurement, or other operational management processes.

Required

Advise the board on the following:

(a) Recommend the benefits of implementing a formal cybersecurity risk governance framework and policies at Relax Hotels.

(b) Consider the benefits of applying the following data analytical methods at Relax Hotels.

(c) Explain how artificial intelligence (AI) could automate or improve operational processes at Relax Hotels.

Suggested answers

Question 1

(a) **Benefits of implementing a formal cybersecurity risk governance framework and policies**

   (i) **Enhanced protection of guest data:** Implementing cybersecurity policies will help Relax Hotels safeguard sensitive guest information, such as personal data and payment details, from cyber threats like data breaches and hacking attacks. By establishing protocols for data encryption, access control, and incident response, Relax Hotels can mitigate the risk of unauthorised access and data theft, ensuring the privacy and security of guest information. Demonstrating a commitment to cybersecurity through robust policies and governance frameworks instils confidence in guests and stakeholders, enhancing Relax Hotels' reputation as a trusted and secure hospitality provider.

   (ii) **Business continuity:** A formal cybersecurity risk governance framework enables Relax Hotels to identify, assess, and mitigate cybersecurity risks systematically, enhancing the organisation's overall risk management strategy. By conducting regular risk assessments and implementing controls to address vulnerabilities, the hotel can proactively manage cyber threats and minimise the impact of potential security incidents on its operations and reputation. This will help Relax Hotels to avoid business disruption by reducing the likelihood of third-party system hacking or other cyber-attacks. By implementing cybersecurity policies and protocols for incident response and recovery, the hotel improves its ability to maintain operations and recover quickly from cyber incidents, minimising downtime and financial losses.

   (iii) **Regulatory compliance:** Adhering to cybersecurity best practices and regulations will ensure that Relax Hotels meets legal and industry standards for data protection and privacy, reducing the risk of regulatory penalties and reputational damage. Compliance with regulations such as the General Data Protection Regulation (GDPR) demonstrates the hotel's commitment to protecting guest rights and maintaining trust in its brand.

   (iv) **Competitive advantage:** By prioritising cybersecurity, Relax Hotels can differentiate itself from competitors and attract customers who prioritise data security and privacy when choosing accommodation options. Promoting the hotel's commitment to cybersecurity as a unique selling point can help attract discerning guests who value peace of mind and protection of their personal information.

(b) **Benefits of applying data analytical methods at Relax Hotels**

   (i) **Customer insights:** Data analytics can provide Relax Hotels with valuable insights into guest preferences, booking patterns, and satisfaction levels, enabling the organisation to tailor its services and offerings to meet customer needs effectively. By analysing guest feedback, reviews, and demographic data, the hotel can identify trends and opportunities for improvement in its amenities, facilities, and customer service.

   (ii) **Operational efficiency:** Analysing operational data can help Relax Hotels identify inefficiencies, streamline processes, and optimise resource allocation, leading to cost savings and improved productivity. By tracking key performance indicators (KPIs) such as occupancy rates, average room revenue, and staff productivity, the hotel can identify areas for improvement and implement targeted strategies to enhance operational efficiency.

   (iii) **Revenue optimisation:** By analysing booking trends and demand forecasts, Relax Hotels can implement dynamic pricing strategies and targeted marketing campaigns to maximise revenue and occupancy rates. By leveraging data analytics tools to identify peak demand periods, seasonal trends, and customer preferences, the hotel can optimise pricing strategies and promotional offers to attract and retain guests while maximising profitability.

(iv) **Fraud detection and prevention:** Data analytics tools can detect unusual patterns or anomalies in transaction data, helping Relax Hotels identify and prevent fraudulent activities, such as payment fraud or unauthorised access to guest accounts. By monitoring transactional data for signs of suspicious activity, the hotel can implement fraud detection algorithms and security measures to protect guest information and financial assets.

(v) **Personalised guest experiences:** Utilising data analytics, Relax Hotels can create personalised guest experiences by offering customised recommendations, promotions, and services based on individual preferences and behaviour. By analysing guest data such as past booking history, dietary preferences, and leisure activities, the hotel can tailor its offerings to meet the unique needs and preferences of each guest, enhancing satisfaction and loyalty.

(c) **How AI could automate or improve operational processes at Relax Hotels**

(i) **Chatbots for customer service:** AI-powered chatbots can handle guest inquiries, booking requests, and room reservations, providing 24/7 customer support and improving response times without human intervention. By leveraging natural language processing (NLP) and machine learning algorithms, chatbots can interact with guests in real-time, answering questions, providing recommendations, and assisting with booking inquiries.

(ii) **Predictive maintenance:** AI algorithms can analyse equipment and facility data to predict maintenance needs, schedule repairs proactively, and minimise downtime, ensuring uninterrupted guest services and operational efficiency. By monitoring sensor data from HVAC systems, elevators, and other critical infrastructure, AI-driven predictive maintenance systems can detect early signs of equipment failure and alert maintenance staff to take corrective action before issues escalate.

(iii) **Personalised marketing:** AI-driven analytics can segment guests based on demographic, behavioural, and transactional data, allowing Relax Hotels to deliver targeted marketing campaigns and promotions tailored to individual preferences and interests. By analysing guest data such as past booking history, spending patterns, and demographic profiles, AI algorithms can identify opportunities for upselling, cross-selling, and personalised offers, maximising revenue and customer engagement.

(iv) **Dynamic pricing optimisation:** AI algorithms can analyse market trends, competitor pricing, and demand forecasts to adjust room rates dynamically in real-time, maximising revenue and occupancy rates while remaining competitive in the market. By leveraging machine learning models to predict demand fluctuations and price elasticity, Relax Hotels can optimise pricing strategies to capitalise on peak demand periods and maximise revenue potential.

(v) **Predictive analytics for demand forecasting:** AI models can analyse historical booking data, seasonal trends, and external factors to forecast future demand accurately, enabling Relax Hotels to optimise inventory, staffing levels, and resource allocation to meet anticipated demand levels. By leveraging predictive analytics to anticipate fluctuations in demand, the hotel can optimise operational efficiency, minimise overbooking or under booking, and ensure optimal guest satisfaction levels.

Managing ethical issues in MDCS

Topic list	Syllabus reference
1 Introduction to ethics for MDCS	All LOs
2 Code of Ethics for professional accountants	"
3 Corporate codes of ethics	"
4 Ethics for accountants in business	"
5 Ethical dilemmas	"
6 Frameworks for dealing with ethical dilemmas	"

Introduction

MDCS will examine ethical issues faced by professional accountants by considering some of the complex ethical issues that may arise during the course of their careers. This chapter will explain the role of the Code of Ethics in ensuring that professional accountants in practice uphold the fundamental principles, as well as the role that a company's code of ethics can play in ensuring that accountants in business are able to apply ethical principles. For the exam, you will need to identify ethical dilemmas and practise **applying** ethical guidelines in given scenarios to resolve these. Before we can understand how to address ethical issues, we need to fully appreciate the nature and range of potential ethical issues faced by professional accountants.

1 Introduction to ethics for MDCS

Ethics are a code of moral principles that people follow with respect to what is right or wrong. Ethical principles are not necessarily enforced by law, although the law incorporates some moral judgements – for example, stealing is wrong ethically and is also punishable legally.

As finance professionals, we will be faced with problems which cannot be solved by applying a reporting standard or legal principle. There may be a moral dilemma or a potential problem, created by a situation or certain behaviours. To resolve these, we may need to apply an ethical code to understand the nature of the problem and the approach required to address it.

1.1 Role of ethical theory

Ethics is concerned with right and wrong and how conduct should be judged to be good or bad. It is about how we should live our lives and, in particular, how we should **behave towards other people**. It is therefore relevant to all forms of human activity.

Business life is a fruitful source of ethical dilemmas because its primary purpose is **material gain**, the making of profit. Success in business requires a constant, avid search for potential advantage over others, and business people are under pressure to do whatever yields such advantage.

It is important to understand that if ethics is applicable to corporate behaviour at all, it must therefore be a fundamental aspect of **mission**, since everything the organisation does flows from that. Managers responsible for strategic decision making cannot avoid responsibility for their organisation's ethical standing. Organisations should aim to consciously apply ethical rules to all of their decisions as part of their mission in order to filter out potentially undesirable developments.

2 Code of Ethics for professional accountants

Key term

> **Professional Codes of Ethics:** Apply to the **individual behaviour** of professionals and are often based on principles, supplemented by guidance on **threats and safeguards**.

2.1 Contents of professional codes

The International Ethics Standards Board for Accountants (IESBA), which is part of the International Federation of Accountants (IFAC), issued an International Code of Ethics for professional accountants (including International Independence Standards) which became effective in June 2019. It provides a good illustration of how codes, not just for accountants, but for other professionals too, are constructed:

(a) The Code begins by stating that it reflects the acceptance by the accountancy profession of the responsibility to act in the **public interest**.

(b) The detailed guidance begins with establishment of **fundamental principles of ethics**.

(c) The guide then supplies a **conceptual framework** that requires accountants to identify, evaluate and address **threats to compliance**, apply **safeguards** to eliminate the threats or to reduce them to an acceptable level.

2.1.1 Advantages of professional codes

IFAC suggests that requiring use of a principles-based framework, rather than a set of specific rules, is in the public interest for the following reasons:

(a) Codes represent a clear statement that **professionals** are expected to act in the public interest, and act as a **benchmark** against which behaviour can be judged. They should thus enhance public confidence in the professions.

(b) Codes emphasise the importance of professionals **considering ethical issues actively** and seeking to comply, rather than only being concerned with avoiding what is forbidden.

(c) The IFAC code states that they can be **applied internationally.** Local differences are not significant.

(d) Codes can include detailed guidance, which should **assist ethical decision-making.**

(e) Codes can include **explicit prohibitions** if necessary.

(f) Codes prescribe **minimum standards of behaviour** that are expected.

2.1.2 Disadvantages of professional codes

(a) Professional codes, with their **identification of many different situations,** can lose focus on key issues.

(b) Evidence suggests that some treat codes as a set of rules to be **complied with and 'box-ticked'**.

(c) **International codes** such as the IFAC code cannot fully capture **regional variations in beliefs and practice.**

(d) The value of international codes may be limited by their not being legally enforceable around the world (although professional accountancy bodies can **enforce sanctions** against members for serious breaches).

(e) **Illustrative examples** can be interpreted mistakenly as rules to follow in similar circumstances.

(f) Giving a lot of illustrative examples in codes may give the impression that ethical considerations are **primarily important** only when accountants are facing decisions illustrated in the codes. They may **downplay the importance of acting ethically** when facing decisions that are not clearly covered in the codes.

2.2 Contents of professional codes

IFAC suggests that the sheer variety of threats to compliance with the fundamental principles mean that no guidance can cover every situation where there is a potential threat.

2.2.1 Advantages of principles-based guidance

IFAC suggests that requiring use of a principles-based framework, rather than a set of specific rules, is in the public interest for the following reasons:

(a) It places the onus on the professional to **consider actively** relevant issues in a given situation, rather than just agreeing action with a checklist of forbidden items. It also requires them to **demonstrate** that a responsible conclusion has been reached about ethical issues.

(b) It **prevents professionals interpreting legalistic requirements narrowly** to get around the ethical requirements. There is an extent to which rules engender deception, whereas principles encourage compliance.

(c) It **allows for variations** that are found in every **individual situation**. Each situation is likely to be different.

(d) It can accommodate a **rapidly changing business or technological environment**, where specific rules can soon become outdated.

(e) It can include **examples** to illustrate how the principles are applied.

2.2.2 Disadvantages of principles-based guidance

(a) As ethical codes cannot include all circumstances and dilemmas, accountants need a very good understanding of the **underlying principles**.

(b) A principles–based code can be difficult to enforce legally, unless the breach of the code is blatant. Most are therefore **voluntary** and perhaps therefore less effective.

2.3 The fundamental principles for professional accountants

These principles are designed to ensure that the accountant fulfils the public interest and meets the expectations of society.

Fundamental principles	
Professional competence and due care	Members have a continuing duty to maintain **professional knowledge and skill** at a level required to ensure that a client or employer receives competent professional service based on current developments in practice, legislation and techniques. Members should act diligently and in accordance with applicable technical and professional standards when providing professional services.
Integrity	Members should be **straightforward** and **honest** in all business and professional relationships.
Professional behaviour	Members should comply with relevant laws and regulations and should avoid any action that discredits the profession.
Confidentiality	Members should respect the **confidentiality of information** acquired as a result of professional and business relationships and should not disclose any such information to third parties without proper or specific authority, or unless there is a legal or professional right or duty to disclose. Confidential information acquired as a result of professional and business relationships should not be used for the personal advantage of members or third parties.
Objectivity	Members should not allow **bias**, **conflicts of interest** or **undue influence** of others to override professional or business judgements.

2.4 Ethical threats to compliance with the fundamental principles for professional accountants

There are various ethical threats to compliance with the fundamental principles.

Threat	Definition	Examples
Self-interest	Financial or other interests of a professional accountant or of an immediate family member inappropriately influence judgement or behaviour	Having a financial interest in a client
Self-review	Evaluation of a judgement by the accountant who made the judgement, or a member of the same organisation	Auditing financial statements prepared by the firm

Threat	Definition	Examples
Advocacy	Accountant promoting a position or opinion to the point where objectivity may be compromised	Advocating the client's case in a lawsuit
Familiarity	A close relationship resulting in excessive trust in, or sympathy for, others	Audit team member having family at the client
Intimidation	Accountant not acting objectively because of actual or perceived pressures	Threats of replacement due to disagreement

As we shall see in the next section, these threats are particularly relevant in the context of threats to independence.

2.5 Ethical safeguards for accountants in practice

There are two general categories of ethical safeguard identified in the guidance:

- Safeguards created by the profession, legislation or regulation
- Safeguards within the assurance client/the firm's own systems and procedures

2.5.1 Examples of ethical safeguards created by the profession, legislation or regulation

- Educational training and experience requirements for entry into the profession
- Continuing professional development requirements
- Corporate governance regulations
- Professional standards
- Professional or regulatory monitoring and disciplinary procedures

IFAC issues ethical standards, quality control standards and auditing standards that work together to ensure independence is safeguarded and quality audits are carried out.

2.5.2 Examples of ethical safeguards in the firm's own systems and procedures

If AIA members work for an accountancy practice, the firm should have the following safeguards in place in relation to its systems and procedures.

- The firm's leadership stressing compliance with fundamental principles
- Leadership of the firm establishing the expectation that employees will act in the public interest
- Quality control policies and procedures
- Documented policies on identification and evaluation of threats and identification and application of safeguards
- Documented policies covering independence threats and safeguards in relation to assurance engagements
- Documented internal procedures requiring compliance with fundamental principles
- Policies and procedures enabling identification of interests and relationships between the firm's team and clients
- Policies and procedures to manage reliance on revenue from a single client
- Using different teams for non-assurance work

- Prohibiting individuals who are not team members from influencing the outcome of the engagement
- Timely communication of policies and procedures and appropriate training and education
- Designating a senior manager to be responsible for overseeing quality control
- Advising staff of independence requirements in relation to specific clients
- Disciplinary measures
- Promotion of communication by staff to senior management of any ethical compliance issue that concerns them

There should also be safeguards relating to specific assignments:

- Involving an additional professional accountant to review the work done or otherwise advise as necessary
- Consulting an independent third party, such as a committee of independent directors, a professional regulatory body or another professional accountant
- Rotating senior personnel
- Discussing ethical issues with those in charge of client governance
- Disclosing to those charged with governance the nature of services provided and extent of fees charged
- Involving another firm to perform or reperform part of the engagement
- Rotating senior assurance team personnel

2.6 Ethical threats to compliance with the fundamental principles for accountants in business

Threat	Examples
Self-interest	Financial interests, loans and guarantees, incentive compensation arrangements, personal use of corporate assets, external commercial pressures, acceptance of a gift
Self-review	Business decisions being subject to review and justification by the same accountant responsible for making those decisions or preparing the data supporting them
Advocacy	Furthering the employer's cause aggressively without regard to reasonableness of statements made. (Furthering legitimate goals of employer organisation would not generally create an advocacy threat)
Familiarity	Long association of a business contact
Intimidation	Threats of dismissal from employment, influence of a dominant personality

2.7 Ethical safeguards for accountants in business

The safeguards created by the profession, legislation or regulation also apply to accountants in business.

2.7.1 Ethical safeguards in the workplace for accountants in business

- The employer's oversight systems
- The employer's ethics and conduct programs
- Recruitment procedures

- Strong internal controls
- Appropriate disciplinary processes
- Leadership that stresses ethics
- Policies and procedures that promote and monitor employee performance
- Timely communication of the employer's policies and procedures to all employees
- Training and education of employees
- Whistleblowing provisions
- Consultation with another professional accountant

In other words, a strong control environment.

However, if these safeguards are ineffective, the professional accountant may have to seek legal advice or resign.

2.8 Threat to ethics by management

The power held by directors and management can be a threat to good ethical behaviours, particularly where this power is concentrated in the hands of one or a few individuals, who can override decisions made by personnel lower in the organisational hierarchy. As a result, senior management could make unethical decisions that remain unchallenged, exposing the company to risks from unethical business practices.

Internal controls and corporate governance principles aim to address this threat as follows:

- Segregation of duties and other internal controls aim to limit the powers of individuals.
- The separation of the CEO and chairperson of the board of directors enables the decision of the CEO to be challenged by an equal ranking company officer.
- The presence of independent, non-executive directors on the board provides the ability to challenge significant decisions.
- The requirement of an independent audit committee, made up of non-executive directors, should ensure compliance with accounting and audit standards, internal control requirements and corporate governance code.
- A separate and independent ethics committee can independently monitor and enforce the company's code of ethics.
- The role of an internal audit department can spot check company actions and behaviours.

2.9 Business ethics

An individual's approach to professional ethics is, to some extent, determined by the business ethics of the organisation that they work for. Business ethics set the tone for the culture and behaviour of management and employees; they are clearly linked to corporate governance. Some companies have an ethical code that sets out their ethical objectives – for example, to be honest in all business transactions and to treat employees well.

In other companies, it may be the norm to deviate from the rules in order to achieve a particular outcome. In the next section, we consider examples of companies throughout the world that have not behaved ethically and as a result, have issued misleading financial statements, sometimes leading to their downfall. In many cases, it was not a single individual at these companies that resulted in problems, but an underlying unethical culture.

In recent years, there have been a number of examples of companies collapsing or suffering financial loss as a result of adopting misleading accounting practices.

 **Case Study**

In September 2015, the EPA (Environmental Protection Agency) revealed that models of Volkswagen cars sold in the United States effectively cheated emission testing in order to yield lower emissions within acceptable standards. In actual fact, the cars' emissions exceeded US standards, which should have prevented the cars from being sold. The cars were fitted with a device that could improve its emissions results when being tested, so this was an active decision made by some Volkswagen employees to cheat emissions testing.

Volkswagen publicly admitted to cheating on its emissions tests in the United States. Consequently, Volkswagen had to pay a $18 billion fine from the EPA and some senior employees lost their jobs as a result. The immediate impact on Volkswagen's share price was significant as it fell by over 30%, removing over $25 billion in shareholder value.

Some stakeholders place the blame on the Volkswagen board of directors for a perceived lack of sufficient independence, as it was dominated by Ferdinand Piech and his wife, and several non-independent non-executive directors who had close personal and business relations to the Piech family. Collectively, this group own over half the voting shares and voted in a bloc under a family agreement. Following public criticism, Ferdinand Piech was forced to resign. The question for academics is whether this lack of board independence allowed for a clear breach in Volkswagen's own ethical code.

3 Corporate codes of ethics

Organisations have responded to pressures to be seen to act ethically by publishing **ethical codes**, setting out their **values and responsibilities** towards stakeholders.

Professionals should look to their organisation's corporate code for guidance on how to resolve potential ethical issues.

3.1 Company code of ethics

An **ethical code** typically contains a **series of statements setting out the organisation's values and explaining how it sees its responsibilities towards stakeholders.**

Codes of corporate ethics normally have the following features:

- They focus on regulating individual employee behaviour.
- They are formal documents.
- They cover specific areas such as gifts, anti-competitive behaviour and so on.
- Employees may be asked to sign a declaration, stating that they will comply.
- They may be developed from third party codes (eg regulators) or use third parties for monitoring.
- They tend to mix moral with technical imperatives.
- Sometimes they do little more than describe current practices.
- They can be used to shift responsibility (from senior managers to operational staff).
- A company code of ethics will make clear prohibited business activities. This may be due to law, regulation or governance requirements or could be a strategic choice.

3.1.1 Purposes of code of ethics

(a) **Establishment of organisation's values**

Ethical codes form part of the organisation's underlying environment. They develop and promote values that are linked to the organisation's mission statement.

(b) **Promotion of stakeholder responsibilities**

Codes also demonstrate whom the organisation regards as important stakeholders. They show what action should be taken to maintain good stakeholder relationships (such as keeping them fully informed). They can show external stakeholders that they are dealing with people who do business fairly. Drafting parts of the code to comply with customer wishes demonstrates that businesses are responsive to customers.

(c) **Control of individuals' behaviour**

By promoting or prohibiting certain actions, ethical codes form part of the human resources mechanisms by which employee behaviour is controlled. All staff should be aware of the importance of the ethical code and it should be referred to when employee actions are questioned.

(d) **Promotion of business objectives**

Codes can be an important element in a company's strategic positioning. Taking a strong stance on responsibility and ethics and earning a good ethical reputation can enhance appeal to consumers in the same way as producing the right products of good quality can.

(e) **Conveying values to stakeholders**

The code is a communications device, not only acting to communicate between partners and staff, but also increasing the transparency of the organisation's dealings with its stakeholders. The code should provide clarity and transparency of what business activities are accepted by the company and which activities are prohibited or where approval must be gained before the company proceeds. This communication and transparency allows external stakeholders to challenge the company on its ethical position and provide guidance and clarity to internal stakeholders on precisely what are acceptable business practices and behaviours.

3.1.2 Example of code of ethics

- The company conducts all of its business on **ethical principles** and expects staff to do likewise.
- **Employees** are seen as the most important component of the company and are expected to work on a basis of trust, respect, honesty, fairness, decency and equality. The company will only employ people who follow its ethical ideals.
- **Customers** should be treated courteously and politely at all times, and the company should always respond promptly to customer needs by listening, understanding and then performing to the customer requirements.
- The company is dedicated to complying **with legal or regulatory standards** of the industry, and employees are expected to do likewise.
- The company's relationship with **suppliers and subcontractors** must be based on mutual respect. The company therefore has responsibilities that include ensuring fairness and truthfulness in all of its dealings with suppliers in areas such as pricing and licensing; fostering long-term stability in the supplier relationship; paying suppliers on time, and in accordance with agreed terms of trade; and preferring suppliers and subcontractors whose employment practices respect human dignity.

- The company has a responsibility to: Foster open markets for trade and investment; promote **competitive behaviour** that is socially and environmentally beneficial and demonstrates mutual respect among competitors; and refrain from either seeking, or participating in, questionable payments or favours to secure competitive advantages.
- A business should protect and, where possible, improve **the environment**, promote sustainable development, and prevent the wasteful use of natural resources.
- The company has a responsibility in **the community** to: Respect human rights and democratic institutions, and promote them wherever practicable; recognise government's legitimate obligation to the society at large and support public policies and practices that promote human development through harmonious relations between business and other segments of society; collaborate with those forces in the community dedicated to raising standards of health, education, workplace safety and economic well-being; respect the integrity of local cultures; and be a good corporate citizen, through charitable donations, educational and cultural contributions and employee participation in community and civic affairs.

Question

Required

How can an organisation influence employee behaviour towards ethical issues?

Answer

Here are some suggestions:

- Recruitment and selection policies and procedures
- Induction and training
- Objectives and reward schemes
- Ethical codes
- Threat of ethical audit

4 Ethics for accountants in business

The accountant in business may face a variety of difficulties, including conflicts between professional and employment obligations, pressure to prepare misleading information, whether the accountant has sufficient expertise, financial interests or inducements.

4.1 Conflicts between employment and professional obligations

Ethical guidance stresses that a professional accountant should normally support the **legitimate and ethical obligations** established by the employer. However, they may be pressurised to act in ways that threaten compliance with the fundamental principles. These include:

- Acting contrary to law, regulation, technical or professional standards
- Aiding unethical or illegal earnings management strategies
- Misleading auditors or regulators
- Issuing, or being associated with, a report that misrepresents the facts

If the accountant faces these problems, they should obtain advice from inside the employer, the professional body or lawyers, or use the formal procedures within the organisation.

4.2 Preparation and reporting of information

As well as complying with financial reporting standards, the professional accountant in business should aim to prepare information that **describes clearly the nature of the business transactions, classifies and records information in a timely and proper manner** and **represents the facts accurately.** If the accountant faces pressures to produce misleading information, they should consult with superiors. The accountant should not be associated with misleading information and may need to seek legal advice, or report to the appropriate authorities.

4.3 Acting with sufficient expertise

Guidance stresses that the professional accountant should only undertake tasks for which they have **sufficient specific training or experience.** Certain pressures may threaten the ability of the professional accountant to perform duties with appropriate competence and due care:

- Lack of time
- Lack of information
- Insufficient training, experience or education
- Inadequate resources

Whether this is a significant threat will depend on the other people the accountant is working with, their seniority and the level of supervision over their work. If the problem is serious, the accountant should take steps to remedy the situation by consulting with others, undergoing further training or outsourcing to an expert.

4.4 Financial interests

Ethical guidance highlights financial interests as a self-interest threat to objectivity and confidentiality. In particular, the temptation to **manipulate price-sensitive information** in order to gain financially is stressed. Financial interests may include shares, profit-related bonuses or share options.

This threat can be countered by the individual consulting with superiors and **disclosing all relevant information.** Having a remuneration committee composed of **independent non-executive directors** determining the remuneration packages of executive directors can help resolve the problems at senior levels.

4.5 Inducements

Ethical guidance highlights the possibility that accountants may be offered inducements to influence actions or decisions, encourage illegal behaviour or obtain confidential information. We cover bribery and corruption in more detail below.

4.6 Conflict of interest

Individuals within an organisation may also face their own conflicts of interest. These may include conflicts between loyalty and responsibilities to their bosses and to staff who work for them.

Question

Bricks plc is a public limited company. The current year end is 31 December 20X9. The finance director is remunerated with a profit-related bonus and share appreciation rights. Bricks plc owns a significant number of properties, which historically have been held under the revaluation model. Recently, due to an economic downturn, property prices have been falling. The finance director is proposing to switch from the revaluation model to the cost model.

Shortly before the year end, the CEO of Bricks plc, who holds a large number of share options, mentioned to the finance director that they were hoping to retire within the next year and were hoping to maximise Bricks plc's share price by their retirement date.

Required

(a) Discuss the view that the board of directors should be remunerated with profit-related pay and share-based payments to align directors' and stakeholders' interests.

(b) Discuss whether the finance director of Bricks plc would be acting ethically if they revised the accounting policy for its properties from the revaluation model to the cost model.

(c) Discuss whether the CEO's comment to the finance director is ethical and what action, if any, the finance director should take.

Answer

(a) **Directors' remuneration**

There is an argument that, as the directors should be acting as the agent for the stakeholders, their interests should be aligned. The key stakeholder, the shareholder, is interested in profitability and returns. By linking the remuneration of directors to profits and share price, it will incentivise directors to try to maximise profits and share price, thus aligning their interests with those of the stakeholders.

However, bonuses based on short-term profits could encourage directors to adopt strategies and accounting policies that maximise profits in the short term, but are detrimental to the company's profitability, liquidity and solvency in the long term.

Share-based payments, with vesting periods and vesting conditions based on performance and share price, would be preferable to bonuses based on short-term profits, as they would ensure that directors act with a longer term goal. However, there is still a danger that strategies and accounting policies are manipulated to obtain maximum return on exercise.

On the other hand, if remuneration was purely cash with no link to the company's performance, there would be a danger that the board of directors would not act in the best of their ability to maximise return for the stakeholders.

(b) **Accounting policy for properties**

IAS 1 *Presentation of Financial Statements* requires financial statements to present fairly the financial position, financial performance and cash flows of an entity. This fair presentation is assumed if an entity complies with accounting standards and the IASB's *Conceptual Framework*.

IAS 8 *Accounting Policies, Changes in Accounting Estimates and Errors* only allows a change in accounting policy where required by a standard or if it results in financial statements providing reliable and more relevant information.

The IFAC Code of Ethics requires professional accountants, which would include the finance director, to act with integrity and professional competence. Professional competence includes complying with accounting standards and the *Conceptual Framework*.

If the finance director of Bricks plc is revising the accounting policy to maximise his remuneration, rather than provide reliable and more relevant financial information, then they could be considered to be acting unethically due to non-compliance with IAS 1 and IAS 8. However, the cost model would not necessarily lead to improved profits (and improved remuneration). This is because, under the revaluation model, losses are first written off to the revaluation surplus (and reported in other comprehensive income) and then to profit or loss, so might not impact profits at all. Also,

even under the cost model, assets need to be written down where there is evidence of an impairment.

If the motivation of the finance director is that the economic downturn is causing volatility in market value of properties and that, therefore, the more stable cost model would provide a truer and fairer view, then they could possibly be considered to have acted ethically.

(c) **CEO's comment to the finance director**

The CEO and the finance director, as directors, should be acting in the best interests of the shareholders.

However, it appears as though the CEO is more concerned with self-interest and maximising the gains on his share options by manipulating the share price.

This pressure from the CEO is a threat to the integrity and objectivity of the finance director. The finance director is in a difficult position ethically, as they report directly to the CEO and the CEO has direct influence over their job security and remuneration.

The finance director could speak directly to the CEO and seek clarification of the intent of their comments, explaining that they are unable to change Bricks plc's accounting policies just to maximise Bricks plc's share price in the short term and that they are bound by the IFAC Code of Ethics to act with professional competence. However, if they felt under too much pressure from the CEO to speak to them directly, they could raise their concerns with the non-executive directors and/or the audit committee.

The problem here is that the threats to both the CEO's and the finance director's objectivity and integrity are similar, so there is a danger that the finance director reacts to the CEO's comments by changing accounting policies to maximise profits and share price, rather than acting in the company's and stakeholders' best long-term interests. This would definitely constitute unethical behaviour.

5 Ethical dilemmas

MDCS questions concerning ethics will often be founded on what should be done if breaches of laws, regulations or ethical guidelines occur or where there are close relationships between the parties, or other conflicts of interest exist.

Case Study

An accountant joined a manufacturing company as its finance director. The company had acquired land on which it built industrial units. The finance director discovered that, before they had started at the company, one of the units had been sold and the selling price was significantly larger than the amount which appeared in the company's records. The difference had been siphoned off to another company – one in which their boss, the managing director, was a major shareholder. Furthermore, the managing director had kept their relationship with the second company a secret from the rest of the board.

The finance director confronted the managing director and asked them to reveal their position to the board. However, the managing director refused to disclose their position to anyone else. The secret profits on the sale of the unit had been used, they said, to reward the people who had secured the sale. Without their help, they added, the company would be in a worse position financially.

The finance director then told the managing director that unless they reported it to the board, they would have to inform the board members themselves. The managing director still refused. The finance director disclosed the full position to the board.

The problem here is the managing director being in breach of their directorial duties regarding related party transactions not to obtain any personal advantage from their position of director without the consent of the company for whatever gain or profit they have obtained. The managing director has legal obligations as a director of the company. They have ethical obligations not to ignore their legal obligations. The finance director behaved ethically by disclosing the full position to the board after giving the managing director the opportunity to do so.

5.1 Ethical dilemmas caused by existing relationships

Relationships should never be permitted to affect ethical judgement. If you knew that your best friend at work had committed a major fraud, for example, integrity would demand that in the last resort, you would have to bring it to the attention of somebody in authority. But note that this is only in the case of last resort. Try to imagine what you would do in practice in this situation.

Surely your first course would be to try to persuade your friend that what they had done was wrong, and that they themselves had an ethical responsibility to own up? Your second option, if this failed, might be to try to get somebody (perhaps somebody outside the organisation) that you knew, to exert pressure on your friend to persuade them to own up.

5.2 Actions

In spite of the difficulties, your aim will usually be to reach a satisfactory resolution to the problem. **The actions that you recommend** will often include the following:

(a) **Informal discussions** with the parties involved.

(b) **Further investigation** to establish the full facts of the matter. What extra information is needed?

(c) The **tightening up of controls or the introduction of new ones**, if the situation arose due to laxity in this area. This will often be the case and the principles of professional competence and due care and of technical standards will usually be relevant.

(d) **Attention to organisational matters** such as changes in the management structure, improving communication channels, attempting to change attitudes.

Question

The finance director has asked you to join a team planning a takeover of one of your company's suppliers. An old school friend works as an accountant for the company concerned; the finance director knows this, and has asked you to try and find out 'anything that might help the takeover succeed, but it must remain secret'.

Required

Outline the ethical issues which arise as a result of the finance director's request.

Answer

There are three issues here. Firstly, you have a **conflict of interest** as the finance director wants you to keep the takeover a secret, but you probably feel that you should tell your friend what is happening, as it may affect their job.

Secondly, the finance director is asking you to deceive your friend. Deception is unprofessional behaviour and will break your ethical guidelines. Therefore, the situation is presenting you with **two conflicting demands**. It is worth remembering that no employer should ask you to break your ethical rules.

Finally, the request to break your own ethical guidelines constitutes **unprofessional behaviour** by the finance director. You should consider reporting him to the relevant body.

6 Frameworks for dealing with ethical dilemmas

FAST FORWARD

In a situation involving ethical issues, there will often be practical steps that should be taken. Any actions should be justified on the basis of an analysis of the situation and will often involve striking a compromise between different interests and considerations.

It is important to bear in mind that when it comes to ethics, there is frequently no single right answer, but rather a multiplicity of views with many shades of grey between them. What matters then is the quality of your discussion and the extent to which you are able to weigh the differing aspects of a decision against one another. The watchword of ethics is complexity.

This section covers the following two frameworks can be applied to evaluate and resolve ethical dilemmas.

- The American Accounting Association model (also, considered to be a practical framework for dealing with ethical dilemmas)
- Tucker's five question model

6.1 American Accounting Association (AAA) mode

The AAA model was set out in a report by Langenderfer and Rockness back in 1990. They recommended a seven-step model.

Step	Question	Approach to use in answers
1	What are the facts of the case?	The aim is to show clearly what is at issue. A brief summary should suffice, maybe just one sentence.
2	What are the ethical issues in the case?	These should be based on the facts.
3	What are the norms, principles and values related to the case?	This means placing the decision in its social, ethical and professional behaviour context, including considering professional codes of ethics or social expectations of the profession. Use the terminology of the ethical guidelines (for example, fairness, bias and influence) when discussing objectivity. Do not be afraid to use the term justice if that is most appropriate.
4	What are the alternative courses of action?	State each course without making reference at this stage to the norms, principles and values. To generate ideas, consider the issue from the points of view of the 'guilty' party and the organisation.
5	What is the best course of action that is consistent with the norms, principles and values identified in Step 3?	Combine Steps 3 and 4 to see which options accord with the norms and which do not.
6	What are the consequences of each possible course of action?	This is to ensure that each of the outcomes is unambiguous.
7	What is the decision?	This is based on the analysis in Steps 1–6.

6.1.1 Example of AAA model

Isuru, a senior accountant, is assigned to the audit of Shan plc, a major client of his firm. During the audit, Isuru discovers a material cut-off error that causes Shan's income to be significantly misstated. According to his firm's policy, any potential material misstatement must be documented in the working papers, with the final determination of materiality made by the partner overseeing the audit. However, Shan plc is unwilling to make the necessary adjustment.

Before finalising the fieldwork, Gihan, the audit manager, instructs Isuru, saying, 'Let's not mention this. Since there are no tax implications, the partner has decided not to force an adjustment. Shan is our largest client.' This places Isuru in an ethical dilemma.

Application of AAA model

Step 1: What are the facts of the case?

Isuru, during the audit of Shan plc, uncovered a material misstatement in the financial statements. However, he has been instructed by his audit manager, Gihan, to ignore this finding. The firm has a policy that requires documenting any material misstatement, and the decision to adjust lies with the audit partner. Shan plc, a major client, does not wish to make the adjustment, and the partner appears to have prioritised the client relationship over addressing the error.

Step 2: What are the ethical issues in the case?

The key ethical issue is whether Isuru should remain silent about the material misstatement or document his findings in line with professional standards. Ignoring the error could amount to negligence and compromise the integrity of the audit. Isuru faces pressure to prioritise the client relationship, potentially conflicting with his duty to present an accurate and fair view of Shan plc's financial position.

Step 3: What are the norms, principles, and values related to the case?

Auditors are bound by principles of integrity, objectivity, and professional competence. They must ensure that financial statements provide a true and fair view of a company's financial position. Isuru has a professional responsibility to adhere to auditing standards and ethical codes, which dictate that any material misstatement should be addressed, documented, and communicated, regardless of client relationships.

Step 4: What are the alternative courses of action?

Option 1: Isuru could comply with Gihan's instructions and refrain from documenting the misstatement.

Option 2: Isuru could refuse to comply, document his findings in the audit workpapers, and escalate his concerns to the audit partner or a higher authority within the firm.

Step 5: What is the best course of action consistent with the norms, principles, and values identified in Step 3?

The course of action that aligns with the ethical norms and principles identified is for Isuru to document the misstatement in the audit workpapers and escalate the issue, if necessary. This step upholds the integrity and objectivity required of his professional role, ensuring transparency and protecting the interests of shareholders and other stakeholders.

Step 6: What are the consequences of each possible course of action?

Option 1: If Isuru remains silent, the misstatement will go unreported. While this might preserve the client relationship in the short term, it exposes the firm to potential accusations of professional negligence and could damage the firm's reputation if the misstatement is discovered later. It also compromises the audit's integrity and fails to serve the shareholders' interests.

Option 2: If Isuru documents the misstatement and communicates his concerns, there might be tension with Shan plc, potentially risking the client relationship. However, this approach maintains professional

integrity, ensures compliance with ethical standards, and protects the firm's reputation. It also serves the interests of shareholders by ensuring that the financial statements provide an accurate view of the company's position.

Step 7: What is the decision on which course of action to take?

The ethical decision is to implement Option 2: Isuru should document the material misstatement in the audit workpapers and communicate his concerns. This action supports the values of integrity and transparency, ensuring that any necessary corrective actions are taken to benefit shareholders and other stakeholders, thereby upholding the trust placed in the auditing profession.

Also, it can be beneficial to consider the following five conflicts of interest when considering an ethical dilemma in MDCS, as follows.

- **Self-interest** – This occurs when an individual could benefit from a financial interest in a decision, they are called upon to make.

- **Self-review** – This occurs when an individual is reviewing subject matter for which they have been responsible.

- **Familiarity** – This occurs by virtue of a close relationship with an individual being affected by the decision.

- **Advocacy** – This occurs when the individual has been perceived to have promoted a particular stance in the past and may be reluctant to change their opinion, even in the light of new evidence relating to a decision.

- **Intimidation** – This occurs when an individual is deterred from acting objectively or exercising professional scepticism by threats, actual or perceived, from one or more parties affected by the decision.

Notice that these five threats do not necessarily appear in isolation, as often in a scenario, there may be two or more issues in play.

Question

AAA model 1

World Tea plc has prepared draft financial statements for the year ended 31 March 20X2, revealing a significant drop in operating profits compared to the previous year. This decline has also negatively impacted operating cash flow in the statement of cash flows. The directors attribute this downturn to a key customer experiencing financial difficulties and an overall reduction in trade during the latter half of 20X1. Despite these challenges, they believe that trading conditions improved in the final two months of the reporting period.

The directors are concerned that the reduced operating cash flow might lead to breaches of loan covenants and a subsequent drop in market confidence. They are also aware that the decline in operating profits will adversely affect performance-related pay for directors and senior management. To mitigate these effects, they have suggested to the financial controller that a portion of operating expenses be reclassified as extraordinary items in the statement of profit or loss, presented after operating profit. This reclassification could artificially inflate the operating profit and improve key performance metrics.

Required

Explain the ethical responsibility of the financial controller in respect of the directors' suggestion by applying the AAA model.

Answer

Step 1: What are the facts of the case?

The draft financial statements for World Tea plc show a significant drop in operating profits and cash flows. The directors, worried about potential breaches of loan covenants and market perception, have suggested the reclassification of some operating expenses as extraordinary items. This adjustment would manipulate the presentation of the company's financial performance. The financial controller has been asked to implement this adjustment, placing them in a challenging ethical position.

Step 2: What are the ethical issues in the case?

The ethical issues centre around whether the financial controller should comply with the directors' suggestion to alter the financial statements. Adjusting the accounts to misrepresent the operating profit violates ethical principles of honesty, integrity, and transparency. It would also involve deliberate manipulation of financial information, leading to potentially misleading statements to shareholders, creditors, and other stakeholders. Accepting this adjustment could breach the financial controller's professional responsibilities and ethics.

Step 3: What are the norms, principles, and values related to the case?

The relevant ethical norms and principles include:

Integrity: The financial controller must be honest in all professional dealings. Manipulating the accounts to present a false view of the company's financial position compromises this integrity.

Objectivity: The financial controller should avoid bias, conflicts of interest, and undue influence from others. Accepting the directors' suggestion indicates a lack of objectivity, particularly if the financial controller is eligible for performance-related pay.

Professional competence and due care: The financial controller has a duty to comply with applicable accounting standards, regulations, and ethical codes. Misclassifying operating expenses as extraordinary items undermines the professionalism required in the preparation of financial statements.

Professional behaviour: The financial controller must avoid any conduct that discredits the profession. Adjusting the financial statements to manipulate performance indicators would be an unprofessional and potentially fraudulent act.

Step 4: What are the alternative courses of action?

Option 1: The financial controller could comply with the directors' suggestion and reclassify the operating expenses as extraordinary items.

Option 2: The financial controller could refuse to implement the suggested adjustments, explaining to the directors why the reclassification is not permissible under accounting standards and ethical guidelines.

Option 3: If the directors insist on making the adjustments, the financial controller could document the dispute and escalate the issue internally or externally, such as notifying the internal or external auditors of the misstatement.

Step 5: What is the best course of action that is consistent with the norms, principles, and values identified in Step 3?

The course of action that aligns with professional ethics is **Option 2**: the financial controller should refuse to implement the adjustments and explain the requirements of accounting standards. This approach maintains integrity, objectivity, and professionalism. If the directors continue to pressure for the adjustments, the financial controller should document the situation and escalate it to the appropriate parties, such as the internal or external auditors (**Option 3**).

Step 6: What are the consequences of each possible course of action?

Option 1: Accepting the directors' suggestion would result in a deliberate misstatement of the financial statements. This action could lead to potential legal and regulatory consequences if the manipulation is discovered. It may also damage the financial controller's professional reputation and the firm's credibility.

Option 2: Refusing to make the adjustments may strain the relationship between the financial controller and the directors. However, it ensures compliance with ethical standards and protects the integrity of the financial statements, serving the best interests of shareholders, creditors, and other stakeholders.

Option 3: Escalating the issue may create further tension within the company and could potentially jeopardise the financial controller's position. However, this step ensures transparency and provides an opportunity for independent review by the auditors, ultimately safeguarding the company's reputation and adhering to ethical standards.

Step 7: What is the decision on which course of action to take?

The ethical decision is to implement **Option 2** initially: the financial controller should refuse to make the suggested adjustments, citing the requirements of accounting standards and ethical guidelines. If the directors continue to insist, the financial controller should escalate the issue to the company's internal or external auditors (**Option 3**). This course of action upholds the principles of integrity, objectivity, and professional behaviour, ensuring that the financial statements accurately reflect the company's performance and protecting the interests of stakeholders.

Question — AAA model 2

Cadge, a European-based clothing manufacturer, has seen a decline in profits over the last two years. The company attributes this decline to the loss of significant contracts and a general reduction in demand for its clothing. Industry experts point out that Cadge's failure to innovate in its clothing designs has contributed to its troubles.

Recently, Cadge's design director received an unsolicited offer from an unknown factory owner outside Europe, who introduced himself only as 'Mr Sim.' Mr Sim proposed selling Cadge the latest designs of a key competitor, which are currently being manufactured in his factories. The sum of money requested for these designs seems reasonable, and acquiring them could give Cadge a much-needed competitive edge. If Cadge launches these designs ahead of their competitor, it could significantly boost the company's profitability for the coming year. However, the ethical implications of this transaction are questionable, given that the designs seem to have been obtained without the competitor's consent.

Required

Analyse, using the American Accounting Association model, the decision of whether to accept Mr Sim's offer.

Answer

Step 1: What are the facts of the case?

Cadge has experienced a fall in profits due to lost contracts and decreased demand for its products.

Industry opinion suggests that Cadge's decline is due to a lack of innovation in clothing designs.

Mr Sim, a factory owner based outside Europe, has contacted Cadge's design director, offering to sell designs belonging to a competitor that are being manufactured in his factories.

The offer from Mr Sim is financially appealing, and using these designs could provide Cadge with a significant market advantage.

There is no clear information about how Mr Sim obtained the designs, but it is implied that these designs have been obtained illegally or unethically.

Step 2: What are the ethical issues in the case?

The central ethical issue is whether Cadge should take advantage of potentially stolen designs to gain a business advantage. Accepting Mr Sim's offer would likely involve intellectual property theft, violating principles of honesty, integrity, and fair competition. It also raises questions about the ethical implications of exploiting another company's hard work and innovation for Cadge's benefit. Additionally, there is a risk of legal and reputational consequences if this transaction is uncovered.

Step 3: What are the norms, principles, and values related to the case?

Legality: Acquiring designs that belong to a competitor is likely illegal under both Cadge's national laws and international intellectual property laws. Accepting this offer could expose Cadge to legal action.

Integrity: Accepting stolen designs would compromise Cadge's integrity, as it would involve using another company's intellectual property without consent or rightful payment.

Honesty: Utilising designs obtained through unethical means is deceptive, especially towards customers, stakeholders, and the market at large.

Fair competition: Engaging in fair competition involves relying on one's innovation and capabilities. Using stolen designs to get ahead undermines the competitive process and violates the industry's norms.

Reputation: Upholding the company's reputation is crucial. Engaging in questionable business practices can damage customer trust, shareholder confidence, and long-term business relationships.

Step 4: What are the alternative courses of action?

Option 1: Reject Mr Sim's offer, maintain ethical business practices, and consider notifying the competitor about the potential breach of their intellectual property.

Option 2: Accept Mr Sim's offer, pay for the designs, and use them to gain a competitive advantage, despite the potential legal and ethical implications.

Step 5: What is the best course of action that is consistent with the norms, principles, and values identified in Step 3?

The best course of action is **Option 1**: Reject Mr Sim's offer. This choice aligns with ethical norms, including honesty, integrity, and respect for intellectual property laws. Additionally, rejecting the offer maintains fair competition in the market. The directors of Cadge should also consider whether to escalate the matter by reporting Mr Sim's offer to the relevant authorities or the competitor whose designs were compromised. By taking this step, Cadge not only avoids unethical behaviour but also actively demonstrates its commitment to ethical business practices.

Step 6: What are the consequences of each possible course of action?

Option 1 (Reject the offer): Cadge will not benefit from an immediate competitive edge. However, the company will maintain its integrity, avoid potential legal troubles, and preserve its reputation in the market. This ethical decision could also lead to greater long-term success by building customer trust and reinforcing positive business relationships.

Option 2 (Accept the offer): Cadge may gain a temporary competitive advantage, potentially boosting profitability in the short term. However, if the transaction is discovered, the consequences could be severe. Cadge could face legal action for intellectual property theft, substantial fines, and reputational damage. Customers, business partners, and shareholders are likely to view this behaviour unfavourably, which could jeopardise existing contracts and future business opportunities. Additionally, Cadge's board may come under pressure from shareholders who find such behaviour unacceptable, potentially leading to internal turmoil.

Step 7: What is the decision?

The ethical decision is **Option 1**: Cadge should refuse Mr Sim's offer. This choice is consistent with upholding integrity, honesty, and legal compliance. Furthermore, Cadge should consider informing the affected competitor or relevant authorities about the potential intellectual property breach to demonstrate its commitment to ethical business practices. By rejecting unethical opportunities, Cadge sets a precedent for ethical conduct, promoting long-term trust and sustainability in its business operations.

As illustrated in the above scenario, it is not always essential to delve into philosophical theories of ethics when addressing practical questions. What matters most is adopting a logical, practical approach to assess the situation and form a sound judgment that resolves the ethical dilemma effectively. By focusing on clear principles like integrity, honesty, and fairness, one can navigate complex issues and arrive at the best possible decision.

6.2 Tucker's five question model

Tucker's model is conceptually different from the AAA model, and needs to be applied carefully to each situation. The model can be used to determine the most ethical outcome in a particular situation, generally an ethical problem for business. It focuses on five key questions that should be asked of a response to an ethical dilemma:

- Profitable?
- Legal?
- Fair?
- Right?
- Sustainable?

Not all of Tucker's criteria will be relevant in every situation. In addition, there are complications with each criterion.

Is the decision:	
Profitable?	Compared with what? Use of profitability as criteria also implies the Tucker model may be more useful for business decisions than for individuals' moral dilemmas.
Legal?	This obviously depends on the jurisdiction(s) involved.
Fair?	In whose perspective? There is a need to consider who stakeholders are and the impact of the decision on them.
Right?	This depends on the ethical position; in particular the distinction between deontological and teleological approaches to whether account should be taken of the consequences of the transaction is significant.
Sustainable?	Is the decision environmentally sound, or sustainable in other ways (eg the long-term success of the company)?

Question — Tucker's five question model 1

Refuse Recycling (RR) is a large recycling company, which collects waste and recycles a large variety of products. Its most profitable product for recycling is glass, although it also collects other materials including plastics. Most of the plastics it collects are under local government contracts for domestic waste collection and recycling. Because RR lacks facilities and expertise in the recycling of plastics, the plastic waste it collects is sorted by item/type and transported long distances to specialised plastic recycling plants operated by other recycling companies.

For some time now the board of RR has been concerned about reduced margins. As a result of a study initiated by the finance director, the company has established that the collection and recycling of plastics is proving unprofitable. Transportation costs have been extremely high, as many recycling operators have not been accepting plastics collected by RR in the hope that this would make the contracts less profitable for RR. They believed this would increase their own chances of winning future tenders.

The chairperson of RR recently called a board meeting to examine the terms of the company's existing contracts with local governments for domestic waste collection and recycling. At this meeting, the finance director stated that, though they felt strongly about the value of recycling to society as a whole, they also felt that RR simply should not continue to perform unprofitable activities if there was 'a way out'.

On examining the contracts, the board discovered that several specified an overall percentage of material collected that must be recycled of 70% (others specified 80%). Based on the volumes of paper, glass, metal and plastics collected over the past year, the board decided that in some locations RR could meet a contractual obligation of 70% without recycling any plastics at all. Plastic collected under these '70% contracts' could simply be dumped at landfill sites, with significant savings from reduced sorting and transport costs. Some board members had reservations about implementing this policy, but were swayed by the strength of the finance director's reasoning.

The dumping of plastics is about to start. Although the board of RR feels the company's actions do not breach the terms of their contracts, it was decided that the vehicles involved in the dumping process would not carry the RR name.

Required

Analyse the board's decision to dump plastics at landfill sites, using Tucker's five question model.

Answer

Using Tucker's five question model, we have to ask, is the decision:

Is it profitable?

The main justification for the decision is to **increase short-term profitability** and if the finance director's figures are correct, that aim has been achieved. However, the effect on long-term profitability may be very different if what RR has done becomes public. A recycling company, even one operating in a commercial environment, must be seen as **caring about the environment** if it is to attract and retain customers. Some local government customers may try to cancel existing contracts on the grounds that RR is not abiding by the spirit of these contracts. In any case local government agencies are likely to be unwilling to renew contracts and RR may be unable to win other new contracts.

Is it legal?

Clearly RR is using **legal landfill sites**. Assuming the board has interpreted the contracts correctly, the company has not breached the strict legal terms of the contract even if it has possibly breached the spirit. Transporting the waste in unmarked vans may be questionable legally though.

Is it fair?

If the view is taken that the customers are vital stakeholders, then what RR is doing is unfair to them, as they may have made **claims** about the support, they are giving to recycling which are unintentionally misleading. Any loss of reputation that local authorities suffer in the fallout that follows discovery of what RR has done may be particularly serious, as it may impact on re-election chances of local councillors. The only mitigation for RR under this heading is that the problem has arisen because of other recycling operators refusing to take RR's waste. They too appear to be putting their commercial interests ahead of the objective of supporting recycling.

Is it right?

The fact that the waste is being **transported in unmarked vans** is effectively an admission by the board that what they are doing is indefensible on moral grounds. Any mitigation may be based on other criteria,

that RR is acting within the law and doing its best for its shareholders, but it is nearly impossible to defend the actions on these grounds.

Is it sustainable?

This is potentially the easiest criterion of them all, as what RR is doing appears to be going against environmental best practice. Apart from anything else, RR's ability to continue doing this depends on the **availability of landfill sites**. In some countries they are running out. The only environmental justification is that by using the landfill sites, RR is cutting down the miles plastics are transported, and is reducing its carbon footprint to that extent.

Question — Tucker's five question model 2

John Tse Building Ltd is a construction company based in London, UK, specialising in commercial and residential projects. The company, founded by John Tse, has operated successfully for over a decade, building a solid reputation for quality and reliability in the construction industry. However, the business has faced significant financial challenges over the past year due to a combination of factors. The economic downturn has hit the construction sector hard, causing a slowdown in new projects. Additionally, one of John Tse Building Ltd's largest clients went into administration, leaving a substantial unpaid invoice that has further strained the company's cash flow.

Currently, John Tse Building Ltd has several outstanding obligations to its suppliers. These suppliers include companies providing raw materials (such as bricks, cement, and timber), equipment rental services, and skilled subcontractors. The company had established good working relationships with these suppliers, with payment terms typically ranging from 30 to 90 days. However, due to the company's recent financial difficulties, it has accumulated a significant amount of unpaid invoices over the past six months.

To avoid further financial deterioration, John Tse has made a unilateral decision to contact all his company's suppliers and inform them that they will only receive 50% of the amounts they are owed.

This decision has been made without prior consultation or negotiation with the suppliers. John plans to make these partial payments, if at all, towards the end of the current financial year, which could be up to nine months away. John believes that this move is necessary to stabilise the company's finances, preserve cash, and potentially return to profitability. However, this decision could have significant repercussions for the suppliers, many of whom are small businesses that rely on timely payments to sustain their operations.

Required

Evaluate the ethical dilemma in this scenario by applying Tucker's five questions model.

Answer

Applying Tucker's five questions model.

(a) **Is it profitable?**

The decision to pay only 50% of the amounts owed would, in the short term, help John Tse Building Ltd retain cash and potentially improve its profitability. By limiting cash outflows, the company might be able to cover other operational costs, meet payroll obligations, and continue ongoing projects. This approach could potentially prevent insolvency, buying the company more time to recover from its financial downturn. However, while this may seem profitable in the short term, the decision could result in long-term financial costs. Suppliers, faced with partial payments, might impose stricter credit terms, demand cash upfront for future transactions, or refuse to supply materials altogether. These outcomes could lead to increased costs and operational delays, potentially affecting future profitability.

(b) **Is it legal?**

In the UK, companies are legally obligated to pay their suppliers according to the terms agreed upon in their contracts. Unilaterally deciding to pay only 50% of the amounts owed without a formal agreement from the suppliers breaches these contractual obligations. This action could expose John Tse Building Ltd to legal claims, as suppliers may choose to pursue the outstanding amounts through legal channels, such as the UK's small claims court or a winding-up petition for unpaid debts. Additionally, the company's directors have a legal duty to act in the best interests of creditors when the company is in financial distress, especially when insolvency is a risk. Failure to act responsibly could result in personal liability for John Tse and the directors, potentially leading to disqualification from future directorships or financial penalties.

(c) **Is it fair?**

From an ethical standpoint, the decision to pay only 50% of the owed amounts is unfair to the suppliers. Many of these suppliers are likely to be small or medium-sized businesses that rely on timely payments to manage their own cash flow and cover operational costs, such as payroll and procurement of materials. By withholding half of what is owed, John Tse Building Ltd is effectively transferring its financial burdens onto its suppliers, potentially putting their businesses at risk. Furthermore, this decision was made unilaterally, without any consultation or effort to negotiate with the suppliers to find a mutually acceptable solution. Fairness would dictate that John Tse engages in open discussions with the suppliers, explains the financial situation, and attempts to agree on a realistic payment plan that considers both parties' interests.

(d) **Is it right?**

The decision raises serious ethical concerns about honesty and respect for contractual agreements. John Tse is knowingly choosing to disregard his company's financial obligations, acting in a manner that is not only potentially illegal but also morally questionable. The suppliers entered into agreements with the expectation of full payment for goods and services provided, and John Tse's decision to pay only half violates the trust inherent in these business relationships. Additionally, the lack of transparency and communication with the suppliers exacerbates the ethical violation. It is ethically wrong to impose financial hardship on others to solve one's own problems, especially without seeking their input or attempting to reach a fair compromise. An ethical approach would involve John Tse being forthright with the suppliers, acknowledging the company's financial difficulties, and seeking to negotiate revised payment terms rather than unilaterally imposing a solution.

(e) **Is it sustainable?**

This decision is not sustainable in terms of business relationships and long-term reputation. By opting to pay only 50% of the amounts owed, John Tse Building Ltd risks damaging its reputation with suppliers, many of whom might refuse to work with the company in the future. This damaged reputation could extend beyond the immediate circle of suppliers, affecting potential future partnerships, client relationships, and the company's overall standing in the construction industry. Furthermore, suppliers might share their negative experiences with other businesses, further tarnishing the company's reputation. In the construction industry, a company's reputation for reliability and financial integrity is crucial for securing contracts and maintaining a steady supply chain. The short-term financial relief gained by withholding payments could lead to long-term operational challenges, supply shortages, and increased costs due to stricter credit terms imposed by wary suppliers.

Conclusion

Using Tucker's Five Questions Model, it is evident that John Tse's decision to pay only 50% of the suppliers' owed amounts is **not ethical**. While it may provide short-term financial relief and improve cash flow, it fails to meet ethical standards in terms of legality, fairness, rightness, and long-term sustainability.

The company is legally bound to honour its contracts, and failure to do so can lead to legal consequences and damage relationships with suppliers and other stakeholders.

The ethical approach for John Tse Building Ltd would be to engage openly with its suppliers, explain the company's financial difficulties, and attempt to negotiate new payment terms that are fair and manageable for both parties. This approach may involve proposing a payment plan that spans a longer period or seeking a partial waiver of debt with the suppliers' consent. By opting for transparency and mutual agreement, John Tse can work towards resolving the financial issues while maintaining its ethical standards and business relationships.

6.3 Managing ethical issues through stakeholder engagement

Gray, R., Owen, D., and Adams, C. (1996) emphasise that organisations have a broader responsibility to engage with a diverse set of stakeholders, not just shareholders.

They argue that companies must acknowledge their impact on society and the environment, addressing ethical issues as they engage with various groups.

This approach to stakeholder engagement is grounded in accountability, transparency, and ethical responsibility, which are crucial for managing and mitigating ethical concerns within and around the organisation.

This idea of managing issues through stakeholder engagement can be applied to managing ethical dilemmas' as follows.

Managing ethical issues through stakeholder engagement

(a) **Define a relevant and broad range of stakeholders**

Gray, Owen, and Adams suggest that managing ethical issues begins with recognising the wide array of stakeholders affected by an organisation's activities. This includes employees, customers, suppliers, communities, governments, and where relevant, environmentalists.

- **Societal and environmental impact:** By expanding the definition of stakeholders, companies are compelled to address the social and environmental impacts of their actions. For example, an ethical issue such as environmental damage cannot be overlooked when the environment itself is considered a stakeholder. Recognising these diverse interests ensures that ethical considerations are embedded in business decisions.

- **Holistic responsibility:** Gray, Owen, and Adams argue that when companies understand their duty to a broad stakeholder base, they are better equipped to identify ethical dilemmas and proactively manage them. This approach shifts the focus from merely satisfying shareholders to balancing the needs and rights of all impacted parties.

(b) **Accountability and transparency**

One of the ways to manage ethical issues, according to Gray, Owen, and Adams, is through accountability and transparency. They advocate for companies to be open about their practices and impacts, holding themselves accountable to stakeholders.

- **Social and environmental reporting:** Gray, Owen, and Adams propose that organisations adopt comprehensive reporting practices that go beyond financial disclosures to include social and environmental impacts. By regularly reporting on issues like labour practices, environmental stewardship, and community engagement, companies can address ethical concerns head-on and provide stakeholders with insight into their ethical performance.

- **Clear communication:** Transparent communication helps in addressing ethical issues by providing stakeholders with the information they need to make informed judgments. It allows stakeholders to understand how the company manages its operations ethically and gives them the opportunity to raise concerns, thereby fostering a culture of accountability.

(c) **Dialogue-based engagement**

Gray, Owen, and Adams stress that ethical management requires more than just informing stakeholders; it requires active dialogue. Ethical issues often arise from a lack of understanding or inclusion of stakeholder perspectives in decision-making.

- **Two-way communication:** Engaging in meaningful conversations with stakeholders is vital for managing ethical concerns. Through dialogue, companies can listen to stakeholder feedback, understand the ethical implications of their decisions, and incorporate diverse perspectives. This engagement helps identify potential ethical risks and facilitates finding solutions that align with stakeholder values.
- **Building trust and addressing concerns:** A dialogue-based approach builds trust with stakeholders, which is essential when ethical issues emerge. By allowing stakeholders to voice their concerns and participate in the decision-making process, organisations demonstrate a commitment to ethical practices, which can mitigate conflicts and foster long-term relationships.

(d) **Ethical considerations in decision-making**

Gray, Owen, and Adams argue that stakeholder engagement should be driven by ethical considerations. Companies must approach engagement not as a strategic tool for reputation management, but as a moral obligation to act responsibly toward those affected by their operations.

- **Moral obligation:** Businesses have a duty to respect and respond to the interests of their stakeholders. This includes addressing ethical issues such as workers' rights, environmental sustainability, and fair business practices. When companies engage stakeholders with a sense of moral responsibility, they create an environment where ethical dilemmas are openly discussed and addressed.
- **Balancing interests:** Managing ethical issues effectively requires balancing conflicting interests of various stakeholders. Gray, Owen, and Adams argue that companies should strive for equitable solutions, ensuring that their actions do not unjustly favour one group at the expense of another. By acknowledging ethical obligations, organisations can make decisions that reflect a genuine concern for all affected parties.

(e) **Sustainable development and long-term ethical management**

Gray, Owen, and Adams highlight that ethical stakeholder engagement is integral to achieving long-term sustainability. Managing ethical issues is not just about addressing immediate concerns, but also about considering the long-term social, economic, and environmental impact of organisational actions.

- **Sustainable decision-making:** They stress that for a company to be truly sustainable, it must consider stakeholder perspectives in its strategic planning and operations. By incorporating stakeholder input, companies can identify potential ethical pitfalls and work towards solutions that promote social equity, economic viability, and environmental protection.
- **Preventing future ethical issues:** Engaging with stakeholders on matters of sustainability helps companies anticipate and prevent future ethical challenges. By addressing issues such as resource use, labour practices, and community impact, organisations can develop ethical standards that support ongoing stakeholder trust and business resilience.

The following question demonstrates active stakeholder engagement to develop a response to an ethical dilemma.

Question — Managing ethical issues through stakeholder engagement

GreenEarth plc, a well-known publicly listed UK company, specialises in eco-friendly packaging solutions, including biodegradable materials and recycled packaging and a wide range of eco-friendly consumer goods, including reusable household items like bamboo toothbrushes, beeswax wraps, and plant-based cleaning products, reusable coffee cups, water bottles, solar-powered garden lights and organic cotton bedding.

GreenEarth was founded on the principle of protection of the environment in 1996 and since then has built a strong brand reputation for its commitment to sustainable practices and environmental consciousness, attracting a loyal customer base that values ethical products. Over the past few years, GreenEarth's market share has increased significantly, resulting in pressure to scale up production to meet growing demand.

GreenEarth operates a major production facility in northern England, which is key to meeting the company's output targets. Due to rising demand, the facility has been working at maximum capacity. However, during a recent internal audit, it was discovered that the facility has been emitting pollutants at levels slightly above the legal and regulatory limits set by UK environmental regulations. While these emissions are not immediately harmful, prolonged exposure could have negative effects on the local environment and community health.

The board of GreenEarth now faces a challenging ethical and business dilemma. An immediate upgrade to the facility's emission control systems would require an investment of approximately £20 million and could cause temporary production downtime. This, in turn, would impact quarterly profits, reduce shareholder dividends, and possibly weaken the company's stock price. On the other hand, delaying the upgrade would help maintain short-term profitability and allow the company to build up funds for future improvements, but it risks regulatory penalties and potential damage to the company's reputation for environmental responsibility.

To assist the board to move forward with a decision, various stakeholders have been consulted, as the results are summarised as follows.

Shareholders – GreenEarth's shareholders have varying interests. Profit-focused investors are primarily concerned about the company's profitability and returns, worrying that the immediate investment and potential production halt will affect the company's financial performance. However, ESG-focused and ethical investors are more concerned about the company's long-term sustainability and integrity, arguing that delaying the upgrade would undermine GreenEarth's reputation.

Customers – GreenEarth's customer base consists largely of environmentally conscious consumers who trust GreenEarth for its ethical stance. A focus group has indicated that a company's failure to comply with environmental regulations, there could be a significant backlash, including boycotts and a potential loss of market share.

Employees – Employees, especially those working at the production facility, may have mixed reactions. While they take pride in the company's sustainability commitments, they also fear the potential impact on job security and wages if production halts for the facility upgrades. However, some employees have advocated for immediate compliance to uphold the company's ethical standards as they see this is the best way to secure long term employment.

Local community – The facility is situated near a residential area, and residents have noticed changes in air quality, although they are not fully aware of the long-term risks. A community leader expects the company to act responsibly and is worried that prolonged non-compliance could lead to public protests and increased pressure on local authorities to enforce stricter regulations.

Regulators – The UK's Environmental Agency requires companies to comply with emission regulations. While GreenEarth's emissions are only slightly over the legal limit, continued non-compliance could result in fines, penalties, and legal action. Whilst the regulator has not been directly consulted, an environment consultant has advised that unless GreenEarth takes immediate corrective action to align with environmental standards, then there could be consequences from the regulator.

Board of directors – Some board members argue for delaying the upgrades to protect short-term profits, while others believe in addressing the issue immediately to preserve the company's ethical standing and brand value.

Required

(a) Identify the key ethical dilemmas facing GreenEarth plc and consider the different perspectives of the stakeholders listed above.

(b) Based on your analysis of the ethical issues and stakeholder perspectives, recommend a course of action for the board of directors.

Answer

(a) The key ethical dilemma facing GreenEarth plc revolves around balancing environmental responsibility with financial performance.

On one hand, there is the immediate need to address the emission control issue to comply with environmental regulations and uphold the company's commitment to sustainability.

On the other hand, the required investment of £20 million and potential production downtime could negatively impact short-term profitability, shareholder dividends, and market confidence.

GreenEarth must decide whether to prioritise immediate compliance with environmental standards at the risk of financial strain or delay the upgrades to preserve short-term profits, knowing that such a delay could harm the company's reputation and result in regulatory penalties.

It is important that the board of GreenEarth consider the perspective of each of GreenEarth's main stakeholder groups in reaching a decision of how to proceed.

Shareholders

From the perspective of shareholders, there is a split between profit-focused investors and ESG-focused investors. Profit-focused shareholders are primarily concerned about the financial implications of immediate upgrades, fearing that reduced profits and production downtime will adversely affect the company's stock performance and dividend payouts. Conversely, ESG-focused investors prioritise long-term sustainability and believe that delaying the upgrade would undermine GreenEarth's ethical standing and long-term value, potentially resulting in reputational damage that could impact shareholder value over time.

Customers

Customers, who largely consist of environmentally conscious individuals, are likely to view non-compliance as a serious breach of trust. A focus group has already indicated that a failure to meet environmental standards could lead to backlash, boycotts, and a significant loss of market share. Customers' loyalty to GreenEarth is built on the company's ethical stance, and continued emissions over the legal limit would betray that trust, potentially harming the company's brand and customer base.

Employees

Employees have mixed feelings about the situation. While many take pride in GreenEarth's sustainability ethos, there is concern about job security if production is halted for facility upgrades. Some employees advocate for immediate compliance, arguing that maintaining the company's ethical standards is the best way to secure long-term employment. Others, however, are wary of the financial repercussions of production downtime and its potential impact on wages and job stability.

Local community

The local community is also affected, especially as the facility is located near a residential area where residents have observed changes in air quality. While they may not be fully aware of the long-term health risks, they expect GreenEarth to act responsibly. Failure to address the emissions could lead to public protests and pressure on local authorities to enforce stricter regulations, thus damaging the company's relationship with the community and potentially causing more severe regulatory intervention.

UK Government environmental regulator

Regulators expect compliance with environmental laws, and while GreenEarth's emissions are only slightly above the legal limit, the company risks fines, penalties, and legal action if it continues to operate out of compliance. An environmental consultant has warned that unless GreenEarth takes immediate corrective action, regulatory consequences are likely. The regulators' stance makes it clear that delaying the upgrades is not a risk-free option.

The board of directors faces internal divisions, with some members advocating for delaying the upgrades to safeguard short-term profits and others pushing for immediate compliance to uphold the company's ethical standing and brand value. The board must consider both the financial implications and the long-term sustainability of the company when making its decision.

(b) Based on the analysis of the ethical issues and stakeholder perspectives, the most appropriate course of action for the board of directors would be to proceed with the immediate upgrade of the facility's emission control systems. This decision aligns with GreenEarth's brand values and ethical commitments, maintaining trust with customers, ESG-focused investors, and the local community, while also fulfilling its strategic objectives and promises on environmental sustainability, which is the principle on which GreenEarth was founded.

While this approach will involve a substantial short-term financial cost and temporary production downtime, the investment would mitigate the risk of regulatory penalties and potential long-term reputational damage, which could be far more costly in the future.

Failure to take this action could result in potential harm to the environment and local communities and would betray its environmentally conscious customers.

To address shareholder concerns, the board should clearly communicate the rationale for this decision, emphasising its alignment with GreenEarth's core values and long-term sustainability goals. The board could also explore options to secure funding for the upgrade, such as green financing or government grants aimed at promoting environmental compliance. Engaging employees in the process and providing support during production changes would help manage internal concerns about job security.

By taking this immediate and transparent action, GreenEarth can reinforce its ethical stance and strengthen its reputation as a leader in sustainable business practices.

End of chapter question

A UK-based manufacturing company, facing severe financial strain due to an economic downturn, has decided to make 250 of its 500 employees redundant. In a recent meeting, management informed the workers that there are 'insufficient funds' to cover the statutory redundancy payments.

This has come as a shock to the workforce, many of whom have long-standing service and depend on these payments for financial stability. Despite the economic situation, the company's directors claim that retaining cash is crucial to avoid insolvency and safeguard shareholder value.

Required

Explain why the company's action is unethical by applying Tucker's five questions model.

Suggested answer

Applying Tucker's five questions model.

(a) **Is it profitable?**

Not paying redundancy would retain cash in the short term, potentially stabilising the company's finances and helping to preserve shareholder value. However, while this decision might seem profitable, it comes at a significant ethical cost and risks damaging employee morale, public image, and long-term profitability due to potential backlash and loss of trust.

(b) **Is it legal?**

No, it is not legal. Under UK law, employees with two or more years of service are entitled to statutory redundancy payments. By withholding these payments, the company breaches employment law, exposing itself to legal action, including potential lawsuits and penalties. Directors could also face personal liability if they knowingly ignore legal obligations.

(c) **Is it fair?**

This decision is inherently unfair. Employees, having contributed to the company's success, deserve to be treated justly, especially during layoffs. Denying them legally due payments shifts the company's financial burden onto them. Fairness would involve at least attempting to negotiate a realistic payment plan or providing additional support to those affected.

(d) **Is it right?**

The company is knowingly ignoring its legal and ethical obligations, failing to support its employees during a time of need. Ethically, the company should seek to honour its commitments or at the very least, explore alternatives like payment plans or government support. This decision reflects a lack of care and respect for the employees' well-being.

(e) **Is it sustainable?**

This approach is unsustainable for future business operations. Failing to pay redundancy could damage the company's reputation, erode trust, and make it difficult to recruit talent in the future. Negative publicity could also harm relationships with customers and partners, impacting long-term business viability.

In conclusion, the company's decision to avoid redundancy payments is **unethical**, failing on multiple counts: legality, fairness, moral responsibility, and sustainability. While short-term financial relief may be gained, the long-term consequences for reputation and trust are severe. The company should explore more ethical options, such as payment plans, seeking external funding, or government aid, to fulfil its obligations and maintain its integrity.

Practice Case Study 1: Pre-seen material

Topic list	Syllabus reference
1 Practice case study 1: Pre-seen case information	All LOs

Introduction

This chapter contains the pre-seen material relating to Case Study 1 (Sophie McCloud Chocolate Heaven Ltd).

It includes:

(1) Sophie McCloud's Chocolate Heaven Ltd background information
(2) Financial data for the year ended 31 March 2020
(3) Extract from board meeting minutes, February 2019
(4) Audit file note: SMCH sales system, November 2019
(5) Extract from *New Food Magazine*, December 2019
(6) Emails between Iain Maxwell, chief operations manager and Philip Slack, purchasing director, January 2020
(7) Email from Philip Slack, purchasing director, to Amanda Jamieson, creative director, January 2020
(8) Extract from board meeting minutes, February 2020

Exhibit 1: Sophie McCloud's Chocolate Heaven Ltd background information

Sophie McCloud's Chocolate Heaven Ltd (SMCH) is a rapidly expanding family run company that has been trading since 2010. The company manufactures handmade chocolates, chocolate cakes and desserts based on closely guarded family recipes. Each recipe specifies the origin of the cocoa to be used and it is important that the cocoa beans are sourced in the correct country, since different locations grow beans of different genetic heritage and quality. SMCH prides itself on its fair trade philosophy in sourcing its cocoa beans.

The company was founded by Jess McCloud, who named her original chocolates after her daughter Sophie. She is a renowned chocolatier who learnt her trade in Belgium but subsequently worked for Chocolat Gourmande in France and Chocelicious plc in the UK. She started the company to have a job with flexibility when her children were young and expanded the business once her children grew up. Initially, the company supplied only local delicatessens. It received a major boost when a big department store in Newcastle discovered its wares and it now wholesales to a number of premium department stores around the country, as well as to specialist cookery shops. Retail sales are also made directly to consumers through the SMCH website.

The company incorporated in 2016 but has retained its stakeholder philosophy towards its customers, employees and suppliers. It plays an active role in promoting fair trade and recently received an Ethical Business Award. Jess McCloud was awarded North East Business Woman of the Year 2019.

Board membership

Name	Position	% shareholding
Jess McCloud	Managing director	35%
Steve Jones AAIA	Finance director	15%
Amanda Jamieson	Creative director	15%
Geoff Tomlinson	Marketing director	
Christine Hind	Human resources director	
Philip Slack	Purchasing director	

The remainder of the shares are owned by a venture capitalist, the employee share scheme, sundry small investors from Jess's family and friends and a trust fund set up for Jess's children.

A venture capitalist invested £12.5m in the company in October 2018. As a result, three new directors, Geoff Tomlinson, Christine Hind and Philip Slack were appointed to the board and a new reporting regime was introduced. The new regime emphasises profitability margins as a management indicator, rather than the measures based on number of customers and number of return customers that were previously used.

The new appointments continue to cause tension in board meetings and these tensions are affecting the morale of employees in the company.

Exhibit 2: Financial data for the year ended 31 March 2020

Year ended 31 March	2020	2019	2018
Revenue	£32.42m	£32.56m	£16.70m
Gross profit	£4.24m	£4.16m	£3.60m
Interest cover	2.1 times	2.8 times	4.9 times
Inventory holding period	47 days	29 days	28 days
Receivables collection period	66 days	46 days	47 days

Exhibit 3: Extract from board meeting minutes, February 2019

Attendees: Steve Jones (SJ), Geoff Tomlinson (GT), Christine Hind (CH), Philip Slack (PS), Amanda Jamieson (AJ)

Apologies: Jess McCloud (JM)

Corporate Governance

SJ confirmed the intention to formalise the system of corporate governance at SMCH. This is in anticipation of achieving a listing on the Alternative Investment Market in the future. He said that JM had expressed support for the plan in earlier discussions.

SJ explained that SMCH has followed elements of the guidance contained in the UK Corporate Governance Code in revising its policies on risk identification and mitigation. GT and CH identified that this represents a challenge for the board as members are inexperienced in formal risk assessment.

High Street presence

GT outlined a new retail strategy to the board, involving opening SMCH shops with integral cafes. This strategy was supported by CH and PS.

GT explained that he envisaged the shops having both a café and a shop floor selling consumable chocolate products and non-consumable products related to chocolate, such as mugs for hot chocolate. PS confirmed that he would make initial contact with suppliers of non-consumables in order to ascertain what products would be a good fit.

GT confirmed that any SMCH shops opened would operate in direct competition to Chocolat Gourmande outlets. However, he believes that SMCH can differentiate itself by emphasising certain aspects of its business which he thinks make it a premium brand.

It was agreed that two shops should be opened initially; SJ agreed to explore funding options, review customer data in order to identify possible target locations and initiate a search for suitable leased premises.

Website

CH proposed that the existing SMCH website be updated and improved. GT and PS supported the proposal and GT reiterated the importance of an effective and user-friendly website, explaining that it would allow access to lucrative overseas markets and reduce dependency on the UK market. GT further identified that a new website could be used to improve the communication with the venture capitalist and other shareholders and to present a slick 'designed' image to the world.

SJ and AJ agreed, and AJ said that she would explore options and costs further. She felt that a new website could provide an opportunity to rebrand the company and this theme could be taken into all corporate communication, including the statutory financial reports which, she felt, have been dull and uninspiring historically.

SJ agreed that there was room for improvement and said he would like to include an upbeat business review in the annual report, together with pictures of products and staff. He said that this would not be possible for the 2019 report, but could be considered for 2020. GT felt the report could be improved to better portray the company as caring and committed to ethically sourced and fairly traded cocoa.

GT remarked that his sister is a director and the majority shareholder at Rufus Lakes Ltd, a well-established and highly thought-of company, with both branding and website design departments. He felt sure that a good deal would be available for SMCH.

Exhibit 4: Audit file note: SMCH sales system, November 2019

A different sales system is operated, depending upon whether the customer is retail or wholesale.

Retail (online and retail shops)

Until September 2019, all retail sales directly to consumers were made via the SMCH website, with payment through secure credit card/debit card transactions. The system will be redeveloped in 2020 with the aim of being more user-friendly.

In September 2019, two retail shops, each named the Emporium of Chocolate Heaven, opened in Newcastle and Leeds. These shops have a café space upstairs and a retail floor downstairs.

Wholesale

Wholesale transactions are handled by the sales department, who negotiate bulk discounts or extended credit terms to secure customer loyalty. The remuneration package of the sales staff has recently been changed to a reduced basic salary, supplemented by bonuses based upon new customer orders and the level of repeat customer orders (item quantities rather than value), which reflects the previous emphasis on customer satisfaction and retention.

Wholesale customers range in size from small to large, which a concentration of customers in the small category:

Customer profile – Credit customers (wholesale)	As at 30 September 2019	As at 31 March 2019
Sales > £250,000	10	15
Sales > £100,000	19	16
Sales > £25,000	154	132

Exhibit 5: Extract from *New Food Magazine*, December 2019

Chocolate Heaven is a Place on Earth – An interview

Jess McCloud barely pauses for breath as she tells me about Sophie McCloud Chocolate Heaven's new venture, such is her excitement. Jess, managing director of the company named after her daughter, has, over the last six months, nurtured the concept of an Emporium of Chocolate Heaven from an idea to reality. It's no understatement to say that she's absolutely delighted with the outcome.

There are actually two Emporia – one in the grand and imposing Victorian Quarter of Leeds; and the other, in Newcastle's historic Grainger Town. Both have the same format – a vintage style café upstairs, where customers can try out chocolate cakes and desserts made to McCloud family recipes, and a retail floor downstairs selling boxed and individual chocolates, chocolate desserts and chocolate-related goods, including the new Sophie McCloud crockery range. Jess explains that the shops opened just two months ago, in September, and already they're drawing in the crowds, eager to try the delicious goodies on offer.

Jess said 'Moving onto the high street has given me back my zest for business. I feel just as I did when I first started getting orders for my chocolates – I hadn't realised how stale the company had become to me – a series of meetings about finance with so little creativity and excitement. I feel energised by taking on new challenges and stretching myself and the company into new areas. I believe strongly that the accounting team and the three new directors are quite capable of looking after the business side of things, leaving me to be creative. I've even stopped attending board meetings because they are doing such a good job.'

And creative Jess has been. The Emporia are warm and welcoming, with beautiful interiors inspired by the ocean-going liners of the early 20th century. The staff are charming and knowledgeable, eager to explain the provenance of the cocoa beans used in each recipe and product, and are themselves full of praise about the products, which they are encouraged to test at regular staff tasting sessions.

I have a feeling that this venture will be a resounding success – after all, who doesn't want to go to Chocolate Heaven?!

Exhibit 6: Emails between Iain Maxwell, chief operations manager and Philip Slack, purchasing director, January 2020

From: Philip Slack, purchasing director
To: Iain Maxwell, chief operations manager
Date: 13 January 2020
Subject: Re: Cocoa Supplies

Hi Iain

Thanks for the email and for highlighting the problem.

I have spoken to our account manager at Chocolate Globe Inc and she has disputed sending cocoa of a poorer quality than that specified in our contract. She won't accept returns and so if we can't use the cocoa because of quality issues, then we're likely to see a build-up of raw materials, which is obviously a problem. I've escalated the issue to Chocolate Globe Inc's sales director and am trying to cancel our three-year agreement with them, but they're threatening to sue us for breach of contract. I'm going to talk to our legal advisers to see what we can do.

In the meantime I've also spoken to Jess about this. She is really keen that we return to SMCH's original small suppliers and she has authorised me to negotiate new contracts with these suppliers, which I will attempt to do. The key problem with that is that I understand there may be reduced availability due to stockpiling activities by some of our larger competitors. It may therefore take some time, so please bear with me.

I'll keep you updated,

Thanks

Phil

>>>>>>>>>>>>>>>>>

Original message
From: Iain Maxwell, chief operations manager
To: Philip Slack, purchasing director
Date: 10 January 2020
Subject: Cocoa Supplies

Hi Phil

Happy New Year!

I meant to touch base with you before Christmas, but it was a little hectic and I didn't have a chance.
I'm a little concerned about our cocoa supplies and the possibility that the ethos of the company may be being undermined.

I know that the move to dealing with large suppliers has resulted in access to some very attractive bulk discounts and I realise that this is important from a profit perspective, particularly given price rises in cocoa beans over the last six months, but I think this represents a move away from the high quality, fairly traded ingredients that are a key part of the brand.

This seems to be becoming a bigger problem – some of the cocoa that we're being sent is simply not up to standard and today I have had to refuse a couple of deliveries from Chocolate Globe Inc. In the short term, I think it would be worth you contacting them to discuss quality, and in the longer term, I think we should consider moving back to smaller suppliers.

Thanks

Iain

Exhibit 7: Email from Philip Slack, purchasing director, to Amanda Jamieson, creative director, January 2020

From: Philip Slack, purchasing director
To: Amanda Jamieson, creative director
Date: 15 January 2020
Subject: Sourcing problems

Hi Amanda

Iain Maxwell recently identified problems with the quality of cocoa beans from one of our suppliers. As a result, I've spent quite a bit of time on the phone with Chocolate Globe Inc, and I've found that it cannot trace the source of its cocoa beans back to individual farmers, meaning that it can't guarantee that child labour has not been used. Chocolate Globe Inc's supplies form at least some of the cocoa content in about 80% of our products. That means that we can only guarantee ethically sourced ingredients for 20% of our output over the last year.

I realise this will potentially create a huge branding issue so wanted to give you a heads up before next month's board meeting.

We are in the process of moving back to using smaller suppliers who we know meet our ethical standards, but this may take some time.

Phil

Exhibit 8: Extract from board meeting minutes, February 2020

Attendees: Steve Jones (SJ), Geoff Tomlinson (GT), Christine Hind (CH), Philip Slack (PS), Amanda Jamieson (AJ)

Apologies: Jess McCloud (JM)

Food labelling

GT reported that legislation regarding food safety is becoming increasingly strict. Quality auditing is putting an increasing burden on the company, as is the need for accurate food labelling. As many of the products made by the company use nuts, care has been taken to ensure that this is clearly shown on all products. The company has also come under pressure to give details of the nutritional content (including nutritional values) of its products. This has required a redesign of the packaging costing £587,345 during the year.

Online sales

SJ identified that online sales leading up to Christmas were 7% lower than those in the equivalent period in 2018. This was due to a fall in consumer confidence after severe weather in the UK in November and December 2019 disrupted deliveries of orders to both direct customers and to retail outlets.

Referring to SMCH's money back policy for late delivery, AJ asked whether customers had generally exercised their right to ask for their money back. SJ confirmed that the majority had, resulting in additional unbudgeted costs in December 2019. GT asked why this policy remained in place. CH felt that the policy should be aligned with the industry norm of charging a premium for fast delivery and not guaranteeing next day delivery. SJ and AJ felt that this goes against the philosophy of customer service so enshrined in the company. It was agreed that GT would discuss with JM.

Funding requirements

SJ explained that as a result of the move into retail, the company has increased its borrowings by extending the use of its overdraft to the full amount made available by the bank. Bank borrowings are due for renegotiation in May 2020. SJ remarked that the bank may not feel inclined to increase the borrowing facility at this time and that this would expose the company to a £4.3 million cash deficit. He confirmed that the venture capital company has indicated that it would be willing to inject capital if required, subject to the satisfactory negotiation of an increased shareholding in the company.

Currency fluctuations

SJ explained that purchases of cocoa beans are made in US dollars and the weakening pound, together with increases in the price of cocoa beans, are causing financial pressure. In order to go some way to addressing this SJ confirmed that he has asked Sasha Chan (financial controller) to explore hedging opportunities. GT asked why this hadn't been considered sooner. SJ replied that it was a case of timing, with the finance department being under pressure in the year due to the launch of the new retail division and associated activities including lease negotiations.

Effectively reading and planning using Pre-seen information for Case 1

Topic list	Syllabus reference
1 Reading and planning using pre-seen Case 1	All LOs

Introduction

In this chapter, we discuss how you would apply the principles in Chapter 5, Research and analysis of the MDCS pre-seen and exam, to the pre-seen material of Case Study 1.

1 Reading and planning using pre-seen Case 1

1.1 Summarise

There's lots of detail in the pre-seen material and it's easy to get overwhelmed.

Your first step should be to skim through the material, noting down the major points to get an overview of what's happening.

The following table notes some key points extracted from the case material and their significance:

	Point noted	Significance
Extract 1		
1	'Rapidly expanding family run company'	There could be issues relating to expansion and putting good systems in place as the company grows.
		To what extent is family involved?
2	Manufactures chocolate products	Where do ingredients come from and how powerful a player in the market is SMCH?
		Cocoa beans are a commodity and subject to price fluctuations.
		We'd like to know who they sell to and what are the routes to market, who are their competitors?
		Chocolate may be seen as a luxury product and so, sales could decline rapidly when the economy is weak.
		May want to research some real-life luxury chocolate manufacturers to gain knowledge about the industry generally.
3	Genetic heritage of beans important, as is fair trade philosophy	Potential or damage to SMCH's credibility if problems in this area.
		Inventory may be overvalued.
4	Jess McCloud key entrepreneur	We'd want to know more about her continuing involvement in the company, her management philosophy/operating style, as she is a key part of the control environment.
		How is she coping with the rapid expansion? Does she have the appropriate skills?
		Does she intend to continue in the business or does she have an early exit strategy?
5	Sell to retailers and to public via website	Having a good website and brand is important to grow consumer sales, reliable delivery and quality is important for retailers as well as competitive price.
		Who maintains and manages the website? Sales are reliant on reliable website.

	Point noted	**Significance**
6	Stakeholder philosophy/ethical business credentials	Could be resentment by stakeholders, especially employees, if rapid expansion leads to less emphasis on stakeholders
		Business brand/reputation could be damaged if not seen as being ethical
7	Names of directors	Three of them are also shareholders, three do not appear to be
8	Venture capitalist	Three new directors who are not shareholders (see 7)
		Pressure on company to meet venture capitalist's expectations
		Tensions/resentment of new directors, Jess could feel resentful at loss of control. Tensions could affect the morale of employees lower down the company.
Extract 2		
9	Revenue almost doubled in 2019 but then declined in 2020	What did the company do in 2019 to achieve that expansion?
		What went wrong in 2020? Or was 2019 simply an exceptional year?
		What are future expectations for revenue?
10	Gross margin 21.6% in 2018, 12.8% in 2019, 13% in 2020.	Presumably increase in sales achieved by cutting prices. Can SMCH continue to do this? Will this damage the perception of the brand as a premium product?
11	Interest cover declined since 2018	Have loans increased as well as shares bought by venture capitalist?
		When must these loans be repaid?
		Is this due to loans or overdraft?
		Low interest cover in 2020 is sensitive to falls in profit as a result of increasing costs. Future cover may fall below 2
12	Inventory days over 50% higher in 2020	What's the reason – is SMCH struggling to sell its stock? Has the company stocked up ahead of a contract?
		Is chocolate perishable? Could some items require writing off?
		Inventory may be overvalued
13	Receivables days almost 50% higher	Why are retailers taking longer to pay? Is there a problem with products supplied? Have new customers been given extended credit terms?
		Are these debts actually recoverable?
		Receivables may be overstated

	Point noted	Significance
Extract 3		
14	Planning to list on AIM	Corporate governance requirements will become important
		Will require a rising profit trend to make listing a success, danger of creative accounting to achieve that
15	Board members inexperienced in formal risk assessment	If risks are not properly managed, they could ultimately lead to going concern problems
16	New shops/cafes planned	New area of business, no experience in that area (especially cafes)
		Would presumably need cash to finance
		Has market research been conducted? Is there a business plan to support the expansion?
		The high street is experiencing a downturn generally, so is this strategy wise?
17	Branching out into non-consumable products such as crockery	No experience in this business, poor products/decisions could damage SMCH's reputation/brand
		Inventory of non-consumables may be overvalued
		Is SMCH selling these as agent or principal?
18	Strong competition in retail business such as Chocolat Gourmande.	The stores may struggle to generate sufficient sales to be profitable
19	Leased retail premises planned	Need to ensure can service lease commitments
		May account wrongly for leases
20	New website planned	New slick 'designed' image may conflict with SMCH's traditional image/focus, could damage reputation/brand and relationship with existing customers
		May account wrongly for website costs
21	'Upbeat' business review planned	May be overly optimistic, could be management bias in the accounts
		Could be CSR measures, may require audit
22	Website development may be performed by Rufus Lakes Ltd, connection with director of SMCH	May have been selected on basis of family relationship, rather than competence
		May not properly disclose related party transactions
Exhibit 4		
23	Retail system to be redeveloped in 2020	Teething problems could lead to annoyance for customers or errors in processing
24	Two new retail stores in Newcastle and Leeds	See 16, 17, 18, 19
		Why were these locations chosen?

	Point noted	**Significance**
25	Sales department negotiate terms with wholesale customers	Could negotiate prices/terms that are not good for company. Is there a company policy for sales department staff to follow?
		Sales staff could commit fraud, offer better terms to friends, accept bribes
26	Bonus to sales staff	Staff could offer low prices to attract new customers, SMCH could make losses
		Staff could record fictitious orders to get bonus then reverse/issue credit notes
27	Customer mix changed from larger to smaller	Smaller customers may be less financially stable, receivables may not be recoverable
		Why have larger customers been lost?
Exhibit 5		
28	Jess McCloud has lost interest in the business side of things	Reduced management supervision could lead to poor decisions and an absence of common strategic direction
		Poor corporate governance to have uninterested managing director
29	Beautifully decorated stores	Could be expensive, if do not generate adequate profits/cash flows, then shops may be impaired
Exhibit 6		
30	Poor cocoa quality	Could damage reputation
		Prices charged to customers may need to be reduced to reflect this
		Inventory of finished goods and raw materials may be overstated
31	Possible legal action	Damages could have serious impact on profits
		Provision/contingent liability may not be treated correctly
32	Delays in sourcing cocoa from smaller suppliers	Could affect ability to produce inventory, damage reputation
33	Rises in cocoa prices	Profits would be reduced unless can increase sales prices
		Hedging strategies may be necessary
		Hedging may be accounted for incorrectly
Exhibit 7		
34	Problems with accurate sourcing of cocoa beans.	Could damage brand
		Could lead to breaches of regulations about ethical/accurate food labelling, possible fines
		Fines/penalties may not be properly provided/disclosed

	Point noted	Significance
Exhibit 8		
35	Legislation on food labelling becoming stricter	See 34
36	Christmas sales reduced	Important season for chocolate sales, falling sales will impact on profits
37	Money back policy for late deliveries	Impacts on profits May not be properly accounted for
38	Bank borrowings due for renewal	If not renewed may be cash flow problems Could lead to management bias
39	Venture capitalist offered more cash for more shares	Could increase tensions between old/new directors, could be perceived as taking over
40	Foreign currency risk and increasing cocoa prices, suggestion of hedging needed	Hedging may be done/accounted for incorrectly
41	Finance department under pressure	Increases risk of errors in financial statements

1.2 Organise

The next step is to try to organise all this information into themes and, as we saw in Chapter 5, some sort of mind map diagram can be useful to do that.

Here is a mind map, organising the information in the summary table above into themes, but you could easily have organised it in a different way. (The numbers in the boxes refer to the numbered rows in the table.)

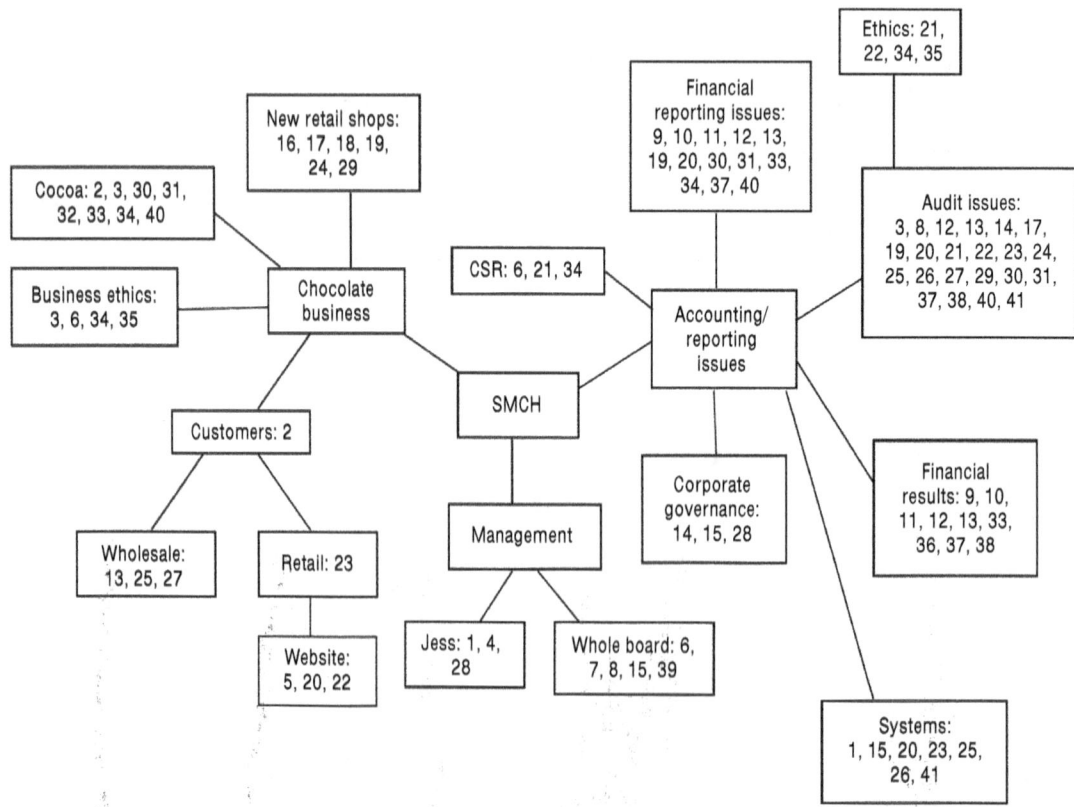

1.3 Further research

Having organised the information, you may have realised that you need to refresh your memory on a number of areas prior to the exam. Based on the case, you might want to research:

- Financial reporting standards: Based on the information in the case, you should ensure you are familiar with:
    - IAS 2 *Inventories*
    - IAS 24 *Related Party Disclosures*
    - IAS 36 *Impairment of Assets*
    - IAS 37 *Provisions, Contingent Liabilities and Contingent Assets*
    - IAS 38 *Intangible Assets*
    - IFRS 9 *Financial Instruments*
    - IFRS 15 *Revenue from Contracts with Customers*
    - IFRS 16 *Leases*
    - SIC 32 *Intangible Assets – Web Site Costs*

- Ethics Code

- Corporate Governance Code

- Auditing knowledge: You need to make sure you're familiar with the audit process, in particular risk-based auditing.

1.4 Practise

As said in Chapter 5, it's a good idea to perform some kind of risk assessment, as many past questions require analysis of business and/or audit risk and/or business strategy.

Many of the points in the summary relate to risk. Go through the table and prepare notes on the following categories of risks. Note that you may identify risks other than those highlighted above:

- Business risks – Events or actions that, if not managed, could damage the company's ability to make profits and could eventually lead to business failure (eg problems in proving genetic heritage of the cocoa beans)

- Risk management – Suggestions as to what the company might do to manage the risks (which will fall into categories of avoidance, acceptance, transfer, control) (eg change supplier to manage risks relating to quality of cocoa beans)

- Audit risks – Risks that could lead to material misstatements in the financial statements which the auditor fails to detect (eg inventory might be overstated if recorded at cost when selling prices of products is reduced due to unauthenticated beans)

- Response to risk – What the auditor will do in response to those risks (eg review sales invoices after the year end and compare selling prices with costs)

Practice Case Study 1: Unseen case information and exam requirements

Topic list	Syllabus reference
1 Practice case study 1: Unseen case information	All LOs
2 Practice case study 1: Unseen information	All LOs

Introduction

This chapter contains the exam requirements relating to Case Study 1 (Sophie McCloud Chocolate Heaven Ltd) and the unseen material. In the real MDCS, you will also be given another copy of the pre-seen material (which, for this Case Study) is in Chapter 7.

Exam requirement

You are a qualified accountant working for a multi-office national accountancy firm, Glenton Haines. You have recently been promoted to a junior audit partner and have taken over the role as engagement partner for a prestigious local company, Sophie McCloud's Chocolate Heaven Ltd (SMCH).

The company has been undergoing significant expansion and is interested in extending the services provided by your firm to include advice on risk management and internal control development as part of its commitment to formalising its corporate governance systems. The management has also asked you if you could provide an internal audit service.

You are also planning the audit for the company for the year ended 31 March 2020.

You have organised a preliminary audit meeting with Jess McCloud, the managing director and Steve Jones, the finance director. This is scheduled to last 45 minutes and they have indicated that they would like to explore the opportunities for extending the engagement terms as well as the logistics of the upcoming audit.

You will be moving from that meeting to a briefing meeting with the audit team who will be performing the audit field work.

Required

You should prepare notes which:

(a) Describe <u>seven</u> business risks facing SMCH and explain how they could impact on the audit for this year. **(28 marks)**

(b) Discuss whether you could accept the extension to the engagement terms which the directors have requested, explaining any relevant ethical guidance. **(6 marks)**

(c) Explain the effect of the activities to develop a new website and rebrand the company on the financial statements of SMCH in the year ended 31 March 2020. **(15 marks)**

(d) Explain the key roles of the audit partner in connection with quality control of your firm's audits generally and the audit of SMCH. **(6 marks)**

(e) Explain what is meant by professional judgement and scepticism and why each is vital in the conduct of the audit of SMCH. **(5 marks)**

(f) Explain how you would expect Sasha Chan to respond to Steve Jones in reply to his email of 31 January 2020. **(20 marks)**

(g) Explain the effect of the mezzanine floor on profit or loss as requested by Geoff Tomlinson in his email of 31 August 2019. **(5 marks)**

Professional Communication marks will be awarded for the quality of the presentation of the report.

Professional Marking Criteria (15 marks):

Report is presented in a style suitable for the audience articulated in the scenario. **(2 marks)**

Structure of the paper is logical and clearly articulated to enable ease of navigation and discussion. **(2 marks)**

Ideas are expressed clearly and in language accessible to the audience identified in the scenario. **(2 marks)**

Technical terms are used accurately and explained where appropriate. **(2 marks)**

Issues are appropriately prioritised within the structure of the report and the body of the discussion. **(2 marks)**

Issues are assessed in a balanced and reasoned manner. **(3 marks)**

Rationale behind assessment of issues and recommendations of responses is clearly articulated and alternative actions explored where appropriate. **(2 marks)**

(15 marks)
(Total 100 marks)

Unseen material

Contents:

(1) Memo to directors from Amanda Jamieson, creative director, 30 March 2020
(2) Email from Steve Jones to Sasha Chan, 31 January 2020
(3) Email from Geoff Tomlinson to Steve Jones, 31 August 2019

Exhibit 1: Memo to directors from Amanda Jamieson, creative director, 30 March 2020

To: All directors
From: Amanda Jamieson
Subject: New website
Date: 30 March 2020

As you know I have spent significant time over the last year developing our new website. The website is now in the testing phase before going live to the public in May 2020 and I wanted to update you on what has been achieved and the associated costs.

I commissioned local web designers, Rufus Lakes Ltd, to design and develop the website, and at the same time, re-brand SMCH. Its focus in terms of the website was to make the online shopping experience smoother and make the website easier to navigate. The website is primarily a selling tool. However, we have included a history of the company and a blog, which will be continually updated with stories and anecdotes from our shops, our suppliers and our customers. We think that these pages will attract customers to the website and are effective forms of marketing our ethos.

Rufus Lakes Ltd invoiced its full contract costs of £1.7 million for the website and £1.2 million for the rebranding exercise on 10 March, giving us one month's credit. The rebranding exercise is considered complete and the website is 90% complete with the final 10% contracted work relating to the testing phase and any necessary tweaks as a result. In addition, before passing the website project to Rufus Lakes Ltd, my team and I spent several hours planning the project and writing content for the history and blog pages. I have asked all staff members to keep a timesheet and have calculated an allocation of salary costs to the website project to be £350,000. We are paying a third party £300 per month for dedicated website hosting services.

The website testing phase is going well and we are making test sales to a small number of customers who have been allowed early access to the site. We have generated £8,400 from these test sales to date and have also gathered feedback from the test customers on the presentation and performance of the website.

Exhibit 2: Email from Steve Jones to Sasha Chan, 31 January 2020

From: Steve Jones, finance director
To: Sasha Chan, financial controller
Date: 31 January 2020
Subject: Hedging options

Hi Sasha,

I think it's time that we start thinking as a company about options to hedge purchases of cocoa beans. It's not so much the price of cocoa beans that worries me, but the fact that we pay for them in US dollars. The pound has weakened against the US dollar recently and I think will continue to do so. We're definitely going to be reporting exchange losses this year and we need to try to avoid that going forward.

I'm not really up to date on hedge accounting – we've never done it here at SMCH and it's been years since I studied accounting standards!

It's highly probable that we'll be buying US$4 million cocoa beans at the end of April. The agreed price is payable on delivery and I'm keen to lock in the current exchange rate before it falls any further. I think we could hedge this using a forward exchange contract to buy US$4 million on 30 April, but I've no idea how to account for it. I don't think we have to pay to obtain a forward exchange contract and there is no liability yet in respect of the purchase, so I just don't know what the accounting entries would be.

Can you prepare a briefing note for me that outlines what I need to know, including any conditions that are required to be met and what the accounting treatment is. If it's a lot of hassle, I'm wondering whether it's even worth hedge accounting. I don't think we have to use hedge accounting even if we hedge in practice.

I've done a bit of research and I think the following information is useful. For illustrative purposes, please assume that a forward contract would be entered into today:

	Spot exchange rate	Forward exchange rate for delivery 30 April 2020
31 January 2020 (actual)	£1: $1.25	£1: $1.23
31 March 2020 (forecast)	£1: $1.18	£1: $1.16

Give me a call if you need any more information,

Steve

Exhibit 3: Email from Geoff Tomlinson to Steve Jones, 31 August 2019

From: Geoff Tomlinson, marketing director
To: Steve Jones, finance director
Date: 31 August 2019
Subject: Lease on Leeds store

Steve

I've just been reviewing the lease documents that you circulated for the new Leeds store. I see that we have to 'put right' any alterations that we make to the property at the end of the lease term. I remember you saying that we'd build a mezzanine floor for the café, so won't we have a huge hit on profits at the start of the lease term when we build the mezzanine and again at the end when we remove it?

Geoff

13: Effectively reading and planning using unseen Case 1 information and exam requirements

Topic list	Syllabus reference
1 Using the unseen material and planning exam requirements	All LOs

Introduction

This chapter takes the guidance in Chapter 5 and applies it to the unseen material and requirements of Case 1, Sophie McCloud Chocolate Heaven Ltd.

1 Using the unseen material and planning exam requirements

1.1 Reading the information

1.1.1 Reading the requirements

Chapter 5 recommended that you read and analyse the question requirements before you read the unseen material.

Applying this approach to the requirements of SMCH:

Requirement	Points to note
(a)	'Describe <u>seven</u> business risks facing SMCH and explain how they could impact on the audit for this year.'
	The requirement asks for business risks but also asks how they could impact on the audit. Risks will impact on the audit if they are audit risks (the financial statements could be materially misstated, but the auditor may fail to detect that fact) or there could be ethical/practice management issues that affect the performance of the audit. So you're required to describe/explain business AND audit risks.
(b)	'Discuss whether you could accept the extension to your role which the directors have requested, explaining any relevant ethical guidance.'
	You need to look out for something in the case about extending your role (at this point, having started with the requirement, you don't know what your role is) and make a note that it's something involving ethics, so something involving independence/threats to independence perhaps. The mention of extending role and hint of ethics (independence) probably means that you are an auditor in this case.
(c)	'Explain the effect of the activities to develop a new website and rebrand the company on the financial statements of SMCH in the year ended 31 March 2020.'
	The pre-seen mentioned the development of a new website in Exhibit 3 and also that one of the companies that might be hired to do this has a connection to SMCH. There's not really enough detail there to write an answer, so we suspect that there must be more detail in the unseen material.
(d)	'Explain the key roles of the audit partner in connection with quality control of your firm's audits generally and the audit of SMCH.'
	We know this is an audit requirement and that you'll be required to demonstrate your knowledge of quality control requirements. It provides more evidence that you are the auditor of SMCH.
(e)	'Explain what is meant by professional judgement and skepticism and why each is vital in the conduct of the audit of SMCH.'
	More auditing, and again looks like you are the auditor of SMCH.
(f)	'Provide the detail that you would expect Sasha Chan to have provided to Steve Jones in reply to his email of 31 January 2020.'
	This requirement doesn't really give you any clues at all! You may recall that Steve Jones is the finance director, but you may not, and you wouldn't recognise the name Sasha Chan, as this is a new character. Make a mental note to look out for this email when you read the unseen material and re-read the pre-seen material.
(g)	'Explain the effect of the mezzanine floor on profit or loss, as requested by Geoff Tomlinson in his email of 31 August 2019.'
	Again, this won't be giving you any clues, as this email wasn't in the unseen material, so you know you need to look out for it.

1.1.2 Reading the preamble

The following points can be identified from reading the text immediately before the requirements: Numbering starts at 42 to continue from the 41 points noted from review of the pre-seen.

	Point noted	Significance
42	You're a junior audit partner in a multi-office firm	You are fairly senior in the firm and it's quite a big firm. This means that it will likely offer a wide range of services to its clients.
43	You are the engagement partner for SMCH	We now know from which perspective we're answering the questions. The use of 'prestigious' hints that we need to be careful to avoid ethical issues, as this client will be quite significant for our firm.
44	You have been asked to extend your services to provide advice on risk management/internal control development plus provide an internal audit service.	This tells us the additional services which are included in requirement (b) and we can see straight away that there may well be ethical conflicts in providing these extra services.
45	You are planning the audit for the year end, which is 31/3/20	The year end puts all the financial information into context. Some of the data given in the pre-seen was at 31/3/20 but did not say 'draft,' so it's likely that 'today's date' is shortly after the year end.
46	You are about to have a planning meeting with the client, then brief the audit team	The question is going to cover aspects of planning (eg risk) and performing the audit (checking the accounting is done correctly, so we need to consider the correct accounting).

1.1.3 Reading the unseen information

	Point noted	Significance
Exhibit 1		
47	Website in testing phase	Development complete. It's good that there is a testing phase, rather than going live immediately and it's a sign of good control.
48	Rufus Lakes used	Potential related party transaction to disclose
49	Detail on different types of pages	A clue that you need to use this detail in your answer in some way
50	Details of different aspects of the costs	A clue that you need to perhaps account for different costs in different ways
51	Details of revenue from test sales	The fact that you're told this must mean that it's significant in some way – start thinking about whether test sales are treated differently from other sales.

	Point noted	Significance
Exhibit 2		
52	Email from Steve Jones to Sasha Chan	This was the email mentioned in requirement (f).
53	Cocoa prices increasing, but bigger concern is that cocoa is paid for in US dollars, considering hedging	It appears that SMCH wants to hedge purchases of cocoa. Probably to hedge currency risk, rather than movements in cocoa prices.
54	Want to avoid reporting exchange losses	Accounting treatment chosen must try to avoid losses.
55	Steve Jones 'not up to date on hedge accounting'	It's looking like the email to Sasha is asking about hedge accounting, and therefore the reply is explaining it (requirement (f)).
56	Details of cost/date	To use in calculations
57	'I don't think we have to pay', 'there is no liability yet.'	A few clues on the accounting treatment to help you work out your answer
58	Briefing note includes conditions to be met, accounting treatment, speculates whether must be used.	Guidance as to the structure of your answer
59	Details of rates	To be used in calculations
Exhibit 3		
60	Email from Geoff Tomlinson to Steve Jones	This is the information to answer requirement (g).
61	'Put right' alternations to leased property	It looks like you are being asked to explain the accounting implications of the lease clause, so IFRS 16 *Leases* is relevant.
62	Don't want a 'huge hit' on profits at start and end of the lease	Need to explain how costs of installing mezzanine are accounted for and how costs of removing it are accounted for. You are provided with a clue that neither will be an immediate expense to profit.

1.2 Organising and synthesising the information

You may remember that in Chapter 8, we drew a mind map of the pre-seen information. Let's now add the new information in the unseen material to that mind map to help give you an overall picture.

(Don't forget that you can't take any material into the exam, so you'll be doing this based on your memory of the structure of your mind map which likely won't be very detailed.)

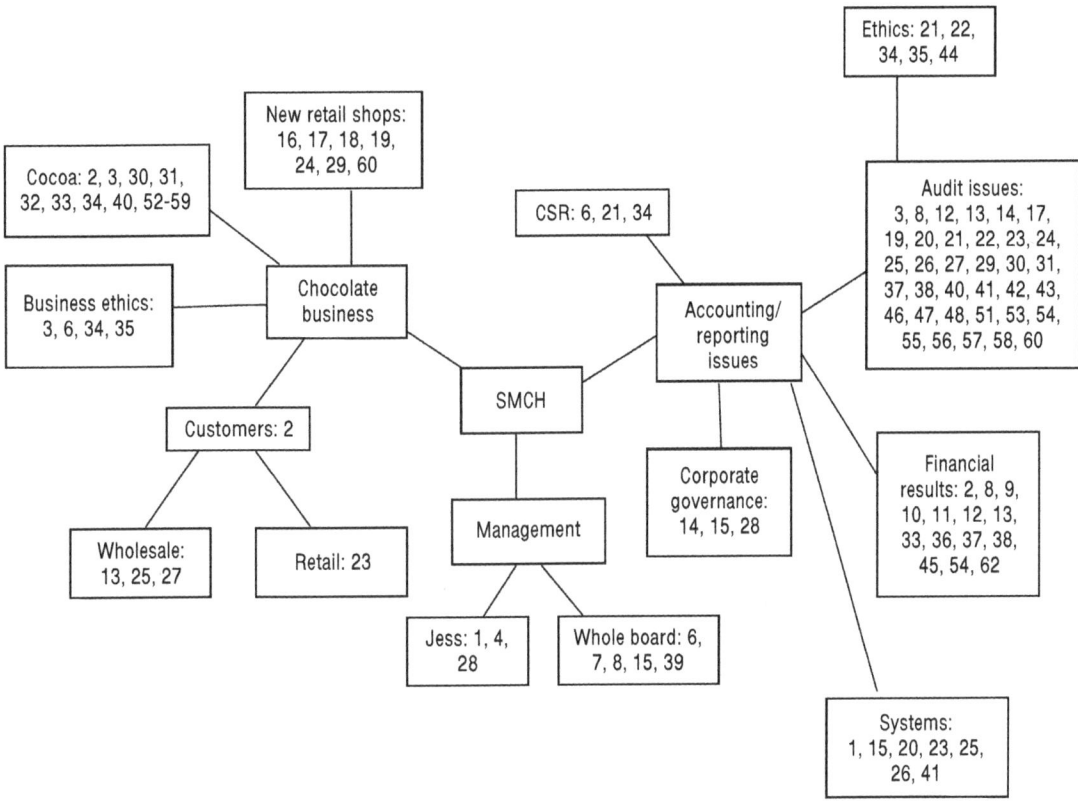

1.3 Planning your answer

Now go back and look at the requirements.

As a general principle, the best parts of the question to do first are short and knowledge-based (not based too much on the case itself) so that you can start writing straight away without going through all that information again.

Try doing (d) and (e) first, because then you can gain some marks quite quickly.

Next try part (b) which is partly based on the Case Study, but also on your knowledge of the ethics code; then (g) which, although based on the case, has all the information you need in Exhibit 3 of the unseen material.

You're then left with (a) (28 marks), (c) (15 marks) and (f) (20 marks). With requirements that have lots of marks, the more you can break it down into different sections, the easier it is to answer as it's less overwhelming.

So for part (a), break down into seven risks. For each risk, you need to write 2 marks worth for business risk (1 for identifying the risk, 1 for describing how it damages profit, 2 for audit risk (1 for explaining how it affects the financial statements, 1 for discussing in what way the financial statements could be wrong (ie fail to meet the requirements of the financial statement assertions)).

When you come to start writing your answer to part (a), there are lots of risks to write about. Try to select business risks where you can easily see the impact on the financial statements and so can write about audit risk too.

For part (c) you might break you answer down into (i) website development costs, (ii) rebranding exercise, (iii) internal writing costs, (iv) test sales and (v) related party transactions based on the information in Exhibit 1.

For (f) you might have sections on (i) what is hedging? (ii) what is hedge accounting? (iii) conditions for hedge accounting, (iv) accounting treatment if use hedge accounting and (v) whether you'd recommend it, given that the company is trying to avoid exchange losses.

1.4 Start writing

It's now time to start writing! Be careful not to run out of time, and bear in mind that there are 15 professional marks for the quality of your writing and structure of your report (see Chapter 11).

Demonstrating professional judgement, commercial awareness, effective writing and time management

Topic list	Syllabus reference
1 Professional judgement	LO 5
2 Commercial awareness	LO 5
3 Further MDCS exam techniques: Interpretation of requirements and answer planning	LO 3
4 Effective writing	LO 4
5 Managing your time effectively in the MDCS exam	All
6 Advice on final MDCS exam preparation	All

Introduction

As we have already seen, you will be often be required to give advice or make a recommendation in the MDCS examination, and your answers will be assessed, not just on their factual accuracy but also on your ability to exercise professional judgement. This chapter considers professional judgement, commercial awareness and developing of MDCS exam techniques and includes a number of examples to illustrate the level of performance expected of you as a candidate at the final level before qualification.

In MDCS, you should include a focus on skills development in every question you attempt as part of your exam preparation. Developing skills requires more than listening and reading – it requires you to try for yourself, use guidance and feedback to consider whether you have met the skills objective, then plan for further improvement.

1 Professional judgement

There are three essential elements to demonstrating professional judgement as part of your analysis and evaluation:

- The first is the ability to **probe deeply** into the underlying reasons for issues and problems, beyond what is immediately apparent from the usual sources and opinions available. It seems sensible to consider judgement as an enhanced form of professional curiosity where you do not simply take what you are told at face value but instead, look beneath the obvious and consider what questions and queries you might have from a given situation.

- The second is to **question facts, opinions and assertions**, by seeking justifications and obtaining sufficient evidence for their support and acceptance. Again, this seems logical once you have started to probe something more deeply: are you happy with what you have been told or does it need something else to satisfy you that all is as it should be?

- The third and final approach to demonstrating professional judgement is to **challenge information presented in the Case Study**, such as the current strategy or assumptions made by management, where this is clearly justified, in a professional and courteous manner.

Assumptions and estimates are necessary to make forecasts and predictions. They should be reasonable, but they could be wrong. There is no magic formula for making a correct forecast! Professional judgement does not involve a confrontational approach – rather it seeks to gain insight into how a conclusion was arrived at and to seek clarification of the underlying assumptions that have been used as part of the analysis presented. Since forecasts are always questionable, it is essential that an accountant is able to identify which seem reasonable and perhaps more importantly, those which appear suspect.

When analysing the pre-seen and attempting the MDCS exam, you should aim to demonstrate, where appropriate, a suitable degree of professional judgement. You should question the information and the assumptions or estimates that you have used in your analysis. Where has the basic information come from? Who provided the estimates?

The questions that should be asked, to demonstrate professional judgement, may be remembered as seven questions beginning with the letter P, as shown in the following table.

Question		
1	**Preparer?**	Who prepared the information or provided the estimates?
		Was it an 'internal' person, with a vested interest in the decision?
		What amount of knowledge or skill does the preparer of the information possess?
2	**Purpose?**	Why has the information been provided?
		Is it a standard set of financial statements, or was it prepared for a specific purpose?
		If it was prepared for a specific purpose, what is the possibility that it may contain bias, given its purpose and the person who prepared it?
3	**Precision?**	What is the likely level of accuracy in the information provided?
		Does it come from an audited source, or from formal management accounts?
		Is it an extrapolation of historical performance into the future?
		Does it come from a new source?
4	**Predictions?**	Are the time frames realistic?
		Are the assumptions realistic about future levels of activity?
		To what extent are predictions in the information provided based on speculation?

Question		
5	Problems?	Are the problems purely financial, or are there non-financial issues to consider?
		Are the problems short-term in nature or more long-term and fundamental to the success of the business?
		Are the problems outside the control of the company and its management? Or do they relate to an internal issue that management can deal with?
6	Priority?	What priority should be given to the issue?
		Is it a high priority problem requiring urgent attention?
		Or is it a problem that can be dealt with less urgently, and dealt with instead over time?
7	Perspective?	From whose perspective should the problem be considered?
		Does the information suitably reflect the interests of the client?
		Be aware of who your client is, what the client is expecting from you and how the interests of the client are affected by your analysis.
		What might other stakeholders think?

From the answers to these questions, you will be able to assess the quality of the information presented in the pre-seen or exam. Your assessment will demonstrate the quality of your professional judgement which is an important aspect of financial analysis and data analysis, and an essential quality of a professional accountant.

Making an assessment on the reliability of the information provided does not mean that you should reject all the numbers and assumptions. You are making an assessment of the quality of the information provided and the level of confidence that you can have in each element of the information. You may need to recognise that some elements of information are more reliable than others.

2 Commercial awareness

There are three essential elements to demonstrating commercial acumen as part of your analysis and evaluation:

- The first is the ability to demonstrate **awareness of organisational and wider external factors** affecting the work of an individual or a team in contributing to the wider organisational objectives. Given that this is a strategic professional exam, it should come as no surprise that you need to consider the 'bigger picture' when producing answers to questions.

- The second is to **use judgement to identify key issues** in determining how to address or resolve problems and in proposing and recommending the solutions to be implemented. Again, demonstrating higher level skills (often in conjunction with higher level question verbs such as 'recommend' or 'evaluate') is crucial for success at this level. Professional marks will be awarded in this area for demonstrating sensible and appropriate solutions that reflect the context of the case overview and exhibits

- The third and final approach to demonstrating commercial acumen is to **show insight and perception** in understanding work-related and organisational issues, including the management of conflict and demonstrating commerciality in arriving at appropriate solutions or outcomes. This means using facts within the case study, and determining whether suggestions and opportunities are practically feasible and will deliver the expected financial and non-financial benefits in the real world.

We will now look at a question which requires a focus on commercial acumen and professional scepticism.

Question

Uptown is considering ways of stimulating the local economy and has invited local businesses to submit proposals for projects which are expected to be both economically viable and able to contribute to the local community in which it will be based. As part of the viability assessment, the local government requires any such project to have a payback period of no more than four years.

One such proposal has been submitted by Good Investments Ltd (a local company which has performed work on behalf of the local government for a number of years) for the construction of a new community centre, the business case for which is shown below.

	Year 1 £	Year 2 £	Year 3 £	Year 4 £	Year 5 £
Costs: Initial	600,000				
Costs: Recurring	60,000	60,000	60,000	60,000	60,000
Benefits: Rental savings	144,000	144,000	144,000	144,000	144,000
Benefits: Energy savings	30,000	30,000	30,000	30,000	30,000
Benefits: Increased income	20,000	20,000	70,000	90,000	90,000
Benefits: Better staff morale	25,000	25,000	25,000	25,000	25,000
Cumulative net benefits	(441,000)	(282,000)	(73,000)	156,000	385,000

Figure 1: Costs and benefits of the business case for the community centre

New buildings built under the local government investment policy must attain energy level targets and this is the basis for the estimation, above, of the **energy savings**. It is expected that the new centre will attract more customers who will pay for the centre's use, as well as increasing the use of facilities such as the cafeteria, shop and business centre. These benefits are estimated, above, under **increased income**. Finally, it is felt that staff will be happier in the new building and their motivation and morale will increase. The centre currently employs 20 staff, 16 of whom have been with the centre for more than five years. All employees were transferred from the old to the new centre. These benefits are shown as **better staff morale** in Figure 1.

The local government official charged with deciding to authorise the investment is unsure about the proposal and has come to you as a recently qualified accountant for advice.

Required

Evaluate the proposal and recommend whether the investment should proceed or not.

Answer

Perhaps the first thing to consider is what the response of a *weak* candidate would be. At its most simplistic, an assessment of the project would include something like:

'Since the payback period of the project is less than four years, it should be allowed to go ahead.'

However, what the MDCS exam requires is more in-depth analysis. Imagine that you are being paid to give advice – you need to bring in a little more than a simple calculation. To do this, firstly, we need to plan out what has to be done.

This investment could be considered to be strategic in nature, and so one would expect to have to use the suitability, acceptability and feasibility approach – but in this case, we have been given very little information to go on with. Realistically, it is unlikely that any organisation would undertake a substantial investment on such a thin business plan, but in this instance, as is so often true in life, we have to work with what we've got.

Focus on professional judgement

In the context of the exam, it is important that a candidate is able to show that they can act and think like a qualified accountant. This means that when looking at this or any other plan, it is important to be able to detect anything that looks questionable, and to identify what further information is needed. Insight may be required to enable you to pinpoint why something has been done in the way it has.

Also, bear in mind that when people are putting a business case together, they will very rarely be completely objective – often they are motivated by self-interest or some other conflict of interest. Ask yourself, does anything look odd? We shall take each item of the business plan in turn and consider whether we have confidence in it.

(a) **Recurring costs** – Notice that the figures remain the same for each of the five years. There is nothing to indicate that these figures are expressed in real terms, and so it might be expected that there would be at least some measure of inflation leading to the costs rising each year. Alternatively, there could be the possibility of increasing efficiency in the running of the centre which might lead to reduced costs as time goes by.

However, it does have to be noted that the probability that these two conflicting forces would cancel each other out exactly is almost vanishingly small. So perhaps the first question to be asked of the firm presenting this business proposal is - how does this peculiar situation arise?

(b) **Rental savings** – Again, these figures are the same every year, but these figures may be more reasonable, since this could be made up of savings that arise from no longer having to pay rent on another privately-owned building, on which an agreed rental has been decided in advance. This therefore will lead to savings – as long as we can actually get out of the lease on the old premises.

(c) **Energy savings** – Again, these figures are constant each year, which may be suspect, but if it is the case that these arise because of a change in the new building, perhaps made with better quality materials with greater insulation capacity, then it may well be reasonable.

(d) **Increased income** – This looks odd. Notice that it is £20,000 in the first two years, then it rises rapidly to £70,000 and then again to £90,000. This begs the question – why? Clearly, we need to know the reason for this substantial increase – is it due to increased footfall, or because we expect to be able to let the premises out to interested parties, or because of something else?

It is not unreasonable for the number of visitors to a community centre to increase after it has been upgraded, but the pattern of the increase seems odd. An analyst reviewing the figures would almost certainly want to know the assumptions that these forecasts have been based upon, so that the reasonableness of those forecasts can be assessed.

(e) **Better staff morale** – This looks the most suspect of all. Again, it is the same amount for each of the five years and rather looks as if it has been included for one reason and one reason only – to make the project seem economically viable. Of course, with a new building, it is to be expected that staff morale would increase – but the question arises as to how a value has been placed on such a benefit.

Focus on commercial awareness

We will now consider this last point relating to staff morale in rather more detail and think about how an analyst might decide if the figures can be trusted or not. Since we do not have much in-depth information about the situation, we are limited as to what we can say about the matter - but we can still make some useful comments, if we are prepared to make some assumptions and indulge ourselves in a little scenario planning.

To do this, we need to use a little professional acumen to think about what the situation might actually be like in practice. What would be the reason for the savings due to an increased level of staff morale? Just because people are happier or more satisfied in their work, it does not automatically follow that financial benefits will inevitably accrue. We might want to imagine what would give rise to the financial benefits, so we can decide for ourselves whether to actually trust the figures. It might be, for instance, that a happier workforce is more likely to stay – so there will be less need for recruitment. Or it might be that people's performance will improve, and this might lead to the need for fewer staff. You do have to be careful though – a reduction in the number of staff needed may well have already been included in the reduction of 'Recurring costs', and so by including it here, one would be double counting the savings.

Let's consider something that may be easier to quantify – staff turnover, and the need to recruit staff that arises from that. The cost of recruiting somebody will vary according to how difficult it is to find someone to fill that role, and the level of training they need after they have started work. It will also be affected by the level of salary they receive – typically, recruitment consultancy agencies may charge somewhere between 20 and 40% of the first year's salary. It will also be affected by the cost of the advertising for the role – say in a national or local newspaper. Notice that in the question, we are given very little information about any of this – we simply have to make some reasonable assumptions and carry out our analysis based upon those assumptions.

How many people might work in a community centre? Of course, it depends on a wide range of variables – how big it is, how many hours a week it is open, what range of services it provides and so on. In this instance, the question tells us that there are twenty, and of that twenty people, sixteen have been there for more than five years – that tells us that the level of staff turnover is actually pretty low.

What sort of pay might they receive? In my personal experience, I would have to say probably not much. There would probably be a manager of some description, but other than that, most people would be on a pretty low wage – they might be part time, and probably fairly low-skilled workers. This last point would make them relatively easy to replace – especially since the local economy has been going through a recession, which would mean higher levels of local unemployment and therefore a large pool of people willing to take such jobs on.

Recruiting people in such a scenario would hardly be a difficult or expensive task – you wouldn't need to use a recruitment consultant, so it's unlikely that you would have to pay expensive fees to actually find a range of candidates.

An advert in a newspaper would probably be sufficient. What sort of cost would that incur? Well, consider the nature of the role – it's probably not a very high level of salary, and therefore it's unlikely that an individual would relocate to fill this position, so there would be little benefit in advertising in a national paper. A local newspaper would almost certainly be the way to go, which would mean that the costs associated with advertising the post would be much lower.

Of course, you may be able to advertise the role online which may be even cheaper, but then you need to ensure that the people you are looking to recruit would actually be likely to look online when looking for work. If not, then you may be placing your advert in the wrong place. If there is a local employment exchange, then that might be a better alternative.

How much would that cost- £100? £200? No more than that.

How often would you have to do that? Twenty staff, most of them low skilled, in an area of potentially high unemployment? Maybe five times a year, at most. So, if the new premises improved morale and staff do not leave as the new building is such a good place to work in, then this might save 5 x £200. So, £1,000 per year, which casts doubt on the validity of £25,000 per year.

Of course, our assumptions might be out, but being out by a factor of twenty five seems unlikely. There could be other reasoning that underpins this number – but it is difficult to see where it has come from.

Conclusion

In conclusion, a figure of £25,000 would be nothing more than an amount included within the business case purely to make the proposal seem economically viable and hence, get the green light to go ahead.

Many of the figures in the analysis appear, on the face of it, to be questionable, with the last line appearing to be nothing more than something that has been included simply to mislead the local government into financing a project that will not satisfy its funding criteria.

At the very least, the management of Good Investments should be invited to explain the basis of their business case – they may, after all, have very sound reasons for their calculations – but no approval should be given until the figures have been shown to have been based upon objective criteria.

A further point to consider is that there may be a number of projects currently being undertaken by Good Investments that have been approved in the past and based upon equally suspect business cases. Consideration should be given for the need of a review of past decisions with a view to identifying weaknesses in the approval process, and the need for improvements.

The answer above is more depth than anything you might be expected to consider in the MDCS exam, but the points it draws out reflect the need to question analysis presented to you in the exam, and the need to avoid being too superficial in your answers.

We will return to this example later on in this chapter, but for now, we need to consider the issue of ethical behavior in professional judgement.

3 Further MDCS exam techniques: Interpretation of requirements and answer planning

MDCS requires the demonstration of many skills, which include correct interpretation of requirements, so you provide an answer which directly responds to the given task and so aligns to the examiner's expectations. Answer planning is then essential in order to complete each task successfully in the time available to ensure you prioritise your answer to the most relevant points, and provide a focused and logical response in your written answers.

3.1 Correct interpretation of requirements

You will have heard the advice 'read the question' or 'RTQ' many times as part of your studies so far, and we are not going to change that now! However, some task requirements may prove difficult to understand due to long, complex sentences and multiple verbs, which indicate a series of tasks instead of just one. It is therefore critical that you can deconstruct the task requirement to isolate each verb and ensure you plan to supply a suitable response in each case.

3.2 Answer planning

Once you know what the task requirement is looking for, you can start to search for answers to the list of things you need to do. Reading the case with this list in mind will help you quickly isolate the important things and discount the rest. At this stage, you will also aim to work out the number of marks available for each task requirement, which should allow you to start considering the number of points a good answer should contain to score well.

4 Effective writing

The MDCS examination not only tests your technical ability; it also tests your business communication skills, and you need to prepare and present a clear and well-structured professional answer in the format required. Additionally, your answer should also succeed in demonstrating your other skills including financial analysis, strategic analysis and professional judgment.

4.1 Structuring your answer

The main body of your report should be divided into sections and each section should have its own heading. There should be one section for each different requirement set out in the pre-seen and you may decide to divide each requirement into sub-sections.

You may know from experience that headings within a report break up the text and make the structure of the report easier to understand – and this makes the report easier to read.

You may be required to make a recommendation or reach a conclusion. If so, you can introduce a sub-heading within each section titled: 'Recommendation' or 'Conclusion'.

4.2 Logical structure and clear points

As a general guide, each main section of the report will:

- Provide a short introduction which references the task.
- Present the arguments and analysis in response to the requirement.
- Where relevant, reach a considered conclusion or recommendation, based on the arguments and analysis that you have presented.

Presenting the arguments and analysis is a big test of your communication skills. When preparing your answer plan, list the points that you consider relevant. Use your judgment to prioritise them and put them into a logical sequence.

You should then write the section of the report using the structure you have chosen for your answer plan. Where the section involves financial analysis, present the key figures in your report, but do not include excessive amounts of figures – refer the reader to an Appendix for the details.

Keep your sentences and paragraphs short, so that the clarity of your argument is not lost in excessive words. Keeping your points brief will also help you to complete the report within the available time. Clarity, however, is the most important requirement for good communication.

The quality of your report will be judged largely by the conclusions or recommendations that you make in each section of your report; so use common sense when making judgments. Any recommendations that you make should be:

- Realistic/realisable/feasible
- Acceptable
- Suitable/relevant to the purpose of the report and the readers of the report

4.3 Professional use of language

Using an appropriate professional tone is an important aspect of communicating the message in your report and will help you to engage your reader.

Whenever possible, use an active rather than passive construction to your sentences, as the active voice is more direct, it is generally shorter and easier to comprehend. Using an active voice signals the confidence you have in your analysis, conclusions, and recommendations. For example, it is better to state: 'The forecast shows that [...]' rather than 'It is shown in the forecast that [...]'.

It is essential as a qualified accountant to communicate in a professional manner, and to exhibit a respect for the other person's point of view. It includes both verbal and written communication – and of course, in today's environment, extends into the realm of social media. While there are various subtleties that arise due to cultural or social norms, there are some key points that are common to virtually all modes of communication. When you use a confident and professional tone, the reader is more likely to agree and accept the message you are conveying.

Firstly, it is important that what is being said is accurate, complete and understandable, and also that it is true. It is therefore important that any claims being made can be backed up by evidence and are not claimed to be facts when they are simply opinions. When presenting a report, it is usually helpful if there is a title outlining what the report is about; if it's a letter that's being written, it should be headed up properly.

A report should have a title, and also state the name of the recipient, the name of the sender, the date, and a brief explanation as to what it's about.

A business letter should be laid out clearly with a title and at the top right, it should have the sender's address and contact details, followed by the date. Where applicable, it should also state a reference

number. On the left hand side, it should have the recipient's details. If you know the name of the person you are writing to, it should begin with their name (Eg 'Dear Mr Tan'). If you do not know the name of the person the letter is being sent to, then begin with 'Dear Sir'. If it's to a firm of, say, accountants it would begin 'Dear Sirs'.

Written communication is nearly always easier to understand if the sentences are short and to the point – otherwise, it gives the impression that the writer is unclear about what they are trying to say, or, perhaps more worryingly, is trying to confuse the reader of the document.

Secondly, if it is written communication, it is important that it is presented correctly, and does not contain errors of spelling or punctuation – such things make the writer seem lazy or indifferent to the matter being discussed and also give the impression that the recipient is not important. As a consequence, the recipient is likely to give the message less attention than it might deserve.

When replying to another's communication, it is important that the specific topics mentioned in the original communication are discussed respectfully, and not in a dismissive or flippant manner. After all, it mattered enough to the sender for them to sit down and compose a letter or email to you, so it is only good manners that you do the same for them. It is always useful to remember that just because a topic or issue seems obvious to you, it might not seem that way to someone else.

On a related note – people often forget that emails and texts do actually live forever, stored on some distant system, just waiting to be recovered when it suits somebody's agenda. Anything that can be misconstrued will be, and often at the expense of the sender, so it is always important to reread anything before it is sent – and if it is anything of a sensitive nature, it is usually a good idea to get someone else to check it before you press 'Send'.

Additionally, it is usually a good idea to remember that, no matter how well you get on with your boss, they are not your friend; you work for them, and it is important not to let work communication start to look like something you would send to a friend or relative. So, for instance, kisses at the end of a work email never look professional – it looks far too familiar and will end up either offending or alienating the recipient.

Finally, it is essential that one is aware of intercultural communication: that is, communication between and among individuals and groups across national and ethnic boundaries – it could also arise when communicating across the generational divide - and it is always important to ensure that what you are sending will not be misinterpreted by the recipient.

Things to avoid:

- Do not use jargon, slang, vague or emotional language in your report.
- Never use language that is discriminatory, offensive, or culturally insensitive.
- Although it is important to convey strength and confidence in your report, you must also avoid coming across as being over-confident, condescending, or arrogant.

4.4 Appendices

The Appendices should present calculations for financial statement analysis and data analysis. They should contain your detailed workings in response to the requirements in the Examination Day Documents.

If an Appendix includes tables of figures, then remember to give each table a clear title.

You must decide what Appendices to include in your answer and what each Appendix should contain. The information in each Appendix should be presented clearly.

As good practice, you should always refer to each Appendix in your answer.

4.5 Writing your report: concluding comments

As with all examinations, time pressure and time management are important factors. You must plan your time properly, giving sufficient weight to each requirement in the MDCS exam. Having planned your time, stick to it.

Failure to finish a requirement in MDCS could be critically important and make the difference between success and failure.

Overall, you should aim to produce a report that:

- Uses relevant information from the unseen and pre-seen
- Provides suitable analysis
- Shows appropriate professional judgement
- Provides good conclusions and recommendations
- Covers all the requirements in a reasonable depth given the time restriction

5 Managing your time effectively in the MDCS exam

To maximise you chance of exam success, it is crucial you attempt all tasks set out in the unseen, or as many as possible. By attempting all requirements, you are effectively accessing more of the available marks and so increasing your chance of passing the exam.

Therefore, it is critical to prepare yourself thoroughly for the MDCS exam by practising the four MDCS Practice Case Studies in this Workbook, and attempting the specimen mock exam made available by AIA. The investment required in study and preparation is significant, but this will pay off in the examination, as you will be able to respond and plan more quickly to exam requirement, and effectively write up your answers in the time available.

Once, you have completed the reading and planning of the unseen, determine your remaining time available in the exam, and allocate this time to each exam requirement. As you progress through these requirements, keep a check on the time remaining for that requirement. Once the time you have allocated to a requirement has expired, you should move onto the next requirement. You will need to be ruthless with your time and approach, however – this exam strategy will ensure you have attempted all requirements. With any time remaining, you can go back and complete any unfinished areas.

The following advice on avoiding pitfalls and approaching the MDCS exam will help you to manage your time more effectively.

5.1 Avoiding pitfalls

Our experience of case study exams enables us to predict a number of weaknesses that are likely to occur in many answers. These pitfalls will eat into the time you have available. You will enhance your time available if you practise beforehand to ensure you avoid these mistakes in the exam.

- **Failing to interpret the requirements correctly and provide what the question verbs require** (discussion, evaluation, recommendation) or to write about the topics specified in the question requirements. It is vital that you read the question requirement very carefully so that you understand exactly what you are being asked to do.

- **Repeating the same comments** and making similar points in different parts of answers.

- **Stating technical knowledge theories and concepts** rather than applying them. MDCS aims to provide a realistic workplace scenario so you are not required to explain a theory or model used. You are expected to select an appropriate model for the scenario, if this is relevant, and use it to plan and structure your answer.

- **Quoting chunks of detail** from the question that don't add any value. Your solution should focus on answering the question and be 'future focused' so you are explaining what the company could be and the benefits of business change, rather than what the company currently is.

- **Forcing irrelevancies into answers**, for example irrelevant definitions or theories, or examples that don't relate to the scenario, as these will **not** score available marks.
- **Giving long lists or writing down all that's known** about a broad subject area, without considering if it's relevant or not. You are required in MDCS to prioritise and filter relevant information to provide focused and relevant answers to each requirement.
- **Making unrealistic or impractical recommendations** means you are not demonstrating commercial acumen. Your recommendations should be suitable for the size and nature of the business in the scenario and the financial and operational capacity of the organisation you are advising.
- **Making vague recommendations**. Instead of just saying, 'improve risk management procedures', you should discuss precisely **why** the recommendation is required, **what** problem it will solve and **how** you would improve them.
- **Failing to answer sufficient questions**, or all parts of a question, because of poor time management. This simply limits the available marks to you, making it harder to pass the exam. Improving your exam success skills so you can attempt all questions and all requirements must be a central goal in your learning, which is why question practice, **and more question practice**, is such an important element of your MDCS exam preparations.
- **Failing to allocate sufficient time to those requirements with higher marks potential**. Many of us make the mistake of seeking perfection of spending too much time chasing few marks. A skill to develop is understanding where to focus time and effort to maximise marks in the available time. This only comes with question practice, which is why it is vital that the remaining practice case studies in this Workbook are attempted, rather than just read through.

5.2 Step by step guide to approaching MDCS requirements

You'll improve your chances by following a step-by-step approach to the case study along the following lines:

Step 1 **Read the introductory paragraphs to the unseen**

The first couple of paragraphs will provide some brief background of what to expect in the unseen and what has changed from the pre-seen. This will help frame the unseen and quickly put the requirements which follow into context.

Step 2 **Read the unseen requirements**

There is no point reading the detailed information in the unseen until you know what it is going to be used for. Don't panic if some of the requirements look challenging – identify the elements you are able to do and look for links between requirements. Use your knowledge of the pre-seen to understand what each task will require you to do.

Step 3 **Identify the action verbs**

These convey the level of skill you need to exhibit and also the structure your answer should have. A lower level verb such as 'define' will require a more descriptive answer; a higher level verb such as 'evaluate' will require a more applied, critical answer. It should be stressed that **higher level requirements and verbs** are likely to be most significant in this paper.

Step 4 **Identify what each part of the requirement requires you to do**

Use your knowledge of the pre-seen and practice cases to consider what is required. When planning, you will need to make sure that you aren't reproducing the same material in more than one part of the question. A requirement may ask you to explain X and discuss Y. You must ensure that you **fulfil both requirements** and that your discussion of Y shows greater depth than your explanation of X (for example, by identifying problems with Y or putting the case for and against Y). Once you have familiarity with the requirements, you can actively read the unseen material as you will be able to understand how new information is relevant to answering each part of each requirement.

Step 5 **Check the mark allocation for each part**

This shows you the depth anticipated and will help you to allocate remaining time.

Step 6 **Read the whole unseen case study through**

Put points under headings related to requirements (eg by noting in the margin to what part of the question the exhibit detail relates). With an understanding of the tasks outlined in each question, you are able to read each exhibit and determine what information and data is important and relevant to each part of each question.

Step 7 **Consider the consequences of the points you've identified**

Remember that you will often have to provide recommendations based on the information you've been given. However, it is important that these recommendations are practical and appropriate to the context in the case study. For example, will the recommended course of action help an organisation to solve a problem it is facing? Does the organisation have the resources and capabilities to implement the course of action? Will the proposed course of action be acceptable to key stakeholders?

Step 8 **Write a brief plan for each question**

Your plans should be produced within your answer book and contain sufficient detail of the scope of your planned numerical analysis, the headings and points you plan to include in your written answer. This process is critical to good time management and should always be included in your approach to answering questions, so this is done automatically and efficiently during the exam itself.

Step 9 **Complete numerical analysis, where relevant**

The results from your numerical analysis is likely to impact or change what you plan to write, so it is important this is completed first. If you struggle to complete the analysis, all is not lost, as you can use your judgement and estimate a reasonable outcome which you can explain and use as a basis for your written answer.

Step 10 **Write up your answer in the prescribed report format**

Make every effort to present your answer clearly, ensuring you only use the time you have allocated to each requirement in your plan. Once you have used this time, be ruthless, leave some space if you are unfinished and move on to the next requirement. You can use any time at the end to return to unfinished requirements. The best way to demonstrate what you're doing is to put separate points into separate paragraphs. This will help the marker clearly identify the separate points you are making and make it easier for the marker to award marks earned.

6 Advice on final MDCS exam preparation

The following advice will help you to maximise the remaining study time you have available before you sit the MDCS exam.

6.1 Attempting further questions and case study exams as part of your preparations

Self-review is a very powerful learning tool as it allows you to review and consider the quality of your work like a marker will when your report is assessed. This is most effective where some time has passed between attempting the exam and a review of the completed report.

It is suggested that you review your own attempt of Practice Case Study 3 (in this L&P Workbook) on the day after you attempt it, so your review is fresh. Be critical and consider how well you managed the issues flagged by the examiner, the quality of your response to the issue or problem and how you managed the time available.

It is advised that you reflect on your own performance – both good and not so good – by reading through your report once again, against the suggested answer and note your strengths as well as points for improvement.

You can then write down the top five mistakes you think you made and reflect on how you can improve your exam performance in each of these areas. It is often a valuable exercise to rewrite or refine parts of the report which have been identified as requiring improvement. Time spent reworking aspects of your answers helps you to understand how you can achieve a quality and sufficient answer.

6.2 Further MDCS preparation

The next step is to focus on your top five areas for improvement in your further question practice – you should use Practice Case Study 4 (in this L&P Workbook) and the specimen MDCS mock exam provided by AIA.

You should thoroughly review your analysis of the pre-seen on the day before your MDCS exam as this will significantly improve your familiarity with the pre-seen and improve your response time to new unseen information and help you to understand the nature of the MDCS exam requirements.

If you have followed this advice, you should now be prepared to attempt the MCDS exam and manage your time effectively.

End of chapter question

Guidance note

This is a comprehensive example aimed at developing commercial awareness and professional judgement. Note, that in the MDCS exam, you will not have to face such an extensive question, as this is for illustration and learning purposes only, but it is likely that you will be expected to identify the key issues and suggest how they might be dealt with, and responded to, in a realistic commercial way.

This example considers the strategic development for a fictitious shoe-making company. They have been experiencing difficulties in the last few years and are looking for advice on what they can do in the future.

Introduction

The Dhawan family founded their company over 100 years ago, and since then, the company has maintained a set of beliefs that stressed the social obligations of employers. Their beliefs guided their employment principles – education and housing for employees, secure jobs and good working conditions. Dhawan Shoes expanded quickly, but it still retained its principles. Today, the company is a private limited company whose shares are still wholly owned by the Dhawan family. Dhawan Shoes still produces footwear in Manchester, but they now also own almost 100 retail shops throughout the UK, selling their shoes and boots. The factory (and surrounding land) in Manchester is owned by the company and so are the shops, which is unusual in a country where most commercial properties are leased. In many respects, this policy reflects the principles of the family. They are keen to promote ownership and are averse to risk and borrowing. They believe that all stakeholders should be treated fairly. Reflecting this, the company aims to pay all suppliers within 30 days of the invoice date. These are the standard terms of supply in the UK, although many companies do, in reality, take much longer to pay their creditors.

The current Dhawan family members are still passionate about the beliefs and principles that inspired the founders of the company.

Recent history

Although the Dhawan family still owns the company, it is now totally run by professional managers. The last Dhawan to have operational responsibility was Ken Dhawan, who commissioned and implemented the last upgrade of the production facilities over 20 years ago. In the past five years, the Dhawan family has taken substantial dividends from the company, whilst leaving the running of the company to the professional managers that they had appointed. During this period, the company has been under increased competitive pressure from overseas suppliers who have much lower labour rates and more efficient production facilities. The financial performance of the company has declined rapidly and as a result, the Dhawan family has recently commissioned a firm of business analysts to undertake a SWOT analysis to help them understand the strategic position of the company.

SWOT analysis: Here is the summary SWOT analysis from the business analysts' report.

Strengths

Significant retail expertise: Dhawan Shoes is recognised as a successful retailer with excellent supply systems, bright and welcoming shops and shop employees who are regularly recognised, in independent surveys, for their excellent customer care and extensive product knowledge.

Excellent computer systems/software expertise: Some of the success of Dhawan Shoes as a retailer is due to its innovative computer systems, developed in-house by the company's information systems department. These systems not only concern the distribution of footwear, but also its design and development. Dhawan is acknowledged, by the rest of the industry, as a leader in computer-aided footwear design and distribution.

Significant property portfolio: The factory in Manchester is owned by the company and so is a significant amount of the surrounding land. All the retail shops are owned by the company. The company also owns a disused factory 50 miles north of Manchester. This was originally bought as a potential production site, but increasingly competitive imports made its development unviable. The Manchester factory site incorporates a retail shop, but none of the remaining retail shops are near to this factory, or indeed to the disused factory site in the north of the country.

Weaknesses

High production costs: The UK is a high labour cost economy.

Out-dated production facilities: The actual production facilities were last updated over 20 years ago. Current equipment is not efficient in its use of either labour, materials or energy.

Restricted internet site: Software development has focused on internal systems, rather than internet development. The current website only provides information about Dhawan Shoes; it is not possible to buy footwear from the company's website.

Opportunities

Increased consumer spending and consumerism: Despite the decline of its manufacturing industries, the UK is a prosperous country with high consumer spending. Consumers generally have a high disposable income and are fashion conscious. Parents spend a lot of money on their children, with the aim of 'making sure that they get a good start in life'.

Increased desire for safe family shopping environment: A recent trend is for consumers to prefer shopping in safe, car-free environments where they can visit a variety of shops and restaurants. These shopping villages are increasingly popular.

Growth of the green consumer: The numbers of 'green consumers' is increasing in the UK. They are conscious of the energy used in the production and distribution of the products they buy. These consumers also expect suppliers to be socially responsible. A recent television programme on the use of cheap and exploited labour in Zealandia was greeted with a call for a boycott of goods from that country. One of the political parties in the UK has emphasised environmentally responsible purchasing in its manifesto. It suggests that 'shorter shipping distances reduce energy use and pollution. Purchasing locally supports communities and local jobs.'

Threats

Cheap imports: The lower production costs of overseas countries provide a constant threat. It is still much cheaper to make shoes in Zealandia, 4,000 kilometres away, and transport the shoes by sea, road and train to shops in the UK, where they can be offered at prices that are still significantly lower than the footwear produced by Dhawan Shoes.

Legislation: The UK has comprehensive legislation on health and safety, as well as a statutory minimum wage and generous redundancy rights and payments for employees. The government is likely to extend its employment legislation programme.

Recent strategies: Senior management at Dhawan Shoes have recently suggested that the company should consider closing its Manchester production plant and move production overseas, perhaps outsourcing to established suppliers in Zealandia and elsewhere. This suggestion was immediately rejected by the Dhawan family, who questioned the values of the senior management. The family issued a press release with the aim of re-affirming the core values which underpinned their business. The press release stated that 'in our view, the day that Dhawan Shoes ceases to be a Manchester company, is the day that it closes'. Consequently, the senior management team was asked to propose an alternative strategic direction.

Financial information: The following financial information is available for selected recent years for Dhawan Shoes manufacturing division, as follows.

Income statement	20X9	20X7	20X5
	£m	£m	£m
Revenue	700	750	850
Cost of sales	(575)	(600)	(650)
Gross profit	125	150	200
Administration expenses	(95)	(100)	(110)
Other expenses	(10)	(15)	(20)

	20X9	20X7	20X5
	£m	£m	£m
Finance costs	(15)	(10)	(5)
Profit before tax	5	25	65
Income tax expense	(3)	(7)	(10)
Profit for the year	2	18	55
Extracted from statements of financial position			
Trade receivables	70	80	90
Share capital	100	100	100
Retained earnings	140	160	170
Long term borrowings	70	50	20

In 20X5, Dhawan Shoes paid, on average, their supplier invoices 28 days after the date of invoice. In 20X7, this had risen to 43 days and in 20X9, the average time to pay a supplier invoice stood at 63 days.

Requirement

You have been hired as an external consultant by the Dhawan family to produce a report examining the following two strategic options that Dhawan Shoes could consider to secure its future position and recommending what the company should do in the future.

Proposal 1. Using the internet to sell shoes directly to customers

Proposal 2. Specialising in the designing and production of premium quality children's shoes and fashion shoes

Suggested answer

It not unreasonable to consider the suitable, acceptable and feasible (SAF) approach when evaluating a strategy. A SWOT analysis has been provided, so it makes sense to use this when generating strategies.

For each proposed strategy we will need to consider the following points:

(a) **Suitability – Will it allow us to deal with the key threat?** In this case, the key threat is losing customers to competitors selling low-priced shoes imported from countries where labour and other costs are lower.

(b) **Acceptability – Will it be seen as acceptable by the key stakeholders?** In this scenario, the key players are the Dhawan family, and we have to consider what they want. There are two things to consider – the family says that they are keen to stick to the company's founding principles of maintaining production in Manchester, but shareholders are usually also very keen to see a high level of return.

There is evidence in the SWOT analysis that little in the way of investment has been undertaken in the last twenty years – perhaps an indication of a lack of long-term commitment to the industry by the family. Additionally, the payables days has started to creep up – maybe the strict adherence to the principles of treating all stakeholders equitably has started to weaken, meaning the family commitments to other principles may be weakening too.

(c) **Feasibility – Is there the ability, resources and time to do it?** Do we have the resources and competences to carry out a particular strategy?

Proposal 1. Using the internet to sell shoes directly to customers

Suitability

The problem that Dhawan Shoes has, is that its shoes are more expensive than those of its competitors that manufacture overseas in lower-cost countries and import them into the UK; it needs to reduce its costs significantly if it wants to remain competitive. By selling directly to customers via a website, it would no longer need to maintain as many stores as it currently does – in fact, it could consider closing them all and selling only through the internet.

A number of factors should be considered.

Firstly, would the closure of the stores and the decision to sell purely through the website result in savings that would be large enough to compensate for the high cost of manufacturing in the UK?

Additionally, we are told in the SWOT analysis that a major threat is the extension of employment legislation, with the prospect of further increases in costs, so any reduction in costs caused by the elimination of shops may well be offset by increases in costs of labour.

Secondly, would they be able to sell in high numbers through a website? One of their strengths is that they provide exceptional customer service, and that might not be something they could adapt to a website.

For the first point - we don't know the specific costs associated with the high street shops themselves, and without that information, we would not be able to come to a definitive conclusion. However, we can say that their competitors would be able to sell through the internet as well, meaning Dhawan would be matching them in terms of sales and distribution costs, but still facing higher costs in manufacturing. It seems unlikely that they would be able to match their competitors for price using the internet.

For the second point – Dhawan would expect that some of their customers would be happy to migrate to the website, but of course, the big question is how many customers would be lost to other high street retailers. Also, it is worth pointing out just how competitive the online marketplace actually is – customer loyalty should never be taken for granted, and just one highly publicised error can alienate customers very quickly.

We have been seeing a fall in turnover in the last four years, so it may well be the case that the move away from the high street would simply accelerate that fall. They may be able to pick up new customers, but one of their big selling points in the past has been their excellent customer service, and that would be difficult to replicate online. If Dhawan can attract new customers from new countries, this could be a significant source of growth, but that is a big 'if', since they are not familiar with overseas markets and would struggle (at least initially) to establish out brand.

In terms of suitability, I think this strategy would fail.

An analyst at this point would probably move onto a different strategy, but for the purpose of illustration, we shall now move on to consider acceptability and feasibility.

Acceptability

The key stakeholders in this scenario would seem to be the Dhawan family, who still own all the shares in the company.

On the face of it, this would be likely to be acceptable to them, since it does not entail the cessation of manufacturing in Manchester.

However, one must also consider what the family members *really* want from the company. They may pay lip service to the beliefs of the founders of the company, but just about every shareholder in a company wants to see an adequate level of return. Since the family seems to have been taking substantial levels of dividends from the company, it is likely that before any proposed strategy could be considered acceptable, it would have to be shown to have a strong chance of being profitable. Since this strategy has so many unknowns associated with it, not least of which is the highly competitive nature of the online marketplace, it is questionable whether the family would accept it.

Feasibility

Setting up a website is not in itself a particularly difficult or expensive task and, with the highly skilled IT team in place, it is unlikely to be a significant obstacle. A bigger problem is likely to be the establishment and development of distribution systems – something they have no experience of in respect of delivery of individual items to the customer's home. Again, Dhawan should be able to overcome this, but shoes are something that people may want to return for a variety of reasons – they may not fit, may not look as good as the customer was hoping, may be a slightly different colour to what the customer was expecting etc.

This could result in the costs of returns decreasing the profit margins at Dhawan Shoes or they would have to be borne by the customer – something that could hamper any attempts to develop an attractive brand identity in new countries.

Conclusion

This proposal is not suitable, may not be acceptable to the family but may be feasible. Overall, it is unlikely that this strategy would be successful.

Proposal 2. Specialising in the designing and production of premium quality children's shoes and fashion shoes

Suitability

The key to this strategy is a move to focus differentiation and, as such, it represents a move away from the low-cost competitors who are taking so much of Dhawan Shoes' market share. Since it appears unlikely that Dhawan Shoes will be unable to compete on price with low cost importers, it makes commercial sense to shift the battle to differentiation, rather than price.

The UK is a prosperous country, with high consumer spending, and consumers have a high disposable income and are fashion conscious. Additionally, parents spend a lot of money on their children, with the aim of making sure that they get a good start in life.

It is therefore not unreasonable to think that there will be strong demand for well-made children's shoes, since parents are prepared to spend a lot of money on their children. Also note that children's feet grow quickly, so the likelihood of regular repeat business is high.

This is an appealing market as children's feet grow quickly, meaning that their shoes must be regularly replaced, and parents wish to avoid the permanent damage to their children's feet that could arise as a result of wearing inappropriately sized shoes. Retail strengths, such as the extensive product knowledge of Dhawan Shoes staff and excellent customer care, could be employed to support this approach. Re-branding of Dhawan Shoes as primarily a children's shoe supplier would reinforce the new message, while a scaled back selection of adult shoes would still be available as cross-sale products which could be purchased impulsively by parents visiting with their children.

Similarly, fashion shoes will change on a regular basis, so the demand for repeat purchases is likely to be high, as what is seen as desirable in one time of the year will change, leading to consumers buying new shoes, even if their current shoes have not actually worn out yet.

Another point to bear in mind is that, with fashion products, the fickle nature of customers may lead to changes in customer tastes at short notice. This gives Dhawan Shoes an advantage in that the products are made in the UK, with a much shorter supply chain and a much shorter lead time. This means that they can respond to changes in customer tastes much more quickly than a competitor manufacturing shoes several thousand miles away.

Both children's shoes and fashion shoes will be bought by consumers who want good service in shops when buying the product which, of course, Dhawan Shoes has a strong reputation for.

Equally, as part of the differentiation of the product, Dhawan Shoes can emphasise the environmentally friendly nature of its policies, which, while it may not be the main reason for buying the shoes, will nevertheless make people think of Dhawan Shoes in a more favourable light.

Acceptability

The key stakeholders are the Dhawan family members, and they would (at least on the face of it) be happy to support a strategy that maintained production in the UK.

This strategy would require no major investment in plant and equipment, or in land and buildings since they already have the infrastructure in place – this would mean that the family would not be required to invest heavily and, indeed, should be able to continue taking dividends out of the company.

Customers are prepared to pay more for high quality shoes, so this strategy would seem to be acceptable to them

Feasibility

Can we do this? Will we have the skills in terms of 'retail expertise, bright and welcoming shops and shop employees [...] recognised [...] for their excellent customer care and extensive product knowledge'?

IT – 'Excellent computer systems and software expertise'. We are also told that Dhawan Shoes is 'acknowledged, by the rest of the industry, as a leader in computer-aided footwear design and distribution.' So using IT to design innovative shoes is something that should not pose any major difficulties.

This strategy would seem to be eminently feasible – but we have not considered the actual process of making shoes. In the SWOT analysis, we noted that the machinery is old and outdated; it is not efficient in the use of materials, labour or energy, and it is likely that significant investment is well overdue. We may well be able to borrow the funds to invest in newer machinery, but it would perhaps reduce the capacity of the firm to pay dividends in the short term – and this, in turn, might lead the family to reject it as a strategy. Of course, there are other sources of capital – they might be prepared to sell off and lease back the properties they own; but this depends on the risk appetite of the Dhawan family shareholders. We are told that in the past, they have been risk averse, and so the proposal to sell off some of the firm's assets may well be considered unacceptable. It should be noted though that Dhawan Shoes has been taking on considerable levels of debt recently, so maybe the family's aversion to risk is not as strong as it once was.

It would therefore seem that this strategy is suitable and feasible, but it may not be acceptable to the family.

None of the above strategies seem overly compelling, mainly because the company needs investment, and at the moment, the Dhawan family seems more inclined to take money out of the business, rather than to invest in it.

Conclusion

The position Dhawan Shoes finds itself in is challenging, but not impossible to deal with.

The recommendation would be to move into becoming a specialised manufacturer of children's and fashionable shoes, and to upgrade the manufacturing equipment to take advantage of increasing efficiencies in production.

If the family shareholders can be persuaded to invest in this venture, or to allow assets to be sold to fund it, then this will provide them with a sustainable source of income for the long term.

Practice Case Study 1: Suggested solution with tutorial commentary

Topic list	Syllabus reference
1 Practice case study 1: Suggested solution	All LOs

Introduction

This chapter contains the suggested solution to the SMCH Case Study.

Suggested answer

(a) **Business risks**

> **Note.** Be careful in answering this question. You are required to identify business risks AND you also have to state the impact on the audit. This means that you need to consider how those business risks lead to audit risks, that is the risk that the financial statements will be materially misstated but the auditors will fail to identify the misstatements.
>
> In general, business risks are likely to lead to audit risks in the following ways:
>
> - A business risk could mean that a particular number in the financial statements could be misstated, eg falling demand could mean that the net realisable value of inventory falls below cost so that, if recorded at cost, it is overstated.
>
> - Business risks could adversely affect the business's ability to generate profits and cash such that the company may no longer be a going concern. If the company's going concern issues are not properly disclosed, then the financial statements may be materially misstated.
>
> - Business risks may lead to management bias, which could affect many different account balances. For example, if the directors are paid a bonus which is based on profits, then there is a risk that they might wish to overstate profits and so there is a risk that revenues are overstated and any expenses are understated.
>
> It's important that you address both the business risk and the audit risks in your answer; otherwise you can only gain a maximum of 50% of the available marks.

Business risk	Impact on audit
Related party	
The contract to redesign the website and rebrand the company was awarded to Rufus Lakes Ltd (RL). The sister of Geoff Tomlinson, a director of SMCH, is a director and major shareholder at RL. The contract may have been awarded on the basis of that relationship, rather than RL's suitability and expertise, and so the quality of the website design and branding may be poor, which could lead to lost custom or the amount paid for the service may be more than the going market rate, which will result in additional expenses and therefore reduced profit.	IAS 24 *Related Party Disclosures* requires that SMCH should disclose the fact that there is a related party transaction, details of the relationship between the parties, the amount of the transactions that occur, any outstanding balances at year end and any amounts written off to expenses in the year. Failure to adequately disclose these details would lead to the financial statements being materially misstated. **Note.** Discussion could also have focussed on ISA 240 *The auditor's responsibilities relating to fraud* if the contract price is inflated
Cocoa bean source	
It is important to SMCH that it can trace the origin of its cocoa beans and that it complies with its fair trade philosophy. If the cocoa beans used fail to meet these requirements, they may not be able to be used in manufacturing which may lead to additional costs if the cost of purchase needs to be written off or cause delays in the manufacturing process if suitable replacements cannot be sourced on a timely basis. If the cocoa beans are used, there could be reputational damage to the company's brand and therefore sales if this becomes known.	The inventory of cocoa beans or finished goods made from those beans may be overstated if the items are written off or sold at a discounted price but have not been written down to net realisable value. **Note.** The damage to the brand is not an audit risk as the internally generated brand should not be recognised in the financial statements.

15: Practice Case Study 1: Suggested answer

Business risk	Impact on audit
Rising cocoa bean prices Prices for cocoa, the company's main raw material, are rising. As cocoa beans are priced in US dollars, adverse changes in currency rates are only exacerbating the problem. If these costs cannot be passed on to customers by way of higher prices, then SMCH's profits will fall, which will also reduce cashflows and could lead to going concern problems in future.	If costs of cocoa beans continue to rise but sales prices do not, then net realisable value may be below cost. Inventory may be overstated if it has not been written down to net realisable value, resulting in the valuation assertion not being met. The company may not correctly retranslate the outstanding liability for cocoa beans at the year end, resulting in misstatement of liabilities due to the valuation assertion not being met. There may be doubts about whether the use of the going concern basis is appropriate but the company may fail to adequately disclose any going concern uncertainties. The requirements of ISA 570 *Going Concern* must be met.
Receivables Receivables collection period has increased from 46 to 66 days. This may be related to the change in customer mix towards smaller customers, who are typically slower payers. If customers take longer to pay, this damages the company's cash flow, which could lead to operational difficulties and eventually going concern problems.	Some amounts owing may not be recoverable. If expected credit losses are not correctly assessed and an appropriate allowance is not created, then the receivables balance and profit will be overstated because the existence and/or valuation assertions are not met.
Legal dispute A supplier, Chocolate Globe Inc, has threatened to sue SMCH for breach of contract. If SMCH loses the case, it will have to pay damages, which may be substantial and will have a negative impact on both profit and cash flow.	If it is probable that SMCH will lose the case, then IAS 37 *Provisions, contingent liabilities and contingent assets* should be applied, and a provision should be made for the likely damages. Failure to include this provision will lead to understatement of liabilities. If it is only possible that the case will be lost, then disclosure should be made. ISA 560 *Going Concern* should be considered if the impact is so severe that it could threaten the going concern status.
Food safety legislation SMCH could be in breach of food safety legislation, for example, due to errors in labelling country of origin of raw materials, nut content or nutritional content. Bad publicity surrounding this could damage the company's reputation, which will reduce sales. If fines are payable or a customer takes legal action as a result of the mislabelling, this would negatively impact profit and cash flow. There may also be additional costs in scrapping the existing labels and creating the corrected labels, which will also negatively impact on profit.	If SMCH fails to provide for any probable fines or legal action, then liabilities will be understated. If the company fails to disclose any possible fines, then the financial statements could be materially misstated due to failure to inadequate disclosure. ISA 250 *Consideration of Laws and Regulations in an Audit of Financial Statements* must be applied.

Business risk	Impact on audit
Renewal of borrowing facilities The company's borrowing facilities are due for renewal in May 2020 and they may not be renewed. The company may not be able to borrow money on equivalent terms elsewhere.	There may be management bias because the directors may want to give a favourable impression of the company's position to increase the chances of the borrowing facilities being renewed. This could lead to assets being overstated, liabilities being understated and profits being overstated. ISA 570 *Going Concern* should be applied in the event that the borrowing facilities are not renewed.

Note. You may have identified other risks and credit would be given for any reasonable, well explained risk that is relevant to the scenario. Make sure that for business risk, you discuss the impact on profitability/cash flow and for audit risk, you discuss the impact on the financial statements and likely audit assertions at risk, plus refer to relevant ISAs, IFRS Accounting Standards and IASs.

(b) **Extension to role**

> **Note.** You could approach this question by type of service, as has been done in this answer, or by working through the threats to independence and considering whether these potential services create such threats. Either way, you need to discuss why such a threat may arise, what potential safeguards there may be, and give advice on whether the work may be accepted.

Two services have been requested by SMCH:

- Advice on risk management and internal control development
- Provision of internal audit services.

Advice on risk management and internal control development

The responsibility for identifying and managing risks and developing internal controls in response to those risks lies with the management of SMCH. If that role was to be performed by Glenton Haines, then it would be assuming management responsibility. The International Ethics Standards Board for Accountants (IESBA) Code of Ethics specifically prohibits audit firms from assuming management responsibilities for their audit clients as they would be unable to be sufficiently independent and objective if that were the case. This is sometimes referred to as a management threat, although it is not called that in the IESBA Code.

If Glenton Haines were to perform such services, then there is also a self-review threat. The firm would be reviewing the internal control system as part of the audit and may be unwilling to highlight weaknesses in internal control to the management if it has itself developed those controls.

Glenton Haines should politely decline to perform these services.

Internal audit

If Glenton Haines were to provide outsourced internal audit services, this could give rise to a self-review threat. As external auditor, Glenton Haines would try to rely on the work of the internal auditor and, if that work was performed by its own staff, may not check that work as thoroughly as it should.

Since SMCH is not a listed company, Glenton Haines may perform these services but with safeguards. Note that if the company does become listed on the Alternative Investment Market in future, then this will not be possible.

To safeguard against the self-review threat, Glenton Haines must ensure that the internal audit services are not performed by members of the external audit team.

If the internal audit services are to be performed, the firm must take care not to assume management responsibility; it must ensure that the management of SMCH directs the work programme of internal audit and makes decisions as to which recommendations of internal audit should be implemented.

Both services

The provision of extra services to an audit client will generate additional fees and these may give rise to self-interest or intimidation threats; the higher the amount of money that is received from a specific client, the less likely it is that the auditor would be willing to give a qualified audit report for fear of losing the client and the fees. In deciding whether this threat is too high, both quantitative and qualitative factors should be considered. We are not given information as to the percentage of the firm's fees which the external and internal audit of SMCH would represent, but we are told that the audit is 'prestigious,' which is an important qualitative factor.

Conclusion

The internal audit work may be accepted, provided the safeguards above are implemented and the total fees are not thought to be high enough to create a self-interest threat. Once SMCH becomes listed on the AIM, additional ethical requirements apply when the fees from a client exceed 15% of the firm's total fees.

(c) **Website and rebranding**

> **Note.** There is a lot of information given about the various costs relating to the website development, testing and operation. You need to be very clear in your answer as to the different treatments that apply to the different components of cost, bringing in knowledge of IAS 38 *Intangible Assets* and SIC 32 *Intangible Assets – Web Site Costs*. To get a good mark, remember that it's mentioned elsewhere in the case that a director and majority shareholder of Rufus Lakes Ltd is a director of SMCH, so you need to also consider IAS 24 *Related Party Disclosures*.

Website costs

Costs associated with the website that are incurred in the year include:

- £1.53 million (90% × £1.7m) payable to Rufus Lakes Ltd for design and development
- £350,000 allocation of internal salaries.
- £300 per month for website hosting services

A website is an intangible asset and therefore IAS 38 *Intangible Assets* applies. SIC 32 *Intangible Assets – Web Site Costs* interprets this standard and applies it to website development.

An internally-developed intangible asset is considered as having a research and a development phase. IAS 38 requires that all research costs are recognised in profit or loss as incurred; and development costs are recognised as an asset only if they meet specific recognition criteria, including a need to generate probable future economic benefits.

A website is only able to generate future economic benefits when it is an ecommerce site on which orders can be placed and therefore revenue can be generated. Therefore, the costs associated with a website developed for advertising or marketing purposes must be recognised as an expense when incurred.

As a result, the accounting treatment to be applied to expenditure on website development depends on the nature of the activity to which the expenditure relates and the stage of development of the website.

Some of the internal salary costs relate to planning the website. Planning activities take place at an early stage of the project and are similar to research activities. Therefore, these costs are recognised as an expense when incurred.

SMCH's website is part for selling purposes (the online shop) and part for marketing purposes (the blog and history). Only those costs associated with the development of the online shop can be recognised as an asset. The amount payable to Rufus Lakes Ltd should be analysed according to the stages of website development and part of the website to which it relates in order to determine what amounts are recognised as an asset.

The internal salary allocation should not be capitalised because this relates to writing content for the history and blog pages, which are not selling pages.

The cost of the hosting services must be recognised as an expense when incurred.

Website testing

The testing costs are included in the £1.7 million payable to Rufus Lakes Ltd. SIC 32 does not specifically refer to testing costs, however, IAS 38 refers to the costs of testing whether an asset operates as intended as directly attributable costs that form part of the cost of an intangible asset. Since testing relates to ecommerce and online selling (rather than advertising, which is not recognised as an asset) it follows that the testing costs should be capitalised as part of the cost of the website asset.

Revenue is earned during the testing phase. Neither IAS 38 nor SIC 32 refer to revenue earned during a testing phase. IAS 8 *Accounting Policies, Changes in Accounting Estimates and Errors* states that when an accounting standard does not specifically apply to a transaction, the requirements of standards dealing with similar issues should be considered. IAS 16 *Property, Plant and Equipment* states that net proceeds from selling items during a test period should be deducted from the costs of testing that are capitalised. It is appropriate to extend this guidance to the development of SMCH's website.

> **Note.** Students would also be given credit for being aware of the guidance in the 2020 amendment to IAS 16, Property, Plant and Equipment – Proceeds before Intended Use. This amends IAS 16 to require that the proceeds from selling items during a testing phase are included in the statement of profit or loss, rather than deducted from the initial cost of an asset. The amendment is effective from 2022.

Rebranding costs

The rebranding exercise creates an internally-generated brand. IAS 38 is clear that internally-generated brands may not be recognised as an intangible asset. Therefore, the associated costs of £1.2 million must be recognised as an expense in the year ended 31 March 2020.

Transactions with Rufus Lakes Ltd

Rufus Lakes Ltd is a related party of SMCH because the sister of Geoff Tomlinson, a director of SMCH, controls Rufus Lakes Ltd.

This means that the presumption of a normal commercial arms-length transaction is not valid and there is the possibility that the interests of the shareholders of SMCH have been put aside in order that the transaction benefits Rufus Lake Ltd to a greater extent than it might otherwise have done.

IAS 24 *Related Party Disclosures* applies and details of the relationship and of the transaction between the two parties, which are necessary for an understanding of the effect on the financial statements, should be disclosed in the SMCH financial statements for the year ended 31 March 2020. Disclosed details should include:

- The cost incurred in the year of £2.73 million
- The total transaction price of £2.9 million
- The outstanding amount, being the full £2.73 million

The nature of the relationship between SMCH and Rufus Lakes Ltd should also be disclosed. SMCH should not declare that the purchase was made at arm's length, unless this can be substantiated.

15: Practice Case Study 1: Suggested answer

(d) **Role of the audit partner in quality control**

> **Note.** This requirement should have been quite a quick one to answer since it is based on your knowledge of quality control procedures generally, rather than you having to apply information from the case. Make sure that you answer in relation to quality control generally and this particular audit, with reference to ISQC 1 *Quality Control for Firms that Perform Audits and Reviews of Financial Statements, and Other Assurance and Related Services Engagements.*

Quality control generally

The ultimate responsibility for the system of quality control always lies with the firm's managing partner and in a firm such as Glenton Haines (with more than one office), it is vital that the firm has procedures that are standardised and applied on a consistent basis.

It is important that all partners give consistent messages regarding quality control importance and lead from the top. This should include ensuring that commercial considerations never override quality of performance and that the firm is always sufficiently independent and approaches audits with a mindset of professional scepticism. This should also involve stressing the importance of quality control in audit meetings and staff appraisals for example.

It is vital that partners act ethically and are seen to act ethically in accordance with the Code of Ethics.

In accepting clients, partners should ensure that they consider the integrity of the client, the competence of the firm to perform the engagement and whether compliance with ethics can be achieved.

Partners will be involved with the management of staff and are collectively responsible for creating a culture that recruits, develops and supports capable and competent staff.

Quality control of audit of SMCH

The partner is in charge of the overall management of the audit and for directing, supervising and reviewing the audit work. The partner will be responsible for ensuring timely audit planning (and that the knowledge gained from the planning process is disseminated to all audit staff), appropriate and timely use of technical specialists and effective post audit reviews. The partner must ensure that the engagement documentation is adequate in order that the firm can prove the quality of its audit work in the event of a negligence claim.

(e) **Professional judgement and scepticism**

> **Note.** This question requires knowledge of the key auditing concepts of judgement and professional scepticism. As well as discussing the importance of these concepts generally, don't forget to explain why they are important in the audit of SMCH.

The ISA 200 *Overall Objective of the Independent Auditor, and the Conduct of an Audit in Accordance with International Standards on Auditing* highlights professional judgement and states that it is essential to the proper conduct of an audit. It requires that the auditor exercises professional judgement in planning and performing an audit.

Professional judgement is defined as the application of relevant training, knowledge and experience in making informed decisions about appropriate courses of action. This must be in a sound, consistent and justifiable manner. It must not be used as a justification for decisions that are not otherwise supported by evidence.

Professional judgement involves the use of appropriate consultation and this should be clearly documented. Regulators and lawyers reviewing the audit files will seek to understand how judgement has been exercised and so thorough documentation of the thought processes is vital. The documentation should be such that an experienced auditor, having no previous connection with the audit, could understand the significant professional judgements made reaching conclusions on significant matters, as per ISA 230 *Audit documentation*.

Scepticism is defined as an attitude that includes a questioning mind, being alert to conditions that may indicate possible misstatement due to error or fraud, and a critical assessment of audit evidence.

ISA 200 includes an explicit requirement for the auditor to plan and perform an audit with professional scepticism. This involves the questioning of contradictory evidence and challenging the reliability of responses.

These concepts are important in the audit of SMCH as there are several areas of risk where the use of judgement and scepticism will be required. For example, the fact that SMCH's borrowing facilities are due for renewal means that management has an incentive to be overly optimistic in the preparation of the financial statements and may exhibit management bias. The audit team should be alert to this, and design and perform suitable procedures to reduce the risk of material misstatement as a result of the management bias to an acceptable level.

(f) **Details on hedging arrangement**

> **Note.** This requirement tests IFRS 9 *Financial Instruments*, a standard which many students find difficult. Break your answer down into sections: What is a hedging arrangement? What is the purpose of hedging? When can hedge accounting be used? An explanation of the accounting treatment if hedge accounting is/is not used. There are a few clues in the question: SMCH is trying to avoid reporting exchange losses, there is zero cost for the forward exchange contract, hedge accounting is optional.

Hedging arrangement

Hedging activities reduce exposure to risk; in this case, the risk that foreign exchange rates will move adversely before the purchase of the cocoa beans, thereby making the purchase more costly than expected. Steve Jones is considering using a forward exchange contract to fix the pounds sterling cost of transferring US$4 million.

Hedge relationship

IFRS 9 allows hedge accounting where there is a designated hedging relationship between a hedging instrument and a hedged item. Hedge accounting reflects in the financial statements the hedging activities that are undertaken by a company. It is not mandatory, and the use of hedge accounting is a choice.

If a hedging arrangement were entered into on 31 January 2020, the hedged item would be the highly probable forecast purchase of goods for $4 million. This is an eligible hedged item in a cash flow hedge. The hedging instrument would be the forward contract to buy US Dollars. Derivatives are eligible hedging instruments.

Conditions to hedge account

Hedge accounting is only permitted where certain conditions are met. Firstly, the hedging relationship must consist of eligible hedging instruments and eligible hedged items, as is the case here. In addition, at the inception of the hedge, there must be formal designation and documentation of the hedging relationship and the entity's risk management objective and strategy for the hedge. SMCH would be required to prepare this documentation before applying hedge accounting. The hedging relationship must also meet hedge effectiveness requirements:

- An economic relationship must exist between the hedged item and hedging instrument, such that they are expected to have offsetting changes in fair value. In this case, if the pound becomes weaker against the dollar, the cost of the purchase will increase (so increasing the fair value of the unrecognised liability) and the derivative will be 'in the money,' so creating an asset.

- The effect of credit risk should not dominate changes in fair value. There is no indication that this would be the case here.

- The hedge ratio (quantity of hedging instrument vs quantity of hedged item in the accounting hedge) should be the same as that actually used in practice. In this case, both hedged item and hedging instrument would be US$4 million dollars in practice and for accounting purposes.

Hedge accounting treatment

In a cash flow hedge, the hedged item is a future cash flow and therefore, only the hedging instrument is initially recognised. This should be remeasured to fair value at each reporting date and:

- A gain or loss arising from an effective hedge is recognised in other comprehensive income; and
- A gain or loss from any ineffective hedge is recognised in profit or loss.

Any amounts recognised in other comprehensive income are accumulated in a cash flow hedge reserve and reclassified to profit or loss when the expected future cash flows (the hedged item) affect profit or loss. In this case, the hedged transaction results in the recognition of a non-financial asset (inventories) and so, the cash flow hedge reserve will be transferred to profit or loss as part of the initial cost of the inventories.

The effective gain or loss in reserves at the reporting date is the lower of:

- The cumulative gain or loss on the hedging instrument since the inception of the hedge; and
- The cumulative change in fair value of the expected future cash flows.

Accounting entries

The derivative hedging instrument has no cost and initially, has no fair value and therefore, no accounting entries would be required at 31 January 2020.

At the year end, 31 March 2020, the fair value of the hedging instrument is dependent on the value of the future cash flow in pounds sterling, based on the contracted exchange rate, compared to the value at the forward exchange rate that could be obtained at 31 March 2020 for delivery on 30 April 2020:

	£
Cash flow at contracted rate ($4m/1.23)	3,252,033
Cash flow at forward rate available at 31 March 2020 ($4m/1.16)	3,448,276
Change in fair value (gain)	196,243

In order to determine what part of the change in fair value is effective and so recognised in profit or loss, the change in fair value of the forecast future cash flows must be calculated. The fair value of the forecast purchase is dependent on the value of the future cash flow in pounds sterling, based on the measurement date spot exchange rate, compared to the rate when the contract was made on 31 January 2020:

	£
Cash flow at spot rate 31 Jan 2020 ($4m/1.25)	3,200,000
Cash flow at spot rate at 31 March 2020 ($4m/1.18)	3,389,831
Change in fair value (loss)	189,831

At 31 March 2020, the gain on the derivative is £196,243, but only £189,831 of this is effective, and so recognised in OCI, with the balance recognised in profit or loss:

Dr	Financial asset at FVTPL (SOFP)	196,243	
Cr	Other comprehensive income		189,831
Cr	Profit or loss		6,412

The effect on SMCH's reported profit or loss in the year ended 31 March 2020 is therefore a small gain of $6,412. If hedge accounting were not applied but the forward contract was still entered into, then the gain would be $196,243.

The larger gain would obviously increase reported profits this year. However, it should be remembered that if the exchange rate does not move as expected, there may be a loss on the derivative, in which case, hedge accounting limits the loss reported in profit or loss.

In the year ended 31 March 2021, the amount recognised in OCI and accumulated in reserves will be transferred to be part of the cost of the cocoa beans purchased. Assuming that reserves show a credit entry, this will reduce the cost of the purchase and so the carrying amount of inventories. The carrying amount will therefore reflect an exchange rate closer to that which applies when the hedging arrangement is entered into. The lower carrying amount of inventories will result in higher profits when the products that the beans are used in are eventually sold.

Without hedge accounting, the purchase of cocoa beans would be recorded at a higher amount and this, in turn, would lead to lower profits in the future. Thus, not using hedge accounting results in greater volatility ie higher profits in 2020 and lower profits in future years.

(g) **Effect of mezzanine floor on profit or loss**

> **Note.** Lease improvements and restoration costs are common features of many commercial leases. If you're not sure where to start, be guided by the fact that Geoff asks if there would a large expense at the start of the lease and another at the end. It's unlikely that a question would require you to agree with the treatment given, so you know you need to be writing about something different.

The construction of the mezzanine floor is a leasehold improvement and should be recognised as an asset by SMCH. IAS 16 *Property, Plant and Equipment* applies, and the leasehold improvement is initially measured at the costs directly attributable to bringing the mezzanine floor into a condition in which it can be used to operate a café. The leasehold improvement asset is subsequently depreciated over the lease term.

At the start of a lease arrangement, a right-of-use asset is recognised. This is measured at the present value of future lease payments (the lease liability), subject to certain adjustments. One of these adjustments is the estimated dismantling and restoration costs that will be incurred at the end of the lease term. In this case, this is the cost of dismantling the mezzanine floor. The expected cost is discounted to present value and recognised as part of the cost of the right-of-use asset and as a separate provision. Subsequently, the right-of-use asset is depreciated over the shorter of the lease term and the useful life of the asset and the discount on the provision is unwound over the same period, resulting in a finance cost every year over the lease term. The lease term is likely to be shorter than the useful life of the building.

Therefore, the effect of the construction of the mezzanine and its subsequent removal are not recognised in profit or loss at a single point in time; both are recognised over the term of the lease, as depreciation (on the cost of the construction of the mezzanine and the present value of the cost of dismantling) and as a finance cost.

16

Practice Case Study 2: Pre-seen material

Topic list	Syllabus reference
1 Practice case study 2: Pre-seen case information	All LOs

Introduction

This chapter contains the pre-seen material relating to Case Study 2 (Shoe Designers plc).

It includes:

(1) Shoe Designers background information

(2) Extracts from Shoe Designers plc draft consolidated financial statements 2020.

(3) Email from Pritesh Malik, 18 August 2020

(4) Extract from *Apparel*, a trade journal for clothing manufacturers, September 2019

(5) Extract from *Business News Weekly*, March 2020

Exhibit 1: Shoe Designers background information

Shoe Designers plc is an expanding company that designs and manufactures shoes for the womenswear market. It has been trading for 15 years. Initially, the company concentrated on designing and manufacturing high quality shoes on behalf of other retailers, including supermarkets and department stores in the UK, Europe and Asia (the wholesale business). In 2018, the company expanded its operations and launched its own premium brand of footwear, which it sold through a network of Shoe Designers shops in the UK and Europe (the retail business). The company also sells its shoes through a joint venture in Russia.

Board and staffing

The company was founded by Pritesh Malik and Victoria Lawrence after they qualified from Northumbria University with degrees in fashion design. The management team has expanded with the company and now includes 6 directors:

Pritesh Malik	Managing director
Victoria Lawrence	Creative director
Rob Da Silva	Finance director
Eloise Howard	Sales and marketing director
Maria Mateos	Human resources director
Neil Newell	Operations director

Each director has an experienced team working under him or her. Rob Da Silva has recently appointed a new financial controller, Lucy Chatfield, to replace Bob Mason who left due to ill health. Lucy has previously worked as financial accountant at a private limited company operating within the UK fashion manufacturing and retail industry and is the daughter of Adam Chatfield, the former audit partner.

Funding

The company was originally financed by backing from Pritesh Malik's family but, since 2013, much of the funding has been sourced from venture capitalists FourVC, plus bank facilities and private equity investment. The retail side of the business is funded by significant leases to finance high street stores.

Growth

Shoe Designers has expanded through both organic growth and acquisition. Initially, the company concentrated on design and outsourced all production to third party manufacturers. However, in 2010, it acquired a small footwear manufacturer. It has subsequently acquired further UK manufacturers, a European distributor and European retailers, making it vertically integrated. All subsidiaries acquired to date are wholly owned.

Production and supply

The company prides itself on high quality design and manufacture using premium materials and skilled labour. From 2010 to 2019, all manufacturing took place in the UK at Shoe Designers' own factories, with production overseen by Neil Newell and his team. Recently the company's designs have been receiving considerable press attention and demand has expanded significantly. In order to manage increased production levels and also to maintain margins in spite of downward pressure on selling prices, the company has outsourced some of its mass production into Bangladesh and Spain. It has contracted with two factories in Bangladesh that have the capacity to produce the significant volume required and have a good reputation for quality of production and staff welfare. Approximately 60% of the manufacture of shoes for the wholesale business has been moved to Bangladesh with 15% manufactured in Spain and 25% remaining in the UK.

Quality control is a significant challenge for the company. Shoe Designers considers its own-brand shoes to be positioned in the market as an affordable 'Jimmy Choo' and the average retail price point is £105.

The wholesale business supplies ranges to retailers for an average selling price of £35. Retailers are able to charge an average mark-up of 85%. Wholesale selling prices are constantly under pressure from the retailers and the directors fear that they may struggle to maintain quality.

Exhibit 2: Extracts from Shoe Designers plc draft consolidated financial statements 2020

Statement of profit or loss
For the year ended 30 September 2020

	Note	2020 £'000	2019 £'000
Revenue		261,975	222,358
Cost of sales		(95,740)	(83,419)
Gross profit		166,235	138,939
Distribution costs		(111,357)	(82,358)
Administrative expenses		(42,197)	(28,163)
Exceptional costs		(2,614)	(2,814)
Other operating income		234	142
Operating profit	3	**10,301**	**25,746**
Finance income	4	34	45
Finance expenses	4	(5,707)	(3,406)
Share of profit of joint venture, net of tax		198	149
Profit before tax		**4,826**	**22,534**
Income tax expense		(1,303)	(6,698)
Profit for the year		**3,523**	**15,836**

Statement of Comprehensive Income
For the year ended 30 September 2020

	£'000	£'000
Profit for the year	3,523	15,836
Other comprehensive income that may be reclassified to profit or loss:		
Cash flow hedges	(320)	(190)
Cash flow hedges reclassified to profit or loss	723	26
Exchange differences on translating foreign operations	152	(92)
Other comprehensive income for the year	555	(256)
Total comprehensive income for the year	**4,078**	**15,580**

Statement of Financial Position
As at 30 September 2020

	Note	2020 £'000	2019 £'000
ASSETS			
Property, plant and equipment	11	35,412	35,680
Right-of-use assets		48,944	55,936
Goodwill		984	968
Investment in joint venture		692	494
Deferred tax assets		4,523	3,418
Prepayments		674	695
Total non-current assets		**91,229**	**97,191**

	Note	2020 £'000	2019 £'000
Inventories		77,673	51,872
Trade and other receivables		44,124	30,587
Amount due from joint venture		225	407
Derivative financial assets		544	411
Cash and cash equivalents		-	8,560
Total current assets		**122,566**	**91,837**
Total assets		**213,795**	**189,028**
EQUITY AND LIABILITIES			
Share capital		2,160	2,160
Share premium		9,137	9,137
Other reserves		91	(312)
Translation reserve		296	144
Retained earnings		85,113	82,335
Total equity		**96,797**	**93,464**
Trade and other payables		40,793	25,281
Bank overdraft		20,039	6,790
Income tax payable		4,360	3,353
Derivative financial liabilities		269	1,063
Lease liabilities due within 12 months		6,948	6,617
		72,409	43,104
Deferred tax liabilities		497	1,420
Lease liabilities due over 12 months		44,092	51,040
Total liabilities		**44,589**	**52,460**
Total equity and liabilities		**213,795**	**189,028**

Selected relevant notes to the financial statements

3. *Operating profit*

Operating profit is stated after charging:	2020 £000	2019 £000
Depreciation of PPE	9,040	7,656
Depreciation of right-of-use assets	6,992	6,992
Exceptional costs	1,114	814
Net impairment reversal of property, plant and equipment	–	(352)
Loss on sale of property, plant & equipment	102	30
Fees paid to auditors of the company		
– Audit of the parent company	9	9
– Audit of subsidiaries and joint venture	101	76
– Interim financial statements review	20	20
– Audit related assurance services	18	20
– Taxation compliance services	9	-
– Other tax advisory services	31	-
– Due diligence services	165	-

The exceptional costs incurred during the year of £1.114 million (2019: £0.814m) include an impairment charge of £0.765 million in respect of retail assets, notably a retail development in the UK that has failed to deliver on its potential. The remaining amount relates to finders' fees and legal fees in respect of the lease of a new store in Edinburgh.

The exceptional costs incurred during 2019 were in respect of set-up costs in relation to manufacturing products in Bangladesh and provision for bad and doubtful debts in respect of our exposure in Spain.

4. *Finance income and expenses*

	2020 £000	2019 £000
Finance income		
– Interest receivable	34	7
– Foreign exchange gains	–	38
	34	45
Finance expenses		
– Interest payable	(2,646)	(208)
– On lease liabilities	(2,883)	(3,198)
– Foreign exchange losses	(178)	–
	(5,707)	(3,406)

11. *Property, plant and equipment*

	Leasehold improvements £000	Fixtures Fittings office equip £000	Motor vehicles £000	Assets under construction £000	Total £000
Cost					
At 1 October 2019	44,279	37,358	126	3,725	85,488
Additions	13,302	8,431	–	(1,876)	19,857
Disposals	(120)	(395)	(25)	–	(540)
Exchange rate movement	(22)	(10)	–	(212)	(244)
At 30 September 2020	57,439	45,384	101	1,637	104,561
Depreciation					
At 1 October 2019	26,282	33,410	116	–	59,808
Charge for the year	4,098	4,941	1	–	9,040
Impairment	513	252	–	–	765
Disposals	(84)	(327)	(18)	–	(429)
Exchange rate movement	(28)	(7)	–	–	(35)
At 30 September 2020	30,781	38,269	99	–	69,149
Carrying amount					
At 30 September 2019	22,997	8,948	10	3,725	35,680
At 30 September 2020	26,658	7,115	2	1,637	35,412

Additions included within the assets under construction category are stated net of transfers to other property, plant and equipment categories.

Impairment of property, plant and equipment

The group has determined that for the purposes of impairment testing, each store and outlet is a cash-generating unit. Cash-generating units are tested for impairment if there are indications of impairment at the reporting date.

Recoverable amounts for cash-generating units are based on value in use, which is calculated from cash flow projections using data from the group's latest internal forecasts, the results of which are reviewed by the board. The key assumptions for the value in use calculations are those regarding discount rates, growth rates and expected changes in margins. Management estimates discount rates using pre-tax rates that reflect the current market assessment of the time value of money and the risks specific to the cash-generating units. Changes in selling prices and direct costs are based on past experience and expectations of future changes in the market.

The pre-tax discount rate used to calculate value in use is derived from the group's weighted average cost of capital.

The impairment losses relate to stores whose recoverable amounts (value in use) did not exceed the asset carrying values. In all cases, impairment losses arose due to stores performing below projected trading levels.

The impairment charge for the year to 30 September 2020 includes a charge in respect of some retail assets, notably a retail development in the UK that has failed to deliver on its potential.

The net impairment credit of £352,000 in 2019 relates to the reversal of an impairment charge of £743,000, incurred during the year ended 30 September 2018, in relation to the carrying value of retail assets in the Republic of Ireland and offset by an impairment charge relating to retail assets in the year of £391,000.

Exhibit 3: Email from Pritesh Malik, 18 August 2020

To: Victoria Lawrence, Rob Da Silva, Eloise Howard, Maria Mateos, Neil Newell
From: Pritesh Malik
Date: 18 August 2020
Subject: Arundels contract and new lease

Hi All

I have two pieces of great news to pass on! Firstly, I have just taken a phone call from Lauren Flynn at Arundels department stores to confirm that we've won the contract to design and supply shoes for its premium ranges. This is a huge boost to the company, and the agreed contract lasts five years with the potential to renew for a further five, depending on performance.

One of the conditions of the contract is that we produce an annual CSR (corporate social responsibility) report in order to assure Arundels that we are acting within the parameters of its internal CSR plan, known as Plan X. I've been through Arundel's Plan X and I've pulled out the key areas that I think we'd be expected to contribute to and listed them in the attached document. I think we'll need to discuss these seriously at the next board meeting, so please can you all start thinking about what steps we can take to achieve compliance. I've mentioned all this to the auditor and they've not audited CSR reports before but say they're up to the challenge.

The second piece of good news is that we've secured the lease on the store on Edinburgh's Princes Street. Although I think that high street presence continues to work well for us at the moment, and this is a prime site, I can see that almost all retail is heading in the direction of online sales, so I think we should try to keep leases short term and aim to terminate early, if possible. The lease starts on 1 September 2020 and we'll aim to open the store in the first week of October.

Many thanks,
Pritesh

Email attachment

> **Youth unemployment**
>
> **Aim:** By 2023, we aim to work with 100 of our suppliers and share best practice in order to open up more vocational training and work placement opportunities for young unemployed people. We aim to collaborate with other companies to encourage them to do the same.
>
> **Progress: On plan.** This new commitment is designed to address youth unemployment through collaboration with our suppliers, partners and other companies to create more opportunities for young people. We helped to set up Movement to Work with some of the UK's biggest employers who have all pledged to run placements and encourage their suppliers to do the same. Between them, Movement to Work members aim to offer 100,000 vocational training and work placements over the next two years. So far, 90 Arundels suppliers have signed-up to support Movement to Work and many are participating at several locations.

Employee diversity

Aim: We will report on gender diversity in the UK, Republic of Ireland and our wholly owned businesses worldwide by 2022, we will aim for 30% female board members and 35% women in senior roles.

Progress: On plan. We've extended this commitment and set new targets. As of March 2020, 29% of our board and 39% of employees in senior management roles were women. In 2019, we were again listed in The Times top 50 Employers for Women.

Employee wellbeing – Wellness

Aim: We will establish measurements and report on wellness for Arundel employees by 2022 to supplement the more traditional measures of employee engagement, considering external best practice.

Progress: On plan. This is a new commitment. Using data from our Tell Us employee survey, we've established a Wellness benchmarking measurement of 81%. This will act as a baseline for future years. We're also working with Business in the Community's Wellbeing Workwell Index to improve the way we measure and report about wellbeing-related matters.

Living wage

Aim: Implement a process to ensure our clothing suppliers are able to pay workers a fair living wage in the least developed countries we source from, starting with Bangladesh, India and Sri Lanka by 2020. We will achieve this by ensuring that the cost prices we pay to our suppliers are adequate to pay a fair living wage.

Progress: Achieved. We developed and used a buying tool that allowed us to take into account a fair living wage when we set the cost price for products made in Bangladesh, India, Sri Lanka and other locations. However, this didn't automatically result in factories paying a fair living wage, so we're involved in a number of collaborative programmes to address this issue.

Supply chain training

Aim: Work with our suppliers and partners to provide a training and education programme for 500,000 workers by 2020. This will cover employee's roles, responsibilities and rights, basic health care and where possible, numeracy and literacy.

Progress: Achieved/ongoing. We've now achieved this existing commitment. By April 2020, we'd provided training to around 506,000 workers in our General Merchandise supply chains since 2015.

Energy efficiency at top 100 clothing suppliers

Aim: Require our top 100 clothing factories to install energy efficient lighting, improved insulation and temperature controls, to reduce their energy usage by an estimated 10% by 2021. These are factories that have featured in a rolling top 100 between 2015 and March 2020.

Progress: On plan. This is an existing commitment. Eighty-five (last year 48) of our clothing suppliers that have featured in our top 100 suppliers by turnover between 2015 and 2019 have now adopted energy efficiency best practices on lighting, insulation and temperature control. Of these, 53 (last year 35) have gone further and achieved our more demanding Eco-Factory standards.

Chemical and effluent management in dyeing

Aim: We will launch a further Model Eco Dyehouses programme by 2023 to focus on developing best practice for chemical and effluent management. The best practice will help to define new standards to be extended across our supply base.

Progress: Not started. We've yet to start to work on this new commitment. We aim to introduce a method for measuring and recognising our best performing dye houses in order to encourage more general improvements. We're also working with other companies as a member of the collaborative Roadmap to Zero Discharges of Hazardous Chemicals (ZDHC) group.

Exhibit 4: Extract from *Apparel*, trade journal for clothing manufacturers, September 2019

Reveal: Are we looking after our manufacturers well enough?

In this latest in our Reveal series, we consider whether western fashion companies are doing enough to protect workers at manufacturing facilities in Bangladesh.

On the evening of 12 September 2019, a 10-storey building in Bhaluka, Bangladesh, housing 4 clothing factories, and around 6,000 workers collapsed. Over 1,100 workers were killed, and thousands of people were hurt, with many suffering life-changing injuries. Labour rights groups and trade unions in Bangladesh and internationally are calling for immediate action from international brands following the collapse.

During the rescue and recovery operation, activists from local labour rights group, Bhaluka Worker Support, discovered labels from high street fashion brands including MissFash and Blue, indicating that these companies were sourcing garments from the factories.

This collapse follows the Sreepur factory fire in a neighbouring district that killed 112 workers in 2018, and the Akhtar Factory collapse of 2015, which caused the death of at least 78 workers. The speed of the garment industry expansion in Bangladesh is an ongoing and pressing concern. The country has seen significant growth in garment factories in recent times, with factories being built on swamp land and without proper building regulations in place. Labour rights groups say unnecessary deaths will continue, unless and until, brands and government officials agree to an independent and binding fire and building safety program.

'Tragedy after tragedy shows that corporate-controlled monitoring is completely inadequate,' says Aadya Dewan of Bangladesh Workers Action Group (BWAG). 'The families of the victims and the hundreds injured in the collapse, are without income and without support. Compensation must be provided by the brands who were sourcing from these factories, and responsibility taken for their lack of action to prevent this happening.'

BWAG is calling upon all major brands sourcing from Bangladesh to sign the 'Bangladesh Fire and Building Safety Agreement' immediately to stop future tragedies from happening. The Clean Clothes Campaign, together with local and global unions and labour rights organisations, has developed this sector-wide program that includes independent building inspections, worker rights training, public disclosure and a long-overdue review of safety standards. This transparent and practical agreement is unique in that it is supported by all key labour stakeholders in Bangladesh and internationally.

Exhibit 5: Extract from *Business News Weekly*, March 2020

TRV rents rise as retail confidence returns

3 March 2020, 10:18

TRV Properties, owner of the sprawling Roberts Centre shopping mall and city centre mall, Northside, completed 71 leases, worth a total of £13 million a year, in the four months from 1 November 2019 to 28 February 2020 across its portfolio.

The mall investor said it enjoyed 'continued improvement in retailer demand', with rents 5% up compared to previous passing rents and in line with valuations. Year-to-date footfall was up 1% and occupancy marginally reduced since 31 October 2019 at 95%, due largely to the loss of Mobile Phone Co and La Femme, with 39 units and 1% of annual rent who failed and closed in the period.

TRV also announced a new £350 million bond issue today to repay other debt. TRV recently refinanced £453 million of bank facilities and agreed £763 million of new facilities. The current development pipeline will cost £1.2 billion. Net external debt was unchanged at £3.9 billion as of 28 February 2020, and the debt to assets ratio based on 28 February valuations was 44%.

TRV has started working up asset management plans at the recently acquired TRV Bristol Mall and TRV Waterside Mall, where new lettings exceeded expectations.

Roger James, chief executive, said: 'We are pleased to see continued improvement in retailer demand for space, particularly evident in centres where we are undertaking investment and development projects. The benefits of last year's rebranding as TRV have been enhanced by further customer service and digital initiatives in the period. The balance sheet is in good shape, strengthened by recent financing transactions and we have a wide range of organic growth opportunities with strong momentum in our £1.2 billion development pipeline.'

James continued: 'The UK economic environment has continued to improve with a seventh consecutive quarter of GDP growth, a sustained increase in consumer confidence and like-for-like non-food sales, now positive for over two years. According to the IPD retail property index, this is now beginning to translate into an uplift in retail rental values, with the index showing rental value growth for the last four months, the first positive period of this length since 2014. At TRV, we continue to see areas of increased interest from retailers, including for new brands and flagship stores, particularly in centres where we have been undertaking or have plans for capital expenditure.'

Shares in TRV were unchanged at 339p.

Practice Case Study 2: Unseen case information and exam requirements

Topic list	Syllabus reference
1 Practice case study 2: Unseen case information	All LOs
2 Practice case study 2: Unseen information	All LOs

Introduction

This chapter contains the exam requirements relating to Case Study 2 (Shoe Designers) and the unseen material. This practice case study is 80 marks, rather than 100 marks, as this is practice case to get you started.

In the real MDCS, you will also be given another copy of the pre-seen material (which, for this Case Study) is in Chapter 13.

Important note: Practice Case Study 2 is applicable for MDCS students following the accounting route, but its practice requirements are suitable for all MDCS students

Exam requirement

You are a qualified accountant working for an accountancy firm, Slack and Rizk, which, until recently, had just three partners.

The company has been undergoing significant expansion and has been approached by Arundels plc to supply shoes for its premium ranges.

You have been invited to a meeting with the directors, Victoria Lawrence and Pritesh Malik. Following this, you will hold a briefing meeting with the audit team who will be performing the audit field work.

Required

(a) Identify and explain five business risks facing Shoe Designers. **(15 marks)**

(b) Calculate the following ratios for both years: operating profit margin, interest cover, inventory turnover days, receivables collection period, payables payment period. For each ratio, identify a business risk which may be indicated and outline how the board of Shoe Designers should respond to the risk. **(15 marks)**

(c) Explain, with supporting calculations, how the new Edinburgh store lease should be reflected in the financial statements in the year ended 30 September 2020. **(15 marks)**

(d) Identify and explain the accounting implications of Eloise Howard's two suggestions in her voice message to Rob Da Silva. **(10 marks)**

(f) Calculate and explain the goodwill arising on the acquisition of El Zapatero Andaluz and the goodwill that should be reported in the consolidated financial statements at 30 September 2020. **(15 marks)**

Professional Communication marks will be awarded for the quality of the presentation of the report.
(10 marks)

(Total 80 marks)

Note. This practice case study is limited to 80 marks to get you started.

Professional Communication marks are allocated as follows:

Professional Marking Criteria (10 marks):

Report is presented in a style suitable for the audience articulated in the scenario **(1 marks)**

Structure of the paper is logical and clearly articulated to enable ease of navigation and discussion
(1 marks)

Ideas are expressed clearly and in language accessible to the audience identified in the scenario **(1 marks)**

Technical terms are used accurately and explained where appropriate **(1 marks)**

Issues are appropriately prioritised within the structure of the report and the body of the discussion
(2 marks)

Issues are assessed in a balanced and reasoned manner **(2 marks)**

Rationale behind assessment of issues and recommendations of responses is clearly articulated and alternative actions explored where appropriate **(2 marks)**

(10 marks)

Relevant exchange rates:

1 August 2020	£1: €1.15
30 September 2020	£1: €1.17

Unseen material

Content:

(1) Memo from Lucy Chatfield to Rob Da Silva, 23 October 2020
(2) Voice message from Eloise Howard to Rob Da Silva, 17 August 2020
(3) Email from Neil Newell to Pritesh Malik, 1 July 2020
(4) Extract from Shoe Designers (SD) board meeting minutes, 2 October 2020

Exhibit 1: Email from Lucy Chatfield to Rob Da Silva, 23 October 2020

To: Rob Da Silva
From: Lucy Chatfield
Date: 23 October 2020
Subject: New lease

Hi Rob,

I've run off a set of draft financial statements, as you requested, but I've realised that they don't include the acquisition of the Spanish supplier or the lease on the new Edinburgh store, other than the initial fees associated with the lease agreement, which have been expensed. I'll leave the acquisition to you as discussed but I'll work on the new lease.

All of the other lease agreements are included in the draft financials – I worked from the schedules that Bob prepared before he left – but I'm a bit stumped on how to account for the new lease. As you know, I used to work at a much smaller, private company and we applied UK GAAP rather than IFRS, so I'm not really up to speed with IFRS 16, although I do know that simplified accounting is available in some circumstances. Would we be able to use that?

I was hoping that you could spend a few minutes with me to point me in the right direction.

I've added below relevant information from the lease agreement and notes that I've found written in the file.

Thanks,
Lucy

Details of the lease agreement

- The lease commencement date is 1 September 2020.
- The lease term is 12 years; lessee has the option to terminate after 6 years
- Fixed lease payments are £1.1 million per annum, payable in arrears
- A penalty of £400,000 is payable on exercise of the early termination clause
- There is a residual value guarantee of £10.8 million

Notes

1. There is no indication of an interest rate implicit in the lease. I have asked the lessor to provide one, but they said that this is not information that they make public, as it is sensitive.

2. Our current borrowing cost is 6.75%. New borrowings would probably attract interest at 7%.

3. According to surveyors, an estimation of the residual value of the property after 6 years is £10.75 million

4. It will cost £450,000 to fit out the shop unit prior to opening the store. We'll pay a premium in order to ensure a quick turnaround. GGT Properties who own the shop has agreed to reimburse £100,000 of the refitting costs as a sweetener.

Exhibit 2: Voice message from Eloise Howard to Rob Da Silva, 17 August 2020

Hi Rob, it's just Eloise. I'm at the airport reading *Business Week* and I've had some ideas. We have a great brand, but I'm thinking about how we can really boost consumer confidence and make ourselves stand out from the competition. I think that we should be offering one of two things to our retail customers. Firstly, we could allow customers to return goods for a cash refund, or a different product, at any time up to a month after purchase. That will allow women to buy shoes, take them home and try them on with various outfits. It shows that we understand consumers and the flexibility that they want. Alternatively, we could offer a 'refund pledge' that we'll refund the cost of any shoes that fail to survive normal wear and tear in the first six months after sale. That would show customers how confident we are in the quality of our footwear. I'm sure that both of these ideas will have some sort of accounting impact, so I thought I'd better keep you in the loop as your input might help me to decide which initiative would work best from a financial perspective. Give me a ring if you want to discuss them.

Exhibit 3: Email from Neil Newell to Pritesh Malik, 1 March 2020

To: Pritesh Malik
From: Neil Newell
Date: 1 March 2020
Subject: Supplier news

Hi Pritesh

As you asked, I've been keeping my ear to the ground for any opportunities to grow the business through acquiring suppliers. I've had a few in-depth discussions with Juan Pablo Almodóvar at the Spanish manufacturer that we've outsourced some wholesale production to, and it's clear that he wants to retire and sees a sale of the business as his exit route. He currently owns 75% of equity shares in El Zapatero Andaluz SL (EZA) and is looking to offload all of them.

It seems like he's looking at a price of €9 million in cash plus 500,000 ordinary shares in Shoe Designers. He'd also like to build in an earnout clause whereby he'd receive a further €2 million if certain sales targets were met within 24 months of the sale. I've had a look at the latest EZA accounts and it looks like the company has a balance sheet value of €11 million.

I can put you in touch with Juan Pablo if this is something that you think you'd like to progress.

Neil

Exhibit 4: Extract from Shoe Designers (SD) board meeting minutes, 2 October 2020

In attendance: Pritesh Malik (PM), Victoria Lawrence (VL), Rob Da Silva (RDS), Eloise Howard (EH), Maria Mateos (MM)

Apologies: Neil Newell (NN)

Acquisition of El Zapatero Andaluz (EZA)

RDS confirmed that the acquisition of a 75% holding in EZA was completed on 1 August 2020 when the share price of SD was £2.50.

After due diligence work, it was agreed that the price demanded by the vendor was fair and Shoe Designers agreed to pay the requested amount. An amount of €2 million payable on meeting earnout targets was assessed to have a fair value of €1.5 million at acquisition, although this was reassessed at €1.65 million at 30 September 2020 as a result of EZA's post-acquisition performance.

RDS explained that it is unusual for SD to acquire less than a 100% holding in a subsidiary and that this acquisition will result in the recognition of a non-controlling interest (NCI) in the consolidated financial statements. He identified that there are two options available to measure such an interest at acquisition and that his choice was driven by a desire to keep the reported NCI at a minimum.

The reported net assets of EZA at 1 August 2020 was presented to the board as follows:

	€'000
Property, plant and equipment	24,300
Intangible asset	250
Inventories	5,700
Receivables	9,600
Cash	4,300
Loan	(13,000)
Payables	(11,600)
Taxes and other payables	(8,100)
Total net assets	**11,450**

RDS identified the following:

- The reported net assets did not include an order backlog with a fair value of €750,000.

- The recognised intangible asset is the amortised cost of a patent to protect manufacturing processes; these processes (excluding the patent) have a fair value of €2.95 million.

- EZA has an unrecognised contingent liability relating to a court case brought by a former employee. The employee is seeking damages of €500,000 for injury, however lawyers have advised that there is no present obligation because it is probable that the court will throw out the case due to lack of evidence.

- The factory premises have a fair value that is €1 million in excess of carrying amount and receivables have a fair value of 80% of their carrying amount due to expected non-collectability.

Practice Case Study 2: Suggested solution

Topic list	Syllabus reference
1 Practice case study 2: Suggested solution	All LOs

Introduction

This chapter contains the suggested solution to the Shoe Designers plc Case Study.

Suggested solution

(a) **Business risks**

(i) **Outsourcing**

The company has recently outsourced much of its production; 60% of the manufacturing for the wholesale business has been outsourced to factories in Bangladesh; and 15% to Spain.

The company will find it much more difficult to maintain control over the quality of production, compared to the production in its own factories. If the quality of the production is poor, Shoe Designers may lose customers or may have to reduce prices in this very competitive market. This could lead to a fall in the company's profits. Shoe Designers will also find it more difficult to ensure that suppliers have behaved ethically.

There will also be longer delivery times for the overseas suppliers, which will mean that Shoe Designers will be able to respond less quickly to changes in demand.

(ii) **Foreign exchange risk**

The company pays suppliers in foreign currency and sells to customers in a variety of countries. The company is exposed to foreign exchange risk on its purchases which could lead to higher (and lower) purchase costs. The company also sells to customers overseas. The sales may be in foreign currencies, which could mean that Shoe Designers receives less than expected, or in sterling. If they are in sterling, then Shoe Designers is not exposed to foreign exchange risk, but if the pound strengthens, this will make purchases more expensive for overseas customers, and so they may buy less. Foreign currency movements could lead to foreign exchange losses.

Shoe Designers also has overseas subsidiaries and a joint venture which could lead to exchange differences on translation.

(iii) **Pressure on margins**

The company's wholesale customers are constantly squeezing the company's margin, resulting in downward pressure on revenue. At the same time, there is upward pressure on costs; rents are rising, and scrutiny from labour rights groups such as Bhaluka Worker Support and BWAG and future scrutiny by Arundels could lead to increased labour costs in Bangladesh.

Decreasing revenue and increasing costs will adversely impact on profits.

(iv) **New Edinburgh store**

The company has opened a new store in Edinburgh. Retail stores are generally performing poorly, and the company has had to recognise impairment charges in relation to some of its retail premises. Even so, the company has committed to a 12 year lease, which will only be cancellable after six years.

The company's operating profit has fallen by around £15 million to £10 million this year, and the lease commitment represents a large proportion of the company's profits. If the Edinburgh shop is not profitable, then this obviously damages the company's profits.

(v) **Contract with Arundels**

The contract to supply shoes to Arundels is obviously good news for the company, but it comes with the condition that Shoe Designers produce a CSR report and operate within the parameters of Arundel's Plan X. If Shoe Designers fails to comply with these two conditions, then Arundels could cancel the contract. This could lead to Shoe Designers having inventory that it cannot sell elsewhere, potentially having to pay penalties to Arundels, and suffering damages to its reputation if this becomes public knowledge.

If Shoe Designers does comply with these conditions, there will be costs, possibly substantial, attached. To comply, Shoe Designers will have to:

(1) Offer vocational training and placement opportunities to young unemployed people
(2) Hire more women into senior roles
(3) Introduce wellness programmes
(4) Pay a living wage in Bangladesh
(5) Provide training and education opportunities to workers in its supply chain
(6) Introduce energy efficient equipment
(7) Introduce best practice in chemical and effluent management

If the company is not already meeting these conditions, then there could be substantial costs incurred in meeting them.

It is likely that Shoe Designers will need to have an assurance engagement on its CSR report in order to give credibility to the measures reported and this will obviously cost money.

Note. You may have identified other risks in the scenario. Make sure that, as you are asked for business risks, you discuss the impact on profitability/cash flow.

(b) **Analytical procedures**

	2020	2019
Operating profit margin	= 10,301/261,975 × 100 = 3.9%	= 25,746/222,358 × 100 = 11.6%
Interest cover	= 10,301/(5,707 − 34) = 1.8	= 25,746/(3,406 − 45) = 7.7
Inventory turnover days	= 77,673/95,740 × 365 = 296 days	= 51,872/83,419 × 365 = 227 days
Receivables collection period	= 44,124/261,975 × 365 = 61 days	= 30,587/222,358 × 365 = 50 days
Payables payment period	= 40,793/95,740 × 365 = 156 days	= 25,281/83,419 × 365 = 111 days

	Potential business risk	Suggested response by the board of Shoe Designers Ltd
Operating profit margin	Operating profit margin has fallen significantly from 11.6% to 3.9% due to increases in distribution costs of 35% and administrative expenses of 50% compared to only 18% increase in revenue. These could be genuine increases but could also be an indication that operating costs are overstated. Since cost of sales has only increased by 15% it may be that some costs of sale have been misclassified as distribution costs or administrative expenses.	Request a detailed breakdown of costs in distribution and administrative expenses categories, comparing them to the prior year. Investigate individual nominal ledger accounts showing significant increases and confirm proper classification. Investigate whether costs related to sales have been misclassified into other categories. Implement cost-control measures and negotiate better terms with suppliers or distributors. Improve efficiency in distribution and consider outsourcing non-core administrative functions. Regularly monitor cost allocations to prevent misclassifications and inefficiencies.

	Potential business risk	**Suggested response by the board of Shoe Designers Ltd**
Interest cover	The interest cover ratio has decreased significantly from 7.7 to 1.8 due to a decline in profits and an increase in finance costs. If borrowings or interest rates increase, the company may not be able to generate adequate profits and cash to make the interest payments. Failure to make the interest payments could lead to banks putting the company into receivership.	Review loan agreements and terms of borrowings, including interest rates, and assess how interest rate changes would impact the company's ability to service debt. Review loan covenants related to interest cover and confirm compliance with required terms and conditions of the loan. Establish contingency plans for rising interest rates. Proactively renegotiate loan terms to secure better rates. Improve profitability through cost-cutting measures or focusing on higher-margin products. Consider alternative financing options to reduce the company's reliance on high-interest debt.
Inventory turnover days	The increase in inventory days from 227 to 296 days may be due to the overstatement of inventory in the statement of financial position. This may be due to stock quantities being overstated or valuations being too high. If inventory is slow moving, then the selling price may need to be reduced below cost and, as a result, inventory measured at cost would be overstated.	Review and enhance inventory management processes, focusing on reducing inventory days by improving stock movement and sales forecasting. Investigate slow-moving or obsolete stock and consider appropriate discounting to move inventory. Implement just-in-time (JIT) inventory strategies to avoid overstocking. Negotiate better lead times with suppliers and enhance sales forecasts to manage inventory levels efficiently. Improve stock control processes and regularly review stock valuation methods to ensure they are accurate.
Receivables collection period	Receivable days have increased from 50 to 61 days, suggesting customers are taking longer to pay, which could indicate that some amounts from customers are not recoverable. If no allowance is made for irrecoverable receivables, then trade receivables will be overstated.	Strengthen the credit control function by implementing more rigorous follow-up procedures for overdue payments. Review customer payment terms and identify any that require renegotiation to better align with the company's cash flow needs. Introduce early payment incentives for customers, and tighten credit checks for new clients. Regularly review receivables aging reports and address overdue payments promptly. Ensure that an adequate allowance for doubtful debts is established and monitored regularly.

18: Practice Case Study 2: Suggested answer

	Potential business risk	**Suggested response by the board of Shoe Designers Ltd**
Payables payment period	Shoe Designers was already taking a long time to pay its suppliers, but this year sees a substantial increase from 111 days to 156 days. It could be that payables is overstated or it could be that Shoe Designers was close to its overdraft limit and so did not make a payment run at the year end. It could also be that Shoe Designers are taking advantage of its strong bargaining power relative to the supplier in Bangladesh and are maximising payment terms. If SD are deliberately paying slowly, and this unethical behaviour continues, then it could lead to the cancellation of the contract with Arundels, with the consequential financial impacts.	Review the company's payment policies to suppliers, ensuring they are ethical and aligned with long-term supplier relationships. Engage with the key supplier in Bangladesh to renegotiate payment terms if necessary, ensuring this will not impact the ongoing relationship. Strengthen supplier relationships by adhering to agreed payment terms. Consider early payment discounts to improve goodwill. Regularly review cash flow projections and manage payment schedules to avoid cash flow issues and the risk of contract cancellation.

(c) **Lease**

IFRS 16 *Leases* requires that a single lessee accounting model is applied to all leases, with limited exceptions. Those exceptions are short-term leases (leases with a term of 12 months or less) and leases for low value assets. Low value is not defined but is suggested in the IFRS 16 *Basis for Conclusions* as being US$5,000 when new. In these cases, a lessee may elect to apply a recognition exemption, sometimes referred to as simplified accounting. The Edinburgh store lease is neither short-term, nor for a low value asset and this option is therefore not available to Shoe Designers.

The standard lessee accounting model must therefore be applied, and a right-of-use asset and lease liability must be recognised by Shoe Designers at the commencement of the lease on 1 September 2020.

In order to calculate the initial measurement of the asset and liability, the lease term must be determined. The lease agreement for the new Edinburgh store stipulates a lease term of 12 years with the option for Shoe Designers to terminate the agreement after six years on payment of a penalty. IFRS 16 states that the lease term includes the non-cancellable period of a lease term plus any period covered by an option to terminate, but only if the lessee is reasonably certain not to exercise that option. Pritesh Malik has indicated that leases should be terminated early if possible and so it follows that Shoe Designers is likely to exercise the termination option. The lease term is therefore six years.

The lease liability is initially measured at the present value of future lease payments. These include the fixed annual payments and also, because the period covered by the termination option is not included in the lease term, the termination penalty. In addition, Shoe Designers guarantees a minimum residual value of £10.8 million at the end of the lease term. However, it is estimated that the actual residual value will be just £10.75 million. Therefore, Shoe Designers will be required to pay £50,000 to the lessor, GGT Properties.

These lease payments are discounted to present value at the interest rate implicit in the lease, or where this is not available, as is the case here, the lessee's incremental borrowing rate. The lease liability is therefore calculated as:

Year	Cash flow £	Discount factor	Present value £'000
1	(1,100,000)	$1/1.07$	1,028
2	(1,100,000)	$1/1.07^2$	961
3	(1,100,000)	$1/1.07^3$	898
4	(1,100,000)	$1/1.07^4$	839
	(1,100,000)		
	(400,000)		
	(50,000)		
5	(1,550,000)	$1/1.07^5$	1,105
Lease liability			4,831

The lease liability subsequently accrues interest and is reduced by annual payments. In the first 12 months of the lease term, interest arises of £338,000 (7% × £4,831,000). This is allocated into two financial years as follows:

Financial year ended	b/f £'000	Interest 7% £'000	Payment £'000	c/f £'000
30.9.20 (1/12 months)	4,831	28	–	4,859
30.9.21 (11/12 months)	4,859	310	(1,100)	4,069

One month of interest, being £28,000 (4,831 × 7% × 1/12), falls within the year ended 30 September 2020. The year-end liability is therefore £4.859 million and this is presented split between a current liability of £0.79 million (1,100k – 310k) and a non-current liability of £4.069 million (4,859k – 790k).

The lease liability forms part of the initial measurement of the right-of-use asset. This is increased by the initial direct costs of £0.349 million. These costs are finders and legal fees, and they were incorrectly recognised as an expense in the draft financial statements. In addition, Shoe Designers received a lease incentive of £100,000, this being the reimbursement of refitting costs. This amount decreases the carrying amount of the right-of-use asset. The asset is therefore initially measured at:

	£'000
Lease liability	4,831
Initial direct costs	349
Lease incentive	(100)
Right-of-use asset	5,080

The right-of-use asset is depreciated over the lease term of six years, giving a carrying amount of £5.009 million (5,080k – (5,080k/6 × 1/12)) at 30 September 2020 and a depreciation charge for the year of £0.071m.

The £450,000 costs to fit out the store are classified as leasehold improvements and are within the scope of IAS 16 *Property, Plant and Equipment*. They are recognised at cost and depreciated over the six-year lease term. The depreciation charge for the year ended 30 September 2020 is therefore £6,250 and the carrying amount at the year-end is £443,750.

(d) **Warranty and refund liability**

Eloise Howard has suggested two initiatives:

(i) Allowing customers to return goods for a cash refund up to one month after purchase

(ii) Refunding the cost of shoes that fail to survive normal wear and tear in the six months after sale

Allowing customers to return goods for a cash refund up to one month after purchase

Guidance on accounting for sales with a right of return is provided by IFRS 15 *Revenue from Contracts with Customers*. The same treatment applies, regardless of whether returns can be made for cash refunds, credit notes or another product.

If this initiative were put in place, Shoe Designers would only recognise revenue on sales to the extent that it expected to be entitled to it. Any consideration received from a customer that the company expected to refund would be recognised as a refund liability in the statement of financial position.

Measurement is likely to be based on expected levels of returns. For example, if the company sold £100,000 of shoes in a week and expected the returns level to be 5%, it would recognise £95,000 revenue and £5,000 as a refund liability.

As well as recognising a refund liability, Shoe Designers would recognise an asset representing the right to recover products provided to customers. This asset should be measured at the former carrying amount of the shoes sold, less any expected decreases in value and costs to recover the products. It should be presented separately from the refund liability. When the asset is recognised (at the point of sale), a corresponding adjustment is made to cost of sales. Thus, neither revenue nor cost of sales reflect the sale of shoes that are expected to be returned.

Refunding the cost of shoes that fail to survive normal wear and tear in the six months after sale

The refund pledge amounts to a warranty that provides assurance that a product will function as intended. This type of standard warranty is within the scope of IAS 37 *Provisions, Contingent Liabilities and Contingent Assets* and does not affect revenue recognition. Therefore, when shoes are sold, the amount of cash received would be recognised as revenue in full.

At the point of sale, a warranty provision would also be recognised to reflect the expected liability as a result of the refund pledge. A provision is only recognised if there is a present obligation as a result of a past event, a transfer of economic resources is probable, and the provision can be reliably measured. All of these conditions are met:

- In this case, the past event that gives rise to an obligation is the sale of the shoes. The obligation is constructive, ie Shoe Designers would create a public expectation that the refund pledge would be honoured, rather than it being a legal requirement.
- It is probable that some returns would be made if the refund pledge were launched.
- The level of returns could be estimated in order to measure the provision.

In the first year of providing the refund pledge, the measurement of the provision would be less reliable than in future years, when there would be historic returns data to refer to. Estimations in the first year could, however, be based on expected values estimated using existing knowledge of customer complaints.

In making a warranty provision, Shoe Designers would recognise a liability in its statement of financial position and a corresponding expense in the statement of profit or loss. Any refunds would reduce the liability, rather than be expensed at the time of payment.

Comparison

In both cases, profit would be reduced. However, in the case of returns within one month, reported revenue would be reduced. This would not be the case if the refund pledge were adopted, since a warranty provision is recognised as an expense, rather than a reduction of revenue. Practically, it is likely that the level of returns would be much higher under the option to return goods within one month and, as a result, that would have a greater effect on the financial statements.

(e) **Goodwill**

Shoe Designers achieved control of a Spanish manufacturer, EZA, on 1 August 2020. Goodwill is calculated on this date, initially in Euro (€) before being translated into pounds sterling (£) at the acquisition date. It is subsequently treated as a foreign currency asset and must be retranslated at the closing exchange rate at 30 September 2020, giving rise to an exchange difference.

Goodwill on acquisition

Goodwill is initially calculated as the difference between (i) consideration plus the non-controlling interest; and (ii) the fair value of the net assets of the acquiree at the acquisition date:

	€'000	€'000
Consideration:		
– Cash		9,000.0
– Shares (500,000 × £2.50 × 1.15)		1,437.5
– Contingent cash consideration		1,500.0
		11,937.5
Non-controlling interest (25% × €14,230)		3,557.5
Net assets of acquiree:		
– As reported at acquisition date	11,450.0	
– Order backlog	750.0	
– Manufacturing processes	2,950.0	
– Fair value adjustment to property	1,000.0	
– Fair value adjustment to receivables (20% × 9,600)	(1,920.0)	
		(14,230.0)
Goodwill		**1,265.0**

Consideration includes cash payable immediately, shares in Shoe Designers and cash payable dependent on an earnout clause being met. All elements of consideration are recognised at their acquisition date fair values. In respect of the shares, this is the share price on the acquisition date (translated at the spot rate).

Rob Da Silva has elected to use the measurement option for the NCI that results in the lowest carrying amount. Therefore, the NCI is measured as a proportion of the fair value of the net assets of the acquired, rather than at fair value.

All identifiable assets and liabilities of EZA should be included in the goodwill calculation, measured at their fair values. As a result, certain intangible assets that are not recognised in EZA's separate financial statements are recognised on consolidation. An intangible asset is identifiable if it is capable of separate sale or arises from contractual or legal rights. Therefore:

- The order backlog is included because this arises from sales contracts and so is the result of a contractual right. This is recognised at acquisition, even if the orders can be cancelled.

- The fair value of the manufacturing processes is included (as well as the recognised patent that protects them) because these are protected legally and so meet the legal rights criterion.

In addition, adjustments are made to the carrying amount of property and receivables, so that fair value is reflected.

The contingent liability of EZA is not recognised as a liability of EZA at acquisition. A contingent liability is defined as either:

- A possible obligation arising from past events and whose existence will be confirmed in the future, or
- A present obligation arising from past events that can be measured reliably and that is not probable of payment.

IFRS 3 requires that a contingent liability is recognised as a liability of the acquiree only if falls into the second category (ie it is a present obligation). In this case, EZA has a possible, rather than probable, obligation.

The resulting goodwill of €1,265,000 is translated at the acquisition date at the spot exchange rate of £1:€1.15, giving initial recognised goodwill of £1,100,000.

Goodwill at the reporting date

At the reporting date, goodwill is not recalculated to reflect the revised value of the contingent consideration because the revision is due to EZA's performance after the acquisition date. Goodwill therefore continues to be measured at €1,265,000 (assuming there are no impairment losses between 1 August 2020 and 30 September 2020).

Goodwill must be retranslated using the exchange rate at 30 September 2020. Goodwill reported in the consolidated statement of financial position is therefore £1,081,197 (1,265,000/1.17).

The resulting exchange loss of £18,803 (1,100,000 – 1,081,197) is reported as other comprehensive income in the consolidated statement of profit or loss and OCI. Since recognised goodwill relates only to Shoe Designers (and not to the 25% NCI), the loss is allocated to the owners of the parent in its entirety and is accumulated in a separate reserve within equity.

Practice Case Study 3: Pre-seen material

Topic list	Syllabus reference
1 Practice case study 3: Pre-seen case information	All LOs

Introduction

This chapter contains the pre-seen material relating to Case Study 3, Triticum Polymers plc (TPP)

Exhibit 1: Corporate background

Exhibit 2: TPP Key performance indicators (KPIs)

Exhibit 3: TPP Key products

Exhibit 4: Key customers

Exhibit 5: Notes of meeting with Cuiting Zhang – Head of research and development

Exhibit 6: Article - Science behind the products

Exhibit 7: Future research interests for TPP

Exhibit 8: Triticum Polymers plc, statement from the chair, October 2022

Exhibit 9: Notes from preliminary meeting with Irene McEvoy – Commercial development director

Exhibit 10: Key commodity information

Exhibit 11: Environmental impacts of textiles

Triticum Polymers plc

Exhibit 1: Corporate background

Triticum Polymers plc (TPP) was founded in 2015 by Arthur Spencer and Irene McEvoy in the UK. Both were research scientists with specific interests in pharmacognosy (the use of plants in pharmaceuticals). As a by-product of their joint research, they discovered a technique of using wheat as a polymer source and developed their first beauty polymer which acted as an effective lubricant for use in a wide range of products from cleansers through to foundation. Backed by funding from Esme Lyn and La Beaute (two international cosmetics companies), the company has expanded rapidly and now has a range of products in both the health and beauty and bio-packaging industries.

As the world moves to a reduction in the extraction of oil, and oil prices become ever higher, industrial science is seeking to replace oil as the basis of polymers and ethanol leading to a rise in plant based or green biotech companies. It is in this market that the enthusiasm of the team at TPP find themselves competing.

The rationale behind using wheat as a raw product was the relative abundance of the crop and its lower price volatility when compared with other commodities. As it was readily available in the EU, supply to the original factory in the UK was also straightforward. Once the UK voted to exit the EU, it became more difficult for supplies to reach the UK factories. TPP founded a factory in mainland China to access local wheat supply and also to allow easier supply into the main manufacturing sites for the beauty industry.

Company history

The rapid growth of the company has been through innovative partnerships with Esme Lyn as a key loan provider to support the scaling up of the initial technology into beauty products. Arthur and Irene refused to go into a joint venture with any company as they are committed to maintaining full control over the research direction and application of their science. This model is not unusual in the bio-technology field.

In 2018, the company acquired ZedCo run by Cuiting Zhang who is now director of research and development. The consideration paid reflected the future potential in the bio-film field and allowed TPP to develop its Triticumfilm through Zhang's work on bio-films and wood pulp.

The company was floated on the London Stock Exchange in September 2019 with 40% of the equity being offered to the public and the remainder owned by Arthur (20%), Irene (20%), Yiming (15%) and the TPP staff share scheme (5%).

Exhibit 2: TPP Key performance indicators (KPIs)

The directors believe that the key performance indicators (KPIs) for the group are:

- Revenues
- Adjusted EBITDA, the earnings before interest, tax, depreciation, amortisation, and exceptional items
- Cash

	2022 £000	2021 £000	2020 £000	2019 £000
Revenue	2,596	3,292	1,288	881
Gross profit	700	1,154	450	140
Adjusted EBITDA	(1,640)	(993)	(2,457)	(5,370)
Cash used in operations	(2,023)	(1,157)	(1,831)	(6,973)
Net cash at the year-end	683	1,448	765	2,655

Income Statement for the year ended 31 March 2022

	2022 £000	2021 £000
Revenue	2,596	3,292
Cost of sales	(1,896)	(2,138)
Gross profit	700	1,154
Other operating income	203	50
Administrative expenses	(2,911)	(2,595)
Group operating loss before exceptional items	(2,008)	(1,391)
Exceptional income/(expense) on revaluation of contingent consideration	1,560	1,560
Operating loss before tax from operations	(448)	(1,639)

Exhibit 3: TPP Key products

Health and beauty:

Triticopol – This is a range of polymers of varying weights which are either used as lubricants, silicone-like substitutes or as petroleum jelly substitutes.

BioPlastics:

Triticumfilm – This is a bio-based material made from wheat. As with the competitor, Biolife produced by Polystar, wheat effectively produces a cellulose which can be converted into a green polymer and used in the production of **shrink film** and other polythene **wrapping and hooding**, like polythene mailing bags and films.

Exhibit 4: Key customers

- **Health and beauty** – Prestigious customers include Lancome, Estee Lauder, L'Oreal, Procter and Gamble, Unilever.
- **BioPlastics** – Prestigious customers include the health and beauty retailers plus supermarket chains.

Key competitor

Green technology is split between the two sectors served by TPP:

Health and beauty:

P2Science Inc

Key competing product: Citropol® 1A is a low molecular-weight liquid polymer that is made from terpenes derived from the forest. Citropol® 1A imparts distinct lubricating properties in skin-care and hair-care formulations. Even in concentrations as low as 1%, the result is a slippery, silky formulation. Citropol® 1A is a valuable component in a range of applications in the beauty industry: cosmetics, skin care, hair care, fragrance, deodorants, and moisturisers.

(**Source**: PE. [Online] Available from: https://p2science.com/citropol/ [Accessed 3 October 2024])

BioPlastics:

Polystar Inc

Key Competing Product – Biofilm™ is a bio-based material made from sugar cane. It is the process of photosynthesis as the plant grows that makes this product carbon positive. The sugar cane actively captures CO_2 from the atmosphere, while at the same time releasing oxygen – making this material not just green, but proactively green. Biofilm™ is a material that can be used in the production of **collation shrink film** and other polythene **wrapping and hooding**, like polythene mailing bags and films.

(**Source**: Polystar. [Online] Available from: https://www.polystar.co.uk/exclusive-materials/biofilm/ [Accessed 3 October 2024]

Exhibit 5: Notes of meeting with Cuiting Zhang – Head of research and development

Current projects

The research and development projects broadly split into four key areas:

(a) Continued developments around beauty applications of Triticum Polymers with plans to patent Velasoft as hair growth and strengthening products in early 2023. Additional uses for Triticum Polymers in facial serums and as a suspension for delivering active botanicals to the skin are scheduled for commercial launch for Christmas 2023.

(b) Continued developments around the bio-plastics with a range of new clingwraps and bio-degradable packages for beauty products including skin care, hair care and make-up on behalf of premium brands are ongoing with most looking to launch in the next 12 to 18 months.

(c) Development of the new Polywaste technology which is taking bio-food waste as a source of carbon for polymerisation into polymers for either packaging or textiles.

(d) Preliminary work on a greener way to recycle plastic plant pots from the horticulture business into clothing polyesters.

Research and development (R&D) budget

Annually, TPP spends £5.6 million on R&D of which £1 million is funded by the company and the remainder is funded through direct grant partnerships with Estee Lauder, L'Oreal and Unilever. In common with other technology companies, TPP capitalises development costs and then amortises the balance once the product moves to full commercial production. The standard useful economic life of a development is taken as ten years.

As at 30 September 2022, the research and development balances listed in the accounts were:

Under development:

Beauty	
Velasoft	£65,450
Triticopol B456	£34,755
Triticopol A 67	£89,750
Triticopol Ser 43	£25,670
Packaging	
Triticum Polymers 569	£45,600
Polywaste	
PW 25	£56,800
Completed projects	£221,975

Exhibit 6: Article – Science behind the products

Why are polymers so important in health and beauty?

Due to their high efficacy, polymers are typically used in small quantities to fulfil various functions in formulations, including acting as: rheology modifiers (eg thickeners); surface active modifiers such as surfactants, emulsifiers and wetting agents; solubility modifiers including coupling agents and dispersants; bulking agents; preservatives; skin and hair conditioners; sunscreen agents; film-formers; aesthetic modifiers; coating agents/encapsulants; and abrasives/exfoliants.

(**Source**: Cosmetics & Toiletries. [Online] Available from: https://www.cosmeticsandtoiletries.com/cosmetic-ingredients/blog/21837598/polymers-in-personal-care [Accessed 3 October 2024])

Exhibit 7: Future research interests for TPP

Researchers from the University of Birmingham, UK, and Duke University, US, have created a new family of polymers from sustainable sources that retain all of the same qualities as common plastics, but are also degradable and mechanically recyclable.

The scientists used sugar-based starting materials rather than petrochemical derivatives to make two new polymers, one which is stretchable like rubber and another which is tough but ductile, like most commercial plastics.

The researchers made the new polymers using isoidide and isomannide as building blocks. Both these compounds are made from sugar alcohols and feature a rigid ring of atoms. The researchers found that the isoidide-based polymer showed a stiffness and malleability similar to common plastics, and a strength that is similar to high-grade engineering plastics such as Nylon-6. Despite isoidide and isomannide only differing by the 3D spatial orientation of two bonds, known as stereochemistry, the isomannide-based material had similar strength and toughness but also showed high elasticity, recovering its shape after deformation. Notably, the materials retained their excellent mechanical properties following pulverisation and thermal processing, which is the usual method for mechanically recycling plastics.

(**Source**: University of Birmingham. [Online] Available from: https://www.birmingham.ac.uk/news/2022/a-sweet-breakthrough-scientists-develop-recyclable-plastics-based-on-sugars [Accessed 3 October 2024])

Exhibit 8: Triticum Polymers plc, statement from the chairperson, October 2022

'We look back on 2022 as a year of important progress for Triticum Polymers. We have consolidated our customer base, entered into a new and exciting partnership with L'Oreal, and continue to expand our technology platform contributing to a broader base of recurring revenues. These advances continue to strengthen our ability to contribute meaningfully to the greening of many consumer products and help to provide a critical force for environmental responsibility in both the health/beauty and packaging sectors.

'Our polymers' commercial base is now well-established, and they are currently used in over 50 consumer products. Our patent-protected processes, used to produce the plant-based polymers we sell, are sustainable, effective and have the capacity to cheaply address the move from oil-based technologies. They use readily available wheat to create polymers needed by our modern world and in the process reduce carbon dioxide emissions. Through our innovative polymers, our intellectual property generates revenue in two core areas: health/beauty and packaging.

'Our progress has not translated into higher revenues and our financial results did not meet our plans for 2022. As detailed in our chief executive officer's statement, the volatility in wheat prices has eroded our margins and meant that our planned up-scale for packaging was delayed. Although demand for health and beauty has recovered somewhat since the Covid-19 pandemic, this temporary decline in cleaning revenues caused a 21.1% decline in revenues overall.

'As our polymers lead to new generations of more sustainable everyday products, our efforts were recognised in May 2022 by the London Stock Exchange. Triticum Polymers was awarded the LSE's Green Economy Mark, which identifies companies that are contributing to environmental objectives. We are very proud of this achievement, and this pride is shared by all our employees. I would like to extend special thanks to them for their valuable work and devotion to our mission of decarbonising the planet with proprietary plant-based products that enhance consumer products.

'In 2022, we continued to strengthen the foundation of our business through new customers, applications, and products. This progress is already manifesting itself in the current financial year and we look forward to the rest of the year and beyond with continued confidence and optimism.

'Thank you to all our stakeholders for your ongoing support. Together we are making a real difference.

Durak Pence
Chairperson 7 October 2022'

Exhibit 9: Notes from preliminary meeting with Irene McEvoy – Commercial development director

The company's products are formulated as key ingredients in a growing range of consumer products. They are now used in over 50 brands worldwide across a widening variety of beauty uses and are being sold in an increasing number of retailers. This increase in use, however, did not translate into higher revenues in 2022.

Health and beauty

Beauty revenues were £0.2 million in 2022 compared to £0.4 million in 2021, representing a 48.2% decline. The ongoing issues with the supply chains have fundamentally shifted customer purchasing patterns. Year-to-year revenues for the company's foundation ingredient sold through Estee Lauder were skewed by a large re-stocking order delivered in late 2021 that met a significant portion of their needs for much of 2022. This pattern of ordering to stockpile is being replicated through the sector and is making it difficult to manufacture to agreed-upon timescales. As we become more used to the revisions in order patterns, we should be able to manage these demand fluctuations more effectively.

Pressure from consumers for more sustainable products continues to grow and create opportunities for our ingredients. As described above, we see an attractive market in hair care for our technology platform and have filed a patent application for new plant-based hair care technology that we plan to launch as VELASOFT® BR 300 early in 2023.

Health revenues increased but as discussed revenues in beauty declined.

The most significant issue was in the packaging segment, where the impact of pandemic-driven inventory stocking by customers in late 2021 and early 2022 was followed by rebalancing of inventories later in 2022. These actions created low monthly volumes in the middle of 2022, which have since recovered as more regular order patterns have returned.

Despite these disruptions, the company continued to add important new brands and new uses to its commercial base. A major North American consumer brand launched a new cling wrap product that set a new level for sustainability and performance. A leading European sustainable cling wrap brand is using Triticum Polymers® TSI™ 569 in its new formulation that will launch in 2023.

New uses for Triticum Polymers include initial orders in a sustainable fashion application to replace fossil-based polymers although this may create a demand that is difficult to supply without expansion in wheat production. Negotiations with the National Farmers Union in the UK and the China Wheat Growers in China are very promising, and we are confident that wheat availability should increase from 2025. Although 2022 revenues were down, the company is well positioned for growth in the coming years.

Exhibit 10: Key commodity information

Wheat production 2020/21

Country	Production ('000 Tonnes)
China	134,256
India	107,590
Russian Federation	85,896
USA	49,691
Canada	35,183
France	30,144
Pakistan	25,248
Ukraine	24,912
Germany	22,172
Turkey	20,500

(**Source**: World Population Review. [Online] Available from: http://worldpopulationreview.com/country-rankings/wheat-production-by-country [Accessed 3 October 2024])

Key commodity information

The impact of Russia's 2022 invasion of Ukraine on global wheat production

Russia and Ukraine together account for nearly **30% of the global wheat trade**. Russia's 2022 military invasion of the Ukraine sent global wheat prices soaring, with Ukraine's production ability compromised and many countries restricting or shutting down trade relations with Russia. Russia is also a major supplier of fertiliser, vital to maximising crop yields, which adds another layer of complication for farmers

(**Source**: World Population Review. [Online] Available from: http://worldpopulationreview.com/country-rankings/wheat-production-by-country [Accessed 3 October 2024])

Chicago wheat futures edged higher to above $10.7 per bushel, rebounding from the two-week low of $10.3 earlier in June amid news of unfavourable growing conditions in North America, while geopolitical tension and food security concerns continue to hamper global trade. Prolonged dry weather posed a threat to harvests of winter wheat in US growing belts. Meanwhile, investors continued to monitor diplomatic developments regarding possible Ukrainian grain shipments. Expectations for the resumption of exports from Ukraine declined further as economic ties between the West and Moscow deteriorate, leaving the Kremlin unlikely to open trade corridors in the Ukrainian Black Sea and Sea of Azov ports. 22 million tonnes of Ukrainian grain are estimated to be stuck in port silos since shipments were halted on February 24. Prices are also supported by India's export ban. Despite news that the government may open trade with Indonesia, exports to other buyers remain halted.

(**Source**: Trading Economics. [Online] Available from: https://tradingeconomics.com/commodity/wheat [Accessed 3 October 2024])

Sugar beet

Country	Production ('000 Tonnes)
Russian Federation	42,066
France	39,580
USA	30,069
Germany	26,191
Turkey	18,900
Poland	14,303

Country	Production ('000 Tonnes)
Ukraine	13,968
China	12,078
Egypt	11,223
UK	7,620

(**Source**: Science Agriculture. [Online] Available from: https://www.scienceagri.com/2023/02/10-worlds-biggest-sugar-beet-producers.html [Accessed 3 October 2024])

Key commodity information

Summary of key factors impacting on beet production and pricing:

Weather conditions impact on both beet and cane production and so any fluctuations in overall sugar supply from either source will impact on the prices for sugar and therefore of beet. Beet pulp is the waste product from sugar beet refining and is traditionally used in the animal feed sector.

The demand for beet is also driven by the bio-fuel sector where it is one of the raw materials in bio-ethanol production.

Current geopolitical problems are adversely affecting the supply of beet as production in Ukraine will be only 67% of usual volumes and supply lines from that country are disrupted.

Commodity pricing

Wheat

	2022/23 prediction per bushel	2021 Average	Increase from 2020
Price in $	$11.81	$6.00	+ 57.4 %

Sugar beet

	2022 predicted	2021	2020
Price per tonne $	$262	$242	$251

Textile exchange 2025 recycled polyester challenge

Textile Exchange and the United Nations Framework Convention on Climate Change's Fashion Industry Charter for Climate Action are launching a joint initiative to further spur a shift in the market towards the uptake of recycled polyester (rPET) and the associated reduction in greenhouse gases (GHGs).

The 2025 Recycled Polyester Challenge serves as an important catalyst for change in the apparel and textile industry. We are challenging the apparel industry to commit to bringing the percentage of recycled polyester up from 14% to 45% at 17.1 million metric tons by 2025. The Challenge will continue the successful acceleration that began with Textile Exchange's 2017 Recycled Polyester Commitment.

We encourage brands to commit to the most ambitious uptake target possible. 80%–100% recycled polyester commitments from the brands in our community will be essential to reaching our 2025 45% recycled volume target and for building critical mass to reach an absolute 90% recycled volume share by 2030

Today, mechanically recycled polyester from plastic water bottles makes up the vast majority of recycled polyester; however, chemical recycling and, more specifically, textile-to-textile recycling will be a necessary part of reaching our goal. We recognise that more data are needed on the GHG reductions associated with chemical recycling and that even with less significant reductions compared to mechanical recycling, it is a key part of the solution. We will continue to explore roadmap scenarios as impact data evolve and as the textile-to-textile recycling market matures.

(**Source**: Textile Change. [Online] Available from: https://textileexchange.org/2025-recycled-polyester-challenge/ [Accessed 3 October 2024])

Exhibit 11: Environmental impacts of textiles

Environmental impacts of EU consumption of textiles and clothing are difficult to estimate due to their diversity and the fact that they occur around the globe. A 2006 Joint Research Centre (JRC) report estimated that while food and drink, transport and private housing account for 70% to 80% of the environmental impact of EU consumption, clothing dominates the rest with a contribution of 2% to 10% depending on the type of impact. A 2017 report by Global Fashion Agenda (GFA) estimated the EU's environmental footprint caused by the consumption of textiles at 4% to 6%. Going into more detail, the 2017 Pulse of the Fashion Industry report, put together by GFA and the Boston Consulting Group, estimated that in 2015, the global textiles and clothing industry was responsible for the consumption of 79 billion cubic metres of water, 1,715 million tons of CO2 emissions and 92 million tons of waste. It also estimated that by 2030, under a business-as-usual scenario, these numbers would increase by at least 50%.

Raw materials

The production of raw materials is responsible for a large share of the environmental impact of the textile and clothing industry, not least from growing crops for natural fibres. Cotton, which according to a 2015 report by European Clothing Action Plan (ECAP) accounts for more than 43% of all fibres used for clothes on the EU market, is considered especially problematic because it requires huge quantities of land, water, fertilisers and pesticides.

The environmental impacts of bio cotton can be drastically reduced compared to conventional cotton, as it uses less water and pollutes less. According to a Textile Exchange report, the share of sustainable cotton increased from 6% in 2012–2013 to 19% in 2016–2017. According to the 2017 Pulse of the Fashion Industry report, natural fibres have the highest environmental impact, with silk having an especially detrimental effect regarding depletion of natural resources and global warming, cotton contributing excessively to water scarcity and wool to greenhouse gas (GHG) emissions. However, the industry is also testing less frequently used natural fibres, such as hemp, flax, linen and nettle, that require less water, fertilisers and pesticides. Polyester, which is made of fossil fuels and is non-biodegradable, accounted for 16% of fibres used in clothes according to ECAP. Its main advantages are that, unlike cotton, it has a lower water footprint, has to be washed at lower temperatures, dries quickly and hardly needs ironing, and it can be recycled into virgin (new) fibres. Recycled polyester, made mainly from plastic bottles, increased its market share from 8% in 2007 to 14% in 2017. However, several studies have recently also shown that one load of laundry of polyester clothes (also nylon and acrylic) can discharge 700,000 microplastic fibres, which release toxins into the environment and can end up in the human food chain.

Estimates show that every year approximately half a million tonnes of plastic microfibres from washing clothes end up in the ocean. The industry is currently experimenting with bio-based polyester (also known as bio-synthetics), made at least partly from renewable resources such as starches and lipids from corn, sugar cane, beet or plant oils. While the challenge is to find feedstocks that do not compete with food production and that do not require large amounts of water and pesticides. Man-made cellulosics (MMCs), derived from cellulose made from dissolved wood pulp of trees, make around 9% of fibres used in clothes on the EU market. Most commonly used is viscose, also known as rayon. They are made from renewable plants and are biodegradable, but the main challenge is also the sustainable sourcing of cellulose, as the global production of MMCs more than doubled from 1990 to 2017. The industry is therefore working with innovative materials that are more sustainable, such as lyocell (also known under brand name of Tencel, made of cellulose from eucalyptus, which grows quickly and requires no irrigation or pesticides), bemberg (also known as cupro, made of cotton linter that cannot be used to spin yarn), and Piñatex (made of pineapple leaves).

(**Source**: EU Parliament. [Online] Available from:
https://www.europarl.europa.eu/RegData/etudes/BRIE/2019/633143/EPRS_BRI(2019)633143_EN.pdf [Accessed 3 October 2024])

A key player in the market for sustainable production of Viscose in the fashion industry is Lenzing Eco-Vero Viscose

As stated in their website:

'The introduction of LENZING™ ECOVERO™ branded viscose fibers marks a new milestone in Lenzing's sustainability journey. LENZING™ ECOVERO™ branded viscose fibers give you confidence your fashion choices are environmentally responsible and have a low environmental impact.

'LENZING™ ECOVERO™ Viscose fibers are derived from sustainable wood and pulp, coming from certified and controlled sources. LENZING™ ECOVERO™ fibers have been certified with the EU Ecolabel for textile products (license no. AT/016/001) as meeting high environmental standards throughout their life cycle: from raw material extraction to production, distribution and disposal. LENZING™ ECOVERO™ fibers can be robustly identified in the final product, assuring you that your purchase contains genuine LENZING™ ECOVERO™ Viscose fibers.

'Lenzing's wood sourcing policies for Viscose production are audited annually for their contribution to forest conservation, transparency, and commitment to sustainability. The introduction of LENZING™ ECOVERO™ is a major step towards these goals.'

(**Source**: EcoVero. [Online] Available from: https://www.ecovero.com/benefits-b2c [Accessed 3 October 2024])

Practice Case Study 3: Unseen case information and exam requirements

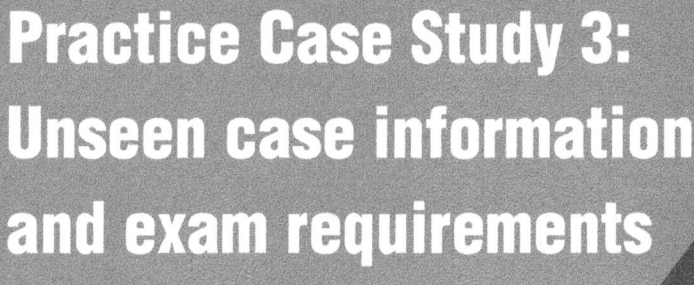

Topic list	Syllabus reference
1 Practice case study 3: Unseen case information	All LOs
2 Practice case study 3: Unseen information	All LOs

Introduction

This chapter contains the exam requirements relating to Case Study 3, Triticum Polymers plc, and the unseen material. In the real MDCS, you will also be given another copy of the pre-seen material which (for this Case Study) is in Chapter 19.

Important note: This practice case study is applicable for MDCS students following the accounting route, but its practice requirements are suitable for all MDCS students

Exam requirement

Triticum Polymers plc

You are an AIA professionally qualified accountant working for Triticum Polymers plc (TPP) which is a large multinational company listed on the UK Stock Market.

You have been seconded from the finance department where you work as a financial controller, into a newly formed Risk and Resilience Project which has been set up to support the work of the board in identifying and developing appropriate strategies to mitigate emerging risks and opportunities facing the company.

The project team contains four colleagues located around the world and you have been drafting the inaugural report for the board. As the most senior team member it has fallen to you to pull together the findings of the Team for this report.

Required

Draft the risk and resilience report for the board which:

(a) Identifies the key strategic risks facing TPP over the next five years. **(10 marks)**

(b) Critically appraises the viability of and the accounting and ethical issues arising from:

    (i) Polywaste development **(25 marks)**

    (ii) Purchase of Mangelwurzel Technology Ltd **(25 marks)**

For each project you must ensure that you address any issues raised specifically by the directors in their discussions and you must explore how each project resolves any of the strategic risks currently facing the company. You must ensure that any technical issues referred to are explained so that the directors can understand the implications of your advice or comments.

(a) Advises, with justification, the concerns you have regarding the internal control environment in Mangelwurzel and the steps which should be taken to resolve these if the purchase is to be recommended. **(15 marks)**

(b) Concludes, with reasons, what the next critical steps should be for TPP. **(10 marks)**

Professional marks are awarded for the quality of the professional skills demonstrated in this report.

(15 marks)

(Total 100 marks)

Professional marking criteria (15 marks):

- Report is presented in a style suitable for the audience articulated in the scenario. **(2 marks)**
- Structure of the paper is logical and clearly articulated to enable ease of navigation and discussion. **(2 marks)**
- Ideas are expressed clearly and in language accessible to the audience identified in the scenario. **(2 marks)**
- Technical terms are used accurately and explained where appropriate. **(2 marks)**
- Issues are appropriately prioritised within the structure of the report and the body of the discussion. **(2 marks)**
- Issues are assessed in a balanced and reasoned manner. **(3 marks)**
- Rationale behind assessment of issues and recommendations of responses is clearly articulated and alternative actions explored where appropriate. **(2 marks)**

Unseen material

Triticum Polymers plc (TPP)

Exhibit 1: Unseen contents

Exhibit 2: Email Exchanges

- Email One – Mangelwurzel culture
- Email Two – Concerns about Yiming Zhou
- Email Three – Concerns over cybersecurity
- Email Four – Discussion of board position for Mangelwurzel directors
- Email Five – Polywaste viability concerns

Exhibit 3: Polywaste

- Project details
- Budgeted costings
- Current progress report

Exhibit 4: Mangelwurzel Technology Ltd

- Outline of proposed purchase
- Details of technology
- Corporate governance statements
- Results of media search into company and directors

Summary of key personnel

Triticum Polymers plc (TPP)

Arthur Spence – Founder and CEO
Irene McEvoy – Founder and commercial development director
Cuiting Zhang – Research and development director and head of research
Yiming Zhou – Head research (waste technology)

Mangelwurzel Technology Ltd

Rinke Stena – CEO
Cathy Patel – Operations director
Christoff Schmidt – Research and development director
Ally Stena – Finance director

Exhibit 2: Email Correspondence

Email One – Mangelwurzel culture

Sender: Arthur Spencer
Recipient: Cuiting Zhang

Hi Cuiting,

Thank you for establishing the link with Mangelwurzel's team – it certainly looks like a very interesting synergy with TPP. I saw the results of the search done by the risk and resilience team into Mangelwurzel and the key players, but I am concerned that this is not picking up some of the issues that I have heard down the grapevine.

Irene had a meeting with a former employee of Mangelwurzel for the post of senior researcher with us. This conversation revealed some stark contrasts between the culture here at TPP and that experienced at Mangelwurzel. Although it may be that this is not the most objective assessment of working conditions, it does seem to support the findings of the BBC report, but it added in some other worrying context. When Irene explored the reason for leaving the prior employer the researcher cited an aggressive culture with a major focus on profit at all costs. He also discussed some issues over the probity of ingredients where he felt that short cuts were being taken which was leading to some misleading product descriptions. When he raised this with the team, his concerns were dismissed as 'being idealistic in a difficult global context.' She got the distinct impression that he would not be willing to work with TPP if the management or management culture of Mangelwurzel were with us.

That being said, I wonder if there are methods by which we could obtain the rights to Mangelwurzel's products without bringing across their management culture – with the strong culture we have at TPP, I would have thought that this would be possible, or am I being naive here? I did hear that Rinke and Cathy are wanting to take a step back from Mangelwurzel to start their retirement which is part of the rationale in seeking new partnerships. If this was the case, perhaps a contingent payment plan could be worked out for them, dependent on the performance of the new products.

We are having a meeting next week with the risk and resilience team and perhaps we can get a better feel for this then.

Best wishes,

Arthur

Email Two – Concerns about Yiming Zhou

Sender: Irene McEvoy
Recipient: Arthur Spencer

Hi Arthur,

I meant to let you know this morning over coffee that the rumour mill is in overdrive regarding Yiming Zhou. It seems that Polystar are very interested in recruiting Yiming to work on moving towards an extended bio-life product portfolio. As you know, they are very much larger than we are and have a significant international profile and it would potentially be an excellent career development and I am very concerned about the attractiveness of the offer. I was wondering whether we need to have a meeting with Cuiting and consider improving our remuneration package through share options and think about offering a board position. What do you think?

I am concerned that we are going to struggle to attract new high calibre staff as we continue to expand, and I think we need to develop a clear progression path for our critical personnel so that we show that we are serious about retention and development. My concern is, as always, our cash position – could we look at offering share options do you think? I know you hate the idea of diluting your control, but I think it may be a price we have to pay for the good of the future of the company.

My other concern regarding this project is the level of involvement that SAI Waste will have in the future revenues of the company – and our dependence on the working capital provided by this company.

I am also concerned about the current level of surety we have regarding the figures – I know you believe that payback period is the appropriate way of assessing viability of the projects but I would prefer using the more scientific discounted cashflow approach.

Perhaps we can raise this with the risk and resilience team in the next meeting?

Best wishes,

Irene

Email Three – Cybersecurity concerns

Sender: Cuiting Zhang
Recipient: Arthur Spencer

Hi Arthur,

I had a meeting last week with Yiming regarding the ongoing collaboration with SAI Waste on scaling up the Polywaste project. We seem to have some issues in getting the e-links between TPP and SAI Waste to function effectively due to our fire wall. Whilst I understand that IT are currently working on this, I am really concerned that this is leaving our systems vulnerable to cyberattack and the theft of our intellectual property.

Our first mover advantage is critical to obtain sufficient market share before the larger companies get involved – whilst we have excellent relations with some of the significant players in the industry, I fear that some international parties are not so ethical and would be happy to take advantage of any breaches.

I had a chat with the head of the risk and resilience team last night who alerted me to some issues with the probity of SAI Waste and has rather set alarm bells ringing for me on this partnership – what degree of due diligence and research have we done about this partnership? Do we really know who we are dealing with here? I know that there are some great green wins from going down this path, and some nice social benefits too but I am getting a bit worried about how this might read publicly. I know you hate all this concern about virtue signalling but I really think we need to take a little step back to ensure we have really thought it through – before we commit too much investment.

I am looking forward to the risk and resilience team meeting next week – I certainly think we have a lot to explore in it. Never a dull moment with TPP, is there?

Best wishes,

Cuiting

Email Four – Discussion of board positions for Mangelwurzel team

Sender: Irene McEvoy
Recipient: Arthur Spence; Cuiting Zhang

Dear Arthur and Yiming,

I have just had a meeting with Ally Stena, the FD of Mangelwurzel, regarding the accounts and the internal control structures currently in place. I am a little concerned at the information that Ally revealed.

She has alerted me to some issues regarding the valuation of research and development and, when I queried why these had been included in the accounts, she disclosed that Christoff has been very aggressive in his position regarding the recognition of the worth of the company. I saw the recent article in *East Today* regarding Christoff, and with the comments of that potential senior researcher, I am getting uneasy about the fit between us and this team.

I would be reluctant to offer the Mangelwurzel directors seats on the board and am certainly erring towards the second option with them of taking over the technology and not the company.

I am interested to see what the risk and resilience team have to say on our meeting next week.

Best wishes,

Irene

Email Five – Polywaste viability concerns

Sender: Cuiting Zhang
Recipient: Yiming Zhou
Cc: Arthur Spencer; Irene McEvoy

Dear Yiming,

I trust all is well with you and I hope you enjoyed your recent break.

I am dropping you this note before the risk and resilience meeting next week as I am a little concerned about the acceptance of the Polywaste technology. The technology is really exciting and the ability to take packaged waste from supermarkets and turn it into viscose polymers without sorting is fabulous. I can also see that it means that landfill waste would also be a possible source of the raw materials and that this has driven you to partnerships with SAI Waste but I am concerned that we are focusing the development in the wrong direction.

There is some evidence from focus groups that consumers may find the idea of wearing recycled food waste more difficult than the idea of clothing made from recycled plastics. This resistance is particularly evident when the source of the waste is from mixed and unclean sources. Although consumers in the focus group can accept the benefit of turning trash mountains into a useful polymer, the idea of wearing fabric derived from something perceived as dirty is more challenging than the idea of wearing fabrics which come from clean recycled uneaten food and waste.

I am also concerned that SAI Waste does not have the reputation as an ethical company and this may also increase resistance to the product and to our ethical reputation.

Can we discuss this in the risk and resilience meeting next week?

Best wishes,

Cuiting

Exhibit 3 – Polywaste technology project

The Polywaste technology allows the breakdown of food waste and petrochemical plastics into polymers which can be used to make viscose for fashion and also polymers for bio-packaging. This has a significant advantage over current viscose sources in that it doesn't require the use of land crops and would enable materials which would go to landfill to be put into use.

There are two key routes for generating the polymer commercially that TPP can pursue.

(a) **Partnership with SAI Waste**

This is currently under negotiation with SAI Waste who ship waste products from Europe for processing in Lokistan. Where the materials become contaminated SAI Waste has a number of very large land dumps where staff are employed sorting this into any recyclable elements by hand. They are very excited by the technology as they believe it will remove the need to dump waste on land and it would be able to be processed immediately. They are also keen to develop sites in Europe to process the waste, thus reducing the transportation costs and associated carbon footprint – and the costs to their company. SAI Waste are prepared to provide working capital of £750,000 to get the first UK site in the north-east of England operationalised with the proviso that they receive 25% of any revenues from future use of the technology for this waste processing from TPP. If sites are developed in Lokistan, SAI Waste have committed to providing the working capital for their development on their land – again with a split of the revenues streaming from the processes.

(b) **Supermarket packaged waste**

This waste processing was the initial focus of the technology developed by Yiming Zhou, who worked with Gold Supermarket and Hope University in the UK to develop the prototype technology. Unfortunately, neither the University nor Gold Supermarket are able to support TPP financially to take the next steps of scaling up the project to a commercially viable process and all of the costs will need to be funded by TPP. This approach allows a more piecemeal development and retains all of the financial benefits with the company. It is anticipated that the overall costs to develop a commercial process are £225,000 which the company is struggling to raise from its current financing arrangements.

There has been a preliminary meeting with Tesco and also Spar to see if they might be interested in a partnership and Marks and Spencer have also expressed interest in the project.

Projected costings

	Polywaste and SAI Waste partnership (costs)/operating profit	Polywaste for supermarket packaged waste (costs)/operating profit
2022/23	(£130,000)	(£75,000)
2023/24	(£130,000)	(£75,000)
2024/25	£50,000	(£75,000)
2025/26	£250,000	£85,000
2026/27 and onwards	£1,000,000 pa	£1,250,000 pa

Limitations with the figures relate to the actual adoption of the technology in the fashion industry or in bio-packaging. Some preliminary research showed some customer resistance to the idea of generating materials from food waste – or more concerningly landfill waste. Although environmentally very favourable, the idea of wearing recycled animal products did not sit well with potential customers who may be vegan or have religious restrictions around animal usage.

Child labour and landfill

'The kids are growing up in New Delhi's 70-acre Ghazipur landfill, a post-apocalyptic world where hundreds of pickers climb a 100-foot-high trash pile daily, dodging and occasionally dying beneath belching bulldozers that reshape the putrid landscape.

On 'trash mountain,' families earn $1 to $2 a day slogging through waist-deep muck. But the residents also marry, have children on their dirt floors, pray and celebrate life's other milestones.

'I am very proud to be a rag picker; we keep you healthy,' said Jai Prakash Choudhary, who has spent years scouring Delhi's dumps in search of cast-off bottles, metal, and even human hair.

An outgrowth of India's rapidly expanding middle class with its embrace of Western-style consumerism is ever more waste: New Delhi produces about 9,200 tons of trash daily, up 50% from 2007. The garbage is expected to double by 2024, leaving Ghazipur and two other landfills overflowing.

That's afforded the country's 1.7 million rag pickers – with 350,000 in New Delhi alone – more pickings, allowing some to dream of one day joining those middle-class ranks. Rising expectations and hunger for a better life are seen in small ways at Ghazipur, charity workers said. Children balk at donations of unfashionable clothing.

Twentysomethings sport stylish haircuts. Many listen to the latest pop tunes on cheap cellphones.

Choudhary is a symbol of that slow rise to the middle class, the desire for more. The rag picker, who's in his 30s, ran for councilman in this month's municipal elections here. Although he lost, his candidacy is an inspiration to other rag pickers, and he's promised to try again in a continuing effort to fight for their rights.

'Dirt comes from the top,' Choudhary said. 'Politics is a noble profession, but Indian politicians are not. I won't disappoint people.'

The first rung for many, including Choudhary, is trash mountain. Most of those living in the shanties ringing the garbage dump are Muslims from impoverished central Bihar state or illegal immigrants from Bangladesh, who learn quickly which wholesalers will pay the most for their trash, how to scratch out a few feet of living space, and where to scrounge for water and power.

In the trickle-down world of trash, they're at the bottom. Because New Delhi has no real door-to-door waste-collection system, the most 'desirable' refuse is snapped up by domestic workers or neighbourhood pickers, who then take the leftovers to select waste sites around the city. From there, trash trucks dump the rest at Ghazipur, where residents pick over the leavings.

'No one wants to be here if they can help it,' said Ram Karan, 35, as several sheep munched on trash nearby. 'It's a necessary evil.'

(**Source**: Stop Child Labour. [Online] Available from: https://stopchildlabor.org/many-children-in-india-live-and-work-in-landfills/ [Accessed 3 October 2024])

SAI Waste

SAI Waste is accused of complicity in the use of child labour in rag picking in a number of its key sites throughout Lokistan. Waste is taken from European countries for recycling but finds its way into the huge trash mountains owned by the company which cast a blight on major cities in the country. This reflects practices recently highlighted by the campaign group Stop Child Labour

Although there are strict laws prohibiting child labour a key child charity has exposed the practice by SAI Waste and has accused the company of window-dressing illegal activities as green practices allowing European countries to green wash their waste at the expense of the children of Lokistan.

Exhibit 4 – Mangelwurzel Technology Ltd

Mangelwurzel Technology

Company details

The company was founded in 2010 by Rinke Stena, Cathy Patel and Christoff Schmidt. All were working in research and development at Europe Green Systems when they discovered the method of making polymers from sugar beet pulp. However, Europe Green Systems decided against investing in the idea and the three scientists decided to set up Mangelwurzel Technology and develop the idea.

Since its incorporation, the company has grown slowly and is supplying raw polymers to 20 international customers in the health and beauty industry. The polymer is now widely used in solid shampoo and cleansing bars and in beauty balm moisturisers.

Mangelwurzel has been operating from a medium-sized factory in Poland which allowed easy transport access to Russian sugar beet pulp and was inside the EU with access to key personnel and easy trade links to customers in the EU. The factory was adapted from a food manufacturing plant but requires some considerable upgrade and extension if capacity is to be increased beyond the current operations. The equipment installed is able to be relocated but will also require upgrade and additional development to scale up activity.

The company employs 45 staff in Poland, 15 of whom have been trained with this specific technology through a schools' apprenticeship scheme.

Financial key performance indicators

	2022	2021
Revenue £'000	540	500
Gross profit £'000	170	154
Gross profit margin	31.4%	30.8%
Adjusted EBITDA £'000	40	22
Cash used in operations £'000	(233)	(215)
Net cash at the year-end £'000	45	278

Revenue is projected to increase by 45% in 2023, maintaining its gross profit margins.

Outline of proposed purchase

Mangelwurzel Technology have approached TPP with a proposal that the two companies merge with all of the directors of Mangelwurzel becoming full board members of the new company – TMP. In the course of the negotiations the idea of a merger has been abandoned and the options under discussion are:

(a) Purchase of 100% of share equity of Mangelwurzel for £2,575,000. In this option, they would also take over the final two years of the lease for the Polish factory, full ownership of the equipment and the patents for the technology. This option would value goodwill and intellectual property in the company at £2,350,000. Effectively, Mangelwurzel would become a fully owned overseas subsidiary of TPP.

(b) The payment would be financed partly in cash and through shares in TPP. As yet, the split of this has not been agreed and neither has the timing of the consideration.

With this option the current directors of Mangelwurzel would all be offered a seat on the board.

(c) Purchase of the patents for the technology and the equipment and the customer list. This would cost £2,400,000 split as follows:

Intellectual property and patents: £2,350,000
Equipment: £50,000

The total consideration again would be split between shares in TPP and cash and the timing for the payment is also a subject for ongoing negotiation.

With this option, none of the existing directors would take a place on the board although Christoff Schmidt would be offered a senior position in the research and development team and Ally Stena would be offered the position of group financial controller.

The manufacture would be transferred to a factory in the UK which TPP has access to for a peppercorn rent of £10 pa as it is currently lying idle near a key sugar beet processing plant in Lincolnshire. The owner of this factory is also the owner of the beet processing plant and is hoping that this incentive will persuade the team to move production to the UK and use the beet pulp from this producer. This would safeguard the future of 35 staff at this plant and create 40 new positions in an area of significant social deprivation.

Details of technology

Mangelwurzel Technology has developed the technique of producing polymers from the sugar pulp by-product of refining sugar beet. Traditionally, this is used as an animal feedstock. Due to changes in consumer meat consumption, Mangelwurzel anticipates that there will be surplus supply of this in the EU and UK over the next decades. This is disputed by some analysts, who believe that the increased demand from China for meat products will uplift beef, lamb and pork demand internationally and inflate sugar pulp prices.

The polymerisation of sugar beet pulp is efficient and uses little water in its processing and has proved successful at scale through the factory in Poland. The staff in Poland are well trained and committed to the company but are unable to transfer to work in the UK due to the new restrictions on immigration caused by Brexit.

Corporate governance arrangements

- CEO – Rinke Stena
- Operations director – Cathy Patel
- Research and development director – Christoff Schmidt
- Finance director – Ally Stena (cousin of Rinke)

The company was founded through a collaboration between Rinke, Cathy and Christoff with Ally joining once the company had expanded. It employs 45 staff in the Polish factory and 15 staff in the research and development arm of the business, currently located in the UK.

Neither Rinke nor Christoff have felt the need to establish a formal organisational structure in the research part of the business and the Polish factory is managed by an on-site senior manager supported by three teams of staff working eight-hour shifts and headed by a shift manager. The remuneration of the shift managers and the on-site senior manager are linked to productivity and there are concerns that this is leading to unfair employment practices.

Rinke and the management team are informal in their style. Christoff does not believe in 'sugar coating' criticisms of staff or fellow board members and Ally has found his personal style difficult to adapt to.

Ally Stena is a new finance director and has been concerned about the quality of the information in the financial statements. She has identified that the research and development capitalised has included a considerable value of general overheads and that it can't be related back specifically to the individual projects. She has some concern that the amortisation policy of 15 years is overly generous and has inflated the statement of financial position.

Her other key concern is regarding the strength of the internal control systems. The other board members regard the company as their baby and have a tendency to ignore the approval systems for petty cash, company credit card use and approval of purchases. Both Rinke and Christoff believe that research and innovation are the key to success and that the research team should have access to everything they require which has led to budgets being ignored and some occasional unplanned cashflow problems which Ally has struggled to manage.

Media search results: Mangelwurzel

Mangelwurzel new productivity in Poland

'Mangelwurzel Technology has initiated a new employment monitoring scheme in its manufacturing operations in Poland. New targets on productivity have been reported as 'putting an impossible pressure on workers' as they monitor the production of sugar beet pulp polymers and support the packaging processes, attempting to meet their targets. One anonymous source told our reporter, 'You can do it if you're basically a machine' they commented, before pondering how one could stand and concentrate for ten hours straight. 'I've never done a job like this […] the pressure is unbelievable,' they said.

'Other worrying employment practices emerged. Jobs at Mangelwurzel operate on a 'three strikes and you're out' system. If an employee is sick, they gain a point; if they are late, they gain half a point. This means employees are always desperately close to losing their jobs and are constantly aware of the precarious nature of their employment.

'We contacted **Professor Mike Marts**, who is a leading expert on stress at work. Shocked by the working conditions, he suggested they could cause 'increased risk of mental and physical illness' and noted that a job at Mangelwurzel offered 'all the bad stuff at once.'

'Mangelwurzel say that they 'comply with all relevant legal requirements' and their employees are their number one priority.'

Article in *Technology Today*, published 27 February 2022

Interview for *East Today* with Christoff Schmidt July 2022

'Christoff Schmidt is part of the founding team of Mangelwurzel Technology, a company based here in Lincolnshire. The innovative team at Mangelwurzel have developed technology to turn sugar beet pulp into polymers with a wide range of use in the plastics and beauty industry and are a key part of the Green Economy here in the east of England. I was therefore very interested to sit down with a key player in the developing green economy and explore his motivation and hopes for the future.

'Christoff appeared less focused on the green credentials of the business and much more interested in the potential profit that can flow from using an undervalued raw material and finding a valuable use for it. He was keen to explain that, in his opinion, realism in business is critical and the only successful companies are those which provide an excellent product at an excellent price – being able to exploit the green revolution to secure the future of the beet production here in Lincolnshire is not a main driver – without the issues regarding the acceptability of Russian beet the factory would not be considering moving back to the UK – although the proximity to the main customers here is a definite incentive now that Brexit has made cross-border European trade so difficult.

'I asked about the recent rumours of quality systems being reduced or ignored to speed up processing as revealed by a whistle-blower. Although these accusations were denied, he revealed that one of the issues with processing beet in Europe is the stringent and – to his mind – unnecessary safety and hygiene requirements which he is hoping will be reduced as the UK unpicks its alignment with Europe. In my supporting research I did not find any evidence that our government is intending to reduce such requirements and so I am concerned that the advantages of the move to the UK may not be as great as Christoff believes.'

Practice Case Study 3: Suggested solution

Topic list	Syllabus reference
1 Practice case study 3: Suggested solution	All LOs

Introduction

This chapter contains the suggested solution to the Triticum Polymers plc Case Study.

Suggested solution

Draft report to board of Triticum Polymers plc

(a) Introduction

This report articulates the initial findings of the cross departments Risk and Resilience Projects, convened in April 2022. This project has been commissioned to strengthen and support the work of the risk committee and the finance departments and to provide a forum in which new innovations can be robustly critiqued prior to presentation to the board.

This report reflects the initial analysis of the critical strategic risks facing TPP and then explores the viability of two projects – Polywaste and Mangelwurzel – in addressing these problems. The report analyses the internal control environment and makes recommendations regarding actions that TPP board should consider improving our competitive position.

Strategic risk analysis

Effective risk management is critical to the success of TPP and, given the volatility of current geo-politics and global economics, this risk and resilience project aims to support the ability of the company to identify emerging risks and to develop appropriate risk mitigations. As an innovative company. TPP's key success criteria is to provide effective and economic environmentally sensitive solutions to the beauty and packaging industries as part of its contribution to decarbonising the world. Therefore, risks relate to the ability of our products to meet this mission yet provide sufficient levels of financial reward to our investors.

Competition and technology

Our technology currently uses wheat as the raw material to our innovative products. As a key innovator, we have an extensive portfolio of research to extend the uses and efficacy of our current products and to seek new opportunities and applications for our current and emerging ideas. There is a risk that current lines of research prove expensive but unfruitful, or we are beaten to the market-place by a competitor.

Additional risk is posed by the work of P2 Science in terpene technology and Polystar with their work in sugar cane. These raw materials may offer increased or different efficacy and may be subject to different less significant commercial pressures.

Raw material supply and pricing

Our founding principle was the use of an abundant and readily available raw material as the source of our plant polymer. Material supply chains are currently under pressure from the political disruption in Ukraine which is threatening the availability of 30% of the world's wheat for 2022 and into 2023. This has caused future pricing of wheat to have increased by 57% this year and is predicted to rise further over the next few years. This pressure on wheat availability cannot be met entirely from other sources and, although China is increasing its production, it will still not fully meet its needs and therefore may not provide a reliable and cheap source.

Customer retention

The ability to retain key customers is critical to maintaining revenue streams. The loss of key customers could impact business results adversely. This may happen if there are reputational questions regarding the appropriateness of our technology versus that of our competitors. We are competing directly with P2 Science products derived from conifers which are not part of the food chain and the excellent reputation these are having with high-end brands, including Chanel, may tempt our beauty customers away. Any disruption with supply or increase in costs may force customers to refocus away from wheat and towards other sources from different raw materials.

Dependence on key personnel

The group depends on its ability to retain highly qualified managerial and scientific personnel. There are a limited number of candidates with the experience and skills to replace these key personnel. Attracting the best candidates can be highly competitive. Although TPP has conventional employment arrangements with key personnel aimed at securing their services for minimum terms, their retention cannot be guaranteed. This risk is exacerbated by the need to replace the skills of Arthur and Irene if they do decide to take a step back from the business.

Law and regulatory risk

Regulatory bans on the use of chemicals in beauty and other products are continually changing and evolving as our understanding of our environmental impact increases. Therefore we must ensure that our understanding of the possible impacts of our ingredients is up-to-date and we continually innovate to reduce our impact. The recent report by the EU into the environmental consequences of plant polymers indicate that there may be restrictions placed on the use of plant sources as polymers where it impacts on either the food supply to developed and particularly developing nations and where it may impact on bio-diversity.

Inflation risk

Global economies have experienced significant inflation during 2021 and 2022. The cost of raw materials increased as costs for shipping, energy and ingredients increased. These increases were partially recovered in selling price increases to customers, but the company may continue to struggle to pass these price rises on to customers. These pressures may also create recessive pressures in our key markets and demand from our customers may therefore reduce.

Foreign exchange risk

The Group's primary operations are in the UK, Europe and China. Revenue and costs are exposed to variations in exchange rates and therefore reported losses. As much of the manufacturing is in the UK, there are threats as Stirling weakens against the US$ and Euro.

(b) **Polywaste**

Financial viability

The financial viability of both routes for the technology looks favourable with both generating a stream of income around £1,000,000 per annum within the medium term.

The development of the commercial factory requires an initial investment of £1,500,000 and a potential site in the north-east of England has been identified if the operations are to be based in the UK. This would be depreciated over 20 years, as per the usual accounting policy, and this has been factored into the operating profit for the decision making. The amortisation of the development costs over ten years have NOT been factored into the profits and the accounting policy of ten years would require an additional cost of £26,000 in the SAI Waste partnership and an additional cost of £22,500.

The capital spend is not approved by the board as the funding source is unclear – and the potential cost of the plant may increase due to inflationary pressures.

There is, however, some considerable risk with the option of using supermarket waste as none of the potential partners have committed to providing the capital required to build the commercial plant.

There is less risk in the option to partner with SAI Waste as they have committed to provide £750,000 of investment in the UK plant development. If the option of building the factory in India is pursued this cost is reduced to £300,000, which would all be borne by SAI Waste.

Considering the Pay-back Periods:

- SAI Waste Partnership India Plant – Total investment costs = £260,000. Payback in Year 2.
- SAI Waste Partnership UK Plant – Total Investment Costs = £1,010,000. Payback in Year 3.
- Supermarket Partnership UK Plant – Total Investment Costs = £1,755,000. Payback in Year 4.

Please note, the development costs of the technology to date have been omitted from this consideration as they are sunk costs and the decision-making is on the costings going forward.

However, these figures are subject to some considerable uncertainty as, at present, it is unclear whether the commercial development will be completed for these costs, the pricing of the factory and the value of the revenue stream.

Discounted cashflow consideration

Although discounted cashflow is a recognised approach to project appraisal, the level of accuracy regarding these figures doesn't lend itself to the use of this approach and the variability in the inflation rate and cost of capital also introduces additional approximations.

As the payback period is over a short number of years, we believe that this is a more appropriate and reliable approach to take.

Strategic synergy

This strategy will move TTP away from its organic plant based raw materials and will allow the company to offer a wider environmental solution to waste – although this waste may not always be from natural sources which may impact on the green imagery widely used in brand development. Having a polymer that is derived from waste may also be more difficult to position in the beauty industry unless the brand communication is carefully handled.

Therefore, it may indeed be more sensible to regard this approach as a product diversification strategy and consider it concentric diversification (Ansoff's Growth Model) and move the customer base away from the health and beauty focus and into a replacement for industrial polymer uses – including fashion. There is evidence from the articles highlighted by our wider research, that there is appetite in clothing for materials generated from waste plastics and this could position itself in that arena.

This development is consistent with the organic growth that the company traditionally engages with and reflects the corporate mission of 'Innovate to Re-instate.'

Strategic risk resolution

Polywaste addresses the current risks in raw material supply and commodity costing that affect the wheat-based polymer. The raw materials for the process are readily available – and indeed there is an argument that they will not only be free but could be contributing to the income since they resolve the waste issue for many countries.

Risk issues

The technology is as yet unproven at scale and requires considerable additional resources to complete. The viability of the product therefore is not completely certain. The estimated time-scale is uncertain and the estimated costs are also uncertain.

As a concentric diversification project, Polywaste retains a focus around technical issues and eco-branding that the company is familiar with but moves into a new customer base where current strong customer relationships will not be helpful. Entry into these new customer markets may be more difficult to penetrate as the company does not have a track record of product success or a reputation upon which they can build.

There is also a key personnel risk – now that the innovation is in the public domain there is a risk that Dr Yiming Zhou may be approached by competitors to complete the work.

There are also risks that the technology is stolen via cyber-attack – it appears that there are vulnerabilities in the computer systems which could increase the likelihood of such an attack being successful.

The final key risk is that patent protection is not applied sufficiently quickly to protect the intellectual property allowing competitors to develop similar products at lower cost as they will have avoided the development costing element of the work.

Accounting issues arising

The key challenge for the accounting of Polywaste currently is around the recognition as development capital in intangible assets.

Under IAS 38 *Intangible Assets,* development costs may only be recognised where:

- It is technically feasible to complete the asset so that it will be available for use;
- Management intends to complete the asset and use or sell it;
- There is an ability to use or sell the asset. It can be demonstrated how the asset will generate probable future economic benefits;
- Adequate technical, financial, and other resources to complete the development and to use or sell the asset are available; and
- The expenditure attributable to the asset during its development can be reliably measured.

There is a significant problem with the final criteria as much of the initial work was common to three projects and so the start date for the recognition of the costs may be subjective. There will also be challenges in the attribution of the staff time to the project and the apportionment of overheads into this.

As explored in the risk discussion, there is some uncertainty over the technical feasibility of the project at scale.

Ethical issues

A key issue for the company is around sourcing the waste materials and the ability that the company has to influence the conditions that supplier employees are subjected to. The debates within the company show the level of concern felt by Cuiting.

The use of child labour is strictly prohibited and therefore the idea of using the Lokistan supplier would be problematic for the reputation of TPP. Additionally, the notion that this would enable SAI Waste to claim increased environmental credentials whilst still contributing to a growth in open waste sites and the associated environmental and public health issues presented by this would not support TPP's brand identity and may compromise its position in the FTSE4Good index.

The alternative sourcing from the supermarkets is more attractive, although it is only resolving issues of waste management in more affluent and well organised societies.

Mangelwurzel Technology

Financial viability

Profitability of product

The current profitability is higher than our existing wheat polymer at 31% over 27.1%. The key financial pressures on raw materials are likely to be less serious than experienced with the wheat as the international prices for sugar beet pulp appear less volatile and less susceptible to the current geo-political pressures and so this should be maintained in the short to medium term.

However, there is the risk that demand for animal feed rises and this may drive increases in raw material costs which could erode the profit margins reported.

Payback periods

Taking the second option, with a cost of £400,000.

Strategic synergy

The purchase of the Mangelwurzel Technology represents a new method of product portfolio development by the company as this will be the second time a product that was not researched and developed in-house by TPP will be manufactured and sold in the TPP family.

The product is however an excellent fit with the Triticum Polymer system, using an existing commodity crop, sugar beet and its cultivars, in a new form. Since it is another alternative plant-based polymer there should be no issues in using this in the health and beauty sector and so this allows existing customer base to be serviced from this new product.

Strategic risk resolution

In line with Polywaste, this would reduce dependence on the volatile wheat market and there is evidence that there is some additional capacity in beet pulp production internationally and prices have generally been decreasing prior to the issues with Russian Federation and Ukraine.

As the approach is to manufacture the polymer in the UK from UK beet, the currency fluctuations caused by a weakening pound are resolved and problems with supply logistics are removed.

Risk assessment

The addition of a new and unfamiliar technology into the business may require additional skills that are not possessed by the current staff. Although two key personnel will be joining the company, there will be significant training needs for the production team in the UK.

The approach requires new supply arrangements with new suppliers which may be difficult to develop at speed and at scale.

There is the ongoing risk of international sugar market volatility and an impact on beet pulp prices with the geo-political instability in Europe. As Russia and Ukraine supply into the world market is unstable – and for many countries Russian supply is being avoided – there may be comparable shortages in supply as we are experiencing with wheat.

The main competitor with this technology is Polyfine although this is not currently their major business focus and there is a risk that their current product has better efficacy and first mover advantage in the market.

Accounting issues arising

Technical background IFRS 3 *Business Combinations*: **Contingent consideration**

Contingent consideration must be measured at fair value at the time of the business combination and is taken into account in the determination of goodwill. If the amount of contingent consideration changes as a result of a post-acquisition event (such as meeting an earnings target), accounting for the change in consideration depends on whether the additional consideration is classified as an equity instrument or an asset or liability (IFRS 3.58):

- If the contingent consideration is classified as an equity instrument, the original amount is not remeasured.

- If the additional consideration is classified as an asset or liability that is a financial instrument, the contingent consideration is measured at fair value and gains and losses are recognised in either profit or loss or other comprehensive income in accordance with IFRS 9 or IAS 39 *Financial Instruments: Recognition and Measurement*.

- If the additional consideration is not within the scope of IFRS 9 (or IAS 39), it is accounted for in accordance with IAS 37 *Provisions, Contingent Liabilities and Contingent Assets* or other IFRS Accounting Standards as appropriate.

Where a change in the fair value of contingent consideration is the result of additional information about facts and circumstances that existed at the acquisition date, these changes are accounted for as measurement period adjustments if they arise during the measurement period.

The key accounting issues will be dependent upon the approach taken to finance the purchase of the intellectual property and associated fixed assets which will impact upon the calculation of the fair value of the assets acquired. There will also be challenges in deciding the valuation split between the assets and the appropriate amortisation and depreciation policies to be applied. By acquiring 100% of the equity of MT, the accounting treatment will fall under IFRS 3.

Fair value accounting requires that the assets are recognised at their fair value consideration on acquisition and then this fair value is reviewed to ensure that any impairments are reflected annually.

The fair value of the consideration is the total of the cash consideration and the value of the shares on the purchase date plus an estimate of the contingent consideration payable to the CEO and Founder, Rinke Stena and the other technical staff.

The contingent arrangements for payments to Cathy Patel and Christoff Schmidt will be treated as remuneration as both will be working for the company and it is dependent upon their successful continued developments of products.

The consideration to Rinke Stena will depend upon whether the consideration is considered to be an equity instrument or a financial instrument. Given the current information on the arrangements being negotiated, it would appear more likely that this would be treated as a financial instrument under IFRS 9 *Financial Instruments* and therefore this will be valued at fair value and restated through the income statement leading to fluctuations in performance. Although the directors may prefer to recognise this as an equity instrument as it would allow all success of the new acquisition to appear in the income statement and therefore in the KPIs, this would not be permitted.

Ethical issues

The key ethical issue in the purchase of Mangelwurzel Polymers is the impact on the existing employees and suppliers as TPP focus on gaining the maximum economies of scale.

TPP could elect to purchase the existing factory based in Poland and use the beet pulp from this production. However, to maximise return on the purchase, TPP may not include the factory and the staff in the purchase. This would make the current loyal and competent workforce redundant. Transferring production into the UK, where there is a surplus of beet pulp production in Lincolnshire would have environmental and social benefits. This would also safeguard the jobs of a key beet pulp supplier in Lincolnshire, reduce the fuel requirements to transport commodities and, as the main customer is based in the UK, significantly reduce wider risks and environmental costs in the supply chain.

(c) **Internal control environment challenges**

Internal control environment in TPP reflects the attitudes, awareness and actions of those charged with governance and management concerning the internal controls.

As defined by ISA 315 *Assessment of Risk* (revised 2020), there are five key principles which should be considered in the assessment of this control environment.

- The organisation demonstrates a commitment to integrity and ethical values:
    - The effectiveness of controls cannot rise above the integrity and ethical values of the people who create, administer, and monitor them;

- Integrity and ethical behaviour are the product of the entity's ethical and behavioural standards or codes of conduct, how they are communicated (eg through policy statements), and how they are reinforced in practice (eg through management actions to eliminate or mitigate incentives or temptations that might prompt personnel to engage in dishonest, illegal, or unethical acts);
- The communication of entity policies on integrity and ethical values may include the communication of behavioural standards to personnel through policy statements and codes of conduct and by example.

- The board of directors demonstrates independence from management and exercises oversight of the development and performance of internal control.
- Management establishes, with board oversight, structures, reporting lines, and appropriate authorities and responsibilities in the pursuit of objectives.
- The organisation demonstrates a commitment to attract, develop, and retain competent individuals in alignment with objectives.
- The organisation holds individuals accountable for their internal control responsibilities in the pursuit of objectives.
- Mechanisms to communicate and hold individuals accountable for performance of controls responsibilities and implement corrective actions as necessary.
- Establishing performance measures, incentives and rewards for those responsible for the entity's system of internal control, including how the measures are evaluated and maintain their relevance.
- How pressures associated with the achievement of control objectives impact the individual's responsibilities and performance measures, and how the individuals are disciplined as necessary.

Critical issues in internal control environment at Mangelwurzel and its impact on TPP

There are three critical challenges facing the internal controls of the company from the acquisition of Mangelwurzel which can be summarised as:

- **New personnel.** New personnel may have a different focus on or understanding of the entity's system of internal control and the integration of the shift managers from Poland into a quality focus over a profit/productivity focus may be difficult. Depending upon the positions assumed by Rinke, Cathy and Christoff, these issues may be exacerbated. As Christoff has revealed a focus on profit and a disregard for quality and the green ethos, this could create real conflict at senior level in the direction and development of the products. If the personnel in Poland are retained, the change in culture to quality green products may be especially difficult.

- **Corporate restructurings.** Restructurings may be accompanied by staff reductions and changes in supervision and segregation of duties that may change the risk associated with the entity's system internal control. As explored above, this will be impacted by the positions that the Mangelwurzel directors take up in TPP and will need to be carefully managed. If the Polish factory is closed and production moved to the UK, there may be real challenges in recruiting and training competent individuals who have their values aligned with TPP's vision. This will be exacerbated if, as planned, the shift managers from Poland would be retained and used to train the workforce.

- **New technology.** Incorporating new technologies into production processes or the information system may change the risk associated with the entity's system of internal control.

From the information obtained by Irene and the issues raised in the interview there are clear issues with Mangelwurzel from the integrity and vision of the team and the problems with how individuals are held accountable for their actions around internal controls. The mission and values of Mangelwurzel appear to be very focused on the maximisation of profit, seeing the environmental pay-offs' as incidental to the work of the company rather than core. As well as potentially damaging the reputation of TPP and compromising its recognition by the LSE, this may cause conflict within the board and make decision making more difficult.

The recent adverse treatment of the staff in Poland and the decision to use Russian Federation beet at a discount all point to a management team whose integrity may not be consistent with that of TPP. Additionally, questions regarding the compliance with accounting policies in the treatment of research and development expenses do not support a team who can be relied upon.

The issues raised by Ally seem to suggest that the management team will not easily integrate into the values of TPP.

Suggested resolution

The key resolution of these issues would involve a clear articulation of the mission and values of TPP embedded through transparent and monitored quality assurance systems with the day-to-day management of the Mangelwurzel business transferred to a TPP senior manager to ensure that these values are communicated effectively to new staff.

It would therefore be much better if the second option were pursued and none of the directors of Mangelwurzel were offered seats on the board.

(d) **Conclusion and recommendations**

Both of the options for development at TPP are financially viable and address critical strategic issues for the company.

The advantages of Polywaste are the extension of the environmental solutions offered by the company in the ability to reduce plastics and food waste and have a significant impact on reducing greenhouse gas production from human consumption. This technology, once successful, will be very valuable and will position the company for the future. It also retains the tried and tested ethos of the company in organic growth and avoids many of the challenges with diluting leadership and vision on the board which could result from the purchase of Mangelwurzel.

Another significant advantage will be the ability to move into textile raw materials and to take advantage of the opportunities in green fashion although this will require new customer and supply chains.

The risks in this project are however the risk that it fails to scale up and the potential loss of the financial investment.

As there is evidence that additional investment in the company from current backers in the beauty business may not be forthcoming against this risk, and there is little available liquidity to move quickly forward it is proposed that we file for patent protection of this technology and then seek alternative partnership to finance the development to scale production.

The advantage of purchasing Mangelwurzel Technology is that there is certainty over the viability of the technology at scale and the polymer will meet the potential shortfalls caused if the world wheat capacity is compromised and prices continue to rise. This product sits easily in the company's customer base and will enable TPP to expand at increased pace.

The disadvantage of the purchase is around the impact on the culture and leadership of the company and the risks involved in moving the production from Poland into the UK and the costs of such rationalisation.

However, with careful management of the rationalisation and its impact on our ethical reputation, together with the implementation of the internal control recommendations above, this option should be further investigated by the board with intention to complete the purchase by 31 December 2022.

Practice Case Study 4: Pre-seen material

Topic list	Syllabus reference
1 Practice case study 4: Pre-seen case information	All LOs

Introduction

This chapter contains the pre-seen material relating to Case Study 4, Whoosh.

It includes:

(1) Whoosh plc – background information
(2) Extracts from the audited consolidated financial statements for the year ended 30 September 2019
(3) Extract from minutes of Whoosh board meeting, 13 May 2019
(4) Extract from minutes of Whoosh board meeting, 12 July 2019
(5) Emails between Gillian Sanderson, CFO, and Bryan Ibid, financial controller, 23 July 2019
(6) Email from Emily Sage, corporate affairs manager, to John Dwight, CEO, 22 June 2020
(7) Inter-office memorandum, Eaton Associates, 15 July 2020
(8) Two articles from *Flying Today*
(9) Notes from presentation to the board by Vicky Hunt, chief people officer, 29 September 2020

This case study was written in February 2020 when the implications of Covid-19 on the airline industry, public health and the world economy were only starting to be understood. Given the rapidly changing situation, and the fact that the lasting implications will not be known until after the publication of this book, you should **ignore** any issues relating to Covid-19 in your answer.

Exhibit 1: Whoosh plc – Background information

It is 2 October 2020.

Whoosh plc (Whoosh) is a low-cost airline which was formed in 2005 by British businessman, John Dwight. Whoosh has a head office in Castle Donington, close to East Midlands Airport, and operates flights to 40 destinations within Europe.

Selected financial and operating data is provided below:

	2019	2018	2017	2016	2015
Total operating revenues (£'m)	1,540	1,480	1,330	1,295	1,150
Profit before taxation (£'m)	170	258	265	243	169
Operating margin	12%	18%	18%	17%	15%
Break-even load capacity	85%	76%	76%	78%	80%
Total revenue per booked passenger (£)	59.65	60.55	62.35	64.15	67.70
Number of employees	3,407	3,216	3,165	3,080	2,918

Whoosh prepares its financial statements to 30 September each year.

The directors of Whoosh are as follows:

Director's name	Responsibility
John Dwight	Chief executive officer
Gillian Sanderson	Chief financial officer
Colin Partridge	Chief operations officer
Vicky Hunt	Chief people officer
Tony Ruffleson	Chief commercial officer
Kiran Kothari	Chief risk and compliance officer
Admiral Patrick Clayton	Non-executive chairperson
Lady Lucy Swires	Non-executive deputy chair
Lord Shail Vaz	Non-executive director
William Bates	Non-executive director
Carol Beacham	Non-executive director
Steven Li	Non-executive director

Whoosh has a subsidiary which provides in-flight catering. In July 2019, in order to reduce costs, a decision was made to outsource its customer service call centre. In May 2020, Whoosh set up a 50:50 joint venture with BrasovAir, a charter airline based in Romania, to set up a call centre in Bucharest, which will provide customer service support to both airlines.

Further details regarding the joint venture are as follows:

- The joint venture company invoices both of its shareholders (Whoosh plc and BrasovAir) for call centre services on a monthly basis, based on call volumes and using a normal industry mark-up on costs.

- Whoosh plc and BrasovAir have appointed a board of directors for the joint venture who make the key strategic decisions for the company and are all based in Romania.

- The joint venture is registered for VAT in Romania.

- The functional currency of the joint venture is the Romanian Leu.

- Romania is a member of the EU and the corporate tax rate is 16%.

Whoosh is audited by Eaton Associates, a medium-sized audit with national and international affiliations. BrasovAir is audited by Baciu & Co and the joint venture will be audited by the same firm.

Exhibit 2: Extracts from the audited consolidated financial statements for the year ended 30 September 2019

Whoosh plc
Consolidated statements of profit or loss for years ending

	30.9.19 £m	30.9.2018 £m
Operating revenues	1,540.2	1,479.7
Operating expenses		
– Fuel and oil	490.1	429.2
– Airport and handling charges	243.7	229.1
– Staff costs	198.4	169.8
– Route charges	139.2	124.4
– Depreciation	126.9	119.6
– Marketing and distribution	101.2	89.8
– Maintenance and repairs	36.2	28.7
– Aircraft rentals	19.3	17.9
Total operating expenses	(1,355.0)	(1,208.5)
Operating profit	185.2	271.2
– Finance charges (net)	(14.2)	(13.8)
– Foreign exchange (loss)/gain	(0.9)	0.6
Total other income/(expenses)	(15.1)	(13.2)
Profit before taxation	170.1	258.0
– Tax charge for the year	(32.4)	(48.9)
Profit for the year	137.7	209.1

Whoosh plc
Consolidated statements of financial position as at

	30.9.19 £m	30.9.18 £m
ASSETS		
Non-current assets		
– Property, plant and equipment	1,996.8	1,675.0
– Intangible assets	27.3	18.9
– Derivative financial instruments	46.8	60.4
Total non-current assets	2,070.9	1,754.3
Current assets		
– Inventories	0.5	0.4
– Trade receivables	11.4	10.8
– Derivative financial instruments	64.9	53.7
– Financial assets: cash > 3 months	216.8	198.1
– Cash and cash equivalents	101.3	199.2
Total current assets	394.9	462.2
TOTAL ASSETS	2,465.8	2,216.5

	30.9.19 £m	30.9.18 £m
LIABILITIES AND SHAREHOLDERS' EQUITY		
Current liabilities		
– Trade payables	130.5	101.2
– Accrued expenses and other liabilities	389.2	385.4
– Current amount of debt owing	60.2	76.3
– Current tax	6.2	6.6
– Derivative financial instruments	76.9	78.7
Total current liabilities	**663.0**	**648.2**
Non-current liabilities		
– Provisions	29.2	15.1
– Derivative financial instruments	1.4	87.2
– Deferred tax	96.3	75.1
– Other creditors	0.2	0.8
– Non-current portion of debt owing	684.2	421.6
Total non-current liabilities	**811.3**	**599.8**
Shareholders' equity		
– Issued share capital	1.6	1.6
– Share premium	115.6	115.6
– Retained earnings	814.6	805.2
– Other reserves	59.7	46.1
Shareholders' equity	**991.5**	**968.5**
TOTAL LIABILITIES AND SHAREHOLDERS' EQUITY	**2,465.8**	**2,216.5**

Exhibit 3: Extract from minutes of Whoosh board meeting, 13 May 2019

New aircraft purchase

Colin Partridge has estimated that we need to increase the fleet size by 20 over the next five years. We currently operate from a single aircraft – the Airspace 500 – but there are plans to begin to also operate the new Airspace 500 MAX (which has a much bigger capacity) in the near future. It has been suggested that we acquire five new aircraft by 1 October 2019 to add to the 5 Airspace 500 MAX that we're expecting to take delivery of in 2023. Initial estimates of the options to achieve the acquisition in 2019 are:

Buy outright

Colin reported that the cost of a new Airspace 500 MAX starts at US$102 million, so around US$105 million with our modifications. However, John Dwight pointed out that we would need to have ordered these several years ago as there is significant lead time, plus we don't have enough cash to buy outright. Colin reported that Airspace 500s generally (not the MAX model) are around US$85 million to purchase new and unmodified.

Traditional lease

Colin stated that we could lease an Airspace 500 MAX on a 10-year lease for US$1,015,000 per month. (Assumed conditions: Paid in arrears, interest rate of 3% p.a.) Or we could lease an Airspace 500 on the same terms for $820,000 per month. We would own the aircraft outright after 10 years.

Wet lease

We could lease aircraft and crew using some kind of wet lease when we need them in order to accommodate seasonal increases in capacity. Colin reported that terms will depend on how many hours we use. Colin estimates that we can lease an Airspace 500 for US$2,750 per hour. If we commit to 400 hours guaranteed usage per month, that comes to $1.1 million per month.

Exhibit 4: Extract from minutes of Whoosh board meeting, 12 July 2019

Financing

In order to finance the lease of five new aircraft in the next financial year, the board made a preliminary decision to consider one or more of the following options:

(a) To hold a rights issue

(b) To issue corporate bonds

(c) To close down the call centre and outsource overseas, perhaps to Eastern Europe where costs are cheaper

(d) Replace part of the remuneration of directors and senior management with share options.

Responsibility: John to research and report back on option (c), Gillian to research and report back on (a), (b) and (d).

WhooshGives

The board decided to extend the WhooshGives community involvement programme by increasing the level of funding allocated to it by 10%. As a result, more Whoosh employees will be able to take paid leave in order to spend time making a difference working on community projects of their choosing. To date, Whoosh has sponsored over 4,000 projects, most recently building shelving at a food bank, planting fruit trees in a community orchard and redecorating a community centre.

Exhibit 5: Emails between Gillian Sanderson, CFO and Bryan Ibid, financial controller, 23 July 2019

From: Gillian Sanderson, CFO
To: Bryan Ibid, financial controller
Date: 23 July 2019
Subject: Re: Wet leases

Hi Bryan

No problem, it takes all of us a while to get up to speed with industry jargon.

Basically, a wet lease involves leasing an aircraft that is fully staffed, maintained and insured. In other words, the lessor, which is often another carrier, provides the flight crew, cabin crew and ancillary services, as well as the aircraft. This contrasts with a dry lease, which is simply the lease of an aircraft. In this case, the lessor is usually a specialised aircraft leasing company such as Aerofund or Avilease Holdings. Just to confuse you even further, a damp lease is the lease of an aircraft, flight crew and maintenance services, but no cabin crew!

Wet leasing is not a structure which we've used in the past, but it's very flexible, which is why John is thinking of using this type of lease on some of the newer routes where we're not sure about demand. When the routes are established, we might switch to a dry lease, or possibly buy new aircraft, and recruit our own flight and cabin crew, but until then we can avoid incurring fixed staff costs.

Let me know if you want to meet to talk a bit more about this and any accounting implications.

Gillian

>>>>>>>>>>>>>>>>>

Original message

From: Bryan Ibid, financial controller
To: Gillian Sanderson, CFO
Date: 23 July 2019
Subject: Wet leases

Hi Gillian

I'm sorry if this is a daft question, but what are wet leases? John mentioned them in the meeting today, but I wasn't quite sure what he meant. I'm guessing this is an airline specific thing?

Thanks

Bryan

Exhibit 6: Email from Emily Sage, corporate affairs manager to John Dwight, CEO, 22 June 2020

From: Emily Sage, corporate affairs manager
To: John Dwight, CEO
Date: 22/6/20
Subject: Environmental reporting

Hi John

I've just been reading *Flying Today*, which has covered a consultancy report produced by Brighter Globe on air travel carbon and energy efficiency. It showed Robinair and Orange Jet to be two of the most energy efficient airlines, which it seems has resulted in a big increase in their share prices. I know that historically we've been reluctant to get bogged down in environmental reporting, but I think the time has come where we have to seriously consider it. It's not like we're not doing this stuff anyway – the report said that Robinair reduces carbon emissions by flying smaller planes with higher load rates, which is exactly what we're doing too. I'd suggest that if we do go down this route, we go a step further and look into <IR> Integrated Reporting, which is becoming more widespread. I appreciate that you may not be familiar with this, so I'd be happy to give a presentation to you and the rest of the board. If we make a decision soon on the way we want to do this, we could work on making the 2021 Annual Report an integrated report.

Let me know what you think.

Emily

Exhibit 7: Inter-office memorandum, Eaton Associates, 15 July 2020

Eaton Associates
Inter-office memorandum

From: Daniel Brevwood, International Liaison partner
To: Siobhan Armitage, Senior Partner, Nottingham Office
Date: 15 July 2020
Subject: Whoosh overseas call centre

Hi Siobhan

Hope you're well and the heat isn't too bad up there? It's verging on tropical in London at the moment!

I've heard back from Peter Asparov in Budapest. I'm not sure how much contact you've had with the Eastern European affiliates, but he's in charge of Hungary, Romania and Albania. Apparently, the Romanian-affiliated firm left the network in March on bad terms, so I'm afraid we're not going to get much help from them.

One of our Hungarian staff also speaks Romanian (and English, clever chap) and has had a look at BrasovAir's website. Apparently, it is audited by a firm called Baciu & Co, but he said they had a very sparse website, so he couldn't find out much.

Sorry not to be of more help.

Dan

Exhibit 8: Two articles from *Flying Today*

Flying today

Dream becomes a reality for Whoosh

By Staff Writer, 2 April 2015

Ten years ago, John Dwight had a dream; the self-professed flying nerd had always wanted to own his own airline and so, after 20 years of successful hedge-fund management, he launched Whoosh.

He's a brave man. He took on the established giants of the low-cost flight industry, including Robinair and Orange Jet, and earned himself lots of attention, both positive and negative, from the bosses of both.

Like its European low-cost competitors, Whoosh followed the low-cost strategy developed by Northwest Airlines in the US. Unlike full-service airlines, such as GB Airways, Whoosh charges separately for everything except the ticket; passengers pay extra for checked baggage, seat allocation, food and beverages and entertainment.

Whoosh also reduces costs by operating a single type of aircraft, the Airspace 500, which cuts down on maintenance costs. It also operates via smaller regional airports, which charge lower landing fees. Other measures, such as only accepting online booking, removing seat-back pockets to reduce weight and cleaning costs, and steeper take-off and landing trajectories to utilise less fuel, have combined to produce an impressive operating margin of 15%.

And Dwight does not plan to stop there. His next brainwave is to offer businesses the right to paint planes in their corporate colours and logos, to have naming rights to planes, and to advertise on seat backs. He also plans to use Whoosh's online traffic to help affiliates sell related services such as hotel rooms, hire cars and luggage, taking a percentage of each sale as commission.

Whoosh currently flies to 30 European destinations and Dwight has ambitious plans to double that within the next decade, helped by a new loyalty scheme, WhooshMiles. After the achievements of the last decade, only a fool would question his chances.

Flying today

More problems for Airspace's 500 MAX

By Staff Writer, 21 February 2020

The return to service of Airspace's crisis-hit 500 MAX jetliner was thrown into doubt after debris was found in the fuel tanks of several new planes which were in storage, awaiting delivery to airlines. It comes as the 500 MAX remains grounded after two fatal crashes.

A company spokesman told Flying Today: 'In the process of conducting maintenance, we discovered Foreign Object Debris (FOD) in undelivered 500 MAX airplanes currently located in our storage facility. That finding led to an in-depth internal investigation and immediate corrective actions in our manufacturing system.'

The revelation is the latest in a series of problems affecting what was once Airspace's best-selling plane. The 500 MAX was banned from flying after two separate crashes killed 279 people, leading to the plane being grounded by regulators around the world in December 2018.

An Airspace spokesperson said the company didn't expect the issue to cause any fresh delays to the 500 MAX's return to service, which the company said could happen by the middle of this year.

John Dwight, CEO of Whoosh, said: 'Although we are concerned at the latest revelations, we remain confident in the quality of manufacturing at Airspace and in the long-term future, of the 500 MAX. We believe this aircraft will be revolutionary in the next phase of low-cost airline travel, offering as it does a lighter plane with more seats, thereby slashing fuel cost per passenger and offering exciting possibilities for reduced fares for passengers. We are looking forward to receiving the five planes we have on order that are scheduled for delivery in 2023.'

Exhibit 9: Notes from presentation to the Whoosh board by Vicky Hunt, chief people officer 29 September 2020

People function

Whoosh depends on the high level of skills and professionalism of its people. Over the past two years, the People Function has evolved from an administrative unit to a professional value-added service partner. The People Function is delighted to have been nominated for an HR Excellence Award in recognition of this achievement.

Headcount and people initiatives

Executive directors

The executive board has remained unchanged throughout the financial year. We do not expect any board members to leave the company during the next two years.

Senior management

The senior management tier has undergone some changes in this financial year, with the headcount reduced from 63 to 61 as a result of retirement. We elected not to fill the vacant positions and instead, took the opportunity to streamline certain areas of management. This has released funds to support the recruitment of more ground staff in order to provide customers with a smoother airport experience.

In addition to the reduction in senior management headcount, which arose due to these retirements, two other senior managers left Whoosh, both transferring to competitors' operations. We were able to recruit high calibre individuals with extensive experience in their areas of expertise to replace these leavers.

In the coming two years, we expect the staff turnover rate at a senior management level to be low, thanks to the new share option scheme. We are currently budgeting for one leaver per year.

Ground staff

We have applied our new 'Jobs4All' policy to increase ground staff headcount by 10% in our home airport and selected other locations. This policy has allowed us to recruit senior citizens, disabled individuals and ex-offenders into appropriate positions within the organisation. We continue to actively recruit individuals who bring vital skills and knowledge to Whoosh, yet struggle to find employment due to their circumstances.

In the coming year, we will implement the new integrated Whoosh computer system which deals with all aspects of operations from reservations to crew flying schedules. All ground staff will be extensively trained in the system and we anticipate a resulting increase in efficiency and reduction in personal stress.

Flight and cabin crew

Whoosh has maintained a steady headcount of flying staff over the last year. Staff turnover has been at 2-3%, with leavers generally retiring or leaving due to family commitments. Our Pilot Recruitment Programme has continued to focus on the 'WhooshWings' programme, which sponsors high calibre individuals through university before putting them through standard and advanced commercial pilot training.

The first phase of a new capability development programme has been implemented in the year for cabin crew. This entails customised classroom and project-based training in order to develop competencies. Feedback received to date is positive and the phase two roll out will commence in the next financial year.

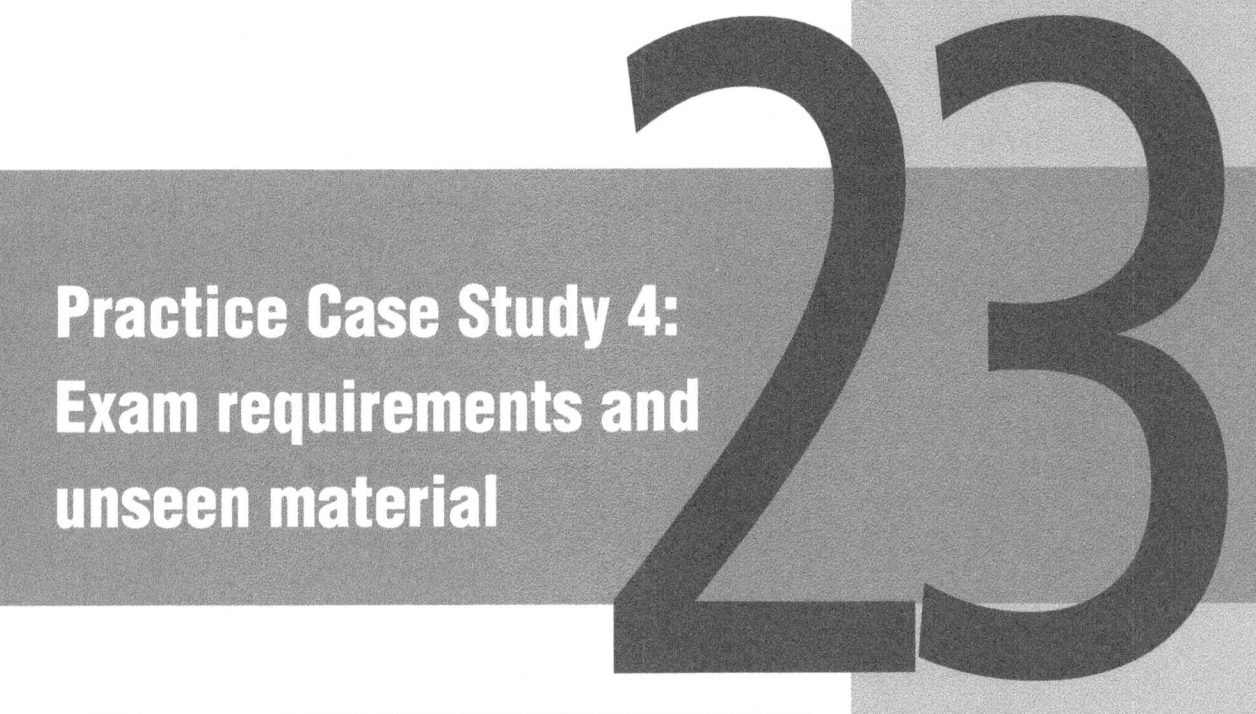

Practice Case Study 4: Exam requirements and unseen material

Topic list	Syllabus reference
1 Practice case study 4: Unseen case information	All LOs
2 Practice case study 4: Unseen information	All LOs

Introduction

This chapter contains the exam requirements relating to Case Study 4, Whoosh, and the unseen material. In the real MDCS, you will also be given another copy of the pre-seen material. For this Case Study, the pre-seen material is in Chapter 19.

Important note: *This practice case study is applicable for MDCS students following the audit route, but its non-audit practice requirements are suitable for MDCS students following the accounting route.*

Exam requirement

You are an audit manager with Eaton Associates which has audited Whoosh plc (Whoosh) for a number of years.

John Dwight, the CEO of Whoosh, is concerned about the risks facing the company in the current uncertain environment and also any changes that should be made to the company's investor reporting. In addition, there are some key accounting issues on which the company requires guidance.

It is currently 2 October 2020. You are planning the final audit for the year ended 30 September 2020. The audit partner has asked you to write a briefing note covering the areas below, which will assist in planning the audit and enable the firm to assess the appropriate accounting treatment for some key financial reporting issues this year.

You should prepare a briefing note in which you:

(a) Identify FIVE key business risks facing Whoosh, including an analysis of the importance of each risk to the business, and a suggested response which the company should make to address each of these risks. You may find it helpful to present your answer as a table but it is not compulsory.

(15 marks)

Note. This analysis may be used by Eaton Associates to offer additional consulting services to Whoosh in future.

(b) Analyse whether the contract with Jetstream is a lease arrangement and determine the amounts to be recognised in the financial statements in relation to the contract. **(20 marks)**

(c) Explain the audit work which Eaton Associates should perform in respect of Whoosh's contract with Jetstream. **(7 marks)**

(d) Discuss a suitable content for the business model section of Whoosh's integrated report, referring to the underlying concepts of an integrated report, including the capitals. **(10 marks)**

(e) Describe the work you would undertake as part of an assurance report on the Key Performance Indicators (KPIs) given. **(5 marks)**

(f) Explain and calculate how you would expect the executive share option schemes to be reflected in the financial statements. **(10 marks)**

(g) Evaluate the matters that Eaton Associates will need to consider and describe the work which will need to be performed in relation to Baciu & Co to determine the extent to which the audit work of Baciu & Co may be relied upon. **(8 marks)**

(h) Explain whether the profits of the joint venture company will be liable to UK corporation tax, either on the joint venture itself or on Whoosh plc as a 50% equity shareholder, and explain the UK VAT treatment of the payment for call centre services by Whoosh plc to the joint venture company.

(5 marks)

(i) Explain the impact on the consolidated financial statements of the investment in the joint venture call centre. **(5 marks)**

Professional Communication marks are allocated as follows:

Professional Marking Criteria (15 marks):

Report is presented in a style suitable for the audience articulated in the scenario **(2 marks)**

Structure of the paper is logical and clearly articulated to enable ease of navigation and discussion
(2 marks)

Ideas are expressed clearly and in language accessible to the audience identified in the scenario **(2 marks)**

Technical terms are used accurately and explained where appropriate **(2 marks)**

Issues are appropriately prioritised within the structure of the report and the body of the discussion
(2 marks)

Issues are assessed in a balanced and reasoned manner **(3 marks)**

Rationale behind assessment of issues and recommendations of responses is clearly articulated and alternative actions explored where appropriate **(2 marks)**

(15 marks)

(Total 100 marks)

Unseen material

Contents:

(1) Email from Gillian Sanderson to other board members, 12 August 2019
(2) Letter from Baciu & Co to Eaton Associates, 14 August 2020
(3) Email from Vicky Hunt to other board members, 31 August 2020
(4) Email from Bryan Ibid, financial controller to David Newell, Long & Co, 1 October 2020
(5) Email from Emily Sage, corporate affairs manager to John Dwight, CEO, 30 September 2020
(6) Inter-office memorandum, Eaton Associates, 15 September 2020

Exhibit 1: Email from Gillian Sanderson to other board members, 12 August 2019

To: Board members
From: Gillian Sanderson
Date: 12 August 2019
Subject: Executive incentive programme

Dear all

Following the preliminary discussion we had at the July meeting about switching from fixed remuneration to share options for part of the remuneration of senior management and executive directors, I can confirm that we will run two schemes:

- **Scheme A:** The 63 staff who are part of the senior management team will be granted 20,000 share options each.
- **Scheme B:** The six executive directors will be granted 60,000 options each.

All awards will be granted on 1 October 2019 and will vest on 30 September 2022, on the condition that the participant still works for Whoosh.

I estimate that the fair value of each option will be around £3.70 when the options are granted, but will have risen to around £8.70 by the vesting date if the targets in our strategic plan are met.

We can obviously discuss this in more detail in the meeting and I can answer any questions, but I wanted you to have a heads up in advance, so you can give it some thought.

Cheers,

Gill

Exhibit 2: Letter from Baciu & Co to Eaton Associates, 14 August 2020

Baciu & Co
Calea Victoriei 219A
București 010061
Romania

Paul Eaton
Eaton Associates
16 Park Row
Nottingham
NG2 1DH

14 August 2020

Dear Paul

Thank you so much for your communication and I am very happy to answer your questions. Please feel free to send the questionnaire you mentioned.

All of us at Baciu & Co are very proud of our involvement with BrasovAir. It is actually our biggest client by far, as we tend to specialise in small businesses. It is great to see the success of my dear friend, Marcel Gheorghiu, and the joint venture with Whoosh can only help to build on that success.

I am also happy to advise you about Romanian accounting standards if necessary, unless you already have knowledge of these? We are lucky that BrasovAir is not a public company, as it means we don't need to study IFRS. Although I'd quite like to know more, especially if I could get a trip to the UK to study them, it's not really necessary in our business to know IFRS and our staff are already working at full capacity as it is.

Please let me know when you have an idea of when you need the audit work for year ended 30 September 2020 to be done, so we can plan how to fit it all in with the staff we have available.

Yours sincerely,

George Baciu
Senior Partner
Baciu & Co

Exhibit 3: Email from Vicky Hunt to other board members, 31 August 2020

To: Board members
From: Vicky Hunt
Date: 31 August 2020
Subject: Gillian's illness – CONFIDENTIAL

Dear all

I am sure that, like me, you were saddened to hear of Gillian's illness. For privacy reasons, I am unable to reveal too many details, but she has asked me to tell you that the prognosis is good and that she hopes to begin a phased return to work in November and be back to full time work by Christmas.

In the meantime, she assures me that although Bryan Ibid is perfectly capable of handling day-to-day matters, there are a couple of areas in relation to the year-end accounts where he might need a bit of help. She contacted Charlotte Miles, the audit partner at Eaton Associates, about this but Charlotte is unable to offer accounting advice herself due to the need to remain independent. Gillian has arranged with accounting firm, Long & Co, to provide some guidance where necessary. Gillian feels, and I agree, that we don't need a full-blown secondment, just a hand-hold for Bryan where needed.

I'll keep you updated. In the meantime, if you want to visit, she's in the QMC until Saturday and then will be transferred to the Park Clinic for a couple of weeks. Her daughter Emily is on 07123 456789 if you want to check on how she's doing.

Vicky

Exhibit 4: Email from Bryan Ibid, financial controller, to David Newell, Long & Co, 1 October 2020

To: David Newell, Long & Co
From: Bryan Ibid
Date: 1 October 2020
Subject: Whoosh accounting issues

Hi David

It was good to chat last week, and again thanks for offering to advise on the accounting treatment applicable to some of Whoosh' transactions whilst Gillian is on sick leave.

As promised, here are further details of the two issues that I would appreciate your view on.

Aircraft leases

We entered into an agreement with another carrier, Jetstream, starting on 1 October 2019. This provides us with the use of five fully crewed Jetstream aircraft for a period of 18 months whilst we establish our new North African routes. Jetstream ground staff will also provide all maintenance services and the aircraft will be insured by Jetstream throughout the 18 month period. The terms of the agreement are as follows:

- Payments are made to Jetstream on 1 October 2019, 31 March 2020, 30 September 2020 and 31 March 2021.

- The first payment is a single non-refundable deposit of £3.1 million relating to all five aircraft.

- Subsequent payments depend on aircraft usage in the previous six-month period. A per-flying-hour rate of £2,100 is payable subject to a minimum guaranteed 2,000 hours for each aircraft per six-month period.

- Whoosh may use the aircraft on routes to any destination within a 2,200 mile radius of its home airport in the UK.

Actual flying hours were:

Aircraft	1	2	3	4	5	Total
6m ended 31 March 2020	1,850	1,930	2,100	2,035	2,140	10,055
6m ended 30 Sept 2020	2,120	2,011	1,990	2,300	2,760	11,181

Prior to the start of the lease, Whoosh also paid Jetstream a total of £585,000 to have the five aircraft painted in Whoosh livery. Occasionally, if one of the aircraft is out of service for maintenance purposes, we will have to fly an alternative aircraft under Jetstream livery.

I've currently recognised the painting costs as an intangible asset, since it equates to a brand. I have recognised the payments to Jetstream as an operating expense as I don't believe the contract meets the definition of a lease. I think this will please Gillian as she's always keen to keep recognised liabilities to a minimum, within the constraints of IFRS requirements.

Before she left, Gillian sent me a note with further details. I'm not sure whether these are of use to you:

- Aircraft only hourly rental rate £1,550
- Flight and cabin crew hourly rate £390
- Insurance cost (averaged to be hourly rate) £120
- Maintenance cost (averaged to be hourly rate) £440
- Whoosh incremental six-month borrowing rate 3%

Executive share option schemes

This year, the company started two share option schemes, the basic details of which I gave to you last week. I know we must recognise a staff expense in respect of these, but I'm a little confused as to how much it should be and when it should be recognised. Having read the terms and conditions of Scheme B in more detail, I've also noticed that it has a feature whereby Whoosh will withhold shares from the settlement of the award at an amount equal to the directors' tax liability. It will then pay the relevant cash amount to tax authorities. Have you come across this before? I'm not sure whether it has a bearing on the accounting. My last concern about the share option schemes relates to deferred tax. I'll admit it's not my strong point and I'm not entirely sure whether I need to account for it. I know that tax relief is given on the intrinsic value of the options, but it's not given until settlement. Can you help please?

I have confirmed that the fair value of a share option at 1 October 2019 was £3.75 and it was £4.30 at 30 September 2020. The intrinsic value of an option at 30 September 2020 is expected to be £3.95. Whoosh pays tax at 19%.

Again, thanks for your help and do give me a call if you'd like to discuss anything or need more detail,

Bryan

Exhibit 5: Email from Emily Sage, corporate affairs manager, to John Dwight, CEO, 30 September 2020

From: Emily Sage, corporate affairs manager
To: John Dwight, CEO
Date: 30 September 2020
Subject: Integrated reporting

Hi John

As requested I've been investigating the concept of integrated reporting a little bit more. An integrated report would replace our annual report. It would still need to contain financial statements, but would also contain certain key content elements, including information on our governance structure, our business model, risks and opportunities and outlook for the future.

I think the part of the report that we should start thinking about first is the business model, because that seems core to our story. A key theme of an integrated report is value creation in terms of the capitals, and I think we can bring that out in a discussion about our business model. Maybe we could both have a think about how best to approach this and then catch up for a chat next week?

Emily

Exhibit 6: Inter-office memorandum, Eaton Associates, 15 September 2020

Eaton Associates
Inter-office memorandum

From: Siobhan Armitage, senior partner, Nottingham Office
To: All members of audit team, Whoosh plc
Date: 15 September 2020
Subject: Whoosh audit – KPIs

Dear all

John Dwight just called to say that Whoosh is planning to publish some key performance indicators (KPIs) this year as a precursor to a full Integrated Report next year.

They're planning to disclose:

(a) Revenue per booked passenger
(b) Number of WhooshGives projects per year
(c) Number of employees employed under Jobs4All programme
(d) Number of pilots graduating from the WhooshWings programme
(e) Average crew per flight

We've agreed that we'll perform an attestation engagement on these.

So good work, team! The fact that he's asked us to do this is a credit to all your hard work on the interim audit in July.

Kind regards,

Siobhan

Practice Case Study 4: Suggested answer

Topic list	Syllabus reference
1 Practice case study 4: Suggested solution	All LOs

Suggested answer

(a) **Key business risks**

Business risk	Likely impact	Recommended response
Price competition Whoosh is facing price competition from new and/or existing competitors. This is illustrated by the decreasing revenue per passenger, which in 2019 was 12% lower than in 2015.	If revenue per passenger continues to fall then Whoosh will only be able to maintain current levels of profit by increasing the volume of tickets sold or reducing costs. Increasing sales volume will require high levels of capital costs to establish new routes or increase service to existing routes. As Whoosh is a low-cost airline already, there may be limited opportunities to reduce costs without adversely affecting service or safety.	Whoosh might be able to increase overall revenue by increasing the prices it charges for ancillary services, such as baggage and seat reservations, as that is likely to be less obvious to customers than an increase in ticket prices which the market is unlikely to support. Whoosh could also introduce new ancillary services and enter into new revenue-sharing arrangements with companies selling travel incidentals, such as car hire companies.
Falling operating margin Although Whoosh's revenue increased by 4.1% from 2018 to 2019, all of its expenses have increased by more than this, leading to a reduction in operating margin from 18% to 12%. The largest percentage increases relate to maintenance and repairs (26.1%), staff costs (16.8%), fuel and oil (14.2%), marketing and distribution (12.7%) and route charges (11.9%).	If Whoosh is unable to bring these costs under control, there could be a serious impact on future profits and cash flow. If revenue increases by 4.1% in 2020 and overall operating expenses increase by 12.1% (as has happened in 2019) then revenue would be £1,603.3m, operating expenses £1,519.0m, and operating profit £84.3m. This would reduce the operating profit margin to 5.3%. If this pattern continued into 2021 it would lead to an operating loss of £33.8m.	Route charges are likely to be out of Whoosh's control, although the company could consider changing its routing to use smaller, cheaper airports, where this is possible, though there would be a risk of reduced volumes and having to reduce ticket price to encourage customers to use these airports. Oil prices, which drive fuel costs, are also outside the company's control but the company could consider hedging to reduce this risk. Staff costs may decrease in 2020 anyway as a result of the outsourcing of the call centre. Staff costs and maintenance may be reduced by the use of the new wet leases and the flexibility which they offer. With respect to marketing, the management should carefully review the marketing

24: Practice Case Study 4: Suggested answer

Business risk	Likely impact	Recommended response
		channels being used and whether they offer value for money and consider if there are more cost effective methods, for example the use of social media.
Outsourced call centre Whoosh's call centre is to be outsourced to a 50:50 joint venture with BrasovAir. Although this entity will be jointly controlled by Whoosh, the fact that it is situated overseas may limit the amount influence that Whoosh has over day to day operations. There is a risk that poor quality operations may damage the company's reputation. There is also the risk that costs in the new venture may be higher than expected and adverse changes in the exchange rate between the pound and the Romanian Leu may worsen this.	The call centre is unlikely to be a major part of Whoosh's operations as bookings are made online so the call centre will only deal with non-routine issues. Since it seems that price, rather than quality of service, is the most important issue for customers of low-cost airlines, it is unlikely that poor service will have much impact on the company's reputation.	Whoosh should review the actual costs of the joint venture against budget on a regular basis and follow up major differences with the managers of the joint venture. Whoosh could enter into forward contracts or exchange rate swaps to manage the risk of volatile exchange rates. Whoosh could perform customer service surveys of call centre users to establish whether service standards are met and could recommend training where necessary.
Financing methods (new aircraft) The rights issue may fail (the rights may not be taken up) if shareholders do not have faith in the company's prospects or like the terms of the rights issue. This would mean that more money has to be raised by way of corporate bonds, which will lead to increased gearing. If the company's prospects are in doubt then any loan is also likely to have higher interest charges to reflect its higher risk.	The board discussed the need for an additional 20 planes over the next five years and a variety of financing options. Whoosh chose to lease five planes on 18 month wet leases which resulted in a contracted minimum cost of £66.7m (£3.1m + (5 × 2,000 × 3 × £2,100) + £585,000). It is not clear what the company intends to do once those lease contracts end. If these leases were extended for 10 years at the same rates, then over 10 years the total cost would be £444.7m (£66.7m × 12/18m × 10yrs) Assuming this was all borrowed at the start, this would increase Whoosh' gearing (calculated as debt/equity) from 75%	The company should try to reduce the amount of the loan. This could be done by increasing the amount of financing obtained from other sources; the rights issue should be structured to make it very attractive to the shareholders, and the company should consider expanding the share option scheme to cover more of the employees and replace a larger proportion of their salaries. If, say, 20% of the salary cost is replaced by share options, this would free up cash of around £40m, compared to the annual leasing cost of £44.5m (£66.7m × 12/18m). It may also be worth the company considering whether it can

Business risk	Likely impact	Recommended response
	((£684.2m+ £60.2m)/£991.5m) to 120% (£1,189.1/£991.5m). These calculations do not reflect the lease liability recognised at the start of the five leases. Gearing would increase even further as a result of this liability. This is a substantial increase in financial risk that will only get worse if a further 15 planes are purchased/leased over the next 5 years.	afford such aggressive expansion plans, and the best approach may be to scale back the number of planes acquired in the medium term.
Environmental issues Increasing awareness of environmental issues and the impact of plane travel on carbon emissions could reduce demand in future. Customers who do continue to travel by plane may be more concerned about the relative energy efficiency of different airlines and select an airline on that basis. Gathering data for environmental KPIs and having those KPIs audited could prove to be expensive for Whoosh. If the results shown by those KPIs are poor then this could damage demand further.	It seems that societal awareness of environmental issues is only likely to increase over the next few years as people become more aware of the critical issues impacting on the environment. With the company's operating margin being only 12% and an 85% load capacity required to break even, the company's profitability is very vulnerable to falling demand.	It appears, based on Emily Sage's email to John Dwight, that Whoosh is already operating in a relatively energy efficient way. If this is the case then publicising environmental KPIs could be to the company's benefit. If Whoosh's environmental performance is poor then the company should take steps to improve it. Whatever the company chooses to do, it should actively promote its positive environmental steps to help limit public focus on its negative issues.
Brexit The economic uncertainty concerning the impact of Brexit has impacted on demand and is likely to continue to do so. The transition period following Britain's exit from the EU ends on 31 December 2020 and the regulatory requirements that will apply to British-owned airlines operating within EU airspace are as yet unknown.	As discussed above, falling demand could have a seriously detrimental effect on the company's profitability. The cost of complying with new regulations could be high, and there may be some regulations with which the company is unable to comply, for example relating to the nationality of share ownership.	The company has already increased its adaptability by entering into wet rather than traditional leases. The company should regularly monitor its routings and adjust schedules according to demand (as above). The company may also wish to research some potential new destinations that do not involve EU airspace, such as Iceland and the North American Eastern Seaboard.

24: Practice Case Study 4: Suggested answer

Business risk	Likely impact	Recommended response
Natural disasters In April 2010 the Eyjafjallajökull volcano in Iceland erupted, producing giant ash clouds which resulting in the closing of European airspace for 6 days with resulting disruption to worldwide air schedules. There have been several similar but smaller incidents in Bali. There is a risk that other natural disasters could occur in future which impact on flight schedules.	The impact on the global economy of the Eyjafjallajökull eruption was estimated at US4.7bn with, for example, it costing low cost carrier Ryanair about £42m. A similar cost for Whoosh in relation to future events would reduce operating profit by 23%.	There is little that Whoosh could do by way of introducing controls, other than maintaining its adaptability in terms of changing schedules. It is uncertain whether Whoosh would be able to insure against such events but it may not be cost effective anyway. Although this is a high impact risk, the likelihood of an event like this occurring is relatively small and so Whoosh may need to just accept the risk.
Airspace 500 MAX problems The Airspace 500 MAX is currently grounded and it is not known when it will be operational. This has implications for current and future flight schedules.	Since Whoosh has five Airpace 500 MAXs on order, if the grounding continues for too long or there are other production delays then this will severely inhibit the flight schedule which Whoosh can offer.	It is likely that Whoosh will receive some compensation from Airspace over this matter if delivery is delayed. The company may have insurance to cover any additional losses. The more adaptable the business is, in terms of lease types etc., the easier it will be to adjust the flight schedules.

Note. Only five risks are required. Credit will be given for other well-explained risks which relate to the scenario.

(b) **Contract with Jetstream**

Nature of the contract

A contract is a lease or contains a lease if it conveys the right to control the use of an identified asset for a period of time in exchange for consideration.

Whoosh has entered into a contract to obtain the use of five aircraft for a period of 18 months in exchange for payment related to usage levels.

The aircraft are painted with Whoosh livery and are therefore specified identified assets. Jetstream will only substitute these liveried aircraft if any of them is out of service for maintenance purposes. This is not a substantive substitution right because it would not benefit Jetstream economically.

Whoosh can control the use of the aircraft if it has the right to obtain substantially all economic benefits from them and it can direct their use. The aircraft are painted in Whoosh livery and so could presumably not be used by other airlines during the 18 month period. They can be used to fly any route within a 2,200 mile radius of the UK home airport. Within this parameter, Whoosh can direct the aircraft use. Therefore Whoosh can control the use of the aircraft.

The definition of a lease contract is met and therefore the arrangement with Jetstream is within the scope of IFRS 16 *Leases*.

Components of the contract

The contract with Jetstream provides access to the aircraft and several ancillary services (flight and cabin crew, maintenance and insurance). It therefore contains both lease components (the aircraft) and non-lease components (the ancillary services).

IFRS 16 requires that these components are separated and the contract payments allocated to each component. Non-lease components are considered in aggregate and the payments are allocated on the basis of standalone prices.

The standalone prices of the aircraft and services based on hourly rates total £2,500 (£1,550 + £390 + £120 + £440). The lease components represent 62% (£1,550/£2,500) and the non-lease components represent 38%.

Therefore £1,302 (62% × £2,100) of each hourly payment relates to lease components and £798 (38% × £2,100) relates to non-lease components.

Accounting for the lease components

IFRS 16 must be applied to account for the lease components. There is no option to use the recognition exemption since the aircraft are not of low value and the lease term exceeds 12 months.

Therefore at the commencement of the lease on 1 October 2019 a lease liability and right-of-use asset must be recognised.

The lease liability is measured at the present value of the future lease payments. These include fixed payments and any variable payments that are in-substance fixed lease payments or that are variable due to a rate or index. They do not include any other variable payments.

The contract with Jetstream requires the payment of variable amounts every six months, based on usage. There is however a minimum guaranteed usage which equates to a minimum guaranteed six-monthly payment. This minimum payment is therefore an in-substance fixed lease payment.

The three payments are discounted at the rate implicit in the lease or, where this is unavailable, the lessee's incremental borrowing rate.

Whoosh's lease liability is therefore initially measured at:

	Cash flow £'000	Discount factor	PV £'000
6m ended 31 March 2020 (£1,302 × 2,000 × 5)	13,020	$1/1.03$	12,641
6m ended 30 September 2020	13,020	$1/1.03^2$	12,273
6m ended 31 March 2021	13,020	$1/1.03^3$	11,915
			36,829

This is subsequently amortised during the year as follows:

6m ended	B/f £'000	Interest 3% £'000	Payment £'000	C/f £'000
31 March 2020	36,829	1,105	(13,020)	24,914
30 Sept 2020	24,914	747	(13,020)	12,641
		1,852		

The year-end liability is classified as a current amount since the lease has only 6 months left to run.

The right-of-use asset is initially measured at the lease liability of £36.829 million plus the initial deposit of £3.1 million and the up-front payment of £585,000 in respect of painting Whoosh livery on the airframes. This cost of painting livery is not an intangible asset, but part of the cost of the right-of-use asset. The total right-of-use asset initially recognised is therefore £40.514 million.

The right-of-use asset is depreciated over the 18 month lease term, giving a depreciation charge in the year of £27.009 million (£40,514 × 2/3). The carrying amount of the right-of-use asset at the year-end is therefore £13.505 million.

Any variable lease payments that are not fixed-in-substance or related to an index or rate are recognised in profit or loss as they are incurred. These payments amount to:

	£'000
6 m ended 31 March 2020 (£1,302 × (*100 + 35 + 140))	358
6 m ended 30 Sept 2020 (£1,302 × (*120 + 11 + 300 + 760))	1,551
	1,909

* Variable lease payments relate to the hours in excess of 2,000 for each aircraft, as follows:

Actual flying hours were:

Aircraft		1	2	3	4	5
6m ended 31 March 2020	Actual	1,850	1,930	2,100	2,035	2,140
	Minimum	2,000	2,000	2,000	2,000	2,000
	Excess	–	–	100	35	140
6m ended 30 September 2020	Actual	2,120	2,011	1,990	2,300	2,760
	Minimum	2,000	2,000	2,000	2,000	2,000
	Excess	120	11	–	300	760

Accounting for the non-lease components

The non-lease components are accounted for as if these services were obtained under a separate service contract ie the related cost is recognised in profit or loss as incurred.

The operating expense recognised in the year is £17.130 million ((((2,000hrs × 5) + 100 + 35 + 140) + ((2,000 hrs × 5) + 120 + 11 + 300 + 760)) × £798).

Option to use the practical expedient

IFRS 16 allows a practical expedient in which the total lease payments are not allocated between lease and non-lease components and the full amount is treated as a lease payment. The initial lease liability would therefore increase, as would the initial right-of-use asset. It follows that finance costs and depreciation charge would be greater, however there would be no operating expense in relation to the non-lease components.

Electing to use this option would, however, reduce the level of work required to account for this and future wet or damp leases. Any election made would apply to all wet or damp aircraft leases as it applies to the entire class of underlying assets.

Gillian Sanderson is keen to minimise recognised liabilities in the financial statements and is therefore unlikely to apply the IFRS 16 practical expedient.

Amounts in the financial statements

Assuming that the practical expedient is not used, amounts to be recognised in the financial statements of Whoosh are therefore:

Statement of financial position (£'000)

- Right of use asset of £13,505
- Current lease liability of £12,641

Statement of profit or loss (£'000)

- Depreciation charge £27,009
- Operating expenses £17,130
- Variable lease payments £1,909
- Finance cost £1,852

(c) **Audit work on contract with Jetstream**

Eaton Associates should:

- Review the contract with Jetstream and confirm the key terms, namely that it:
    - Commenced on 1 October 2019 and was for 18 months
    - Was for five aircraft and included flight and cabin crew, maintenance services and insurance
    - Required a guaranteed minimum 2,000 hours per aircraft per six-month period
    - Allowed Whoosh to use the aircraft on routes to any destination within a 2,200 mile radius
    - Did not provide Jetsteam with a substantive right to substitute the aircraft

    It is important that the terms in the contract agree to the terms used within the leasing calculations otherwise the amounts calculated will be misstated and the categorization of the contract as a lease may be incorrect.

- Agree the amount of the deposit and payments used in the calculations to the lease contract to provide assurance that the figures have been correctly extracted and used in the lease calculations.

- Agree the deposit and the lease payments which were scheduled to be paid on 31 March 2020 and 30 September 2020 to the cashbook and bank statements in order to establish that the terms of the lease contract are being met. If the payments were not made on time penalties or additional interest might be payable.

- Agree flying hours per aircraft to flight operations records to ensure that the variable lease payments have been calculated correctly for recognition in profit and loss.

- Review the invoice/contract for livery painting to confirm the amount is accurate when it is in included in the amount recognised for the right-of-use asset.

- Agree the payment of £585,000 to the cashbook and bank statements to confirm that the amount was actually paid and is not an outstanding liability.

- Agree the details of the standalone rates charged for the aircraft and the ancillary services to quotations/correspondence which the chief finance officer had received. Recalculate the proportions represented by the lease and non-lease components and the respective hourly rates of £1,302 and £798. This is to confirm that the lease payments have been correctly allocated to lease and non-lease components and that the amounts taken to profit and loss as incurred for the ancillary services is correct.

- Discuss the estimate of incremental borrowing rate with the finance department and agree to correspondence with banks. If the rate used in the lease calculations is incorrect then the calculations of finance charge and lease liability will be misstated.

- Recalculate the initial lease liability and the right-of-use asset. Recalculate the finance cost for each period and the year-end liability. This is to check the mathematical accuracy of the amounts initially recognised and recorded at the year end.

- Recalculate the variable lease component to confirm that the correct amounts were taken to profit and loss.
- Recalculate the depreciation for the year and the carrying amount of the right-of-use asset at the year end to confirm that the asset value at the year end is correctly stated.
- Review the disclosures in the draft financial statements in order to confirm they are in accordance with IFRS 16 *Leases*.

(d) **Integrated reporting**

The International Integrated Reporting Council has issued the Integrated Reporting (<IR>) Framework which identifies that the fundamental concepts which underlie integrated reporting are:

- Value creation for the organisation and others
- The value creation process, and
- The capitals, being the resources and relationships used and affected by an organisation.

The capitals are categorised as financial, human, social and relationship, intellectual, manufactured, and natural.

Whoosh's integrated report should explain its business model in the context of these fundamental concepts. A business model is a system of transforming inputs, through business activities, into outputs and outcomes that aim to create value over the short, medium and long term. Therefore the report should identify Whoosh's material inputs, indicating how they relate to the capitals, and explain how the business creates value in them or otherwise affects them. The description of outcomes should refer to both internal and external outcomes and both positive and negative outcomes.

The content should be concise, as required by the <IR> Framework. An effective description of a business model might be presented in a diagrammatic or tabular format.

Whoosh

Inputs to Whoosh's business model that are part of financial capital are share capital and reserves, cash and cash equivalents and borrowings, including lease arrangements. Financial capital enables value creation in terms of all other capitals, as it is used to fund People initiatives such as WhooshWings and develop and acquire manufactured assets, such as the new integrated computer system for ground operations. It is also used to acquire the use of new aircraft in order to expand operations and fly new routes which, in turn, creates value for passengers and local communities in new destinations. Financial capital also allows investment in initiatives such as WhooshGives which benefit the community and so create value in terms of social and relationship capital. Whoosh operations are profitable and there has been a growth in operating revenues. The company is therefore also creating value in a financial capital sense – an outcome that the other capital inputs all contribute to.

Human capital inputs include leadership, employees that are skilled in specific areas (such as engineers and pilots) and HR policy and processes. Whoosh is a service organisation and therefore its people are a critical asset. Through its human capital Whoosh can foster relationships with customers and achieve customer loyalty. This in turn leads to customer loyalty and allows Whoosh to achieve profits and so create financial value.

Social and relationship capital inputs include relationships with customers and suppliers, dealings with the government and regulators, a positive relationship with employees, and proactive interaction with communities, citizens and the media as well as shareholders and lenders. The WhooshMiles scheme helps Whoosh to understand the movements and habits of its regular passengers and rewards them for their loyalty, so enhancing the relationship with them. The company maintains a good relationship with employees and has achieved a move to become a value-added service partner rather than an administrative function. The introduction of new employee incentive schemes and policies such as Jobs4All further contributes to the relationship with employees and the wider community. The community also benefits in numerous ways from the WhooshGives scheme.

Intellectual capital includes standard operating procedures, policies, frameworks and processes, tacit knowledge and employee development, including the cabin crew capability development programme and ground staff training in the new computer system. Through these Whoosh is able to create tangible monetised value in the form of revenue and profits and intangible value in the form of brand value. Whoosh's operating procedures, including online booking, removal of seat back pockets and steeper take-off and landing trajectories create financial capital by improving profits. Its focus on smaller planes with higher load rates, reduces the company's negative impact on natural capital.

Manufactured capital inputs to the business model include Whoosh's owned and leased aircraft as well as other property, plant and equipment. In the year ended 30 September 2021 manufactured capital will be increased through expenditure on the new ground operations computer system. Through these manufactured assets Whoosh is able to create financial value in the form of revenue and create infrastructural value for the wider economy. Whoosh understands that flying adversely affects natural capital through emissions and it seeks to reduce this negative impact through using only Airspace 500 models and increasing load rates.

Natural capital inputs include water, air, biodiversity and eco-system health. Whoosh operates its aircraft across several countries with diverse eco-systems and its operations effect eco-system health. They also generate waste and emissions which in turn contribute to global warming. Natural capital outcomes include environmental stewardship whereby Whoosh is aware of and manages its impact on the environment.

(e) **Work to be performed on KPIs**

As this is to be an attestation engagement, Whoosh will calculate and state the KPIs and we will check the measures stated and the working papers to support them.

KPI	Assurance work
Revenue per booked passenger	(1) Agree the total revenue to the audited financial statements (2) Agree the number of passenger bookings to data from the booking system (3) Recalculate (1)/(2) and ensure the result is the KPI stated
Number of WhooshGives projects per year	(1) Agree the total number of projects disclosed to a list of projects produced by the client (2) Select a sample of projects and review details of project, including correspondence as to the nature of the project (3) Review cashbook to confirm funds contributed to the project
Number of employees employed under Jobs4All programme	(1) Agree the total number of employees disclosed to a list of employee names (2) Select a sample of employees on the list, review their HR files to confirm that they meet the criteria to be part of the Jobs4All programme

KPI	Assurance work
Number of pilots graduating from the WhooshWings programme	(1) Agree the total number of graduates disclosed to a list of employee names (2) Select a sample of employees on the list, review their HR files to confirm their employment history and that they successfully completed the WhooshWings programme (3) Review details of any pilot graduation ceremonies and agree the names of graduates to the list in (1)
Average crew per flight	(1) Agree number of flying crew (pilots and cabin crew) to HR/payroll data (2) Agree number of flights in the year to operational flight records (3) Recalculate (1)/(2) to confirm it is equal to the amount disclosed

(f) **Executive share option schemes**

Scheme type

Both Scheme A and Scheme B involve the issue of share options to staff members. A share option is an equity instrument and schemes involving payment for services in the form of share options are classified as equity-settled share-based payment schemes.

Scheme B has a feature whereby some of the share options will be withheld by Whoosh at 30 September 2022 (the settlement date) and instead the company will use its own cash to directly settle with the tax authorities the directors' tax obligations which will arise as a result of the scheme. This has the same net effect as making part settlement to the directors in cash and the directors then using the cash to settle their tax bill. This raises the question of whether a scheme with this feature can still be classified as equity-settled.

IFRS 2 *Share-based Payment* refers to this as a net settlement feature. It says that if all other characteristics of the scheme indicate that it is equity-settled, it remains accounted for as equity-settled in its entirety. Therefore Scheme B is treated as an equity-settled share based payment transaction.

Total measurement

Each scheme is measured based on:

(i) The number of options granted that are expected to vest on 30 September 2022; and
(ii) The fair value of an option at the grant date.

The number of options that are expected to vest depend on the number of leavers, since options will not vest if an employee leaves Whoosh before 30 September 2022. The number of leavers considered at the 2020 year end is those that have left to date and those expected to leave in the remaining two years of the vesting period. Therefore at 30 September 2020 the schemes are measured in total as follows:

Scheme A: (* 63 − 4 − 1 − 1) × 20,000 options × £3.75 = £4.275 million
Scheme B: 6 × 60,000 × £3.75 = £1.35m

* Calculated as 63 senior managers at the start of the year minus two retirees and two to competitors during the year. Staff turnover rate budgeted at one leaver per year.

Recognition

Bryan is correct that each scheme must be recognised as a staff cost in profit or loss. The corresponding entry is made to equity. IFRS 2 is not specific as to which account the credit entry should be made and it may be made to retained earnings or a separate account, such as a share option reserve.

The total expense is recognised over the vesting period. Therefore in the year ended 30 September 2020 the share-based payment expense is:

	£'000
Scheme A: £4,275/3 years	1,425
Scheme B: £1,350/3 years	450
	1,875

The same amount will not necessarily be recognised in the years ended 30 September 2021 and 2022 as the total measurement will be updated for leavers at each date. It is not, however, updated to reflect changes in the fair value of the share options; these remain measured at the grant date.

Deferred tax

The share option schemes result in the recognition of a deferred tax balance. This is because an expense is recognised in profit or loss in each year of the vesting period but tax relief is not given until settlement. This results in a deferred tax asset (because future tax payable will be reduced by the relief given).

The carrying amount of an equity-settled share-based payment scheme is always nil therefore the temporary difference is equal to the tax base, which is the amount that will be deductible for tax purposes. This is an estimated amount based on the year-end intrinsic value of the share options and the vesting period to date.

At 30 September 2020 the tax deduction is expected to be:

	£'000
Scheme A: (63 – 4 – 1 – 1) × 20,000 options × £3.95/ 3 years	1,501
Scheme B: 6 × 60,000 × £3.95/3 years	474
	1,975

This will result in tax relief of £375,250 (£1.975m × 19%) which is recognised as a deferred tax asset. Deferred tax income recognised in profit or loss is limited to the amount of tax on the cumulative IFRS 2 expense ie £356,250 (£1.875m × 19%). The balance is recognised in equity:

Dr	Deferred tax asset	£375,250
Cr	Deferred tax (P/L)	£356,250
Cr	Deferred tax (equity)	£19,000

The deferred tax asset is subject to IAS 12 *Income Taxes* restrictions on recognition ie it can only be recognised to the extent that it is probable that a taxable profit will be available against which it can be utilised.

(g) **Work performed in relation to Baciu & Co**

The work to be performed will be dependent on whether the Romanian joint venture represents a significant component of the Whoosh group. Given that the call centre does not have a big role in the operations of Whoosh (bookings being made online) and it is only 50% owned by Whoosh, it is unlikely to be a significant component. This means that Eaton Associates is unlikely to need to audit the call centre directly but instead will rely on the work performed by Baciu & Co.

Areas that Eaton Associates will need to consider include:

(i) Ethical requirements: Eaton Associates will need to review the ethical requirements in Romania against the IESBA requirements which are relevant to Whoosh. Eaton Associates must confirm that Baciu & Co is independent of the Romanian joint venture and any other companies/key personnel in the group and so will need to supply Baciu & Co with a list of those parties. George Baciu states that BrasovAir is the firm's biggest client so there may be issues of financial dependence which could result in self-interest and/or intimidation threats. The letter from Baciu & Co refers to a 'dear friend Marcel Gheorghiu' who is presumably somebody at BrasovAir so there may well be independence concerns in relation to the joint venture.

(ii) Whether Baciu & Co has sufficient professional competence. The letter from George Baciu says that BrasovAir is the firm's biggest client, that it specialises in small businesses and that it is unfamiliar with IFRS (and possibly ISAs). The firm may not therefore have the technical knowledge needed to perform the audit. There are also hints about difficulties in having sufficient resources to staff the audit, which could mean that it is not done properly.

Eaton Associates should perform the following work:

(i) Obtain and review the ethical code applicable to Baciu & Co, and compare it to that followed by Eaton Associates.

(ii) Obtain a statement from Baciu & Co that it has adhered to this code.

(iii) Establish through discussion or questionnaire whether Baciu & Co is a member of an auditing regulatory body, and the professional qualifications issued by that body.

(iv) Obtain confirmations from the professional body to which Baciu & Co belongs as to whether there have been any disciplinary complaints.

(v) Enquire whether Baciu & Co is a member of a network of audit firms.

(vi) Discuss the audit methodology to be used by Baciu & Co in the audit of the joint venture and compare it with those used under ISAs (eg how the risk of material misstatement is assessed).

(vii) Ask Baciu & Co to complete a questionnaire or checklist with a summary of audit procedures used.

(viii) Ascertain the quality control policies and procedures used by Baciu & Co, both firm-wide and those applied to individual audit engagements.

(ix) Request any results of monitoring or inspection visits conducted by the regulatory authority under which Baciu & Co operates.

(x) Communicate to Baciu & Co an understanding of the assurances that Eaton Associates will expect to receive, to avoid any subsequent misunderstandings.

(h) **Tax and joint venture company**

Corporation tax

The Joint venture company will not be liable to UK corporation tax, as it is not UK resident. Its profits will instead be liable to Romanian corporation tax at 16%.

To be UK resident, a company must either be incorporated in the UK, or its central management and control must be in the UK. Central management and control is usually deemed to be exercised where the board of directors meet.

The joint venture company is incorporated in Romania, and, while Whoosh plc was involved in appointing the directors, they are based in Romania and key strategic decisions are taken by the Romanian directors. Therefore its profits are outside the scope of UK corporation tax.

Whoosh plc would be entitled to 50% of any dividends declared by the joint venture, and this would be shown as income in Whoosh plc's separate company accounts. However dividend income (including dividends from overseas companies) does not form part of taxable total profits for UK corporation tax.

VAT

The supply of call centre services by the joint venture company is a business to business (BTB) supply between two VAT-registered companies. The place of supply of BTB services is where the customer (ie Whoosh plc) belongs, so this is a UK supply.

Because the JV company will be registered for VAT in Romania and not the UK, Whoosh plc will be responsible for accounting for the VAT on its purchases via the 'reverse charge' mechanism - ie the appropriate VAT at 20% on each invoice from the joint venture is added to Whoosh plc's output VAT for the relevant period. This can be recovered as input VAT in full, as all of Whoosh plc's supplies (flights and associated services) are taxable.

(i) **Impact on the consolidated financial statements of the investment in the joint venture call centre**

In the consolidated financial statements equity accounting must be applied to Whoosh's investment. This means that the investment is initially recognised as a non-current asset in the statement of financial position, measured at cost and is subsequently increased by Whoosh's 50% share of the joint venture's post-acquisition total comprehensive income and decreased by any dividends received and any impairment losses.

In the consolidated statement of profit or loss and other comprehensive income, the joint venture is reported as two separate line items:

- Share of profit of joint ventures, in which 50% of the company's profits are reported, and
- Share of other comprehensive income of joint ventures, in which 50% of the company's OCI is reported.

Since the functional currency of the joint venture is Romanian Leu, its financial statements must be translated to pounds sterling prior to applying equity accounting. Assets and liabilities should be translated at the exchange rate at 30 September 2020 (the closing rate) and income and expenses at the average rate between May 2020, when the venture was set up, and 30 September 2020.

This will give rise to an exchange difference, which the joint venture must report as other comprehensive income and accumulate in a separate reserve in equity in its individual company financial statements in pounds sterling.

When equity accounting is applied it follows that 50% of this exchange difference is brought in to the Whoosh consolidated financial statements. This continues to accumulate in a consolidated reserve until such time as the joint venture is disposed of. At this time the cumulative exchange difference is reclassified to consolidated profit or loss.

Practice Case Study 5: Pre-seen material

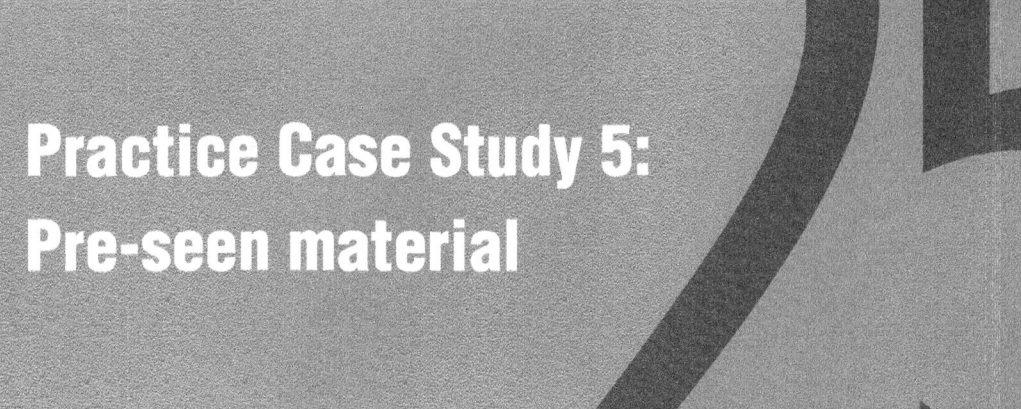

Topic list	Syllabus reference
1 Practice case study 5: Pre-seen material	All LOs

Green Housing plc

Company background

Green Housing plc was founded as a sustainable, community focused homebuilder with the specific aim to build homes and neighbourhoods across previously industrial sites. It specialises in brownfield regeneration (which consists of reviving previously developed but currently underused land) to create unique, sustainable and nature-rich places where communities thrive and people of all ages and backgrounds can enjoy a great quality of life.

Green Housing plc is the only international homebuilder delivering brownfield regeneration at scale. It works in partnership with governments and corporates to identify under-utilised sites and supports the delivery of corporate and government partners' sustainable promises. It has developed an international reputation in the ability to transform the most heavily polluted and difficult brownfield sites, creating nurturing and thriving communities. This regeneration of brownfield land to community use is a priority for many governments and the experience acquired from the UK past projects positions the company to compete internationally to help repurpose cities throughout the world which helps to meet local housing needs, support community cohesion through investment in deprived areas, stimulating local economies and reducing urban sprawl.

Green Housing has built more than 15,000 houses in the last five years, created more than 25,000 jobs per year through the supply chain and contributed over £1 billion to the economy of the communities it serves.

The following information has been extracted from information contained in the Green Housing website and their relevant published reports.

Green housing corporate vision

"Our vision is the rebirth of the urban environment through a partnership between nature and mankind to build vibrant, happy, sustainable communities. Our purpose is to build high quality homes, strengthen local communities and make a positive difference to people's lives. This driving purpose shapes everything we do and is fundamental to our long-term value-added approach.

Our focus is on large-scale, capital intensive brownfield regeneration projects. We develop challenging and complex sites over the long-term, bringing urban land back into community use. Green Housing is the only international residential developer regenerating brownfield land at scale."

Key stakeholder engagement

Investors

We ensure our financial strength reflects the prevailing macro environment, and we invest in opportunities for the business. Green Housing makes returns to shareholders through either dividends or share buy-backs.

We recognise the cyclical nature of the housing market and the high operating risk of our complex, long-term developments and therefore keep financial risk low at all times. We prioritise financial strength ahead of annual profits. This enables Green Housing to invest, both in new land and in our sites, at the right time in the cycle.

We have a strong track record of generating sustainable returns for shareholders, with annual returns committed through to 2025.

Nature

Leading nature's recovery

We are proud to have pioneered nature recovery within our industry and played a proactive role in reversing biodiversity loss within the communities we serve, which is the other great environmental challenge of our time.

We were the first homebuilder to commit to delivering a measurable net biodiversity gain on every new site back in 2017 and have since built up a pipeline of 46 developments, which together will create over 500 acres of new or improved natural habitats, not including the 155-acre country park planned for our Newcastle (United Kingdom) site.

These projects will create or measurably enhance approximately 100 acres of nature-rich grassland, 70 acres of woodland and 50 acres of living roofs. This focus on biodiverse and beautiful natural landscapes has been of great benefit to the health and well-being of the communities within and around our sites, as well as to the natural environment.

The success of our programme has led the Government to mandate biodiversity net gain of 10% for all developments, which is expected to occur in late 2023. The average net biodiversity gain we expect to deliver across our 46 sites is over 400%. We remain committed to supporting nature recovery on a national scale and are proud to have become a founding member of the Blue Recovery Leaders Group, set up in 2021 by the Wildfowl and Wetlands Trust and supported by then Royal Highness The Prince of Wales, to create networks of healthy wetlands across the UK. 37 of our current developments have planned or completed wetland features, which will amount to 52 acres of valuable blue habitats.

Financial key performance indicators

Profit before tax (£m)

2022	2021	2020	2019	2018
551.5	518.1	503.7	775.2	977.0

Our core measure of profitability is our absolute return from the sale and delivery of new homes in the year.

Definition: Profit earned by the Company during the year, including any finance income and costs and share of results of joint ventures, but before any tax expense.

Pre-tax return on equity (%)

2022	2021	2020	2019	2018
17.5	16.5	16.6	27.9	41.9

The efficiency of the returns generated from shareholder equity in the business.

Definition: This is measured by calculating profit before tax as a percentage of the average of opening and closing shareholders' funds.

Net cash (£m)

2022	2021	2020	2019	2018
268.9	1,128.2	1,138.9	975.0	687.3

This provides a measure of the financial strength of the Group.

Definition: Cash and cash equivalents, less total borrowings.

Non-financial key performance indicators

Net Promoter Score (NPS) (Rate).

2022	2021	2020	2019	2018
77.2	77.9	78.8	73.5	73.9

Our six-month rolling NPS is an indicator of the success of our efforts to provide world-class housing and customer service. Our NPS significantly exceeds the sector average of 45 (HBF, March 2022) and compares favourably with top-performing consumer brands.

Definition: Customers register a score between 0–10 of their assessment of the quality of their living experience in our homes and how likely they are to recommend us to a friend; 9–10 being classified as promoters, 7–8 being passive, and 0–6 being detractors. The NPS is the percentage of promoters less the percentage of detractors.

Annual injury incidence rate (Rate per 1,000 people)

2022	2021	2020	2019	2018
0.72	1.24	1.17	1.14	1.42

This measure shows the number of reportable injuries during the year, in relation to the number of Green Housing employees and on-site contractors. It significantly outperforms the construction industry average of 2.72 (HSE, October 2021).

Definition: This rate is calculated by taking the number of reportable injuries and dangerous occurrences across our operations throughout the year, multiplied by 1,000, divided by the average number of people working across our activities in the year.

Greenhouse gas emissions intensity (tCO2e/100 sq m)

This measure relates to our annual scopes 1 and 2 (market-based) greenhouse gas (GHG) emissions resulting from our direct activities to the floor area legally completed in the year.

2022	2021	2020	2019	2018
0.61	0.95	1.24	1.16	0.84

Definition: This is calculated by dividing the level of greenhouse gas emissions, from our activities, by the floor area legally completed in the year.

Affordable housing subsidies and wider contributions (£m)

2022	2021	2020	2019	2018
556	204	270	525	420

This measures our contribution to affordable housing subsidies and wider community and infrastructure benefits delivered or committed to during the year. The value in any one year is influenced by the number and mix of homes delivered.

Definition: This is the total value of affordable housing and wider community and infrastructure benefits delivered or committed to during the year.

Key financial notes

2022 financial statements

Accounting policy – Revenue

Revenue represents the amounts receivable from the sale of properties, comprising private and affordable residential homes and commercial properties, ground rent assets and other income directly associated with property development.

For the significant majority of residential and commercial property sales, properties are treated as sold and profits and revenues are recognised when all performance obligations under the contract have been satisfied, following which control of the unit is passed to the customer. This is determined as the point of legal completion.

Where revenue arises on contracts where the customer controls the property during construction and for which the Group has a right to payment for work performed, the Group recognises revenue over time. Revenue and costs are recognised with reference to the stage of completion of the contract.

Ground rent assets are treated as sold when contracts are exchanged, all material conditions precedent to the sale have been satisfied and control of the ground rent assets have passed to the customer.

	2022	2021
	£m	£m
Residential revenue	2,202.0	2,100.3
Commercial rental revenue (afford housing)	146.0	101.9
Total	2,348.0	2,202.2

Included within revenue is £356.6 million (2021: £279.6 million) of customer deposits for units that legally completed in the year.

Also, included within residential revenue is £114.7 million (2021: £115.8m) of revenue recognised in relation to the stage of completion of the contract. This relates to the ongoing Can Gas Construction Development (see page 8).

Notes from the meeting of the environment committee

9 January 2023

(a) Climate action disclosure

Whilst GH supports the recommendations of the Financial Stability Board's Task Force on Climate-related Financial Disclosures and the accounts for 2022 reflect our diligent attempt for compliance with these.

(b) Review of progress

GH set its first carbon reduction targets for our operations in 2010. Having identified flooding, over-heating and water shortage as key issues in our 2014 risk identification exercise, GH focused on climate change adaptation, creating new homes and places that are more resilient to the challenges of a warmer climate, which embrace the great potential of nature-based solutions.

Currently our direct business operations are carbon neutral in the UK, which represents 70% of our activity. We procure 100% renewable electricity in the UK, have set science-based targets for reducing our scopes 1, 2 and 3 greenhouse gas emissions by 2030 and have been awarded an A-rating for Climate Action and Transparency by CDP. Looking forward, Climate Action remains a key strategic priority for the business.

GH is playing a full role in addressing this global challenge and our climate action programme is holistic, involving transformational changes to our business operations and to the ways in which we design and create new places in partnership with our supply chain.

(c) Reducing negative impacts and working towards environmental net gain

The committee note that GH has considerable evidence of its consideration regarding our impact on the environment.

Key monitoring areas:

- Site-specific consultation and engagement strategies seek out contributions from a representative mix of local people and stakeholders on environmental issues at both a local level and a global scale.
- We liaise with local planning authorities, who in turn directly consult relevant regulators such as the Environment Agency, Natural England, other relevant national agencies and local water authorities on development proposals.
- We register every site with appropriate environmental authorities and are subject to regular external audits which cover our approach to environmental protection on behalf of our neighbours and the communities in which we work.
- We engage with industry organisations and initiatives focused on improving how companies in the built environment sector impact the natural world. These include being a

partner member of the UK Green Building Council and the Supply Chain Sustainability School, together with being an active member of the Construction Leadership Council's Green Construction Board and a founding member of the Wildfowl and Wetlands Trust Blue Recovery Leaders Group.

- We support and contribute to consultations, research and innovation, for example through the UK Green Building Council's Net Zero Programme, and Government consultations on changes to the Building Regulations and Biodiversity Net Gain.

- We engage with materials suppliers and trade contractors purchasing materials on our behalf to understand the environmental credentials of materials and their supply chains.

(d) Key issues for 2023

There is evidence that climate change is accelerating the number and severity of heat waves and flooding, and this may impact on the development of the business in a number of ways.

The first impact is upon government policy around planning and approval of buildings where failure to address sustainability issues could affect the GH's ability to acquire land, gain planning permission, manage sites effectively and respond to increasing customer demands for sustainable homes and communities, with access to green spaces and nature.

The second issue relates to our social housing rental portfolio. Although the Afford Homes property rental aspect of our business represents only 15% of our annual sales, the problems of extreme weathers may create additional management issues for us as landlords. The summer of 2022 demonstrated the problems that heat can create for urban homes and the need for heat mitigation measures to ensure the safety of tenants. Our strategies for our current portfolio in respect of heat and flooding require an urgent review by July 2023.

Another key issue relates to the ability to report upon scope 3 greenhouse gases (those indirect emissions as a consequence of our supply chain activity) the which will require detailed work with our suppliers and our customers.

The final issue relates to our developments overseas, where local regulation and infrastructure around environmental issues is not currently as well developed as in the UK. We are unfamiliar with local regulatory systems and issues and the information that is available from suppliers and sub-contractors to support our environmental monitoring is not always available. This reflects the issue of reporting scope 3 greenhouse gases, but also our effectiveness in mitigating local environmental and ecological challenges. Depending upon the strategic direction of the company regarding international opportunities for regeneration, this issue may become more pressing.

Can Gas Corporation Development project

In 2017 GH entered into a partnership with the Can Gas Corporation to redevelop a heavily polluted former gas works at a site in Chongqing near the confluence between the Jianling and Yangzi rivers (China).

The project involves the clean-up of the brownfield site over three years, followed by the construction of three phases of housing comprising a total of 1,570 apartments.

The Can Gas Corporation site will be developed under the UrbanEco model of urban planning. UrbanEco regeneration specialises in unlocking some of the most technically complex regeneration sites at the heart of communities, creating homes for everyone.

On every site, this starts with the landscape. This opens up and reconnects inaccessible private spaces for public use and responds to the challenges of congestion and density mega cities.

It offers us a way to create welcoming, sociable, beautiful places at the same time as building the additional housing that people urgently need. At GH, we always think about people first, the spaces they need and how they will use them. We fit the buildings to the landscape, not the other way round.

GH first used this design concept for Elizabeth Housing in south-west London, also on the site of an old gas works. This created 740 homes, inspired by that area's unique blend of industrial heritage and green landscape. The design fused the elegance of Victorian mansion blocks with the strength of 19th century gasholders which once stood on the site and the serenity of Battersea Park (United Kingdom) nearby.

In the Chongqing site, the architectural inspiration comes from the majesty of the Yangzi River, the industrial heritage of the site, the traditional architecture of the Great Hall of the People and the modern aesthetic of Raffles City, to which it sits in close proximity (China).

The regeneration of the site will include devoting 40% of the land to ecological restoration and other landscaping. This will use natural wetlands to alleviate flood risk and restore habitat as well as significant woodland and meadow plantings to reduce heat build-up.

The environmental landscaping will offer residents outdoor areas for recreation and socialising supporting the creation of a new community within the centre of the city.

In total, 1,570 apartment units will be built in three phases. Much of the development will be lower rise than the surrounding blocks, with communal roof gardens on all blocks, and balconies on all units.

New funding model

The project will use a new funding model, common to Chinese property development, but less usual for Green Housing. Although 25% of the land clearance will be financed by the Chongqing local authority, the remainder of the cashflow will be provided by the deposits paid for the apartments (usually of 30% payable on reservation, 30% payable on phase completion, 20% payable on possession) and then 20% finally settled as the site is fully landscaped and completed. The final settlement is subject to a late penalty clause whereby an overall reduction to this settlement of 10% is given if the final landscaping of the site is incomplete 12 months after possession.

Can Gas Corporation development costings – Budget projections at 2017

Land clearance costs	£287.2m	
Flood mitigation costs	£127.3m	
Site landscaping costs	£153.5m (completion 31 January 2025)	
Phase One – 870 units – Completion date 30 September 2022.		
Total income		£1,202m
Total costs	£510m	
Phase Two - 400 units – Completion date 31 January 2024.		
Total income		£554m
Total costs	£270m	
Phase Three – 300 units – Completion date 31 October 2024.		
Total income		£416m
Total costs	£219m	
Total estimated contract value		£2,172m
Total estimated contract costs	£1,567m	
Total estimated profit		**£605m**

Background economic and social information

(a) Chinese Real Estate Market
(b) UK Real Estate Market
(c) UN Sustainable Development Goal 11 – Human settlements
(d) OECD Better Policies for Better Lives – Housing
(e) Newspaper Article regarding recent flooding in Chongqing
(f) Advantages of Green construction

China's real estate sector goes south

18 October 2022

Author: Alicia Garcia-Herrero, Bruegel

The mortgage boycott in China is a direct consequence of the bankruptcies of an increasing number of developers. In 2021, real estate giant Evergrande left behind 1.3 million incomplete **housing units** for which Chinese households had already used their savings to make large down payments.

Some Chinese households have stopped servicing their mortgages for homes that remain incomplete. According to public data, the average delay in home completions has reached 14 months. Luckily, only a fraction of these cases triggered mortgage payment boycotts.

The problem may spread to other developers, supply chains, banks and local governments as land sales plummeted by 35% in August. Defaulted developers will suffer the most as their unfinished projects are behind almost all mortgage boycott cases, including Evergrande, SUNAC and Greenland. Homebuyers have lost confidence in the completion of new real estate projects and are refraining from buying new properties.

Housing prices are falling in more than half of China's cities. New home sales are also plummeting, dropping 23% year-on-year as of August. A drop in pre-sales is important because they account for 86 per cent of Chinese developers' funding.

Chinese developers are excessively dependent on household financing by international standards. That is a direct consequence of the 'three red lines' enforced by Chinese regulators in 2020, prohibiting banks from extending additional lending to developers.

Barring a bailout scenario, there are four important implications for China and Asia. The most general is the increase in systemic risk with a downward effect on China's low growth rate. Real estate investment will act as a major drag on the Chinese economy in 2022 and 2023, detracting at least 1 per cent of growth from an increasingly **low potential growth rate** of around 4%–5%.

The only way to soothe the impact of the necessary correction of this huge sector is to find other engines of growth with the help of innovation and the development of the service industry. The lifting of zero-COVID-19 policies is also essential to achieving this goal. The Chinese real estate sector will also be increasingly state dominated, which does not bode well for the role of the private sector in China's economic model.

The consequences for Asia are gloomy. The slowdown of the Chinese economy means its imports may further weaken, which is problematic for commodity **exporters**. With weaker domestic demand for property construction, China is importing less iron ore and other inputs for construction.

The demise of China's real estate sector, pushed by developer defaults and mortgage boycotts, is a major risk for the Chinese economy. Over time, its collapse might prove an even bigger shock than Beijing's current zero-COVID policies.

(**Source**: East Asia Forum. [Online] Available from: https://www.eastasiaforum.org/2022/10/18/chinas-real-estate-sector-goes-south [Accessed 3 October 2024])

Why UK house prices could plunge by 20% after the latest interest rate hike

Larry Elliott, economics editor

Property market has defied gravity for years, but analysts say rising mortgage rates will mirror the 1980s price crash

Analysts agree that 2023 will see further falls in house prices, with one predicting a peak-to-trough fall of more than 25% once inflation is taken into account.

There are structural reasons why house prices tend to go up in the UK – tough planning laws, a tax system that rewards home ownership, a sharp fall in the number of new homes being built since the 1950s and 1960s – but occasionally there are breaks in the trend.

This year is on course to be one of those break periods. A long boom driven by record-low interest rates has run its course.

The party was always going to end sooner or later as, even with rock-bottom interest rates, finding a deposit for a home and meeting mortgage payments became more and more of a struggle. Figures from the Halifax Bank [a key provider of household mortgage lending in the UK] this week showed a first-time buyer was paying just over £300,000 to get a foot on the property ladder and needed a deposit of £62,000. More than 60% of mortgage completions were in joint names last year.

But two other factors have contributed to the rapid cooling in demand: the steady increase in official interest rates since late 2021 and the impact of Liz Truss's brief premiership, which involved mortgage rates rising to almost 6%.

(**Source**: Guardian, The. [Online] Available from: https://www.theguardian.com/business/2023/jan/28/ [Accessed 3 October 2024])

Sustainable Development Goal 11 – Human settlements

Make cities and human settlements inclusive, safe, resilient and sustainable.

Given the importance of this topic to global development efforts, recent movements pushing to address sustainable development from an urban perspective have taken place throughout the world. Results from this movement can be seen in the inclusion of a stand-alone goal on cities and urban development in the 2030 Agenda, Sustainable Development Goal 11, 'make cities and human settlements inclusive, safe, resilient and sustainable'. There is also recognition of the cross-cutting nature of urban issues, which have an impact on a number of other Sustainable Development Goals, including SDGs 1, 6, 7, 8, 9, 12, 15, and 17, among others. UN-Habitat's complementary New Urban Agenda, adopted as the outcome document from the Habitat III Conference in 2016, seeks to offer national and local guidelines on the growth and development of cities through 2036.

Prior to the adoption of the 2030 Agenda, Millennium Development Goal 7.D made a call for efforts to achieve, 'a significant improvement in the lives of at least 100 million slum dwellers' by 2020.

Sustainable human settlements development was also discussed at the second and third sessions of the Commission on Sustainable Development. 'Promoting sustainable human settlements development' is the subject of Chapter 7 of Agenda 21, which calls for (1) providing adequate shelter for all; (2) improving human settlements management; (3) promoting sustainable land-use planning and management; (4) promoting the integrated provision of environmental infrastructure: water, sanitation, drainage and solid waste management; (5) promoting sustainable energy and transport systems in human settlements; (6) promoting human settlements planning and management in disaster-prone areas; (7) promoting sustainable construction industry activities; and (8) promoting human resource development and capacity-building for human settlements development.

Paragraph 89 of the 2030 Agenda calls on major groups and other stakeholders, including local authorities, to report on their contribution to the implementation of the Agenda. Local and regional governments have a wealth of valuable experience in the 'localization' of the 2030 Agenda, where they provide leadership in the mobilization of a wide range of stakeholders, the facilitation of 'bottom-up' and inclusive processes, and the formation of multi-stakeholder partnerships.

(**Source**: UN. [Online] Available from: https://sdgs.un.org/topics/sustainable-cities-and-human-settlements [Accessed 3 October 2024])

OECD Better Policies for Better Lives – Housing

Reconciling housing and the environment

The nexus between the residential sector and environmental quality is reciprocal and complex. The residential sector generates environmental impacts via land and materials use, energy consumption, and the transportation activity it engenders. Environmentally motivated policies on land use, construction and energy efficiency, and transport seek to alleviate these impacts by incorporating the cost of environmental externalities into housing prices. Sustainability in the housing market can be promoted according to social welfare approach that accounts for housing affordability, as well as the environmental and economic impacts of policies.

(**Source**: OECD. [Online] Available from: https://www.oecd.org/housing/policy-toolkit/data-dashboard/housing-environment/ [Accessed 3 October 2024])

Massive flooding hits Chongqing

7 September 2021

By Deng Rui and Tan Yingzi in Chongqing for ChinaDaily.com

On Monday, the Cuntan hydrologic station in the upper reaches of the Yangtze River saw the biggest flooding this year, as the Jialing River's No 2 flood and the Yangtze River's No 1 flood had formed in the Qujiang River. Qujiang is a tributary of the Jialing River.

Following the heavy rainfall, major floods occurred in Minjiang, Tuojiang and Jialing rivers, three Yangtze tributaries. The flood in Qujiang exceeded the warning level, forming the Jialing River's No 2 flood at 8 am on Monday. Yangtze is the longest river in China.

The Yangtze River No 1 flood was formed in the upper reaches at 2 pm on the same day, due to the increase of upstream and interval water inflow. The rapidly growing water inflow in the Three Gorges Reservoir reached 54,000 cubic meters per second, which was unprecedented being the first flood to exceed the magnitude of 50,000 cubic meters per second this year.

According to the Upper Reaches Bureau of the Changjiang Water Resources Commission, as of 5 pm on Monday, the water flow at the Cuntan hydrologic station was 46,800 cubic meters per second and the water level exceeded the alarming level of 0.05 meter. The water level is still rising.

As of 7 pm on Monday, the water flow at the Luoduxi hydrologic station in Qujiang was 19,100 cubic meters per second. The water level exceeded the alarm level of 0.09 meter and is still rising.

Relevant departments, sub-bureaus and stations of the Upper Reaches Bureau of the Changjiang Water Resources Commission are doing hydrological forecasting and paying close attention to multiple circumstances to better address the two overlapping floods.

(**Source**: China Daily. [Online] Available from: https://www.chinadaily.com.cn/a/202109/07/WS61372027a310efa1bd66dec6.html [Accessed 3 October 2024])

Ten benefits of sustainable construction

As the benefits will become more apparent during the next years, the **advantages of green construction** fall into three main categories:

- Environmental benefits;
- Financial benefits; and
- Social benefits.

This categorization depicts the multi-aspect contribution of sustainable building and is one of the first solid steps of construction to focus on the full building life cycle, combining utility with insightful resource management.

Here are the 10 essential benefits of sustainable construction:

(1) COST REDUCTION

Construction is a $10 trillion industry, but its financial struggles can't be ignored. With its efficiency and rework rate up to 30%, smart and functional alternatives are considered to be more than necessary. Sustainable construction can provide great help in that direction. Overall, a green building costs less than a normal building because fewer resources (eg water and energy) are required for the completion of the project. On top of that, sustainable buildings have great ROI, as well. Simply put, the value of the property is significantly increased with sustainable building.

(2) INCREASED PRODUCTIVITY

As reported by *The Guardian*, environmentally friendly workspaces help employees perform better while reducing absenteeism. The better the environment, the easier it is to concentrate and work effectively toward the completion of tasks.

(3) IMPROVED HEALTH

Green buildings can be beneficial to health. According to the Environmental Protection Agency, **outdoor air is two to five times less polluted than indoor air**. Building and furnishing materials, such as paints, cleaning products and carpets, can be dangerous for human health. The use of sustainable materials can help with the purification of the air.

(4) WASTE MINIMISATION

In Europe, the construction industry is responsible for 34.7% of the continent's total waste. Green buildings minimise waste with their lower environmental impact and use of renewable sources and materials. Products such as demolition debris, sand and burnt coal can be used with excellent environmental and aesthetic results.

(5) BETTER USE OF MATERIALS

Sustainable buildings manage water in a more effective and environmentally friendly manner. Sustainable buildings can be equipped with systems that recycle water, such as collecting rainwater for toilet cleaning. Sustainable buildings can collect and preserve natural energy, such as solar or wind energy, storing it and reusing it accordingly.

(6) ENVIRONMENTAL PROTECTION

Recycled materials used during the construction process are contributing significantly to the protection of the environment and to the reduction of waste. Moreover, sustainable construction takes into serious consideration a number of critical elements. The installation of well-insulated windows, ceilings and walls can ensure that no energy is going to waste. Additionally, the use of solar heaters, insulated air-conditioning pipes and photovoltaic panels can make buildings more energy efficient and less harmful to the environment.

(7) NOISE AVOIDANCE

Noise can have a significant effect on a person's well-being. Sustainable construction put extra attention to noise avoidance in the following ways:

- Distance augmentation between the source of the noise and the subject;
- Planting of more trees close to the noise source in an effort to absorb it; and
- Creating noise barriers (between a building and a highway for example).

(8) BETTER QUALITY OF LIFE

Sustainable construction has a plethora of benefits in every stage of a construction project. Improved health due to safer materials, increased productivity thanks to better surroundings and more effective noise protection are only a few of the advantages. Green buildings can improve life quality.

(9) A NEW MARKET IS EMERGING

The advent of sustainable building has helped the market evolve and unlock new possibilities.

(10) ROOM FOR EXPERIMENTATION

Sustainable construction can be an excellent opportunity for creative experimentation in the industry. New materials are being used and as a result, more innovative techniques are being developed and implemented, such as the ski slope opening on a new **power plant in Copenhagen**.

Sustainable construction is developing day by day and opportunities are opening up for the industry. Keeping an open mind and a well-functioning plan can result in further groundbreaking changes.

(**Source**: CE. [Online] Available from: https://www.constructionexec.com/article/ten-benefits-of-sustainable-construction [Accessed 3 October 2024])

The methods and benefits of sustainable construction

Chris Jackson 2/11/21

The construction industry is one of the most prominent consumers of minerals and natural resources by its very nature. The need and significance of sustainability in construction have become a debated topic due to the growing concerns over global warming and the finite nature of resources. This conventional truth caused increased pressure on construction firms to reduce their environmental impact.

But what exactly is sustainable construction, and how does one transition into a more renewable development method? Are there any benefits, and what are the appropriate methods? Learn more by reading the guide below.

What is sustainable construction?

Sustainable construction involves using renewable and recyclable materials on building projects to reduce energy consumption and toxic waste. The primary goal of this initiative is to decrease the industry's impact on the environment by utilising sustainable construction procedures, practising energy efficiency, and harnessing green technology.

While several companies from different business sectors are doing ways to be more environmentally responsible, many focus their attention on the construction industry since it is considered the largest user of global resources. This sector alone is responsible for approximately 50% of the worldwide consumption of raw materials and is a significant waste producer. It makes construction unique because by changing outdated practices, the industry can significantly reduce the effects of global warming.

Sustainable construction methods

Many construction firms are now recognising the importance of sustainable and green building methods. With the increased interest in sustainability and energy conservation, new advances in technology, materials, and practices have been developed over the past decade to enable and promote overall efficiency.

One of the best ways to implement sustainability in construction is through materials. Technological advancements have paved the way for a new generation of more robust, lighter, and renewable building materials such as **insulated access doors and panels**, which can help push traditional practices to be more environment-friendly.

These ecological materials also help promote a cleaner Earth by reducing the carbon footprint of the buildings that utilise these elements. They have the same purpose as their non-renewable counterparts while also aesthetically pleasing and much more efficient.

Ergonomic construction isn't just about using renewable materials; it's also about implementing methods that enhance sustainable efforts. Some of these methods include:

- Limiting the materials used to reduce waste;
- Controlling waste management, such as separating and recycling waste;
- Constructing green buildings;
- Adaptive reuse projects that transform old buildings;
- Managing construction sites to improve conservation efforts;
- Examples include treating water on-site, no smoking, recycling food containers, etc;
- Conserving energy;
- Choosing sustainable and recycled materials.

Benefits of sustainable construction

Construction sustainability isn't just beneficial for the environment, but it also supports the well-being of individuals and communities. There are many proven benefits of adopting the green initiative in the building industry, and these include:

(a) **Promotes healthier living**

   It's no secret that our surroundings significantly impact our physical, mental, and emotional health. Over the past decade, designers and builders have developed a sustainable architecture that substantially affects the inhabitants' overall state in green buildings. The modern age has allowed us to branch out and modernise everyday appliances such as lighting and power sources, thermal conditions, ergonomic features, and even air quality. Occupants residing or working in sustainable buildings have experienced a noticeable improvement in their health, stress levels, and overall quality of life.

(b) **Reduces waste**

   Over the past decades, global warming has remained a steadfast concern due to its increasing evident effects on our planet. Pollution and the depletion of our natural resources are at an all-time high. While we are almost at the point of no return, we can still minimise or slow down the imminent effects of climate change with our sustainable technological advancements. Construction firms have started relying on renewable resources and methods, which are beneficial for us and promote a cleaner environment.

(c) **Boosts the economy**

   The construction industry is a known economic driver in the United States. The US Green Building Council (USGBC) stated that the green building industry contributes more than $134.3 billion in labor income to working Americans. It is safe to say that the green initiative in construction helps boost the economy by creating more jobs due to an increased demand for construction workers.

(d) **Promotes cost efficiency**

   One of the most substantial benefits of sustainable buildings is their lower maintenance costs with specially engineered design elements that help reduce water and energy bills. Reduced maintenance and operational costs mean huge savings invested elsewhere, such as higher employee wages or product development.

Although the cost required in building such structures may be initially higher than the traditional non-renewable forms of architecture, these efficient layouts can save corporate and building owners down the line.

(e) **Decreases material cost**

Sustainable building methods utilise eco-friendly materials without compromising quality or structural integrity. Many of these materials are recycled and reused. Among which are biocomposites that are commonly substituted as sustainable building materials have proven to be as reliable and durable as their non-renewable counterpart.

For green architects, energy efficiency remains their number one priority and goal in building design. Building structures that obtain their energy from natural resources - such as the wind, sun, and water - are exceptionally favorable to our environment.

(f) **Enables carbon footprint reduction**

There has been an increase in large corporations supporting and adopting green initiatives. The Environmental Protection Agency (EPA) stated that buildings are responsible for 30% of all greenhouse gas emissions in the United States. Property owners and large businesses have taken heed, as imposing sustainability is an opportunity to do something positive for the company and society.

Importance of sustainable construction

The demand for a more sustainable and economical solution has significantly grown due to the evident effects of global warming. The construction industry has already caused unfathomable damage to the environment. According to the United Nations Environment Programme (UNEP), 'the increased construction activities and urbanization will increase waste which will eventually destroy natural resources and wildlife habitats over 70% of land surface from now up to 2032.'

It is deeply unsettling for us and our future generations, and therefore, the need for sustainability in the construction sector is growing. Over the years, the building industry has primarily contributed to the continuous eradication of our ecosystem, whereas it accounts for:

- 45% of total CO2 emissions in the UK (27% from domestic buildings and 18% from non-domestic).
- 72% of household emissions are due to space heating and the provision of hot water.
- 32% of landfill waste from construction and demolition of buildings.
- 13% of construction waste is sent directly to the landfill without being used.

Resolving this situation has become a priority for construction firms and critical decision-makers to minimise the consumption of raw materials and natural resources and reduce their carbon footprints.

To meet these objectives, numerous firms have started practicing necessary steps towards designing, renovating, or building structures in compliance with environmental rules and sustainable methods.

Although the cost of renewable construction is higher in all stages of the project, mainstream contractors and renowned firms are undertaking sustainable development in construction. The adaption of sustainable methods and materials has dramatically increased over the past few years, that the cost of sustainability in construction has come down.

Large construction firms and companies aren't the only ones to improve their methods and practices to better the environment. Regular people working on their building projects can do their part by choosing renewable materials and practicing sustainable techniques. Whether using the proper equipment or implementing reliable engineering geared towards conservation, simply doing your best to be energy efficient can help progress sustainability efforts.

(**Source**: Construction21. [Online] Available from: https://www.construction21.org/articles/h/the-methods-and-benefits-of-sustainable-construction.html [Accessed 3 October 2024])

Practice Case Study 5: Exam requirements and unseen material

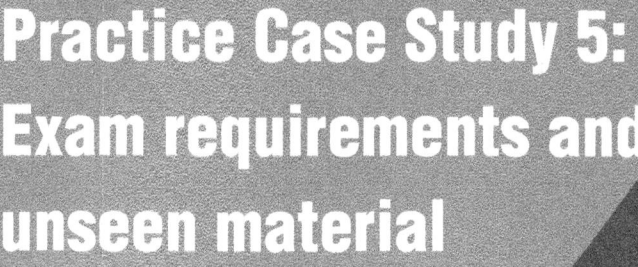

Topic list	Syllabus reference
1 Practice case study 5: Exam requirements and unseen material	All LOs

Important note: This practice case study is applicable for MDCS students following the accounting route, but its practice requirements are suitable for all MDCS students

Exam requirement

Green Housing plc

Scenario

You are an AIA professionally qualified accountant working for Green Housing plc (GH) which is a large multinational company listed on the UK Stock Market.

You have been seconded from the finance department where you work as a financial controller, into a newly formed Green Vision Team which has been set up to support the work of the board in identifying and developing appropriate strategies to mitigate emerging risks and opportunities facing the company and to develop the strategic reports and other information issued with the financial statements.

Within this role, you are also required to provide analysis and recommendations regarding potential future actions for the company.

The Green Vision Team comprises six colleagues from the finance, operational and quality assurance aspects of the business and you have been drafting the inaugural report for the board. As the most senior team member it has fallen to you to pull together the findings of the Team for this report.

Required

Draft the Green Vision Report for the board which:

(a) Identifies the key strategic risks facing GH over the next five years. **(20 marks)**

(b) Critically explores potential contributions to the business, exploring, where appropriate, the risk and financial viability, strategic fit, accounting and ethical issues, of:

    (i) Can Gas Corporation Development **(30 marks)**
    (ii) Sale of Afford Housing South to Happy Homes plc **(5 marks)**
    (iii) Sale of Can Gas Corporation Development to Peony Buildings **(10 marks)**

(Total 45 marks)

(c) Advises, with justification, the response that the board should make to the criticisms regarding GH Vision, Culture and CSR made by the fund manager of Gold Investment Trust. **(5 marks)**

(d) Critically appraises the ethical implications of the report and articulates this clearly to the board within the report. **(5 marks)**

(e) Concludes, with reasons, how the board should develop the company in the medium term.
(10 marks)

The draft report should be in a format suitable for presentation to the board.

(Total 15 marks)

Unseen material

Background to the Green Vision Team

The Green Vision Team has been founded to support the executive board with their strategic and risk analysis and to appraise new investment and business opportunities within the sustainability vision of the company. The team members are from a range of business backgrounds including planning and development, environmental compliance and finance. As an experienced AIA qualified accountant, you are leading the financial aspects of the work and collating the information into a useful report to inform board discussions.

It is currently May 2023 and you are due to report to the board for the first time at the June board meeting.

The board has been approached by Happy Homes plc who has expressed an interest in either entering into a joint venture with GH or buying out the Afford Housing sector of the business.

Happy Homes plc (HH) is a commercial property rental company which operates on a Campus model, whereby they develop and let office space to prestigious clients, frequently in financial services although lately also in technology, supported by housing and retailing to provide an attractive work and living environment for staff.

As GH has three sites next to HH Campuses, HH is seeking to purchase or control the rental housing in these areas to allow for flexibility and expansion of the living options for businesses.

Details of HH business model and an outline of the proposal are attached below.

The board is also concerned about the performance of the redevelopment of the Can Gas Corporation Developments (CGCD) site in China. The project is not meeting budgeted targets and the board is anxious to evaluate how GH should reduce their risk exposure here.

Relevant Email Correspondence

Exhibit 1: Email One

From: Sarah Chan – Contracts costing accountant
To: Nirali Patel – CFO Green Housing
Subject: Can Gas Corporation Development contract progress

Dear Nirali,

I have forwarded the minutes of the last project meeting for Con Gas Corporation Development. As requested, I am emailing you directly with a summary of the cost implications discussed.

The current position is less favourable than we had hoped when we celebrated the project agreement with the Chongqing City Authority in October 2017. Enduring the turmoil of the Covid pandemic and the recent local lock downs and recovering from the flooding has delayed our work by at least 18 months, but with renewed impetus from the city and workforce we are starting to catch up and progress has been good.

There are two critical concerns for the project which I will deal with in turn:

(a) Sales

The level of sales has been depressed, in part due to the impact of Covid, but also due to the issues arising from Evergrande which continue to affect market confidence. We would have anticipated reservations of 85% of phase one, 70% of phase two and some uptake, around 20% for phase three at this stage of the development. Currently we are around 50% down on all areas. This is out of line with the market.

Current reservations by phase are:
Phase One   420 units
Phase Two   200 units
Phase Three   75 units

(b) Costs

The costs are escalating at a somewhat alarming rate. The current cost increase for the land clearance was 17% (in part due to the additional £20m required to repeat work as a consequence of the flood). The City Authorities are requiring additional flood mitigation measures which will increase this cost from £127.3m to £143.6m.

The current over-spend on the construction costs for Phase One have been £47m with a predicted £16m to complete this phase.

Phases Two and Three are not really started and the current projected overrun is anticipated to be 16% and we expect the landscaping costs to increase by 22%.

Hope all of this information proves useful in the next meeting.

Best wishes,
Sarah.

Exhibit 2: Email Two

From: Carl Porter – Marketing executive (international)
To: Green Vision team leader
Subject: Customer confidence

Dear team leader,

As requested, I pulled the latest information for the CGCD development sales feedback.

We have held a number of open days on the site, now that we have a couple of units complete to show as show homes. We have had a lot of interest with these, but they are not converting into reservations at the rate we were led to expect would be normal for the Chinese market.

There are a number of concerns routinely arising in discussions with potential owners. One concern is around the proximity to the river confluence and the potential for future flooding. Although we have presentations detailing the flood mitigations for the site and the specific protections for the apartments, this is not entirely assuaging doubts. The other concern that we hear a lot relates to a lack of confidence in our ability to clean the site of potentially dangerous heavy metal residues. We don't have a sufficient track record in China to convince potential purchasers that we will deliver on our promises. Finally, there is a lot of concern that we won't fulfil our landscaping commitments and that the site will not be a safe and attractive place to live.

Our market research indicates that a reduction in unit sales price of around 15% would reflect the change in market conditions going forward.

I hope that helps in moving the project forwards.

Best wishes,
Carl.

Exhibit 3: Email Three

From: Andreas Schill – CEO Green Housing
To: Nirali Patel – CFO Green Housing
Subject: Revisions to CGCD release schedule

Dear Nirali

Thank you for your update regarding the costs on the CGCD project. I do concur with concern at the delays and cost overruns, but I remain committed to the Chongqing City Authority partnership and have faith that, despite the setbacks, it will prove successful.

I received a schedule of revised timings from the project team yesterday which I have summarised for you. They represent the best estimate and I think are achievable – although you know that their project team do have a tendency towards optimism – a good thing given the challenges the site has thrown at them!

Phase One completion – 30 September 2023
Phase Two completion – 31 October 2024
Phase Three completion – 31 January 2025
Final landscaping – 31 December 2025

As you can see, this represents quite a slippage for Phase One but some catching up on the timetable for the housing. The final landscaping will however be a year late due to the impact of the additional flood mitigation measures.

You correctly indicated that there is a problem with the potential for late penalties resulting from the landscaping delays, but I feel strongly that we will need to honour this to maintain our reputation in this market. I also think we need to look at reducing the sales price per unit across the board by 7% and reflecting that in the settlement of the customers who have already reserved their units.

I know that this will put pressure on the financial viability of the development, but I think we should remain committed as a gesture of good faith to our new suppliers, partners and customers and for the future opportunities it affords us.

Best wishes always,
Andreas.

Exhibit 4: Email Four

From: GH Compliance Team
To: Green Vision Team
Subject: Grant conditions from Chongqing City Authority

Hi Team,

We have had a good look at the contract and memorandum of understanding that we signed with Chongqing City Authorities.

The 25% land clearance funding was granted on the following conditions:

(a) That the resulting development created a new community supported by critical outdoor landscaped infra structure with 30% of the site devoted to ecological restoration

(b) That the development reduced ambient temperatures through the use of tree cover and other plant materials

(c) That biodiversity was restored

(d) That the flooding risk was mitigated through natural wetland

(e) That all building materials were of the highest safety specifications

In the event that any of these conditions are breached, the funding will be repayable back to City in full.

Andreas signed off on this with confidence as all of our projects can demonstrate exceeding these criteria.

By the way, we have heard that the CFO is seriously looking at the sale of CGCD to Peony Buildings as she has heard that your figures indicate this could be a sensible option. Have you managed to obtain detailed revisions to the cost schedules and specifications at all? We haven't been able to get finalised versions from Sarah's team as she is so busy and the information she has seems to be very broad brush.

If you need any additional information, please do not hesitate to contact us.

Best wishes,
GHCT.

Exhibit 5: Email Five

From: Andreas Schill
To: Nirali Patel
Subject: Approach from Happy Homes and Peony Investment Trust

Hi Nirali.

Per our meeting yesterday, I can confirm that we have received tentative offers from both organisations as follows:

Happy Homes plc

They would like to explore the possibility of purchasing the Afford Housing South property portfolio. They are willing to pay around £1,275 million and would acquire ten sites, five of which are adjacent to their proposed new campuses in London.

Peony buildings

They would be willing to buy out the Can Gas Corporation Development from us, in its current state of completion for £625 million.

Peony Buildings is not an organisation I am familiar with – my research indicates that it is a well-established company in southeast Asia but has little experience in the Chinese market. Its developments have a good reputation, but they don't have a track record in re-developing challenging sites and they seem to be very profit driven. In our initial discussions, the CEO believes that the market is about to rebound so is unconcerned about the current reservation levels and would not be proposing a price reduction. He also believes that costs can be reduced in the landscaping and that would speed things up – removing the need for late penalties. I am a bit concerned that he places little value on ecological restoration and would like to increase the density of the housing. None of this makes me feel that this is a viable option to us – but I promised you I would see what could be done to reduce our exposure here!

I know that you have been very concerned about the state of our cashflow since the pandemic, and the risks we are exposed to in China, so I thought you might like to pass this onto the Green Vision Team for their risk appraisal and advice.

I am not in favour of either option if avoidable but would be happy to see the figures the team comes up with to take to the board to inform our next strategic discussions.

Best wishes,
Andreas.

Exhibit 6: Email Six

From: Yuming Zheng – Head of investment – Gold Investment Trust*
To: Andreas Schill – CEO Green Housing
Subject: Sustainable business focus

Dear Andreas,

I have recently analysed your latest figures and am concerned with the direction of Green Housing. Whilst I agree that climate change is a critical issue for the world, and that helping nature is a laudable ambition, I am concerned that your growth is stalling, and I am very concerned with the drop in your cash resources. It is my belief that CSR is an issue for rich companies when times are good, and that, in these difficult days, companies should be much more focused on their primary job – creating returns for the shareholders.

I did hear a rumour that you were considering cutting prices for units in China retrospectively and giving around a 10% discount because the site isn't on time – this seems to be foolhardy in the extreme – and ignores the needs of your investors. I have also seen a media article where you boast that 40% of the regeneration sites are devoted to ecological restoration. This seems to be another area where you are choosing to reduce profits by 40%.

I would like this matter to be discussed at our next investor forum and I believe that many other trust fund managers may share my concerns.

Best wishes,
Yuming
Head of Investment Gold Investment Trust

Footnote – Gold Investment Trust is a significant shareholder in Green Housing and has been very proactive in its investor engagement with the company.

Afford Homes sector analysis

Afford Homes, as part of Green Housing plc, delivers affordable and thriving communities. Afford Homes consists of two aspects of GH business, namely the construction of affordable homes (committed to be 35% of GH annual build) and management of lettings for some of this social housing, focused on providing affordable rental homes.

We deliver social outcomes and a positive impact on communities by taking a commercial approach. All our profits go back into providing homes that are safe and secure, helping people to achieve their aspirations and making places work for everyone. For us, 'ESG' is not a policy or a programme, it is everything we do.

We own or manage more than 12,500 properties in communities across the UK that are homes to around 300,000 customers. In addition, we provide a vast range of services for those customers, including money and energy advice to help sustain tenancies. We build homes for people at every stage of their lives, ranging from students, first-time buyers and young renters right through to those seeking to retire. Our focus is on creating inclusive places where people can afford to live and with facilities that help build thriving communities.

Using the power of partnership, we forge strategic relationships with like-minded organisations, including local authorities, public sector bodies, community groups, other housing providers, developers and investors. By working collaboratively, we create communities that provide people with opportunities and choice in a way that few organisations can match.

Social housing income breakdown

	2022 £m	2021 £m
Affordable housing sales	71.7	63.4
Afford homes rental income	146.0	101.9

Rental Income Location Breakdown

	2022 £m	2022 Properties
Afford south	71.5	5,250
Afford north	38.1	3,850
Afford west	36.4	3,400
Total	146.0	12,500

	2022	2021
Average residential home size	100 square metres	100 square metres
Average tenure	11 years 3 months	11 years 4 months
Average occupancy rates	84%	83%

Happy Homes plc

Happy Homes plc (HH) is a commercial property rental company with an international portfolio, specialising in the short and medium-term lettings in London, Hong Kong, Beijing and Singapore. The company initially provided short to medium term lets to support the financial and business communities to provide housing for staff on secondment. The business then expanded to include key worker accommodation and some student letting. Typically leases last between one and three years with many of the renters being under the age of 30. There is a limited family and middle-aged occupancy.

Happy Homes mission statement

Happy Homes

Our purpose is to create and manage outstanding places which deliver positive outcomes for all our stakeholders on a long term, sustainable basis. We do this by understanding the evolving needs of the people and the organisations who use our places, and the communities who live around them. The deep connections we create between our customers, communities, partners, and people help our places to thrive.

Happy Homes development and rental model

Campus model

The international office market requires more than a place to work. As well as modern and high-quality environments, business occupiers want spaces which enhance wellbeing and support the needs of a sustainable future. Our experience shows that our prestigious partners prefer places which allow staff to live close to work, are well connected and have a range of amenities nearby for people to enjoy outside of office.

We have developed a unique Campus model of commercial development for busy urban commercial centres and through this we have the premier office portfolios for our cities – and partner with the most prestigious financial and corporate clients allowing them to move their staff seamlessly around the world.

We own the spaces between our buildings, and have a mix of commercial office, retail and housing within a campus, we can curate an engaging public realm and our placemaking activities help to foster a sense of community amongst our occupiers and with local people.

The Campus model also enables occupiers to grow with us – occupiers can upscale on or between our Campuses and we actively plan our development in conjunction with our occupiers' needs.

Happy Homes KPIs

	2022	*2021*
Residential letting annual Income £ per square foot	£335	£325
Average residential home size	75 square metres	75 square metres
Average tenure	2 years 2 months	1 year 11 months
Average occupancy rates	87%	84%

Additional economic information.

Exhibit US 1

Reduced revenue potential and spending in an uncertain economy

A recent **Deloitte survey** collected revenue data from the CFOs of prestigious investment companies and commercial real estate owners. The data showed that expected revenue in 2023 was ambiguous. 12% of those surveyed expected no changes in revenue, whilst 48% expected revenue decreases, and 40% anticipated increases. Off the back of this uncertainty, 33% plan to cut costs in 2023, where only 6% had such plans the year before.

It is evident that factors such as recession, escalating interest rates and higher levels of inflation have all negatively impacted growth potential in the commercial property market. These implications mean that the climate has become more difficult for property, so we might expect to see reduced investment in 2023. That said, experts are predicting that the recession should pass quickly, seeing the beginning of a more promising economy towards the end of this year.

Investors will need to plan carefully for when and where is best to put their money this year. The location and sector are likely to play a significant role in how profitable a particular property investment may be, so it is essential to thoroughly do one's research before investing. The industrial sector in particular is expected to see continued strong growth in 2023.

Affordable housing and renters' reforms

Back in June 2022 the national government published a white paper entitled 'A Fairer Private Rented Sector' proposing a new deal to ensure fairness and affordability to renters.

As the demand for affordable housing increases, and with rental reforms likely in the near future, landlords will need to look at how they can meet any new requirements and whether their properties will remain profitable. It is likely this may feed the existing trend of private landlords selling up, leading to a reduction in the overall stock of private rental properties.

(**Source**: Longmores. [Online] Available from: https://www.longmores.law/articles/what-to-expect-from-the-uk-commercial-property-market-in-2023 [Accessed 3 October 2024])

Exhibit US 2
Building to net zero – Costing carbon in construction
UK Government – House of Commons Committee Report 2022–23

Introduction

(a) 25% of the UK's total greenhouse gas emissions are attributable to the built environment. Greenhouse gases are emitted at every stage of the construction and use cycle, from the manufacture of materials through construction and maintenance to eventual demolition. Emissions from the built environment must be reduced if the UK is to meet net zero by 2050. More pressingly, the UK's Sixth Carbon Budget requires carbon emissions to be reduced by 78% by 2035, compared to 1990 levels. At COP26 the UK Government committed the UK to achieving a 68 per cent reduction in the UK's carbon emissions by 2030, compared to 1990 levels. This is only seven years away.

(b) There is little government guidance as to how these targets are to be met by the built environment industry. Moreover, to date, policy has focused entirely on operational emissions; emissions resulting from energy consumption in the day-to-day running of a property, like heating. In comparison, emissions from the construction process, maintenance and demolition of buildings, known as embodied emissions, have been ignored. Embodied carbon emissions are not required by current policy to be assessed or controlled, other than on a voluntary basis. These emissions amount to some 40 to 50 million tonnes of CO_2 annually, more than emissions from aviation and shipping combined. We have been struck by the lack of evidence of overall planning for how the built environment will contribute to the net zero target. In this report we examine how best to reduce emissions from the built environment, so that the UK Government can start to meet its pressing and numerous carbon targets in relation to this sector.

(c) The Government has set itself the ambition of building 300,000 homes a year by the mid-2020s. Construction of these homes is required to meet housing needs, but will have significant carbon impacts: firstly, in terms of the up-front embodied carbon used to construct buildings, and secondly in how the fabric and energy efficiency of these buildings affect energy use, and how much repair and maintenance is required over the buildings' lifetime. The housing sector is lagging behind other sectors in reducing these carbon emissions; housing emissions were cut by 1 million tonnes CO_2 equivalent from 2018 to 2019 compared with cuts of 8.5 million tonnes from energy supply, 2.2 million from transport and 2.5 million by businesses.

(d) Finding the appropriate balance between demolition and new build versus reuse and retrofitting of existing buildings is crucial to a built environment policy which delivers sustainable outcomes. Changes have recently been made to permitted development rights to help stimulate housing delivery by making it easier to demolish or repurpose vacant and redundant buildings and rebuild them as domestic properties. Considerable emissions are involved in demolition and rebuilding of properties, especially when measured under a whole-life carbon approach: under this approach, it becomes more debatable whether the replacement of properties is a sustainable approach to take.

(e) In this report we consider the best routes to net zero for the UK's future building needs, from the use of low-carbon materials and retrofitting through to policies to minimise the whole-life carbon (WLC) impact of new buildings.

Background to the inquiry

(f) We launched this inquiry in March 2020. Our aim was to examine the Government's progress on sustainable building measures since the Climate Change Committee's 2019 report on *UK Housing Fit for the Future*. During the inquiry, we sought to examine:

- Accounting methods for embodied and whole-life carbon in buildings;
- How materials can be employed to reduce the carbon impact of new buildings;
- The role of the planning system, permitted development and building regulations in delivering a sustainable built environment;
- The balance between reuse and retrofit of buildings versus demolition and new build; and
- Government action to incentivise greater sustainable construction, repair, and retrofit.

As local government, planning and housing policy is devolved, this report focuses principally on sustainability in construction policies in England promoted by the UK Government.

(**Source**: UK Parliament. [Online] Available from: https://publications.parliament.uk/pa/cm5803/cmselect/cmenvaud/103/report.html [Accessed 3 October 2024])

Practice Case Study 5: Suggested answer

Topic list	Syllabus reference
1 Practice case study 5: Suggested answer	All LOs

Suggested answer

Rationale behind the Green Housing plc Multi-disciplinary Case Study

The inspiration for Green Housing plc is Berkeley Group plc, which is focused on the regeneration of heavily polluted inner city brown field sites in the UK to provide low carbon environmentally sensitive re-development which creates sustainable communities. Much of the pre-seen information is developed from this corporate disclosure around its environmental credentials and its social mission.

However, the case study explores the difficulties of maintaining this focus when economic challenges create a conflict between the corporate mission and vision and the need to secure cashflow and maintain investor confidence. This allows an exploration of the student's understanding of problems with corporate strategy and recognition of strategic risk (part a); the appreciation of the difficulties that inflation and economic uncertainty create for the application of IFRS 15 *Revenue Recognition* on long term contracts in the Can Gas Corporation and the problems of moving a development model into another culture (namely China) (part bi); the issues arising from a joint venture with another company with conflicting values around social rentals – Happy Homes is based upon British Land plc and their Campus Model of corporate development (part bii); a justification of environmental engagement exploring the students understanding of different ideas around stakeholder engagement; an analysis of the ethical risks in developing information for decision making (part d) and then an overall synthesis and assessment of the correct future actions (part e).

The structure of the paper has deliberately reflected experience from the first two sittings but is assessing the understanding of strategic and accounting issues in the context of the construction industry. Again, this company is rooted in the needs for more sustainable business requiring students to apply some of the ideas from their ethics module to real life scenarios supporting the AIA stated education objectives and commitments.

Draft Green Vision report to the board of Green Housing plc

Introduction

This report articulates the initial findings of the cross departmental Green Vision Team, convened in January 2023. This project has been commissioned to strengthen and support the work of the board in identifying and developing appropriate strategies to mitigate emerging risks and opportunities facing the company and to develop the strategic reports and other information issued with the financial statements and to provide a forum in which emerging issues can be robustly critiqued prior to presentation to the board.

This report reflects the initial analysis of the critical strategic risks facing GH and then explores the viability of two projects. Can Gas Corporation (CGC) and the refocusing of the business away from acting as a social rental landlord with the sale of the Afford Homes portfolio to Happy Homes plc in promoting the Green Housing vision. Additionally, the report analyses the criticisms of the current strategy made by a key investor, Gold Investment Trust and makes recommendations regarding actions that GH board should consider to ensure our continued success.

(a) **Strategic risk review**

MDCS Textbook Chapter 2

As noted in the financial statements for the year ended 31 December 2022, the company has continued to enjoy robust performance despite the challenges presented by the last two years of economic uncertainty. However, the profit and profitability remain considerably lower than in 2018 and the following risks may compromise future growth.

Economic outlook

Uncertainty in housing demand

As a property developer, GH business is sensitive to wider economic factors such as changes in interest rates, employment levels and general consumer confidence. Changes to economic conditions in the UK and worldwide may lead to a reduction in demand for housing – although the current assessment of the way in which these pressures may impact on the property marker is mixed (US1) – which could impact on the Group's ability to deliver its corporate strategy.

There is evidence that interest rates are rising internationally, and particularly in the UK. From the predictions of analysts, it appears that these rate rises will not reverse in the short to medium-term which may impact on the affordability of property as these rates feed into mortgage and borrowing costs and therefore monthly housing costs. This squeeze on affordability of housing, and therefore demand, is being exacerbated by other pressures on household budgets and may ultimately serve to reduce property values and potentially make current development projects less profitable.

We have sales to both house owners and to buy-to- let landlords and appear exposed in both markets and we may find ourselves unable to meet our budgeted transaction levels, causing difficulties with cashflow management and liquidity over the short to medium term.

Inflationary pressures on costs

Energy pricing

There is an inherent risk that as energy prices increase, property buyers will favour lower carbon homes and expect greater operational energy efficiency. Conversely, with our strong environmental-related credentials evidenced this should improve the prospects of higher demand for GH's homes.

However, as energy prices rise internationally, these costs will feed into the supply chain, causing inflationary pressures on transportation of materials, and raw materials costs themselves as steel, concrete, cement and glass all have energy intensive production which could require increased energy input costs.

Raw materials and labour

As noted above, build costs are affected by the availability of skilled labour and the price and availability of materials, suppliers, and contractors.

We are experiencing a reduction in the availability of a skilled workforce in the UK and internationally. The costs of labour are increasing, also exacerbated by wage inflation and changes to these prices may start to impact on our build programmes – both in our capacity to meet contract deadlines and the profitability of our schemes.

The inability to attract, develop, motivate, and retain talented employees will have an impact on the GH's ability to deliver our strategic priorities.

Political pressures

Adverse changes to Government policy on areas such as taxation, design requirements and the environment could restrict the ability of the GH to deliver its strategy. In 2022, the national government commissioned The Fairer Private Rental Sector which indicates that reform for the rental sector is likely. Although GH is well positioned in its treatment of private rentals, especially through the Afford Housing division, these reforms may further exacerbate pressures on our margins in this sector of our business.

Compliance with law and building regulations

Failure to comply with laws and regulations could expose the Group to penalties and reputational damage. The recent scandals around non-compliance with materials regulations for fire safety has

reduced consumer confidence in builders and affected some of the demand for apartment living. Much of our urban development is focused on this type of property and therefore there may be additional pressures on demand.

Environmental regulation

Aggressive climate mitigation could lead to the implementation of carbon tax regimes, and an increase in the demand for renewable energy and cost of emissions offset. The cost of raw materials could increase if suppliers pass through the impact of carbon pricing for carbon intensive building materials. For example, steel, concrete, cement and glass all have energy intensive production which could require increased energy input costs.

Environmental risk

Flooding and damage caused by weather related extremes also have the potential to adversely impact on both the building process, increasing costs and extending build times, and on the security of the final homes we deliver. Many of our sites are in inner cities with the issues of aged drainage and flood prevention infrastructure which increases flood risk and may reduce the attractiveness of our development model. As noted in the Environmental Action Plan, our sites are also at risk from the effects of excessive heat. Our strategy of redevelopment with re-wilding and mitigation of environmental risks will reduce this risk, although it may not be totally effective as the effects and impacts of climate change become clearer.

> Additional risks which could be explored by students include those related to land availability, failure with the Can Gas Corporation Development impacting on the reputation of GH and the ability to expand internationally, and loss of key staff/ management. Students may choose to present the answer within PESTEL framework Any other valid and sensible risks will be credited but will be capped at 2 marks if not considered to be key.

(b) (i) **Assessment of Can Gas Corporation Development project**

MDCS Chapter 2 6.2; 9.1; AIA 13 Chp 21 AIA 11 Chp 2

Strategic synergy

It appears that there is a lack of appetite for potential house owners to commit to off-plan purchase of apartments at the Can Gas site.

This may be due to an overall lack of confidence in the Chinese house buyer after the problems with Evergrande caused such a significant number of contractors to fail to complete homes, leaving mortgage commitments on incomplete assets and resulting in the mortgage boycott.

However, from the email from Sarah Chen, our underperformance on sales is greater than the market, at 42% rather than 23%, and this may indicate any issue with the site itself. As noted in the newspaper article, this brown field regeneration represents the first of such a polluted site. There appears to be a lack of confidence in the ability of GH and its subcontractors to effectively clean up the site and re-generate the environment into an attractive place to live. Additionally, the site is positioned next to the river estuary which has seriously flooded in 2021.

Overall, it appears that our first move into China may have failed to consider the cultural difference in the financing of the property market, and impact of recent problems, or the difficulties in building confidence in our environmental business model.

Risk assessment

The risk with this project is significant.

In addition to the problems with the sales levels explored above, there are risks associated with our ability to complete the project on time due to the impact of the flooding in 2021 and the ongoing problems with supplies and labour since our main contractor failed earlier this year. Costs have increased due to both inflation, which has driven raw materials up by an average of 16% and the additional flood mitigation regulations introduced in January 2023.

Our cashflow funding this project is now stretched, and GH is funding this from its cash reserves, as evidenced from the significant reduction in cash reserves for 2022. Any further delays with the completion of phase one and phase two will seriously impact on our ability to attract additional much needed sales for either of these phases and phase three. This is also making the completion of the landscaping of the site problematic, which further affects the desirability of the homes and may expose the risk of penalties, reducing the value of each unit by 10% and impacting on estimated profit by £217m (based on 10% of estimated sales value). These may exacerbate the cashflow difficulties facing the project and further tie up our cash reserves affecting our ability to fund profitable projects.

Overall, the problems with the project are damaging to our reputation and may adversely affect our ability to engage with the regeneration opportunities in China or other overseas markets in the future.

The risks are impacting on the overall profitability of the development as detailed below:

Can Gas Corporation Development costings – Best estimates May 2023

Land clearance costs (287.2 × 1.17)		£336.0m
Flood mitigation costs (per Nirali email)		£143.6m
Site landscaping costs (153.5 × 1.2) £184.2m (completion 31 January 2025)		

Phase One – 870 Units – Completion date 31 September 2022
Total income £1,202m
Total costs (510 + 47 + 16) £573m

Phase Two – 400 units – Completion date 31 January 2024
Total income £554m
Total costs (270 × 1.16) £313.2m

Phase Three – 300 units – Completion date 31 October 2024
Total income £416m
Total costs (219 × 1.16) £254m

Total estimated contract value		£2,172m
Less 7% discount		(£152m)
Less anticipated penalty at 10%		(£202m)
Total revenue		£1,818
Total estimated contract costs	£1,804m	
Total estimated profit		£14m

At current projections there is considerable risk that the project may not be profitable. At the moment the company has only received £288.4m in deposits leaving some £1,530m at risk and the costs may escalate further.

Accounting issues

The key accounting issue relates to the treatment of the contract under IFRS 15 *Revenue Recognition*.

There are two key issues within the CGCD as a result of the economic conditions in China and Internationally.

Certainty of consideration

Doubts over full recoverability of consideration receivable

IFRS 15 includes a 'collectability threshold' which requires that it must be probable (ie more likely than not) that an entity will collect in full the consideration to which it is ultimately entitled from the customer before it can apply the standard to the contract.

If it is no longer probable that the consideration will be received in full, IFRS 15 typically prevents any further revenue being recognised until certain conditions are met. This will impact on some of the units sold under phase one and phase two of the development – but is a matter of subjective judgement to what level sales will not be honoured.

As the delays to the contract have arisen in part due to supply issues and in part as a consequence of the impact of the 2019 flooding, these factors will play into the potential lack of confidence for purchasers to commit to units. However, the evidence that there is a shortage of homes in Chongqing and there is reason to have optimism that, once the development is completed and the flooding risks mitigated, all units will be sold.

Changes in estimates of variable consideration

IFRS 15 requires variable consideration to be estimated and may restrict the amount that can be recognised as revenue when there is a degree of uncertainty; this restriction is generally referred to as the 'variable consideration constraint' and will apply to the recognition of late penalties on completion.

As a result of the uncertainty in the Chinese property market, the estimate of variable consideration may have changed in addition, if there is an increased level of uncertainty, this is likely to lead to greater restrictions on the amount of revenue that can be recognised.

For CGCD contract, the new sales contract with purchasers allocates penalties for late delivery to each individual apartment. Although, an expectation of future late deliveries will typically not affect revenue recognised to date, in circumstances in which it is appropriate to allocate such late delivery penalties to the contract as a whole, expectations of future late deliveries will affect the amount of revenue recognised for deliveries already made. Accordingly, GH will need to decide whether the late penalties resulting from the certain delays of the re-development should impact on both the revenue recognised in the year and adjust for the revenue recognised to date.

It is my considered opinion that, as the delays are to the whole of the site, this latter option would be correct. This will reduce the profits that can be recognised on the contract during its development and mean that the income statement may be less attractive for the next two years.

Costs attributable to inefficiencies or cost base alterations

As a result of the problems with supply and the inflationary factors driving up costs on raw materials and labour, the CGCD contract is incurring additional costs.

When assessing the appropriate impact of such costs, we need to assess whether they should be regarded as attributable to significant inefficiencies in GH's performance. We cannot assume that any costs not initially envisaged will represent inefficiencies.

Where the costs have increased in order to comply with additional flood and health safety requirements these are not inefficiencies – they are additional costs that render the contract as less profitable than GH originally expected.

However, some of our additional costs are attributable to significant inefficiencies in our performance. These costs should be:

- Expensed to profit or loss when they are incurred.
- Excluded from the measurement of progress when recognising revenue over time.

Impact of accounting issues

The impact of these accounting issues relates to the recognition of the profits across years of the development. It appears from this assessment that we will be unable to recognise profits on CGCD during 2023 and may have to write back profits recognised in prior years. This has the potential to impact on our overall profitability and may reduce confidence in our overseas strategy for future development.

Ethical issues

The permissions to regenerate the site of the gasworks in Chongqing were based on the promise of reducing flooding risk to the new homes, creating natural solutions to flooding as an exemplar for future developments and creating a beautiful environment for residents. Should GH alter its approach to the development, or have the development delayed further, then these promises may not be delivered. This has the potential to prevent future brownfield regenerations in China or other overseas countries from attempting to deliver ecological and environmental benefits. This will have adverse impacts of the delivery of future sustainable development.

If GH were to vary the contract design to reduce the ecological and wellbeing benefits to minimise the costs, this would deliver a home which was not consistent with that promised to residents. This may damage well-being of residents, trapping buyers in a devalued asset and meaning they are unable to move away to better quality homes and environments.

The impacts on both customers and the environment as stakeholders would be negative and compromise the delivery of the UN Sustainable Development Goal, which was the key aspect of the planning permission.

> **The suggested points above represent a far more extensive answer than a student could be expected to submit and therefore cover all issues intended by the examiner within the materials presented. However, students who have engaged in wider preparation may have accessed other more recent information that could impact on the strategic synergy of the development and its risks. This is particularly in association with the developments in the Chinese property market. Any other valid and sensible comments will be credited but will be capped at 2 marks if not considered to be key.**

(ii) **Potential sale options:**

MDCS Chapter 4

Sale of Afford Homes South to Happy Homes plc

Financial viability

The sale of the AH division to Happy Homes plc would realise cash and provide needed liquidity to support the completion of the Can Gas Corporation Development. However, although £1,275m does only represent an average sales price of £243,000 per rental unit, it is equivalent to some 17.8 years income. It is debateable whether this price is really competitive and perhaps a higher price could be negotiated.

Strategic synergy

Happy Homes plc espouses a similar commitment to positive lifestyle developments as GH, The sale of Afford Homes South will transfer the role of landlord from a company committed to affordable housing with security of tenure, to a company where tenure is limited and generally linked to well-paid employment. Although some of the focus of Happy Homes is on key worker accommodation and student living, it appears that the main driver for the purchase is to allow increased accommodation to support the Jubilee Campus and the expansion of office leasing to a new Tech company.

Risk assessment

There is a potential reputation risk for GH as this would expose existing tenants to the risk of rising rents, which they may not be able to afford, or the risk of no-fault eviction. This could adversely affect the reputation of GH and reduce the attractiveness of Afford Homes in other locations as tenants may fear this could happen to them. It may also impact on the ability of GH to obtain planning permissions from local authorities where a key consideration is the availability of affordable rental housing. This strategy may create the impression that the social agenda of GH is merely a screen to obtain planning permissions and is not honoured.

> The suggested points above represent a far more extensive answer than a student could be expected to submit and therefore cover all issues intended by the examiner within the materials presented. However, students who have engaged in wider preparation may have accessed other more recent information that could impact on the strategic synergy of the development and its risk assessment. Any other valid and sensible comments will be credited but will be capped at 2 marks if not considered to be key.

(iii) **Sale of Can Gas Corporation Development to Peony Buildings**

AIA 9 Chp 8

Based on current indications the revised contract budget for CGCD is:

Anticipated profit	£14m	
Costs incurred to date		£846m
Costs to completion		
Flood mitigation	143.6	
Landscaping	184.2	
Completion of Phase One (47 + 16)	63	
Cost of Phase Two and Three		567.2
Total costs to complete	958m	

Deposits received:

Phase One 420/870 units @ 30% of budget price 1202m = 174.1m
Phase Two 200/400 units @ 30% of budget costs 554m = 83.1m
Phase Three 75/300 units @30% of budget costs 416m = 31.2m
Total deposits received   288.4m
Funding from Chongqing City Authority 25%   £84m
Total costs incurred in the project to date = 846m − 288.4m − 84m = £473.6m.

The sale of CGCD to Peony Buildings would realise £625m which would provide a much-needed boost to the cashflows and reduce the cash and profit exposure of GH in the

Chinese market. This would realise a profit on the project of £151.4m which is considerably more attractive than the potential £14m from completing the project.

However, it appears that Peony Buildings may not fulfil critical aspects of the project conditions which permitted the development, and that the initial 25% site clear up grant would need to be repaid to the Chongqing City Authority, reducing the cash benefit to £541m. If the sale contract made the compliance with these conditions explicit this could mean that any failure to deliver would enable financial recompense to be sought from Peony, but it would be potentially expensive and damaging.

Peony are also not intending to reduce the price of the units, believing that there will be a boom in demand once the issues around Evergrande resolve. They are also intending to reduce costs of landscaping and not honour the 10% late payment if the project overruns. This creates a more attractive project with good profit opportunities but at the expense of the stakeholders. This may damage the reputation of GH with the City Authority and their Chinese customers.

Withdrawing from the project could damage the reputation of GH and make it very difficult to attempt this type of development internationally, compromising both the growth opportunities for the company and the ability to extend the innovative sustainable housing models.

> The suggested points above represent a far more extensive answer than a student could be expected to submit and therefore cover all issues intended by the examiner within the materials presented. However, students who have engaged in wider preparation may have accessed other more recent information that could impact on the strategic synergy of the development and its risks. This is particularly in association with the developments in the Chinese property market. Any other valid and sensible comments will be credited but will be capped at 2 marks if not considered to be key.

(c) **Response to Gold Investment Trust criticisms**

AIA 3 Chp 1

The criticisms from Yuming Zheng of Gold Investment Trust reflect a pristine capitalist perspective to the responsibility of GH to its stakeholders, whereby the sole purpose of the company is to maximise shareholder's wealth within the requirements of law. The statements made on behalf of Gold Investments Trust imply that safeguarding the environment and dealing responsibly with employees, customers and suppliers reduce the returns to shareholders, whereas the evidence from many sources indicates the opposite.

The mission of GH does take regard of the treatment of its stakeholders – as articulated in its mission statement the purpose of the company is the rebirth of the urban environment through a partnership between nature and mankind to build vibrant, happy, sustainable communities. Our purpose is to build high quality homes, strengthen local communities and make a positive difference to people's lives. This driving purpose shapes everything we do and is fundamental to our long-term value-added approach. This approach puts the interests of the stakeholders at the forefront of the company and through this creates wealth for shareholders. The directors consider this normative approach to customers and nature as a core part of the corporate identity and critical to the business success.

Creating homes which delight occupiers gives us a key competitive position in the market and will protect demand for our developments, as seen from the rising KPI Net Promoter Score. Protecting our reputation with customers, and treating them with fairness, is a key part of the GH brand and changing this practice may cost shareholders in the future.

The report into Sustainable Construction shows that our cost base is also reduced as a consequence of using environmentally sustainable materials, especially energy. It also increases the availability of land and the likelihood of planning permissions enabling the company to access future development opportunities.

It is also likely that environmental regulations will increase over time, and so the way in which GH conducts its business may no longer be an option.

> **The suggested points above represent a far more extensive answer than a student could be expected to submit and therefore cover all issues intended by the examiner within the materials presented. However, students who have engaged in wider preparation may have accessed other more recent information that could impact on their consideration of the role of sustainability in construction and may have alternate evidence to support their appraisal of its impact on corporate performance. Students may consider the answer using the ideas of Donaldson and Preston and Instrumental Stakeholders or other models of CSR engagement. Any other valid and sensible comments will be credited but will be capped at 2 marks if not considered to be key.**

(d) **Green Vision Team ethical issues**

MDCS Chapter 6. AIA 11 Chp 5 AIA 7 Chp 4

As a team, the board has delegated the responsibility for appraising the risks and business options for the company in these difficult times. I have become aware that the board are considering the sale of the Can Gas Corporation Development to Peony Funding as an alternative to the sale of Afford Housing. We are concerned that the figures we have provided regarding the potential risk and cost implications of this contract, and our rough appraisal of the impact of the sale, may be used to inform this decision.

The figures we have developed to consider the level of loss currently within the contract reflect the approximate information provided by Sarah in her brief memo and do not constitute sufficiently detailed costings to inform your sales decision. This would require more detailed consideration of the future costings and a full schedule of costs to date.

In my professional judgement, permitting the information from our report to be utilised in such a way would be a breach of professional standards. It is a key part of my professional duty to act with integrity whereby I must ensure that information I provide is fit for purpose and not reckless or misleading – and I must ensure that the information used to justify any such sale does not misrepresent the facts.

Although the information we have provided here does indicate that the completion of the contract may compromise our cashflow in the short-term or may make a loss, the information is subject to considerable estimation uncertainty – not least due to the volatility and uncertainty in raw materials and energy costs and with future demand from the Chinese property market.

> **The suggested points above represent a far more extensive answer than a student could be expected to submit and therefore cover all issues intended by the examiner within the materials presented. However, students may apply the ideas from the IFAC Code of Ethics more explicitly and explore the threats to ethical behaviour presented in the production of the report. Additionally, the problems caused by predicting the impact of inflation could be explored in depth here to support the need for caution.**
>
> **Any other valid and sensible comments will be credited but will be capped at 2 marks if not considered to be key.**

(e) **Recommendations**

AIA 10 Chp 4

Based on the information provided to the Green Vision Team the following options seem open to the company:

Continuation of the CGCD project

There is some risk around the overall viability of the CGCD project although there is considerable uncertainty around the actual profit that may be realised. On current conservative projections, the project appears to break even whilst delivering the high-quality homes and ecological restoration envisaged at its inception. It could act as an excellent reputation building project for this new and emerging market for us and it supports our commitment to UN sustainable development goal 11 and takes our innovative approach into a new area.

However, this is impacting negatively on our cashflow and may be hampering our ability to engage in other development opportunities going forwards.

Sale of Afford Homes to Happy Homes

This would realise much needed funding to support the CGCD project, but it exposes our tenants to the risk of no-fault evictions or increased rents due to the focus of Happy Homes. It appears that the motivation for the purchase is to support the development of new campuses in London which increases the risk of rent rises/evictions. This is not in line with our strategic vision and the proposed consideration seems to under-value the asset.

We do not believe that this sale represents a viable option to the company.

Sale of CGCD to Peony

This would enable us to realise a profit on this project and avoid further cash outflow on a risky project but again the purchaser does not seem to align with our mission and values and may adversely affect the Chongqing City Authority. Although the consideration proposed does seem to offer value to the investors, this compromises our stakeholder values and is based on insufficient information at present.

Recommendation of Green Vision Team

It is recommended that the board revisit its commitment to its mission and values and explore and articulate where these may be compromised in the face of risk and poor performance. There is some considerable risk in continuing with the CGCD project, but, if the risk inherent with this does not exceed the appetite of the board, and more detailed costs and sales projections are produced, the retention of this should be considered.

In the medium term, the mission and values of the company and its commitment to sustainable development are consistent with the development of the industry and the needs of society and government and therefore should be retained.

The suggested points above represent a summary of the findings of the examiner. Credit will be given for synthesis of the students own findings and opinions, where supported by valid evidence. Any other valid and sensible comments will be credited but will be capped at 2 marks if not considered to be key.

Practice Case Study 6: Pre-seen material

Topic list	Syllabus reference
1 Practice case study 6: Pre-seen material	All LOs

Chocolate Artist plc
Pre-seen material

Chocolate Artist plc background

Chocolate Artist plc was founded by Mathilde Betram and Ben McDowd in 2009 after a holiday in St Lucia at the Rabat Estate owned by Hotel Chocolat. As a passionate foodie, Mathilde trained as a chocolatier in Belgium and started making artisanal chocolates on a small scale for sale at farmers' markets and then online both directly and through Amazon.

The company has grown very rapidly, winning an extensive and impressive range of awards for the quality of its products and its customer service.

The company was listed in 2016 as Mathilde and Ben focused on their ambition to transform the sustainability of cacao production and create a truly ethical brand that does good to the planet, its creatures, its suppliers, and wider society whilst tasting delicious.

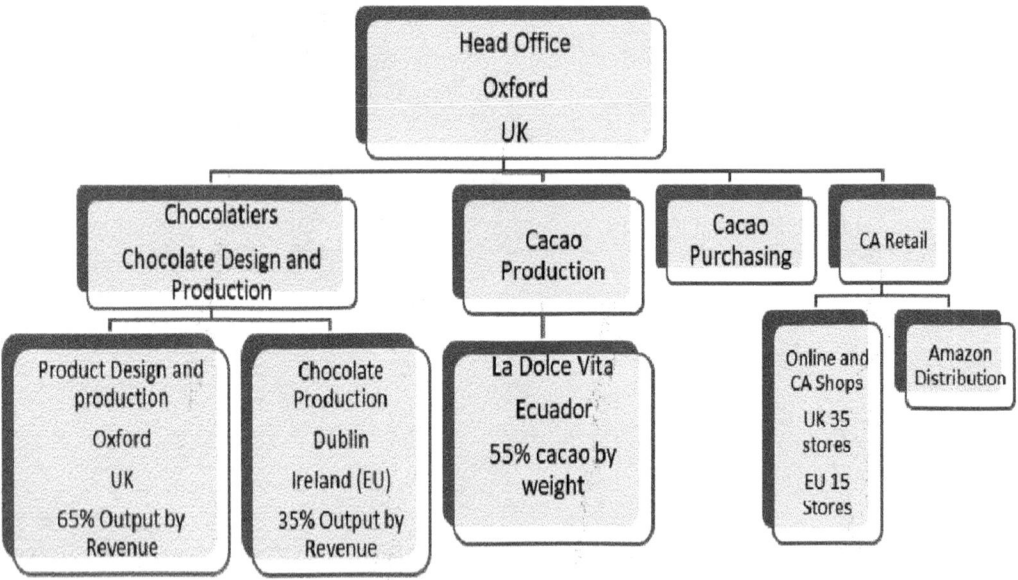

Organisational chart of Chocolate Artist plc

Chocolate Artist products

It has focused on the development of premium single estate chocolate from its La Dolce Vita Estate in Ecuador. This provides 55% of the raw cacao currently used in production, the remainder being sourced from West African and Indonesian estates and combined into either single estate or single country of origin products.

> Extract from an interview with Mathilde Bertran for *Chocolatier Magazine*
>
> 'Hardly any chocolatiers get involved in the bean any longer, buying all their chocolate ready made from specialist bean converters. And, unfortunately, cocoa growing has plummeted in Ecuador and the West Indies as bananas and tourism have taken its place. However, the beans from this part of the world are of a really high quality.
>
> I thought – why don't we grow our own cocoa and do the opposite of everyone else? As it is working so well for Hotel Chocolat I believe we can use this as a way to lead the industry to real accountability for its ethics. It also allows us to develop single estate chocolates with their unique taste from the plantation of origin as well as from the bean – as with wine and coffee.

'It's a bold move growing our own cocoa and it's one that goes against the overall trend in the chocolate industry – to specialise more and more in a particular part of the chocolate making process. But La Dolce Vita allows us to create a direct connection between our customers and the very origin of chocolate, cocoa. We're one of the few in the world able to do this – and the proof of the benefits to the consumer are in the awards we have won.'

Chocolate Artist recent awards

Academy of Chocolate Awards 2022

Dark Bean to Bar under 80%

Gold – Ecuador Dolce Vita Growers 70% Dark

Dark Bean to Bar 80% and over cocoa solids

Silver – Ecuador Dolce Vita Growers 85% Dark

Milk Bean to Bar

Silver – Ghana Sweetness Estate 55% Milk

Bronze – Indonesian Blue 65% Milk

White Bean to Bar

Gold – Indonesia 40% White

Chocolate Artist mission statement

Acting as an ethical company is the very essence of the Chocolate Artist, and it's a key part of our founding philosophy.

We act with kindness, fairness and compassion and aspire to improve life for our stakeholders and our planet.

We are always learning and aim to lead the industry in the most sustainable and effective ways to help our planet and those we work with - from our cacao farmers in Ghana and Ecuador, to our staff internationally.

As a chocolatier and cacao grower, we've learned about taking care of the environment – from organic farming and sustainable packaging to reducing waste and our carbon footprint.

We have a culture which empowers success for all with the opportunity for all our staff and stakeholders to achieve their goals.

In our ten-year history we have become the market-leaders in ethical business practices and sustainability. But we will never be complacent, and we will continue to benchmark, review and improve.

We also recognise the impact that our business has on the environment and set ourselves two targets. One is achieving Net Carbon Zero by 2030. The other is having 100% recyclable or re-usable packaging by the end of 2024 – we're proud to have achieved 96% and we're working hard to reach 100% as soon as we can.

We want to leave things better than we found them – and think our chocolate tastes better for it.

Chocolate Artist key metrics

Annual revenue	£216 million	£197 million
Cacao usage – Tonne	50	47
Cacao production – Tonne	27.5	23.8
Cacao sourcing – West Africa single estate Tonne	8.6	9.7 Indonesia Single Estate Tonne
	13.9	13.5

Chocolate Artist plc income statement – Management format

	2022	2021
	£000	£000
Revenue	216,000	197,000
Cost of sales	98,800	87,900
Gross profit	117,200	109,100
Sales and distribution*	71,300	65,800
Administration	31,100	27,300
Research and development	5,900	4,600
Operating profit	8,900	11,400

- Sales and Distribution Costs include the costs of the retail infrastructure, its running costs and sales staff salaries.

Research and development expenditure 2022:

Sustainable farming	£2,176,000
New product development	£3,728,000

Sustainability investment 2022

Sustainable farming research	£2,176,000
Cacao productivity subsidy	£157,000
Community investment programme	£250,000
Carbon off-set – Estate tree planting and diversity	£1,350,000
Fair employment programme	£360,000

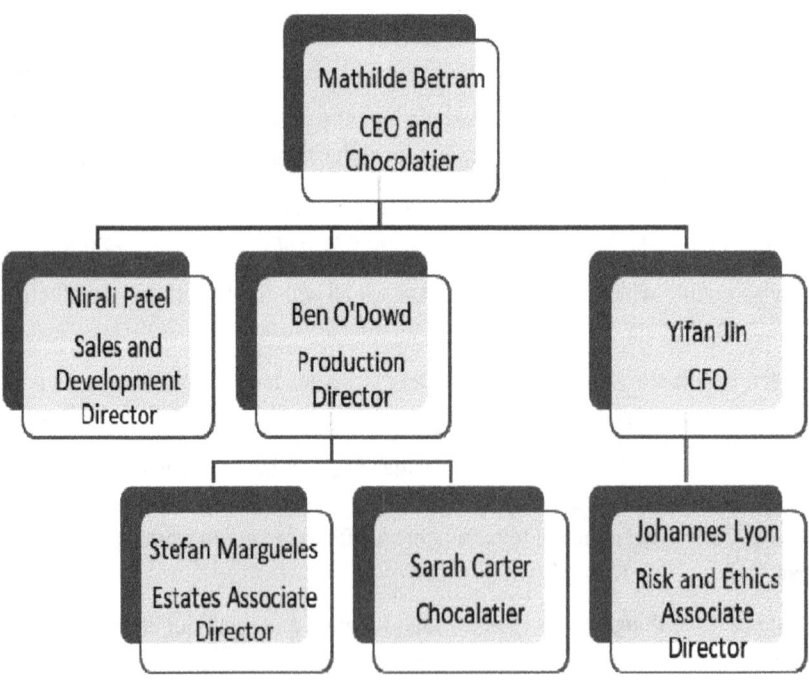

Chocolate Artist plc overview of operational management team

Chocolat Paradiso

Chocolat Paradiso is a very large estate located in Ecuador, bordering on the south of the La Dolce Vita Estate. It has recently come to the market after being in the ownership of the same family since 1947. It produces chocolate on a small scale but also has a range of well-regarded beauty products which are sold internationally. The estate is also run as a hotel and exclusive spa.

It is currently run as a cacao plantation but does not engage with modern growing techniques and has worked with nature by preserving the forest and growing the cacao under the forest canopy. This is regarded as a more sustainable practice and is favoured by the Rainforest Alliance (see below) although the estate does not have Rainforest Alliance accreditation. This approach has reduced the productivity of the estate to around 75% of more commercial estates in the region but has been more resilient to recent droughts.

The Rainforest Alliance is an international non-profit organization working at the intersection of business, agriculture, and forests to make responsible business the new normal. We are building an alliance to protect forests, improve the livelihoods of farmers and forest communities, promote their human rights, and help them mitigate and adapt to the climate crisis.

Summary of recent awards

Global Green Beauty Awards 2022

Salt & Cocoa Bean Body Scrub won gold in Best Salt Based Product.

Aloe Vera, Frankincense and Cocoa Butter Body Wash won gold as Best Body Wash.

Top Sante Beauty Awards 2021

Cacao and Brazil Nut Body Butter won silver in the Best Moisturiser Category.

Natural Health Beauty Awards 2021

Almond Chocolat Lip Balm won Best Lip Balm.

Salt and Cocoa Bean Body Scrub won Best Body Scrub.

La Dolce Vita Hotel

Conde Nast Traveller, Readers' Choice Awards 'No.1 Hotel in the Central America 2021'

2021 Travellers' Choice by Tripadvisor 'Best Small Rainforest Hotel 2021'

Tripexpert Expert's Choice Awards 2021 'Expert's Choice Award'

Booking.com 2021 Traveller Review Awards '9.7 out of 10'

World Travel Awards – 'Ecuador's Leading Hotel 2021: La Dolce Vita *also nominated for 2022

Key performance indicators

	2022	2021	2020
Cacao production (tonnes)	6.2	6.4	6.7
Hotel and spa revenue	$9.3million	$7.6 million	$7.5 million
Beauty sales	$1.2 million	$1.5 million	$1.4 million
Overall net profit	$430,000	$200,000	$187,000

Background economic and social information

(a) Child slavery in West Africa
(b) European Union Council adopts new rules to cut deforestation worldwide
(c) Cocoa sustainability guide
(d) Hotel chocolat sinks into the red
(e) European chocolate market analysis
(f) Cocoa commodity information as at 30 June 2023
(g) Academic papers on the environmental impacts of the cocoa industry

Child slavery in West Africa – understanding cocoa farming is the key to ending the practice

Steven Vass Business and Economics Editor – The Conversation

'Cocoa farming once involved the consecutive phases of boom and bust, followed by a shift to a new forest area (production shift), a different product in the same area (diversification) or a different system of cocoa cultivation requiring extra production factors. Studies of cocoa cultivation in West Africa have provided evidence of planters' migrating to new forest after exhausting existing forestland, resulting in shifts in production centres within and between countries.

However, accessing new forestland is becoming ever more difficult, and far more labour is needed to replant cocoa than to plant on pioneer forest soil.

This labour problem is particularly pronounced in cocoa cultivation areas that depended on migrant labour in the past (such as Ivory Coast). Here, a reduction in migration over time, coupled with deforestation, has resulted in a labour crisis: although post-forest cultivation requires more labour than pioneer planting, less labour is now available. To continue cultivating cocoa, planters in these areas have turned to cheaper sources of labour, such as family members and children.

This change in labour relations seems to have led to an increase in child slave labour.

Investing time

Chocolate producers such as Mars and Nestlé are well aware of the labour problem in cocoa cultivation. Historically, this problem has led to diversification: when cocoa has become difficult to cultivate, planters have turned to other products. Although such diversification may be good for farming communities, it spells bad news for buyers of the raw material. This has led to multinationals intervening under the banner of sustainability to prevent diversification away from cocoa. Their 'sustainability' programmes are ostensibly designed to combat child labour, slavery or trafficking or labour. They are, however, in fact productivity-boosting programmes with token anti-slavery components.

It is no longer sufficient merely to show that child slavery exists in cocoa farming in West Africa. To have any chance of combating these practices, campaigners must invest time and effort to truly understand the processes and conditions that create them.'

(**Source**: Conversation, The. [Online] Available from: https://theconversation.com/child-slavery-in-west-africa-understanding-cocoa-farming-is-key-to-ending-the-practice-170315 [Accessed 3 October 2024])

European Union Council adopts new rules to cut deforestation worldwide

Today, the Council gave the final go-ahead to a regulation that aims to minimise the risk of deforestation and forest degradation associated with products that are placed on or exported from the EU market.

The EU is a large consumer and trader of commodities and products that play a substantial part in deforestation. The new rules aim to ensure that the EU's consumption and trade of these commodities and products don't contribute to deforestation and further degrading forest ecosystems.

Due diligence

The regulation sets mandatory due diligence rules for all operators and traders who place, make available or export the following commodities from or into the EU market: palm oil, cattle, wood, coffee, cocoa, rubber and soy.

The rules also apply to a number of derived products such as chocolate, furniture, printed paper and selected palm oil based derivates (used for example as components in personal care products).

Operators will be required to trace the commodities they are selling back to the plot of land where they were produced. At the same time, the new rules aim to avoid duplication of obligations and reduce administrative burden for operators and authorities.

There is also a possibility for small operators to rely on larger operators to prepare due diligence declarations.

The regulation sets a cut-off date for the new rules on 31 December 2020, meaning that only products that have been produced on land that has not been subject to deforestation or forest degradation after 31 December 2020 will be allowed on the EU market or to be exported from the EU.

Checks on products

The regulation creates a benchmarking system, which assigns a level of risk related to deforestation and forest degradation (low, standard or high) to countries within and outside the EU.

The risk category will determine the level of specific obligations for operators and member states' authorities to carry out inspections and controls. This will facilitate an enhanced monitoring for high-risk countries and simplified due diligence for low-risk countries.

Competent authorities will have to carry out checks on 9% of operators and traders trading products from high-risk countries, 3% from standard-risk countries and 1% from low-risk countries, in order to verify that they effectively fulfil the obligations laid down in the regulation.

In addition, competent authorities will carry out checks on 9% of the relevant commodities and products placed, made available on, or exported from their market by high-risk countries.

The EU will enhance the cooperation with partner countries, in particular those classified as high risk.

Human rights aspects

The new rules also take into account the protection of human rights related to deforestation and a reference was added to the principle of free prior and informed consent of indigenous peoples.

Dissuasive penalties

The regulation includes provisions on penalties, which member states should ensure are effective, proportionate and dissuasive.

Fines proportionate to the environmental damage and the value of the relevant commodities or products concerned should be set at the level of at least 4% of the operators' annual turnover in the EU and include a temporary exclusion from public procurement processes and from access to public funding.

Background and next steps

The Commission published its proposal for a regulation on 17 November 2021. The Council adopted its general approach on 28 June 2022. The Council and the European Parliament reached a provisional political agreement on 6 December 2022. The Parliament adopted the regulation on 19 April 2023. Now that the Council has in turn adopted the regulation, it will be published in the EU's Official Journal and enter into force 20 days after.

The main driver of global deforestation and forest degradation is the expansion of agricultural land, which is linked to the production of the commodities included in the scope of the regulation. As the EU is a major consumer of such commodities, it can reduce its contribution to global deforestation and forest degradation by making sure these products and related supply chains are 'deforestation-free'.

(**Source**: Consilium. [Online] Available from: https://www.consilium.europa.eu/en/press/press-releases/2023/05/16/council-adopts-new-rules-to-cut-deforestation-worldwide/ [Accessed 3 October 2024])

Cocoa and the tropical ecosystem

Grown properly, cocoa can play a positive role in protecting the environment. Cocoa grows best under the shade canopy of mature rainforest trees. A cocoa farm can provide a safe, nurturing home to many different types of animals.

But it will not happen automatically. The World Cocoa Foundation supports efforts to protect and enhance the environment in which cocoa farmers grow their crop.

World Cocoa Foundation programs help farmers select pest control methods that are effective, economically feasible and cause minimal impact to the environment.

World Cocoa Foundation-supported programs also educate farmers on growing cocoa responsibly within existing forests – rather than 'clear cutting' the land.

Other World Cocoa Foundation-supported efforts include training on growing cocoa together with other crops and forest trees.

The World Cocoa Foundation also works with partners to provide grants to organizations developing better farming techniques that are environmentally responsible, safer and more economically rewarding.

(**Source**: Cocoa Initiative. [Online] Available from: https://www.cocoainitiative.org/sites/default/files/resources/ECA_-_2011_-_Cocoa_Farming_an_overview%20(1).pdf [Accessed 3 October 2024])

Cocoa sustainability guide

'Chocolate is one of the world's favourite treats, worth over **$100 billion in retail sales globally**. Western Europe, North America and Asia Pacific (including Australia) are the biggest chocolate consumer markets accounting for 70% of sales worldwide (**Source**: Euromonitor).

Cocoa, or cacao is the key ingredient in chocolate, and it typically grows far from where the chocolate lovers enjoy their treat. Approximately **5 million tonnes of cocoa are grown every year**, and the two largest producing countries are Côte d'Ivoire and Ghana, which means **West Africa accounts for more than two thirds of the world's cocoa production**.

Understanding this dynamic between where cocoa is grown, and where chocolate is consumed, is key to understanding cocoa sustainability and what can be described as 'sustainable chocolate'.

What are the issues in cocoa?

Right now, the picture of the cocoa industry is not one of sustainability. At Barry Callebaut, we have identified 5 key interlinked issues that need to be tackled:

- **Farmer poverty** – The majority of farmers are living below the **World Bank's benchmark for extreme poverty**.

- **Poor productivity** – This productivity is driven by a number of things including **poor agricultural practices**, **ageing cocoa trees** that lead to declining yields, and **lack of quality inputs.**

- **Child labor** – It is estimated there are about **1.6 million children in child labor** in Côte d'Ivoire and Ghana, mostly working on their family farms (**Source**: NORC report). The term 'child labor' is defined as work that deprives children of their childhood, their potential and their dignity, and that is harmful to physical and mental development (**Source**: ILO). Common activities include using sharp tools, carrying heavy loads, or not being in school in order to help out on the farm.

- **Deforestation** – Some farmers encroach on **protected areas** that are more productive whilst cocoa *can* be grown in a way that protects the environment.

- **Climate change** – Deforestation makes cocoa a contributor to climate change. Cocoa farmers' livelihoods are also at risk to any changes in drought and rain patterns, due to climate change as cocoa is primarily a **rain-fed crop.**'

(**Source**: Barry-callebaut. [Online] Available from: https://www.barry-callebaut.com/en-GB/manufacturers/cocoa-sustainability-guide-understanding-sustainable-chocolate [Accessed 3 October 2024])

Hotel chocolat sinks into the red

'Hotel Chocolat posted a full-year loss of £9.4 million this morning after its botched international expansion plans led to tens of millions of pounds being written off, while the chairperson and CFO have said they'll be quitting in the new year.

The Hertfordshire-based chocolate maker was forced to write off almost £30 million after its Japanese business went through insolvency. The firm blamed the collapse on pandemic restrictions in Japan and supply chain woes and said it was seeking to localise supply chains in the country through working with local manufacturers.

Hotel Chocolat boss Angus Thirlwell told the Standard: 'We thought we should take that on the chin and write the cost off and change the way we approach international opportunities and contain the capital spend and work with partners rather than try to do it ourselves. 'Nobody gets international right the first time straight out of the blocks – it's very much a case of adapting and taking the learnings and making your work smarter as you go on.'

CFO Matt Pritchard is now set to leave the business in 2023 'to pursue other opportunities,' while the chairperson Andrew Gerrie is also planning to step down.

The Company saw sales grow 37% in the year to June 2022 to £226 million as shoppers flooded back to its high street stores, leading to a softening in online sales, Thirlwell said. The firm increased its customer database by 15% to two million, while its subscription service also saw growth. 'What we're seeing really go well is our drinking chocolate both in our café and stores,' Thirlwell said. 'We launched a mince pie drinking chocolate as well and that seems to be pressing the button for a lot of people.'

Hotel Chocolat shares rose 1% to 147p. The stock is down 72% since the start of the year'.

(**Source**: Evening Standard. [Online] Available from: https://www.standard.co.uk/business/hotel-chocolat-sinks-into-the-red-over-botched-japan-expansion-b1044034.html [Accessed 3 October 2024])

Europe chocolate market analysis

The Europe chocolate market was valued at USD 44,762.65 million in 2022, and it is projected to register a CAGR [compound annual growth rate] of 4.79% during the forecast period (2022–2027).

During COVID-19 pandemic mainstream chocolate consumption has remained stable; however, the craft chocolate segment witnessed a sluggish growth in European Market. As per a survey conducted by the Fine Cacao and Chocolate Institute (FCCI) to better understand the impact of COVID-19 on small chocolate businesses, the cancellation of industry events was a major cause for the decline in craft chocolate sales. Additionally, the lower consumer demand played an important role.

The European chocolate market is highly competitive, with numerous leading players accounting for the majority of the market share. The increasing demand and growing popularity of dark and organic chocolates are fuelling market growth. Furthermore, seasonal demand plays an important role in chocolate sales. Various companies are launching a wide range of chocolate varieties during occasions like Easter. Factors such as the shape, innovation, mix of multiple flavours and packaging of chocolates are the key strategies adopted by companies to attain maximum sales during a festive season.

Health concerns related to high sugar content are restraining the market, but dark and premium chocolates are taking over the market share. Companies evolve with innovative models and new trends that are shifted to health and human well-being, attracting a customer base and brand equity.

Europe chocolate industry segmentation

Chocolate is a preparation of roasted and ground cacao seeds that are made in the form of a liquid, paste, or in a block, which may also be used as a flavouring ingredient in other foods. The market is segmented by product type into softlines/selflines, boxed assortments, countlines, seasonal chocolate, moulded chocolate, and other chocolate confectionery.

By distribution channel, the market is segmented as supermarkets/hypermarkets, specialist retailers, convenience stores, online channels, and other distribution channels.

By geography, the market studied is segmented into France, Germany, United Kingdom, Spain, Italy, Russia, and the Rest of Europe.

(**Source**: Mordor Intelligence. [Online] Available from: https://www.mordorintelligence.com/industry-reports/europe-chocolate-market [Accessed 3 October 2024])

Cocoa commodity information as at 30 June 2023

Cocoa futures hovered above $3,300 per tonne, remaining near the 7-1/2-year high of $3,324 touched on June 30th amid persistent concerns of low supply from the world's top producers. Above-average rain in the Ivory Coast flooded plantations and threatened the start of the main crop in October. Poor weather conditions also hurt crop prospects in Ghana. The dent in supply from the globe's top two producers drove the International Cocoa Organization to forecast a global supply deficit of 142,000 tonnes, more than twice of previous estimates of a 60,000 shortfall.

Cocoa is traded on New York Mercantile Exchange (NYMEX) and the Intercontinental Exchange (ICE) in London. The prices in New York are based on the South-Asian market and prices in London are based on cocoa from Africa. The size of each cocoa contract on the NYMEX is 10 metric tons. The biggest producers of cocoa are Ivory Coast and Ghana which together account for more than 60% of the world's output. Other major producers include: Indonesia, Nigeria, Cameroon, Ecuador and Brazil. Although cocoa is one of the world's smallest soft commodity markets, it has global implications on food and candy producers, and the retail industry. Cocoa prices displayed in Trading Economics are based on over-the-counter (OTC) and contract for difference (CFD) financial instruments.

Actual	Previous	Highest	Lowest	Dates	Unit	Frequency
3,290.00	3,277.00	5,379.00	211.00	1959 - 2023	USD/MT	Daily

Academic papers on the environmental impacts of the cocoa industry

The cocoa industry – The environmental impacts

Anna Gardner 7 May 2022

ClimaTalk

'Cocoa farming has a very specific geography. It is grown close to the equator because the cacao trees benefit from a warm and humid climate [1]. West Africa accounts for 70% of cocoa production worldwide, with the largest producing countries being Cote D'Ivoire and Ghana [2]. The industry forms the backbone of these countries' agricultural economies, employing about 60% of the agricultural labor force in Ghana and contributing the majority of income for these households [3].

The cocoa value chain is complex and has multiple stages connecting farmers to chocolate manufacturers through local buyers, local processors or large international buyers. The longer the value chain, the less contact farmers have with the manufacturing giants that profit from low cocoa prices [4].

The environmental effects of the cocoa industry emerge across the value chain, from the extraction of raw materials and production of farming inputs through to the industrial processing of beans into cocoa powder or cocoa butter. Some of the effects are direct, like water pollution or loss of biodiversity from the application of artificial pesticides [5]. Other effects are less visible, like greenhouse gas emissions from the fossil fuels used to transport the beans to the processing factory.

A particularly damaging local environmental consequence of the cocoa industry is deforestation, especially where cocoa farmers clear tropical forests and plant new trees rather than reusing the same land. In terms of scale, it has been estimated that 70% of illegal deforestation in Cote D'Ivoire is related to cocoa farming [6]. Another localised effect is the depletion of soil fertility and quality where unsustainable farming practices are deployed [7].

The environmental consequences of cocoa farming cannot be separated from other forms of exploitation. One of the most severe is the use of child labor in growing, harvesting, and transporting cocoa beans. There is also evidence of slave labor in the industry, where people work on plantations but are not paid [8].

Despite these forms of ecological and social exploitation, there are reasons to be hopeful about the cocoa industry.

For example, the role of tropical forests in carbon sequestration is gaining attention in the climate discussion and this has contributed to interventions to protect tropical forests [9]. One possible solution to deforestation is to invest in farming techniques that boost the productivity of existing farms, therefore reducing the incentive to clear more forests [10]. Moreover, agricultural and state banks can finance the transition period to make rehabilitating forests economically viable for smallholders [11]. Further along the value chain, the use of natural gas rather than diesel in cocoa processing factories can reduce acidification potential and greenhouse gas emissions [12].

Another solution is to increase the use of certified cocoa. Analysis has shown that certification of cocoa production through bodies like the Rainforest Alliance and Fairtrade lead to more efficient use of agrochemicals and less severe impacts on biodiversity, but currently only 16% of the world's chocolate products are made from certified cocoa [11].

10 years ago, large chocolate companies including Mars and Nestle pledged to limit deforestation in their supply chains by 2020. Unfortunately, no company has managed to eliminate forest destruction from their supply chain and the purchase of cocoa from intermediary suppliers like Cargill makes it difficult to trace cocoa back to specific farms [9]. One chocolate company which is tackling the problem head-on is Tony's Chocoloney. Tony's mission is to make 100% slave free chocolate the norm, linking social and environmental outcomes by increasing awareness among farmers and consumers and investing in long-term partnerships with farmers to improve farming techniques [8]. For programmes like this, it is evident that stakeholder engagement is key to making ecologically sustainable innovations effective [13].

In this way, it is feasible that consumer demand will put pressure on chocolate companies to provide more sustainable cocoa. In the long-term, it also makes financial sense because of the harmful effects of environmental degradation on productivity [14].

Overall, sustainability improvements are of strategic importance for the cocoa industry. Looking to wider themes, an environmental analysis of the cocoa industry is illustrative of the impacts of other agricultural commodities, especially in the context of the United Nations Sustainable Development Goal 15 to promote the sustainable use of terrestrial ecosystems [15]'.

Reference list

(a) Konstantas, A., et al. (2018) Environmental Impacts of Chocolate Production and Consumption in the UK. *Food Research Internation*, 106, 1012–1025. [Online] Available from: https://doi.org/10.1016/j.foodres.2018.02.042 [Accessed 3 October 2024]

(b) Putri, A. S., et al. (2015) Value Chain Improvement for Cocoa Industry in Indonesia by Input-Output Analysis. *Proceedings of the IMECS*, 2. [Online] Available from: https://www.iaeng.org/publication/IMECS2015/IMECS2015_pp947-952.pdf [Accessed 3 October 2024]

(c) Appiah, M. R. (2004) *Impact of Cocoa Research Innovations on Poverty Alleviation in Ghana.* Academy of Arts and Sciences Publications, Ghana.

(d) Rolden, M. B., et al. (2013) From Producers to Export Markets: The Case of the Cocoa Value Chain in Ghana. *Journal of African Development,* 15 (2), 121–138. [Online] Available from: https://ideas.repec.org/a/afe/journl/v15y2013i1p121-138.html [Accessed 3 October 2024]

(e) Takyi, S. A., and Amponsah, O. (2020) Ghana's Cocoa Production Relies on the Environment, Which Needs Better Production. *The Conversation*. [Online] Available from: https://theconversation.com/ghanas-cocoa-production-relies-on-the-environment-which-needs-better-protection-134557 [Accessed 3 October 2024]

(f) WWF (2017) Bittersweet: Chocolate's Impact on the Environment. *World Wildlife Magazine.* [Online] Available from: https://www.worldwildlife.org/magazine/issues/spring-2017/articles/bittersweet-chocolate-s-impact-on-the-environment [Accessed 3 October 2024]

(g) Tondoh, J. E., et al. (2015) Ecological Changes Induced by Full-Sun Cocoa Farming in Cote d'Ivoire. *Global Ecology and Conversations*, 3, 575–595. [Online] Available from: https://doi.org/10.1016/j.gecco.2015.02.007 [Accessed 3 October 2024]

(h) Tony's Chocoloney (n.d.) Our Missing Explained in 5 Simple Steps. [Online] Available from: https://tonyschocolonely.com/uk/en/our-mission [Accessed 3 October 2024]

(i) Tompkins, L. (2021) Hundreds of Companies Promised to Help Save the Forests. Did they? *New York Times.* [Online] Available from: https://www.nytimes.com/2021/12/02/climate/companies-net-zero-deforestation.html [Accessed 3 October 2024]

(j) Ingram, V., et al. (2019) The Impacts of Cocoa Sustainability Initiatives in West Africa. *Public Private Partnerships for Sustainable Development, MDPI.* [Online] Available from: https://doi.org/10.3390/books978-3-03897-833-6 [Accessed 3 October 2024]

(k) Nieburg, O. (2015) Chop Chop: Cocoa Dependents Must Finance Farm Training Before More Forests Are Axed. *Confectionary.* [Online] Available from: https://www.confectionerynews.com/Article/2015/04/29/What-is-the-environmental-impact- [Accessed 3 October 2024]

(l) Ntiamoah, A., and Afrane, G. (2008) Environmental Impacts of Cocoa Production and Processing in Ghana: Life Cycle Assessment Approach. *Journal of Cleaner Production,* 16 (16), 1735–1740. [Online] Available from: https://www.sciencedirect.com/science/article/abs/pii/S0959652607002429?via%3Dihub [Accessed 3 October 2024]

(m) Yamoah, F. A., et al. (2020) Stakeholder Collaboration in Climate-Smart Agriculture Production Innovations: Insights from the Cocoa Industry in Ghana. *Environmental Management,* 66 (4), 600–613. [Online] Available from: https://link.springer.com/article/10.1007/s00267-020-01327-z [Accessed 3 October 2024]

(n) Peprah, K. (2019) Cocoa Plant, People and Profit in Ghana. *Theobroma Cacao - Deploying Science for Sustainability of Global Cocoa Economy.* [Online] Available from: https://www.intechopen.com/chapters/67474 [Accessed 3 October 2024]

(o)   UN (n.d.) Goal 15. *UN Department of Economics and Social Affairs.* [Online] Available from: https://sdgs.un.org/goals/goal15 [Accessed 3 October 2024]

Climate change could threaten cocoa production: Effects of 2015-16 El Niño-related drought on cocoa agroforests in Bahia, Brazil

- Lauranne Gateau-Rey
- Edmund V. J. Tanner
- Bruno Rapidel
- Jean-Philippe Marelli
- Stefan Royaert

Abstract

Climate models predict a possible increase in the frequency of strong climate events such as El Niño-Southern Oscillation (ENSO), which in parts of the tropics are the cause of exceptional droughts, these threaten global food production. Agroforestry systems are often suggested as promising diversification options to increase farmers' resilience to extreme climatic events. In the Northeastern state of Bahia, where most Brazilian cocoa is grown in wildlife-friendly agroforests, ENSOs cause severe droughts which negatively affect forest and agriculture. Cocoa (Theobroma cacao) is described as being sensitive to drought but there are no field-studies of the effect of ENSO-related drought on adult cocoa trees in the America's; there is one study of an experimentally-imposed drought in Indonesia which resulted in 10 to 46% yield loss. In our study, in randomly chosen farms in Bahia, Brazil, we measured the effect of the 2015–16 severe ENSO, which caused an unprecedented drought in cocoa agroforests. We show that drought caused high cocoa tree mortality (15%) and severely decreased cocoa yield (89%); the drought also increased infection rate of the chronic fungal disease witches' broom (Moniliophthora perniciosa). Our findings showed that Brazilian cocoa agroforests are at risk and that increasing frequency of strong droughts are likely to cause decreased cocoa yields in the coming decades. Furthermore, because cocoa, like many crops, is grown somewhat beyond its climatic limits, it and other crops could be the 'canaries in the coalmine' warning of forthcoming major drought effects on semi-natural and natural vegetation.

(**Source**: Gateau-Rey, L., Tanner, E. V. J., Rapidel, B., Marelli, J. P, and Royaert, S. (2018) Climate Change Could Threaten Cocoa Production. [Online] Available from: https://journals.plos.org/plosone/article?id=10.1371/journal.pone.0200454 [Accessed 3 October 2024])

Climate change, combined with unsustainable farming techniques, have caused a crisis in cocoa production—in fact, some regions have already been rendered totally unsuitable for growing cocoa. Longer dry seasons and less rainfall, as well as new pests and diseases can reduce yields and quality, which translates into reduced income for farmers and their families. But by using climate-smart agriculture (CSA) methods, farmers can build more resilient livelihoods and farming systems and help secure the future of chocolate. The Rainforest Alliance is working with farmers in Indonesia and West Africa, the world's key-producing areas, to do just that.

(**Source**: Rainforest Alliance (n.d.) Preparing Cocoa Farmers for Climate Change. [Online] Available from: https://www.rainforest-alliance.org/insights/rainforest-alliance-certified-cocoa/ [Accessed 3 October 2024].

Practice Case Study 6: Exam requirements and unseen material

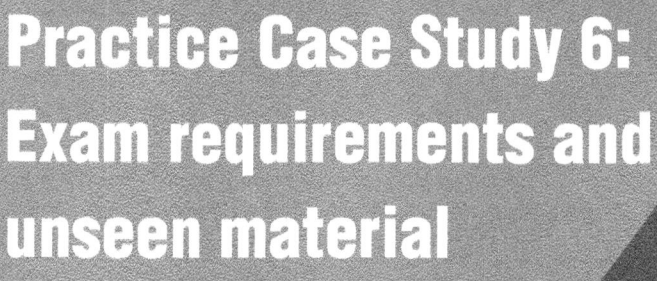

Topic list	Syllabus reference
1 Practice case study 6: Exam requirements and unseen material	All LOs

Important note: This practice case study is applicable for MDCS students following the accounting route, but its practice requirements are suitable for all MDCS students.

Exam requirement

Chocolate Artist plc

Question briefing

Scenario

You are an AIA professionally qualified accountant working for Chocolate Artist plc (CA) which is a large multinational company listed on the UK Stock Market.

The company has been the target of an unwelcome take-over speculation in the financial press and the CEO, Mathilde Bertran, is anxious to show that the company is on track to deliver market-leading growth and dividend streams.

You are currently working as head of management accounts and project costings. Mathilde Bertran has asked your team to explore a number of possible options available to CA to future-proof the company's success.

Required

Draft the Chocolate Artists Future-Proof Report for the board which:

(a) Identifies the key strategic risks facing CA over the next five years. **(15 marks)**

(b) Critically appraises the suitability, acceptability and feasibility of the purchase of a new estate. This should contrast the desirability of either Chocolat Paradiso in Ecuador or the Sweetness Estate in West Africa. **(30 marks)**

For each project you must ensure that you address any issues raised specifically by the directors in their discussions. You must ensure that any technical issues referred to are explained so that the directors can understand the implications of your advice or comments.

(c) Advises, with justification, the approach that CA should take to ensure that they comply with the developing sustainability issues facing the chocolate industry, discussing the role of a code of ethics and whistleblowing in the supply chain for CA and any implications for the existing governance at CA. **(10 marks)**

(d) Explores the key performance indicators that CA should consider focusing on to drive business development and the delivery of the CA Mission. This discussion should highlight the advantages of using a mix of non-financial and financial indicators to a business such as Chocolate Artist and explain some of the difficulties which may be encountered in their development. **(20 marks)**

(e) Concludes, with reasons, what the next critical steps should be for CA. **(10 marks)**

Professional marks are awarded for the quality of the professional skills demonstrated in this report.

(15 marks)

(Total 100 marks)

The draft report should be in a format suitable for presentation to the board.

Unseen material

Unseen case study materials

Contents

Media reports

- The almost sustainable brand – Chocolate Artist plc
- Power prices in Britain predicted to remain high
- Firms warn of price rises as energy costs soar
- Traders double down on interest rate rise bets as pound hits 15 month high

Emails:

- One – Ben O'Dowd – Reducing margins
- Two – Johannes Lyon – Big Forest Estate
- Three – Yifan Lin – Investor profile
- Four – Nirali Patel – Chocolate sales trends
- Five – Ben O'Dowd – The Sweetness Estate

Media reports

> **Chocolate Artist plc – Our new guilt(less) pleasure!**
>
> At *Family Life Magazine* we are all very keen on chocolate but knowing the ethical issues around our favourite treat we were delighted to hear that Chocolate Artist – a relatively new UK brand – has been awarded 'the almost sustainable chocolate' award by the Rainforest Alliance for 2022. This follows their investment in single estate origin chocolates produced from their own Ecuadorian La Dolce Vita.
>
> The brand was founded by chocolatier Mathilde Bertran to specifically address the problems with cacao farming by becoming a grower as well as a producer. This is certainly paying off as the sales are growing and the list of awards grows ever longer – for the quality of the chocolates as well as the kindness to their suppliers and the planet.
>
> The company has ambitions to extend their sustainability credentials further and rumours abound that they are looking to invest in some new estates – although whether this is in Ecuador or West Africa remains to be seen.
>
> However, there have been some nasty rumours that all may not be as virtuous as it seems as Chocolate Artist may have been using some cacao beans from West African sources where another child labour scandal was uncovered last month – and where there is evidence that productivity is being prioritised over the environment with new plantations being developed resulting in deforestation.
>
> It will be interesting to see if Chocolate Artist and other ethical chocolate brands can really drive a clean-up in this somewhat murky trade.

> Power prices in Britain are predicted to remain high until the late 2030s.
>
> That's according to the latest forecast unveiled by consultancy Cornwall Insight, which highlights the surging demand for power as a key factor driving this trend, [caused by] the increased adoption of electric heating and transportation, [leading to] a strain on the [power] grid.
>
> Experts say that in the near term, the introduction of low carbon energy sources is expected to bring prices down.
>
> It is projected that prices will fall below £100/MWh by 2028, two years earlier than previously anticipated.
>
> Approaching 2030, the transition to cost-effective renewable energy sources will coincide with the expanding electrification of the economy.
>
> Tom Edwards, Senior Modeller at Cornwall Insight, said: 'The challenges of rising power demand, increasing exports and reliance on gas continue to keep our power price forecasts above historical levels

for many years to come. Despite these concerns, we continue to be optimistic about the positive impact of low carbon, cost-effective energy sources and favourable gas price trends.'

(**Source**: Energy Live News. [Online] Available from: https://www.energylivenews.com/2023/07/07/uk-energy-prices-to-stay-high-until-late-2030s/#:~:text=UK%20energy%20prices%20to%20stay%20high%20until%20late%202030s%20%2D%20Energy%20Live%20News [Accessed 3 October 2024])

Andrew Large, director general of the Confederation of Paper Industries, said: 'This is a highly inflationary situation for the British economy and members will clearly be in a position where they do try to pass those costs on to consumers where they can.'

One paper manufacturer, the Northwood Group, said the industry had been 'left to fend for itself' in the face of 'horrendous' knock-on effects from the gas price rise.

'The spike [in gas prices] that we have seen since January is equivalent to a 550% price increase, which of course destroys any industrial planning,' said chairperson Paul Fecher.

Laura Cohen, chief executive of the British Ceramic Confederation, said many of her member firms could even be forced to stop production 'due to uneconomic higher energy costs'.

This could cause 'severe damage' to production facilities such as brick kilns, which could not easily be turned off at short notice, she said.

(**Source**: BBC News. [Online] Available from: https://www.bbc.co.uk/news/business-58840537 [Accessed 3 October 2024])

Traders double down on interest rate rise bets as pound hits 15-month high

Michael Hunter and Daniel O'Boyle

Evening Standard

The pound hit its highest level in 15 months today and City traders doubled down on bets for more Bank of England rate hikes after data on wage rises powered through forecasts.

Sterling peaked at $1.2913 after the wages data, taking it up by over half a cent on the day.

The rally came as financial markets moved to factor in a higher peak for UK rates, with inflation looking likely to stick at high levels and both the Chancellor and the Governor of the Bank of England repeating their determination to tame the upward spiral in prices.

Traders were placing bets that the BoE would go for another super-sized half-point rate rise at its next meeting in August. That would be the fourteenth consecutive hike of any size and the second straight half-point hike.

Markets were also pricing in an interest rate peak of 6.5%, probably early next year. The outlook faces its next test from the number at the centre of the BoE's bitter struggle: consumer price inflation (CPI) data due next week.

James Smith, developed markets economist at ING, said the numbers 'could push the Bank of England into another [half-point] rate hike,' adding: 'These trends have been on display for several months now, and policymakers are losing confidence that they will translate into lower inflation. The BoE is focused squarely on the official pay and CPI data as it emerges.'

(**Source**: Evening Standard. [Online] Available from: https://www.standard.co.uk/business/city-nterest-rate-rise-bets-pound-high-dollar-inflation-bank-of-england-currency-sterling-mortgages-b1093559.html [Accessed 3 October 2024])

Exhibit 1: Email One

From: Ben O'Dowd – Production director
To: Yifan Jin CFO
Subject: Reducing margins

Hi Yifan,

Further to our chat in the meeting yesterday, I can confirm that the key driver for the uplift in production costs in the factory in Oxford has been the rise in electricity costs. As documented in the media, prices have been rising significantly in the UK since autumn 2021, although there is some evidence that this is now resolving.

In addition to the rise in energy costs impacting on our margins I am also aware that the rapid rise in interest rates is impacting on our borrowing costs which may make investing in new plant and machinery more expensive next year. On the plus side it is benefiting the costs of imported cacao that we need to buy on the open markets – although the price of cacao is rising, the strengthening of the pound is serving to offset this a little.

The effect of these increases in our costs are to reduce our gross margins but Nirali has been resistant to starting to really increase our prices – although we may have to succumb to the overall inflationary trends.

There is little I can see that we can do in terms of improving our efficiency in the Oxford or Dublin factories and I know Mathilde is very resistant to reducing our spend around the sustainability agenda – but I can see that this is creating issues for you and your department.

Best wishes
Ben.

Exhibit 2: Email Two

Email Two.

From: Johannes Lyon – Risk and ethics associate director
To: Ben O'Dowd – Production director
Subject: Issues with Big Forest Estate West Africa

Dear Ben,

I have been following up on the information I received about Big Forest Estate but am struggling to locate the initial informant – the contact-name on the supplier invoices is unknown to the estate and it appears they may have disappeared. The allegations are very serious – it seems that we may have used cacao from a plantation which has caused several hectares of new deforestation, and which does not honour the UN guidance on child labour or fair wages to farmers.

It seems that the supplier was not vetted before we signed the purchase contract with them, and that the decision was entirely based on the price offered. I know we are under pressure on the margins. but I would not have expected this to have been the only criterion upon which such a decision was made.

I did look at our system around supplier vetting and we don't appear to have a written policy or set of guidelines for supplier vetting other than the usual credit checks and money laundering requirements. I am also concerned that we can't locate the whistle blower and I don't know if they are an employee of ours who is afraid to speak out or whether this is an employee of Big Forest Estates who has been harmed or gone into hiding.

I am wondering whether this is indicating a deeper issue around our staff familiarity with our ethical values. Although I have ethics in my title, I am not clear that designing systems for ethical compliance would only fall to me and my department as it will affect all parts of the business – and especially your team.

I think we need to liaise with Nirali and Mathilde around a possible response to this information – and whether we need to withdraw our Big Forest Estate chocolate from the shelves – or whether that will create other issues of sustainability – namely waste! This might also not be beneficial to our reputation in a cost of living crisis.

Let me know your thoughts.
Best wishes
Johannes.

Exhibit 3: Email Three

From: Yifan Jin
To: Mathilde Bertran
Subject: Investor comments

Dear Mathilde,

As promised, I have the analysis of our investor profile following the recent purchasing activity – you may be correct in thinking that we have an unwelcome approach developing from Peacock Investment Trust and Fortune Favour Trust.

The significant shareholders can be summarised as:

Internal shareholders		External shareholders	
Mathilde Bertran	22%	Peacock investment trust	10%
Ben O'Dowd	18%	Fortune favour trust	8%
Chocolate Artist employee shares	11%	Ethical equity	7%
		Others (under 2% holding)	24%

The correspondence that I received from Peacock Investment implies that they have been liaising with both Fortune Favour Trust and some of the other smaller shareholders. They are expressing concern that the cost of our sustainability agenda is eroding the profit margins and reducing our dividends. Unlike Hotel Chocolat, we did pay a small dividend this year, but I fear that we may not be able to sustain the re-investment in the company over returns to shareholders with this pressure.

Perhaps we need to have a more robust discussion around our key performance indicators to help balance these developing conflicts.

Best wishes
Yifan.

Exhibit 4: Email Four – market development – actions of competitors.

From: Nirali Patel
To: Mathilde Bertran and Ben O'Dowd
Subject: Chocolate market trends

Dear Both,

I have been examining our recent sales data which is showing very healthy growth in filled chocolate boxes and in the small novelty offering but a slight slowing in our premium single estate range. This is most evident in the UK where the inflationary pressures on households are most extreme – but there is a slowing in Germany and other parts of the Eurozone too. Sales to the US and China remain more buoyant although they are only 27% of our overall sales – so an opportunity for growth but not offsetting the issues in the UK and Europe.

I suspect that some of the slowing is due to some new entrants into the single estate market from the large global players – and we can't compete easily with their distribution channels and volumes. However, this does confirm that single estate may be a way to continue our product differentiation.

On another note, the new Chocolate Taster loyalty scheme is creating a lot of repeat custom and some lovely buzz on social media. We have been working with the estates team in Ecuador on identifying specific terroir notes for different bar ranges and I am very hopeful that, in common with coffee and wine, we may be able to really create an interest in the premium nature of our product.

I note in the board agenda that we are discussing the possible purchase of a new estate – I have the information for Chocolat Paradiso which looks really interesting, but I don't have any information around the productivity of the estate or the cost. Could I have that sent over before we meet next week?

Best wishes
Nirali

Exhibit 5: Email Five

Report from Ben O'Dowd and Yifan Lin to board of Chocolate Artist plc
Subject: New estate purchase

Investment objectives

To expand the single estate offering

To secure sustainable cacao supply for CA

Current shortfall of cacao production

In 2022 we needed to purchase 22.5 tonnes of cacao and we believe that we will need 50.5 tonnes in total for 2023 and 2024 which will create a larger volume to be purchased from the open market.

The Sweetness Estate – Purchase cost $7.5 million

The Sweetness Estate is located in West Africa and grows excellent cacao which is used widely in Belgian premium chocolates and rarely comes to the UK. Last year the yield of the estate was 23.1 tonnes which is a productivity of 475kg/hectare. The estate productivity is declining, and the production methods do not reflect our agroforestry model, but this can be developed over time.

The Estate is farmed by three families and follows traditional West African family practices and so child labour would need to be addressed. The estate has been run commercially and quite aggressively by a global cacao processor which has allowed the chocolatiers to remain distant from the more unpleasant consequences of profit at any cost.

Chocolat Paradiso – Ecuador – Purchase cost $13.2 million

Chocolat Paradiso is located in Ecuador and grows outstanding cacao which is used internationally in some premium ranges. The yield of the estate is 10.1 tonnes and has productivity of 300kg/hectare. This estate has embraced agroforestry, is RainForest Alliance-certified and has a progressive employment policy without child labour and with fair wages.

Funding

Both options will require funding from loans which will be raised from UK lenders.

Issues for discussion:

- Should we purchase a new estate?
- Do either of the estates under consideration represent a sensible investment approach?

Practice Case Study 6: Suggested answer

Topic list	Syllabus reference
1 Practice case study 6: Suggested answer	All LOs

Suggested answer

Chocolate Artist plc

Background to paper

Chocolate Artist plc is inspired and loosely based on Hotel Chocolat and is positioning the students in the sustainability debate around both UN Goal 15 (Life on Land) with particular emphasis around deforestation issues, UN Goal 12 (Responsible Production and Consumption) and UN Goal 8 (Decent Work and Economic Growth). The scenario is explicit around the issues of child labour and the difficulties in establishing decent working practices in the cacao industry in West Africa and the pre-seen case study materials gives background to the specific concerns of global regulators around these issues. This further develops the AIA agenda around ensuring that sustainability issues are at the core of their education. This also allows a discussion around issues of whistle blowing and the role of the accountant in business to act as an ethical leader – and the potential difficulties that this may pose.

The projects suggested are based on the recent initiatives explored by Hotel Chocolat which have not been entirely successful and although the information given in the materials would allow candidates to assess the ideas as viable, those who have taken the time to read the pre-seen materials will appreciate that these are not without risk. The performance of the Chocolat Paradiso Hotel and Spa is taken from Langdale Estate and Spa in the Lake District.

The report required is an exploration of where CA currently is, what opportunities, risks and uncertainties are facing CA, a discussion and recommendation for where CA should aim to be in the medium term and suggestions for actions to deliver these goals, (MDCS Chp 2) and should be the mindset for all candidates for this examination.

MDCS Chapter 2/AIA 4 Chapter 1/AIA 3 Chapters 1,2 ,3, LO 1, 2

(a)   Identifies the key strategic risks and opportunities facing CA over the next five years.

Chocolate Artist is a leading ethical producer of artisanal chocolates although it is a relative new entrant to the global market. It currently represents only 1% of the revenue of the major global players in the market and has a similar turnover to Hotel Chocolat. Nevertheless, the media interest in the company's ethical stance has caused an upturn in sales and supports the company's ambitions to have an impact in the industry.

Our opportunities relate to our well-established reputation for chocolate excellence and our market leadership in high ethical standards.

Our single estate chocolate ranges command a significant price premium which gives an excellent operating margin when compared to single origin chocolates and the global brand leaders. Our extensive range of chocolates covers a wide range of price points without damaging the premium branding and our sales volumes have remained resilient across the economic turbulence caused by the recent Covid 19 pandemic. Seasonal holiday sales have been buoyant internationally, and CA has experienced rapid growth in Germany, China and the United States. As reported by the Chocolate Forum, the three markets are very significant and growing which offers excellent opportunities for growth.

Our market leadership for ethical standards reduces the costs arising to CA from recent changes in regulation around deforestation for goods sold in the EU. The company has been in partnership with the Rainforest Alliance to promote sustainable farming methods and has received significant positive publicity resulting in being named as 'almost sustainable chocolate brand of the year' which provides a unique selling point and some protection against changing consumer demands around sustainability.

The risks facing the company arise from the following external sources:

Commodity volatility

Cacao

There is a projected 142,000 tonne shortage of cacao due to flooding in Indonesia and drought in Ghana which has driven up prices to a 7 plus year high. This illustrates the issues facing the chocolatier in both accessing sufficient cacao to fulfil demand and the risk that significant price rises will pose to the margins earned on products.

Energy pricing

As CA chocolates are produced in Ireland and England, a key constituent cost is that of transportation of cacao from Ecuador and West Africa and the distribution costs to the customer. This exposes the company to the risks in oil price volatility. The factories in England and Ireland also use energy which has seen a significant rise since the geopolitical instability in February 2022. Both factors will add to pressure on margins.

Reductions in productivity – Climate change

Climate change is adversely affecting cacao productivity. Cacao production is limited to areas around the equator and requires high temperatures and humidity but is sensitive to heat extremes and drought. It appears that overall global productivity is reducing due to climate disruption, and this is predicted to worsen in the medium term. As cacao yields become less reliable the traditional response of the small cacao farmer is to diversify away from cacao into other crops which further reduces supply. Managing this will require industry wide initiatives which have currently not been successful or widely adopted.

Economic turbulence

The covid-19 pandemic caused a drop in the chocolate market by 2.9% driven by issues in supply but also in issues of demand as consumer net disposable income came under pressure. This illustrates that chocolate, as a luxury discretionary product, is susceptible to down-turn in demand. The Eurozone and the UK, both significant markets for CA, have been teetering on the edge of recession since the end of the pandemic and, with ongoing inflationary pressures leading to hardening of fiscal policy and rising interest rates, these recessionary forces may continue in the medium term. This could erode demand and reduce the size of the market internationally – although the US and China appear to be more stable in this regard.

Changes in customer taste

There is a risk that the chocolate market may be reduced by changes in consumer taste. The rising health issues created by obesity may lead to government regulations and additional sugar taxes. There is also a rise in interest in more sustainable consumption and cacao is not currently recognised as a sustainable crop. As substitutes are developed there is a risk that market overall is reduced.

Our growth targets are ambitious and meeting these to the satisfaction of our investing stakeholders may be subject to some risks and uncertainties. As noted, some of our investors are unconvinced by our projections in the last investor briefing, and may therefore place pressure on the company to grow more quickly than our current suppliers can support, leading to an erosion of our ethical supply chain and dilution of our USP and reputation.

> **Although this answer is more extensive and beyond that which a candidate may be able to explore within the time constraints of the examination, candidates may choose to approach the analysis using a PESTLE framework or Porter framework which will be fully credited.**

> Additional risks also exist around competition from the large global players including Mars and Nestle and students could explore the difficulties in entering into new global markets. They could also explore the risks around supply chains in more depth. Where candidates have explored the performance of large global players or Hotel Chocolat in depth, discussions may highlight the issues in the margins made by CA.
>
> Answers could also explore what the company does poorly specifically and use this framework to analyse the risks.
>
> Any sensible points will be rewarded.

(b) Critically appraises the suitability, acceptability and feasibility of the purchase of Chocolat Paradiso in Ecuador vs the purchase of the Sweetness Estate in West Africa.

For each project you must ensure that you address any issues raised specifically by the directors in their discussions and you must explore how each project may affect the strategic vision or resolve any risks currently facing the company. You must ensure that any technical issues referred to are explained so that the directors can understand the implications of your advice or comments.

MDCS Chapter 2,3 4 / AIA 4 Chapter 3 LO 1, 2, 3, 4, 5

Purchase of a New Chocolate Estate

This option represents both a market penetration strategy for both estates [1] and a concentric diversification into a related market to chocolate for Chocolat Paradiso.[1]

Suitability: Strategic fit

The purchase of Chocolat Paradiso will further consolidate our focus for cacao from Ecuador and give us another single estate to expand our single estate range.

The estate currently is certified by the Rainforest Alliance. The employment practices of the estate are very progressive with a ban on child labour and a significant focus on fair staff remuneration which would be compatible with our ethical labour practices.

The purchase of the Sweetness Estate adds another estate into the range but offers diversification into another more well-known chocolate producing area. This estate is not certified by the Rainforest Alliance and its employment practices are unclear which may not fit into the ethical position taken by CA.

Advantages of acquisition

Both estates increase our direct access to a dedicated cacao source and will allow our single estate branding to be more firmly focused, in the case of Chocolat Paradiso this is also consolidating the focus at Ecuador, giving the brand further differentiation.

The current productivity of the estates will provide us with either 20% (CP) or 46% (SE) of our 2024 projected requirements and reduce our dependence on the West African open market and its volatile prices.

Chocolat Paradiso offers a diversification opportunity into hospitality and beauty treatments. The Paradiso cacao based beauty brand has a small but niche following and would offer a well respected opening into a potentially lucrative if competitive market.

Acceptability

	Chocolat Paradiso	Sweetness Estate
Purchase cost	$13.2m	$7.5 m
Annual estate yield (Tonne)	10.1	23.1
Productivity per hectare	300 kg/hectare	475 kg/hectare
Compliance with fair employment	Yes	No
Agriforestry in use	Yes	No
Estate profit from other sources	$430,000	No

Risks from acquisition

Both purchases focus the product development at premium single estate chocolate. Although there is evidence that this market is growing, some of the major international competitors are entering this market. As market penetration success depends on the ability of the companies to persuade customers of the virtue of this type of product as well as the quality of the CA brand (and for CP the quality of Equadorian chocolate which is less well known than that of West Africa) advertising and promotion is critical to success – which will require considerable funding and CA may be at a competitive disadvantage compared with the larger players.

The hotel and beauty aspects of Chocolat Paradiso are insignificant against the total revenue of CA and would require considerable investment in an unfamiliar industry to offer a major diversification impact. This could distract the management of CA from their core business and expose the company to dissatisfaction from investors who may believe that this is not a viable contribution to the company. Given the difficulties that Hotel Chocolat experienced with Rabat and the impact this has had on market confidence in their management team, resulting in the loss of the chair and the CFO, this could be a difficult idea with which to persuade the investors.

The CP investment will originate all of our dedicated cacao supply in one country which exposes CA to increased risk if productivity due to climate change is reduced or the harvest is damaged due to flood or drought.

The SE purchase exposes CA to a reputation risk that its stance on sustainable production, with specific emphasis on fair treatment of farmers and avoidance of child labour, is not met. As a key aspect of the unique character of CA, this would erode our differentiation and would be unacceptable to many of our sponsoring stakeholders.

Feasibility

Financial resources

For both options CA will need to fund the purchase using long term bank finance. As finance will be raised in the UK, this may be more expensive than previous borrowings due to the rise in interest rates. It is therefore likely that the bank will require tighter restrictions on the level of borrowings in the company and the bank covenant may restrict the flexibility of ongoing funding for operations. This may put the company under cashflow pressures if the predictions and assumptions around future income prove too optimistic.

> **Although this answer is more extensive and beyond that which a candidate may be able to explore within the time constraints of the examination, it is not exhaustive.**
>
> **Candidates may choose to approach the analysis using a number of possible frameworks to enable a considered conclusion regarding the suitability of the options to be considered. These could include taking the Tuckers Five Questions approach or linking the analysis around the strategic ideas explored in part a.**
>
> **Additional discussions regarding the option to purchase an additional estate at all could be explored in more depth and this could consider the opportunity costs of tying up capital in an uncertain environment. Candidates who have explored Hotel Chocolat in more depth may realise that the beauty aspect of the Chocolat Paradiso option did not make a material differentiation to their business.**
>
> **Answers could also specifically identify the risks facing CA and show how each option addresses these.**
>
> **Any sensible points will be rewarded**

(c) Advises, with justification, the approach that the CA should take to ensure that they comply with the developing sustainability issues facing the chocolate industry, discussing the role of a code of ethics and whistleblowing in the supply chain for CA and any implications for the existing governance at CA.

MDCS Chapter 6/ AIA International Accountant Issue 129 May June 2023/AIA Paper 11 Chapter 3. LO 2, 3, 4, 5

Although CA mission is around the ethical and sustainable production of high-quality chocolates, the company has not articulated this in a code of practice, and it is unclear where responsibility for this critical aspect of the company's identity resides. There are clearly aspects of the ethical and sustainability agenda articulated in the Risk Report and therefore managed by the risk committee and, from recent board minutes, the CEO and production directors both take a lead in this area. This creates the risk that the senior management of the company is out of touch with issues in the business and that sustainability issues fail to be managed adequately.

This is illustrated by the recent issues in the sourcing of beans from the Big Forest Estate in West Africa. This highlights that the link between ethical requirements regarding child labour and farmer remuneration and the need to be able to avoid beans which have caused deforestation in the assessment of suppliers and the purchasing of beans has not been working.

Whilst the board are confident that all staff understand and share the sustainability vision of the company, the lack of detailed training or written policies, or embeddedness in the governance of the company, means that this is not easy to convincingly demonstrate. This could compromise our certification ambitions as a sustainable chocolatier.

The code of ethics provides critical guidance to all staff to explain what it means to 'do the right thing' and promotes a culture of integrity within an organisation. This code is applicable wherever the organisation operates and at all levels of the business. This creates issues for the company where it is expanding its cacao estates or requiring additional sources from West Africa or Indonesia.

To be effective the code must be explicit, clear and relevant but not be seen as legalistic – it must reflect the issues that staff encounter in their work and be reflective of the actions required by the organisation. In CA, this could create a cumbersome document that staff may chose to ignore – or that may feel irrelevant to them in places.

This code must also be supported by clear policies and procedures around farming practice, recruitment and employment practice, selection of suppliers and business partners and in the design and development and manufacture of the product. These need to be articulated in the internal controls of the company and supported by excellent feedback loops to ensure that CA is continually learning and refining its sustainability approach.

For the code to be effective it must be consistent with the behaviours observed in the organisation and staff must see that compliance with the code is rewarded.

Whistleblowing is a key aspect of a robust internal control in this area ensuring the link between sustainability in the supply chain and governance of the company. A whistleblowing policy is essential but needs to be supported by excellent communication through newsletters, staff briefings and within the company HR policies which gives the clear message that whistleblowing is encouraged and valued and that those who speak up against poor practice will be protected.

This must all be supported by the tone at the top set by the directors and supported by managers at all levels in the company – and we must train the managers on how to respond to staff concerns.

> Although this answer is more extensive and beyond that which a candidate may be able to explore within the time constraints of the examination, it is not exhaustive.
>
> Although the question intends students to explore the need for an ethical code with clear whistle blowing procedures and internal controls, discussions could take a more advisory tone around ensuring that the issues of sustainability in cacao production are safeguarded and may explore ideas such as agroforestry, farming subsidies, traceablity systems, fair labour practices and removal of plastics and palm oil from the company.
>
> **Any sensible points will be rewarded**

(d) Explores the key performance indicators that CA should consider focusing on to drive business development and the delivery of the CA Mission. This discussion should highlight the advantages of using a mix of non-financial and financial indicators to a business such as Chocolate Artist and explain some of the difficulties which may be encountered in their development.

MDCS Chp 4/AIA 9 Chapter 8/AIA 4 Chapters 3, 6, 7, 8, LO 2, 3, 4, 5

The mixed indicator approach, such as the balanced scorecard for example, will enable CA to consider the factors beyond profit that are critical to its success. CA is driven by its desire to improve the sustainability of cacao production and to provide ethical leadership in this industry and believes that doing good creates great tasting chocolate – and therefore profit (a triple bottom line approach to sustainable business practice} Ensuring that non-financial strategic measures are incorporated into and measured in the management of the company prevents CA becoming too focused on short term financials at the expense of longer-term strategic measures. This will enable key performance indicators to be better aligned with strategy at all levels of the organisation.

Financial perspective

How do we create value for our shareholders and how should this appear to these shareholders?

Although Mathilde and Ben are significant shareholders (40% in total), Peacock Investment Trust owns 10% of shares, Fortune Favour owns 8% of shares, Share Returns owns 9%, Ethical Equity has a 7% stake and the Employee Share Scheme owns 11%. This means that at least 18% of the shareholding may be more focused on dividend stream and return on capital than the delivery of the ethical mission and we are only certain that the ethical vision is supported by 58% of the shareholders. Our current driver is striving for higher returns but this fails to articulate what return means to our different investors and there may be tension between the delivery of higher ethical standards and their impact on the cost base and profit.

- Possible KPI
- Revenue growth %
- Operating profit %
- Return on equity
- Dividend growth %

Customer perspective

What are the key issues that our customers value?

The quality of the chocolate is a key factor in repeat purchases and our reputation and brand built on ethical single estate products which differentiates the chocolate into a premium and desirable bar. Our current success driver is billed as having a clear differentiated product and engaging experiences but this is too vague to really allow us to track.

Knowing that we are reaching our customers and this is converting into sales means that our key indicators should be focused around:

- Number of new customers on database
- Number of repeat customers
- Average sales value per customer
- Sales values per product line and market segment
- Product awards
- Sustainability accreditations

Internal business processes

What must CA excel at – what operational performance must we be excellent at?

We produce 100% of our chocolate across our two sites in Dublin and Oxford and we grow the cacoa raw materials for 55% of this production in Ecuador. We must excel at both our productivity and quality of the initial bean and the technical consistency and quality of our manufacture – and we need to link this into product development to ensure that we retain our unique market position (see below .

To preserve our ethical status we must also excel at the treatment of our suppliers and farmers and staff and ensure that our sustainability credentials are maintained.

Key performance indicators could consider:

Productivity of La Dolce Vita Cacao – Tonne per Hectare

Species diversity of La Dolce Vita Estate – Number of species (plant and animal) per monitoring period

Learning and innovation

How can CA maintain and develop its competitive position?

This will consider the balance between innovations of cacoa production improving productivity and chocolate products maintaining and growing market share as well as the developments in the sustainability of all business practices which will require investment in the skills of cacao farmers and chocolatiers.

- Key performance indicators
- Area of land under agroforestry management
- Improvements in cocoa yield
- Number of qualified agrifarmers employed or in training
- Number of qualified chocolatiers
- Number of new chocolate products launched into the market

The major issue in developing meaningful performance indicators is ensuring that they are measurable and reflect the operational success factor that is desired without creating possible negative and undesirable behaviour within the business. This will be especially evident in the clash between sustainability measures and productivity measures.

> Although this answer is more extensive and beyond that which a candidate may be able to explore within the time constraints of the examination, it is not exhaustive.
>
> This answer follows the ideas of a Balanced Scorecard which is discussed in the MDCS Study Text, but any sensible mix of financial and non-financial indicators which specifically addresses the tension between the need for profitability and the ethical aspirations of the company will be credited. Students could choose to split the metrics into business performance and sustainability metrics for example. Students could also explore the ideas of Environmental Management Accounting in their discussion.
>
> The metrics suggested in the answer are by no means exhaustive and any sensible suggestions will receive credit.
>
> Any sensible points will be rewarded

(e) Concludes, with reasons, what the next critical steps should be for CA.

LO 2, 3, 4, 5

CA should develop both a code of ethics and whistle blowing policy and agree a new governance structure which explicitly articulates responsibility for sustainable development management.

Developing a clear set of KPI around financial, operational and sustainability performance should also be addressed, and the delivery of these KPIs should also be specifically allocated to managers and directors within the CA Team.

Further work is required to fully appraise whether the purchase of a new estate represents an appropriate use of funds and the level of financial risk this would place into the company.

Whilst the investment in Chocolat Paradiso is less financially attractive, it does offer considerable economies in distribution of cocoa to Europe and CA has considerable experience in working in Ecuador. Additionally, this investment sits more comfortably in the ethical mission of CA. However, it does expose CA to an environmental risk with all of its production in one geographical area which is less well known for its chocolate. Additionally, the opportunities to diversify into hospitality and beauty may be a distraction and less attractive to our investors.

The investment in Sweetness Estate is financially more attractive as it requires less initial financial investment and provides a more productive crop. However, this moves CA into a new geographical location where it has little existing competence and also creates additional logistical issues requiring a new distribution system. It is also not a good cultural fit with the sustainability mission of CA and this creates the risk of an unknown additional cost to ensure a good ethical fit which may compromise the financial benefit.

> **Although this answer is more extensive and beyond that which a candidate may be able to explore within the time constraints of the examination, it is not exhaustive.**
>
> **Students will be credited for any conclusions based upon their own previous analysis of the purchase options and the benefits of KPIs and a Code of Ethics**

Index

Note. **Key Terms** and their page references are given in **bold**.

4Ps, 27
4Ts, 31
7Ps, 27
7Rs, 31

A
Acceptance tests, 287
Accountability, 162
Acquisitions, 21
Acting with sufficient expertise, 305
Addressable market, 26
Ansoff's growth strategies, 22
Artificial intelligence (AI), 240
Assumption, 76

B
Balanced scorecard, 83
Bargaining power of customers, 14
Bargaining power of suppliers, 14
Big data, 255
Blockchain, 244
Brand image, 23
Breakeven analysis, 78
Business risk, 30

C
Cadbury report, 348
Changeover, 288
Cliff risk, 177
Cloud computing, 238
Company code of conduct, 302
Competence, 298
Concentric diversification, 24
Confidentiality, 298
Conflict of interest, 308
Conglomerate diversification, 24
Contrived tests, 287
Correct controls, 200
Cost leadership, 22
Cost-benefit, 282
Cost-volume-profit (CVP), 78
Courtesy, 298
Cybersecurity, 187

D
Data analysis, 252, 258
Data analytics, 256
Data manipulation, 258
Data modelling, 258
Data visualisation, 253
Data, 251
Deep ecologists, 37, 38
Detective controls, 199

Differential advantage, 27
Differentiation, 22
Direct controls, 200
Distributed ledger, 244
Diversification, 24
Due care, 298

E
Emerging risk, 177
Enterprise risk management (ERM), 32, **215**
ESG dependencies, 149
ESG impacts, 149
Estimate, 354, 355
Estimate, 76
Ethical codes, 302
Ethical theory, 296
Ethics, 296
Exception reporting, 210
Executive Share Options Plans (ESOPs), 35
Expedients, 37, 38

F
Feedback from customers, 210
Financial interests, 305
Firm infrastructure, 19
Five competitive forces, 14
Five whys technique, 192
Fixed cost, 77
Forecasting, 82
Free cash flow, 64
Functional strategies, 24
Fundamental principles, 298

G
Gray, Owen and Adams, 37
Growth through acquisitions, 21

H
Human resource management, 19

I
IFAC Code of Ethics, 296
Impact, 190
Inbound logistics, 18
Incremental change, 263
Independence of internal audit, 213
Individual behaviour, 296
Information sources, 208
Information, 251
Inherent risk, 177
Insights, 252
Installation, 285
Intangible assets, 66
Integrity, 298

audit, 211
 uditing Handbook, 214
 ..ionship of variances, 210
.ey performance indicators, **82**
Knowledge, 265

Least-cost producer, 22
Lines of communication, 209
Linkages, 18, 19
Long-term creditors, 34

Market development strategy, 23
Market penetration strategy, 23
Market size, 26
Marketing and sales, 18
Marketing mix, 27
Marketing strategy, 26
Mendelow, 179
Mergers, 21
Monitoring, 204

Objectives of internal audit, 212
Objectivity, 298
Operational financial risks, 31
Operational information, 207
Operational risks, 30, 32
Operational strategies, 24
Operations, 18
Organic growth, 21
Organisation impact analysis, 285
Outbound logistics, 18

PESTEL, 12
Porter's Five Forces model, 13
Positioning strategies, 27
Predictive analytics, 261
Preventative controls, 199
Primary activities, 18
Principles-based guidance, 297
Pristine capitalists, 37, 38
Proactive change, 262
Probability analysis, 192
Process automation, 239
Procurement, 19
Product development strategy, 23
Product differentiation, 27
Product risk, 30
Professional behaviour, 298
Professional competence, 298
Profit pool mapping, 26
Profit-related pay, 35

Proponents of the social contract, 37, 38
Pure risk, 177

Qualitative information, 82
Quantitative information, 82

Radical feminists, 37, 38
Ratios, 65
Reactive change, 262
Realistic tests, 287
Reporting risks, 32
Reports on resolution of weaknesses, 210
Residual risk, 177
Risk appetite, 177, 178, 183
Risk appetite, 31
Risk attitude, 176, 183
Risk auditing, 213
Risk capacity, 177, 183
Risk events, 177
Risk identification, 176, 177
Risk management systems, 31
Risk of non-compliance, 32
Risk profile, 177
Risk quantification, 190
Risk taxonomy, 177
Risk tolerance, 177, 178
Risk, 176, 183, 215
Rivalry amongst current competitors, 14

Safeguards, 299
Security, 34
Self regulation, 35
Sensitivity analysis, 193
Sensitivity analysis, 87
Severity, 190
Share option scheme, 35
Social ecologists, 37, 38
Social responsibility stances, 37
Socialists, 37, 38
Speculative risk, 177
Stakeholders, 34
Stewardship, 162
Strategic analysis, 9
Strategic drift, 23
Strategic financial risks, 31
Strategic information, 206
Strategic planning, 11
Strategic position, 11
Strategic risk, 30, 32
Strategy formulation, 9, 21
Stress testing, 191
Support activities, 19

Sustainable development, 110
SWOT analysis, 15

Tactical information, 207
Tail risk, 177
TARA framework, 196
Target markets, 27
Technology development, 19
Terminate a risk, 197
Testing, 286
The internet of things, 247
Threat of new entrants, 14
Threat of substitute products, 14
Threats and safeguards, 296
Training, 287
Transfer, 196
Transformational change, 263
Tucker's five question model, 315

Uncertainty, 176
Unprofessional behaviour, 309
Unquantifiable risk, 177

Value activities, 18
Value chain analysis, 26
Values and responsibilities, 302
Variable cost, 77
Variance trend, 210
Vertical integration, 24
Volume tests, 287
Voluntary code of conduct, 35

Whole customer experience, 28

INDEX